PROPAGANDA AND
THE AMERICAN REVOLUTION

The Virtuous Patriot at the Hour of Death. Low's Astronomical Diary, *1775.*
By courtesy of the Massachusetts Historical Society.

PROPAGANDA

AND THE

AMERICAN REVOLUTION

1763-1783

PHILIP DAVIDSON

For if the trumpet give an uncertain sound,
Who shall prepare himself to the battle?
I Corinthians 14:8

CHAPEL HILL
THE UNIVERSITY OF NORTH CAROLINA PRESS
1941

To

MOTHER AND FATHER

PREFACE

INTANGIBLE subjects often have an appeal that counterbalances the difficulty of working them out, and so it has been with this, one of the most illusive of the intangibles, propaganda. The difficulties, however, are not ineluctable, and the pleasures are delectable.

We have been helped by many people, this book and I, through its infancy and adolescence to its majority. They have encouraged or chastened, have corrected faults when they could and have shaken their heads sadly when they could not (the faults, some of them, being inherited and ineradicable), and they have done their best for it.

To Professor Marcus W. Jernegan of the University of Chicago we owe an unpayable debt of gratitude; from the inception of the idea to this final phase he has been a sympathetic and stimulating critic. Professor Quincy Wright, also of the University of Chicago, contributed largely to the basic framework of the study and through funds for an investigation of the causes of war made possible much of the research. Dr. Harold D. Lasswell of the William Alanson White Psychiatric Foundation has read the manuscript and has made many helpful suggestions.

The directors and staff members of the libraries in which I have worked have been most courteous. I am grateful to them all and particularly to those of the Massachusetts Historical Society, the New York Public Library, the New York Historical Society, the Historical Society of Pennsylvania, the Library of Congress, the Maryland Historical Society, the Virginia Historical Society, the North Carolina Historical Commission, the South Carolina Historical Society, the Charleston Library Society, and the Rhodes Memorial Home in Atlanta. I am also grateful to the editor of the *American Historical Review* for permission to use freely the material which appeared in my article "Whig Propagandists and the American Revolution," *American Historical Review*, XXXIX, 442-453.

My colleagues and students at Agnes Scott College have likewise been of much assistance. Dr. George P. Hayes, Professor of English, knows how much time and thought he has put on this manuscript; he cannot know how much his help has meant to me.

President McCain has provided the most favorable conditions for my work and has encouraged me at every point. Among the many students who have helped, I must acknowledge particularly the assistance of Miss Rosalyn Crispin.

My wife, Jane Davidson, has shared with me the troubles and pleasures of this undertaking and throughout has been wonderfully patient and inspiring. For a good many years now this study has been our companion, and reluctantly do we let it go to make its own way in the world of books.

Agnes Scott College   PHILIP DAVIDSON
Decatur, Georgia
January, 1941

CONTENTS

ILLUSTRATIONS

INTRODUCTION

THE AMERICAN REVOLUTION, perennially attractive in its complexities, has been subjected to a recurrent examination, and with each change of emphasis our comprehension of it has grown. Some historians have been primarily concerned with institutional developments, others with economic problems, and still others with social and intellectual issues. To further our understanding, it is here purposed to study the Revolution in the light of our modern knowledge of the technique of propaganda.

Propaganda, which is simply an attempt to control the actions of people indirectly by controlling their attitudes, is the object of a lively but anxious interest today. The efforts to describe, analyze, and define it are innumerable; academic and popular treatments abound, and for every author there is a different definition. Sociologists, psychologists, political scientists, educators, advertising agents, professional propagandists, and businessmen have written or talked on the subject, and nearly everyone has a clear idea of what the word connotes to him, and but a vague idea of what it really means. There is a general feeling that propaganda is evil, that it arises from undesirable motives and interests, that its methods are dangerous, and that its results are bad. This feeling is perhaps a natural reaction to the propaganda of the World War. Although justified by current usage, this meaning of the word is entirely too narrow and restricted. The most careful study recently made, lists definitions according to types and from the common elements deduces the following definition: "Intentional propaganda is a systematic attempt by an interested individual (or individuals) to control the attitudes of groups of individuals through the use of suggestion and, consequently, to control their actions."[1] Intentional propaganda arises, therefore, from interested motives, is consciously and systematically

[1] Leonard W. Doob, *Propaganda, Its Psychology and Technique*, p. 89. Quoted by permission of Henry Holt and Company. There is no need to repeat the excellent list of definitions given in Frederick E. Lumley, *The Propaganda Menace*, Chap. II. Doob, *Propaganda*, Chap. VI, discusses these definitions in detail. The Institute of Propaganda Analysis, formed in October, 1937, defines propaganda as "expression of opinion or action by individuals or groups deliberately designed to influence opinions or actions of other individuals or groups with reference to predetermined ends."—*Propaganda Analysis*, Vol. I, no. 1, pp. 1 f.

carried on, and its primary purpose is to obtain public support for a particular idea or course of action. Propaganda must not be confused with the technique of the propagandist. It is not necessary for propaganda to be false or for the propagandist to conceal himself or his motives. Whether the suggestions are to be true or false, whether the activities are to be open or concealed, are matters for the propagandist to decide.

There also are those who without conscious efforts control attitudes through suggestion. These are the unintentional propagandists —the beneficiaries of the existing order who depend in part upon social values traditional in the system to preserve it, who wish to maintain the *status quo*. Those who set about to change some feature of the existing system or the system itself are intentional propagandists; those who defend the system against such attacks are unintentional propagandists.[2] The anti-British leaders in the American Revolution, in so far as they consciously and systematically set about changing the existing laws, were intentional propagandists. The English officials and their supporters were unintentional propagandists until they began to agitate actively against the patriots, when they, too, became intentional propagandists.

Propaganda today is the inevitable accompaniment of every sales campaign, every election, every diplomatic move, and every international crisis. It came into popular consciousness during the World War and has since become the subject of almost daily conversation. Yet it is not new. Throughout human history those who promoted a course of action either had to control directly the actions of people, or they had to win support by suggestion. The use of propaganda in relation to other forms of social control, such as coercion or bribery, depends, therefore, upon the degree of control that the promoters of the new idea have. When their control is weak or when they lack a strong following, propaganda is a primary necessity—it is a prerequisite to demanding action. The more democratic a community, the more need for first marshaling opinion. In a feudal or semi-feudal society, where the noble or the large plantation owner has a high degree of control over his workers, the need for propaganda is at a minimum. In a community of small independent producers, agrarian or industrial, propaganda is of great importance. Histori-

---

[2] This distinction is made by Doob, *Propaganda*, pp. 77 f.

cally, it has increased in volume and importance proportionately to the increased application of the democratic principle, but it has always been present in every society to greater or less degree.

The only differences between modern and ancient promoters are in a greater awareness of the utility of propaganda and in the use of new techniques. There were propagandists in the past as now, whatever they may have called themselves. It is of necessity so. We know today that large bodies of people never co-operate in any complex movement except under the guidance of a central machine operated by a comparatively few people and except, lacking authoritarian control, after a prolonged period of agitation; we know that in all revolutions sufficient unity of opinion is prerequisite to an attempt at rebellion and requisite to the maintenance of the revolutionaries in power once they have rebelled.[3]

In the American Revolution as in all revolutions propaganda was extensively and effectively used. Had the Revolution been the work of a majority, united on methods and objectives, in sure control of the movement throughout, there would have been little necessity for propaganda. That it was not is obvious. It is true that throughout the colonial period there were conditions tending toward a separation of England and America. There was the gradual divergence of institutions, customs, language, and interests; there was the steady infiltration of non-English people who found a freer life in America than they had known in Europe and were at best but indifferent to the mother country of their compatriots; there were the weakness, the confusion, and the selfishness of British policy. The revolution of 1763 in British commercial policy, a change which adversely affected so many colonial interests, destroyed many of the bonds between mother country and colony, and the removal of the French menace in 1763 by the Treaty of Paris broke one of the strongest ties binding the colonies to England. But it is also true that in 1763 there were serious dissensions among the colonists, and that there were still solid benefits of union with England. There was still the British protection of trade and commerce; there was still the imperial defense against the Indians; and there were still the bounties to many colonial producers. It was by no means sure that the million or so straggling settlers, but loosely united in their disparate,

[3] Walter Lippmann, *Public Opinion*, p. 228.

quarrelsome governments, would unite to challenge the greatest empire in the world. The difficulties the leaders faced at every stage of the conflict, the coercion and violence by which thousands were forced into acquiescence or exile, the indifference and malingering of thousands of others, and the constant dissensions which disrupted the leadership itself are sure evidences that the Revolution was at best but the work of an aggressive minority.

Propaganda was thus indispensable to those who first promoted resistance to specific British acts and ultimately urged revolution. Even under such provocation as the Stamp Act spontaneous action is incredible; some there had to be who, sensing the popular but unexpressed opposition, first made articulate the popular attitudes and provided the machinery through which they could express themselves in concrete action. Within a generation the settlers had first united with England to destroy the power of France on the Continent, had then completely nullified British legislation within the colonies, had revolutionized their own governments, and had then united with their ancient enemy France to defeat the mother country. Within a generation a revolution in thought and institutions had crystallized. This was not accomplished by chance. The evidences of a conscious, systematic effort on the part of certain colonial leaders to gain public support for their ideas are unmistakable. "By their fruits ye shall know them."

I

WHIG PROPAGANDA
1763-1776

I

PROPAGANDISTS

THE NUMBER of people who consciously and systematically attempted to arouse anti-British sentiment was not large. The creative
leadership of any movement is always small. The influence of the
small body of propagandists, however, was out of all proportion to
its size. From the Whig propagandists came the ideas which ration-
alized the economic, political, and social interests of those who opposed British legislation, and from them came the popularization of
those ideas.

In the main the propagandists were substantial, propertied people, people of standing in their communities. Assemblymen, merchants, manufacturers, planters, lawyers, writers, and preachers, they
were influential in the life of their colonies long before the Revolution, and had, many of them, assured positions of cultural and intellectual leadership as well. A survey of some of the more important
will demonstrate their understanding of the prior necessity of opinion to action.

Sam Adams owned no superior as a propagandist. No one in
the colonies realized more fully than he the primary necessity of
arousing public opinion, no one set about it more assiduously. His
entire life up to 1763 had equipped him perfectly for the work.
Harvard training grounded him in the classics and gave him an
equally profitable acquaintance with Locke and the liberal writers of
the eighteenth century. He read theology and abandoned the ministry, he read law and abandoned the bar, he entered business and
lost a thousand pounds.[1] Each experience narrowed the field of his
future endeavors and finally forced him into the one field in which
he had any real interest and for which he had any real talent—
politics. But these experiences did more: they gave him a substantial
background for his later efforts. He had absorbed the political im-

[1] W. V. Wells, *The Life and Public Services of Samuel Adams*, gives copious detail;
R. V. Harlow, *Samuel Adams, Promoter of the Revolution*, interprets Adams as suffering
from an inferiority complex; and J. C. Miller, *Sam Adams, Pioneer in Propaganda*,
interprets him as motivated by a Puritan complex.

plications of the eighteenth-century nonconformist thought, he had learned the legal approach to the rights of his colony, and he had seen the effects of British interference in its internal economic and political affairs. Academically he had been thoroughly interested in the eighteenth-century discussions of liberty, and became realistically concerned when an act of Parliament ruined a very promising venture of his father—the ill-fated Massachusetts Land Bank—which nearly resulted in the complete loss of his patrimony.[2] With a group of other young men he had formed in 1748 a club which carried on the political activities of Elisha Cooke, who had for years plagued the royal governors. This club published a newspaper called the *Independent Advertiser*,[3] and at twenty-six years of age Adams was writing essays on liberty in the style of the natural rights philosophers. Two years before this, he held his first office in the town of Boston—clerk of the market—and from then on was a typical office seeker. Through the Boston Caucus Club he was elected to several offices and in turn found the Club an immense service to him later in his political and revolutionary activities in Boston. It does not appear, however, that he managed any of these offices with conspicuous success until he began drafting instructions to Boston's assemblymen and entered the assembly himself in 1765. This was the first field opened to him in which he could use his real abilities. In him are found the elements of the perfect Whig agitator.

His varied career and intimate knowledge of so many aspects of New England's life made him almost a composite of the aggrieved American; he could speak with assurance for the clergyman, the lawyer, and the merchant, and with his secret knowledge of what the people thought, wished, feared, and hated, he could interpret to the public "its own conscience and its own consciousness"—therein lay his strength.[4] In addition to this sureness of knowledge and complete identity of himself with his times there were the will and the qualities to do the task—tremendous physical energy, inexhaustible patience, a burning zeal for the doctrines of liberty, and religious fervor for the tenets of Puritanism.[5] "I will oppose this

---

[2] *Ibid.*, pp. 23 f.
[3] It was published by Rogers and Fowle from January 4, 1748, to April, 1750.
[4] M. C. Tyler, *The Literary History of the American Revolution, 1763-1783*, II, 42.
[5] Miller, *Sam Adams*, particularly emphasizes the influence of Puritanism on Adams' thinking.

tyranny at the threshold, though the fabric of liberty fall, and I perish in its ruins."[6]

To the task of opposing British encroachments on colonial rights, Adams brought his every ability—"All are not dead; and where there is a Spark of patriotick fire, *we* will enkindle it."[7] From the first issue of the *Independent Advertiser* in January, 1748, to the Declaration of Independence he was constantly writing for the press under a variety of pseudonyms—at least twenty-five have been recognized as his.[8] The number of his essays and controversial articles must have run into the hundreds. During the height of the pre-revolutionary struggle he practically filled the pages of the *Boston Gazette,* writing essays, clipping items from other papers, extracting pertinent bits from his private correspondence, editing news items—all with the one idea of arousing anti-British feeling. He carried on a voluminous correspondence with leaders in England and America, insinuating his ideas and gaining support for his policies. He was instrumental in forming revolutionary organizations, such as committees of correspondence, and was a member of many of the more important Boston and Massachusetts committees. His activities were directed toward preparing opinion. He wrote James Warren: as it cannot be foreseen what the British ministry may do, "it will be wise for us to be ready *for all Events,* that we may make the *best Improvement* of them."[9]

He was at his best in writing and in political manipulation; public oratory was never his real field and, although he could speak with force and distinction at times, he was no true mob leader. Moreover, he was no social incendiary. The social institutions of Massachusetts were in no danger from his activities.[10] Although he was

---

[6] Wells, *Life of Adams,* I, 217, citing a manuscript memoir of Adams written by his daughter after his death.

[7] *Warren-Adams Letters,* I, 14, Samuel Adams to James Warren, Dec. 9, 1772.

[8] Wells lists twenty-three, and H. A. Cushing, the editor of *The Writings of Samuel Adams,* includes essays signed by twenty-five different pen names.

[9] *Warren-Adams Letters,* I, 24.

[10] Everyone, of course, spoke of the sanctity of property. That was part of the eighteenth-century philosophy—the rights to life, liberty, and property were inalienable. England by levying taxes in America was invading the sacred rights of property. Adams' whole career is sufficient evidence that he had no love for mass government. He said in 1771: "I am not of levelling principles: But I am apt to think, that constitution of civil government which admits equality in the most extensive degree, consistent with the true design of government, is the best." The true design of government, he thought, was that man might enjoy a greater share of the blessings resulting from his social nature than he would if he

closely identified with the leaders of the working classes in Boston, he made few public appeals to the illiterate. The written appeal was his forte. He did far better work among his own people and in his own assembly than he ever did in the broader field of colonial affairs and in the Continental Congress. His contribution lay in his superb organization of the movement in New England and in the unity of opinion he achieved throughout the colonies by his ceaseless agitation against the colonial policies of Great Britain.

Associated with Sam Adams in Massachusetts was a group which knew and practiced the arts of mass suggestion. John Adams, never the propagandist his cousin was, wrote heavily for the press and gave his aid to the Sons of Liberty, writing inscriptions for their transparencies. He said, many years after the Revolution, of the public addresses of the Continental Congress, "I never bestowed much attention on any of those addresses, which were all but repetitions of the same things, the same facts and arguments . . . I was in great error, no doubt . . . for those things were necessary to give popularity to our cause, both at home and abroad."[11] Yet he bestowed much attention upon his own writing. His earnest desire, he said, was to avoid "all exceptionable scribbling in the newspaper of every kind" and to discuss questions "without all painting, pathos, rhetoric, or flourish of every kind."[12] His essays abundantly prove that he was successful. They are sober, dignified, and at times eloquent in their sincerity.

Different as his appeal was from that of his cousin Sam's, it was still designed to arouse opposition to British legislation. Articles in 1765 attacked the Stamp Act as another instance of the constant tyranny in human history of civil and ecclesiastical authority, which had to be defeated if men were to be happy. Others in 1767 attacked Governor Bernard of Massachusetts, the local tyrant.[13] In the dull days after the repeal of the Townshend Act in 1770, he aided Sam Adams by attacking openly, under his own name, the British plan of paying certain colonial officials out of revenue obtained in Amer-

---

were in a state of nature.—"Vindex," *The Boston Gazette*, Jan. 21, 1771; also in *Writings*, II, 142-153.

[11] *The Works of John Adams*, X, 80, a statement to Jefferson in 1813. On his relations with the Sons of Liberty, see *ibid.*, II, 178 ff., 183, 184.

[12] *Familiar Letters of John Adams and His Wife*, pp. 11, 16.

[13] John Adams' essays are in his *Works*, III, 469-500.

ica. These articles, which ran in the *Boston Gazette* from January 11 to February 22, 1773, bolstered Sam Adams' political theory with a full discussion of the legal aspects of the problem. His controversy with Daniel Leonard in 1774 produced one of the important statements of the legal exemption of the colonies from parliamentary jurisdiction and was of particular influence in its effect on New England opinion. He looked with approval on the efforts of others to keep alive the spirit of liberty by demonstrations and celebrations, although taking no active part in arranging them, and in many other ways showed that he knew the necessity of arousing the people. He intimated to his own minister that he should take politics into his pulpit, he wrote his friends to send him letters that he might publish, and soon after independence was declared he wrote, "A more exalted love of their country, a more enthusiastic ardor for military glory, and deeper detestation, disdain, and horror of martial disgrace must be excited among our people, or we shall perish in infancy."[14]

Then there was Josiah Quincy the younger, emotional and delicate, who for all the weight of his legal learning never burdened his effective essays with heavy detail. He could popularize a constitutional argument as well as anyone in the colonies and knew the central fact of crowd psychology—that emotion, not reason, determined action. Listen to this passage from one of his early essays:

> "Who has the front to ask, wherefore do you complain? . . . Are not pensioners, stipendiaries, and salary-men (unknown before,) hourly multiplying on us, to riot in the spoils of miserable America? . . . Is not the bread taken out of the childrens mouths and given unto the Dogs? Are not our estates given to corrupt sycophants, without a design, or even a pretence, of solliciting our assent, and our lives put into the hands of those whose tender mercies are cruelties? . . . In short, what have we to lose, what have we to fear? . . . By the sweat of our brow, we earn the little we possess; from nature, we derive the common rights of man, and by charter we claim the liberties of Britons: Shall we, dare we, pusillanimously, surrender our birthrights? . . . Is the obligation to our fathers discharged—is the

---

[14] Edmund C. Burnett, *Letters of Members of the Continental Congress*, II, 57. See also John Adams to Moses Gill, June 10, 1775, Revolutionary Letters, Mass. Archives, CXCIII, 349 f.

debt we owe posterity paid?   Answer me, thou coward! who hidest thyself in the hour of trial!"[15]

Therein is contained a summary of almost the entire revolutionary argument. Quincy first began his agitation against British internal regulation of the colonies in 1767 with a series of articles signed "Hyperion" and continued writing all through 1770, 1771, and 1772,[16] for as he said, "Our hemisphere is calm, but the diviners of our political sky see a cloud at the horizon, though not bigger than a hand. They who have reason to fear a storm, will seek a shelter."[17] Although he, together with John Adams, had defended the soldiers accused of the Boston Massacre and triumphantly won his case, not four months later he lamented hearing "so little discourse relative to a decent, manly, and instructive commemoration of the melancholy tragedy of the 5th of March, 1770" and urged an annual speech on that occasion to hold forth the "fatal effects of the policy of standing armies."[18] A tour through the South in 1773, during which he met prominent men in each colony, gave him opportunity to spread his views and those of his fellow workers and to promote the necessary unanimity of opinion: " 'To think justly, is [certainly] not sufficient'—but we must think *alike*, before we shall form a union;—that truly formed, we are invincible. They who have the principles of freemen, feel them;—the sensation once felt, it directs 'the band of the undivided and free.' A spark of fire inflames a compact building, a spark of spirit will as soon enkindle a united people."[19] His last effort in America was the pamphlet, *Observations on the Act of Parliament Commonly Called the Boston Port-Bill*, addressed to the "Freeholders and Yeomanry of my Country," the virtue, strength, and fortitude of a state. He sailed for England in September, 1774, to gain what friendships he could for America and died on the return voyage in April, 1775, just a few days after the battle he had foreseen. The cause lost much that April day.

Even more emotional was Joseph Warren, who knew how to "animate the dejected" by hopeful letters and how to insinuate his

[15] *Boston Gazette*, Oct. 3, 1768.
[16] A good list is in Josiah Quincy, *Memoir of the Life of Josiah Quincy, Junior, of Massachusetts Bay; 1774-1775*, p. 67.
[17] *Ibid.*, p. 147.   (To George Clymer, Aug., 1773.)
[18] *Ibid.*, p. 51.   [19] *Ibid.*, pp. 146 ff.

ideas through others: "it may not be amiss to try how far some further steps for securing our rights might (if absolutely necessary) be approved by our brethren on the continent."[20] The people must be constantly advised of the British program for the complete destruction of all representative government in America, he said. "A fair state of this matter, done by the masterly hand of some of our worthy friends at the Congress, would open the eyes of many."[21] He utilized every position he held for the dissemination of propaganda, and not a committee he served on but became an agency for spreading the ideas of the radical party. The appeal in his letters and essays found even more violent outlet in his speeches. One of these, on the Boston Massacre, contains such incredible passages as this:

"Approach we then the melancholy walk of death. Hither let me call the gay companion, here let him drop a farewell tear upon that body which so late he saw vigorous and warm with social mirth—hither let me lead the tender mother to weep over her beloved son—come widowed mourner, here satiate thy grief; behold thy murdered husband gasping on the ground, and to complete the pompous show of wretchedness bring in each hand thy infant children to bewail their father's fate— take heed, ye infant babes, lest, whilst your streaming eyes are fixed on the ghastly corpse, *your feet slide on the stones bespattered with your father's brains.* . . . We wildly stare about, and with amazement ask, Who spread this ruin round us? What wretch has dared deface the image of his God? Has haughty France or cruel Spain sent forth her myrmidons? Has the grim savage rushed again from the wilderness? Or does some fiend, fierce from the depths of hell, with all the rancorous malice which the apostate damned can feel, twang her deadly arrows at our breast? No: none of these; . . . it is the hand of Britain that inflicts the wound. The arms of George, our rightful king, have been employed to shed that blood which freely would have flown at his command when justice, or the honor of his crown, had called his subjects to the field."[22]

[20] Richard Frothingham, Jr., *Life and Times of Joseph Warren*, pp. 357, 382.
[21] *Ibid.*, p. 340.
[22] Conveniently found in Hezekiah Niles, *Principles and Acts of the Revolution in America*, p. 20. This oration was printed in *Boston Gazette*, Mar. 17, 1775, and *Pa. Journal, Supplement*, Mar. 29, 1775, and in pamphlet form in both Boston and New York.

With such words as these, typical of all his writing and speaking, it is no wonder that minuteman met redcoat by Concord's quiet stream. The only wonder is that they had not met sooner; Warren at least had done his best.

Another was James Otis, whose wild harangues in Boston town meeting did more for the cause among the lower people than did his bitter pamphlets. Although he hated violence, his speeches against British officials were so inflammatory that mob action was almost inevitable. The British called him mad even before he was so badly wounded and said of him that he had "contributed more than any *one* man to bring us into the state of *out-lawry* and confusion we are now in."[23] He exposed constantly in the press what he called designs of "the Cabal against this Country," using both the pamphlet and the newspaper, and spread throughout his circle the doctrine of liberty in internal affairs.[24] Although he did not figure prominently in the movement after 1770, no one did more than he to raise the preliminaries of the storm which finally broke upon the colonies in 1775.

Outside of Boston, Joseph Hawley of Northampton aided in forming the local revolutionary organizations in his community and was closely associated with Sam Adams and the Boston radicals. A first-class lawyer, he did some writing himself, stressing the legal aspects of the controversy. He constantly agitated against any British interference in local affairs, and like other good propagandists he first went about the task of gaining public support for his ideas, determined to take no final steps until he had the "express categorical decision of the continent."[25]

[23] *Boston Gazette*, Dec. 28, 1767. Transcripts of Materials Relating to American History in the British Museum, C. O. 5, vol. 43, f. 121, p. 136. Yet Otis himself said, "no possible circumstances, though ever so oppressive, could be supposed sufficient to justify private tumults and disorders." Quoted in Richard Frothingham, *Rise of the Republic of the United States*, pp. 206 f.

[24] E.g., N. Y. *Journal, Supplement*, Oct. 5, 1769. His brother wrote "Liberty" over the door of his place of business, and his father read to large circles of the common people the *Oration, Upon the Beauties of Liberty* and "recommends it as an excellent production."—*Works of John Adams*, II, 320.

[25] To Thomas Cushing, Feb. 22, 1775, Revolutionary Letters, Mass. Arch., CXCIII, 33. Sam Adams said of him, "if there be a Lawyer in the house in Major Hawley's Absence, there is no one in whom I incline to confide in."—*Writings of Sam Adams*, II, 430. For a discussion of Hawley's legal practice, see E. F. Brown, *Joseph Hawley, Colonial Radical*. Hawley wrote one of the committee reports for the assembly in 1772, and Governor Hutchinson gloomily reported that it was "well adapted to the purpose of inducing the people to believe, that their rights by charter were invaded."—*The History of the Colony of Massachusetts Bay*, III, 358.

One of the ablest of the early New England propagandists was Stephen Hopkins, founder of the *Providence Gazette* and author of one of the best pamphlets against the Stamp Act. He had been governor of Rhode Island as early as 1755 and was a constant political rival of Samuel Ward of Newport. He distrusted Ward and the *Newport Mercury,* which he considered insufficiently patriotic. Therefore, he took a leading part in establishing the *Providence Gazette,* and his articles against the Stamp Act first appeared there. They were later collected in a pamphlet edition, called *The Rights of the British Colonies Examined.* His health was poor, however, and he did not figure after 1776.[26]

William Livingston, New York and New Jersey politician, was a self-confessed propagandist of real ability. Above rather than of the people, he knew them shrewdly and was one of the few who during the war not only realized the urgency of reanimating their enthusiasm but set about it. His finest work was done after the war was declared, not before. The family, politically influential in New York and dour Presbyterians,[27] found their most determined opposition in the wealthier, Anglican De Lanceys. Young Will, studying away in the 1740's at the parentally imposed law books (for he had wanted to paint), saw Anglicans taking over the newly founded King's College, Anglicans arrogantly demanding an American bishop, and Anglican De Lanceys about to wreck the political power of his family. His Presbyterian dislike of establishments fully confirmed by this doleful outlook, Livingston began a long fight on the Anglicans, writing persistently against the plans for an American episcopate, until his essays had, as he said, "an universal alarm. . . . For I take it that clamour is at present our best policy, and that if the country can be animated against it, our superiors at home will not be easily induced to grant so arrogant a claim, at the expense of the public tranquility."[28]

With such ideas and with his background, William Livingston could not conceivably have been a Tory; yet he was in some apparent doubt himself, and it was not until independence was safely declared and he was irrevocably bound to the cause as governor of New Jer-

[26] The Rhode Island leaders are discussed in the second volume of S. G. Arnold, *History of the State of Rhode Island.*

[27] Philip Livingston, William's brother, strongly inclined to Anglicanism.

[28] Theodore Sedgwick, Jr., *Memoir of the Life of William Livingston,* pp. 136 f.

sey that he again called upon his abilities as a propagandist, aware
that the campaign of mind was as hard as the campaign of arms.
He established the first New Jersey newspaper during the Revolution and understood thoroughly its use. When asked by Washington
to write against the proposed reconciliation with Great Britain in
1778, he replied immediately:

> "I have sent Collins a number of letters, as if by different
> hands, not even excluding the tribe of petticoats,[29] all calcu-
> lated to caution America against the insidious arts of enemies.
> This mode of rendering a measure unpopular, I have frequently
> experienced in my political days to be of surprising efficacy, as
> the common people collect from it that everybody is against it,
> and for that reason those who are really for it grow discouraged,
> from magnifying in their own imagination the strength of their
> adversaries beyond its true amount."[30]

His essays, broadsides, and speeches all show a real knowledge
of crowd psychology. The most important motive in war psychosis
is not reason or justice, or even self-interest, but hate, and he knew
it. Compare this paragraph from one of his addresses to the New
Jersey legislature with anti-German propaganda of the World War:

> "They have warred upon decrepid age; warred upon de-
> fenceless youth. They have committed hostilities against the
> possessors of literature; and the ministers of religion: Against
> public records; and private monuments; and books of improve-
> ment; and papers of curiosity; and against the Arts and Sciences.
> They have butchered the wounded, asking for quarter; mangled
> the dying, weltering in their blood; refused to the dead the
> rights of sepulture; suffered prisoners to perish for want of sus-
> tenance; violated the chastity of women; disfigured private
> dwellings of taste and elegance; and in the rage of impiety and
> barbarism, profaned edifices dedicated to Almighty God . . .
> who will not always suffer *the sceptre of the wicked to rest on
> the lot of the righteous. . . .*"[31]

[29] One letter is signed "Belinda."
[30] *Ibid.*, p. 282 (Apr. 27, 1778). Collins was the printer of the *New Jersey Gazette*.
The same day Livingston also wrote Henry Laurens, "Tho' my good friends in New-York
have faithfully promised to cut my throat for writing, which they seem to resent more than
fighting, I have already begun to sound the Alarm in our Gazette in a variety of Letters,
as tho' every body execrated the proposals of Britain."—Henry Laurens Papers.
[31] 2 *New Jersey Archives*, I, 301-305.

That might have been written in 1918.

Even young Alexander Hamilton, not yet turned twenty, realized at this early age the importance of first stimulating the public consciousness. "The tories will be no doubt very artful and intriguing," he wrote John Jay, "and it behooves us to be very vigilant and cautious. I have thrown out a handbill or two to give the necessary alarm, and shall second them by others."[32] He made liberal use of the newspapers, publishing a series of essays in the New York *Journal* beginning with one on the destruction of the tea in Boston harbor and continuing through 1774. In 1775 he published his remarks on the Quebec Act, with the design of proving "that arbitrary power and its great engine, the Popish religion, are, to all intents and purposes, established in that province," with the effect that the king is "like to have no other subjects in this part of his domain, than Roman Catholics." During the war he inspired the Whigs with accounts of the battles, done up with the "usual embellishments of a newspaper paragraph," to use his own phrase.[33] His pamphlets in refutation of the "Westchester Farmer" were written with full knowledge of the important classes in New York to which he must appeal. The first, *A Full Vindication of the Measures of Congress*, was addressed to the farmers of New York, and the closing pages consist of an extremely well-written appeal, in simple yet forceful language, to those "who would lose most, should you be foolish enough to counteract the prudent measures our worthy Congress have taken for the preservation of your liberties." All his work in this period indicated the sure touch of the good propagandist.

Pennsylvania produced some of the best propagandists of the period. Thomas Paine, agitator and propagandist supreme, was not connected with the revolutionary movement by the facts of his condition and environment, as were the great majority of the Whig leaders. His association with it was almost an accident. Introduced to Philadelphia printing circles by Benjamin Franklin after a drab and undistinguished career in England, he began unimportant writing for the *Pennsylvania Magazine* shortly after his arrival in November, 1774. This writing was for the most part not political in character, although Paine did write a poem, "The Liberty Tree,"

[32] *The Correspondence and Public Papers of John Jay*, I, 41.
[33] *The Works of Alexander Hamilton*, I, 85.

which was published in its pages. *Common Sense* and the *Crisis* letters, written during the war, establish sufficiently his claims as a propagandist. He sensed as did few others the radical temper and could express to people what they themselves thought and felt in striking, popular language. He was not an original thinker, and as Adams said of *Common Sense*, there was nothing in it that had not been frequently urged on the floor of the Continental Congress.

He was far more radical in his social theories than the other propagandists of the upper classes and was, of course, not identified with their interests except in the one particular of the revolutionary movement. His northern compatriots did not share his deistic notions, his southern friends did not share his antislavery ideas, and few leaders anywhere shared his ideas of private property. But these were ideas and concepts immaterial to the immediate problem of independence, and the Puritan New Englanders, the slave-holding southerners, and the propertied leaders everywhere had no compunctions about using the crude vigor of Paine's English to further their own objectives. There is still power in the famous essay, read by Washington's order to his troops, which begins "These are the times that try men's souls. The summer soldier and the sunshine patriot will in this crisis, shrink from the service of his country; but he that stands it NOW, deserves the love and thanks of man and woman." The stirring sibilants, the epigrammatic vigor of these lines heartened the discouraged little band of winter patriots left with Washington. So it was with all his writings—each one perfectly timed, perfectly adapted to the needs of the moment.

Aside from Paine there was a small group of Pennsylvania agitators who, while not showing evidences of consistent propaganda activities throughout the entire period, yet aided materially at certain times. Franklin, of course, was a propagandist the equal of Sam Adams, but his work was primarily designed to mold English and French opinion. Even though he was in America only one year between the passage of the Stamp Act and the signing of the treaty of peace, his propaganda activities were of considerable importance in the colonies. He was of course the perfect embodiment of the middle-class American, but more than that, no one of his class had greater influence with the discontented back-country men. He had been largely instrumental in quelling the Paxton riots in 1764, and even when he was in England it is said that he arranged with Herman Husband, North Carolina regulator, for the distribution of pamphlets through the southern back country, where the influence of both men was strong.[34] Some of his most famous pieces—the "Edict of the King of Prussia" and "Rules by which a Great Empire may be Reduced to a Small One"—he himself sent over to be published in American papers. The latter, he said to Cushing, was written "to expose, in as striking a light as I could, to the nation, the absurdity of the measures towards America. . . . These odd ways of presenting Matters to the publick View sometimes occasion them to be more read, talk'd of, and more attended to."[35] He promoted, often at considerable expense to himself, the publication of pamphlets which he thought would be of value in America and was the first to see the real possibilities in the use of cartoons. He saw most clearly that one of the essential propaganda problems was to give the appearance of unity to American protests, "to show that the discontents were really general and their sentiments concerning their rights unanimous, and not the fiction of a few demagogues."[36]

John Dickinson, a quiet, conservative Quaker, is perhaps the very antithesis of the popular conception of a propagandist. Yet a series of letters he wrote in 1767, called "Letters from a Farmer in Pennsylvania to the Inhabitants of the British Colonies," determined the legal argument against the Townshend Acts. Their appearance has been called the most brilliant literary event of the entire Revolution. Earlier, Dickinson had written against the Stamp Act, and in 1768 he composed the "American Liberty Song." In 1773 he answered Sam Adams' request for further efforts with a broadside opposing the Tea Act, not because of the legal principles involved, but because the British East India Company now "cast their Eyes on America, as a new Theatre, whereon to exercise their Talents of Rapine, Oppression and Cruelty."[37]

Thomas Mifflin, Thomas McKean, and Joseph Reed furthered their political aspirations by timely speeches or written appeals di-

---

[34] E. W. Caruthers, *A Sketch of the Life and Character of the Rev. David Caldwell,* pp. 119 f.

[35] The quoted passages occur in two separate letters to Thomas Cushing, Sept. 12, Sept. 23, 1773. See *The Writings of Benjamin Franklin,* VI, 125, 137.

[36] *Ibid.,* p. 115.

[37] The article was signed "Rusticus"; it is conveniently found in *The Writings of John Dickinson, 1764-1774,* I, 460. See also Tyler, *Literary History,* I, 234.

rected against England. Mifflin and McKean both aided the radical movement by addressing large meetings of the people, and Reed wrote for the press in defense of the acts of the Continental Congress, although he adopted reluctantly the idea of independence.[38]

James Wilson, one of the keenest legal minds in the colonies, did not come to America until 1765, but he soon built up a huge law practice (he had studied under John Dickinson) among the Germans in Reading. He became a rabid land speculator and took an active part in the early work of organizing the western counties for the Revolution. He presented one of the ablest of the pamphlets on the subject of internal freedom—*Considerations on the Nature and Extent of the Legislative Authority of Parliament*—but the violence of the Revolution alienated him. He wrote but did not publish an article, designed, he said, "to lead the public mind into the idea of independence," and when the Declaration was passed he voted for it but was dubious about the wisdom of the act. He was completely out of Pennsylvania politics during the Revolution and did not hold office until the conservatives got back into power in 1782.[39]

The most active committeeman and agitator in Maryland was Samuel Chase. An intense partisan and a natural agitator, he depended more upon his violent boldness and tremendous physical energy than upon finesse or shrewd management; a direct frontal attack was his way. He led rioters in Maryland at the time of the Stamp Act and was the most tireless worker of every committee he served on, and he served on many. Little of his work was done through the press, for he relied upon the sheer power of his presence to influence. Once, however, he realized that more was needed. When Maryland was wavering on the matter of independence, Chase hurriedly left Congress on June 14, 1776, to attend the Maryland convention from the twenty-first of June to the sixth of July.

[38] Reed's essays may be found in Reed Papers, III, 31 ff. Mifflin wrote against the Tea Act in *Pa. Journal*, Oct. 13, 1773.—Emmett Collection, No. 2906, a letter from Benjamin Rush to William Gordon, Oct. 10, 1773. Mifflin also made several speeches of importance—see William Hooper to Joseph Hewes, Nov. 30, 1776, Hayes Collection; and Rawle, "A Sketch of the Life of Thomas Mifflin," Hist. Soc. Pa., *Memoirs*, Vol. II, pt. 2, pp. 110 f. Thomas McKean addressed meetings in Newcastle and Lewestown in July, 1774.—*Pa. Gazette*, July 6, 1774; Peter Force, comp., *American Archives: Consisting of a Collection of authentick Records, State Papers, Debates and Letters*, 4th series (hereinafter cited 4 Force, *Amer. Arch.*), I, 658-661.

[39] There are several early editions of Wilson's works and a sketch in John Sanderson, *et al.*, *Biography of Signers to the Declaration of Independence*. The best account of his revolutionary career is in the *Dictionary of American Biography*.

He discovered there that his presence and his voice were not enough and went over the heads of the delegates in a successful popular appeal in behalf of independence. On the twenty-fourth he wrote John Adams: "I have not been idle. I have appealed *in writing* to the people. County after county is instructing. . . . Shall I send you my circular letter?" And triumphantly on the twenty-eighth he wrote, "I am this Moment from the House . . . with an unan:[imous] vote of our Convention for *Independence*. . . . See the glorious Effects of County Instructions—our people have fire if not smothered. . . ."[40]

Thomas Jefferson, now learning the arts of party leadership which were to secure him the presidency, knew how to inspirit the people with words of delusive hope and how best to reach them. Acting under "conviction of the necessity of arousing our people from the lethargy into which they had fallen as to passing events," he got the Virginia assembly in 1774 to recommend a day of fasting, humiliation, and prayer, and saw to it personally that the ministers in his area made the most of the occasion. He saw the value of committees of correspondence as propaganda agencies and knew the power of the press. The Declaration of Independence, surpassed by few if any propaganda efforts, placed within seeming grasp the unattainable aspirations of men, but only as men fought for it did they give meaning to it; each effort should *now* be made to keep up the spirits of the people, said Jefferson on July 1, 1776.[41]

Three of the Lee brothers—Arthur, William, and Richard Henry—had as clear an appreciation of the necessity of mass suggestion as any three men in the colonies. Although Arthur and William were in England the greater part of the time, they kept in close contact not only with their brother Richard Henry but with Sam Adams and other leaders as well, urging on them continually the need for constant agitation. Even in the quiet year 1772, Arthur Lee wrote Adams, "By bending all our attention to keeping alive in the People, a due sense of their wrongs, & by digesting a plan for their redress, we shall meet the first great occasion, perfectly pre-

[40] Burnett, *Letters of Members of Cont. Cong.*, I, 503 n.; *Works of John Adams*, III, 54 n., 56. The next day, Chase wrote R. H. Lee to send his "News to the Southward." —Lee Transcripts, IV, 218.
[41] *The Writings of Thomas Jefferson*, I, 9 ff.; II, 41.

pared."[42] He himself wrote a series of ten articles in 1768 for Rind's *Virginia Gazette*—the "Monitor" series, modeled on the "Farmer's Letters"—and in England wrote another series in 1770 and also two pamphlets, one in 1774 and one in 1775, both of which were sent to America. He and his brother William both urged an American congress and correspondence among the leaders in the different colonies, since "harmonizing in one great & popular measure, would influence all America, & unite it in one absolute, irresistible effort."[43]

William Lee, merchant and sheriff of London, took to himself the task of winning friends for America in London and sent to his brother in Virginia constant advice on stirring public sentiment. "In every Colony incessant pains should be used to engage the yeomanry or people at large in the same spirit of opposition with the principal men, and by degrees lead them on to the last point, if it should be necessary."[44] He sent pamphlets to be distributed, speeches to be printed in the papers, and letters to be extracted for the press. He obtained a copy of a letter Governor Dunmore of Virginia had written the Earl of Dartmouth and sent it back to be printed in Virginia, so that "the minds of men may be disposed in time to seize his person. . . ."[45]

Equally clear in his convictions that the leaders must be beforehand in preparing the people, and with greater opportunities for achieving his purpose, Richard Henry Lee began early with a published address to the people of Virginia on the iniquities of the Stamp Act, is said to have led the group which forced the resignation of Virginia's stamp distributor, and from that time on had clearly in mind the problem of prepared opinion. When Dickinson's "Farmer's Letters" appeared, he realized their value instantly and arranged for a Virginia edition: "It was the benefit of my Country that suggested the measure to me and I accordingly wrote the preface, and the terms, negotiated the whole matter with Rind, and got sev-

[42] Arthur Lee to Samuel Adams, Apr. 7, 1772, Samuel Adams Papers.
[43] *Ibid.*
[44] *Letters of William Lee,* I, 90.
[45] *Ibid.,* p. 127.   Richard Henry Lee did publish the letter, and the county committees raised a storm of protest against Dunmore.—*Virginia Gazette* (Dixon and Hunter), June 10, 1775.   Other aspects of Lee's influence on American leaders may be found in *Letters of William Lee,* I, 85, 91, 152, 155.

eral hundred subscribers for the pamphlets."[46] He knew the power of the press, bewailed the absence of any newspaper whatever in Virginia for some months in 1781, and throughout the war regretted the failure of the leaders to make use of what facilities they had for reaching the people. He supplied editors with propaganda—extracts of letters, pamphlets to be reprinted, articles written by his friends. On occasion he called on his friends for public appeals. To Landon Carter he wrote on sending him a pamphlet, "I would recommend the pamphlet to your attention, not for its merit, but that it may receive a proper answer. And such an one, it easily admits of as would make its Author blush, if it be possible for a Minister to blush. But though an answer might fail to do this, it will certainly have weight with the cool and sensible part of Mankind, and thereby perhaps, prevent the future extension of arbitrary unconstitutional power."[47] Although he did not openly advocate independence until fairly late, there is every indication that he was ready for it himself.

George Mason also engaged in propaganda activities, although not so persistently. "Among the numbers who in their small circles were propagating with activity the American doctrines was George Mason in the shade of retirement. He extended their grasp upon the opinions and affections of those with whom he conversed."[48] But his work was not confined to his own circle. He wrote with the definite purpose, as Washington put it, of stimulating the people to cordial agreements. When nonimportation engagements were being discussed, he wrote Washington that nothing definite could be done until the General Court met, but that "in the meantime it may be necessary to publish something preparatory to it in our gazettes, to warn the people of the impending danger, and induce them the more readily and cheerfully to concur in the proposed measures to avert it; and something of this sort I had begun, but am unluckily stopped by a disorder, which affects my head and eyes."[49] The more obscure Landon Carter of Sabine Hall, whose essays in the press

---

[46] *The Letters of Richard Henry Lee* (ed. J. C. Ballagh), I, 42. Quotations from this work are by permission of The Macmillan Company.

[47] *Ibid.*, pp. 8 f.

[48] Edmund Randolph's estimate of Mason, given in K. M. Rowland, *Life and Correspondence of George Mason, 1725-1792*, I, 178. Thomson Mason, George's brother, wrote a series of articles, signed "A British American," in June and July, 1774.—*Ibid.*, p. 175.

[49] *Ibid.*, p. 141.

were brought home to the people on county court days, tried know-ingly but vaguely, as all good propagandists should do, to convince them "that the case of the Bostonians was the case of all America & if they submitted to this arbitrary taxation begun by the Parliament, all America must, and then farewell to all our Liberties."[50]

Washington himself, although doing no speaking or writing, realized that no plans could be successful unless the leaders would "be at some pains to explain matters to the people, and stimulate them to cordial agreements."[51] As commander in chief of his little army he saw the dampening effect of flagging spirits and constantly urged his more literary friends to act upon the "hopes and fears of the people at large . . . in such manner, as to make them approve and second your views."[52] In the midst of dire military distress, even in the busy days of involved campaigns, he still listened intently to the confusion of voices around him and sagaciously advised Congress to give out information "in a manner calculated to attract the attention and impress the minds of the people." He saw the danger of allowing favorable news items to circulate without pointed statements as to their importance: "As they are now propagated, they run through the country in a variety of forms, are confounded in the common mass of general rumors, and lose a great part of their effect."[53]

Certain North Carolina leaders figured as self-confessed revolutionary propagandists. William Hooper, Boston born and educated, became after 1764 one of the leading lawyers of North Carolina. Aloof, aristocratic in manner, he had no love for plain people and distrusted them. He was a member of Governor Tryon's expedition against the back-country rioters in 1768 and fought the democratic features of the state constitution of 1776. Yet he was radically anti-British and not only took the lead in organizing the opposition but saw to it that his friends made sure of popular support for measures he aided in devising. He wrote Joseph Hewes and John Penn to call a provincial council, urging shrewdly, "I hope nothing will be omitted that may work upon their Reason, or affect their passions.

[50] "The Diary of Landon Carter," *William and Mary College Quarterly*, XIV, 246. See also *Letters of Richard Henry Lee*, I, 8 f., 12. Carter did not like *Common Sense* at first and wrote against it in Purdie's *Virginia Gazette*.—"Diary," XV, 20.

[51] Rowland, *Life and Correspondence of George Mason*, I, 139.

[52] *The Writings of George Washington* (ed. W. C. Ford), VIII, 298.

[53] *Ibid.*, VII, 347.

You well know the avenues that lead to their Hearts. I am sure you will pursue them attentively." When he heard rumors that troops were on the way to North Carolina he wrote again, "therefore write all your friends to stand forth & to exert themselves. Pray press the matter on Mr. Thos. P[erson] urge him to call forth the back Country."[54] John Penn immediately wrote Person, "For God's sake my Good Sir, encourage our People, animate them to dare even to die for their country."[55]

Sam Johnston, moderate though he was, yet sought popular approval for the measures he advocated. In answer to Hewes's request for activity he wrote, "I have this day invited Ned Vail and his family to dine with me that I may have an opportunity of rousing and Animating him, I shall go to Pasquotank tomorrow and will endeavour to infuse a proper spirit in every part of my small Circle."[56]

James Iredell, future dignitary of the Supreme Bench, passed from hand to hand a manuscript he had written on the causes of the war and the necessity for independence. Other pieces of his surveyed the more important aspects of the controversy from 1774 to 1778, and the charges to his grand juries declared that British depravity and cruelty were almost alone responsible for the war. William Hooper knew the value of his work: "whilst I was active in the contest, you forged the weapons which were to give success to the cause which I supported."[57]

William Henry Drayton, effective essayist until his death in 1779, was one of the few South Carolina propagandists. He first set himself against the program of the radical party, and in 1769 he wrote against the nonimportation agreement. However, he soon found himself in distress, his crops unsold or exported at a loss, his appeals for popular support in vain, and himself decidedly unpopular. He was in England for some time after this experience, but when the crisis of 1774 arose he was back in the colonies and took aggressively the popular side. He even reached the astounding position that "The Almighty created America to be independent of

[54] Hayes Collection, 1776. Hooper attended James Lovell's grammar school in Boston and was graduated from Harvard with an A.B. and later with an M.A. degree. He studied law under James Otis and moved to North Carolina in 1764.

[55] *Colonial and State Records of North Carolina*, X, 450 (Feb. 12, 1776).

[56] Hayes Collection (June 11, 1775).

[57] G. J. McRee, *Life and Correspondence of James Iredell*, I, 196.

Britain; let us beware the impiety of being backward to act as instruments in the Almighty Hand, now extended to accomplish his purpose. . . ."[58]

His pamphlets and newspaper articles all showed that he knew the elements of good propaganda. Such passages as this, for instance, have a timeless quality that simply by changing the names fits them for use in any war: "whatever may be the issue of this unlooked for defensive civil war . . . whether independence or slavery, all the blood and all the guilt must be imputed to British and not to American counsels."[59]

The political leaders who have been discussed received great help in their agitation against Great Britain from preachers, many of whom were also propagandists. Most of them no doubt caught their tone from the spirit of the times, as must all whose livelihood depends upon intimate emotional contact with their followers. Some, however, worked clearly and definitely to formulate public opinion, not only in their pulpits but outside them as well. It is significant that almost all the preacher propagandists were nonconformist clergymen associated with the older, wealthier churches.

Two of the Boston ministers were particularly important. Samuel Cooper of the Brattle Square Church exercised great influence because of his associations with the prominent revolutionary leaders—Otis, Hancock, Adams—and with the lower classes in Boston. He not only is said to have written Hancock's Fifth of March Oration but certainly did much to direct the activities of the Sons of Liberty. Charles Chauncy of the First Church, frail though he was, was yet the most influential minister in Massachusetts. He carried the burden of the fight against the establishment of an American bishopric, and in his pulpit and published sermons he attacked the encroachments of the British government on the rights of his colony and of his people.[60]

John Cleaveland of Ipswich, Separatist, soldier in the Seven

---

[58] John Drayton, *Memoirs of the American Revolution*, II, 274.

[59] David Ramsay, *The History of the American Revolution*, I, 63.

[60] Tyler, *Literary History*, II, 279 ff., 303 ff. Only one of Cooper's published sermons between 1763 and 1783 deals with revolutionary affairs. Alice M. Baldwin, *The New England Clergy and the American Revolution*, pp. 93, 156, says it was common knowledge that Cooper wrote the oration. Chauncy published several sermons on revolutionary matters. Andrew Eliot, another influential Boston minister, consistently refused to take politics into his pulpit. Jonathan Mayhew, who took a prominent part in 1765, died in 1766, or undoubtedly he would have figured largely in the development of revolutionary attitudes.

Years' War, was one of the most persistent and violent anti-British propagandists among the New England clergy. He first began to write against the royal government in 1771. A series of articles in the *Essex Gazette*, signed "Johannis in Eremo," attacked Hutchinson for his arbitrary administration, intimating that thereby the political compact had been broken and the colonies thrown back into an original society. These same ideas he developed even more fully in 1774 and 1775, and the battle of Lexington was to him the final violation of faith which dissolved the allegiance of the colonists to George III. Of Gage he said, "Without speedy repentance, you will have an aggravated damnation in hell ... you are not only a robber, a murderer, and usurper, but a wicked Rebel: A rebel against the authority of truth, law, equity, the English constitution of government, these colony states, and humanity itself."[61]

Stephen Johnson of Lyme, Connecticut, began a campaign against the Stamp Act in the fall of 1765. He saw with dismay some disposition to submit to the Act and began at once to point out its true meaning. Napthali Daggett of Yale had written against the distributors of the stamps, but Johnson attacked the very basis of the Act itself in six well-written articles published in the *New London Gazette* and widely copied. Therein he came perilously close to an open advocacy of independence and certainly justified and urged absolute rebellion against unconstitutional legislation.[62] He delivered a fast day sermon on December 18, 1765, which included these same ideas. This was later printed in a pamphlet, *Some Important Observations, Occasioned by, and Adapted to, The Public Fast.*

The Reverend Joseph Lyman and the Reverend Thomas Allen are credited with having almost alone reversed the attitude of their frontier charges, Hatfield and Pittsfield. Lyman not only preached the new doctrines of the eighteenth century on Sundays but addressed the town meetings and wrote for the papers. His influence was dominant by 1774, and the Tory party, led by Israel Williams, was badly demoralized. Thomas Allen exerted even wider influ-

---

[61] *Essex Gazette*, July 13, 1775. Others of Cleaveland's essays are *ibid.*, Jan. 8, Jan. 15, Mar. 26, Apr. 9, 1771; June 7, 1774; Apr. 18, Apr. 25, July 13, 1775.
[62] *New London Gazette*, Sept. 6, Sept. 20, Sept. 27, Oct. 4, Oct. 11, Nov. 1, 1765. See also G. H. Hollister, *The History of Connecticut*, II, 130 f.; and Baldwin, *New England Clergy*, pp. 99 f.

ence than Lyman. The Tory party was particularly strong in Pittsfield, but Allen set himself the task of destroying the power of its leaders, William Williams and Israel Stoddard. He was on the important town committees, wrote most of the town papers on the Revolution, and even engaged in coercive activities. Through the press and in public he agitated continually for the cause: "I have exerted myself to disseminate the same spirit [of liberty] in King's district, which has of late taken surprising effect. The poor tories at Kinderhook are mortified and grieved, and are wheeling about, and begin to take the quick step. New York government begins to be alive in the glorious cause and to act with vigor."[63]

William Gordon, English born, was in such sympathy with the American colonies that in 1770 he left his pastorate and emigrated to Massachusetts. He became pastor of the Third Congregational Church in Roxbury in 1772, and convinced of the justice of the patriot cause he advocated it vigorously on every opportunity. Three of his sermons—"Religious and Civil Liberty" (a fast day sermon in 1774), his election sermon of 1775, and "The Separation of the Jewish Tribes," preached on the first anniversary of the Declaration of Independence—had wide influence in New England and are fine examples of the propagandist's art. He was active in the campaign against Thomas Hutchinson, Governor of Massachusetts, copying his letters and preparing them for the press. He was an early advocate of independence and was made chaplain of both houses of the Massachusetts provincial council in 1775. He retained his influence until 1778, when he was dismissed because he attacked the inept state constitution of 1778. Until then, however, his influence was strong.[64]

Dr. John Witherspoon, president of Princeton, took no open part in the early Revolution. He did not come to New Jersey until 1768 and did not preach his first political sermon until May 17, 1776.[65] Thereafter, however, he supported the cause of independence in college, pulpit, Congress, and the press. More important in the earlier period was George Duffield of the Third Presbyterian

[63] *Ibid.*, p. 161. For accounts of these men see *ibid.*, pp. 159 ff.; and J. E. A. Smith, *The History of Pittsfield, Massachusetts*, pp. 309 f.

[64] A few of Gordon's letters are in Historical Society of Pennsylvania. See Tyler, *Literary History*, II, 423 ff.

[65] This is his own statement in the sermon, "The Dominion of Providence over the Passions of Men," *Works of John Witherspoon*, V, 176-216. His newspaper writings are *ibid.*, IX, and *passim*.

Church in Philadelphia. Although he was a newcomer to Philadelphia in 1774, the members of the Continental Congress frequently went to hear him, so decided was his stand in behalf of the colonies. He was asked to deliver several public addresses outside his own pulpit and was generally recognized by Whig and Tory alike as a powerful influence in the community. Before coming to Philadelphia he had made a missionary tour through the back country of Pennsylvania, Maryland, and Virginia, making contacts and establishing friendships which later gave greater weight to the several letters on the dispute with England which he wrote to the southern presbyteries.[66] His whole career indicates a purposive effort to arouse anti-British sentiment among the colonists.

William Tennent was one of the few southern preachers who give evidence of systematic propaganda activity. A Princeton New-light he served various charges until 1772, when he settled definitely in Charleston. There he openly agitated after 1773 for the radical party, and although he rarely took political matters into his pulpit, he frequently spoke on Sundays at the courthouse and is said to have done a great deal of writing for the press. As one writer put it, "he left no measure untried to reach the ear and heart of the inhabitants of South Carolina."[67] Political leaders recognized his ability; he was put on the local committee of intelligence and later sent with Drayton into the back country to break the hold of the Tories there.

Francis Hopkinson is one of the clearest examples of a literary propagandist. He called his own political squibs "ammunition" and during the war complained that "most of our writers have left the great field of general politics wherein they might have been of considerable service to skirmish & bushfight in the fens & thickets of Party Disputes for which I blame them much."[68] He varied frequently the form of his appeals, now writing poems, now parodies, publishing a pamphlet on this occasion, writing a letter to the press

---

[66] See Joel T. Headley, *Chaplains and Clergy of the Revolution*, pp. 350 ff.

[67] *Ibid.*, p. 117. One sermon, *An Address delivered in Charleston*, 1774, was printed.

[68] Hopkinson to Franklin, *Writings of Franklin*, VII, 351 n. He wrote his wife an account of the destruction of his home by the British, done he thought at the instance of Polly Riché, and said, "I will send some of the enclosed Papers to camp and take care it shall be in every News Paper."—Charles Hildeburn, "Loyalist Ladies of the Revolution," p. 64. A good account of Hopkinson's revolutionary activity is in George E. Hastings, *The Life and Works of Francis Hopkinson*.

on that; songs, ballads, even mock advertisements, many of them anonymous, attest his activity.

John Trumbull likewise knew the value of numerous anonymous contributions to the press and, both in Boston in 1774 and in New Haven later, he contributed to the local papers a running series of satirical comments on the policy of the British government and the official administration. After writing "M'Fingal," he sent it to Silas Deane with instructions to use it as he saw fit without divulging the authorship.[69]

This rapid sketch has shown governors, judges, preachers, writers, and three future presidents uniting to excite the people against Great Britain. They were agitators, but most of them were very dignified agitators. They were not social radicals; with the fewest exceptions they upheld the interests of the property owning, respectable groups from which they came. There were no Marats, no Kropotkins among the list, and only one Tom Paine, and his ideas on social matters did not figure at the time.

Allied with the more conservative leaders, sometimes indeed taking the lead, was an entirely different type, the boss or mob leader. Leaders of this type commanded the agencies of coercion and violence; in addition they were themselves agitators and promoters of the Revolution. Drawn from the working classes in the cities or from the lesser politicians and tradesmen, they provided the most radical opinion and action of the revolutionary movement. Necessary as they were to the upper-class leaders, they were dangerous allies. They were particularly prominent in the commercial centers but were found in agrarian areas as well.

Boston's Thomas Young, William Molineux, and Ebenezer Mackintosh were typical examples of the hierarchy of lower-class leaders. Dr. Thomas Young, Irish born, started his career in Albany, New York, as a bitter opponent of the Stamp Act. The surrounding area was much too lethargic to suit him, and in 1766 he went to Boston, where people had a stronger sense of their grievances. There his radical opinions endeared him to Sam Adams, and he became one of Adams' most trusted assistants. He carried on an extensive correspondence with John Lamb and Alexander McDougall of New York and was instrumental in organizing and directing the Sons of

---

[69] Trumbull to Silas Deane, Oct. 5, 1775, *Deane Papers, 1774-1790,* I, 86 f.

Liberty after 1767. Throughout the period he was one of the most important links between the upper- and lower-class leaders.

Young was clear-headed and independent and had a shrewd sense of revolutionary methods and problems. He encouraged William Goddard's plan for an American post, and when that was well under way he wrote Lamb, "when we have settled the present momentous affair our next Attack will be upon the Custom House. The Ursurpations there are intolerable."[70] In 1774 he went to Newport because his wife was badly affected by the disturbed conditions in Boston, and there he aided in overcoming the Tories by skillful methods. He wrote Lamb of the favorable conditions there and gave him good advice on handling the disaffected in New York: "Military Companies are forming and a great Ambition runs thro all ranks to become skillful in the use of arms. For God's sake endeavor to stir up some such thing in New York! No means which have hitherto been tried have served more to convert young gentlemen of tory sentiments than to get them embodied with the Whigs and begin to taste of their Spirit by being often in their company."[71] Later in Philadelphia he aided in drawing up the Pennsylvania constitution and served in the Continental Hospital; it was there that he contracted the disease of which he died in July, 1777.

William Molineux was one of the most radical of the lesser Boston figures. He was a trader himself, and his particular function in the revolutionary movement was to organize the merchants in the nonimportation movement. He was on the committee of inspection established in Boston in 1768 and was sent with other merchants to recalcitrant importers in Boston and even to neighboring towns where defection was feared.[72] When the economy measures were adopted in 1767, Molineux was put in charge of developing local industries and did a splendid job. He, too, was closely associated with the lower-class leaders, and much of his power as a member of the committee of inspection came from the general belief that behind him was the power of Ebenezer Mackintosh and his mob. The upper-class leaders distrusted him; as Rowe said, he was "known and disliked as an agitator."[73] He died in 1774, and two comments

---

[70] Lamb Papers, p. 40.   [71] Ibid., p. 52.

[72] See *Boston Gazette*, Jan. 22, Aug. 13, 1770, and C. M. Andrews, "Boston Merchants and the Non-Importation Movement," Col. Soc. Mass., *Publications*, XIX, 246.

[73] Ibid., p. 163.

indicate his attitudes and position in the movement: John Andrews wrote: "If he was too rash, and drove matters to an imprudent pitch, it was owing to his natural temper; as when he was in business, he pursued it with the same impetuous zeal. His loss is not much regretted by the more prudent and judicious part of the community." John Eliot wrote Jeremy Belknap more concisely: "General Molineux is dead. Some are glad & some are sorry. *Nil nisi bonum de mortuis.* It's possible he may have been actuated by noble principles."[74]

Still lower in the scale was Ebenezer Mackintosh. He was a cobbler and for a time held a minor office in Boston as a sealer of leather. He ruled over the South End mob and was said to have two or three hundred men at his command. He was the principal mob leader in Boston, and he and his followers did the damage during the Stamp Act riots of August, 1765. He was of particular prominence in the earlier period, but with the more complete organization of the movement in Boston he became of less importance and figured only slightly after 1774.[75]

Three leaders of the New York group correspond somewhat closely to the three in Boston—John Lamb, Alexander McDougall, and Isaac Sears. John Lamb, whose father had been an optician, was engaged in the liquor trade after 1760 and made a considerable sum of money out of it. He was an accomplished linguist (it was said he knew Dutch, German, and French), and was therefore particularly valuable as a leader of the polyglot workers. He was one of the original founders of the New York Sons of Liberty and was important in organizing the movement outside of New York as well. His correspondence with the leaders of the Sons of Liberty in other colonies was of primary importance in co-ordinating their activities.[76] He frequently called and addressed radical mass meetings in New York and was thus a propagandist in his own right. On the declara-

---

[74] "The Letters of John Andrews, Esq., of Boston. 1772-1776," 1 Mass. Hist. Soc., *Proceedings*, VIII, 379; and Belknap Papers, Vol. III, Nov. 8, 1774. He was called "Paoli" Molineux and was referred to by the Tories as the "first Leader in Dirty Matters."—Quoted from J. C. Miller, *Sam Adams, Pioneer in Propaganda*, p. 87, by permission of Little, Brown and Company. On his promotion of spinning, see *Reports of the Record Commissioners of the City of Boston* (hereinafter cited *Boston Town Records*), *1758-1769*, pp. 273 ff.; *1770-1777*, p. 73.

[75] G. P. Anderson, "A Note on Ebenezer Mackintosh," Col. Soc. Mass., *Publications*. XXVI, 348-366.

[76] In addition to the letters themselves in the Lamb Papers, there is also a biography: Isaac Leake, *Memoir of the Life and Times of General John Lamb*.

tion of war he joined the army almost immediately and, wounded at Quebec, was captured. He rose in command to Brigadier General after being paroled, but after the war, although he made a small fortune speculating in confiscated loyalist lands, he lost it all and died penniless.

Alexander McDougall, the so-called John Wilkes of New York, was the son of a milk peddler and a fairly well-to-do woman. He sailed with a privateer during the Seven Years' War and with his profits he set himself up in trade in New York City. He, with Lamb, was one of the originators of the Sons of Liberty but contested with Lamb for pre-eminence in the organization and at one time split the Sons of Liberty. More radical than Lamb he was successfully accused of libel because of an inflammatory handbill, *To the Betrayed Inhabitants of New York*, printed in 1770, and was imprisoned. There, as one of his enemies said, he lay "imitating Mr. Wilkes in everything he can."[77] Two weeks after he was finally dismissed by the court (he had been released from prison some time before), he wrote Joseph Reed, inclosing "very alarming and interesting" news from England and added, "oh that the Spirit of Brutus & Casius Possessed the People of England we might hope for a Better Issue than was effected by their Virtuous struggles. What will become of the much Envied Constitution of England and these Distressed Colonies."[78] He wrote and spoke in an effort to arouse the lower classes and, unlike Lamb, continued his propaganda activities during the war, even though in the army.[79] He and Lamb both consulted William Smith and were themselves called into consultation by the upper-class leaders in times of crisis.[80]

Isaac Sears, the real mob leader in New York, was also a privateer during the Seven Years' War, but he lost his vessel in 1761 and established himself in the West Indian trade in New York. He had much the same type of following in New York as Mackintosh did in Boston and was the leader of most of the riots. He it was who seized the guns when the news of the battle of Lexington and

[77] *Colden Letter Books, 1760-1775*, II, 212.
[78] Joseph Reed Papers (May 15, 1771).
[79] Alexander McDougall to Philip Schuyler, Dec. 12, 1778, Schuyler Papers.
[80] McDougall's manuscripts are in the N. Y. Hist. Soc. There are many references to him in the Diary of William Smith. Information may also be found in Thomas Jones, *The History of New York during the Revolutionary War . . .*, and in the *Dictionary of American Biography*.

Concord reached New York and for days terrified the Tories. He was associated with the merchants and was on some of the merchant committees, but his principal function as a leader of the lower classes was to aid in organizing and directing coercive activities. He was in close communication with upper-class leaders, although they could not always control him, and with Lamb and McDougall he formed the plans for New York's resistance to British legislation and directed the mob activities against the Tories.[81]

Much less is known of lower-class leaders in other communities. Samuel Crandall of Rhode Island appears vaguely as the organizer of the riots against the customs officers in Newport, and Isaac Howell, a liquor dealer in Philadelphia, was known to have influence with the Philadelphia working men. Osborn Sprigg of Annapolis led the crowds which harassed the stamp distributor and much later the Tory preacher, Jonathan Boucher. William Johnson, an influential mechanic, and Christopher Gadsden were the principal leaders of the Charleston working men. Gadsden, the acknowledged leader of the South Carolina radicals, was not of the lower classes himself. He had a plantation, four stores, and a wharf. It was through his commercial connections that he became the leader of the Charleston workingmen, whom he organized in 1766 for political purposes.[82]

[81] The Diary of William Smith contains many references to the relations of Sears, Lamb, McDougall, and Smith. Sears was inspector of pot and pearl ashes for the city of New York and was charged with corruption in office.—N. Y. *Journal*, Apr. 4, 1771. He conceived the idea in 1775 of seizing Governor Tryon and sending him to Hartford, and only Philip Schuyler's persuasion and Washington's express command prevented him from attempting it.

[82] See *Boston Gazette*, Sept. 2, 1765; *Rhode Island Records*, VI, 454 ff.; John Dickinson Papers; Edward McCrady, *The History of South Carolina under the Royal Government, 1719-1776*; *South Carolina Gazette*, Oct. 11, 1773; and Jonathan Boucher, *Reminiscences of an American Loyalist, 1738-1789*, pp. 122 f.

II

PURPOSES AND PROBLEMS

THE PROPAGANDISTS openly began the attack on the British government which ultimately grew into the American Revolution. They were not social incendiaries, and the Revolution was not an internal social upheaval, like the French Revolution or the Russian Revolution. It really began as a home rule movement and ended as a secessionist movement. The leaders of the earlier period, unlike most revolutionaries, were not agitating *for* something, they were agitating *against* something—successive acts of the British Parliament which affected the internal affairs of the colonies. Instead of attempting to change the existing situation, they were trying to maintain it. The purposes and objectives of the propagandists in these activities can be clarified by a brief survey of certain conditions in colonial society just after the Treaty of Paris of 1763.

The majority of the propagandists came from that fairly well-to-do element in colonial society which by 1763 was in virtual control of the internal affairs of the colonies. It was composed of assemblymen, county politicians, judges of colonial courts, lawyers and other professional men, and in the North merchants and in the South planters. They controlled in practically every colony the lower house of the provincial assembly, and with the English officials in the colonies they dominated the internal economic and political life of the colonies. Except that the words connote a sharper division than really existed, this group might be called the provincial ruling class.

Its position in colonial politics had been won by a twofold policy. On the one hand, through their political agency, the assembly, the colonial leaders had encroached so successfully on the authority of the governor and council that by 1750 the only limitations to their authority were the obstructive tactics of the upper house and governor, the royal disallowance of colonial legislation (exercised sparingly), and the English control of foreign affairs. They evaded. nullified, or protested English laws, orders, and instructions which endangered their interests, and yearly they became bolder in their assertions of authority. Definitely they were in the ascendancy. At the same time that they were freeing themselves from internal control above, they were securing their position against any attack from below. The interests of the small farmers and wage earners were flagrantly neglected. They limited suffrage and the right to hold office by property qualifications, and to the newer counties they denied for long periods division or full representation and delayed the privileges of courts, schools, churches, roads, bridges, and even protection from the Indians, except when the older settlements might suffer. The interests of the increasing number of urban workers fared no better—apprenticeship laws, wage laws, debtor laws, all operated directly against them. In all but four colonies (Rhode Island, Delaware, Pennsylvania, and most of New York) there were more or less oppressive religious establishments—Congregational in New England, Anglican elsewhere.

This privileged position, however, was seriously endangered between 1763 and 1775. It was threatened at once with a determined drive from above by the English government to regain its lost authority and with a demand from below to regain rights so long denied.

The British government stunned the merchants, anxiously looking to stabilized and increased trade after seven years of war, with new revenue-raising legislation and trade laws, and manifested every intention of enforcing them. The customs service was tightened, new courts of admiralty were created, and the military and naval power of England put behind them. The easy-going days of the nonenforced regulatory acts were over. The speculator in western lands was caught by the Proclamation of 1763 just when he saw profit from the sale of lands to settlers who would naturally move out, now that the war was over, and the tax-paying class was indignant over legislation designed to make it pay part of the staggering British debt. The currency laws and the restrictions on credit were rigidly maintained and bore still more heavily now that hard money and credit were scarce. The English administration, moreover, threw its weight behind its colonial officials to check the rapid decline in their power and attempted to tighten its hold on the central government of every colony. The increasing cost of royal and proprietary governments, the increased number of English appointees to colonial positions, who thus barred the way for local aspirants, and the increased activity of the Anglican Church in the North added injury and insult.

By such policies of the English administration, members of the provincial ruling class were threatened in their position and thought they faced economic disaster and political ruin. At the same time there came ominous signs of revolt from below. The rudimentary labor organizations being formed in Boston, New York, Philadelphia, and Charleston, under the leadership of such men as Ebenezer Mackintosh, John Lamb, Isaac Sears, and others, had more the appearance of mobs to the wealthier and more conservative elements in society, and the menace seemed obvious. In the rural areas there were even more patent signs of unrest. The necessities of the war and the fear of Indian attacks had kept the underprivileged of the newer areas quiet, but with the treaty of peace in 1763, the whole frontier began an insistent assertion of right, demanding attention to its grievances and threatening revolution. In upstate New York in the spring of 1766 the Levellers—discontented tenants on the larger estates—marched on Albany under William Pendergrast demanding more satisfactory leases and freedom from oppression by their creditors. County court justices and sheriffs were abused and their offices closed. From April to August the situation was dangerous, but Pendergrast was finally sentenced to execution and the movement stopped. Pendergrast is said to have declared that no one on his jury had the right to convict him as a rebel, for all had themselves been guilty of rebelling against the Stamp Act, but the justice of that remark appealed only to Pendergrast.[1]

Two years before these riots, some people of western Pennsylvania, the so-called Paxton Boys, rose against the Philadelphia government because of their political disabilities and the refusal of the Quaker government to protect them from the Indians. They rose first against some peaceful Indians and massacred them, and then in a body moved against Philadelphia. Only Franklin's influence saved

---

[1] Five hundred Levellers marched to Livingston Manor and threatened to destroy the place and to murder the owner unless their leases were modified. As an anticlimax they added that they would pay neither rent nor taxes until the change was made, nor suffer other tenants to pay.—*Montresor Journals*, pp. 360-377. See also R. R. Livingston to John Sargent, May 2, 1765, R. R. Livingston Papers, II, 55.

the city from a major battle. He published a pamphlet describing the atrocities of the rioters, with the idea of turning public opinion against them, and then formed a defense association of the citizens. He, with a committee appointed by the Governor, met the rioters and got them to disband on promise that the assembly would receive a petition. The petition was presented on February 13, 1764, and contained this resolution, prophetic of many a Whig resolution of a later day:

> "First. We apprehend that as Freemen and English Subjects, we have an indisputable Title to the same Privileges & immunities with His Majesty's other Subjects who reside in the interior Counties of Philadelphia, Chester, and Bucks, and therefore ought not to be excluded from an equal share with them in the very important Privilege of Legislation; nevertheless . . . our five counties are restrained from electing more than ten Representatives . . . while the three Counties and City of Philadelphia, Chester, and Bucks, elect Twenty-Six. This we humbly conceive is oppressive, unequal, and unjust, the cause of many of our Grievances, and an infringement of our Natural privileges of Freedom & Equality. . . ."[2]

The debtors of New Jersey were likewise uneasy during the years after 1763, and finally in 1769 they flared out in open rebellion against the oppressive lawyer-creditor class. Governor Franklin had urged some relief in 1768, and a temporary measure was passed; however, the assembly also drew up laws aiding the creditors, and the relief measure was so loosely drawn that it really benefited the creditors rather than the debtors. In 1769 the debtors could stand the oppression no longer and in Essex and Monmouth Counties broke out in rebellion. David Ogden's property was destroyed, and the Governor called the Assembly together. The rioting was stopped, and once again the assembly passed laws aiding the creditors.[3]

---

[2] *Colonial Records of Pennsylvania, 1683-1790,* IX, 138. The name was originally Paxtang from the name of the community.—Max Farrand, "The West and the Principles of the Revolution," *Yale Review,* O. S., XVII, 44-58, lists many similar statements.

[3] E. J. Fisher, *New Jersey as a Royal Province, 1738 to 1776,* pp. 256-262, 402 f. Specifically, the assembly passed the following acts: an act to regulate the militia, an act to prevent dangerous tumults and riotous assemblies, an act to revive the courts in Monmouth County, and an act to *lessen* the cost of recovery of debt, particularly of debts under fifty pounds. Similar "reforms" in New Hampshire also materially aided the creditors.—R. F. Upton, *Revolutionary New Hampshire,* pp. 10 f.

The Regulators of North Carolina—disaffected settlers in the western counties—rose twice against the eastern government and were put down only with military power, and the spread of their principles to South Carolina and Georgia caused much uneasiness. In South Carolina the people in the area between the Broad and the Saluda—old Ninety-Six—were notoriously disaffected to the Charleston government, and under the able leadership of Moses Kirkland, the Cunningham brothers, and Thomas Fletchall, kept up a constant agitation for recognition of their grievances.[4]

In Georgia, Governor Wright wrote Hillsborough, "Your Lordship has undoubtedly been Acquainted with what the back Settlers in North Caroline have done, and we have many in our Back Settlements of the same Stamp . . ."; and James Habersham reported also to Hillsborough, "that several idle People from Northward, some of whom, he is told are great Villians, Horse Stealers &c, and were amongst the North Carolina regulators have setled and built Hutts on the Lands proposed to be ceded by the Indians to His Majesty. . . ."[5]

There was discontent and unrest among the small farmers, petty tradesmen, and plain people of New England, but no actual rebellion. Isaac Backus was organizing the Baptists in pointed protest against the intransigent attitude of the established Congregationalists, and from the small farmers in New Hampshire and western Massachusetts came equally pointed complaints against the domination of the wealthier, older areas.[6]

Faced with this crisis in its affairs, attacked at once from above and below, the provincial ruling class in each of the colonies sought to maintain its position by shrewd tactics. It first combined with the British officials to defeat the lower, and then combined in the Revolution with the lower to defeat the British. The contrast between the

[4] J. S. Bassett, "The Regulators of North Carolina, 1765-1771," American Historical Association, *Report, 1894*, pp. 141-212; McCrady, *S. C. under Royal Government*, has material on the leaders of the South Carolina back-country men.

[5] Colonial Records of Georgia (MS., Rhodes Memorial Home, Atlanta), XXXVII, 502; XXXVIII, 6.

[6] E.g., *Boston Gazette*, July 22, 1765; Boston Committee of Correspondence, Records, 1772-1775, pp. 603 f.; Schlesinger, *Colonial Merchants*, p. 28; J. T. Adams, *Revolutionary New England, 1691-1776*, pp. 253 ff. Miller, *Sam Adams*, describes the distrust of the lower classes for the upper but divides Massachusetts into but two major groups—the Court and Country parties. As he shows later, however, Boston radicals had difficulty in obtaining support from the western farmers.—See especially pp. 137 f., 158 f.

actual coercion of the Levellers in 1766 and the complete failure to control the Stamp Act riots at the same time is illuminating.

Here, then, is one important source of anti-British leadership—the substantial, propertied, politically dominant elements in each colony uniting to obtain complete control of their own affairs.

In the condition and interests of the lower classes in the cities and towns is found the source of another group of anti-British agitators. The city workers were already becoming class conscious, and the events of the next few years were to make them more so. They were becoming politically conscious as well and increasingly demanded a voice in the affairs of the cities. Restless and insistent, they could and did profit from the political divisions created by the revolutionary movement.

Their interests, furthermore, were directly and adversely affected by much of the British legislation. The press gangs of the British warships, the seizure of vessels, and the threat of unemployment occasioned by the activities of customs officials and by the British trade laws injured all those connected with shipping—tidewaiters, stevedores, longshoremen, to use the modern names, laborers in the shipyards and ropewalks, sailmakers, caulkers, and sailors themselves. Some of the worst violence came from this class. The laborers in the thriving liquor industry were also directly affected by legislation which threatened to reduce the business. The interests of all these people, moreover, were dependent upon the welfare of the merchants, and thus they were powerful allies. The petty tradesmen and itinerants, the craftsmen, and the mechanics were likewise to a large extent ancillary to the merchants in the northern cities; in the southern cities legislation which did not materially affect the merchants because of their relations with British firms adversely affected the mechanics. The printers, too, universally hurt by the Stamp Act, took the lead in opposition to it and were thereafter bound to the American side. In the major trading towns then, the bands of laborers, already loosely associated, were eager to join in a movement against Great Britain.

Patently the object of the leaders at each stage of the controversy was the repeal of the British legislation in question—the Grenville Acts, the Stamp Act, the Townshend Acts, the Tea Act, and the like.

Behind that open and declared purpose, two broader ones may be distinguished.

The first of these was to resist the encroachments of the British government and the official ruling class in the internal affairs of the colonies, to obtain for the provincial ruling class what it had practically exercised before 1763—complete control over the internal polity of each colony. That is simply to say that Sam Adams, for example, would have protested against any parliamentary act which adversely affected the internal affairs of Massachusetts, no matter when passed after 1765. As Joseph Hawley wrote: "One thing I want that the southern gentlemen should be deeply impressed with; that is, that all acts of British legislation which influence and affect our internal polity, are as absolutely repugnant to liberty and the idea of our being a free people, as taxation or revenue acts."[7] It was late when Hawley wrote that—1775—and the formal legal argument justifying this position had not been clearly expressed and agreed upon until 1774, but there can be no question of the jealous determination of the assemblymen to protect their right to legislate for the internal affairs of the colonies long before 1774. This might be called the home rule movement.

Home rule had the support of the radical leaders for only a short time. The constructive proposals to make home rule practicable by means of an American congress or by some other method of obtaining internal freedom while remaining within the British Empire came from the conservatives like Joseph Galloway, most of whom turned loyalist in 1776. The aggressive Whigs never seriously proposed a method of home rule. They rapidly abandoned, in fact, their demand for internal freedom in favor of the extreme demand for complete freedom, external as well as internal. This meant secession from the empire.

Secession, or independence, the second broad purpose of the leaders, began to develop slowly after 1773 and transpired with the battle of Lexington and Concord. Only a very few of the propagandists had independence in mind and worked consciously for it before April, 1775. In view of the manifest loyalty to the King of the great majority of Americans in 1774, it would be a matter of

[7] *Works of John Adams,* IX, 345.

considerable surprise if there had been an open movement of any size to promote complete separation. Movements so emotional in character as this come with a rush and accumulate great force in a very short time; witness the growth of war sentiment in America in 1861 and in 1917. Moreover, it is almost a truism that the early phases of any complex affair are always managed by very few persons. It is perfectly natural, therefore, that there should have been only a few who had independence as their conscious goal in the early days of the Revolution, but it is also perfectly true that there must have been some.

Certain obvious difficulties present themselves at once: the word independence was so loosely used in the period that it did not always connote complete legal separation from Great Britain, and in the second place, the leaders would have been the most naïve conspirators imaginable to have given away their treasonable plans before there was a solid chance of success. It was absolutely essential to have reasonable assurance that public opinion would support them before there could be an open declaration of intent. The English treason law was not a pleasant thing to read, as Hawley reminded his friends in a long letter early in 1775, urging that no decisive step be taken until other colonies agreed: "When once the blow is struck, it must be followed, and we must conquer, or all is lost forever. If we are not supported, perseveringly supported, by divers other Colonies, can we expect anything else than in a short time to fall a prey to our enemies? May God make us consider it." "If they get a grand jury," he said, speaking of the Superior Court then sitting at Boston, "then they probably will obtain indictments of high treason; and indictments will not be procured without a view and respect to arrests and commitments, convictions, hangings, drawings and quarterings. What your chance will be I need not tell you." But privately a year before he had written, "We must fight, if we can't otherwise rid ourselves of British taxation, all revenues and the constitution or form of government enacted for us by the British Parliament. . . . It is *now* or never, that we must assert our liberty."[8] Not a leader but agreed that American opposition had to be united,

---

[8] Hawley to Cushing, Feb. 22, 1775, *Revolutionary Letters*, Mass. Archives, CXCIII, pp. 33 f.; *Works of John Adams*, IX, 641.

and not a one but recognized the difficulties in the way of promoting independence. Even as late as March, 1776, with *Common Sense* still the month's best seller, John Adams wrote half-jokingly to Gates: "If a Post or two more, should bring you unlimited Latitude of Trade to all Nations, and a polite Invitation of all Nations to trade with you, take care that you dont call it, or think it Independency. No such Matter. Independency is a Hobgoblin of so frightful Mien, that it would throw a delicate Person into Fits to look it in the Face."[9]

But he was not entirely joking.

The propagandists consequently pursued a shrewd policy: private efforts to work out a concerted program, public denials that they had anything of the sort in mind, a cautious propaganda campaign subtly suggesting the idea, and finally, as the thought took hold, an open campaign in favor of it.

Sam Adams was one of the first to demand complete freedom. He admitted in 1775 that he had had separation in mind since 1768, but there is nothing in his published writings to support the statement.[10] It would be surprising if there were. He and a few of his colleagues were accused by the Tory leaders of seeking independence, and with considerable show of reason. The Boston quadrumvirate was one of the earliest groups to insinuate the idea in its writings. In the letters of the Boston committee of correspondence and in the pages of the *Boston Gazette* there are numerous instances to show that these leaders were attempting to inculcate the idea. There appeared, for instance, the following statement early in 1773:

"Truth and common sense will at last prevail, and if the Britons continue their endeavours much longer to subject us to their government and taxation, we shall become a separate state —This is as certain as any event that has not already come to pass; for the people from every quarter of the world are coming to this country, of all trades arts and sciences, soldiers and

[9] Burnett, *Letters of Members of Cont. Cong.*, I, 406. Gerry wrote James Warren three days later: "I sincerely wish you would originate instructions . . . and give your sentiments as a Court in favor of independency. I am certain it would turn many doubtful minds, and produce a reversal of the contrary instructions adopted by some Assemblies. If you think caution in this respect good policy, change the name."—*Ibid.*, p. 410.

[10] The following statement appeared in the *Boston Gazette*, September 5, 1768: because of the measures already adopted by Parliament, "*political union between Great Britain and the colonies was thereby dissolved.*" This is not in the *Writings of Sam Adams*.

seamen, and in a short time the Americans will be too strong for any nation in the world."[11]

Compare this with a statement attributed to Sam Adams which appeared some months later in the *Boston Gazette:*

"How shall the Colonies force their oppressors to proper terms? This question has often been answered, already by our politicians: 'Form an independent state,' 'AN AMERICAN COMMONWEALTH.' This plan has been proposed, and I can't find that any other is likely to answer the great purpose of preserving our liberties. I hope, therefore, it will be well digested and forwarded, to be in due time put into execution, unless our political fathers can secure American liberties in some other way. As the population, wealth, and power of this continent are swiftly increasing, we certainly have no cause to doubt of our success in maintaining liberty by forming a commonwealth, or whatever measure wisdom may point out for the preservation of the rights of America."[12]

Southward the leaders more reluctantly adopted the idea. Even the aggressive Richard Henry Lee did not openly advocate independence until quite late, although no one who has gone through his letters can doubt but that he himself was prepared for independence long before he publicly advocated it. He demanded, as did many others, the return to the policies of 1763. But this common demand for a return to the situation in which, in short, the provincial ruling class had in practice if not in theory complete control of the internal polity of each colony, was simply good propaganda; the policy of every propagandist was to throw the burden of guilt upon Great Britain and to maintain consistently that America was forced in self-defense to each new position. Never once did the leaders put themselves in the position of forcing the issue—it was always

[11] *Boston Gazette,* Jan. 11, 1773; N. Y. *Journal,* Jan. 21, 1773. See also Boston Committee Records, p. 318.

[12] Oct. 11, 1773. Compare this with the statement attributed to Joseph Warren which appeared in the *Boston Gazette,* Nov. 2, 1772, "To the People of America." This statement is summarized in Frothingham, *Warren,* p. 198. See also *ibid.,* pp. 394 ff. In the resolutions of the town of Abington, Jan. 18, 1774, there occurs this passage: "That such Measures [as the Tea Act] continued and persisted in, will have a direct tendency to alienate the Affections of the Americans from their parent State: and will be the most likely Method to desolve their union, and finally to break and destroy the british Empire."—Boston Committee Records, p. 8. See also *ibid.,* pp. 177 f.

forced upon them. There was no disposition on the part of the radical Whig leaders to accept the terms when offered in 1775.

After the nineteenth of April, 1775, the movement for independence gathered force, and the propagandists began an avowed campaign in favor of it on the grounds that it was the sole method left of preserving the liberties of the colonists. As we shall see in more detail, they persistently declared that they were attempting not to gain new liberties, but to preserve old liberties threatened by British legislation. Because of the work of the propagandists, the demand for independence gathered momentum with an upward surge that left its opponents breathless and bewildered.

The problems the leaders faced in achieving their objectives were different at each stage of the controversy with England. Each successive act of the British Parliament affected different colonial interests; the problem of presenting a united opposition changed, therefore, with each act.

Resistance to the Grenville Acts of 1764, which replaced the prohibitive duties of the Molasses Act with small duties designed to produce revenue, was limited to northern merchants. Important southern support would have been difficult to obtain but for the proposed stamp tax, and southern protests were principally against any form of stamp duty. The Stamp Act itself, which placed a tax on all legal documents, newspapers, diplomas, playing cards, and dice, raised a storm of protest. The propagandists' task here was principally to facilitate expression and to organize the overwhelming popular opposition. The successful attack on the Act, for it was repealed on March 18, 1766, was of great importance in subsequent periods of agitation, when the opposition was not so universal. The experience of working together, the ideas that were inculcated during the agitation, and the sense of accomplishment resulting from united efforts were indispensable. The agitation of each period, in fact, made easier the work of the next.

It might have been difficult, for example, for the leaders to have maintained a common front against the Townshend Acts as long as they did but for the prior activities and achievements of the Stamp Act period. The acts were three: the first levied import duties on glass, paints, paper, tea, and a few other items; the second created four vice-admiralty courts to hear all colonial cases of violation of the trade laws, and in other particulars aided in the enforcement of the trade acts; the third suspended the legislature of New York for its refusal to furnish supplies for British troops. The first two of these acts created consternation among the merchants, but the planters, except as consumers, were not directly concerned. The third act, however, affected the provincial politicians in every colony. Hugh Hughes and John Holt of New York immediately wrote their friends in other colonies urging a public discussion of the scheme to coerce the assembly; if submitted to, they said, this act would "engulf all the Colonies in one Common Calamity; notwithstanding its apparent direction at New-York."[13] Said Richard Henry Lee, astute Virginia politician, the act "*hangs like a flaming sword* over our heads and requires by all means to be removed."[14] Yet at the very moment that northern merchants and southern planters were joining in protest against British legislation, the nonconformists of the North began a violent attack on the Anglican church, for they feared that England was preparing to establish an American bishopric and to set up religious establishments in every colony. The southern planters were almost to a man Anglican. Although many Anglicans did not want an American episcopate, the attitude of the nonconformists did not help at all in creating common sympathies and mutual respect.

The division which really prevented a completely successful attack on the trade act, however, was not one between northern merchants and southern planters but was between the merchants and the political radicals. England repealed all of the duties except that on tea; the merchants were content with the compromise, but the radically anti-British leaders demanded that the boycott of British goods continue until the principle of no taxation had been gained. The merchants won their point, and peace reigned for three years.

The problem of the propagandists when England granted a monopoly of the sale of tea to the British East India Company—the Tea Act of 1773—was again that of winning support from people not directly affected, for only independent northern merchants were immediately concerned. The agitation that was aroused throughout the country was a real triumph for the propagandists. And so it was

---

[13] To Silas Downer, Sept. 24, 1767, Rhode Island Historical Society, Manuscript Collections, Letters and Papers, 1765-1776, XII, 75.

[14] *Letters of Richard Henry Lee*, I, 27.

with the final phase of the controversy. British punishment of Boston for the famous tea party might not have stirred the colonists but for the prior work of the propagandists through ten years of agitation. These four acts of 1774 concerned only Massachusetts—the Port Act, which closed the port of Boston, the Administration of Justice Act, which provided that officers accused of a crime could be taken to any other colony or to Great Britain for trial, the Government Act which changed materially the charter provisions for the government of the colony, and the Quartering Act, which required provisions for the British troops. Acts which affected solely Massachusetts, none too popular as it was, would seem to be poor basis for an extensive propaganda campaign against Great Britain, yet the unwavering answer to the propagandists' plea was that Boston must be supported.

The opening of the war in April, 1775, made independence inevitable, yet it was nearly fifteen months before the act of independence could be passed. The contest which delayed the decision was between those who wished reconciliation and those who demanded independence. In this contest, the propagandists were necessary, and their work was decisive.

It is obvious that the basic problem facing the propagandists in nearly every period was the unification of their own group—the Whigs. There was nothing faintly resembling a Whig party in 1763. The leaders in the different colonies did not even know one another. A few met at the Stamp Act Congress in New York, but many of those in the first Continental Congress had never seen each other. The interests of the different colonies and sections varied widely and were often in conflict, as the leaders soon found when they attempted to form a common government, whether in 1775 or 1787. The internal affairs of the southern colonies, for instance, were dominated by an eastern planter aristocracy, largely Anglican, from the tidewater and piedmont areas. The dominant interests in the northern colonies on the contrary were commercial and nonconformist. To unite under one government southern Anglican planters, opposed in their own colonies to nonconformists, with northern nonconformist merchants, opposed in their own colonies to Anglicans, that was a pretty problem. That the temporary union effected for the immediate purposes of the Revolution soon created major difficulties was to be expected.[15]

Moreover, among the leaders themselves there were divergent interests and attitudes. Most of the leaders might be termed social conservatives. Few had anything more in mind than increased popular rights under aristocratic leadership—the American form of European benevolent despotism. They differed sharply on imperial politics, however, ranging all the way from the conservative who desired little more than complete autonomy and was won over to independence with difficulty, to the extreme revolutionary who early demanded complete separation.

There was a constant fight, in fact, between the more conservative and the more radical for pre-eminence and control. The more conservative in social and political affairs were dismayed by the progress of events after 1774, and many of them abandoned the movement and either withdrew from politics or became loyalists. The northern merchants, who had initiated the earlier opposition to British trade legislation, were disturbed by the idea of separation from the government which had protected their trade for so many years, and many of them deserted the Whigs.

Such complexities were made even more intricate by the problem of the lower classes.

The workingmen in the cities, the craftsmen, and the lesser tradesmen, as we have noted, were eager if somewhat dangerous allies of the provincial ruling class leaders. The rural workers presented a somewhat different problem.

The small farmers in New England, particularly in New Hampshire and Massachusetts, were less concerned than the dominant Congregational merchants by British trade legislation, yet they hated Anglicanism and had no love for England. Acts which directly affected them, such as the Massachusetts Government Act, would arouse their bitter resentment, and in the event of an actual war, they would take the patriot side. But Sam Adams had his troubles when he urged aggressive action on the western counties.[16] The small farmers and tenants elsewhere, many of whom were Scotch-Irish and German, were not directly affected by British legislation. The most

---

[15] E.g., Miller, *Sam Adams*, pp. 137 f., 158 f.

[16] Schlesinger, *Colonial Merchants*, p. 6, says that the fundamental problem of the Revolution was that of getting the two sections to act together.

serious objection to the Proclamation Line of 1763 came from the land speculators, and the Stamp Act created little excitement in the newer areas for no distributors and no stamps penetrated there.[17] The controversy over the Townshend Acts and the enforcement of the nonimportation agreements were obviously affairs of the coastal areas. Some of these people, indeed, had sound reasons to support the British government. Several of the newly arrived Germans and Highland Scots had received from it bounties and land grants and firmly believed that to rebel meant to lose this land. The English government was a strong defense against the Indians, and her Indian agents, particularly Sir William Johnson in the North and John Stuart in the South, exercised a powerful influence over the surrounding territory.[18]

Most of these people, however, were either indifferent or actually hostile to Great Britain. The European elements had no tradition of loyalty to her, and the Irish and Scotch-Irish had bitter memories of mistreatment at her hands. These plain people had cast their lot with America, and there they would live. They certainly knew a freer life than they had ever known back home. After all, if they had grievances against those just above them, they had equal grievances on the same score against the English officials, for they had been party to their oppression in domestic affairs.

The county officials and representatives in the local assembly of these elements in every colony had, moreover, the same interest in preserving the internal rights of the colonies as did the representatives of the upper classes. Through these officials the less privileged had their best opportunity of making gains. Although they might lag behind in the early days, when the Revolution actually came it might mean great changes. Although it was initiated by those that oppressed them within the colonies, although its objectives were not clearly defined, it might be successful, and it might mean more than anyone could foresee. It might mean equal representation, increased suffrage, equal justice, religious freedom—even land might be won.

[17] The Stamp Act was universally condemned, of course, but the people of upstate New York, for example, were distinctly cool toward the method of opposition to it.

[18] Sir William Johnson died in 1774, and it has been said that had he lived the Six Nations would have joined solidly with Great Britain.—J. W. Lydekker, *Life and Letters of Charles Inglis*, p. 150. He certainly had great influence with the Indians. The most active loyalism in Virginia was on the extreme frontier and on the seacoast.—Isaac S. Harrell, *Loyalism in Virginia. Chapters on the Economic History of the Revolution.*

Here was the basis for the radical demand from many western counties in 1775 that the time had come to form new governments. Only where bitterness against the upper classes was intense, as among the Regulators of North Carolina or among the South Carolina back-country men, would there be serious difficulty in obtaining support for a movement against Great Britain.

Of great aid to the aggressive leaders in their efforts to unify the Whigs and to win over the doubtful was the powerful current of the eighteenth-century natural rights philosophy. Here is the familiar basis of the Revolution, the consent or compact theory of government, the right of free man in society to determine the character of the government which in the last analysis he creates. Here is the propagandist's rationalization of his desire to protect his vested interests. But the implications of the new philosophy in its effect on the movement are more far-reaching than that. It was a new way of life, a new attitude toward all the interests of man in society. The current of European thought found perfect home in the American environment, and although the full expression and application of the humanitarian, sentimentalist attitude did not come until later, the new ideas were strong. The concept of the inherently good man, who of himself could do no wrong but only as corrupted by the evil in institutions over which he had no control, and the new interest in the natural world and man's relations to it are seen less in the formal writings of the earlier period than in the daily lives of the people. Merchants who were not to read Adam Smith for another decade believed that the state should aid them, rather than that they should build up the power of the state. Man's natural rights to his religion and his land, and to control over his own interests, were demands even before Rousseau was widely read. These social and economic aspects of the new thought were implied in the frequent assertions that man is inherently vested with the control over his own government. The provincial Whig oligarchies speaking the language of Locke taught it to the lower classes, and soon they too were talking of their rights as freemen, violated "contrary to the Proprietor's Charter and the acknowledged principles of common Justice & Equity."[19] On every issue lower-class argument against eastern oppression paralleled eastern argument against British op-

[19] The Paxton resolutions of February, 1764.

pression.[20] But the very fact that the lower classes knew and understood the new attitudes toward government, even though they used them against their local oppressors, gave the Whig propagandists a powerful advantage over the Tories, because it united both classes in a common philosophical opposition to the outmoded ideas of the English ruling class. The older ideal of the ordered state and society, the doctrine of submission to a higher authority so admirably summed up by St. Peter, "Submit yourself to every ordinance of man for the Lord's sake, whether it be to the King as supreme, or unto Governors as those that are sent by him for the Punishment of Evil Doers and for the Praise of them that do well," the dogma that all economic activity should be subordinated to the interests of the state, these were the tenets of the English ruling class in the colonies. The philosophy of a new freedom permeated America and with triumphant force beat against the ideals of a past day. In time it might free all men from the shackles of the old order, but its immediate victory was to free the provincial ruling class from the domination of a weakened English oligarchy.

[20] See Farrand, "The West and the Principles of the Revolution," *loc. cit.*

III

THE MACHINERY OF PROPAGANDA

THE PROPAGANDISTS kept up a virtually continuous agitation against Great Britain during the decade or more preceding the Declaration of Independence. The quantity of speeches, sermons, demonstrations, and resolutions of the period attest their activity. Yet throughout the entire twenty years of the revolutionary movement there never existed a central propaganda organization to unify the work of the leaders and plan the strategy of the propaganda campaigns. There was nothing even faintly resembling the Bureau of Public Information established by President Wilson in the United States in 1917. The propagandists, however, could concert their plans by corresponding with each other, and there were a number of organizations they could use to get their work done. The agencies of government could unify the official protests of the people by resolutions and addresses, the Sons of Liberty could stage their demonstrations for them, and the churches, schools, and clubs could disseminate propaganda in a variety of ways.

PROPAGANDA THROUGH GOVERNMENT AGENCIES

In the conventional social and political revolution, the revolutionaries are in open conflict with the regular agencies of government and must overthrow them to accomplish their purposes. In the American Revolution, on the contrary, open rebellion against the laws of the British government was carried on through the regularly established legal system of town and county governments, courts, and legislative assemblies.

Whig propagandists controlled the existing agencies of government in every colony—the lower house of the assemblies, the town governments in New England, the county governments in the middle and southern colonies, and the colonial courts. They could therefore use them for the dissemination of authoritative propaganda by inducing them to adopt resolutions incorporating their ideas. Resolutions, memorials, addresses, or petitions, when adopted by the legal agencies of government were of great importance, for they gave the effect of unity and were themselves good propaganda. Patrick Henry, for example, forced his famous Stamp Act resolutions through a reluctant House of Burgesses by a single vote, yet the effect was the protest of an entire colony, not just that of a small group. Every other colony and the British government as well could assume, however unjustifiably, that Virginia was wholeheartedly united in the sentiments set forth in Henry's resolutions. It was of great consequence, therefore, that the influence of the thirteen assemblies and of the more than seven hundred towns be used and that their protests be unified. The propagandists assiduously set about this task. A brief examination, first of the assemblies, then of the towns and counties, will show the devices they used.

Attempts had been made as early as 1764 to unify the assemblies in protest against the Grenville Acts. Several of the assemblies appointed committees of correspondence to write other colonies urging common protest against both the trade act and the proposed stamp duty. Most of the correspondence of these bodies was with the colonial agents in London, but here was the beginning of a system for uniting the colonies.[1] When the Stamp Act was actually passed, the resolutions of the Virginia House of Burgesses, drawn up by Patrick Henry; acted as an "alarum bell." The Massachusetts assembly sent out a circular letter calling for a conference in New York in October, 1765, and these two activities spurred on the other colonial assemblies. The result was a series of resolutions from every colonial legislature attacking the act as an infringement of the assemblies' sole right of taxation.[2]

Little effort was needed in 1765 to arouse the assemblies against so flagrant a violation of what they considered their rights, but more was needed in 1767 when the protest against the Townshend Acts was far less general. Sam Adams, however, worked out a plan for unifying the assemblies. At his suggestion the Massachusetts as-

[1] Carl Becker, *History of Political Parties in the Province of New York, 1760-1776*, pp. 26 f.; "Proceedings of the Virginia Committee of Correspondence, 1759-1770," *Virginia Magazine of History and Biography*, Vols. IX to XII, inclusive; *Colonial Records of North Carolina*, VI, 1261; R. W. Gibbes, *Documentary History of the American Revolution, 1764-1782*, I, 1 ff.; *The Letters of the Honorable James Habersham, 1756-1775*, Georgia Historical Society, *Collections*, VI, 3 f.

[2] E.g., *Maryland Gazette*, Oct. 3, 1765. There is another set of resolutions, almost the same, in *Georgia Gazette*, Oct. 10, 1765.

sembly in January, 1768, directed a series of letters to prominent officials in England—Shelburne, Rockingham, Chatham, Camden— and to the King. On February 11 the assembly sent copies of these letters to other assemblies with a letter urging that each draw up similar protests. Governor Bernard of Massachusetts was pained by this defection of what he had thought was a "complacent" house and ordered the vote approving the letter rescinded. Adams reversed an apparent majority against him by some shrewd political maneuvering and kept control by a wide margin—ninety-two to seventeen. Governor Bernard was even more pained. He saw the real purpose of these letters and dissolved the assembly: "There is no doubt but the principal design in forming these remonstrances was to set an example to the rest of America, and produce a general clamour from every other Assembly against the late acts."[3]

The clamor was general. Even Georgia assemblymen petitioned the King, although humbly.[4] In the same way, the Virginia resolutions of 1769 were sent to other colonies, and once more the assemblies united in condemning parliamentary taxation and the great extension of admiralty courts, which deprived offenders of their right of trial by jury.[5]

The complete plan for unifying the action of the colonial assemblies was worked out by Richard Henry Lee and Thomas Jefferson. In March, 1773, they secured the appointment by the Virginia House of Burgesses of a standing committee of eleven members, all strongly anti-British Whigs. Within a year every assembly except Pennsylvania had set up a standing committee of correspondence, so that even though prorogued by the governor the assemblies could still concert their plans.

This system proved itself when the growing dispute over the

---

[3] Francis Bernard, *Letters to the Ministry*, pp. 6 f.

[4] Charles Colcock Jones, Jr., *History of Georgia*, II, 108. The resolutions of the New Hampshire Assembly declared its hope that the people of the colony would never be faced with the "Dreadful Alternative, either to take the Sword, or submit to give up all English Liberties."—*Documents and Records Relating to the Province [Town and State] of New Hampshire, 1623-1800* (hereinafter cited *Documents N. H.*), VII, 190. Typical of the methods of legislative control were those used by the South Carolina Whigs. Of the fifty-five members of the assembly, only twenty-six voted on the resolutions, and those twenty-six were from the two town parishes and the neighboring areas. The delegates from the western parishes did not vote.

[5] Rhode Island adopted the second, third, and fourth of the Virginia resolutions.— *R. I. Records*, VI, 603 f. See also *South Carolina Gazette*, Aug. 24, 1769; and *Col. Rec. N. C.*, VIII, 123 f.

Tea Act and the passage of the Intolerable Acts demanded united action. The Massachusetts assembly ordered its committee of correspondence to send copies of the Boston Port Act to other assemblies with a letter requesting support. This letter contained the essentials of Massachusetts' propaganda for the next year:

"Though the town of Boston, is now intended to be made a victim to ministerial wrath; yet the insult and indignity offered to our virtuous brethren in that capital . . . ought to be viewed in the same odious light as a direct, hostile invasion of every province on the continent, whose inhabitants are now loudly called upon, by interest, honor and humanity, to stand forth, with firmness and unanimity, for the relief, support and animation of our brethren in the insulted, beseiged capital of Massachusetts Bay."[6]

Every assembly condemned the Port Act and publicly sympathized with Boston.[7] There was hardly a period of the Revolution when it was more important that the assemblies definitely commit themselves and their colonies. The common protest against acts specifically directed against but one colony was of paramount importance to the Whig leaders.

At this point, 1774, the assemblies became almost useless to the Whigs. Although they had control of the lower house in most of the colonies, the royal governors could interfere too successfully with the revolutionary plans of the leaders. The power of the governor to prorogue or dissolve the assembly, to change the place of meeting, and to interfere in the selection of its officers, were obvious and serious difficulties. Governors so frequently dissolved assemblies that not only the revolutionary plans of the leaders, but their position in colonial society as well were endangered. As the people of Monmouth, Virginia, complained: "A savage Enemy ravaging our Frontiers, the publick Creditors unpaid, a stagnation of Justice by Reason of the Lapse of the Free Bill, the Courts of Law occluded, everything that is held sacred in civil Society confounded, the Just

<hr>

[6] This letter may be found in *R. I. Records*, VII, 293; and in *Newport Mercury*, May 16, 1774.

[7] E.g., *R. I. Records*, VII, 246 f.; *Public Records of the Colony of Connecticut*, XIV, 409; Georgia, *Revolutionary Records, 1769-1784*, I, 48 ff.; 4 Force, *Amer. Arch.*, I, 1171.

Creditor deprived of property, and the dishonest Debtor triumphant, these are the bitter Fruits of the late Dissolution."[8]

Even before these people had declared their grievances, Samuel Johnston, leader of the conservative branch of the North Carolina Whigs, had urged that a provincial congress be called: "Without Courts to sustain property and to exercise the talents of the Country," he said, "and the people alarmed and dissatisfied, we must do something to save ourselves."[9]

As a result, in every colony except Rhode Island and Connecticut, where there were no royal governors, provincial congresses were substituted for the colonial assemblies. In every colony these bodies were controlled by the same elements which had dominated the old assemblies. In fact, in several colonies the assembly simply adjourned to another room and constituted itself the provincial congress. The same program for unifying the protests of the new assemblies was naturally continued. Each appointed a committee of correspondence, and with each new development in the controversy with England resolutions and addresses from every provincial congress set forth the common complaints of the thirteen rebellious colonies.

The resolutions and memorials drawn up by the assemblies and the provincial congresses from 1764 to 1776 were important, however, not only in giving the appearance of unity to the colonial complaints. Of equal if not greater importance was the fact that they were good propaganda in themselves. They were definitely written as much for the colonial reader as for the British officials. All were published in the local newspapers, and many of them were reprinted in other colonies.[10] Publication was, in fact, one of the first considerations. When Sam Adams marked for publication in the *Boston Gazette* a letter written by the Massachusetts assembly to Lord Hillsborough, James Otis protested, saying that the public would have it before the minister for whom it was intended. "What signifies that?" replied Adams. "You know it was designed for the people, and not for the minister."[11] Governor Bernard knew what

---

[8] *Virginia Gazette* (Purdie), *Postscript*, July 21, 1774.   [9] *Col. Rec. N. C.*, IX, 968.

[10] Examples abound. See *Ga. Gazette*, Oct. 10, 1765; *S. C. Gazette*, June 28, 1773. The *Newport Mercury* printed practically all of the resolutions against the Stamp Act.

[11] Wells, *Life of Adams*, I, 196. W. E. H. Lecky, *The American Revolution, 1763-1783*, pp. 113 f., says this and other letters written at the same time were intended primarily to win English support. Much of the propaganda was directed to an English audience, but Adams published this letter first in the *Boston Gazette*, not in an English paper.

the propagandists were about. He wrote Lord Hillsborough of this same letter: "As it is professedly intended for the people more than for your Lordship, so it is accompanied with comments much more calculated to prepare the people to resent the disallowance of their pretensions than to induce your Lordship to endeavour to procure an allowance for them."[12]

The comments to which Governor Bernard referred were not straightforward statements designed to influence officials charged with the enforcement of an act. They were founded upon much broader grounds and were much less precise than such protests would have been unless intended to arouse opinion. This is true of most of the resolutions passed from 1764 on. The resolutions of the Massachusetts assembly, drawn up by Sam Adams in 1765, are clearly in point. Adams went beyond anything that had previously been said in his statement that the British Constitution protected the settlers from parliamentary taxation because it was founded on the higher law of nature—William H. Seward's higher law doctrine in colonial form.[13] Practical officials of the British government were not likely to have been impressed with such a doctrine, but the American public would accept it as an unanswerable argument against British taxation.

Just as the propagandists had used the assemblies to further the anti-British movement, so they also used the town and county governments. One of the most familiar features of the revolutionary movement is the New England town meeting. So dangerous was it to the English government in the colonies, that in the Massachusetts Government Act of 1774 all meetings except the annual meeting for the election of officers were prohibited except by special permission of the governor. Governor Hutchinson's experience with town meetings was typical. As he wrote Lord Hillsborough: "We find, my Lord, by experience, that associations and assemblies pretending to be legal and constitutional, assuming powers that belong only to established authority, prove more fatal to this authority than mobs, riots, or the most tumultuous disorders. . . ."[14]

There were over seven hundred towns in colonial America, five hundred and twenty-two of them in New England alone. The New

---

[12] Bernard, *Letters to the Ministry*, p. 57.

[13] *Writings of Sam Adams*, I, 23 f.

[14] Richard Frothingham, "The Sam Adams Regiments in the Town of Boston," *Atlantic Monthly*, XII, 600.

England town was the unit of local government, and the freeholders, or those allowed to vote, were legally competent to regulate the affairs of the community. There was an annual meeting for the transaction of business, and special meetings could be called on petition to the selectmen. The Whig leaders could thus get an endorsement of their program at any time, and actions taken by the town had the force of law.

In the middle and southern colonies, on the contrary, there were only some two hundred towns, and they were not units of local government. The business of towns and counties was not carried on by public meetings, but when endorsement was needed for the Whig program, a popular meeting, extra-legal in nature, could be called. It was not until 1774 that meetings of that sort were generally held throughout the middle and southern colonies.

Town action prior to 1772, and there was a great deal of it, was stimulated by local leaders, for there was no regular system of communication among the towns. The Sons of Liberty, as we shall see in the next chapter, performed that service, particularly in the Stamp Act period. Through the correspondence among the different branches the country was unified, and it was not until after the decline of the Sons of Liberty that a system of town committees was necessary.

The most common method used by town meetings to register their protest against the Stamp Act was not so much in public resolutions as in the regular instructions towns always drew up to guide their representatives in the assembly. These instructions were usually drawn up by a committee and voted on at a regular town meeting. Here was an opportunity for authoritative propaganda of the finest sort. John Adams, for example, drew up the instructions of the town of Braintree to its representative Ebenezer Thayer. This statement in direct and vigorous language declared the Stamp Act unconstitutional and instructed Thayer to join in measures for redress. These instructions were printed in the *Massachusetts Gazette, and Boston News-Letter* and were copied by forty other towns.[15] The importance of this method is obvious.

---

[15] Conveniently found in the *Works of John Adams*, III, 465 ff. His own comments on the instructions are found *ibid.*, II, 152 f. These were reprinted in the *Boston Gazette*, Oct., 1765. For other examples, other than the numerous town records, see *ibid.*, Aug. 19,

During the controversy over the Townshend Acts, towns more commonly adopted previously prepared resolutions condemning the acts. The method of giving the semblance of unified opposition through the adoption of resolutions, and at the same time markedly influencing opinion, is admirably illustrated in a Boston meeting, called in 1768, when it was known that troops were being sent from England to enforce the trade acts. A small group petitioned for a town meeting, and at the meeting called for the appointment of a committee to consider the coming of the troops. When the report was made the following day, there followed, said Governor Bernard, "a set of speeches by the chiefs of the faction, and no one else; which followed one another in such order and method, that it appeared as if they were acting a play, every thing both as to matter and order, seeming to have been preconcerted beforehand." The town officials, most of them radically anti-British, had in the meantime ordered the guns owned by the city cleaned, and they were lying exposed in the town hall during this meeting. "These arms," said Bernard, "were often the subject of discourse, and were of singular use to the orators in the way of action."[16] The guns had their effect. The meeting first passed resolutions against the danger of standing armies in time of peace. It then voted that "as there is at this Time a prevailing apprehension, in the Minds of many, of an approaching War with France" the men of Boston should be armed, "in order that the Inhabitants of this Town may be prepared in case of sudden danger."[17] The Reverend Samuel Cooper, later defending the action of the town, said cautiously that although many people really feared a war with France, "Some however, I do believe were in Favor of this Vote, not Knowing what Excesses the Troops that were then expected might commit."[18] This town meeting is an extreme example, of course, but the method of preconcerting plans is typical.[19]

and *Supplement*, Nov. 4, 1765; *Newport Mercury*, Sept. 2, 1765; and *New York Gazette, or, The Weekly Post-Boy*, Nov. 28, 1765.

[16] Bernard's own account is in *Letters to the Ministry*, pp. 70-75. He was a hopelessly prejudiced reporter, of course, but in this instance at least there was good ground for his statements.

[17] *Boston Town Records, 1758-1769*, p. 264.

[18] Letter to Thomas Pownall, Feb. 18, 1769, "Letters of Samuel Cooper to Thomas Pownall, 1769-1777," *Amer. Hist. Rev.*, VIII, 304.

[19] E.g., Joseph Ward to William Cooper, "Yesterday we had a Town Meeting, previous to which a number of spirited Notes and Resolves were drawn up to be passed at the

Although the number of town resolutions during the period from 1767 to 1770 had really been enormous,[20] there had been no other system of stimulating them than by individual correspondence. Sam Adams, however, had long been interested in establishing a more regular system of committees of correspondence.[21] When Adams proposed that Boston appoint a committee of correspondence, the province was quiet, and all Adams had to go on was the rumor that the British government proposed to pay certain Massachusetts officials out of a civil list, thus making them independent of the colony. So apathetic was the town, that only by a stratagem could Adams force his proposal through. Adams' knowledge of propaganda technique is clearly set forth in the reasons he gave for forcing the issue: to James Warren he wrote, "We have long had it thrown in our faces, that the Country in general is under no such fears of Slavery, but are well pleasd with the measures of Administration." Because of this situation, he explained to Elbridge Gerry, "Our timid sort of people are disconcerted, when they are positively told that the Sentiments of the Country are different from those of the City. Therefore a free Communication with each Town will serve to ascertain this matter; and when once it appears beyond Contradiction, that we are united in Sentiments there will be a Confidence in each

---

Meeting, but there was such a Swarm of stupid Tories . . . to oppose every laudible measure, that nothing was done but chusing a Committee to draw up something to lay before the Town at their next Meeting. . . . Liberty is in its infancy in this Province."—July 13, 1770, Sam Adams Papers.

[20] Random selection of instructions from Marblehead (which had been in opposition to the Braintree resolutions of 1765), Salem, Roxbury, and Leicester, show that the towns were in such accord that their instructions deal with identically the same problems in almost the same language. The *Boston Gazette* for 1769 printed many of these. Resolutions sometimes took the form of letters of thanks to favorite leaders—John Dickinson, James Otis, and others. E.g., Boston, Ipswich, and Salem, Massachusetts; New London, and Lebanon, Connecticut; and Providence, Rhode Island.—*Boston Town Records, 1758-1769*, p. 243, *1770-1777*, p. 22; *Boston Gazette*, Aug. 1, Aug. 15, 1768; *Ga. Gazette*, July 13, Sept. 14, 1768.

[21] This idea was not original with Adams, of course. The assemblies had committees in 1764 as did some of the merchant organizations. Adams had urged the idea several times and had even applied it in a limited way. During the Stamp Act troubles, he had built up a correspondence with Plymouth and the two towns exchanged letters and resolutions.—*Records of the Town of Plymouth*, pp. 166 f., 169 ff.; *Boston Town Records, 1758-1769*, pp. 168 f., 172 ff.; and *Boston Gazette*, Feb. 3, Mar. 31, 1766. Jonathan Mayhew suggested the idea to Adams, and Adams himself had recommended a "union" of writers to the Sons of Liberty in 1766; later Adams was in correspondence with R. H. Lee, Peter Timothy, and others on the same point.—Alden Bradford, *Memoir of the Life and Writings of the Reverend Jonathan Mayhew, D.D.*, pp. 428 f.; Sam Adams Papers, September, 1770; *Letters of Richard Henry Lee*, I, 29. Lee was more interested in inter-colonial committees of correspondence.

other, & a plan of Opposition will be easily formed, & executed with Spirit." To another he wrote to the same effect: "If the Enemies should see the flame bursting in different parts of the Country & distant from each other, it might discourage their attempts to damp & quench it."[22]

The committee Adams recommended was appointed at a town meeting on November 2, 1772. Twenty-one members composed the committee with James Otis as chairman and Sam Adams and Joseph Warren as its most influential members. Of the remainder only six were really active.[23] The town ordered this committee to make a report on the rights of the colony and the violations of those rights. On November 20, 1772, the two statements, together with a letter of correspondence to other towns, were adopted by a town meeting. James Otis, Josiah Quincy, and Samuel Adams drew up the "State of Rights of the Colonies," Joseph Warren, Joseph Greenleaf, and Thomas Young drew up the list of infringements, and Benjamin Church, Nathaniel Appleton, and William Powell wrote the letter of transmissal.[24] The natural rights of the colonists as conceived in the first statement included the right of life, liberty, and property, and the right to protect them by change of allegiance or by force of arms. John Locke would have had no trouble recognizing his child. These fundamental rights had been violated by England, the second statement went on to say, in numerous ways: by the Declaratory Act, the revenue acts, the establishment of a civil list from the revenue so collected, the extension of the power of the vice-admiralty courts, the use of fleets and armies to enforce parliamentary legislation, the abridgment of the right of trial by jury, and the threat to establish an American episcopate.[25] Of these only the establishment of the civil list was an issue at the time, and there was little public concern over that.

[22] *Warren-Adams Letters*, I, 11; and *Writings of Sam Adams*, II, 346 f.

[23] The six were Benjamin Church, Thomas Young, William Molineux, William and Joseph Greenleaf, and Josiah Quincy. Nathaniel Appleton and Caleb Davis might be added. The complete list may be found in the Boston Committee of Correspondence, Minutes, I, 1. Hutchinson said of the committee: "Some of the worst of them one would not choose to meet in the dark,—three or four at least of their Corresponding Committee are as black-hearted fellows as any upon the Globe."—British Museum Transcripts, C.O. 5, vol. 246, f. 48, pp. 62 f.

[24] These three statements may be found in the *Boston Town Records, 1770-1777*, pp. 95-108. The authorship is in Boston Committee Minutes, I, 2.f.

[25] Boston Committee Minutes, I, 3. This letter is listed in the *Writings of Sam Adams* because a copy with corrections in his hand is in his papers.—*Works*, II, 350 n.

The letter of correspondence urged that the towns express themselves and communicate their resolves to Boston, but Adams wrote several of his friends personal notes asking that they have committees appointed in their communities.[26]   James Warren and Elbridge Gerry responded promptly, and, in all, seventy-eight of the five hundred odd towns in New England replied to the letter. Ultimately many more appointed committees. The distribution of these committees shows that about the same proportion of eastern towns as western towns had them; the proportion of those in active opposition, however, was larger in the west and in the extreme east on the coast, that is, just north of Boston and around the Cape.[27]

The results of Adams' plans were excellent. The larger towns replied promptly, but as the letter had not gone out until the last of November many of the smaller towns waited until the annual spring meeting to consider the matter. At these meetings the letter from Boston and the two reports were read, resolutions adopted, a committee of correspondence appointed, and the records of the meeting sent to the Boston committee. The resolutions were all of a type, as they were modeled closely on the Boston statements. Many of the towns drew up instructions to their representatives at the special request of the Boston committee.[28] Unincorporated towns, such as Pearson, out on the frontier, expressed surprise that they had been remembered, and declared the inhabitants firm in support of their rights, about which they had probably just heard. The committee cleverly replied that no matter how small the community or how far from the center of activity, the people were still "Englishmen & Christians, entitled to all the liberties & privileges of such."[29]

Boston answered these replies, stressing those ideas it felt would make the greatest appeal. It urged the people of Duxbury to fill themselves with that ardent zeal "for the support of religious & civil Liberty which animated the Breasts of the first Settlers of the old

[26] *Warren-Adams Letters*, I, 11 f.; *Writings of Sam Adams*, II, 340 ff., 346 ff.

[27] The first seventy-eight towns plotted on a map make a figure T resting on a semicircle. The semicircle is around Boston, the leg of the T extends westward to the Connecticut River, and the arms of the T extend north and south along the valley. When Rhode Island, Connecticut, and New Hampshire towns join the movement, there is no particular configuration.

[28] "The advantage of instructing our Representatives has probably never appeared in so conspicuous a light, as at this time."—Boston Committee to Bradford, Feb. 2, 1773, Boston Committee of Correspondence Records, 1772-1775, p. 96. See also *ibid.*, pp. 318, 435, 688.

[29] *Ibid.*, pp. 599-601.

Colony of Plymouth from whom the native Inhabitants of Dux-
borough have lineally descended," and when the people of Harps-
well declared they abhorred independence, Adams hastily corrected
them; life distinct from England they might abhor, but they surely
did not mean that they favored dependence on England, or subjection to any power not expressly recognized in the charter of Massachusetts Bay.[30] After this first exchange of letters, the Boston committee continued to write disquieting letters on the gradual loss of
liberty in America, "not to agitate the Minds of our Brethren with
groundless Apprehensions, but to excite in them that Watchfullness
which alone will be a Guard against a false Security, forever dangerous to our Rights and Liberties."[31]

This system of town committees did not get outside of Massachusetts to any marked extent prior to the controversy over the Tea
Act. In New Hampshire, for example, only Haverhill in the western area had a committee of correspondence, and by 1774 there were
only seven towns with committees.[32] It was not until after the Boston Port Act created a sensation that Connecticut and Rhode Island
towns became active in appointing committees.

Although it is true that without subsequent British legislation
and blunders, no revolution would have resulted from these town
resolutions, two things of prime importance to the Whig leaders had
been accomplished. In the first place, as Benjamin Franklin said,
"the resolutions of the New England townships must have the effect
they seem intended for, viz. to show that the discontents were really
general and their sentiments concerning their rights unanimous, and
not the fiction of a few demagogues, as their governors used to represent them here. . . ."[33]

The appearance of unity had been gained. In the second place,
an effective system for unifying resistance through town meetings
had already been established. When a real crisis came, it could be
readily set in motion. As Sam Adams had said, it was wise to be
ready for all events.

The crisis soon came. The Tea Act of 1773 produced at the in-

[30] *Writings of Sam Adams*, III, 32 f.; Boston Committee Records, p. 318.
[31] 1 Mass. Hist. Soc., *Proceedings*, XIII, 159.
[32] Upton, *Revolutionary New Hampshire*, pp. 14, 34.
[33] *Works of Franklin*, VI, 115. Franklin had in mind the effect on English official
and public opinion, but the statement applies with equal force to the effect on colonial
opinion.

sistence of the Boston Committee a great many town resolutions condemning the use of tea and agreeing to unite in any rational plan for redress. However, the news of the Intolerable Acts inaugurated the most important period of town activity in New England. Many towns adopted resolutions supporting Boston, in language, said Governor Hutchinson, "calculated to strike the mind and inflame the passions, but qualified with, now and then, a word to avoid a charge of treason, or other high offence."[34] The system of town committees had been proposed by Sam Adams as much to stir up the laggard rural counties as for anything else, and they had done their work well. The rural towns now constantly sent committees to Boston to determine the state of affairs and to quiz the governor, and Hutchinson complained that although he could do very well with the Boston selectmen, "the damn'd country committees plague his soul out."[35]

In this period of intense agitation, the little used county units of Massachusetts were called into action. The Massachusetts Government Act of 1774 provided among other things for a new method of electing judges and other officials of the county courts. In August and September, 1774, county conventions were called at the instance of the Boston Committee of Correspondence to consider the matter and if possible to prevent the sitting of the newly constituted courts. These conventions, frequently nothing more than conventions of the town committees of correspondence, not only took action against the courts, but they adopted resolutions endorsing some type of nonimportation agreement and urged that no obedience be given any officer appointed under the authority of the Massachusetts Government Act. The more famous Mecklenburg resolutions of nine months later were no more rebellious in tone than were those, for example, of a Bristol meeting, which declared that "all civil officers in this province, considered as holding their respective offices by the tenure specified in a late act of the British parliament, deserve neither obedience nor respect."[36] The resolutions of the Suffolk County Convention were endorsed by the Continental Congress, thus committing that body to a more radical position than many of its

[34] *History of Massachusetts Bay*, III, 358.
[35] John Andrews to Barrell, Oct. 5, 1774, 1 Mass. Hist. Soc., *Proceedings*, VIII, 373. See also Boston Committee Records, pp. 219, 353.
[36] *The Journals of Each Provincial Congress of Massachusetts in 1774 and 1775, and of the Committee of Safety*, pp. 626 f.

members wished, for the resolutions declared the Intolerable Acts unconstitutional and void, recommended the formation of new civil governments for the colonies, and urged the establishment of local militia.[37]

It was at this time that the system of town committees inaugurated in Massachusetts finally spread to the middle and southern colonies. The particular occasion was the proposal of the Massachusetts radicals that the colonies immediately boycott all import and export trade with Great Britain. A proposal so serious, thought leaders elsewhere, needed careful consideration, and the result was the counterproposal of a continental congress, to meet in Philadelphia. City and county meetings throughout the country debated these proposals. The committees set up in the middle and southern colonies after May, 1774, became in reality local governments. Three stages in the development of revolutionary committee government appear: (1) From May to September, 1774, the appointment of local committees to decide upon a continental congress and the method of electing delegates. (2) From October, 1774, to April, 1775, the appointment of committees to enforce the general nonimportation association adopted by the Continental Congress on October 20, 1774. (3) After April, 1775, the appointment of committees to organize the local areas for war.

It is not germane to our central purpose to trace the establishment of these different committees, but it is important to note that these committees either did the work of committees of correspondence or appointed subcommittees to do it. By August, 1774, the entire country was covered by the system. The political propaganda machine was complete.

The effect can be seen in the resolutions that were adopted by town and county meetings during the crisis of the revolutionary movement. They are almost identical. Those that were drawn up in the summer of 1774 all professed loyalty to George III but declared the Intolerable Acts "unconstitutional, oppressive, and tyrannous." They denied the right of Parliament to tax the colonies or to interfere in their internal polity. They announced that Boston was suffering in the common cause, and they recommended a continental

[37] Joseph Warren wrote these resolutions. Meetings were held in Berkshire, Bristol, Essex, Middlesex, Plymouth, Suffolk, and Worcester.—*Ibid.*, 609 ff., 615 ff., 621 ff., 629 ff., 750 ff., 776 ff. Others met later.

congress to determine upon a common mode of resistance. The conception of American rights and of the nature of the British Empire, the philosophical background of the ideas expressed, and the remedies proposed were drawn from a common fund of political ideas and experiences, vaguely realized and ill-defined until clarified by the cogent phrases of the propagandists.

When independence was being debated, again the system of town and county committees and the resolutions they sponsored were of major service to the leaders. The provincial congress of Massachusetts and the assembly of Connecticut, for example, called upon the towns to express themselves on the matter, and throughout May and June town meetings were being held and resolutions adopted. And in Maryland, as we have already seen, Samuel Chase testified to the effect of county instructions to the delegates debating independence in the convention.[38]

The system of committees created to unify the protests of the towns and colonies and to arouse the people against British legislation constituted the most important organization for the dissemination of propaganda that was created throughout the entire period.

---

[38] See above p. 17. Caesar Rodney wrote his brother Thomas to see that "proper persons" promoted meetings throughout Delaware, so that when the state convention met in 1776 it would know the sense of the inhabitants.—*Letters to and from Caesar Rodney, 1756-1784*, p. 80. The resolutions of the Massachusetts towns have been printed in 4 Force, *Amer. Arch.* VI, 698 ff.

IV

MERCHANT AND MECHANIC ORGANIZATIONS

ONE OF the most significant movements of the prerevolutionary period is the development of two class-conscious groups, the merchants and the mechanics. Organizations of both were formed during the period, and through these organizations the propagandists could reach, to greater or less degree, two groups directly affected by British legislation.

MERCHANT ORGANIZATIONS

The first group to organize was naturally that most affected by British trade laws, the northern merchants. As early as 1763 some of the merchants in the larger cities began to work more closely together in an effort first, to better their trade relations, and second, to resist British legislation.

The Boston merchants were the first to form what might be called a chamber of commerce. The "Society for Encouraging Trade and Commerce within the Province of Massachusetts Bay" was formed in April, 1763. It proposed that merchants elsewhere form similar societies, each with a committee of correspondence, and that conventions of these committees be held for the discussion of common problems and for the presentation of united protests against the trade acts.[1] Some merchant groups in other Massachusetts towns joined in a protest against the Sugar Act of 1764, but no permanent organization of the merchants in Massachusetts was created.

The New York merchants formed a standing committee in January, 1764, and in 1768 a permanent chamber of commerce was created. Elsewhere the merchants held meetings at times of crisis and appointed committees to act for them. This was the common method in practically all the larger commercial centers. The merchants' purpose in forming these more or less temporary committees was pri-

---

[1] A hundred and forty-seven merchants joined this organization.—C. M. Andrews, "Boston Merchants and the Non-Importation Movement," Col. Soc. Mass., *Publications*, XIX, 161 ff. Schlesinger, *Colonial Merchants*, gives, of course, a complete study of the merchant committees.

marily to obtain commercial reform; that is, to modify, or free themselves completely from parliamentary trade restrictions. Two methods were chosen to effect this purpose: petitions to Parliament asking relief, and failing that, coercive measures, such as nonimportation or nonconsumption agreements. Merchant committees drew up their own petitions to Parliament and, to strengthen their case, successfully urged the colonial assemblies to petition for reform in behalf of the colony.

Petitions had little effect, however, and coercive measures were soon adopted. It was in connection with the nonimportation movements that the merchants built up their organizations to their greatest strength. The first nonimportation agreements were formed to defeat the Stamp Act by forcing English manufacturers and traders to bring pressure on Parliament. Together with the work of the Sons of Liberty, who prevented the enforcement of the act in the colonies, this measure was successful, and the nonimportation agreement became the common method of coercing England.

No difficulties had been experienced in enforcing these first agreements, because everybody execrated the act and gladly deprived themselves. Not so, however, when the traders tried to enforce nonimportation agreements to defeat the Townshend Acts. Not even the northern merchants themselves were in accord with the proposed methods of resistance, and the southern merchants were opposed to resistance of any sort. As commission merchants they made their profit regardless of the tax. The confusion of methods and purposes resulted in a variety of nonimportation agreements, some well enforced, others but poorly.

By 1770 it became apparent indeed that the aims of the merchants were quite different from those of the radically anti-British politicians, who were beginning to take over the movement in the commercial centers and to have an increasing number of positions on the merchants' committees. The merchants had formed the organizations to obtain trade reforms; the political leaders wanted to use the associations to force Parliament to recognize the constitutional freedom of the colonies from taxation.[2] Therefore, when Parliament repealed the duties on all of the articles except tea, the

---

[2] Andrews, "Boston Merchants and the Non-Importation Movement," p. 259, has a splendid discussion of these cross-purposes.

merchants wished to abandon the nonimportation agreements, but the radical politicians demanded that the boycott be kept up until all of the duties had been repealed. The difference in objectives led to a physical split in some of the organizations, as in New York and Charleston, where organizations called "The Friends of Liberty and Trade" were formed.[3] The merchants won out everywhere, and the boycotts were abandoned. This rendered the merchant organizations practically useless to the propagandists, for the divergent aims of the two groups made it almost impossible for them to use the merchants' own organizations to disseminate anti-British propaganda. As a matter of fact, the merchants' organizations had never really been of much value as propaganda agencies. The resolutions and petitions they drew up were primarily intended to obtain relief from the British authorities, and only indirectly did they affect American opinion.

Sons and Daughters of Liberty

In sharp distinction, the finest organization for the dissemination of propaganda among the working classes was the Sons of Liberty. The most remarkable feature of the Stamp Act controversy, in fact, was the work of that organization, which did not exist in the summer of 1765, yet which by November, 1765, practically directed throughout the colonies the entire movement against the act.

An organization made up principally of workingmen was a godsend to the political leaders. Through it they could reach directly those who were suffering from the enforcement of the trade laws at a time of economic distress and widespread unemployment, for times were hard after the Seven Years' War.

The working classes provided perfect material for the Whig agitators, and the organization of these groups into a patriotic society would at once provide the necessary coercive power to enforce the Whig program and, at the same time, direct the restless energies of the underprivileged against Great Britain.

The history of the Sons of Liberty, however, is closely concerned with the gradual appearance of a class-conscious laboring element in colonial society, and much of the activity of the Sons of Liberty and

[3] N. Y. *Journal*, Feb. 8, 1770, Apr. 12, 1770; *S. C. Gazette*, Mar. 21, 1771. There is evidence of a similar spirit in Newport.—*The Literary Diary of Ezra Stiles, D.D., LL.D.*, I, 42.

later workingmen's organizations was intended to obtain political privileges for the mechanic class. The political leaders wanted to use the workingmen's association in their fight against British legislation; the workingmen themselves were eager allies, but they hoped in addition to gain privileges for themselves. The history of the working-class organizations before the Revolution is consequently the history in large part of the conflicts and compromises of these two elements in the larger Whig group.

The first workingmen's association was formed in the late summer of 1765 by what we might call lower middle-class leaders, acting on their own initiative. Originally it was a loose, informal organization; there was not even agreement on the name, for the term Sons of Liberty did not come into common use until November or December, 1765. The first purpose of the leaders was to prevent the enforcement of the Stamp Act by obtaining resignations from those men appointed to distribute the stamps in the colonies. Almost spontaneously, it would seem, bands of men associated themselves together in the colonies for this purpose and from August to November led crowds against the distributors.[4] The crowds were openly led by the mob leaders of the period, Isaac Sears, Ebenezer Mackintosh, and the others. All the evidence points, however, to the conclusion that behind every mob leader there was a small group of men, keeping their identity secret, who had gotten together before the actual outbreak against the stamp distributors. They made their plans for this first step and thereafter charted the course of popular opposition to the act.

The Boston group, first calling itself the Loyall Nine, organized in the summer of 1765. Two distillers, two braziers, two petty merchants, a jeweler, a painter, and a printer comprised the secret plotters who guided the popular disturbances openly credited to Ebenezer Mackintosh.[5] The early New York Sons of Liberty were

[4] Philip G. Davidson, "Sons of Liberty and Stamp Men," *North Carolina Historical Review*, IX, 37 ff., discusses in some detail the activities of the Liberty Boys during the Stamp Act disturbances.

[5] Wells, *Life of Samuel Adams*, I, 63, says the group was formed either in the spring of 1765 or at the time of the August riots. The only direct evidence is in *Mass. Gazette*, Aug. 21, 1765, in which it is stated that on the afternoon of August 14 the people entered the home of Andrew Oliver and there formed their society, by name the Union Club. The Loyall Nine had no doubt been meeting for some time. The Nine consisted of John Avery, Thomas Chase, John Smith, Stephen Cleverly, George Trott, Thomas Crafts, Benjamin Edes, Henry Bass, and Henry Welles.—G. P. Anderson, "A Note on Ebenezer

headed by two or three small merchants, a tavern keeper, a cabinet maker, and even a teacher.[6] There was less interest in Philadelphia in the summer of 1765, perhaps because the city had not yet felt the economic depression. In spite of popular lethargy a small group, principally led by Charles Thomson, William Bradford, the printer, and Robert Morris, associated themselves together to defeat the Stamp Act.[7] In some of the other northern towns there were similar associations. Israel Putnam and Hugh Laddie headed the New London and Pomfret Sons of Liberty; William Goddard, the printer, and a group of Providence merchants had begun to make their plans as early as August, 1765, and Dr. Thomas Young was no doubt as active in Albany as he was later in New York.[8] In the southern colonies some of the more influential leaders initiated the movement. Samuel Chase and William Paca took charge of the work of the Liberty Boys in Annapolis and Baltimore, and Christopher Gadsden was surely the guiding figure behind William Johnson. The formation of groups in other cities is more obscure. It is obvious that they must have existed, and in some instances we can surmise the membership, but there is little to connect some of the familiar revolutionary figures with the Sons of Liberty. Cornelius Harnett, John Ashe, and Hugh Waddell were instrumental in forming the organization in Wilmington,[9] and we know that an organization existed in Georgia without knowing its membership. About the end of October the popular resentment against the Stamp Act increased in Georgia, "and those persons who falsely call themselves the Sons of Liberty began to have private cabals and meetings, and . . .

Mackintosh," Col. Soc. Mass., *Publications*, XXVI, 356. Cf. *Works of John Adams*, II, 178 f. Henry Bass wrote Samuel Savage after the second resignation of Oliver in December, "We do everything to keep this and the first affair Private; and are not a little pleas'd to hear that McIntosh has the Credit of the whole Affair."—Mass. Hist. Soc., *Proceedings*, XLIV, 688 f.

[6] N. Y. *Journal*, May 3, 1770. Hugh Hughes taught an evening school.—*Ibid.*, Apr. 30, 1767. Others of the group were Isaac Sears, John Lamb, Joseph Allicocke, Marinus Willett—called the Paul Revere of New York—Thomas Robinson, and William Wiley. See also N. Y. *Gazette*, Oct. 17, 1765, in which there is an unsigned call for a meeting of the "Friends to Liberty and the ENGLISH CONSTITUTION." No date was set for the meeting. See Herbert Morais, "Sons of Liberty in New York," in *The Era of the American Revolution. Studies Inscribed to Evarts Boutell Greene*, pp. 269-289.

[7] Schlesinger, *Colonial Merchants*, p. 73.

[8] N. Y. *Gazette, or, Weekly Post-Boy*, Aug. 22, 1765; Lamb Papers, p. 35.

[9] *Col. Rec. N. C.*, X, 98; R. D. W. Connor, *Cornelius Harnett*, p. 33. On Gadsden, see Joseph Johnson, *Traditions and Reminiscences, chiefly of the American Revolution in the South* . . ., pp. 37-43.

many had signed an Association to oppose and prevent the distribution of the Stamped papers, and the act from taking effect."[10]

It was with this loose organization that the first five months' work was done. The Liberty Boys as formed in the summer of 1765 comprised small groups of radicals working through mob leaders, whose duty it was to assemble the crowd and carry out plans previously made. No central organization existed, and the only contact among the groups was a rather limited correspondence among the leaders. This was sufficient for the first work of the Sons of Liberty, which consisted of nullifying the Stamp Act by the threefold method of arousing public opinion against it, obtaining the resignation of the stamp distributors, and preventing the use of stamps. The co-ordination of activities among the groups during this first period was in part the result of mere imitation and in part the result of concerted planning. The procedure of Boston in demanding the resignation of Andrew Oliver, the stamp distributor, was quickly followed by neighboring colonies and so spread through all; nothing more was needed than the action itself. But loose as the organization was, a good many activities were concerted. For instance, carefully planned demonstrations were held on August 26 in New London, Lebanon, and Windham, Connecticut, and in Norwich and New Haven within a week. Portsmouth, New Hampshire; Newport; Baltimore; and Wilmington, North Carolina—all buried an effigy of American Liberty on November 1, and there were rumors in New York that "there was a design to execute some foolish ceremony of burying Liberty."[11]

The Sons of Liberty in these early patriotic activities had the good will and actual support of the more conservative Whigs. The historian William Gordon, himself an active participant in the later revolutionary movement, expressed a common point of view:

> "It is not to be supposed, that the disorderly proceedings
> . . . were chargeable solely to the dregs of the colonies—The
> mobs consisted not of mere rabble; but were composed much of
> independent freemen and freeholders. . . . Merchants, assembly-
> men, magistrates, &c. united directly or indirectly in the riots,
> and without their influence and instigation the lower class of

[10] Governor James Wright to Conway, quoted in Jones, *History of Georgia*, II, 61.
[11] See below Chap. X.

inhabitants would have been quiet; but great pains were taken to rouse them into action."[12]

Unwanted violence, however, accompanied all too many of the demonstrations. There was serious rioting in Boston on August 26, and in New York there were ominous signs that the lower classes under Isaac Sears were but insecurely controlled. Really dangerous rioting there on the night of November 1 was prevented with difficulty.[13] The actual or threatened violence and the desire of many to await the outcome of the petition of the Stamp Act Congress to the King caused a general turning against the Liberty Boys. Even among the ranks of those who had first supported the disturbances divisions appeared in the winter of 1765-1766, and there were constant references to the "True-Born Sons of Liberty" as distinct from the "Bastard-kin."[14] The Liberty Boys felt the decline in their influence and determined to strengthen their position. They saw that they must gain the support of the better people and that a strong organization was necessary. Out of this situation came the attempt to form a coherent, intercolonial organization of the working classes which should have the support of the dominant merchant-planter groups.

The first step in the attempt to win over influential Whigs was made by the Boston Loyall Nine, by now the Sons of Liberty. John Adams was invited to attend one of the meetings, and the leaders carefully quieted his apprehensions. Later his advice was often requested, and he was even asked to write inscriptions for some of their placards and transparencies. The Portsmouth, New Hampshire, Boys, after openly forming their organization, obtained the services of Samuel Langdon, later President of Harvard, as their corresponding secretary, and in Newport, Henry Ward, Governor of Rhode Island, Metcalf Bowler, speaker of the House, and Wil-

---

[12] *The History of the Rise, Progress, and Establishment of the Independence of the United States of America*, I, 137. See also Hutchinson, *History of Massachusetts Bay*, III, 126.

[13] See Becker, *Political Parties*, pp. 31 f.; Wilbur C. Abbott, *New York in the American Revolution*, pp. 54 f.; *Montresor Journals*, pp. 337 f.

[14] *Ibid.*, p. 347. The broadside announcing the second resignation of Andrew Oliver on December 17 said that the affair had been carried out by the true-born Sons of Liberty, and the notice of the proposed funeral of Liberty in Newport requested all "True Sons" to meet at the Coffee House, "but if there is any Bastard-kin, it is desired they would not sully his Memory with their Company."—*Newport Mercury, Supplement*, Oct. 28, 1765.

liam Ellery consented to serve on the general committee of the Sons of Liberty.[15] New York leaders had already made contact with at least two members of the Council—John Morin Scott and William Smith—and were in close touch with Philip Livingston.[16]

The effort to effect an intercolonial organization of the Sons of Liberty originated in New York, where the Liberty Boys suffered from popular disapproval. They felt a greater need for the strength that closer association with other groups would give them. The leaders therefore sounded out the Sons of Liberty in other colonies, sending agents late in December into New England to propose an association of the Liberty Boys. Members of this association agreed to defend anyone endangered by a British official, to watch vigilantly all those who might introduce the use of stamps, and to defend those officials who agreed not to enforce the Act. All were to promote a strong union of the colonies.[17] On December 31 two of the agents arrived in New London and entered into conference with the leaders of the Liberty Boys there, telling them of the rumor that troops were coming to enforce the Stamp Act. From New London they went to Norwich with the same story. Two others went to Boston, where they were admitted to the secret councils of the Sons of Liberty. The agents were told that there were three hundred men in Boston ready to arm on a moment's notice (probably a reference to Mackintosh and his followers), and forty thousand more in Massachusetts and New Hampshire. It was about this proposal that the Boston Liberty Boys consulted John Adams. Copies of the proposed association were sent to other New England towns and everywhere there was interest.[18]

The next step in the New York program was the formation of

[15] *Works of John Adams,* II, 178 ff., 183, 184; Belknap Papers, 1745-1776, I, 61, II, 111 f.; R. I. Hist. Soc., Manuscripts, XII, 67.

[16] The Diary of William Smith during this period gives many illustrations.

[17] Gordon, *History of the Rise of Independence,* I, 135 f.

[18] *The Thomas Fitch Papers,* II, 385 f.; *Works of John Adams,* II, 183 f.; Lamb Papers, p. 10. A statement from the Portsmouth Liberty Boys is in Belknap Papers, III, 111 f. Colonel Israel Putnam sent word that he would assist with the militia.—*Montresor Journals,* p. 350. There is evidence of a similar spirit in New Jersey. Allicocke in a letter spoke of rumors of defection in New York and Philadelphia, "whereupon I was informed that our Liberty Boys were more than ordinarily enraged with their wonted Patriotic Fire, and I do verily believe, had there been truth in the assertion, a respectable Body of them would have filed off to the Southward and in their way would have been Join'd with a noble possy of Jersey Folks, beside a succeeding Junction of Eastern Lads kept ready at a moment's warning who upon occasion will swarm like the Industrious Bees."—Lamb Papers, p. 4. South Carolina offered assistance to Georgia.—Jones, *History of Georgia,* II, 65.

local societies. A meeting was held on January 7, and several resolutions were passed against the enforcement of the Stamp Act. On February 4 it was decided to appoint a committee of correspondence, and it was this committee which did so much to unify the Sons of Liberty in the northern colonies. The complete program of the New York society, which it hoped all others would adopt, comprised the formation of associations of Liberty Boys everywhere, an attack on anyone suspected of handling stamps and on the stamps themselves, and an attempt to get the business of courts and customs offices carried on as usual. To carry out this program letters were addressed to the leaders of the Sons of Liberty wherever known, urging them to call a general meeting of their groups and present these plans.[19] Letters were sent to the southern Liberty Boys asking that they form societies in their communities, and these bore fruit later.[20] The Boston Sons of Liberty at the same time instigated an active correspondence among the New England Sons of Liberty advocating practically the same program.[21]

In consequence of the letters sent out by the New York and New England Sons of Liberty, meetings were held all over the country.[22] The program followed in some of the colonies in the spring of 1766 was much more comprehensive than anything that had been undertaken previously, and it is clearly indicated that the framework of a real revolutionary machine was being built.

In some instances, as in Connecticut, nothing more was under way than a general concurrence with the New York and Boston ideas. Delegates from a "great majority" of the towns met in Hart-

[19] An analysis of this correspondence is in Becker, *Political Parties*, pp. 46 ff.

[20] Boston Liberty Boys wrote those in Portsmouth, New Hampshire, that the circulars to the South had "produced the desired effect, as far as we have heard, so that we have the most sanguine hopes of being a united body from South Carolina to New-Hampshire in a few Weeks."—Belknap Papers, III, 119. Notice that Georgia was not included. See also R. I. Hist. Soc., Manuscripts, XII, 67; and Lamb Papers, p. 33.

[21] "We are writing to all the Towns in the Province to know their Dispositions." —Boston Sons of Liberty to those in Portsmouth, Feb. 10, 1766, Belknap Papers, III, 114. An excellent example of this New England correspondence may be seen in the first letter of the Providence Liberty Boys to those in Newport, Mar. 20, 1766: "From Principles of Duty to our Sovereign, from what we owe to ourselves, to our fellow Subjects in America, and to our Posterity, we have associated, and firmly united to risque our Lives and Fortunes in supporting His Majesty's Government in these Colonies, according to its true Form and Texture; and to oppose with all our Might and Strength, any Invasions of our Rights and Privileges from His Majesty's Enemies."—R. I. Hist. Soc., Manuscripts, XII, 64.

[22] A list of towns in which there were recorded groups styling themselves Sons of Liberty is in Davidson, "Sons of Liberty and Stamp Men," *N. C. Hist. Rev.*, IX, 50.

ford on March 25 and drew up resolutions supporting the New York program.[23] Throughout the country there were a good many town meetings of the same sort.

In Maryland, however, a colonial association of more permanence was formed. The attempt to open the courts and customs houses, closed because of the lack of stamped paper, required more strength than the Baltimore Sons of Liberty had. They, therefore, requested each town to send delegates to aid. The convention met and accomplished its purpose.[24]

New Jersey worked out still more completely the details of a revolutionary organization. Each town was to elect delegates to a county convention, which was to appoint a committee of correspondence. From the county committees delegates were to be sent to a provincial convention, and it in turn was to appoint a committee for the colony.[25] This was almost identically the plan followed later when a complete framework of local government was set up in August, 1775.

Although no central organization was ever effected, every independent unit of the Sons of Liberty had a committee of correspondence. These committees tied the colonies together to a really remarkable extent. The resolutions adopted by the meetings, like the resolutions of the New England towns, were all of a piece. They expressed loyalty to George III and abhorrence of the Stamp Act, which they called arbitrary, tyrannical, and unconstitutional. The resolutions announced a willingness to unite with other groups to protect the country from the Stamp Act and its officers; they declared those who would enforce the act "enemies to their country," and those who would carry on business as usual "true friends to Liberty." Recognizing the disapproval with which the better classes viewed them, the Liberty Boys uniformly throughout the country declared themselves the true-born Sons of Liberty, determined to maintain the peace of the community.

So successful was the network of corresponding committees that Sam Adams proposed its continuance, even in the event of the repeal

---

[23] *Connecticut Courant,* Mar. 31, 1766. A suggestion that some such plan be adopted is in *Connecticut Gazette,* Dec. 6, 1765.

[24] *Maryland Gazette,* Mar. 6, Mar. 20, Apr. 3, 1766; Lamb Papers, p. 19; and two broadsides in collections of N. Y. Hist. Soc., both headed *Proceedings of the Sons of Liberty of Baltimoretown,* 1766.

[25] *N. Y. Gazette, or, Weekly Post-Boy,* Mar. 6, 1766; Lamb Papers, p. 14.

of the Stamp Act. A "union" of writers, he said, should be established in every colony "to prevent the cunning & Artifice of some designing Men who perhaps may attempt some other Method to enforce their Scheemes."[26] This idea bore fruit, along with several others, in the committees of correspondence of a later day. Sam Adams was looking well ahead.

The repeal of the Stamp Act brought an end to the activities of the Sons of Liberty. Never afterwards was there such overwhelming, spontaneous joy as then overflowed the colonies. Celebrations, most of them managed by the Liberty Boys, swept the country. The Sons of Liberty and George III had united the country as it had never been united before.

The later history of the Sons of Liberty shows a marked decline in their influence. Originally a semisecret organization of workingmen in a few principal cities, its membership began to change materially even during the Stamp Act controversy. The meetings of the Sons of Liberty, called by local groups in response to letters from New York or Boston, were public meetings, open to all. The resolutions adopted frequently stated that "a number of the principal inhabitants of the town, desirous of being enrolled among the true-born Sons of Liberty" had met to consider the parlous state of affairs and had adopted these their resolutions. The name Sons of Liberty was so loosely used that it came to mean little more than patriot or Whig, and in fact in the colonies south of New York it was actually synonymous with the term American Whig. So complete was the identification that it can hardly be said that an organization called the Sons of Liberty existed in the southern colonies. The absence there of a compact, class-conscious labor group, except perhaps in Charleston, made impossible the formation of any real working-class organization. In the northern cities, on the other hand, there was an actual organization, made up largely of the lower middle classes and artisans, within, but distinct from, the Whig party as a whole. In Newport, for example, it was said that there was a "regular Society, distinguished by that laudable Appelation, THE SONS OF LIBERTY, the more readily to unite, on any Emer-

---

[26] R. I. Hist. Soc., Manuscripts, XII, 67. Mayhew suggested that the colonial assemblies undertake the task.—Alden Bradford, *Memoir of the Life and Writings of Rev. Jonathan Mayhew*, pp. 428 ff. Sam Adams wrote the letter to Providence.

gency, in Defense of their natural and constitutional Rights. . . ."[27]
In both Hartford and Providence the groups were apparently quite
distinct from the ordinary freemen, for both took independent political action on certain occasions.[28] In New York and Boston, of
course, the organization was also distinct.

Differences as important as the above made any effective intercolonial organization of the working classes difficult; the Sons of
Liberty had attempted it and failed. No further attempt was ever
made to create one, and never again did the Sons of Liberty have
the influence they had during the Stamp Act period. The events of
the Stamp Act controversy had demonstrated definitely the absolute
necessity of conservative control of coercive activities. Throughout
the ensuing struggle strong efforts were made to subvert the Sons
of Liberty and similar working-class organizations to the uses of
the Whig party by rigidly controlling their coercive activities and by
transforming them into agencies for the dissemination of propaganda
among the lower classes. These efforts are clearly observable from
the repeal of the Stamp Act on to 1775, when the war gave safer
outlet for the mob spirit. Important changes in the working-class
organizations consequently occurred:

1. The Sons of Liberty became almost exclusively an agency for
the dissemination of propaganda, lost its original character entirely,
and soon died for lack of support. Its name, loosely enough used in
1766, became almost meaningless by 1774.

2. The workers formed new organizations devoted primarily to
obtaining political privileges for the lower classes. In those cities
where the labor interest was strong, rudimentary political parties,
called the Mechanics, the Mechanics' Party, and the like, appeared.

3. The coercive function of the old Sons of Liberty was taken
over by committees of inspection or safety. The secret abettors of
the Whigs now hid behind such fictions as "The Mohawk River
Indians," "Legion," and others.

The repeal of the Stamp Act brought to an end the activities of
the Sons of Liberty, but the individual societies did not always dis-

---

[27] *Boston Gazette, Supplement*, Apr. 14, 1766.
[28] The Hartford Liberty Boys once met to select their candidates for governor and
deputy-governor, not because all of them could vote but to give the freemen a "lead."
—*Conn. Courant*, Mar. 31, 1766. The Providence organization once met at the same time
as the town meeting to approve the instructions to the town representatives in the assembly.
—*N. Y. Gazette, or, Weekly Post-Boy*, Aug. 22, 1765.

band.[29] Skeleton organizations remained in most of the cities where there had been an active group, but only the Boston Sons of Liberty were at all active before the agitation over the Townshend Acts. They alone of the other groups co-operated in arranging for the celebration on the repeal of the Stamp Act and in both 1766 and 1767 celebrated August 14, their own anniversary, the day "when the noble Ardour of Liberty burst thro' its long Concealment, o'er-leaped the Barriers of Oppression, and lifted its awful Crests amid the Group of cowering Dastards, haughty Tyrants and merciless Parricides."[30]

Organizations of the Sons of Liberty elsewhere did not become active until the agitation against the Townshend Acts was well under way. The Boston and Charleston Sons of Liberty were ready to begin work in 1768, but the New York Sons of Liberty were in difficulty. The society had split into two factions, one led by Sears, Lamb, Allicocke, and John Morin Scott, the other by Alexander McDougall. The split had been occasioned in part by personal diffi-culties between Sears and McDougall and in part by local political problems. The Livingston faction had been using the Sons of Lib-erty to further their own political interests in their fight with the De Lanceys, and this tended to split the group. In the summer of 1769 a compromise was reached, and the two factions joined to sup-port the nonimportation agreement, adopted in August, 1768. A broadside on July 7, 1769, announced this fact:

"It must appear obvious to every unprejudiced Mind, that Supineness would prove as fatal to us, as a Disunion; and there-fore, the more effectually to guard against both—A Number of the Inhabitants of this City, have determined to drop all Party Distinction that may have originated from a Difference in Senti-ments in other Matters—to form Ourselves into a Society, under

[29] The New York group apparently disbanded. Nicholas Ray, New York agent in London, answered a letter from the Sons of Liberty in which he recommended that a Liberty Club be formed. Sears, Allicocke, Lamb, and a few others replied that it could not be done "as it is imagined that some inconveniences would arise should such a club be established, just at this time."—Leake, *Life of Lamb*, pp. 36 f. This was October, 1766. The Sons of Liberty was openly formed again in 1769.

[30] *Boston Gazette*, Aug. 18, 1766; Mar. 23, 1767. See also "The Diary of John Rowe," 2 Mass. Hist. Soc., *Proceedings*, X, 63. There is some evidence that the Providence Sons of Liberty maintained their organization.—*Newport Mercury*, Aug. 31, Dec. 14, 1767.

the general and honourable Appellation, of the United SONS of LIBERTY. . . ."[31]

The revived Sons of Liberty in these three cities were of considerable importance in enforcing the nonimportation agreements in their communities, particularly among their own members. They were also of more importance, perhaps, as agencies for the dissemination of propaganda, for they aided greatly by their demonstrations and celebrations to unify the sentiments of the people.

Outside of these three cities, the organization was either dead or dying. The loose organizations of the Stamp Act period were simply not revived in many cases. In several instances, the organizations had become so weak as to be almost useless. The combination of a powerful official class and an unusual and somewhat unique period of prosperity in Portsmouth, New Hampshire, completely defeated the Portsmouth Liberty Boys. The Rhode Island merchants frankly refused to adopt a nonimportation agreement, and the Sons of Liberty in Newport and Providence were even more helpless than their brethren in Portsmouth. The organization survived in a few Connecticut towns, but it was completely dead in Philadelphia.[32] Even in the three cities where there were active branches of the Sons of Liberty there was a gradual tendency to drop the name. It was almost never used after 1773 to refer to a society; it was simply another name for patriot.[33]

The second change in workers' organizations took place some time between 1770 and 1774. During that period the city workers began to form open if somewhat rudimentary political parties, designed primarily to obtain political privileges for themselves. The change resulted in part from the efforts of the Whig leaders to substitute for the old Sons of Liberty coercive organizations under better

[31] N. Y. Public Library, Broadside Collection, 1763-1783.

[32] One letter of what was probably a considerable exchange between the Connecticut and Rhode Island Sons of Liberty has survived. The Middletown Sons of Liberty wrote those in Providence that a violator named Isaac Colten was still at large, but that they had hopes of apprehending him shortly. They also asked to be notified if any of their group traded with any of the Providence merchants.—R. I. Hist. Soc., Manuscripts, XII, 82. Mathew Tallcott, Sam Willis, George Phillips, and Richard Alsop signed this letter.

[33] E.g., the Cape Elizabeth Committee of Correspondence wrote Boston, "we can assure you every Person in this District are true Sons of Liberty."—Boston Committee Records, p. 134. A writer in a southern paper in 1774 said of Goddard's idea of an American post office that it must appeal "to every sensible, clear sighted and real son of Liberty."—*South Carolina and American General Gazette*, May 6, 1774.

control, and in part from the efforts of the working-class leaders to develop better organizations for furthering their interests.

The first real mechanics' association for political purposes originated in Charleston in 1766. Christopher Gadsden called the old Sons of Liberty together in the fall to urge upon them the necessity for maintaining a strict union. He pointed out the danger from the Declaratory Act and the consequent danger of relaxing their efforts in defense of their liberties. This group really constituted a political party. It nominated a ticket in the fall elections of 1768 and put Gadsden in office for the first time in his career. Three of its nominees were elected, and thereafter this mechanics' party formed a substantial element in the political life of South Carolina.[34] It organized the workers in opposition to British legislation and was a powerful ally of the planters in overcoming the merchant influence. One third of the membership of the city committees to enforce the nonimportation agreements was always given to the mechanics, one third to the merchants, and one third to the planters. The mechanics and planters could always outvote the merchants.[35]

The political organization of the workingmen in Philadelphia apparently grew out of an association formed in 1772 called the Patriotic Society. There had been a strong movement, led by the smaller tradesmen and the more substantial mechanics, against the aristocratic control of the colony, but their voting power was so weak that no real gains could be made. The Patriotic Society purposed to preserve "our just Rights and Privileges to us and our Posterity against every attempt to violate or infringe the same, either here or on the *other side the Atlantic*."[36] Neither the Patriotic Society nor the Sons of Liberty appeared by name in the mob activities at the time of the Tea Act, and by 1774 the Patriotic Society had apparently metamorphosed into a mechanics' association. On the ninth of June, 1774, the Mechanics' Association of Philadelphia met in response to letters from the New York mechanics about the Boston

---

[34] The list of those there is in McCrady, *South Carolina under Royal Government*, p. 590 n. An account of the meeting is in Johnson, *Traditions and Reminiscences of the Revolution*, pp. 28 f. On the election of 1768, see McCrady, *op. cit.*, pp. 604 ff.

[35] The mechanics called a meeting in March, 1774, to determine whether they were being taxed without their consent and whether "this reputable Province" would preserve its reputation or would sink into disgrace and contempt.—Broadside, bound with *S. C. Gazette*, Mar. 21, 1774.

[36] *Pa. Gazette*, Aug. 19, 1772.

Port Act. A committee of eleven was appointed to co-operate with the merchants in determining upon a course of action, and this committee met with the political and religious leaders of the city to pre-arrange plans for a city mass meeting. On the committees subsequently appointed by the city, the mechanics had an increasing influence.[37]

The formation of the New York Committee of the Mechanics was a radical and sudden change in the workingmen's organization. The Sons of Liberty had maintained its organization after 1770 but did little more than celebrate the anniversary of the repeal of the Stamp Act by having a dinner at one of the taverns. When the news of the Tea Act reached New York, there was a good deal of uneasiness among several interested groups, and once more the Sons of Liberty came to the front with a definite program. The leaders published on November 29, 1773, proposals for an agreement to boycott anyone who should aid or abet the introduction or use of tea imported under the terms of the Act.[38] The Sons of Liberty then gained popular support for their program by a meeting of the associators on December 16 and ultimately engineered the forcible rejection of the tea.[39] There was, however, objection to the use of force, and there was once more uneasiness among the socially conservative as to the methods being adopted by their fellow patriots. So strong was this feeling when news of the Boston Port Act came that they determined to direct the course of the opposition.[40] It was this situation which undoubtedly caused the leaders of the Sons of Liberty to change their organization. There appeared in the politics of the city for the first time the Committee of the Mechanics, which

[37] *Pa. Journal*, June 15, 1774; Lamb Papers, p. 51; Charles H. Lincoln, *The Revolutionary Movement in Pennsylvania, 1760-1776*, p. 169.

[38] Becker, *Political Parties*, pp. 105 f. William Smith says in his Diary, December 1, 1773, that the people were not upset by the Tea Act until Sears and McDougall received notice of the Boston resolution that the tea should not be landed. There was agitation against the Act in the papers well before this, however. E.g., N. Y. *Journal*, Oct. 14, Oct. 21, 1773.

[39] Sears, McDougall, and other leaders met secretly at a tavern to concert plans for dealing with the tea when it arrived.—Diary of William Smith, Dec. 22, 1773.

[40] There is ample testimony to the growing uneasiness of the conservatives. There is, of course, Gouverneur Morris's much quoted letter to John Penn, May 20, 1774, which should be read in full: "the heads of the mobility grow dangerous to the gentry; and how to keep them down is the question."—4 Force, *Amer. Arch.*, I, 343. See also *Colden Letter Books*, II, 361, and *Col. Rec. N. C.*, IX, 1084. William Smith wrote of the merchants in his Diary, Apr. 29, 1775, that they were "so humbled as only to sigh or complain in whispers. They now dread Sear's Train of armed men." This was written just after the riotous seizure of guns in New York.

thereafter represented not only the demands of the lower classes for political reform but also the revolutionary aims of the more radical propagandists.[41] It acted throughout the next few years as the executive committee of a political party, and its decisions bound the party —a point of great importance. It nominated its own lists of delegates to the various provincial congresses and the Continental Congress, voted on matters relating to the Continental Association, and ultimately was the first organized body in New York to vote for independence.[42]

The change from the Sons of Liberty to a workingmen's party in Boston was much slower and not so complete as in New York. The name Sons of Liberty almost never appeared in Boston after 1773, although the organization had directed several celebrations during the quiet years after 1770. Paul Revere became an important member and Ebenezer Mackintosh left town in the summer of 1774, but otherwise there was no change in the leadership. Much the same coercive activities were carried on; there were the same warnings and threatenings,[43] and it was the same old crowd which threw the tea in Boston harbor and intimidated officials. But the Sons of Liberty did not figure openly. Celebrations of the old anniversaries were now managed by other agencies, and even the anniversaries peculiar to the Sons of Liberty passed unnoticed. The last celebration of August 14 was in 1773, and that appears to have broken up in a riot.[44] There is less and less evidence each month of an active, vital organization, and gradually most of the functions of the old Sons of Liberty were absorbed by the new committees. On the Committee of Sixty-Three, for instance, created to enforce the Association of 1774, the former leaders of the Sons of Liberty were well repre-

[41] Becker, *Political Parties*, pp. 112-120. The organization was not entirely abandoned. There is evidence that Sears and others retained the framework for purposes of mob action and used the Committee of the Mechanics for political purposes. Broadsides bearing the name "Legion," an old pseudonym of the Liberty Boys, appeared warning the printers not to print anything derogatory to the Whigs and threatening public officials. E.g., Library of Congress, Broadsides, New York, Oct. 27, 1774; and Abbott, *New York in the American Revolution*, pp. 165 f. The Sons of Liberty also burned copies of Myles Cooper's *American Querist* and Seabury's *A View of the Controversy.—N. Y. Gazetteer*, Jan. 12, 1775. They also called a meeting to oppose supplying the troops.—N. Y. Pub. Library, Broadsides, Apr. 13, 1775. The name was so loosely used, however, and so commonly used to refer to any group engaged in coercive activities that it probably did not refer to an organization. Sears and his followers did the work, whatever the name they used.

[42] Becker, *Political Parties*, p. 120 and *passim*.

[43] Pseudonyms were used as before—"O. C., secretary," "Determined," "Joyce Jun." Joyce is said to have been John Winthrop, Jr.—2 Mass. Hist. Soc., *Proceedings*, XII, 139 n.

[44] *Boston Post-Boy and Advertiser*, Aug. 23, 1773.

sented. But even though radical leaders had seen their organization lose its prominent part in the movement, they did not develop another, as did those in New York and Philadelphia. The mechanics of Boston did act at least once as an organization: they refused to assist Gage in his efforts to fortify Boston Neck and wrote the New York Committee of Mechanics to refuse aid likewise should he apply to them.[45]

The old leaders of the Sons of Liberty, acting probably for themselves rather than for any organization, attempted in March, 1775, to institute a weekly exchange of news with New York. They offered to send "the earliest and most authentic intelligence of what may be transacted in this metropolis and province, relating to the public affairs and general concerns of America," but they received little encouragement.[46]

Outside of these centers there do not appear to have been any working-class organizations of importance. There are occasional references to the Sons of Liberty as a society, but they are few.[47] In some places the workingmen were joined in semisocial clubs—the Sons of St. Patrick, or the Sons of St. Tammany—but there is no evidence that they committed their membership to the Whig program.[48] In the main the mechanics other than in the commercial centers were not sufficiently class-conscious to form organizations of their own.

No specific agency for the organization of the rural lower classes was created by the Whig leaders. There were organizations of the small farmers and tenants, such as the Regulators in North and South Carolina and the Levellers in New York, but instead of being a possible aid to the Whigs they were a positive menace. Before the

[45] 4 Force, *Amer. Arch.*, I, 803 f.

[46] Leake, *Life of Lamb*, p. 99.

[47] E.g., Wallingford Sons of Liberty erected a liberty pole in 1774—*A Century of Meriden*, p. 268; on December 17, 1774, "a Drum and fife pervaded the Streets of Portsmouth, accompanied by several Committee-men and the Sons of Liberty, publickly avowing their intention of taking possession of Fort William and Mary."—*Documents N. H.*, VII, 423. Ezra Stiles dined in October, 1774, with a number of "Gentlemen, Sons of Liberty from Boston and N. York."—*Literary Diary*, I, 461, 463. The *Ga. Gazette*, Aug. 30, 1774, reported that a "respectable body of Sons of Liberty" tarred and feathered Thomas Brown and drummed William Davis around Liberty Tree three times. The account was signed, John Willson, secretary.

[48] E.g., Charleston Sons of St. Patrick generally celebrated the anniversary of the repeal of the Stamp Act.—*S. C. Gazette*, Mar. 22, 1773. The Sons of St. Tammany in Norfolk celebrated his anniversary in May.—*Va. Gazette* (Purdie), May 19, 1774.

Whigs could make any real accessions in the areas controlled by these organizations it was necessary to destroy them. The Tories, on the contrary, could have used them most effectively, and one of the most serious weaknesses of Tory propaganda was the failure to make use of the existing organizations already in bitter opposition to the Whigs.

Whig leaders did, however, organize the women and with great success. Patriotic societies of women, called Daughters of Liberty, were formed in 1765 in sympathy with their brother organizations of the Sons of Liberty. They passed spirited resolutions, and it was reported, perhaps facetiously, that one group of unmarried women had resolved to marry no man who would use a stamped marriage license.[49]

When the northern merchants and Whig leaders were trying to resist the Townshend Acts, they really began to organize the women in a serious way. Organized women could aid greatly in enforcing the nonconsumption and nonimportation agreements. The early nonconsumption agreements, for example, included many items used and purchased almost exclusively by women—stays, ribbons, hats, women's clothing, muffs and furs, and piece goods. The subscribers in addition, agreed to live frugally and to support local manufactures. The women had to be induced to support these agreements; self-denial had to become a patriotic duty. Associations of women were therefore formed to promote these objects. The Daughters of Liberty, spinning societies, and other voluntary associations began to appear throughout the country. These were simply groups of women more or less loosely associated together. Even children had spinning clubs, and much interest was aroused in their activities. William Molineux was a tremendous success as an organizer of women in Boston, and the spinning bees he arranged made some remarkable records.[50] Of more importance was the fact that societies publicly endorsed the Whig program and as social organizations brought pressure to bear on their members. Every group adopted resolutions

[49] *Newport Mercury*, Dec. 9, 1765. The Boston Sons of Liberty sent their thanks to the Daughters of Liberty in Providence for their patriotic resolves.—R. I. Hist. Soc. Manuscripts, XII, 67.

[50] *Boston Gazette, Supplement,* Feb. 26, 1770; and *Boston Town Records, 1770-1777,* p. 73. The subject is dealt with in Rolla Milton Tryon, *Household Manufactures in the United States, 1640-1860.*

against tea drinking, and some passed resolutions boycotting those merchants who violated the agreements. The same policies were followed when the Continental Association was adopted throughout the colonies, and since women did the buying, such actions were of real importance.[51]

[51] Both the North End and the South End Daughters in Boston, some three hundred women, banned tea, as did the Daughters in Bedford, Virginia.—*Boston Gazette*, Feb. 12, 1770; *Newport Mercury*, Feb. 7, 1774; *Va. Gazette* (Purdie), Mar. 17, 1774. See also Richard Frothingham, Jr., *The History of Charlestown, Massachusetts*, p. 278; *New Hampshire Gazette and Historical Chronicle*, Aug. 22, 1775; *Newport Mercury*, Apr. 11, 1774.

V

CHURCHES, SCHOOLS, AND CLUBS

The most powerful social institution in eighteenth-century America was the church, and it, of all, could be the most effective in the dissemination of propaganda. The Great Awakening had tremendously stimulated religious enthusiasm and had counteracted among the plain people the deism that was spreading among the upper classes in the South. There was certainly a more intense religious life among the lower classes than ever before. The falling off from the high period of Puritanism in New England, moreover, was not so marked but that the churches still exercised more authority than any other social institution. The Whig leaders would gain great moral support for their proposals if they could obtain public endorsements from organized church groups. If political rights and duties could be identified with religious rights and duties, if civil liberties could be identified with religious liberties, if the contest could be tinged with high and holy purposes, then could be enlisted the support of thousands who might not fight for the Whigs but would fight for God. That cause is almost won which can call to its support organized virtue, which can spread itself through those who speak with the authority of the cloth and the lectern—the Book in front of them and God, almost visible, behind them.

There were in 1775 approximately thirty-two hundred churches of eighteen denominations. The Congregational churches were the most numerous, followed in order by the Presbyterian, Anglican, Baptist, Quaker, German Reformed, Lutheran, Dutch Reformed, Methodist and Catholic.[1] The interest and organization of these churches varied widely, and they were therefore of unequal value to the Whig leaders.

The established Congregational Church of New England, of all the churches in America, was the only one that by its principles and

[1] Professor M. W. Jernegan mapped the churches for Charles O. Paullin's *Atlas of Historical Geography of the United States:* total mapped, 3,228; Congregational, 668, Presbyterian, 588, Anglican, 495, Baptist, 494, Quaker, 310, German Reformed, 159, Lutheran, 150, Dutch Reformed, 120, Methodist, 65, Catholic, 56, Moravian, 31, Congregational-Separatist, 27, Dunker, 24, Mennonite, 16, French Protestant, 7, Sandemanian, 6, Jewish, 5, Rogerene (Baptist), 3.

interests might be expected to take an aggressive part in the revolutionary movement. All but seven of its six hundred and sixty odd churches were in New England, and there it was substantially identified with the provincial ruling class. The Edwardian revival had fastened its establishment on Massachusetts and Connecticut for another hundred years and had checked the wane in clerical influence throughout New England. This established church, therefore, was thrown into sharp conflict with those struggling for religious freedom within the colony and with the Anglican Church backed by the British government. The struggle for religious freedom within the colony was largely carried on by the Baptists, drawn from the lower classes, and the position of the church was thus attacked from below at the same time that it feared an attack from above. Wrongly, but none the less firmly and fearfully, church leaders in New England believed that the home government intended to appoint a bishop for all America and to promote a general establishment.[2] This was the one church in America, therefore, which because of its principles and position might be expected to take a positive part in the revolutionary movement. The nonconformist ministers, from their political and ecclesiastical thought and experience, had developed a philosophy which was a perfect counterpart of the eighteenth-century political philosophy. It was the *naturrecht* of John Locke in its religious application: as men could form a government, so men could form a church; as men in society possessed certain inalienable rights, so men in religious societies possessed certain equally inalienable rights—worship after their own fashion, and the liberties wherewith Christ had made them free; as governments were instituted among men to protect their civil rights, so were they to protect religious rights. When governments became subversive of these privileges, it was the right, nay the duty, of Christians to resist. The Anglican controversy and the very real fear of an American episcopate aided greatly in clarifying these politico-religious thoughts, so that by the opening of the controversy with England the ministers had not only developed this philosophy but had begun to expound it.[3] Even so, Samuel Adams could write Elbridge Gerry in 1772:

[2] See A. L. Cross, *The Anglican Episcopate and the American Colonies.*

[3] This whole subject is dealt with extensively in Baldwin, *New England Clergy*, Chaps. III, IV. Just as those demanding civil rights denied them to others, so those demanding religious rights denied them to others.

"I cannot but hope, when you consider how indifferent too many of the Clergy are to our just & righteous Cause, that some of them are Adulators of our Oppressors, and even some of the best of them are extremely cautious of recommending (at least in their publick performances), the Rights of their Country to the protection of Heaven, lest they should give offence to the little Gods on Earth, you will judge it quite necessary that we should assert [and] vindicate our Rights as *Christians* as well as Men & Subjects."[4]

At least, however, the ministers would agitate voluntarily against the English religious policies, and they could therefore be led the more easily into a general protest against imperial policies. In the earlier days of the New England colonies they had led the fight against Great Britain, and in this modern controversy, those who were not propagandists themselves would be willing agents. No central organization existed, however, through which the propagandists, clerical or otherwise, could work. The attitude of the individual minister would determine his response to the propagandist's appeal, for the churches recognized no legal superior.

The Presbyterian Church presented a somewhat more complex situation. Its strength lay in the middle and southern colonies,[5] and its membership was drawn from both the upper and lower classes. In spite of the fact that many of the members in the southern colonies were among the discontented elements, the church rigorously condemned those who promoted rebellion against the colonial governments. In 1768, at the time of the Regulator movement in North Carolina, for example, it sharply rebuked the Regulators, many of whom were Presbyterians with definite religious grievances. A letter signed by four Presbyterian ministers addressed to the leaders of the rebellion deplored the departure from the principles and practices of the church, "which . . . have always evidenced a zealous attachment to the Protestant Succession in the present royal Family, and a spirited opposition to every measure concerted at home or abroad, to shake the present happy Establishment and this on the principles strictly enjoined by the Westminster Confession of Faith and Catechism." Redress, they said, must be sought within the law, not by

---

[4] *Writings of Sam Adams*, II, 349.
[5] Paullin, *Atlas of Historical Geography*, Plate 82, lists only 12 in Massachusetts, 4 in Connecticut, 1 in Rhode Island, and 2 in Georgia.

rebellion: "Submit yourself to every ordinance of man for the Lord's sake, whether it be to the King as supreme, or unto Governors as those that are sent by him for the Punishment of Evil Doers and for the Praise of them that do well." Governor Tryon gratefully reported to Lord Hillsborough, "I have pleasure in acknowledging the utility that the presbyterian ministers' letters to their brethren had upon the then face of public affairs. . . ."[6] It must have been a comfort to the eastern political leaders to know that officially, at least, the Presbyterian Church would support them against social revolution from below.

The Presbyterians, nearly all of them Scotch Calvinists, had no love for England and were naturally hostile to the idea of an American episcopate. The laity was greatly aroused by the supposed threat and looked angrily on the extension of the Anglican Church. The southern membership, however, already lived under an Anglican establishment, and one not maintained by Great Britain but by the colonial leaders themselves. Anglican planters and Scotch Presbyterians would join against England, but it would be at the sacrifice of the Anglican establishments in the southern colonies.

Because there were so many potential revolutionists among the Presbyterians, it was particularly fortunate for the Whigs that a central organization of the church did exist. It might be induced to speak for the membership, thus giving the appearance of unity, and through it the suggestions of the leaders could be spread. The Great Awakening had divided the church at the same time that it greatly stimulated the growth of New Side Presbyterianism. From 1745 to 1758 two synods of the church existed, the Philadelphia, or Old Side, synod, and the New York, or New Side, synod. In 1758 a compromise was effected, and the united church grew rapidly in numbers and influence under the guidance of the triumphant revival party. This united organization gave the Whig leaders an unusual opportunity to reach with an effective appeal the small farmers of the South, which otherwise could be reached only with difficulty.

The situation of the Anglican Church was even more complicated. The Society for the Propagation of the Gospel was making

[6] This letter was signed by Hugh McCaddon, Henry Patillo, James Creswell, and David Caldwell.—*Col. Rec. N. C.*, VII, 814-816, 886.

vigorous efforts to extend the influence of the church, particularly in the middle colonies, and there was the recurrent though ungrounded fear among Americans that England proposed to set up an American bishopric, to have charge of the church in all the colonies. The Anglican Church was completely identified with the English officials in the colonies. Nonconformist New England was therefore in bitter opposition to it, and Anglican clergymen and laity there were willy-nilly thrown into the Tory party.

The Anglican Church in the middle colonies was established in only four New York counties, and there was of course considerable opposition among the other religious groups to the extension of its influence. The clergy, however, were not all aggressively pro-British agitators. The attitude many of them took is admirably illustrated in a letter of the Pennsylvania clergy to the S. P. G., written in 1775. They explained that so far they had been able to keep their pulpits clear of politics, but the time had come when silence would be misconstrued. Congress had appointed a day of fasting and prayer, the people were forming military associations, and increasing pressure was being brought upon the local churches to declare themselves. "Under these Circumstances our People call upon us, and think they have a right to our advice in the most public manner from the Pulpit. Should we refuse, our Principles would be misrepresented, and even our religious usefulness destroyed among our People."[7]

The situation was entirely different in the South. There the Anglican Church was substantially identified with the local leaders, and the church establishments were under colonial control. As the church had no important contacts with the lower classes, it was of no service to the Whig leaders in winning their support,[8] and its relations with the official English class simply complicated the situation. Some clergymen, although a minority, would incline toward England simply because of that connection, whereas others would

[7] W. S. Perry, *Historical Collections Relating to the American Colonial Church*, II, 470. The letter stated that the ministers took turns preaching on the fast days because they really wished to be mediators but lacked sufficient "interest and consequence" to influence the people. The letter was signed by Richard Peters, William Smith, Jacob Duché, Thomas Coombe, William Stringer, and William White. Duché, Coombe, and Smith inclined strongly to the patriot side at this time. See E. F. Humphrey, *Nationalism and Religion, 1774-1789*, p. 40.

[8] Paullin, *Atlas of Historical Geography*, Plate 82, shows that the Anglican churches in the South were concentrated in three areas: tidewater Virginia, northeastern North Carolina, and coastal South Carolina.

remain neutral if they could. Others, however, because closely identified with the Whig politicians, would even actively agitate against
British policies. Of the hundred Anglican ministers in Virginia, for
example, only thirteen showed active loyalty to England and forty-
four had a public record of loyalty to the patriots. Of the twenty-
three Anglican ministers in South Carolina, only five were loyal to
England.[9] In the North the church sought the aid and protection
of England in its efforts to extend its influence and effect a general
establishment; in the South there were many ministers of the church
who did not wish an American episcopate and fought against it.[10]

The German Reformed, Lutheran, and Dutch Reformed churches
had their largest following in the middle colonies and in the south-
west. They, too, were opposed to the extension of the Anglican
Church, and it is obvious that, representing as they did colonial interests and classes, they would be either agents of the Whig leaders
or would remain neutral as their interests dictated. Many individual
ministers of the German and Dutch Reformed churches were actively pro-Whig, but many of the Lutheran churches were pro-
British. The three churches each had at least one synod, primarily
for the training and licensing of ministers, but these synods had little
control over the individual churches. The Lutherans received their
teachers and instructions from either Halle or Hanover and were
thus doubly bound to George III as King of England and as Elector
of Hanover. The membership of all three churches was neither particularly hostile to Great Britain nor particularly friendly to her; it
could be held for the Whigs by adroit methods.[11]

The position of the Baptist Church was somewhat peculiar. It
was identified almost exclusively throughout the colonies with the
underprivileged classes. It therefore suffered in nine colonies from
an established church, and Baptists were actually persecuted as late
as 1774 in Virginia. Moreover, its membership was divided by the
Great Awakening, and the church had no central organization whatever. There were perhaps a few associations of local churches, such
as the Sandy Creek Association in North Carolina, but the propagandists would in the main have to deal with individual ministers,

---

[9] Harrell, *Loyalism in Virginia*, pp. 63 f.; McCrady, *South Carolina under Royal Government*, pp. 450 ff.

[10] See Cross, *Anglican Episcopate*, Chap. X.

[11] Humphrey, *Nationalism and Religion*, pp. 106 ff.

and it was obvious that the Baptists would want value received. However, they had no more love for Great Britain than they had for their local oppressors, and it is significant that in 1769 the Sandy Creek Baptist Association threatened with expulsion any of its members who joined the Regulator Movement.[12]

The remaining churches can be dismissed much more quickly. The pietistic sects—Quaker, Mennonite, and the like—may be disregarded at once, for they constituted a special problem unconnected with the dissemination of propaganda. The Methodist Church was in about the same position as the Baptist, but it was so small as to be negligible. The Virginia Methodists, only about two thousand in number, were in fact loyal to England.[13] The Roman Catholic Church as an organization played no part in the movement; its members did, but not the church. Its sympathies, incidentally, were American rather than English.[14]

The inescapable conclusion to be drawn is that, with the possible exception of some Presbyterian ministers and the Congregationalist clergymen in New England, the ministers would at best be no more than agents, more or less willing, but none the less agents of the propagandists. The propagandist would have to lead the way and arouse church support, and in only a few churches were there central organizations through which he could work. Other means would have to be used, therefore, in enlisting the support of the majority of ministers. There can be little question but that the great work of the clergy in furthering the revolutionary movement was done at the instance of, and on opportunities given by, the political leaders and propagandists.

No effective attempt was made prior to 1775 to commit church members through central agencies. Synodical resolutions approving nonimportation agreements or banning tea would have been of real value, but it does not appear that any effort was made to get the Presbyterian or German synods to take action. In 1775, the Presby-

[12] *Col. Rec. N. C.*, VIII, 655. The Anglicans and Quakers, of course, condemned the movement, as did at least one Dutch Reformed minister.—*Ibid.*, VII, 821, 822.

[13] Humphrey, *Nationalism and Religion*, p. 124.

[14] Jonathan Boucher said of the Maryland Catholics that they "seemed to hesitate and were unresolved" what part to take. "Their principles, no doubt," he continued, "led them to side with Government; whilst their inclinations, and (as they then thought) their interest, made it their policy to be neutral: but it soon became easy to foresee that neither they, nor any others, would long be permitted to enjoy a neutrality."—*A View of the Causes and Consequences of the American Revolution*, p. 241.

terian synods aided greatly in furthering the Whig program. On May 12, 1775, a pastoral letter, written by John Witherspoon, was sent out by the synods of New York and Philadelphia. It exhorted all members of the church to better living in view of the impending crisis, and, while professing loyalty to George III, urged all to demand their rights as Englishmen and Christians, and to maintain the firm union of the colonies.[15]

The clearest example of the propagandists' use of the Presbyterian Church as an organization is the effort made by certain North Carolina leaders to obtain its aid in winning over the reluctant back-country men. Joseph Hewes wrote Samuel Johnston from Philadelphia: "We have prevailed on the Presbyterian Ministers here to write to the Ministers and congregations of their Sect in North Carolina, and have also made application to the Dutch Lutherans and Calvinists to do the same. . . ."[16]

The Philadelphia ministers, Francis Alison, James Spront, George Duffield, and Robert Davidson, responded with an open letter to the ministers and congregations in North Carolina, which was subsequently printed in pamphlet form and generally distributed. It was a very adroit appeal. The letter began with a discussion of the right of Britain to tax the colonies, which, it said, if once established would permit English leaders to lighten their own burdens at the expense of the colonists. The letter then dealt at length with the central theme of propaganda at that time, the need for firm union. Parliament, it said, had asserted the right to bind the colonies in all cases whatsoever. Popery had been established in Quebec; why not in North Carolina? Boston harbor had been closed; why not New York, Philadelphia, Charleston, or any other port? Northern fishing had been stopped; why not domestic manufacturing? The Massachusetts charter had been destroyed; why not all charters? What security have we, it asked, save in united efforts and in God?

Independence, said the clergymen, they did not desire, but the right of revolution no one could deny, and they cleverly inserted an appeal to it:

[15] The record of the church as a whole is found in the official records of the church, but much more conveniently in Humphrey, *Nationalism and Religion*, pp. 81 f. The letter in full is quoted in the *Virginia Gazette* (Dixon and Hunter), Sept. 9, 1775. Shober of New York printed it in a pamphlet.

[16] Burnett, *Letters of Members of Cont. Cong.*, I, 160 (July 8, 1775).

"If we are now wrong in our conduct, our forefathers that fought for liberty at Londonderry and Enniskillen in King James' time, were wrong; nay, they were rebels, when they opposed, and set aside that bigotted Prince, and the Stewart [*sic*] family, and set the Brunswick family on the throne of England. But we hope that such language will never be heard from the mouth of a Protestant, or from an English subject, and much less from any one of our denomination, that have ever maintained the Revolutional Principles, and are firmly devoted to the present reigning family, as the assertors of the British privileges and English liberty."

Two hundred copies of this letter were printed by order of the Provincial Congress of North Carolina and given to the members for distribution—a unique instance of fine propaganda technique.[17]

Yet the church was never asked to take an official vote on independence, the most effective way of utilizing its influence. The church, in fact, lagged considerably behind public opinion on this matter. The first Presbyterian organization to pronounce in favor of independence was the Hanover Presbytery on October 24, 1776, and then only incidentally to its demand that the pledge of religious freedom in the Virginia Declaration of Rights be fulfilled.[18]

The appeal to the German churches, mentioned in Hewes's letter, was likewise successful, for the German Reformed and Lutheran churches in Philadelphia sent a forty-page letter, later printed in pamphlet form, to the Germans in both New York and North Carolina, stating that the Germans in Pennsylvania were solidly behind the movement; militia companies and corps of sharpshooters had been formed, and those who could not serve in the army were ready to contribute in other ways. The Reverend H. M. Mühlenberg, later a militia leader himself, sanctioned this appeal.[19]

The lack of centralized church organizations forced the propagandist to rely upon other methods of enlisting clerical support. The individual church was valuable both as an agency for the dissemination of propaganda and as an organization which could markedly influence its members merely by action. That is, a minister's sermon

---

[17] The letter in full is in *Col. Rec. N. C.*, X, 222-228. It was printed in *Cape Fear Mercury*, Aug. 25, 1775, just a month after it was written.
[18] Humphrey, *Nationalism and Religion*, p. 82.
[19] A. B. Faust, *The German Element in the United States*, I, 287.

in behalf of the Whig cause might win converts either because it was good propaganda or because of the influence of the minister himself, a fact recognized at the time:

"When the clergy engage in political warfare, religion becomes a most powerful engine, either to support or overthrow the state. What effect must it have had upon the audience, to hear the same sentiments and principles, which they had before read in a newspaper, delivered on Sundays from the sacred desk, with a religious awe, and the most solemn appeals to Heaven, from lips, which they had been taught from their cradles, to believe could utter nothing but eternal truths!"[20]

The best method of achieving this double purpose was to provide opportunities for the ministers to declare themselves publicly on the issues of the controversy. Certain opportunities other than the usual Sunday service already existed in New England. There was the annual spring fast and the fall thanksgiving day, the annual spring election sermon, and the annual summer muster day, when the artillery company sermons were delivered. Of these, only militia day was observed with any regularity outside of New England. Ministers were always asked to preach upon these occasions; as the crisis approached and people became more agitated it was inevitable that the sermons should deal pertinently with the state of affairs.[21] In the case of the annual fast and thanksgiving days the common practice was to cite in the preamble to the proclamation the particular conditions which made the day desirable or noticeable, and these proclamations, being read in all the churches, were not only good propaganda in themselves, but conditioned to an extent the tone of the minister's sermons. Massachusetts set aside the usual day of thanksgiving in 1775 because of the firm union of the colonies for which all should be thankful. But, the proclamation added, "in consequence of the unnatural, cruel, and barbarous measures adopted and pursued by the British Administration, great and distressing calamities are brought upon our oppressed Country, and on this Colony in particular."[22]

---

[20] Daniel Leonard in *Massachusettensis*. John Adams' reply is a clear exposition of the right and the duty of clergymen to instruct their congregations on political affairs. —*Works*, IV, 55 n.

[21] The sermons are discussed below, Chap. XI.

[22] 4 Force, *Amer. Arch.*, III, 1351. See also *Conn. Public Records*, XII, 447. Governor Trumbull set aside a spring fast day in Connecticut in 1774 because of the "threatening

The propagandists had not created these opportunities, but they could see to it that the ministers made the best use of them. John Adams sent explicit instructions through Abigail, his wife, to his own minister in Braintree: "Does Mr. Wibird preach against oppression and other cardinal vices of the time? Tell him, the clergy here of every denomination, not excepting the Episcopalian, thunder and lighten every Sabbath. They pray for Boston and Massachusetts. They thank God most explicitly and fervently for our remarkable successes. They pray for the American army."[23]

The propagandist showed his real ability in creating opportunities which the ministers could not ignore. Public meetings were always opened with a prayer, and what minister could fail to invoke the blessings and mercy of God on a people distracted by the loss of their rights? At one of the adjourned meetings of the Suffolk convention, "Good Parson Dunbar gave us the most extraordinary liberty prayer that I ever heard,"[24] and John Adams cleverly enlisted the services of the doubtful Jacob Duché, Anglican minister in Philadelphia, by asking him to deliver one of the opening prayers before the newly-assembled Continental Congress. He reported to his wife later, "Episcopalian as he is, Dr. Cooper himself never prayed with such fervor, such ardor."[25]

Even the reading of notices could become at once a test and an opportunity. In Massachusetts one of Governor Hutchinson's proclamations for a day of fasting and prayer was denounced by the radicals in 1771 as an open insult, because it called for thanks for the *"Continuance of our Privileges,"* whereas, the leaders declared, the people had lost their dearest rights. Such proclamations had always been read in the churches, but several ministers received petitions not to read this one. Dr. Pemberton alone of the Boston pastors read the proclamation, and he did so simply because the Governor was a member of the congregation. He did it with evident embarrassment, and many of the members turned their backs or left the building. It was generally read in the country districts because the

---

aspect of Divine Providence on the Liberties of the People, and the dangers they are menaced with."—Stuart, *Trumbull*, p. 151. See also *R. I. Records*, VII, 249; *Newport Mercury*, Nov. 18, 1765.

[23] *Familiar Letters of John Adams*, p. 50.

[24] A. K. Teele, ed., *The History of Milton, Massachusetts*, p. 424.

[25] *Familiar Letters of John Adams*, pp. 37 f.

clergymen were not sufficiently organized to demand united action.[26]
Governor Hutchinson himself recognized that "a more artful method
of exciting the general attention of the people, which would otherwise, for want of a subject, have ceased, could not have been projected."[27] In 1774 the associated pastors of Boston voted on motion
of Charles Chauncey not to read in their churches any proclamation
which the governor and council might issue.[28]

Much more important in commanding the services of the ministers were the public ceremonies ordered by authority. These were
of two types—celebrations and anniversaries peculiar to the revolutionary movement and special days of fasting, prayer, and humiliation, or of thanksgiving. Ministers had delivered the thanksgiving
sermons on the repeal of the Stamp Act but rarely delivered anniversary sermons. The demonstrations on March 18, the anniversary
of the repeal, were usually in the hands of the Sons of Liberty, who
preferred a picnic or a dance to a sermon. Not even the orations on
the Boston Massacre were delivered by ministers. But throughout
New England, ministers preached on the anniversary of April 19,
1775. The first anniversary produced one of the most bitter and
inflammatory addresses of the whole period. The Reverend Jonas
Clark took as his text, "Egypt *shall be a desolation* . . . because
they have shed INNOCENT BLOOD *in their land*," and, citing
almost every instance of British cruelty and depravity, he made it
perfectly plain that war had made independence inevitable. British
soldiers, he asserted, first drew the sword of violence, more like murderers and cutthroats than the troops of a Christian king:

> "With a *cruelty* and barbarity, which would have made the
> most hardened savage blush, they shed INNOCENT BLOOD!
> —But, O *my* GOD!—! How shall I speak!—or how describe
> the distress, the *horror* of that *awful morn*, that *gloomy day!*—
> *Yond field* can witness the *innocent blood* of our *brethren slain!*
> —And from thence does *their blood* cry unto God for vengeance
> from the ground! There the tender father bled, and there the
> beloved son! There the hoary head, and there the blooming
> youth! . . . *They bleed—they die*, not by the sword of an open

---

[26] "Letters of Samuel Cooper," *Amer. Hist. Rev.*, VIII, 325 f. "Had the ministers
inclined it was not in their Pow'r to read it, a circumstance w'ch never before took Place
among us."—*Ibid.*, p. 326.

[27] Hutchinson, *History of Massachusetts Bay*, III, 347 f.

[28] W. Deloss Love, Jr., *The Fast and Thanksgiving Days of New England*, p. 334.

enemy . . . in the field of battle; but by the hand of those that delight in spoil, and *lurk privily that they may shed innocent blood!*"[29]

Still more important because more generally observed were the special days of prayer and thanksgiving. They might be appointed by any governing agency. The best example of local fast days was the concerted movement in Massachusetts in 1768. Boston, Lexington, Charlestown, Braintree, and probably other towns observed one day in September as a special day of fasting and prayer in protest against the coming of the troops, "The Town," as Braintree said, "having under their consideration the Distressing and Alarming circumstances they are now subjected to as also those impending."[30] Sam Adams was doing his best to prepare for the abortive Convention of September 22, when he hoped strong action would be taken against the troops.

The idea of colonial fast days was introduced into the southern colonies by alert propagandists in 1774. Jefferson reports that he and several others, particularly Patrick Henry and Richard Henry Lee, "were under conviction of the necessity of arousing our people from the lethargy into which they had fallen as to passing events; and thought that the appointment of a day of general fasting & prayer would be most likely to call up & alarm their attention."[31] The House of Burgesses appointed June 1, and every member sent a copy of the resolution to the clergymen of his county. On his return home he invited one of them to address the people on the occasion. Jefferson describes the result: "The people met generally, with anxiety & alarm in their countenances, and the effect of the day thro' the whole colony was like a shock of electricity, arousing every man & placing him erect & solidly on his centre."[32] Other

---

[29] *The Fate of Blood-thirsty Oppressors and GOD'S Tender Care of His Distressed People*, pp. 27 f.

[30] *Records of the Town of Braintree, 1640-1793*, p. 421; Charles Hudson, *History of the Town of Lexington*, p. 94; Frothingham, *Charlestown*, p. 277; and *Boston Town Records, 1758-1769*, p. 264. Westborough appointed a day of fasting in 1774.—Boston Committee Records, pp. 881 f. [31] *Writings*, I, 9 f.

[32] *Ibid.*, 11 f. Jefferson states that his was the first such day since 1755 and that he got the wording of the resolutions from old Puritan forms, modernizing the phrasing. See also "Diary of Landon Carter," *William and Mary College Quarterly*, XIV, 185. Carter said of his clergyman that he "did very pathetically exhort the people in his sermon to support their liberties, concluding with the resolve for the fast & in the room of God Save the King! he cried out God preserve all the just rights and Liberties of America."

colonies later adopted the same idea. The provincial congress of South Carolina set aside February 17, 1775, as a day of fasting and prayer, and appropriate sermons were delivered throughout the colony. The House of Commons attended St. Philip's Church in a body to hear a sermon by the Reverend Robert Smith. Maryland appointed May 11, a day also observed in Massachusetts and Rhode Island, and Georgia followed later with a day in July, 1775.[33]

Churches also appointed fast days. In 1769 the Consociation of Connecticut set aside the last Thursday in August, and in April, 1775, the Anglican Church of New York appointed May 7 as a special day of prayer.[34] The Presbyterian synod appointed the last Thursday and the German Reformed Church the last Wednesday in June, 1775, as days of prayer to be observed throughout the entire churches.[35]

The Continental Congress, however, really unified the prayers of the people. It set July 20, 1775, as a day of humiliation and prayer for the restoration of the just civil and religious privileges of America, and "Congress Sunday," as it was commonly called, was observed throughout America. Copies of the notice were distributed even to the southern back country (where the day was but poorly observed), and in the city churches impressive use was made of the occasion. The next spring Congress set May 17 for national observance as a day of prayer, and thereafter it adopted the New England idea of a spring fast and an autumn thanksgiving day.[36]

A few other methods of enlisting ecclesiastical support were used. The best example, and one which should have been followed in every other colony, was the resolution of the first provincial congress of Massachusetts which called upon the clergy to "assist us in

[33] S. C. Gazette, Feb. 20, 1775; Drayton, Memoirs of the American Revolution, I, 179, 214; Md. Gazette, May 4, 1775; Rev. Rec. Ga., I, 231, 240.

[34] Humphrey, Nationalism and Religion, p. 63; Ecclesiastical Records of the State of New York, VI, 4287.

[35] Humphrey, Nationalism and Religion, p. 113; N. Y. Journal, June 1, 1775.

[36] Journals of the Continental Congress, II, 87. John Adams said that the fast had been kept "more strictly and devoutly than any sunday was ever observed in this City." —Burnett, op. cit., I, 162. Reverend Robert Smith again preached the sermon to the House of Commons in South Carolina and is said to have made a marked impression.—Edward McCrady, The History of South Carolina in the Revolution, 1775-1780, p. 57. The committee of safety in Wilmington, N. C., distributed copies of the resolutions throughout the colony, but the Moravians in Salisbury reported that "there is not the slightest sign that any one has taken any notice of it."—Records of the Moravians in North Carolina, II, 877.

avoiding that dreadful slavery with which we are now threatened, by advising the people of their several congregations . . . to abide by . . . the resolutions of the Continental Congress" and to "make the question of the rights of the colonies and the oppressive conduct of the mother country a topic of the pulpit on week days."[37] The results of this appeal were remarkable.

Another instance of good propaganda technique occurred in Philadelphia. When the news of the Boston Port Act reached the city, a public meeting was called to consider Boston's request for an immediate boycott of British trade. The more moderate Whigs were determined to control this meeting. The leaders held a caucus to which they invited six representatives from each religious group in the city. This caucus agreed upon the officers to be elected at the meeting, the speakers who were to be recognized by the chairman, and the subject of their remarks.[38] The program went through without a break, except that Charles Thomson got excited and fainted. The clergymen who had participated in this bit of political management were so pleased with the results that they wrote the Committee of Fifty-One in New York, then in charge of affairs there, to enlist the aid of the New York ministers. Isaac Low, the chairman, replied that as the Committee had no jurisdiction over such matters he had simply sent copies of the letter to the New York clergymen, telling them to take what action they thought advisable.[39] Low was a poor propagandist.

It should be clear that, although a good many opportunities were overlooked, the propagandists did realize the essential value of the churches and did in many instances effectively gain their united support.

Other social institutions were not so adaptable to the uses of the propagandists. The special pleader today has a complete program for diverting (usually perverting) the purposes of education and ingeniously puts it into effect, but there were a good many difficulties in the way of his predecessor of revolutionary days. In the first

[37] *Journals Mass. Prov. Cong.*, p. 60. The second half of the quotation does not appear in this proclamation; it is given on the authority of Baldwin, *New England Clergy*, p. 123. See 4 Force, *Amer. Arch.*, I, 997. The address is *ibid.*, p. 1000.
[38] Charles Thomson's account in C. J. Stillé, *The Life and Times of John Dickinson, 1732-1808*, p. 344.
[39] 4 Force, *Amer. Arch.*, I, 300.

place, it took a good deal of foresight to make and execute any general program of education in Whig principles before 1774, and even after that date very few realized how long the struggle would be. In the next place, the curriculum did not adapt itself to propaganda purposes as it does today; there were no courses in citizenship, no courses in "problems of democracy," no general assemblies of the students, none of the numerous possibilities of modern curricular and extracurricular activities. Only debating societies and religious services offered opportunity for activities extraneous to the solid round of eighteenth-century subjects.

There is plenty of evidence to show that the colleges fostered American ideals and nurtured a crop of ardent young Whigs, for during the period the students on several college campuses evinced a great deal of spontaneous enthusiasm, although not a great deal of originality. They voted in 1768 to wear homespun, and they burned tea in 1774; they passed resolutions on various occasions, and they debated the most delicate and involved subjects with all the fire and all the confidence of youth.[40] In a few instances it is possible to suspect the influence of authority. Three college presidents— Samuel Langdon of Harvard, Ezra Stiles of Yale, and John Witherspoon of Princeton—were active Whigs. Langdon had written all the letters for the Portsmouth Sons of Liberty and had done a good deal of writing for the press on his own account. Witherspoon, it is even supposed, wrote some of the patriotic orations delivered by students and set some of the debate topics on the rights of the colo-

---

[40] Harvard students voted in 1768 to wear homespun and in 1769 never to deal with John Mein.—Josiah Quincy, *The History of Harvard University*, II, 163; *Boston Gazette*, Sept. 4, 1769. It was in 1769 that Andrew Eliot said of the students there (a good commentary on most of the college students of the day): "They have caught the spirit of the times. Their declamations and forensic disputes breathe the spirit of liberty. This has always been encouraged; but they have sometimes wrought themselves up to such a pitch of enthusiasm that it has been difficult to keep them within due bounds. But their tutors are fearful of giving too great a check to a disposition which may hereafter fill the country with patriots, and choose to leave it to age and experience to correct their ardor." —"Letters from Andrew Eliot to Thomas Hollis," 4 Mass. Hist. Soc., *Collections*, IV, 447. This might just as well have been said of Princeton students, for commencement oratory during Witherspoon's regime became so inflammatory that objection was raised. Princeton boys censured New York for breaking the association of 1768, wore homespun in 1770, burned tea in 1774, and organized a volunteer militia company in 1775.—V. L. Collins, *Princeton*, p. 76. One teacher, William Russel, influenced his students by copybook mottoes—"Wilkes and Liberty," "Liberty! No Stamps," and the like, and James Lovell of the Boston Latin Grammar School adjourned classes on occasions of political excitement and told the boys to go to the gallery of the Old South.—James Kimball, "The One Hundredth Anniversary of the Destruction of Tea in Boston Harbor," Essex Institute, *Hist. Coll.*, XII, 230; *Memoir of Josiah Quincy*, p. 125 n.

nies; Ezra Stiles is said to have made Yale a "seminary of sedition, faction and republicanism."[41]

There were a variety of clubs, social and semisocial in character, which brought pressure on their members by endorsing the Whig program. The Plymouth Society, or Old Colony Club, formed in 1769 to commemorate the landing of the Pilgrims, offered in its annual celebrations an excellent appeal to the trials and heroic efforts of the Pilgrims in defense of their liberties. As the *Essex Gazette* observed: "The breast which had only one spark of patriotism must have been raised to a flame, to see a large circle of venerable old men, in contemplating the difficulties and hardships the first settlers waded through, animated to a degree that would have excited them to bleed at the shrine of freedom."[42]

The speakers had an obvious opportunity to make a present application. What war orator today, addressing the Mayflower Society of America, would fail to contrast the grim and daring courage of the Pilgrims, their exalted faith, and their mighty hardships with the moral decay of the present, or would fail to draw the lesson by urging the lineal descendants of that noble little army to reimbue themselves with their high purposes and simple but unshaken faith? That, in brief, is the outline followed by the annual addresses to the Old Colony Club.

Few other organizations afforded an appeal so obvious and so sentimental. Any organization worth the name had periodic meetings and a dinner with toasts and speeches; it did not matter greatly whether the society cared for the local unfortunates, put out fires, or staged an annual ball, it had some influence over its members. The Fellowship Clubs, those early organizations for the care of unfortunates, toasted all patriots and waved *bon voyage* to Governor Bernard, retiring Governor of Massachusetts, on his way, they audibly hoped, to Tyburn. They were told, no doubt, that their duties were increased by England's ruinous policy, which was rapidly filling the prisons with poor but honest men.[43] Of the Fire Clubs in various cities, only the one in Boston attempted to influence its members

<hr />

[41] F. B. Dexter, "Notes on Some of the New Haven Loyalists," New Haven Colony Historical Society, *Papers*, IX, 29-45.

[42] *Essex Gazette*, Feb. 8, 1774. See also James Thatcher, *History of the Town of Plymouth*, pp. 181 f.; *Boston Gazette*, Jan. 22, 1770, Jan. 2, 1775.

[43] *Newport Mercury*, Sept. 18, 1769.

along political lines. In 1765 it resolved that if the Stamp Office should be on fire it would not put it out, and in 1769 it expelled a member for breaking the nonimportation agreement.[44] Club Number 45 of Charleston ordered and erected a statue of Pitt in 1770, and the members of the Amicable Society of Georgia held a meeting in 1769 to consider the state of affairs, voted themselves greatly distressed by unconstitutional taxation and recommended frugality and the nonimportation of British goods.[45]

The Masonic lodges were important organizations in many communities, and their relationship to the anti-British movement is worth considering in more detail. The exact number of lodges is difficult to determine; in 1775 there were well over a hundred. These lodges derived their authority principally from two sources. One set, called the Moderns, derived from the premier Grand Lodge of England, formed in 1717. The other set, inversely called the Ancients, was authorized, or warranted, by a rival Grand Lodge, formed in 1751. Both of these grand lodges established provincial grand lodges in America with authority to warrant local lodges, and between the two groups thus formed there was great rivalry.

This rivalry showed itself clearly at the time of the Revolution. All of the lodges, of course, owed allegiance to the parent lodge in England, whether Ancient or Modern, and that allegiance was strong. Furthermore, it was and is contrary to the policy of the order to take an open stand on controversial political questions. Marked differences, nevertheless, began to appear in the activities of the lodges. In general, the members of the Ancient lodges were Whigs, those of the Moderns, Tory.

Joseph Warren had been made in 1772 Provincial Grand Master of the Continent of North America, under the authority of the Grand Lodge of England, Ancients. Four years before, John Rowe, the Boston merchant, had been made Provincial Grand Master of all North America under the authority of the Grand Lodge of England, Moderns. Warren was an outstanding Whig, Rowe a rather cautious moderate. What the influence of these two men may have

---

[44] *Boston Gazette, Supplement,* Aug. 11, 1766; *Supplement,* June 5, 1769; Feb. 19, 1770. A writer in the *Pa. Gazette,* June 2, 1768, expressed indignation that the many small clubs in the city did nothing to further the cause and suggested that the members of the Fire Club at least could wear homespun.

[45] *S. C. Gazette,* July 5, 1770; *Ga. Gazette,* Sept. 6, Sept. 20, 1769.

been is, of course, difficult to say. When we take into consideration first, that men normally associate themselves with those congenial to them, and second, that the rivalry between the two lodges was intense, it is understandable that the Ancient lodges should incline to the patriot side, and the Modern lodges to the British. It is also true that the earlier grand lodge in England, the Modern Grand Lodge, had become somewhat aristocratic and was in fact somewhat identified with the court party. On the contrary, the Ancient Grand Lodge had been formed in part in protest against this tendency. This cleavage in England also inclined the Ancient lodges in America to the patriot side.

In New England, for example, the Ancient lodges became closely identified with the Whig cause and continued active work throughout the Revolution. It does not appear, however, that at any time did any lodge by vote or other formal action endorse any item in the Whig program. In sharp contrast, the Modern lodges ceased work entirely, and many of the members became loyalists.

The same situation existed in both New York and Pennsylvania. Sir John Johnson was Grand Master of the Modern Lodges in New York, and in 1775 every lodge except one was under his authority. He himself was a loyalist, and every Modern lodge except St. Patrick's, Johnstown, ceased work. From the scanty records available, it would appear that there was the same division in Pennsylvania. The occupation of Philadelphia by the British troops occasioned many a Mason there to turn loyalist, but in general the Moderns were Tory, the Ancients, Whig. The difference between the two sets was not so marked in the southern colonies. In Virginia and the Carolinas a good many of the Modern lodges were strongly anti-British, as were all of the Ancient lodges.[46]

From the Ancient lodges came some of the most radical leaders of the Whig party. Fifty-two of the fifty-six signers of the Declaration of Independence were Masons, as were many of the lesser politicians. The organization, however, was of little value as an agency for the dissemination of propaganda.

[46] Henry L. Stillson, ed., *History of the Ancient and Honorable Fraternity of the Free and Accepted Masons*, pp. 199 ff. See also Bernard Faÿ, *Revolution and Freemasonry, 1680-1800*; and Sidney Morse, *Freemasonry in the American Revolution*.

VI

THE LAWYER'S PLEA FOR THE RIGHTS OF AMERICA

The influence of the propagandists was out of all proportion to their number. Through the machinery they set up and through other agencies available to them, they agitated almost continuously against the policies of the British government. Their words and activities were so much the model and inspiration for others that their ideas, their actual words, were repeated almost endlessly. In the colonial press, in the resolutions of the towns, counties, and assemblies, and in the correspondence of the committees, there are the same phraseology, the same order of ideas, the same words. The hundreds of town resolutions in New England after 1772, for example, reflected almost as perfectly as a student's examination paper the words of the teacher—the Boston Committee of Correspondence. The few variations are from those who opposed the ideas of the committee. So was it with the resolutions of the towns and counties in the middle and southern colonies and with the resolutions of the Sons of Liberty; their uniformity is striking. The ideas set forth in a newspaper essay by Sam Adams or John Dickinson or any of the familiar essayists of the period can be traced through the colonial press for months, sometimes even years. It is possible to find in the writings of one or the other of the Whig propagandists almost any idea that appeared in the public prints of the day. In a measure, therefore, many of the town resolutions and newspaper or pamphlet essays were the results of propaganda. But they were propaganda themselves, and the fact that, for example, forty towns adopted the instructions which John Adams wrote for the town of Braintree, or that every colonial newspaper but three printed John Dickinson's "Letters from a Pennsylvania Farmer" is certain indication that someone was consciously attempting to influence attitudes.

The full force of anti-British propaganda cannot therefore be estimated by a study of the work of a few leaders. We are concerned here with the total effect of the anti-British appeal upon the individual colonist, with an analysis of the revolutionary argument as propaganda, and with the method of presenting the appeal—straight argument, seriously and forcibly written, satirical essays, fables, allegories, literary hoaxes, imaginary colloquies, dreams, dramatic presentations in symbolical form, pictorial and oral suggestions, all the devices, in fact, by which ideas are presented in striking fashion.

The central problem of the propagandist is to select the most suitable appeals, those most likely to influence the specific groups he has in mind, and to present them as effectively as possible. The specific groups vary with each propaganda situation. In war propaganda there are four major groups: nationals, allies, neutrals, and the enemy. Each of these presents a particular problem. Nationals must be unified in support of a common purpose, and a war psychosis developed and maintained by arousing hatred for the enemy; the friendship of allies must be preserved; the friendship and co-operation of neutrals must be secured; and the enemy must be demoralized.[1] These were the problems of the revolutionary propagandist, but in the period from 1763 to 1775 only the first group was of immediate concern. The Whig propagandist's primary problem of suggestion was to unify as many people within the colonies as possible in support of his program.

In selecting the appeals to his own countrymen, the propagandist has four major aims: (1) to justify the course he advocates; (2) to demonstrate the advantages of victory; (3) to arouse hatred for the enemy; (4) to neutralize inconvenient suggestions. The specific appeals in pursuit of these aims, if they are to be successful, must be in line with the thinking and prejudices of the people. They must fit in, that is, with dominant or central attitudes, for the propagandist cannot create attitudes, nor can he change within a short period of time the basic attitudes of a group. They must be sufficiently general to include many diverse interests and sufficiently specific on occasion to touch specific interests. The art of the propagandist lies in his ability to coalesce diverse, often conflicting groups, into one compact mass vibrating to one hope and to one ideal. He can do this by appeals to aims so general, so vague as to their real meaning, that each group can interpret them to suit its own interests. It can also be done by appeals not in conflict with the interest of any major element of the population but which offer peculiar rewards or warn of

---

[1] H. D. Lasswell, *Propaganda Technique in the World War*, p. 195.

peculiar disasters. The criterion is the appeal so general and yet so succinct that it presents a yes and no situation—Freedom versus Slavery, Democracy versus Dictatorship—that it becomes, in short, a compulsive idea. It is in the light of these basic principles that we must study Whig propaganda. The first objective was to prevent the enforcement of British legislation; the ultimate objective, at least of the radically anti-British, was independence. The dominant suggestions of the twelve years' agitation, changing in emphasis from period to period, show an unmistakable if unconscious knowledge of the technique of the propagandist.

JUSTIFICATIONS

The problem of justifying opposition to Great Britain was simply a problem of fastening upon her, beyond all doubt, the crime of aggression, of proving that she had violated the rights of colonies and colonists, and that she had committed the overt act of war. The undivided burden of the guilt must rest upon the enemy; the Revolution, even in its earliest phases, was made a contest between right and wrong, good and evil, just and unjust. This was the dominant theme for ten years—the violation of colonial rights.

Two types of appeal were used to justify opposition. The first was the lawyer's argument that Great Britain had violated the legally established rights of the colonies; the second was the familiar appeal to colonial self-interest.

The primary rights which the propagandist claimed had been violated by English legislation were legal rights, and no appeal fitted more perfectly the pre-existing attitudes of the people. Colonial controversies with England had always emphasized law, and the legal appeal of this period was but the culmination of a century and a half of argument which had made the colonists so legal minded that the approach was almost instinctive.

The colonial writers, of course, considered themselves the sole judge of their rights and were unembarrassed by legal complexities and uncertainties. They fixed in their own minds the rights guaranteed to them by that shadowy substance, the British Constitution, they determined for themselves the legal relations among the parts of the empire, and they judged English acts by an entirely new philosophy of government, the eighteenth-century compact philosophy. They were supported in many of their contentions, it is true, by a substantial body of English opinion (which they themselves had cultivated in part), but the point is not that they were right or wrong. The point is that with the typical methods of the propagandist they flatly asserted their rights and proved them by principles even then in dispute.

The legal appeal seldom dealt with detailed complexities. It was usually presented in formed conclusions, phrased in vigorous, often crude, and homely language.

THE BRITISH CONSTITUTION

The colonists, claimed the propagandists, were protected as Englishmen by the British Constitution. The constitution they had in mind, however, was not the somewhat vague body of law and principles that had been developed in England over hundreds of years. They were appealing to the kind of document, fixed and unchangeable except by the people, that they themselves were going to make at Philadelphia many years later.

The rights of this fixed constitution had been confirmed in many instances to the colonists by their charters, it was asserted. Even charters long since voided were cited to prove that the settlers had brought with them the rights of Englishmen, for, as Arthur Lee claimed, these rights remained even though the charter which granted them had been abrogated.[2] Therefore, said a writer in the *Boston Gazette:* "The ministerial writers, and all the great and little tools on this and the other side the water, are oblig'd to confess, that the subjects of America are upon an equal footing with regard to Liberty and Right, with those in Britain."[3]

Some of the colonies, however, had no charters. That made no difference, said the propagandists. The British Constitution protected them simply because they were Englishmen, wherever they might live. All colonists of whatever country, wrote Stephen Hopkins, have had the same rights as their mother countrymen: "will anyone suppose the British colonies in America are an exception to this general rule?—colonies that came out from a kingdom renowned for liberty, from a constitution founded on compact, from a people of

[2] *S. C. Gazette*, June 27, 1768; *Pa. Evening Post*, May 30, 1776.
[3] July 15, 1765.

all the sons of men the most tenacious of freedom?"[4] Indeed, said the people of a little Rhode Island town, "the only true glory and unfading grandeur of the British monarch consists in governing his extensive empire with equal and impartial law, founded in reason, and rendered sacred by the wisdom of ages; and that every attempt to impair that noble constitution, which hath ever been the envy and terror of Europe, constitutes the blackest treason."[5]

Sam Adams, as usual, summed the matter up completely:

"The *absolute Rights* of Englishmen, and all freemen in or out of Civil society, are principally, *personal security personal liberty* and *private property*. All Persons born in the British American Colonies are by the laws of God and nature, and by the Common law of England, *exclusive of all charters from the Crown*, well Entitled, and by the Acts of the British Parliament are declared to be entitled to all the natural essential, inherent & inseparable Rights Liberties and Privileges of Subjects born in Great Britain, or within the Realm. . . . These are some of the first principles of natural law & Justice, and the great Barriers of all free states, and of the British Constitution in particular."[6]

The rights to life, liberty, and property, so solidly founded in the British Constitution and so unquestionably guaranteed by it to the colonists were constantly being violated by parliamentary acts, charged the propagandists. Trial by jury, one of the oldest of them all, was violated in the Sugar Act, the Stamp Act, and the Townshend Acts, for offenses were cognizable in admiralty courts, and the new court set up in Philadelphia in 1767 made the presiding judge the "party, judge, and jury."[7] Thus were the colonists illegally deprived of their property: "If we are Englishmen, on what footing is our property? . . . Is not our property, after being seized by a numerous swarm of horse-leaches, who never cease crying, Give! Give! to be thrown into a prerogative court? a court of admiralty?"[8]

[4] *The Rights of the Colonies Examined*, p. 8.

[5] *R. I. Records*, VII, 303.

[6] From the "Rights of the Colonists" drawn up in 1772 by Sam Adams, *Writings*, II, 356, 357.

[7] *Pa. Journal*, Jan. 5, Jan. 26, 1774; 4 Force, *Amer. Arch.*, I, 394 f.

[8] *Boston Gazette*, July 15, 1765. See also *N. H. Gazette*, June 7, 1765; *Newport Mercury*, Sept. 9, 1765; *N. Y. Gazette, or, Weekly Post-Boy*, Oct. 31, 1765; and *Boston Gazette, Supplement*, Nov. 4, 1765. There had been, of course, vice-admiralty courts long before this. The new vice-admiralty courts set up in Boston, New York, and Philadelphia had increased jurisdiction.

Long-established methods of legal procedure were carelessly abandoned for new and illegal methods. The Administration of Justice Act, according to the Whigs, completely destroyed fundamental civil rights. Before they had even read it carefully, some of them seized on it as a glaring example of parliamentary violation of established rights. This act, they stated, deprived persons accused of murder of their age-old right to witnesses, for it put it in the power "of every American Governor to take such person from all his friends, neighbors, connections, and acquaintence, and send him moneyless and friendless three thousand miles off, and to prejudiced judges." The innocent had no redress. "To be hanged or buried in this case is the only alternative left to such unhappy victims."[9]

Shrewd Tories promptly and gleefully pointed out the errors. The Act applied only to Massachusetts, and only to crown officers who in pursuit of their duty should kill a person. The trial could be held in any other province, or England, and witnesses were to be taken at the expense of the crown to the scene of the trial. The Whigs with equal promptitude changed their argument completely. This, they said, was an even greater injustice. Did it comport with the constitution to have different trials in different sections of the country? Under the terms of this act, there was never any possibility of obtaining justice from government officials. They could now murder at pleasure, for the British government could take the case from the place where the murder could be proved to one where it could not, and there was no safety for the American citizenry where troops were stationed.[10]

That very matter of stationing troops in the colonies was viewed as another gross injustice. Englishmen had fought for centuries against the evils of a standing army in time of peace and the enforced billeting of troops, and these rights had finally been secured in England. Yet Parliament and the ministry without hesitation ordered

[9] *Ga. Gazette,* July 27, 1774; *S. C. Gazette,* June 27, 1774.

[10] *Ga. Gazette,* Aug. 17, 1774. One Whig had still a different idea of the terms of the Act: "a third Act places every Crown Officer above the Reach of Law in the Country where he lives, declaring him amenable only to the Courts of Justice in England, at the same Time that every Person in the Massachusetts Government who happens to be obnoxious to the Ministry (that is, every honest and intelligent Friend to his Country) is made liable to be transported to the King's Bench in England for trial . . . where, unhappily for the Prisoner, the Prosecution must be altogether Persecution, there being no Prospect of Evidence but on one Side, and the Chance of the accused for escaping, however innocent, as small as the Act itself is certainly void of every Particle of Reason and Justice."—*Va. Gazette* (Purdie), June 30, 1774.

the colonists to provide supplies for a standing army and suspended the legislature of New York when it refused to do so. "Good God! Are there no watchful guardians of our liberties left? Are there no remains of those noble patriots who struggled so hard against standing armies?"[11]

The fundamental right of all Englishmen, the propagandists claimed, was the right to give and grant their own, to be taxed only with their own consent. But the colonists were not, and, by the very nature of things, could not be represented in the British Parliament, they said, and had never, therefore, given their consent to be taxed by it. They were scornful of the nice distinctions between American and English representation, and mocked at the idea that they were "virtually" represented in Parliament:

> "Yet learn hence ye wise ones, ye ass ones & goose ones,
> Ye rich ones and poor ones, and fast ones and loose ones;
> By this virtual Hodge podge fresh cook'd up in London,
> And cramm'd down our Throats, we are virtually undone.
> *Since good Things and bad Things, and great Things and*
> *small Things,*
> *Are here reconciled and virtually all things.*"[12]

"Our *privileges* are all *virtual*," declared the "Monitor," "our sufferings are *real*." He continued:

> "When we are to be taxed, we are in *America;* when duties are laid upon the commodities we purchase from *Great-Britain;* when our governments are to be suspended . . . we are then in *America;* but when we are to *chuse our Representatives,* our trustees, who are bound thereby in duty and interest to treat us with the same justice and tenderness, with which they would treat themselves, then, my countrymen, we are unhappily in the *manor of Greenwich.*"[13]

An "Address to the Citizens of New York" summed up the indictment against those who violated the legal rights of the colonists:

[11] *N. Y. Gazette, or, Weekly Post-Boy,* May 30, 1765; Library of Congress, Broadsides, Connecticut, Vol. III, *No Standing Armies; Boston Gazette,* Dec. 5, 1768.

[12] *N. Y. Gazette, or, Weekly Post-Boy,* July 4, 1765.

[13] *Va. Gazette* (Rind), Mar. 10, 1768. See also *N. Y. Gazette, or, Weekly Post-Boy,* May 16, 1765; *Ga. Gazette,* Sept. 19, 1765; *Va. Gazette* (Purdie), Oct. 20, 1774.

"General warrants, violation of the rights of election, the disfranchisement of the proprietors of the East-India Stock, murders committed, murderers pardoned, encouraged, rewarded, and the other overt acts (of treason, I may say) which the ministry have been guilty of against law, Magna Carta, and the English constitution, are so notorious, that it is almost impertinent to mention them."[14]

The British Constitution itself was in danger from these obvious efforts of the English officials to sap its foundations. The real criminals were those who attempted "to abolish the antient & established modes of deciding property; and to introduce in their room, a method odious, unconstitutional, & unfriendly to liberty."[15] "Who were the better Christians," queried a writer in the *Newport Mercury*, "those that attempted to blow up the parliament of Great Britain on the 5th of November, 1605,—or those who endeavoured to destroy the British constitution in N. America, in the—year 1765?"[16]

Parliamentary acts which violated the British Constitution were unconstitutional and were thus null and void; resistance to them was not rebellion, it was brave defense of the basic principles of English liberty. That this was a legal principle not even now established in Great Britain was of little concern to the propagandists; they believed it. According to the British Constitution itself, declared one inspired writer, acts contrary to Magna Carta were void, and others frequently stated that acts contrary to the Petition of Right and the Bill of Rights were unconstitutional. The Stamp Act in fact was no more binding on the colonists than if it had been the decree of the Sultan of Turkey, for no obedience was ever due "arbitrary, unconstitutional edicts, calculated to enslave a free people."[17]

Propagandists thus bound Parliament by the terms of a constitution they themselves practically framed and certainly interpreted. But still other legal grounds were used to justify resistance to British legislation.

---

[14] *Boston Gazette*, Aug. 1, 1774.   [15] *Ibid.*, Aug. 12, 1765.
[16] *Newport Mercury*, Oct. 23, 1769. See also N. Y. *Journal*, Dec. 1, 1768; Apr. 4, 1771; Feb. 4, 1773.
[17] N. Y. *Gazette, or, Weekly Post-Boy, Extraordinary*, Dec. 27, 1765; Johnson, *Some Important Observations*, p. 21; *Boston Gazette, Supplement*, Oct. 21, 1765; N. Y. *Journal*, Sept. 3, 1767; 4 Force, *Amer. Arch.*, II, 918.

IMPERIAL LAW

Whig propagandists viewed the legal relationships of the different parts of the empire and found, to their satisfaction, that the colonies had certain rights which Parliament could no more abrogate than it could those of the colonists. The British Constitution and the charters, which had confirmed to the people the rights of Englishmen, likewise confirmed to the separate and individual colonies certain rights. Parliament thus became bound by this constitution and these charters in its relations with the colonies, just as it was bound by them in its relations with the colonists. It was a new view of imperial relations, a new framework of the empire. It was a framework in which the colonial assemblies had the same relations to the colonies that Parliament had to England itself; the British Parliament, therefore, had no authority whatever to legislate for the colonies, which were united to the mother country only in the person of the King. It was a federal empire of divided but not conflicting authorities.

As early as 1765 the startling view was put forth that Parliament had usurped the authority of the King in passing the Sugar Act and the Stamp Act, and a few months later it was contended that the colonial legislative authority was distinct from that of Parliament. Parliament, therefore, had no right to change the governmental basis of any colony without the consent of the people.[18] Clear statements that parliamentary legislation invaded the rights of the colonial assemblies were increasingly frequent, and by 1774 the theory was generally accepted by the Whigs.

A variety of arguments were used to substantiate this view of the empire. Parliamentary acts were void, said Thomas Jefferson in his *Summary View of the Rights of British America*, because of the very method of settling the colonies. The settlers came out of their own choice and owed no allegiance to the mother country:

"That settlements having been thus effected in the wilds of America, the emigrants thought proper to adopt that system of laws under which they had hitherto lived in the mother country, and to continue their union with her by submitting themselves to the same common Sovereign, who was thereby made the central

[18] *N. Y. Gazette, or, Weekly Post-Boy*, Jan. 9, 1766; Broadside signed "C. P.," New York, 1765, Library of Congress, Broadsides.

link connecting the several parts of the empire thus newly multiplied. . . . The true ground on which we declare these acts void is, that the British parliament has no right to exercise its authority over us."[19]

The old argument that Parliament could not tax the colonists because they were not represented in it was extended to prove that Parliament could not legislate for the colonies in any particular. "The Parliament of England cannot justly make any laws to oppress, or defend the Americans, for they are not the representatives of America, and therefore they have no legislative power either for them, or against them." Thus the author of the *Oration, Upon the Beauties of Liberty* in 1773. "For my part," he added, "I cannot see how any Man in America, can properly break the Laws of England."[20] "That 'supreme power over America is vested in the estates in parliament,' is an affront to us," declared John Adams in 1774, "for there is not an acre of American land represented there; there are no American estates in parliament."[21]

Parliamentary acts were therefore *ultra vires*, and the colonists were not bound by them. "We owe no Obedience to any Act of the British Parliament, that is, or shall be made, respecting the internal Police of this Colony," declared a meeting in Spotsylvania County, Virginia,[22] and a Massachusetts county convention formally resolved that neither obedience nor respect was due officials who held office under the Massachusetts Government Act.[23]

REVOLUTIONARY PRINCIPLES

Still a third basis for justifying resistance to British legislation was found in entirely new principles of government, the principles of the eighteenth-century natural rights philosophy, the philosophy of government by compact and consent. The writings of Locke and Montesquieu, Vattel and Sydney, went into the propaganda against Great Britain to prove that she was violating the rights of the colonists not only as Englishmen but as men. These were their rights to life, liberty, and property, and their right to consent to the gov-

---

[19] *Writings*, I, 431, 434. The priority of ideas is not a matter of concern at the moment. Richard Bland, *An Inquiry into the Rights of the British Colonies*, 1766, asserted this point in a confused and contradictory manner.
[20] Pp. x, 26.
[21] *Works*, IV, 107.
[22] *Va. Gazette* (Purdie), July 7, 1774.
[23] *Journals Mass. Prov. Cong.*, p. 627.

ernment under which they lived, to exercise continuing control over it, and to withdraw from it when it became subversive of those rights. These were their inherent rights, wrote young Alexander Hamilton; they needed no charter to confirm, no written constitution to guarantee. "The sacred rights of mankind are not to be rummaged for among old parchments, or musty records. They are written as with a sunbeam, in the whole volume of human nature, by the hand of the Divinity itself, and can never be erased or obscured by mortal power."[24] Propagandists first showed that England had violated these rights in certain of her acts and then appealed to this philosophy to justify their positive acts of resistance.

The very first revenue acts were tested by this philosophy and found to violate its principles. "A man's own is his own," and it cannot be taken from him without his consent. Sam Adams, in his statement of the rights of the colonists and the infringements of them, summed up the natural rights of the people more clearly than anyone had as yet done. He showed that by levying a tax on the colonists Parliament had deprived them of that inherent right "which every man has to keep his own earnings in his own hands until he shall in person, or by his Representative, think fit to part with the whole or any portion of it."[25] And the author of the *Oration, Upon the Beauties of Liberty* wrote: "No doubt, my Lord, but they have a right to tax the strangers, that come to dwell in their country; but to tax the children, which are free in their own native country, this will not do! Nature forbids it; the law of GOD condemns it. And no law, but that of tyranny, can desire it."[26]

The fundamental right of a free people to control their own government was threatened in the Townshend Acts, which provided that the money raised could be used to pay crown officials in the colonies. Wrote Sam Adams under his pseudonym "Brittanus Americanus": "*Governors* INDEPENDENT! What a sound is this! It is a discord in the ear of a Briton. *A power without a check!* What a Solecism in a free government!"[27] And again: "Is it possible to form an idea of *Slavery*, more compleat, more miserable, more *disgraceful*, than that of a people, where justice is administer'd, gov-

[24] *The Farmer Refuted*, p. 38.
[25] *Writings*, II, 360. See also *Boston Gazette*, Sept. 14, 1767.
[26] P. xi.   [27] *Boston Gazette*, Aug. 17, 1767.

ernment exercis'd, and a Standing army maintain'd, at the expense of the people, and yet without the least dependence upon them?"[28]

Thus by the law of nature parliamentary acts were "illegal" and need not be obeyed. Indeed, said one Benjamin Aiken: "It Appears to me, if there is any force in the Late acts of Parliament, they have Sett us afloat. that is have thrown us into a State of Nature: we now have a fair oppertunity of choosing what form of government we think proper: and, Contract, with any Nation . . . for a King to rule over us . . . it would be Best for us to form a New Charter for ourselves."[29]

The new philosophy was not simply a touchstone by which to test the legality of parliamentary acts; it was positive justification for the rebellious acts of the colonists themselves. To it they appealed as they approached revolution.

Christopher Gadsden as early as 1769 had answered the charge that the nonimportation agreements were illegal by saying that whether or not they were illegal, they were justifiable. In times of oppression people had the right, he claimed, to exert "those *latent*, though *inherent* rights *of* SOCIETY, which *no climate, no time, no constitution, no contract*, can ever destroy or diminish."[30] Hamilton took identically the same position when the Continental Congress was condemned by the Tories as an illegal body:

"Granting your supposition were true, it would be a matter of no real importance. When the first principles of civil society are violated, and the rights of a whole people are invaded, the common forms of municipal law are not to be regarded. Men may then betake themselves to the law of nature. . . . In short, when human laws contradict or discountenance the means which are necessary to preserve the essential rights of any society, they defeat the proper end of all laws, and so become null and void."[31]

[28] *Ibid.*, Oct. 7, 1771, reprinted in *Writings*, II, 246 ff. A Boston town meeting in 1772 used the words "An Exterior power claims to govern us."—*Town Records, 1770-1777*, p. 83. See also Boston Committee Records, pp. 574 f.; N. Y. *Journal*, Nov. 18, 1774.

[29] Boston Committee Records, p. 198.

[30] *S. C. Gazette*, Oct. 18, 1769. This is usually attributed to Gadsden, but William Henry Drayton in the preface to *A Letter of a Freeman of South Carolina* says John McKensie, a planter, wrote it. One radical even defended mob violence: "May *American* mobs be crowned with success, and all posterity will revere them as the glorious conservators of the rights of mankind."—4 Force, *Amer. Arch.*, II, 159.

[31] *The Farmer Refuted*, pp. 52 f.

The doctrine of the right of revolution had been indirectly taught for years by the New England divines. They had decided in the seventeenth century that no obedience was due a civil magistrate when his acts violated the will of God as set forth in the Bible. When somewhat the same question now arose in the eighteenth century, the same answers were given. The Biblical story of the revolution against Rehoboam, son of Solomon and King of Israel, who unjustly burdened his people with taxes, was recounted to prove that rebellion against tyranny was lawful in the sight of God.[32] The influence of the clergy is further seen in the resolutions of the town of Marlborough in 1772. They affirmed the right of a people to form such civil contracts as they wished, and when any ruler violated the agreement, it was not necessary to obey him: "when he grows haughty, Unjust, & a Tyrant, Using Arbitrary Power, Introducing Popery, & all Manner of Debauchery & Wickedness; Then that free-born people are not required by the Religion of Jesus-Christ to submit themselves as Slaves to such Irreligious Tyranny."[33]

This identification of religious and political philosophy was a common one in the minds of the colonists. "Be not intimidated by any insolent, traitorous and illegal proclamations," said "An Address to the Farmers, mechanics, and tradesmen of Rhode Island," "GOD has given you a right to preserve your liberties, lives and property, and no power under heaven has a right to deprive you of either without your consent."[34] The law of nature, in the minds of the New Englanders at least, was the law of God. Otis had declared that the true foundation of government was the "unchangeable will of God," and writer after writer from 1765 on had used the phrase, "the law of God and nature." In the resolutions of the little frontier town of Ashfield, Massachusetts, adopted late in 1776, there is the same confusion. They voted that "as the Old Laws that we have Ben Ruled by under the British Constitution have Proved Inefectual to Secuer us from the more then Savige Crualty of tiranical Oppressars and Sense the God of Nature hath Enabled us to Brake that yoke of Bondage we think our Selves Bound in Duty to God and our Country to Oppose the Least Appearance of them Old Tiranical

[32] *Boston Gazette*, July 15, 1765. The Biblical reference is to II Chronicles.
[33] Boston Committee Records, pp. 493 ff.
[34] *Newport Mercury*, July 11, 1774.

Laws taking Place again," and resolved that they would take the "Law of God for the foundation of the forme of our Government . . . it is our opinion that we Do not want any Govinor but the Govinor of the Univarse. . . ."[35]

The Bible and the New England preachers had taught the people that the laws of God permitted revolution; Locke and the Boston Committee of Correspondence taught them that the laws of nature permitted it. Wrote the Chelsea committee to its Boston teacher:

"We have no doubts at all of the natural right of Colonies to form into a government by themselves whenever they think it expedient, and therefore, if our grievances should not be redressed, impartial reason must justify British America in separating from a State, that after many fruitless attempts to enslave its subjects at home, would fain intail bondage on these Colonies."[36]

Thus did the colonists determine, on the good authority of Locke and the Bible, that the tyrannous acts of the British government had violated the compact made with them, and that they had the right at any time to set up a government of their own.

Violation of the compact was sufficient reason to terminate the agreement, yet propagandists found still broader grounds in this philosophy of rebellion to justify the course of opposition. When Jefferson declared in the Declaration of Independence that all men were entitled to life, liberty, and the pursuit of happiness, he was but stating in better form what others had already said. As early as 1768 John Dickinson in his "Farmer's Letters" reasoned thus:

"Let these *truths* be indelibly impressed on our minds— *That we cannot be happy without being free*—that we cannot be free, *without being secure in our property*—that we cannot be secure in our property, *if without our consent, others may, as by right, take it away*—that *taxes imposed upon us by parliament* do thus take it away—that *duties laid for the sole purpose of raising money* are taxes—that attempts to lay such duties *should be instantly and firmly opposed*."[37]

[35] Quoted from J. T. Adams, *Revolutionary New England*, p. 443, by permission of Little, Brown and Company.
[36] Boston Committee Records, p. 176.
[37] N. Y. *Journal*, Apr. 21, 1768.

And much later, another writer put the whole matter of independence entirely upon the inherent right of people to happiness: "the first and great question, and that which involves every other in it, and from which every other will flow, is happiness. Can this Continent be happy under the Government of *Great Britain* or not? Secondly, can she be happy under a Government of her own?"[38]

[38] 4 Force, *Amer. Arch.*, V, 1020. See also *ibid.*, pp. 1078 f.; *Pa. Gazette*, Feb. 18, 1768; Boston Committee Records, pp. 25 f.

VII

COLONIAL SELF-INTEREST

FAR MORE important than a strictly legal argument, even when popularly phrased, is the appeal to self-interest, to fear of the future. Colonial propagandists spread the alarm to all classes and to all groups in colonial society, warning that unless all joined the fight against arbitrary government none would be secure in life, liberty, or property.

Every basic economic interest of the colonists was threatened by British pretensions. The point emphasized by the propagandists was not so much that any particular act worked hardship on the colonists, although they said that clearly enough.[1] The particular point they stressed was that the *right* to lay revenue acts was the central danger, for it threatened every interest. The emphasis was upon future penalties rather than present hardships.

There would be no end, they said, to parliamentary taxation once the right was granted. "If once the Americans submit," wrote a Bristol merchant to a friend in Philadelphia, "I forsee a Train of Evils ready to light upon them: Taxes, Impositions and Oppressions, without Moderation or End."[2] Indeed, said a Virginian, "it is a Fact perfectly understood both in Britain and America, that the Tax on Tea, when imported here, was laid, and has been continued, with the declared Intention, to establish a Precedent for the further unlimited Extension of Taxes on America by the British Parliament."[3] Once admit the right, wrote "Zeno," "and there is Nothing we possess, whether Lands, Houses, Cattle, Money, or any Thing

---

[1] "Let this Act but take Place, Liberty will be no more—Trade will languish and die—our cash will be sent into his Majesty's Exchequer—and Poverty come upon us like an armed Man."—Resolutions of the town of Cambridge, *Boston Gazette*, Oct. 21, 1765. Beggary and ruin would be the result if the revenue acts were enforced, was the common charge. See Maurice Moore, "The Justice of Taxing the American Colonies, in Great Britain, considered," in *Some Eighteenth Century Tracts Concerning North Carolina; N. H. Gazette*, Dec. 27, 1765; N. Y. *Journal*, Dec. 24, 1767; *S. C. Gazette*, June 1, 1769; *Pa. Journal*, Nov. 24, 1773.

[2] First printed in *Pa. Packet* and reprinted on a broadside. American Antiquarian Society, Broadsides, Oct. 3, 1774. The point is not that the Bristol merchant made the statement but that a local propagandist used it to further the cause.

[3] *Va. Gazette* (Purdie), Mar. 3, 1774. Similar statements were common; e.g., *Pa. Gazette*, May 12, 1768; N. Y. *Journal*, Sept. 27, 1770; Oct. 21, 1773; May 26, 1774.

else, which we can *then* call our own."[4] Stephen Johnson in his letters to the *New London Gazette* in 1765 drew up a specific list of possible taxes. His list was repeated time and again through the following years: if Parliament had the right to lay a stamp tax, it had the right to lay a "poll tax, a land tax, a malt tax, a cider tax, a window tax, a smoke tax; and why not tax us for the light of the sun, the air we breathe, and the ground we are buried in?"[5] Another essay, called the "American Looking Glass," listed specimens of taxable articles in Great Britain as an object lesson for America:

> "First, a small Specimen of the taxable and dutiable Articles in Great Britain at this Day, viz. The Land Tax, Poor Tax, Tavern and Alehouse Licenses, &c. with Taxes and Duties on Tea, Coffee, Leather, Plate, Soap, Candles, Beeswax and Wax Tapers. . . . Now if we once submit to the landing of the infamous Tea . . . [it] certainly will establish a Modus, by which arbitrary Power may Saddle us with such a dreadful Catalogue of grievous Taxes as are above enumerated."[6]

Landholders and land speculators were warned to unite with the merchants in opposing taxes on trade, for a land tax was certain to follow if the right of taxation was admitted. Sam Adams recognized the strength of this appeal, and in the instructions he wrote to the Boston representatives in the assembly in 1764 he said, "If our Trade may be taxed why not our Lands? Why not the produce of our Lands and every Thing we possess or make use of?"[7] And in the statement on the rights of the colonists, written in 1772, he returned to the same threat: "Hitherto many of the Colonists have been free from Quit Rents; but if the breath of a british house of commons can originate an act for taking away all our money, our lands will go next or be subject to rack rents from haughty and relentless landlords who will ride at ease, while we are trodden in the dirt."[8] *The American Alarm* continued the charge: "What, my

---

[4] N. Y. *Journal*, Dec. 23, 1773. In one piece the author tells a dream he had, in which a man was trying to brand some horses. A bystander remarked, "Have you never heard that branding is a mark of property? If the brand was once put on, I should not wonder if your next errand here was for the beasts—or their hides."—Quoted in Tyler, *Literary History*, I, 63.

[5] *New London Gazette*, Sept. 6, 1765. Many of the Germans in Georgia protested that they had been told that unless they subscribed to the Savannah resolutions of Aug. 10, 1774, a stamp tax would be laid on them.—*Ga. Gazette*, Sept. 21, 1774.

[6] *Va. Gazette* (Purdie), Jan. 6, 1774; also in N. Y. *Journal*, Dec. 16, 1773.

[7] *Boston Town Records, 1758-1769*, p. 121.

[8] *Ibid., 1770-1777*, p. 99.

dear Americans, will nothing but an immediate LAND TAX alarm you . . . Will the respectable Americans, land-holders, and farmers tamely submit to this?"[9] But not only was there threat of a land tax, even the lands themselves and the status of the farmers as free-holders were in danger. The Westborough committee of correspondence wrote Boston: "the cruel & vindictive measures of the british Parliament respecting the Town of Boston, are a formal Declaration of their intentions to reduce all british America to a passive submission to their unrighteous Exactions, should they succeed in this arrogant this execrable Design, the Land holder must look upon himself to be a Tenant at Will, and may be ejected from his Freehold, whenever his british masters shall think proper."[10] The Boston committee itself furthered this idea: "that they should succeed, which God forbid, slavery would be the consequence, this good land would be divided into lordships, and instead of being masters, we should be servants to as an abandoned set of men as ever the earth produced."[11] Could any appeal to a New England audience have been more effective?

Another certain penalty of submission to British acts was the swarm of pensioners, placemen, customhouse officers, and similar officials who would fill the new offices and thrive upon American taxes. I know the consequences of submission, said a Boston propagandist, "the *worthy* Commissionors of the customs will be *continued*, and the *troops* which have so *eminently protected the lives, and reformed the morals* of the people, will be reinstated; so that the *well-affected* may enjoy their *places* and PENSIONS without molestation from the vulgar."[12] Indeed, cannily asserted a writer in the *Pennsylvania Journal*, "*The* Ministry *have already begun to give away in* PENSIONS, *the* Money THEY *have* lately *taken out of* OUR Pockets,

---

[9] Pp. 11 f., 20. "It has been lately proposed, by some writers in England, to have an American LAND TAX, equal to what it is in Great Britain."—*Boston Gazette*, June 20, 1774.

[10] Boston Committee Records, p. 883.

[11] 4 Mass. Hist. Soc., *Collections*, IV, 247. See also *Mass. Gazette, and the Boston Post-Boy and Advertiser*, July 11, 1774. It was rumored that a heavy tax would be raised by the establishment of a new post office, and also that the quartering of troops would in time mean a yearly expense of sixty pounds on each housé.—*Ga. Gazette*, Aug. 15, 1765; *S. C. Gazette*, Nov. 22, 1773.

[12] *Boston Gazette*, Nov. 26, 1770. "We know the consequence following, it will be poverty and the most servile subjection to PENSIONED MISCREANTS."—*Pa. Journal*, Nov. 3, 1773.

WITHOUT OUR CONSENT."[13] *The First Book of the American Chronicles of the Times* put it well:

> "Behold yonder I see a dark cloud, like unto a large sheet, rise from the NORTH, big with Oppression and desolation, and the four corners thereof are held up by the four great beasts, BUTE, MANSFIELD, BERNARD, and HUTCHINSON; Carrying a large swarm, like unto locusts, of sycophants, Commissioners, duty-gatherers, customhouse officers, searchers, tide-waiters, placemen and pensioners innumerable; The bastards and spurious breed of noblemen, and the children of harlots, enveloped in smoke and big with destruction; and they seem as it were moving on towards the westwards, guided by the light of the star Wormwood."[14]

The penalties the propagandists thus foresaw were sufficiently general to affect most of the colonists in one or more of their interests. In addition the propagandists appealed directly to the self-interest of minor groups. South Carolina planters were asked to consider what Parliament might do to them if such acts as the Boston Port Act were permitted:

> "What are you to expect from such a Precedent as this? Have not the Parliament as good a Right to pass an Act that *Rice* and *Indico* shall be made only in such Parts of this Country as the King shall direct? For my Part, I should not be surprized even to see an Edict restricting the making of these Articles to the Colony of Georgia, and imposing heavy Fines upon those who should presume to make them here."[15]

Wharf owners in both Charleston and Boston were told that this same act greatly endangered their private property. The first Boston letter sent out regarding the act declared that even in the event of complete submission to it and full restitution for the tea, "the private Property, in most of the Wharves which surround this great Town, is ravished from the rightful Owners, and rendered useless,

---

[13] July 7, 1768.

[14] P. 12. Other examples may be found in *Pa. Gazette*, Feb. 13, 1766; *Pa. Journal*, May 18, 1774.

[15] *S. C. Gazette*, June 20, 1774. They were also told that if they entered into a non-importation association they could extricate themselves from the debts they owed the merchants.—*Ibid.*, July 4, 1774.

to the utter Ruin of many worthy Citizens."[16] South Carolina propagandists took the cue from Boston. One of them, perhaps Christopher Gadsden (who owned a wharf), declared: "The Design of this is three-fold. 1st, to establish a Precedent of parliamentary Right even to dispose of our Lands, 2dly, To promote a new Wharf-Office, for the Support of a thousand more Bloodsuckers in America. And, 3dly, To give the King Power to punish, by these Wretches, any Wharf-Holders who shall hereafter prove Patriotic."[17]

Merchants warned that the act granting a monopoly on the sale of tea to the East India Company was but the beginning of such acts. "The establishing *Tea-Ware-Houses* in America, by the India Company, 'tis said, is intended to pave the way for introducing large *Factories* for other goods, at all the principal ports, and then to bring in an *Honorable Board* of EXCISE."[18]

The foundations of civil and religious freedom were as insecure as property rights, charged the propagandists. The civil rights of the colonists had already been invaded by acts of the British Parliament, and the cumulative effect of such invasions, if allowed to continue, would result in the complete destruction of all civil liberty.

The claims of Parliament would render, as one South Carolinian asserted, "assemblies of your representatives *totally useless*."[19] The American judicial system would be destroyed by such efforts as England was making to render the Massachusetts judges dependent upon the crown for their support: "For if once the judges of the court of *judicatory* of this province become dependent for their support, or salaries, upon the favour of the crown, or ministry at Home, you become a nation of slaves to ministerial power; for thereby you submit the key of all your essential rights as Americans, to be in the hands of your enemies. . . . Where is the security of your lives, or your property?"[20]

[16] This letter was printed on a broadside for distribution. Mass. Hist. Soc., Broadsides, May 12, 1774.

[17] S. C. Gazette, June 20, 1774. "If Restitution was to be made, is that a sufficient Reason, that the Land, Wharves and Property of Thousands should be given to the King forever?"—Ibid., July 4, 1774.

[18] Ibid., Dec. 6, 1773, June 17, 1774; Mass. Spy, Oct. 14, 1773. People were told that the act would raise prices, for although a low rate might be set at first, when the monopoly was well established the East India Company, which had a bad record, would set what rates it pleased.—N. Y. Journal, Oct. 28, 1773.

[19] S. C. Gazette, Nov. 29, 1773. See also, among many others, N. Y. Journal, Dec. 22, 1768.

[20] Oration, Upon the Beauties of Liberty, p. 22. See also Boston Committee Records, p. 944; American Alarm, pp. 10 f.

Liberty of the press was clearly endangered, it was said time and again, by obvious efforts of the British government. And once that happened, wrote Isaiah Thomas in 1772, "farewell the remainder of our invaluable rights and privileges! We may next expect padlocks on our lips, fetters on our legs, and only our hands left at liberty to slave for our *worse than Egyptian taskmasters,* or—or—FIGHT OUR WAY TO CONSTITUTIONAL FREEDOM."[21]

More serious to the entrenched religious interests would be a threat to their established churches. Almost every act of the British government, propagandists warned, threatened religious liberty. Puritan New Englanders, denying liberty to all but their own sect, warned of an Anglican establishment and joined with Anglican southerners, who likewise denied liberty to everyone but themselves, in frightening the people with the bogy of popery.

Civil and religious liberties were mutually interdependent, affirmed the propagandists; the loss of one entailed the loss of the other, and both were in danger from parliamentary invasion of American rights. The propagandists had an appeal here in perfect accord with the pre-existing attitudes of the people, for the Great Awakening had spread the doctrines of religious freedom, and establishments were increasingly criticized. Colonists everywhere had a traditional dislike, distrust, and even fear of Roman Catholicism, and the New England and middle colonies had always been nervous about the establishment of an Anglican episcopate in America. Within the decade preceding the Revolution there were two periods of intense agitation in these colonies against the suggested creation of an American bishopric, one from 1763 to 1765 and the other from 1767 to 1769.

Although there was no real danger of the establishment, the agitation was most timely for the anti-British propagandists. Thus an appeal which warned of the danger of an Anglican establishment and of the introduction of popery was certain to arouse the people, particularly in the North and in the southern back country. The propagandists constantly scared up rumors of an American episcopate and scented popery in many an act innocent of religious designs, and, throughout the writings on this subject, there was an intentional confusion of Anglicanism and Roman Catholicism.

[21] *Mass. Spy,* Oct. 8, 1772.

John Adams, for instance, based his objection to the Stamp Act principally on the ground that it was simply another attempt on the part of corporate authority to establish a civil and ecclesiastical tyranny in America. Throughout history, he said, the laws of the church and the laws of the state had buttressed each other, and the Stamp Act was but another instance of the ceaseless effort of those in authority to intrench themselves more firmly. The land of America had been designed "for the illumination of the ignorant, and the emancipation of the slavish part of mankind all over the earth." Unless the colonists united against the Stamp Act, however, there would be established in that land the same civil and ecclesiastical tyranny from which men had freed themselves by the Protestant Reformation.[22]

Preachers and politicians alike urged that the loss of civil liberty meant the loss of religious liberty. "The Religion and public Liberty of a People are intimately connected," wrote Sam Adams in 1772, "their Interests are interwoven, they cannot subsist separately; therefore they rise and fall together. . . . How greatly then does it concern us, at all Events, to put a Stop to the Progress of Tyranny."[23] The Boston radicals saw in the Port Act a direct attack on both civil and religious freedom. A two-page broadside published on June 8, 1774, well before the news of the Quebec Act had reached America, warned of the danger: "Gentlemen, The evils which we have long foreseen are now come upon this town and Province, the long meditated stroke is now given to the civil liberty of this country? How long we may be allowed the enjoyment of our religious liberty is a question of infinite moment. Religion can never be retained in it's purity where tyranny has usurped the place of reason and justice."[24]

The rumored creation of an American bishopric was viewed as an attempt against the religious liberties of the other sects. Jonathan Mayhew flatly charged that the establishment of an American episcopate, regardless of the present modest plans of the Anglicans, would in all probability lead to their complete political and religious domination of the colonies. Although Charles Chauncy in 1768 attacked

[22] *Works of John Adams*, III, 445-464.
[23] "Valerious Poplicola," *Boston Gazette*, Oct. 5, 1772, reprinted in *Writings*, II, 332-339.
[24] Listed in Israel Evans, *American Bibliography*, No. 13,157.

the establishment simply as unnecessary, the newspaper essayists returned to Mayhew's old threats. William Livingston, in his series "The American Whig," took the issue straight to the people in a violent attack on the proposal:

> "You are yet to be chastised *only* with *whips* [referring to the title chosen by one of his antagonists, "Whip for the American Whig"] but depend upon it, when the *apostical monarchs* are come over . . . you, and such as you, will be chastised with scorpions. But this is not all: the *bellum episcopale* will doubtless be declared with every circumstance of awful pomp; and this extensive continent may soon be alarmed with the thund'ring signal, *the sword of the Lord, and of the Bishop.* Then, O dreadful! The torrent of episcopal vengeance! . . . The soft bleatings of the lamb will be changed into the terrible howling of the wolf; and every poor parson whose head never felt the weight of a bishop's hand will soon know the power of his pastoral staff, and the arm of the magistrate into the bargain. . . . Give the reins to one of the bookworms, and he will attempt to drive the chariot of the sun: let him be an ecclesiastic besides, and impelled by the two irresistible momentums of the *glory of God and the salvation of souls,* and how can he refrain from adopting the Popish comment upon the text, *compel them to come in!*"[25]

Even after the agitation of 1768 had died down, the propagandists recalled it to the minds of the people and renewed their warnings. "For my part," said one in 1773, "being rather of an easy temper, bordering upon indolence, I could wish to see those halcyon days, when freed from the labour of managing or thinking of our own political concerns, which serve only to sour the temper, and roughen the manners; England shall send us grenadiers for governors, and New Gate solicitors for judges,—when we shall have nothing to do but swallow competent doses of passive obedience and non-resistance, administered by the courtly and dignified clergy in lawn sleeves, with whom this land will in due season if the people should deserve it, be blest."[26]

To arouse the fear of Anglicanism was good propaganda in New England and the middle colonies, but the appeal would alienate the

[25] *N. Y. Gaz., or, Weekly Post-Boy,* Apr. 4, Apr. 18, 1768. This series was reprinted in *Boston Gazette* and *Pa. Journal.* [26] *Pa. Journal,* Nov. 10, 1773.

southern colonies. Anglican and Congregationalist alike, however, could join in an attack on popery. This element was first injected into the Anglican controversy in 1768 by the newspaper, not the pamphlet writers. The newspaper articles were more definitely popular appeals than were the pamphlets of Charles Chauncy, and they stressed, as he did not, that aspect of the question which would have the greatest public appeal—the danger of Romanism. "The Puritan" wrote a series of essays in the *Boston Gazette,* occasioned, he said, by the evident lack of concern over religious problems: "I confess I am surpriz'd to find so little attention is given to the danger we are in, of the utter loss of . . . religious Rights. . . . To say the truth, I have from long observation been apprehensive, that what we have above everything else to fear, is POPERY."[27] The essays which followed simply pointed out the actual evidences of Romanism within New England itself. "Bless me! could our ancestors look out of their graves and see so many of *their own* sons, deck'd out with the worst of *foreign Superfluities,* the ornaments of the *whore of Babylon,* how it would break their sacred Repose!" Others joined in the hunt and reported their findings in the *Boston Gazette.*[28] One discovered a parson who had turned Romish and wrote a poem on his apostasy; the last stanza shows the typical association of Anglicanism and Romanism:

"But if he from Rome greater Profit had hop'd,
He who now is be-bishop'd, would have been be-pop'd,
And equally run, to avoid being Poor,
To the arms of the church, or of Babylon's Whore."[29]

Open charges that there was a Catholic plot against the liberties of America, a plot abetted by the British government, were frequent and vehement. As early as 1770 a writer in Boston stated that the Crown's permission to the Roman Church to send missionaries to Nova Scotia was one of the most "daring Violations of Law, and

[27] *Boston Gazette,* Apr. 4, 1768.
[28] *Ibid.,* Apr. 25, 1768. "Edvardus Non-Episcoparias" and "Anti-Pope." "Anti-Pope" named Cambridge, Reading, Duxbury, and Chelmsford as in danger.
[29] *Ibid.,* May 9, 1768. In the eighteenth century, whore was pronounced whoor to rhyme with poor. The Whore of Babylon referred either to the Pope himself or to the church as a whole in the popular writing. "A Master-Key to Popery" was advertised for sale by the *Newport Mercury,* Apr. 12, 1773, in a box headed "To all Protestants, of every Denomination throughout America, and all other Friends to religious and civil Liberty."

attacks upon the PROTESTANT RELIGION, which have disgraced the Annals of the Present Reign."[30] The Quebec Act gave the propagandists their real opportunity to play upon the colonial hatred of Rome. The object of the Act, said the Reverend John Lathrop, was to "cut off all the liberties of the rest of the colonies," and the *Newport Mercury* printed a song, supposed to have been sung by "goody" North to that foundling, the popish Quebec Act:

> *"Then up with the Papists, up, up,*
> *And down with the Protestants, down-e,*
> *Here we go backwards and forwards,*
> *And all for the good of the crown-e."*[31]

The propagandists relied extensively upon the seventeenth chapter of Revelation in their religious appeals, for it contained a perfect association of ideas. Quotations from two sermons show the application of these verses to the revolutionary problem. Henry Cumings preached a sermon in Billerica in 1775 in which he said:

> "We can have no security of enjoying our religious privileges, should that ministerial system of oppression, which has lately been planned against us, be once established among us. For civil and ecclesiastical tyranny are nearly allied; and the latter follows close at the heels of the former. From the Canada bill, and some other things favourable to popery, we have grounds to fear, that should the present schemes of arbitrary power succeed, the Scarlet Whore would soon get mounted on her Horned beast in America, and, with the CUP OF ABOMINATIONS in her hand, ride triumphant over the heads of true Protestants, making multitudes DRUNK WITH THE WINE OF HER FORNICATIONS."[32]

Samuel Sherwood's great sermon, "The Church's Flight into the Wilderness," printed in New York in 1776, showed how many rulers of England in the past had succumbed to the lure of the Scarlet Woman and then said of the present government:

> "How far the present ministry have walked in this enchanting road, and how fond they are of the kind embraces of this

---

[30] *Boston Gazette*, Nov. 19, 1770.
[31] John Lathrop, *A Discourse Preached Dec. 15, 1774*, p. 28; *Newport Mercury, Extraordinary*, Mar. 15, 1775. This whole subject is completely dealt with in Charles Henry Metzger, *The Quebec Act; A Primary Cause of the American Revolution*.
[32] *A Sermon, Preached in Billerica, On the 23d of November, 1775*, p. 12 n.

The Mitred Minuet. A Paul Revere engraving. Royal American Magazine, October, 1774.
By courtesy of the New York Public Library.

old filthy harlot, the world will judge from their open attempts to propagate and establish popery, that exotic plant, in these northern regions; which is not a native to our benign soil, nor of our heavenly Father's planting; and their gathering up of armies professedly Roman catholics to dragoon us into slavery, and bondage, or massacre and butcher us and our families, and lay our pleasant country in desolation and ruin."[33]

Throughout the country there was a shouting campaign against the popish designs of the British government. A South Carolinian recounted at length the horrors that had been committed in the past in the name of the Pope—the Massacre of St. Bartholomew, the Gun Powder Plot, the horrors of Bloody Mary—and warned the people against the dangers of "suffering Popery to be introduced and established among us."[34] Francis Lightfoot Lee wrote Landon Carter, who was definitely opposed to independence, "the Roman Catholic Lords, Bishops & gentry are extremely active in procuring recruits. . . . The establishment of Popery will no doubt be the reward of the exertions of the Roman Catholics."[35] Others, too, saw a Catholic plot in America. The Wilmington committee of correspondence was the author of the surprising information that captured letters of Gage to Carleton contained the request that "his good friends the Catholics may be sent to assist him in cutting the throats of all the hereticks."[36] The Tryon County (New York) committee of safety made the danger more imminent, in a letter to the Albany committee reporting that Johnson Hall, Sir William Johnson's old home, was fortified and that his son had gathered "about 150 Highlanders (Roman Catholics)," who were armed and ready to march against Albany.[37] An appeal was directed to the British soldiers, urging them not to support these plans:

"You are about to embark for America, to compel your fellow-subjects there to submit to POPERY and SLAVERY. . . .
"You will be called upon to imbrue your hands in the blood of your fellow-subjects in America because they will not admit to be slaves, and are alarmed at the establishment of popery and arbitrary power in one half of their country.

[33] Pp. 16 f.
[34] S. C. Gazette; and Country Journal, Feb. 7, 1775.
[35] Lee Transcripts, II, 74 f.   [36] Ga. Gazette, Aug. 30, 1775.
[37] The Minute Book of the [Tryon County] Committee of Safety, p. 8.

"Whether you will draw those swords which have defended them against enemies, to butcher them into a resignation of their rights, which they hold as the Sons of Englishmen, is in your breasts."[38]

The result of the establishment of Catholicism, said the propagandists, was that King George had absolved the allegiance of the colonists to him, for he had broken his coronation oath. "I will not say that our King *hath* committed wilful and corrupt Perjury . . . neither do I assert that the People are now *absolved from their allegiance;* but . . . *nobody can be hanged for thinking*," wrote a bold Virginian in 1774.[39] Samuel and Jacob Williams of North Carolina both testified that members of the Anson County committee of safety told them that "Lord North was a Roman Catholick, that the King's Crown tottered upon his shoulders, for he had established the Roman Catholick Religion in the Province of Quebec, and that the King and Parliament did intend to establish Popery on all the Continent of America, and that the King was forsworn."[40] Throughout the colonies this idea was assiduously propagated. It did much to prepare people for the Declaration of Independence, for the hatred of Roman Catholicism was real, both in the Anglican South and the dissenting North. Propagandists had effectively related that feeling to the political problem of the Revolution.

The personal freedom and actual lives of the colonists, said the propagandists, were no more secure under British domination than were their property and their religion. British troops were being sent to enforce the new trade laws, and tragedy was in store for America. The billeting of troops in private homes was but the least dangerous consequence of submitting to Great Britain. "I am certain," said "The Watchman," "that there is not a more effectual method of augmenting the number of martyrs to their country than a submission of any Colony, or a part of any Colony, to the tools of Administration . . . who can answer for the numbers that shall be slain in battle, and in cold blood?"[41] Hanging work will begin,

---

[38] Mass. Hist. Soc., Broadsides, Salem, July 19, 1775; and *Ga. Gazette,* July 5, 1775.
[39] *Va. Gazette* (Purdie), Oct. 13, 1774.
[40] *Col. Rec. N. C.,* X, 127 ff. See also *Ga. Gazette,* Sept. 28, 1774. Sears and McDougall spread the idea in New York.—*N. Y. Gazetteer,* Jan. 12, 1775; and 4 Force, *Amer. Arch.,* I, 1230.
[41] 4 Force, *Amer. Arch.,* V, 994. Enoch Huntington in a sermon called *The Happy Effects of Union,* expressed the same fear: "And if we are once subdued to her will, and

said a clergyman; and a British friend of America wrote that if the colonists submitted, "sixty of you are to be hanged in *Philadelphia,* and the same Number in *New-York.*"[42] And William Stearns in a fast day sermon delivered in Marlborough on May 11, 1775, described in all its gruesome detail the old English law providing for the punishment of traitors:

> "If they gain a victory, then we are to be treated as *Traitors,* which (by the law of England) is as follows; we are to be drawn on hurdles . . . to the place of execution—then hanged a while by the neck—then taken down, and our bowles taken out and burnt before our eyes—then beheaded and quartered, and our heads and quarters disposed of at the King's pleasure! (God Almighty be merciful to our souls!)—then ensue a confiscation of estates and corruption of blood, so that our posterity never can inherit, to the latest generation."[43]

Philip Freneau's bitterness was admirably adapted to such appeals:

> "If Britain conquers, help us, Heaven, to fly!
> Lend me your wings, ye ravens of the sky.
> If Britain conquers,—we exist no more;
> These lands shall redden with their children's gore,
> Who turned to slaves, their fruitless toil shall moan—
> Toils in these fields that once they called their own!

> "Haste! to your tents in fetters bring
> These slaves that serve their tyrant of a king.
> So just, so virtuous, is your cause, I say
> Hell must prevail—if Britain wins the day!"[44]

In short, as the propagandists put it, the safety and security of all America were at stake; complete disaster, the ruin of all the col-

---

should be subjected to the controul and power of her exasperated, brutal soldiery, such cruel and dreadful scenes would take place, as every good and benevolent man . . . might well desire to hide himself from the sight of."—P. 20. In 1768 a writer warned of the dangers of a press bill: "Our *money* only is seized upon now, to *relieve the debt* of *Great-Britain,* and will not our *youth* be ravaged from us next to *fight* her battles, in the fields of *Germany,* or in the *Indian* Ocean? . . . then must we prepare to see our property ravished from us, our houses broken open, our wives, our daughters, violated, ourselves torn from the tenderness and caresses of our families, and dragged with every circumstance of violence and barbarity, to hardships, labour, insults, and oppression."—*Va. Gazette* (Rind), Mar. 24, 1768.

[42] 4 Force, *Amer. Arch.,* II, 1607; Niles, *Principles and Acts of the Revolution,* p. 323.
[43] P. 20.   [44] Quoted in Tyler, *Literary History,* I, 417.

onies would inevitably follow from submission to the claims of Great Britain. The issue as they presented it to the people was simplified and rarefied in the single phrase, Liberty or Slavery, so vague that the hopes and fears of each individual and each group could be encompassed in its ample connotations. In this, the commonest appeal of the entire movement, the issue was reduced to its simplest, most elementary terms. Constantly presented in a variety of forms, it was the epitome of the propagandist's appeal.

Slavery was the fate of America if she did not resist, and once the monster Slavery was let in:

> "He will debauch your Wives and Daughters, devour your Cattle, Swine, Corn and Poultry: He will set Fire to your Woods, trample on the tender Plants in your Gardens, break down your Fences, and make your pleasant Fields desolate. Whenever he reigns among you, he will make Dastards of brave Men, and Fools of the Fearful; Thieves of the Honest, and Whores of the Modest; Reprobates of the Religious, and Madmen of the Moral. In short there is no diabolical Change, which the infernal Monster, called SLAVERY, cannot accomplish."[45]

That was the issue, an issue even more important than life or death "We are obliged to say," resolved the Middlesex County, Massachusetts, meeting of August 30, 1774, "that the Question now is Whether . . . we are contented to be the most abject Slaves . . . or by a manly, joint and virtuous Opposition assert & support our Freedom. . . . LIFE & DEATH, or what is more, FREEDOM & SLAVERY, are in a peculiar Sense now before us."[46] Poetic versions of the same theme were frequent:

> "There is a Tide, in the Affairs of Men,
>   Which, taken at the Flood, leads on to FREEDOM!
>   Omitted,—all the Voyage of their Life
>   Is bound in Shallows and in Slavery."[47]

There were worse imitations of Shakespeare in Revolutionary America than that one. The opening lines of "HOPE: A Rhapsody" belied its name:

[45] *Conn. Gazette,* July 12, 1765.
[46] Mass. Hist. Soc., Broadsides, Aug. 30, 1774. See also *Va. Gazette* (Purdie), July 28, 1774; Samuel Roads, *The History and Traditions of Marblehead,* p. 97—two of many examples.   [47] *Conn. Gazette,* July 12, 1765.

"Mourn, Yankey, mourn, the dreaded loss deplore,
For Freedom bleeds, and Liberty's no more.
Let Massachusetts sons neglect the toil,
Of reaping plenty from their grateful Soil;
Throw up to desert waste the vast domain,
And give confusion universal reign."[48]

THE ADVANTAGES OF VICTORY

In presenting the other half of the phrase Liberty or Slavery to the people of America, the propagandists moved into the second line of attack against England—the advantages of victory. They proved her guilty of unjust and illegal invasions of American rights, and they showed that her acts adversely affected the interests of every important group in the colonies. They now presented the enemy as a bar to the future progress of America, as a hindrance to the realization of new colonial hopes.[49] The propagandists stressed as the principal advantage of victory the freedom to develop the ideals of American life, but they rarely were specific. They had specified the dangers, but they rarely specified the advantages.

The most specific statement of advantages was made by the radically anti-British propagandists when urging independence. Even so, much of the argument in favor of independence was in refutation of Tory arguments against it. Tom Paine's famous *Common Sense*, for example, is almost entirely an attack on hereditary monarchy and a denial of the advantages of reconciliation with Great Britain. Powerful as the essay is, the list of positive advantages of independence which closes it is weak and repetitive:

1. Until America declares her independence, no foreign power can mediate the dispute between the two.

2. Spain and France will certainly not give America aid unless she is independent.

3. The Americans are rebels in the eyes of the world until they break away from England.

4. Petitions to the courts of Europe asking their support will do more good than a boatload of petitions to Britain.

[48] N. Y. Hist. Soc., Broadsides, July 26, 1774. Compare this couplet:
"When FREEDOM'S Day of Grace is once past by
Vile *Slaves* you'll live; like *Malefactors* die."
          —*Newport Mercury*, Jan. 25, 1773.
[49] Lasswell, *Propaganda Technique*, pp. 58 f.

Elsewhere in the essay he had flatly stated that "nothing but independence, i.e. a continental form of government, can keep the peace of the continent and preserve it inviolate from civil war." This idea he amplified in an imaginary dialogue between the ghost of General Montgomery and a delegate to the Continental Congress.[50] The two arguments he principally urged in support of a declaration of independence—the possibility of obtaining foreign aid and the preservation of domestic peace appealed strongly to the cautious and the conservative. There were many who feared to tackle the power of the British empire singlehanded and who feared the disorders which might follow the collapse of British authority in the colonies.

A list of advantages published in the *Pennsylvania Evening Post* is typical of many others:

1. The colonies would be delivered from two governments directly opposed to each other.

2. They would be delivered from the disorders of unlimited, undescribed, and arbitrary powers of conventions, committees of safety, and committees of inspection.

3. Criminal correspondence with the enemy would be stopped.

4. The people would be delivered from the danger of crown officers.

5. The British Constitution could be restored to each colony with the added advantage of a governor and council elected by the people.

6. France would immediately attack England in her most defenseless regions, thus drawing off the British fleets and armies from America.

7. No power would join with England in the fight against America because they would have such respect for the love of freedom in America that they would not want to aid England in destroying it. (This obviously was in refutation of the Tory argument that England would obtain continental allies.)[51]

There were many who added to this list the benefits of a free and unlimited trade with the world and the resulting benefits to all classes of people:

[50] 4 Force, *Amer. Arch.*, V, 128 ff.
[51] Apr. 20, 1776. See also *Pa. Evening Post*, Feb. 17, 1776; and 4 Force, *Amer. Arch.*, V, 854 ff.

"What will be the probable benefits of independence? A free and unlimited trade; a great accession of wealth, and a proportionable rise in the value of land; the establishment, gradual improvement and perfection of manufactures and science; a vast influx of foreigners, encouraged by the mildness of a free, equal, and tolerating government to leave their native countries, and settle in these Colonies; an astonishing encrease of our people from the present stock. Where encouragement is given to industry, where liberty and property are well secured, where the poor may easily find subsistence, and the middling rank comfortably support their families by labour, there the inhabitants must encrease rapidly; to some of these causes we owe the doubling of our numbers in somewhat more than twenty-five years. If such hath been the progress of population under the former restraints on our trade and manufactures, a population still more rapid may be reasonably expected when these restraints come to be taken off. . . . WE CANNOT PAY TOO GREAT A PRICE FOR LIBERTY, AND POSTERITY WILL THINK INDEPENDENCE A CHEAP PURCHASE AT EIGHTEEN MILLIONS."[52]

As in all mass movements where conflicting interests must be harmonized, the propagandists fell back upon loose generalizations. They endeavored to catch up discordant elements in aims so broad that each group could make the war over in its own image and could visualize the achievement of its own aims in an independent America. Thus they stressed not so much the profits from increased trade or lumbering, free from England's baneful restrictions, not so much the opportunity to pre-empt western land and sell it at speculative prices. They rather stressed the future glory of America, which was the last asylum for civil and religious liberty on the face of the earth, the home of the brave and the land of the free. The struggle, said the propagandists, was one between a young, hopeful, and virile nation of high ideals, and an older, effete civilization of low standards and debased morals.

England stood squarely opposed to the full development of the American promise, and if her plans were not resisted, the propagandists asserted, it "will dash the hopes of liberty and empire."[53]

[52] *Pa. Evening Post*, Feb. 17, 1776.
[53] *Newport Mercury*, Feb. 28, 1774. Ezra Stiles was quoted in *S. C. and Amer. Gen. Gazette*, Sept. 29, 1774, as having said, "Plantations may be made with encouragement,

America, they said, was the last asylum of civil and religious liberty for mankind, and it should be saved for freedom.

> "And if any miserable people on the continent or isles of Europe, after being weakened by luxury, debauchery, venality, intestine quarrels, or other vices, should, in the rude collisions, or now-uncertain revolutions of kingdoms, be driven, in their extremity, to seek a safe retreat from slavery in some far-distant climate; let them find, O let them find one in America under thy brooding, sacred wings; where *our* oppressed fathers once found it."[54]

Philip Freneau foresaw the day

> "when strangers rule no more,
> Nor cruel mandates vex from Britain's shore;
> When commerce shall extend her shortened wing,
> And her rich freights from every climate bring;
> When mighty towns shall flourish free and great,—
> Vast their dominion, opulent their state;
> When one vast cultivated region teems
> From ocean's side to Mississippi's streams,
> While each enjoys his vine tree's peaceful shade,
> And even the meanest has no foe to dread."[55]

Even if war should come and the country be devastated, said William Gordon in 1774, the loss would not be great compared with future gains:

> "Should the country be wasted for a few years, and numbers of its inhabitants be destroyed, ere the wished-for salvation is granted, how soon, after having secured its liberties, will it regain its former prosperity; yea, become far more glorious, wealthy, and populous than ever, through the thousands, and ten thousands that will flock to it, with riches, arts, and sciences acquired by them in foreign countries."[56]

---

but cannot successfully be forced. Free policy, free religion, free property and matrimony will soon populate a fertile country in good climate."

[54] Mayhew, *The Snare Broken*, p. 36. Some Tories cut down a Liberty Tree in Boston in 1775, and a patriot improved the occasion: "But be it known to this infamous band of traitors, that the Grand *American* Tree of Liberty, planted in the center of the United Colonies of *North America*, now flourishes with unrivalled, increasing beauty, and bids fair, in a short time, to afford under its wide-spreading branches a safe and happy retreat for all the sons of Liberty, however numerous and dispersed."—4 Force, *Amer. Arch.*, III, 472.

[55] A slightly different form is in *Poems* I, 180 f.

[56] *Religious and Civil Liberty, a Thanksgiving Discourse*, Dec. 15, 1774, p. 35.

Indeed, declared William Livingston in the "American Whig" in 1768, the future greatness of America was inevitable:

"Courage, then Americans! liberty, religion, and sciences are on the wing to these shores: The finger of God points out a mighty empire to your sons. . . . The day dawns in which the foundation of this mighty empire is to be laid, by the establishment of a *regular American Constitution.* All that has hitherto been done, seems to be little beside the collection of materials, for the construction of this glorious fabrick. 'Tis time to put them together . . . before seven years roll over our heads, the first stone must be laid.—Peace or war; famine or plenty; poverty or affluence; in a word no circumstance, whether prosperous or adverse, [that] can happen to our parent . . . no conduct of hers . . . no possible temper on her part . . . will put a stop to this building. There is no contending with Omnipotence, and the *predispositions* are so numerous, and so well adapted to the rise of America, that our success is indubitable."[57]

A Virginia poet in 1774 envisioned the glorious future of America:

"Thus we shall see, and triumph in the Sight,
    While Malice frets and fumes, and gnaws her Chains;
AMERICA shall blast her fiercest Foes,
    Shall brave the dismal Shocks of Bloody War,
And in unrivall'd Pomp resplendent rise,
    And shine *sole* Empress of the WESTERN WORLD."[58]

Yes, said the propagandists, the finger of God pointed the pathway to empire and glory. W. H. Drayton even warned against the "impiety of being backward to act as the instruments in the hand of the Almighty, now extended to accomplish his purpose," and it was even said that as God could no longer flourish in the corrupt east, "we may naturally conclude that America is to be the theatre of this glorious event."[59]

But it was the beauty of liberty the propagandists stressed, liberty which had been gained by blood and treasure of the forefathers, and which must be transmitted undiminished to future generations. It

[57] *N. Y. Gazette* (Parker), Apr. 11, 1768. "There has been, my countrymen, *Liberty* once among us. . . . And is it fled?—No, methinks I see recorded in the will of Heaven! —*My Sons, this* Land, *a* Land *by Heaven designed for* Liberty, *is yours.*"—*Newport Mercury, Supplement,* Oct. 28, 1765.
[58] *Va. Gazette* (Purdie), May 19, 1774. See also *ibid., Supplement,* Nov. 9, 1769.
[59] *Conn. Courant,* Apr. 22, 1776.

was a sentimental appeal to a common background and a common destiny. "It is for liberty, that liberty for which our fathers fought, that liberty which is dearer to a generous mind than life itself, that we now contend."[60] This was the power in the resolves of the Suffolk convention:

"Whereas the power, but not the justice, the vengeance, but not the wisdom, of *Great Britain,* which of old persecuted, scourged and excited our fugitive parents from their native shores, now pursues us, their guiltless children, with unrelenting severity. And whereas, this then savage and uncultivated desert, was purchased by the toil and treasure, or acquired by the blood and valour of those our venerable progenitors; to us they bequeathed the dear-bought inheritance . . . and the most sacred obligations are upon us to transmit the glorious purchase, unfettered by power, unclogged with shackles, to our innocent and beloved offspring. On the fortitude, on the wisdom, and on the exertions of this important day, is suspended the fate of this new world, and of unborn millions."[61]

"The blessings of Heaven attending," said the people of Windham, Connecticut, in 1774, "America is saved; children yet unborn will rise and call you blessed; the present generation will, by future —to the latest period of American glory—be extolled and celebrated as the happy instruments, under God, of delivering millions from thraldom and slavery, and secure permanent freedom and liberty to America."[62] The compulsive appeal of a vague concept was admir-

[60] Arnold, *Rhode Island,* II, 259, quoting the resolutions of the town of Newport, Sept. 3, 1765. The ancestor theme is recurrent; see Mass. Hist. Soc., Broadsides, *Tea Destroyed by the Indians:*

"Could our Fore-fathers rise from their cold graves,
And view their Land, with all their children SLAVES;
What would they say! how would their spirits rend,
And, Thunder-Stricken, to their Graves descend."

See also *S. C. Gazette; and Country Journal,* Mar. 18, 1766, Oct. 3, 1769; and *Newport Mercury,* Apr. 30, 1770.

[61] 4 Force, *Amer. Arch.,* I, 776.

[62] Ellen D. Larned, *History of Windham County, Connecticut,* II, 125. "*We Remember our Ancestors and Posterity.*"—Resolutions of the town of Palmer, Boston Committee Records, p. 597. "For *your country's sake!* then—for *your own,* and *your posterity's sakes*—for the sake of millions of *infants* yet unborn!"—*S. C. Gazette,* Dec. 6, 1773. See also *Two Liberty Songs,* Mass. Hist. Soc., Broadsides, 1776. One stanza of one of them is:

"For your Freedom and lives,
Your children and wives,
To defend is the time, now or never;
Then tyrants oppose,
AMERICA'S foes,
And live Freemen both now and forever."

ably made in Joseph Warren's letter to the committee of the little town of Stonington, Connecticut, in 1774: "we are compelled to support the conflict. When liberty is the prize, who would shun the warfare? Who would stoop to waste a coward thought on life? We esteem no sacrifice too great, no conflict too severe, to redeem our inestimable rights and privileges."[63]

Propagandists thus identified the cause of America with the cause of liberty throughout the world. "We are engaged, my fellow soldiers, in the cause of virtue, of liberty, of God."[64] And Perez Morton in his *Oration on Warren* declared, "the Heights of *Charlestown* shall be more memorable for thy Fall, than the *Plains of Abraham* are for that of the Hero of *Britain*. For while *he* died contending for a single Country, *You* fell in the Cause of Virtue and Mankind."[65] As another summed it up: "Arguments from every quarter, from heav'n, from earth, from the living and from the dead, from all that is to be desired or dreaded in life, hoped or feared at death, from America's vast extended continent, the spacious world, with all the regions in which men reside,—urge us to support, dignify, and with manly fortitude vindicate the invaded rights of humanity."[66]

"For, brethren, ye have been called unto liberty"—it was the call to freedom and a new day, stirring the thoughts of the people with shadowy, ill-defined hopes, and giving them a sense of unity and common purpose. What did liberty mean? Who can tell? To one it may have meant simply freedom from English restrictions, perhaps nothing more than freedom from the Stamp Act; to another it may have meant complete freedom from England; to still a third it may have meant internal freedom from local oppressors. It may have meant political, economic, religious freedom—free governments, free land, free trade, free religion, free liquor, free anything that people want. It meant just as much or just as little as "Liberty, Fraternity, Equality" in another revolution, or the "fruits of the war" in the America of 1867, or "Democracy" in 1918. The power

---

[63] Quoted in Hollister, *Connecticut*, II, 156. "HARK! What's this we hear? The alarm of war. The drums beat, the trumpets sound to arms! to arms! to arms! Liberty waves her flowing banners in the air and calls on her Sons to attend her standard, erected against oppression, fraud and tyranny, the black catalogue of her foes."—*Boston Gazette*, Feb. 26, 1776.

[64] *Va. Gazette* (Pinkney), Dec. 20, 1775.

[65] P. 11.   [66] *Conn. Courant*, Feb. 19, 1776.

of the word was its vagueness. Who would not choose Liberty to Slavery? Some there might have been who would not fight for the merchants, or for the political bosses, some there might even be who would not fight for the preachers, but it was a craven spirit who would not fight for Liberty. "If your HONNORS should call for me I am ready to serve my Country with all freedom and assistance that I am capable of as I think It tis the Duty of all well wishers to Libbity and the North Amarrica, wishing suckess to libbity. . . ."[67]

America was thus presented by the propagandists in contrast to Great Britain as having a truer concept of political right, a greater regard for the well-being of the individual, and a higher type of civilization. They had united her in defense of their common heritage and their common hopes, and in defense of the liberties of all mankind.

[67] *Documents N. H.*, VII, 472.—A letter from a man in Freeworthy, May 13, 1775.

VIII

HATE

THE MOST important motive in war psychosis is not reason or justice, or even self-interest, but hate. An unreasoning hatred, a blind disgust, is aroused not against policies but against people. The propagandists, in proving that acts of Parliament violated fundamental American rights and that Great Britain's plans endangered the welfare of America and its future greatness, made men fearful and angry. It was only necessary to direct these emotions against the people who supported these policies, and the compound of hate, a compulsive emotion, was aroused. For ten years the propagandists unremittingly and with increasing bitterness aspersed the characters and defamed the names of the English ruling classes at home and abroad. By 1775 they had become objects of hatred and disgust. Americans had come to think of themselves almost as a different race of people, and the anti-British movement was practically an "oust the foreigner" movement.

Propagandists thus indicted the British: They were venal and corrupt, seeking only their own profit in the downfall of American liberty that they might continue to live in idleness, luxury, and debauchery. The rude irony of the poem "Oppression," written in England by an American in late 1764, was fitting style for such an attack:

> "When countries groan beneath Oppression's hand,
> And pensioned blockheads riot through the land;
> When colonies a savage excise pay,
> To feed the creatures of a motley day,
>
> .   .   .   .   .   .
>
> When dunce on dunce successive rules our state,
> Who can't love a Pitt, and who a Grenville hate?"[1]

The people of Plymouth, thinking of the trials and sufferings of their forefathers, indignantly resolved that the fair inheritance transmitted to them should never become the prey of "Vultures and

[1] First printed in London, reprinted in Boston in 1765. Tyler, *Literary History*, I, 120 n., suggests Arthur Lee as the author.

Harpies," and in Hatfield the committee of correspondence wrote Boston, "We are daily more and more convinced of the ambitious views of those wicked men who are attempting to parcel our properties amongst themselves and their adherents."[2] A poem on the Tea Act urged all honest men neither to hold nor wish for place

"While Faction reigns, and Tyranny presides
And base Oppression o'er the Virtues rides,
While venal Measures dance in Silken Sails
And Avarice, O'er Earth and Seas prevails,
And Luxury, creates such mighty Feuds,
E'en in the Bosoms of the Demi Gods."

And another poem, "The Unnatural Parent," assured Americans that

"NATIONS unborn shall curse the Men who first
From malice, folly, or ambitious thirst,
The baneful seeds of enmity have sown,
Which now to crops of fatal discord grown,
Our charters, commerce, laws and acts annoys,
The bounds of mutual confidence destroys,
And blasts the parent's and the children's joys."[3]

Enoch Huntington in a sermon in April, 1776, summed up this charge of venality and corruption:

"Already do the avaricious courtiers of *Great-Britain*, with the numerous train of their needy dependents and hangers-on, with the whole tribe of dissolute spendthrifts, and idle deboshee's, feast themselves with the prospect of possessing the fruits of our past industry, and the spoils of our future earnings, and if once subjected to them, we should find them greedy and insatiable . . ."[4]

---

[2] *Plymouth Records*, Nov. 13, 1772, p. 261; 4 Mass. Hist. Soc., *Collections*, IV, 243. The town of Marlborough resolved against "those mercenary wretches who are so sordidly detached from all good" that they would "enslave this country in misery, by stripping the people of their Religious Liberty and Property."—Charles Hudson, *History of the Town of Marlborough*, p. 150.

[3] The first poem is from *Boston Gazette*, Mar. 21, 1774, the second from *Pa. Journal*, Apr. 13, 1774.

[4] *Happy Effects of Union*, p. 25. "If the Estates of Americans are to be at the Disposal of a luxurious Set of Placemen and Pensioners of Great Britain, who give the strongest Proofs of their being both inimical to our Sovereign and ruinous to the Nation, what are Americans to expect will be the Consequences?"—*Essex Gazette*, May 24, 1774.

The internal enemies of America were just as mercenary as their masters in England. Of those who would enforce the Stamp Act it was said:

> "Let therefore all those apostate sons of venality, those wretched hirelings, and execrable parricides, those first-born sons of Hell, who for a little filthy lucre, have thus as far as they were able, betray'd and murder'd their country, with the vile slander of their contagious breath and dire hissing of their forked tongues, conscious of their base perfidious lies, blush and be confounded at the light of the sun, and tremble at the countenance of the sons of honour and vertue."[5]

John Sullivan actually reported to Washington that the Tories of Portsmouth would with their own hands, if given the opportunity, burn the town, "expecting a Reward from the Ministry for such hellish service,"[6] and the Boston committee on donations virtuously wrote the town of Coventry, "we cannot but experience a satisfaction far superior to what those can feel, whose joys arise from the prospect they think they have, of *building their greatness on their country's ruin.*"[7]

The foes of America were frauds, tricksters, and liars. This was a valuable charge because it helped to counteract the Tory suggestions. If the people learn to disbelieve the enemy, its propaganda is discredited.[8] "Our enemies," said the Boston propagandists on the committee on donations, "will use every artifice that hell can suggest and human power can execute, to enslave us";[9] and Alexander McDougall charged that "the Minions of Tyranny and Despotism in the Mother Country, and the Colonies, are indefatigable in laying every Snare that their malevolent and corrupt Hearts can suggest."[10] The Tories had "unwearedly practiced every low artifice to Deceive the more unthinking part of the Community," and had endeavored

---

[5] *Boston Gazette*, Sept. 16, 1765. See also *Conn. Gazette*, Aug. 9, 1765. These were common suggestions.

[6] *Documents N. H.*, VII, 636.   [7] 4 Mass. Hist. Soc., *Collections*, IV, 102.

[8] Lasswell, *Propaganda Technique*, pp. 79 ff.

[9] 4 Mass. Hist. Soc., *Collections*, IV, 55. Cf. Aaron Cleaveland's statement to the same committee praying that the Lord would deliver the people "out of the hands of a wicked and despotic power, who are exerting all the subtility and malice of hell."—*Ibid.*, p. 151.

[10] In the broadside, *To the Betrayed Inhabitants of New York*, McDougall Papers. See also Amer. Antiq. Soc., Broadsides, *Extracts of Private Letters*, Apr. 7, Apr. 8, 1774; Boston Committee Records, pp. 562 ff.; and Hutchinson, *History of Massachusetts Bay*, III, 369 f.

by "base and false insinuation, to frighten others into a tame submission to Ministerial Measures." They were, because of their frauds and their lies, "the most perfidious and serpentine domestic enemies," and in them no confidence could be placed.[11]

The English ruling classes were licentious and immoral. The *American Alarm* denounced the Anglican churchmen, who brought untold sufferings on the people, "only for taking liberty to worship GOD, according to his word, and because they will not give their property to support that worship, which they know has not GOD for its author, nor his word for their rule—This is enough, to make the hills to tremble, and the earth to quake."[12] But such attacks were rare—there were too many Anglican friends of America in the southern colonies. A savage attack published in Rhode Island in 1774 contained ideas more commonly, though not usually so violently, expressed: "BEELZEBUB" published this memento on the Boston Port Act and the other acts of Parliament, that all ought to remember that "*hypocrisy, venality* and *corruption,* with all other immoralities, unthought or unheard of, are the only *favourite principles* of the reigning *administration,*" an administration which had declared "that in the disposal of all offices of trust, and honor" the mockers of religion, the encouragers of false oaths, "the *factious promoters* of *vice* and *sedition* . . . the *worshippers* of that *idol* of *falsehood Hutchinson,* all smugglers, &c . . . shall be considered as fittest objects for such appointment."[13]

But far more important, the English were wantonly cruel and depraved. This, the culminating attack on the enemy, was the prelude to war. The ministry had been pictured in 1765 as Egyptian taskmasters with the fixed design of enslaving the colonists, and had been charged with forming plans and setting them aside simply because they would please America.[14] But when troops were sent to Boston, the attack began in earnest. The Sons of Liberty in Provi-

---

[11] *Worcester Town Records 1753-1783,* p. 215; *Newport Mercury,* Aug. 29, 1774; *Conn. Gazette,* June 7, 1776. The genealogy of a Tory was published in N. Y. *Journal,* Apr. 19, 1770: the Devil begot sin, sin begot error, and so on down the line of ancestors until disaffection was reached; "dissaffection begot a Tory, on the Body of the *Wh—re of Babylon,* when she was deemed *past child bearing.*"

[12] P. 4.

[13] *Newport Mercury, Supplement,* Aug. 22, 1774. See also Library of Congress, Broadsides, Connecticut, *A Poem,* June 23, 1775.

[14] N. Y. *Gazette, or, Weekly Post-Boy,* July 11, 1765; *Conn. Gazette,* July 19, 1765; and *The Pitkin Papers,* p. 104.

dence, on the third celebration of the repeal of the Stamp Act, defended Boston and indicted the ministers of state: Though they repealed the Stamp Act, they have laid new taxes, "and, for the Collection of the Duties, have sent Fleets, Armies, Commissioners, Guarda Costas, Judges of Admiralty, and a Host of petty Officers, whose Insolence and rapacity are become intolerable. Our cities are garrisoned—The Peace and Order which heretofore dignified our Streets, are exchanged for the horrid Blasphemies and Outrages of Soldiers.—Our Trade is obstructed.—Our Vessels and Cargoes, the effects of Industry, violently seized; and, in a Word, every Species of Injustice that a wicked and debauched Ministry could invent, is now practised against the most sober, industrious and loyal People that ever lived in Society."[15] When it was heard that Gage had been instructed to send troops to Rhode Island to support the new commission sent to investigate the burning of the *Gaspee,* the author of the *Oration, Upon the Beauties of Liberty* prefaced his pamphlet with a letter to Lord Dartmouth, which gave his testimony to the "bloody power" of the ministry: "What, my Lord, is bloody Bonner's day so near America? O America! O America! What, the blood[y] power of the sword and death to aid civil magistrates to destroy the people's rights?"[16]

After the passage of the Boston Port Act, attacks of this nature became increasingly common, particularly in the North, where troops were stationed. The South, throughout, heard less of this sort of talk. The town of Boston resolved on May 18, "That the Impolicy, Injustice, Inhumanity, & Cruelty of the Act . . . exceed all our Powers of Expression & Conception, we therefore leave it to the just Censure of others, & appeal to God & the World";[17] and a Pennsylvanian attacked the policy "despicable and detestable as it is, of suppressing the freedom of *America* by a military force, to be supported by money taken out of our own pockets."[18] England had let loose

---

[15] *Boston Gazette,* Mar. 27, 1769.   [16] Pp. xii f.

[17] *Boston Town Records, 1770-1777,* p. 175. Boston complained of the villainy of the local British officials, who refused to allow supplies to be brought in by sea, although it was not prohibited in the act. The wagons which brought in supplies were called "Lord North's Coasters."—*Amer. Hist. Rev.,* VIII, 328; and 1 Mass. Hist. Soc., *Proceedings,* VIII, 330, 336.

[18] *Pa. Journal,* June 15, 1774; and 4 Force, *Amer. Arch.,* I, 703. The Boston committee on donations wrote Middleborough: "What has Boston done to deserve carrying into execution measures so unjust, so oppressing, so cruel, so destructive? It greatly stands in hand the promoters and favorers of such a pernicious plan, instead, to have a satisfactory answer ready, when it shall at another, an infinitely more important day, be required

upon the innocent colonists "banditti of licensed free-booters . . . for the *innocent* and *laudable* purposes of robberies, rapes and murders."[19] "My countrymen," said Moses Mather in *America's Appeal to the Impartial World*, "we have everything to fear from the malignity, power and cunning of our adversaries.

"In a word, are not all our rights and liberties, natural, religious, and civil, made a mark for their arrows, and threatened to be laid in the dust? And to compleat our ruin, are not our harbours blocked up? Our coasts lined with fleets? Our country filled with armed troops? Our towns sacked? Inhabitants plundered? Friends slaughtered? Our pleasant places desolated with fire and sword? All announced rebels? Our estates declared forfeit and our blood eagerly panted for?"[20]

Tom Paine, attacking the idea of reconciliation in *Common Sense*, stressed the cruelty which made separation inevitable:

"But examine the passions and feelings of mankind, bring the doctrine of reconciliation to the touchstone of nature, and then tell me whether you can hereafter love, honor, and faithfully serve the power that hath carried fire and sword into your land? . . . Hath your house been burnt? Hath your property been destroyed before your face? Are your wife and children destitute of a bed to lie on, or bread to live on? Have you lost a parent or child by their hands, and yourself the ruined and wretched survivor? . . . if you have, and can still shake hands with the murderers, then you are unworthy the name of husband, father, friend, or lover, and whatever may be your rank or title in life, you have the heart of a coward, and the spirit of a sycophant. . . . Reconciliation is *now* a fallacious dream. Nature hath deserted the connection, and art cannot supply her place. For, as Milton wisely expresses, 'never can true reconcilement grow where wounds of deadly hate have pierced so deep.' "[21]

---

of them, 'What have the Bostonians done to merit such cruel treatment?' But we forbear."—4 Mass. Hist. Soc., *Collections*, IV, 122 f. See also Lathrop, *A Discourse, Dec. 15, 1774,* p. 38.

[19] 4 Force, *Amer. Arch.*, II, 173. See also, *ibid.*, p. 211.

[20] Pp. 58, 60.

[21] *The Complete Works of Thomas Paine*, II, 26 f.

The general indictment of the nation had to be made particular and personal. The individual, to the simple mind, typifies the group to which he belongs, and the evils of a part are imputed to the whole. Thus, by circular thinking, the individual condemns the group and the group condemns the individual. Because one Englishman was bad, all Englishmen were bad, and therefore any Englishman was bad. The propaganda of hate must be directed against individuals, for just as the crowd demands a god, so it also demands a devil. The Kaiser admirably supplied the devil of the World War, and Wilson the messiah. These parts were played during the Revolution by George III and Washington, but this clear-cut casting did not take place in the popular mind until the war was well under way. In the period from 1765 to 1775 the general charges against the English ruling class were specifically applied to minor English officials, royal governors in Massachusetts, certain of the English ministers of state, and finally the King himself. The minor English officials—stamp distributors and customs commissioners, for instance —were within reach of the coercive agencies, but in the main it was only by suggestion that the propagandists could discredit the higher officials. To describe all the personal attacks made by the Whigs would involve listing almost every important Tory, for by 1775 there was hardly a one that had not been maligned in some way. A few illustrations must suffice.

One of the most striking is the way in which the Massachusetts radicals discredited the three royal governors, Francis Bernard, Thomas Hutchinson, and Thomas Gage. They aroused hatred against them and, by identifying them with the English government, accomplished a transference of this emotion from the individual to the group as a whole.

The attack on Bernard began in 1765 and continued without ceasing until after his departure for England in 1769. From January 5 to May 11, 1767, for example, at least twenty-one articles against him appeared in the *Boston Gazette* alone. It was charged that he had enriched himself at the expense of the province—twenty-two thousand pounds in nine years;[22] that he had consistently opposed salutary legislation, even though it in no way affected English interests; that he would allow no friends of the colonies to hold

[22] *Boston Gazette*, Dec. 8, 1766; July 31, 1769.

office under him; and that he had consciously misrepresented the province in his letters to the Ministry. But there was a noble spirit of liberty in the province, said the propagandists, "so that we doubt not (erelong) to expose that little dirty TALEBEARER, who has done such amazing Mischief in *America*, during his few Years Machinatious Government."[23] By 1769 the attack was much more abusive. His removal was openly agitated in the press and by petition to the home government, and the demand was strengthened by scurrilous journalism. Benjamin Church addressed an eight-page poem to him, "An Address to a Provincial Bashaw":

> "Tell me proud villain! Shameless as thou art!
> Now thine opprobrious Conduct taints the Air;
> Does not Remorse harass thy callous Heart,
> And pour a poison'd Flood of Anguish there?
>
> .   .   .   .
>
> "Hie thee, poor Tyrant! to that happy goal
> Where unsuccessful Malice may repose;
> Where VERRES, ANDROS, from Resentment stole,
> Go share eternal Infamy with those."[24]

"The sooner he embarks the better" wrote "Legion" in June, "and we only wish that in Tenderness to the Colonies, and from a Regard to the Honor of the British Nation, this Land may never hereafter be curs'd with a despicable, avaricious, and arbitrary G——r."[25] A celebration was held at the wharf when he departed, and the *Boston Gazette* remarked: "Tuesday last embarked on board his Majesty's Ship the *Rippon*, Sir Francis Bernard of Nettleham, Bart, who for nine Years last, has been a Scourge to the Province, a Curse to North-America, and a Plague to the whole Empire."[26]

It was proposed that August 1 be thereafter commemorated as the anniversary of his departure, and at a dinner of the Fellowship Club in Providence the toast was drunk, "A speedy Passage to Gov. B-n-d, that he may meet his Reward at T-b-n."[27]

---

[23] *Newport Mercury*, July 25, 1768.

[24] *Magazine of History*, extra number 74, pp. 117-124. Verres, at one time Roman governor of Sicily, was known for his cruelty.

[25] *Boston Gazette*, June 19, 1769.

[26] Aug. 7, 1769. See also *An Elegy to the Infamous Memory of Sir Francis Bernard*, a broadside, listed in W. C. Ford, comp., *Broadsides, Ballads, etc. printed in Massachusetts 1639-1800*. This was a poem of forty-five stanzas.

[27] *Newport Mercury*, Sept. 18, 1769; July 30, 1770. This referred to Tyburn, a place of public execution in London.

The attack on Governor Hutchinson shows even more the careful preparation of the radicals. He had, of course, been the object of mob attack in 1765, but he was also the object of a consistent newspaper attack from 1770 on. After the Boston Massacre, John Adams copied in his diary without comment a supposed address to Hutchinson by Crispus Attucks, the mulatto killed that night:

> "Sir:—You will hear from us with astonishment. You ought to hear from us with horror. You are chargeable before God and man, with our blood. The soldiers were but passive instruments . . . You was a free agent. You acted, cooly, deliberately, with all that premeditated malice, not against us in particular, but against the people in general, which, in the sight of the law, is an ingredient in the composition of murder. You will hear further from us."[28]

The attack on Hutchinson was carried on primarily by printing extracts of his letters to the home government, with fitting comments and headings. Bernard's letters had been published with considerable success, and Sam Adams was extremely anxious to get copies of Hutchinson's. He wrote Stephen Sayre in 1770 to get them for him, but Sayre replied that it was impossible. Franklin finally obtained them.[29] Once the letters were in his possession, Adams published them in the *Boston Gazette*, from which they were copied in papers all over the country, even in South Carolina. The letters were prefaced in the *Newport Mercury* with the statement that they were being published "that the public in general may be more fully informed of the secret machinations, and horribly *dark, infernal* plots, for several years carried on against the dearest liberties of this country, by a set of insidious, venal wretches, in order to enslave this whole continent."[30] The statement which accompanied the series in the *Boston Gazette* connected Hutchinson with all the evils of the past few years:

> "Remember, Sir, your joining with *Bernard!* Paxton! Hallowell! Burch! Hulton! . . . Remember the despicable figure you cut in worrying the General Court, by dragging

[28] *Works*, II, 322. See also N. Y. *Journal*, Dec. 5, 1771.

[29] Sayre's reply is in Samuel Adams Papers, Sept. 18, 1770. See also *Writings of Sam Adams*, II, 66.

[30] June 28, 1773. They also appeared in *Pa. Journal*, N. Y. *Journal*, S. C. *Gazette*, and elsewhere.

them to Cambridge from time to time—the insulting and over-bearing language used to them one day, and the dastardly pusillanimous retreat made the next! Remember saving the life of Richardson . . . Remember that you have not transacted one single thing for the benefit of your Province. . . ."[31]

Adams sent copies of the letters through the committee of correspondence to most of the towns with which the committee regularly corresponded, with gratifying results,[32] and in 1775 it was decided to publish them again. William Gordon wrote Joseph Warren on May 20, "Should the Committee approve of sending me *Hutchinson's* loose letters, with the letter books, on *Monday*, will apply myself to sorting them according to date, reading them over, and notifying everything that shall appear to me of importance to be laid before the public."[33] Those who had any of the letters were asked to send them to the printer of the *Boston Gazette*, and these new letters, together with the extracts of the old ones, were printed in several papers. The *Pennsylvania Journal* headed the column of letters "*Further Account of* Tom. Hutchinson's *Assiduity in rooting up our* ONCE *happy Constitution, and of his Endeavours to disunite the* AMERICAN COLONIES."[34] His name soon became a symbol of English cruelty and despotism, and the little town of Hutchinson, Massachusetts, soon petitioned to have its name changed to Barre.[35]

Thomas Gage, the third governor, was even more roughly treated in the press, for by this time the war was under way. He was called a "profane, wicked-monster of falsehood and perfidy," a "robber, a murderer, a traitor, and a tyrant."[36] When he ordered the people of Boston to disarm, the following address to him appeared in the *Pennsylvania Evening Post*:

[31] Sept. 27, 1773.

[32] The replies of the town committees are in Boston Committee Records. They all expressed great indignation. Cushing wrote Franklin on June 14, 1773: "Nothing could have been more seasonable, than the arrival of these letters. They have had great effect; they make deep impression wherever they are known."—*Writings of Franklin*, VI, 59. The New London committee wrote the Boston committee requesting the letters and asking advice on how to handle affairs in general. The letter is signed Erastus Wolcott, Nathaniel Wales, Jr., Samuel H. Parsons, and Joseph Trumbull.—Emmett Collection, June 16, 1773.

[33] 4 Force, *Amer. Arch.*, II, 664.

[34] Oct. 25, 1775; *Boston Gazette*, June 5, 1775; and Reed Papers, II, 101.

[35] Wells, *Life of Adams*, I, 41 n.

[36] *Pa. Evening Post*, June 27, 1775; *Boston Gazette*, July 17, 1775; and 4 Force, *Amer. Arch.*, V, 1055 ff.

"To the vilest Tool of the most profligate and tyrannical Administration that ever disgraced a Court. . . .

"Now, Sir, waving all that may be said of your hypocrisy, cruelty, villainy, treachery, perfidy, falsehood and inconsistency, are you not ashamed to throw out such an insult upon human understanding, as to bid people disarm themselves till you and your butchers murder and plunder them at pleasure!"[37]

Governor Dunmore of Virginia was treated in somewhat the same fashion. He was accused of impressing a hundred and sixty people into his service; he finally returned all of them, admitted the accuser, except two maidens "detained as bedmakers to his lordship." The following "Extract of a letter from Philadelphia" has a familiar sound to students of anti-German propaganda of the World War: *"I forgot to tell you in my last, that that execrable fellow, Dunmore, had barrelled up some dead bodies of the small pox, and sent them on shore, hoping that the curiosity of the people would propagate the disease."*[38]

The ministry was the object of nearly all the propaganda directed against Great Britain down to late 1775, for the propagandists consistently maintained that good King George had been deluded by his ministers.[39] It is unnecessary to describe the propaganda against them in detail, for all that has been said above in the general indictment of the English administration was applied to them by name. Grenville, Bute, and North were the principal victims. Bute, even though he had not been prime minister since 1763, was reviled until the end of the war. In the popular mind, both English and American, Bute still pulled the political strings which worked the King, and a jack boot commonly accompanied English and American demonstrations against the ministry, long after Bute was out of power. He and Grenville were likened to the beast in the thirteenth chapter of Revelation, and though neither one of their names added up to the mystic number 666 as did the Kaiser's, there were marked similarities to the beast, said the propagandists. Together with

[37] June 27, 1775. This was clipped from a New England paper.
[38] *Va. Gazette* (Pinkney), Dec. 30, 1775; *Conn. Gazette*, July 26, 1776.
[39] "Jacob," *Boston Gazette*, Oct. 21, 1765, expressed this very common idea in another fashion: "tand trong agins all tamps our crate and good king Chorge vil love us, and peal the Tamp Ax, and remove al the scare crose, screach ouls, an vultures, to those regans that will sute their constushon petter than this."

North, they were commonly called sordid, profane, wicked, and abandoned men in whom there was neither honor nor virtue.[40]

The personal abuse of the King began mildly at first with such statements as "A good king is a miracle," but did not become common until after the appearance of *Common Sense,* as it was primarily used for war purposes. Paine attacked the idea of monarchy and spoke of the "Royal Brute of Great Britain," and thereafter others came out boldly. Boston in May, 1776, instructed its representatives in these bitter words:

> "We have seen the humble Petitions [of] these colonies to the *King of Great Britain* repeatedly rejected with Disdain. For the Prayer of Peace he has tendered the Sword;—for Liberty, Chains;—for Safety, Death! He has licensed the Instruments of his hostile Oppressions to rob us of our Property, to burn our Houses, & to spill our Blood—He has invited every barbarous Nation, whom he could hope to influence, to assist him in prosecuting those inhuman Purposes. . . . Loyalty to him is *now* Treason to our Country."[41]

Atrocity stories then as now constitute the outstanding justification for war and the most effective way of making people hate the enemy. The Boston Massacre was the first major incident used to condemn the troops and the administration. The "Journal of Boston Occurrences," a sort of diary of the relations of troops and citizens in 1769, had played up the insolence and brutality of the troops before the Massacre, but after that event the propagandists surpassed themselves. The following quotation is typical of numberless others:

> "A mercenary, licentious rabble of banditti are encouraged to riot uncontrol'd, and tear the bowels and vitals of their brave but peaceable fellow subjects, and *to wash the ground with a profusion of innocent blood* . . . which like the blood of Abel and Zechariah, *still* cries ALOUD for *pointed* vengeance to blast the ORIGINAL PROCURERS as well as the *execrable instruments* of that horrid massacre."[42]

[40] E.g., *Boston Gazette,* Dec. 30, 1765, Jan. 13, 1766; "The Times," a poem attributed to Benjamin Church, *Magazine of History,* extra number 84, pp. 5-20; *Pa. Evening Post,* Mar. 30, 1775.

[41] *Boston Town Records,* 1770-1777, p. 237.

[42] *Boston Gazette,* May 28, 1770. Examples abound.

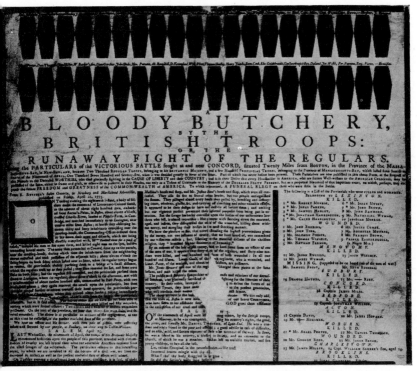

Bloody Butchery by the British Troops. A Broadside Memorializing the men who fell at Lexington and Concord in April, 1775.
By courtesy of the Essex Institute.

And a Salem Whig urged that everyone be ready to sacrifice his life if necessary "in extirpating a profligate, licentious, and blood-thirsty Soldiery, stationed among us with the avowed Intention of rendering ineffectual the present Struggles for preserving all that is dear and valuable."[43]

The battle of Lexington and Concord and the retreat to Boston provided the second major opportunity for emotional appeals dealing with the depravity of the troops. Two illustrations are sufficient to stand for them all—one from Pennsylvania and one from New York. From Pennsylvania came this:

"Americans! forever bear in mind the BATTLE OF LEXINGTON!—when British Troops, unmolested and unprovoked, wantonly, and in a most inhuman manner fired upon and killed a number of our countrymen, then robbed them of their provisions, ransacked, plundered and burnt their houses! nor could the tears of defenceless women, some of whom were in the pain of child-birth, the cries of helpless babes, nor the prayers of old age, confined to beds of sickness, appease their thirst for blood!—or divert them from their DESIGN OF MURDER AND ROBBERY."[44]

The New York specimen was in the form of an address to the inhabitants:

"Alas! would not the heathen, in all their savage barbarity and cruelty, blush at such horrid murder, and worse than brutal rage? Is this the bravery of the *British* Troops? . . . Is it not rather the ferocity of a mad wild beast, from whom they cannot be supposed to differ only in shape? Let every *American* hear and abhor; let every inhabitant consider what he is likely to suffer if he falls into the hands of such cruel and merciless wretches."[45]

[43] *Ibid.*, Mar. 19, 1770.

[44] *Pa. Journal, Supplement*, May 24, 1775.

[45] 4 Force, *Amer. Arch.*, II, 428. Other examples may be found in *N. H. Gazette*, Apr. 28, 1775; N. Y. *Journal*, May 4, 1775; *Ga. Gazette*, June 21, 1775; 4 Force, *Amer. Arch.*, II, 173, 837; *Worcester Town Records*, p. 266. Nathan Fiske emphasized the sacrilegious acts of the troops: "Who are they that with cruel hands, have, the summer past, wantonly made such havoc in our land—plundered and destroyed so many of our villages, and cast fire into so many of our cities?—that have reduced our metropolis to such distress—have profaned the sanctuaries of God, and treated his worshippers with so much perfidy, barbarity and insult?"—*Remarkable Providences to be Gratefully Recollected, Religiously Improved, and Carefully Transmitted to Posterity*, p. 28.

Houses, and indeed entire towns—Charlestown, Falmouth, and others—had been burned simply to make the people miserable, and for no other reason. One of the most atrocious poems of the entire revolutionary period related to the battle of Breed's Hill and the burning of Charlestown:

> "AMERICANS pray lend an Ear
> And you a solemn Tale shall hear
> 'Twas on the seventeenth of June,
> Men were cut down all in their bloom.
>
> .   .   .   .   .   .
>
> "These Savage Troops Charlestown did Fire,
> And it to Ashes did expire,
> The TOWN now in Destruction lies,
> The sight affects our Hearts and eyes."[46]

There were twenty-six stanzas of this particular piece of idiocy.

There can be no question but that the propaganda of hate was effective. The long agitation against the troops prior to 1770 bore fruit in the intense anger which followed the Massacre, so different from the attitude of the people in New York after the so-called Golden Hill affair, when some troops fired on a party of the Liberty Boys. This incident occurred just a few months before the Boston Massacre, yet it passed almost without mention in New York and nothing was said about it elsewhere, although there was little real difference between the two except that the victims in New York were only wounded.[47] The outbreak of hostilities in 1775 was of course sufficient justification in itself for continued war, but the propaganda against the troops had greatly heightened the emotional tension and accounts in large part for the war psychosis so manifest by 1775.

[46] Mass. Hist. Soc., Broadsides. This is bad poetry but good propaganda. It was written by Elisha Rich, a minister. See also 4 Force, *Amer. Arch.*, III, 1168 f.; *Documents N. H.* VII, 558, 623. The troops were constantly accused of stealing. Because they sequestered so many animals for food they were commonly called "sheep stealers." See *Extracts from the Diary of Christopher Marshall*, p. 37; *Boston Gazette*, June 5, 1775; and Frank Moore, *Diary of the American Revolution*, I, 139, quoting one of the Virginia papers, which attacked Captain Squires, of the sloop *Otter*, who frequently made trips up the rivers gathering supplies and frightening the people.

[47] *N. Y. Gazette and Weekly Mercury*, Feb. 5, 1770; Becker, *Political Parties*, p. 82.

IX

COMBATING TORY PROPAGANDA

THE PROPAGANDIST'S task is not done when he has made his appeal for action—the effect of the enemy propaganda must be destroyed by neutralizing its suggestions where they cannot be suppressed. This the propagandists of the Revolution understood. A common method of refuting the pro-British writers was to consider in detail the pamphlets, essays, and proclamations they wrote. Governor Martin's proclamation, issued in 1775, calling upon all loyal people to support the King's cause, for example, was declared false and seductive by the Rowan County committee of safety, and it resolved that "an advertisement be made setting forth the dangerous tendency of said proclamation."[1] The "advertisement" refuted almost sentence by sentence the proclamation. The pamphleteers engaged in debates of this same sort. Alexander Hamilton and Samuel Seabury attacked each other's pamphlets, and John Adams and Daniel Leonard engaged in a newspaper controversy which lasted several months. Often these detailed statements were so detailed that they defeated their own purpose, and the reader was lost in a maze of charge and countercharge. Many of the points were petty, many of the distinctions overfine. Many of the arguments were almost unintelligible, many of the remarks descended to the level of pothouse brawling. But there was able refutation of major issues.

A great deal of the refutation was taken up with temporary or local problems, for each period of the controversy produced its peculiar problems for the propagandists. Three illustrations from the period 1773 to 1775 will show how the leaders met difficult arguments as they arose.

It was commonly said, when the Tea Act was passed, that the monopoly granted the East India Company did not involve the matter of taxation. The tax, if any, would be paid by the Company in England, and thus the colonists were not affected at all. The propagandists in answer clearly and properly pointed out that the old

[1] *Col. Rec. N. C.*, X, 92, 138.

duty on tea had never been repealed and was still in force. They declared that no matter who paid the tax, the amount would be passed on to the American consumer. "You cannot believe," said a writer in South Carolina, "that the *Tea Act*, with respect to its design and tendency, differs in one single point from the *Stamp Act*— If there be any difference, the *Tea Act is the more dangerous*."[2] To the statement that the monopoly would lower the price of tea, the propagandists answered: "Tho' the first Teas may be sold at a low Rate to make a popular Entry, yet when this mode of receiving Tea is well established, they, as all other Monopolists do, will meditate a greater profit on their Goods, and set them up at what Price they please."[3] Others recounted the history of the East India Company to show that it had had a disastrous effect upon the economic life of India and had been guilty of great cruelty there. The author of the New York "Alarm" reasoned that, unable to fasten a tax upon the colonies openly, the ministry had entered into an illicit bargain with the East India Company, by which the tax went to the crown and the profits to the Company, "to support the tyranny of the *lost* in the east, enslave the west, and prepare us fit victims for the exercise of that horrid inhumanity, they have in such dread abundance, and with more than savage cruelty, practiced, in the face of the Sun, on the helpless Asiaticks."[4]

The destruction of the tea in Boston and the passage of the Intolerable Acts presented another problem in rebuttal to the propagandists. There was talk of paying for the tea, and it was said that Boston was being properly punished for her radicalism.[5] The Boston leaders immediately dramatized themselves as "stationed by the providence of God, in the first rank of opposition to the cruel measures of an incensed ministry." The circular letter sent out on May 13 by the committee of correspondence contained statements that determined the character of the appeal for the next nine months: "The Town of Boston is now Suffering the Stroke of Vengeance in the Common Cause of America. I hope they will sustain the Blow with becoming fortitude; and that the Effects of this cruel Act, in-

---

[2] *S. C. Gazette*, Nov. 15, 1773. See also *Pa. Journal*, Nov. 3, Nov. 17, 1773; N. Y. *Journal*, Nov. 4, Dec. 9, 1773; and two broadsides, *A Mechanic*, Hist. Soc. Pa., Broadsides, I, 149, and *A Student of Law*, N. Y. Hist. Soc., Broadsides, Nov. 19, 1773.

[3] *Boston Evening Post*, Oct. 18, 1773; N. Y. *Journal*, Nov. 25, 1773.

[4] *Ibid.*, Oct. 21, 1773; *Newport Mercury*, Jan. 24, 1774.

[5] E.g., 4 Force, *Amer. Arch.*, I, 487 f.

tended to intimidate and subdue the Spirits of all America will by the joynt Efforts of all be frustrated."[6] A broadside was published on the twelfth which appealed for support in the common cause, declaring that in the fight for a cause "which has been hitherto so nobly defended by ALL, we cannot entertain a Thought so dishonourable to our Friends that in this crisis *we* shall be left to struggle *alone.*"[7] Letters to individuals were written by members of the committee of correspondence, and the Boston committee on donations in every letter of thanks for contributions reiterated the appeal. The following letter to Brooklyn is typical:

> "If we shall be pushed to a yet greater extremity, your sentiments are perfectly just, that 'If Boston is subjugated, all British America must fall.' This sentiment cannot be spread too far and wide. It ought to be inculcated in season and out of season. The yoke of bondage is laid upon our necks; a yoke which neither we nor our fathers have borne. In matters of civil liberty and public oppression, all delay is fatal; the times call for very vigorous remedies. God grant that America may never see one Province after another plundered, slaughtered and ravaged with impunity."[8]

From every colony came the reply—"This horrid attack upon the town of *Boston,* we consider not as an attempt upon that town singly, but upon the whole Continent." "Let not any Person imagine that these unexampled Abuses of Boston are intended only for her," wrote a Virginian, "the Rod of Despotism is, in Turn, to be applied for the Punishment of every Colony that moves in Defence of Liberty."[9] A South Carolinian assumed a share of the guilt: "Why is the Attack made only on one Province, when all are equally guilty? Divide and Destroy is the only answer which can be given."[10] Throughout America this idea was propagated by every

---

[6] Both of these were written by Sam Adams, *Writings,* III, 106, 108.

[7] Mass. Hist. Soc., Broadsides.   [8] 4 Mass. Hist. Soc., *Collections,* IV, 53.

[9] The first quotation is from a letter of the Westerly, Rhode Island, committee of correspondence, 4 Force, *Amer. Arch.,* I, 337, the second is from *Va. Gazette* (Purdie), June 30, 1774.

[10] *S. C. Gazette,* July 4, 1774. "Be not deceived, ye unhappy Americans; the ax is laid to the root of the tree, every privilege you at present claim as a birthright, may be wrested from you by the same authority that blockades the town of Boston."—*Ga. Gazette,* July 27, 1774. The *Newport Mercury,* May 16, 1774, headed the following statement with the words "JOIN OR DIE!": "The act of parliament for blockading the harbour of Boston, in order to reduce its spirited inhabitants to the most servile and mean compliances ever attempted to be imposed on a free people, is allowed to be infinitely more alarming

agency and through every medium. The universal answer, "Boston is suffering in the common cause, for we are next in line," was the carefully cultivated product of seeds sown by the propagandists.

When the war broke out in April, 1775, it was deemed essential to prove that British troops had been the aggressors and had fired first. The Continental Congress and the Massachusetts Provincial Congress both ordered depositions to be taken concerning the events, and about twenty were subsequently published.[11] The Connecticut committee of correspondence immediately wrote Hancock on April 21 for authentic information regarding the battle "to frustrate such exaggerated Accts as may go from the army and navy," and Hancock promptly began to collect information. On April 24 he wrote the Massachusetts committee of safety:

> "I beg, by the return of this express, to hear from you, and pray furnish us with depositions of the conduct of the Troops, the certainty of their firing first, and every circumstance relative to the conduct of the Troops, from the 19th instant to this time, that we may be able to give some account of matters as we proceed, and especially at *Philadelphia.* . . . For *God's* sake do not suffer the spirit to subside, until they have perfected the reduction of our enemies."[12]

Connecticut officials were still disturbed, and on the twenty-eighth Joseph Trumbull wrote Gage at the request of the assembly for his account. This letter, although it contained the following statement, "It is feared, therefore, that we are devoted to destruction, and that you have it in command and intention to ravage and desolate the country," alarmed the Massachusetts propagandists, for

and dangerous to our common liberties than even that hydra the Stamp-Act (which was destroyed by our firmness and union)."

[11] These depositions are in 4 Force, *Amer. Arch.*, II, 488-501. See also, *Journals Mass. Prov. Cong.*, May 12, 1775; and *N. H. Gazette,* "BLOODY NEWS," Apr. 21, 1775.

[12] 4 Force, *Amer. Arch.*, II, 384 f. The Connecticut letter was signed William Williams, Nathaniel Wales, and Joseph Trumbull. Revolutionary Letters, Mass. Arch., CXCIII, 54. The Continental Congress appointed John Adams, George Wythe, and Silas Deane a committee to collect authenticated statements of the hostilities committed by the troops since March, 1775, and to write a report on the matter. Adams wrote James Warren, Oct. 19, 1775: "I hope We shall tell a true Story, and then I am sure it will be an affecting one. We shall not omit their Butcheries, nor their Robberies, nor their Piracies. But we shall want Assistance from every Quarter. I want the Distresses of Boston painted by Dr. Cooper's Pencil. Everything must be supported by Affidavits."—*Warren-Adams Letters,* I, 144. No report from this committee was ever printed. The Massachusetts provincial committee of safety ordered William Cooper, William Gordon, and Peter Thatcher to send a report of the same nature to England, but there is no evidence that it was ever sent.— *Journals Mass. Prov. Cong.*, p. 594.

the men who delivered it were authorized to treat with Gage. The second Massachusetts Provincial Congress issued an address to Connecticut expressing its alarm:

"We are greatly alarmed at the unparalleled wickedness of our unnatural enemies, in endeavoring to persuade our sister colony, that the inhabitants of this, first commenced hostilities; a suggestion which, we cannot but think, will appear absurd, when the great inequality of the Lexington company and the detachment of regular troops, which attacked them, is cooly considered. . . . The experience which we have had of general Gage, hath fully convinced us, that but little dependence can be placed in his professions."[18]

On June 12, Gage himself issued a proclamation attacking the Whig incendiaries. He charged them with opening the attack, listed the atrocities they had committed, and then offered pardon to all but Hancock and Adams. Two counter-proclamations were immediately issued by the Massachusetts Provincial Congress. The first was issued on June 14 on a broadside, prefaced by this statement:

"The Following is a copy of an infamous thing handed about here yesterday, and now reprinted to satisfy the curiosity of the public. As it is replete with consummate impudence, the most abominable lies, and stuffed with daring expressions of tyranny, as well as rebellion against the established constitutional authority of the American States, no one will hesitate in pronouncing it [to] be the genuine production of that perfidious, petty tyrant, Thomas Gage."

The remainder was simply a reprint of Gage's proclamation, a clever trick, for it gave the definite impression that the Whigs had nothing to fear from what Gage had to say. The second statement was a detailed refutation and countercharge.[14]

Nor was Gage's account of the battle of Breed's Hill allowed to circulate without refutation. The Wilmington committee of safety discovered the account when Boyd, the printer of the *Cape Fear Mercury*, was ordered to turn over to the committee all the material

---

[18] *Conn. Public Records*, XIV, 440 ff., and 4 Force, *Amer. Arch.*, II, 433 f., 482 f., contain the correspondence of Gage and Trumbull. The Massachusetts letters are in *Journals Mass. Prov. Cong.*, pp. 179 f., 193 f., 532 f.

[14] Evans, *Amer. Biblio.*, No. 14,185; *Journals Mass. Prov. Cong.*, pp. 344 ff. One unofficial propagandist admitted that the colonials had fired first but charged Gage with hiring three or four American traitors to open fire.—*Pa. Journal*, May 24, 1775.

he had received from the Governor. The committee declared the account to be a "base and willful misrepresentation of facts," and ordered that the committee's strictures on it be published in the same paper and immediately following it, and refused to allow separate handbills of it to be printed. The committee probably felt it could not countermand Governor Martin's order to Boyd, otherwise it would have suppressed the account entirely.[15]

There were also recurrent suggestions, common to the entire period and to almost every section, that had to be combated. One of the most common was the statement that the radicals were aiming at independence. A good bit of the time they were, but they could hardly afford to admit it too early, and this allegation had to be denied. It was met simply by flat denials and by professions of loyalty to George III. Such statements were common features of the town resolutions down to 1774, but thereafter they become much more infrequent.

Another tenacious idea that kept cropping up at each period of resistance to England was that the colonists were under such heavy obligations to Great Britain for aid granted them in the early period of settlement and for protection during the recent war with France, that it was utterly unfair for them not to pay their share of the expenses incurred in their behalf. It was not only unfair, it was absolutely wrong for them to object. The Whig propagandists met this argument with three telling points—right or wrong, the people could understand and sympathize with each of them.

They first denied that England had contributed either to the settlement of the colonies or to the expenses of the wars in America. The settlement of America had not been a national act, nor at national expense. The settlers, actually driven out of England, had borne the full brunt of the cost in life and money. "America," said "Candidus" in 1776, "was not sent out a Colony at the charge of *Great Britain*, and, for all the protection afforded her, might well be esteemed an orphan instead of a child; and with all the clamour raised on that head, with intention to lull the people into a submission to the most ruinous exactions, were 'a fair account stated, it would be found that the balance in favour of *America* would amaze all mankind."[16]   Amos Adams, in an extended discussion of the whole point, avowed that the colonists had not "in our most distressed circumstances, received protection or relief from Great Britain," and Judah Champion, using identically the same argument, reached the same conclusion. During King Philip's War, for example, "accounts were transmitted home, yet no assistance was receiv'd. Neither ships, men or money were sent to them, under the intolerable burthen of all those calamities. . . . For more than 120 years they received (as far as I can learn) not the least parliamentary aids."[17]   Thomas Paine stated the matter succinctly in *Common Sense:* "She did not protect us from *our enemies* on *our account,* but from *her enemies* on *her account.*"[18]   The assertion that the French and Indian war was fought for American causes was flatly denied: "This is a vulgar Error. . . . The war was . . . waged in defence of Lands claimed by the Crown, and for the Protection of *British Property.*"[19]   In short, said the propagandists, "We in America, who have supported ourselves above a Century, are no more bound in Conscience to pay one Farthing in Discharge of the national Debt, than we are to contribute towards lessening the *National Debt* of Japan."[20]

In the second place, said the propagandists, America had already borne more than her full share of the war costs. Stephen Johnson said on the public fast day in Connecticut in 1765: "We have had requisition upon requisition, from the British court, even the last war; we were chearfully obedient and ready, even beyond our power; we were (I may say) lavish of our men, our monies, and our blood, for the common cause, 'till we were reduced almost to the brink of ruin. . . ."[21]   It was the colonials who had taken Louis-

[16] *Pa. Gazette,* Mar. 6, 1776. See also, *Boston Gazette, Supplement,* Nov. 4, 1765; *Newport Mercury,* Mar. 15, 1773; *Records of the Town of Tisbury, Massachusetts,* pp. 206 ff.

[17] Amos Adams, *A Concise, Historical View of the Difficulties, Hardships, and Perils, which attended the Planting and Progressive Improvements of New-England,* p. 65; Judah Champion, *A Brief View of the Distresses, Hardships and Dangers our Ancestors Encounter'd, in Settling New-England,* pp. 19, 29. "Philopolis," writing in *Ga. Gazette,* Oct. 19, 1774, had to admit what he could not deny. The bounties which Georgia had received from Great Britain, however, were not granted, he said, from any desire to aid Georgia, but were occasioned by the "accidents" of British politics.

[18] *Works of Thomas Paine,* II, 21.

[19] *An Oration Delivered at the State House, in Philadelphia . . . 1st of August, 1776 . . .,* p. 11.

[20] *N. Y. Gazette, or, Weekly Post-Boy,* Sept. 15, 1765. See also, *N. Y. Journal,* Oct. 20, 1774; Samuel Stillman, *A Sermon preached to the Ancient and Honorable Artillery Company . . . 1770,* p. 21.

[21] *Some Important Observations,* p. 37; *Boston Gazette,* Feb. 24, 1766. Samuel Webster's two sermons, *Rabshekah's Proposals Considered* and *The Misery and Duty of an Oppress'd and Enslav'd People,* contain the same idea.

burg in 1745 and saved Boston from invasion at another time, and what, they asked, has been the return? "What have the *common people*, either in Britain or America, had in return for their so freely lavished blood and treasures in the acquirement of new territories over half the globe? New taxes, new boards of commissioners, with an indefinite train of dependents, to collect and consume them."[22] The American share of the national debt had been paid in American money and American blood.

The closing argument was even more trenchant: England had reaped solid material advantages from the settlement of the colonies and the wars with France—why should the colonists be forced to pay for them? The little town of Bristol, Rhode Island, put the shoe of ingratitude on the other foot: "Considering the vast addition of territory, wealth and power, that the plantations in North America are to the crown of Great Britain; that it was obtained by our ancestors, without any expense to the crown, with the toil of their lives, and expense of their blood and treasure . . . to invade our privileges, is the most cruel ingratitude."[23] Any part of the national debt that might have been contracted in behalf of the colonists had long since been repaid in the profits from colonial trade. These accrued largely, if not exclusively, to England, and except for these profits, "are we bound in justice or gratitude to contribute one farthing to her?"[24] An *Address to the American Army*, published in Salem in verse form showed where the advantages were.

"Let's view *Canada's* border vast, to British Crown annex'd,
America in all these feats for praise may claim pretext.
Such blood and treasure lavished by us in *Britain's* cause,
Sure can't deserve without reserve, such cruel tyrants' laws."[25]

---

[22] *Pa. Journal*, Oct. 11, 1775. "For these above-mentioned Services you have rewarded us with insupportable Taxes, and even infernal ones."—*Boston Gazette*, Dec. 23, 1765. See also *ibid.*, Sept. 16, 1765; and 4 Force, *Amer. Arch.*, V, 211 ff.; *Boston Gazette, Supplement*, Nov. 4, 1765; "Our Youth the Flower of the Country are many of them slain, our Treasure exhausted in the Service of our Mother Country, our Trade, and all numerous Branches of Business dependent on it reduced, and almost ruined by severe Acts of Parliament, and now we are threatened . . . with being loaded with internal Taxes, without our Consent."   [23] *R. I. Records*, VII, 274 f.

[24] *Pa. Journal*, Dec. 15, 1773. See also, *ibid.*, Oct. 12, 1774. "Why then should they command you?" demanded the *American Alarm*, "Is it not enough for the Americans to feed and support England with their trade? (and are willing to do so until the English streets are paved with American gold)."—P. 13.

[25] Mass. Hist. Soc., Broadsides, 1775. See also, Mather, *America's Appeal*, p. 55: "Thus the Americans laboured, fought and toiled; and the Britons reaped the advantage."

The mother country? concluded the propagandists—

> "Spurn the Relation—She's no more a Mother,
>   Than Lewis to George, a most Christian Brother,
>   In French Wars and Scotch, grown generous and rich
>   She gives her dear Children Pox, Slavery and Itch."[26]

A third troublesome suggestion was that England was entirely too powerful, and that the colonists faced certain defeat in any effort to oppose her. This appeal was admirably adapted to the timorous mind so common in every society, and it was furthermore based upon a pretty solid foundation of fact; it was a most inconvenient idea. Defeatist suggestions must be instantly combated and confidence in success engendered, for reason, justice, and interest must be vitalized by hope. The propagandists based their contention that America could not be defeated, whether resisting the Stamp Act or the British army, upon three principal points: the weakness of the enemy, the strength of America, and the help of God.

As to the first, they cheerfully exaggerated the importance of American trade to the commercial strength of England, and asserted that without this trade, England could not maintain her public credit. Six of the seven million people in England, said a writer in South Carolina, were dependent on manufacturing, and half of those were directly dependent, therefore, upon the colonies, which supplied the raw materials. England received, furthermore, two millions sterling in revenue from her exports to the colonies. Cut off the trade with British merchants, and "we would have them at our mercy."[27] It was insisted that the war could not last long because the inevitable decay of English trade would force her to end the conflict.[28]

England, furthermore, was divided within herself. America had many friends in England, said the propagandists, and perseverance would so weaken the administration that her friends could take the lead. The Boston committee on donations wrote Farmington in 1774 that it had received reliable information from England that "the non-consumption agreement, if faithfully adhered to, must be the ruin of the Ministry; and our friends would succeed; when we

---

[26] *Boston Gazette*, Dec. 2, 1765.
[27] *S. C. Gazette*, July 4, 1774; *N. Y. Gazette, or, Weekly Post-Boy*, Jan. 23, 1766. See also Rowland, *Life and Correspondence of George Mason*, I, 385; Moore, "Justice of Taxing the Colonies," *loc. cit.*, p. 173.   [28] *Pa. Evening Post*, Feb. 17, 1776.

might hope for such a constitution from the King, Lords and Commons, as would be agreeable to us, and for the benefit of the whole empire."[29] Disturbances "much in our favour" were reported in England, and the possibility of civil war was suggested.[30]

England was degenerate, and her troops were weak and discouraged. Theodoric Bland had written a long poem in 1765 emphasizing the decline of England's power, and another poem published in Virginia eleven years later applied the same idea more directly to the war:

> "Forgetful of thy ancient glory,
>   Wherein thou so excell'st in story,
>   Degenerate grown! thy mighty arm
>   To neighboring states gives no alarm;
>   Regardless, they thy force defy,
>   Tread under foot thy dignity,
>   And, loading thee with abjuration,
>   Exclaim! how fallen is the nation!"[31]

The propagandists likewise minimized the power and bravery of the King's troops. *The First Book of American Chronicles* introduced the suggestion even before the war was under way. The troops sent by the King to reduce the Amerikanites wrote back:

> "The land thou sent us to subdue, is a land that eateth up thy people; for the men we saw in it are mightier than we in understanding. . . . Moreover they be giants, men of great stature, and we seemed but as caterpillars in their sight; they assemble in such multitudes, and come on so fast, that they seem minded to do us mischief, so maliciously are their hearts set against us."[32]

After April, 1775, propagandists quoted British officers and soldiers to show how disillusioned and discouraged they were. Captured letters from them, said the Hartford committee in June, 1775, "showed how little they were to be feared":

> "Those letters in general are full of complaints and expressions of uneasiness. Some of the officers desire and entreat to

[29] 4 Mass. Hist. Soc., *Collections*, IV, 98 f.

[30] *Ibid.*, pp. 46 f.; *Speech of the Statue of William Pitt*, Amer. Antiq. Assoc., Broadsides, June 5, 1770; 4 Force, *Amer. Arch.*, III, 684; N. H., *Freeman's Journal*, June 29, 1776.

[31] *Va. Gazette* (Dixon and Hunter), July 6, 1776.

[32] P. 9.

sell out, others say they are fighting in a bad cause, and apprehensive of mutiny; others mention a difference between the General and the Admiral, and that the Army in general are disheartened and uneasy."[33]

Another letter, written by an English officer after Breed's Hill, complained that the army had not gained a single solid advantage by the battle; on the contrary, they had learned "one melancholy truth, which is, that the *Americans*, if they were equally well commanded, are full as good soldiers as ours; and as it is, are very little inferior to us, even in discipline and steadiness of countenance."[34]

More effective was the ridicule of the British troops. They were constantly satirized in such poems as Franklin's "The King's own Regulars, and their Triumph over the Irregulars; A New Song to the Tune of 'An Old Courtier of the Queen's, and the Queen's Old Courtier.'" Circulating through the colonies in 1775, it served the colonists in the early part of the war much as did Hopkinson's "Battle of the Kegs" later. The whole is a clever bit of satire on the bravery of the troops and their total inability to defeat the minute-men. A few stanzas will suffice:

"At Prestonpans we met with some rebels one day,
    We marshalled ourselves all in comely array;
    Our hearts were all stout, and bid our legs stay,
    But our feet were wrongheaded and took us away.

"At Falkirk we resolved to be braver,
    And recover some credit by better behavior;
    We wouldn't acknowledge feet had done us a favor,
    So feet swore they would stand, but—legs ran however.

.   .   .   .

"As they could not get before us, how could they look
            us in the face?
    We took care they shouldn't, by scampering away apace.
    That they had not much to brag of, is a very plain case;
    For if they beat us in the fight, we beat them in the race."[35]

---

[33] 4 Force, *Amer. Arch.*, II, 912.   [34] *Ibid.*, II, 1021.
[35] Charles Carroll stated that Franklin was the author.—Carroll to Mrs. Carroll, Apr. 15, 1775, Carroll Papers, VIII, 335. So far as I know it has not been attributed to anyone else. It appeared in the *Boston Gazette*, Nov. 27, 1775, and in *Pa. Evening Post*, Mar. 30, 1776. Similar to it was a poem in the *Boston Gazette*, Nov. 6, 1775:

        "We came, we saw, but could not beat,
        And so—we sounded a retreat:

The second substantial reason for believing in the ultimate success of America, said the propagandists, was her own strength. They pointed to the unlimited resources of the country—inexhaustible supplies of food, mineral deposits of unknown extent, wool and hemp, timber for ships and vehicles—"Resources beyond any part of the World."[36] The country itself gave the colonials a tremendous advantage over the British regulars. "*Nature* and *convenience* has formed your country for defence—believe me it may be defended almost inch by inch, your whole country has *breast works already erected against small arms.* . . ."[37] The mere extent of the continent made it almost impossible for the enemy to overrun it, especially since every commander could "chuse his ground for attacking, in a country with which he is perfectly acquainted, and where every inhabitant, even the children, are standing spies upon all the motions of an adversary."[38] Its distance from England made the improbability of defeat even greater. As George Mason said: "Would there have been no difficulty in raising and transporting a body of troops sufficient to occupy a country of more than two thousand miles in extent? Would they have had no dangers to encounter in the woods and wilds of America? Three millions of people driven to desperation are not an object of contempt."[39]

It was the brave American "yeoman" himself, however, who provided the propagandist with his best appeal. As early as 1772, the author of the *Oration, Upon the Beauties of Liberty* declared that "where his Majesty has one soldier, who art in general the refuse of the earth, America can produce fifty, free men, and all volunteers, and raise a more potent army of men in three weeks, than England can in three years."[40] Propagandists boasted of the number of men available, a hundred and fifty thousand in New England alone, and three hundred thousand, nay five hundred thousand if need be, in America. And these thousands of soldiers were

---

On Roxbury Hill again we saw 'em,
And did like Devils clapper claw 'em,
But warlike casuists can't discuss
If we beat them, or they beat us."

[36] *Speech of the Statue of William Pitt, loc. cit.*, June 5, 1770. See also *S. C. Gazette*, July 4, 1774.
[37] *Boston Gazette*, Sept. 26, 1774; and Oct. 10, 1774.
[38] Gordon, *Religious . . . Liberty, A Discourse*, Dec. 15, 1774, p. 30.
[39] Rowland, *Life and Correspondence of George Mason*, I, 385.
[40] Preface, p. xiv.

trained in the hardy pioneer life of America; they were excellent marksmen—"by which the waste of ammunition will be greatly prevented"—and in actual tests in Pennsylvania sixty men hit a mark the size of a man's nose at a hundred and fifty yards: "General Gage, take care of *your* nose."[41] Moreover, these men were not the downtrodden peasantry of Europe; they were spirited, independent Americans, fighting for their homes, with a will to win far greater than even the flower of the British troops and far greater than the miserable hirelings of a petty German state.[42]

The propagandists exulted after the first battles. British redcoats had actually fled before the fire of the ragged militiamen, and American hopes seemed justified. The propagandists turned from the realm of conjecture to the realm of fact. At Breed's Hill victory came to the superior forces of the British only after an intense engagement lasting all day, and then not until the American ammunition had run out.[43] The *Pennsylvania Packet* listed on January 1, 1776, the remarkable occurrences of the year 1775, and among them were these two items:

"2000 veteran British soldiers were attacked and defeated by 300 peasants, and were saved from total destruction by running 40 miles in one day.

"An army of Americans, commanded by a VIRGINIA FARMER, blocked up 10,000 British troops, commanded by three of the ablest Generals in the British service.

Finally, said the propagandists, America would not be alone in her struggles for freedom. France would come voluntarily to her aid, hoping to ruin her old enemy. In any case, she could be bought with an offer of Canada. Spain perhaps, and the stalwart Dutch, and all the maritime states "will find in their interest . . . to protect a

---

[41] *Pa. Journal*, Oct. 5, 1775; 4 Force, *Amer. Arch.*, II, 1608 f.; Moore, *Diary of the Revolution*, I, 111; 4 Mass. Hist. Soc., *Collections*, IV, 270 f.

[42] See particularly Charles Lee, *Strictures on a Pamphlet Entitled A Friendly Address to all Reasonable Americans*, pp. 7 ff. An address to the Baltimore Independent Company inspirited the members by pointing out that Charles XII had defeated Peter the Great. Since then, it continued, Russia, although a barbarous nation, had become the most powerful nation in Europe: "is it not reasonable to suppose then, that we, who are a civilized people, should become equally popular [powerful?]?"—The Mordecai Gist Papers, Vol. III, signed "Agamemnone."

[43] Conn. Hist. Soc., Broadsides, *Fresh News*, 1775; *Boston Gazette*, Jan. 15, 1776; *N. H. Gazette*, June 2, 1775; *Freeman's Journal*, May 25, 1776; and *Continental Journal*, July 4, 1776.

people who can be so advantageous to them." Europe as a whole would rejoice to see the defeat of perfidious Albion.[44]

But the greatest ally of all, God, was on the side of America. A writer in the *Freeman's Journal* railed against England: "Why do YE suffer YOUR Fleets and Armies again to be sent against America? Are YE not yet convinced that the GREAT JEHOVAH is on her Side? and that God helping her the Gates of Hell shall never prevail against her?"[45] As each year passed, the propagandists reviewed the special favors of Heaven vouchsafed the colonists. They reminded them that God had supported their forefathers through the trials of the early settlement, and that He had continuously supported them throughout the controversy with England. As He had supported them in the past, so He would in the future, for it was clear by these dispensations that the colonists were His chosen people. Indeed, said the Reverend Henry Cumings in a sermon in 1775, it may well have been that God brought about the conflict "with a view to roll the ball of Empire over to this Western World."[46] This is one of the most characteristic suggestions of the entire period; hardly a writer or a speaker failed to make it at some time or other. If reiteration makes for belief, then surely the colonists believed that they were the chosen people of God and invincible.

War and independence produced two other dangerous suggestions which the Whigs had to combat. The first was that war was sinful. This argument found particular reception in Pennsylvania and North Carolina, where there were Quakers and other pacifistic sects in large numbers. Ministers could help substantially in refuting this idea. As early as 1765 Philemon Robbins delivered a sermon in Branford, Connecticut, in which he said, "such as plead the King's prerogative in acts unconstitutional and wrong are going apace to the doctrine of *passive obedience* and *non-resistance,* a doctrine held only by high flying churchmen."[47] Thomas Coombe preached an entire sermon on July 20, 1775, on the twofold proposition that the colonists had acted entirely on the defensive in the war with England and that a defensive war was justifiable. David Jones, in a sermon

---

[44] *Pa. Evening Post,* Feb. 3, 1776; Paine, *Common Sense;* 4 Force, *Amer. Arch.,* V, 992, VI, 1131.   [45] June 1, 1776.
[46] *A Sermon, delivered at Billerica,* p. 9.
[47] Quoted in Love, *Fast Days in New England,* p. 331.

printed under the title *Defensive War in a Just Cause Sinless,* traced the subject through the Old and New Testaments in proof of his contention that *"a defensive war is sinless before* God; consequently to engage therein, is consistent with the purest religion."[48] A writer in the *Pennsylvania Evening Post* said in the same year, "The opposing an arbitrary measure, or resisting an illegal force, is no more rebellion than to refuse obedience to an highway-man who demands your purse, or to fight a wild beast, that came to devour you."[49] More succinctly, Charles Lee declared in his *Strictures on a Pamphlet Entitled a Friendly Address,* "to preach up in this enlightened age . . . passive obedience, is a mark of lunacy. . . ."[50]

The second inconvenient idea originated among the moderates— genuine friends of both England and the colonists, perhaps—who counseled such mild measures of obtaining redress as petitions, objected to the warlike preparations being made in the fall and winter of 1774-75, and finally urged reconciliation with England rather than independence. What good did petitioning do in 1765-1768? asked the propagandists in answer; even if the King could be trusted, they said, his advisors could not. Those who urged moderation were the most dangerous of America's enemies, for that way lay certain failure.[51]

As to the formation of militia companies, the propagandists urged an old argument—"In PEACE prepare for WAR."[52] Civil war, some said, was far less an evil than slavery, for the one was short and sharp, but the other was permanent. Had America been armed in 1774, England would never had attacked her, they said, "for defense is ever the best." Yes, wrote Charles Lee, "being prepared for a civil war, is the surest means of preventing it; that to keep the swords of your enemies in their scabbards, you must whet your own."[53]

The demand from the moderates and Tories for reconciliation was even more dangerous. They jeered at American leaders, they made fun of the Continental Congress, they declared that independence would turn loose upon the colonists a rabble of cheap politicians

[48] P. 7. [49] June 27, 1775.
[50] P. 4. See also John Carmichael, *A Self-Defensive War Lawful.*
[51] E.g., Boston Committee Records, p. 586; and *Pa. Journal,* June 29, Aug. 31, 1774.
[52] *Boston Gazette,* Apr. 9, 1770; Feb. 18, 1771; Sept. 21, 1772.
[53] *Strictures on a Pamphlet Entitled a Friendly Address,* p. 11. See also *Pa. Magazine,* July, 1775, pp. 313 f.; N. Y. *Journal,* Oct. 13, 1774, Nov. 9, 1775.

far worse than England's most incompetent officials, and they urged that the only safety of America lay in effecting a reconciliation with England. To these attacks on themselves, the Whigs steadily replied with eulogies of their leaders, indignant contradictions, and elaborate defenses of Congress. Most of the writers were content to show that Congress had done all that could be expected, that the divisions therein were the best evidence of its representative character, and that in the time of crisis all would unite. Others denied flatly that independence meant the tyranny of the mob; on the contrary, it was the surest way to break the power of the extra-legal committees and return to orderly government.[54]

The British proposals for reconciliation imperiled the success of the Whig plans. The Ministry made several attempts to work out a compromise which would satisfy both the imperialists and the self-determinists, and the Tories wholeheartedly backed their proposals, but at every point their efforts were blocked by a torrent of Whig propaganda. Prior to 1775 there had been suggestions that the tax problem might be solved by requisitions, and in 1775 Lord North definitely proposed that those colonies which made definite provision for paying a share of imperial expenses would be relieved of all taxation. In 1776 commissioners arrived to treat with the colonists. The plan was attacked at once as an effort to divide the colonies and destroy them one by one. The right of Parliament to interfere in the internal adminstration of the separate colonies was denied, and it was specifically pointed out that the sufficiency of the amount voted by the compliant colonies was to be judged by Parliament alone, and that England had not agreed in return to open a free trade with the rest of the world.[55] To return to the status of 1763, they said, would be folly in view of the past ten years; only

---

[54] E.g., 4 Force, *Amer. Arch.*, V, 992, dated Philadelphia, Apr. 20, 1776, in which the writer urges that the colonists would be delivered from the "disorders which arise from the unlimited, undescribed, and sometimes arbitrary powers of Conventions, Committees of Safety, and Committees of Inspection."

[55] *Va. Gazette* (Dixon and Hunter), *Supplement*, June 17, 1775; *Pa. Evening Post*, Feb. 13, 1776; N. Y. *Journal*, Dec. 14, 1775; 4 Force, *Amer. Arch.*, V, 529 ff., VI, 1131. The powers of the commissioners were attacked as inadequate.—*Pa. Evening Post*, Mar. 26, 1776; *Conn. Gazette*, May 3, 1776. The only people in favor of the plan, said some, were Tories and a few renegade Whigs: "All ye timid, irresolute, terrified, and double faced Whigs, who have, by one means or other, crept into authority, open your mouths wide, and bawl stoutly against every vigorous measure until the Commissioners arrive. . . . They will bring pockets well-lined with *English* guineas. . . . Your palms will be first greased. You are the only men who can complete the Parliamentary plans for raising an American Revenue."—"Cassandra," 4 Force, *Amer. Arch.*, V, 41 f. (Mar. 2, 1776).

the cessation of hostilities and the withdrawal of troops and the hoard of placemen and commissioners could secure America: "To be effectually secured from future mischiefs and machinations in case of a reunion, there must not be one Crown-Officer, either civil or military, left on the Continent, nor a *British* Ship-of-war permitted to enter our harbours. From them our present distresses sprang, and by them they will be continued."[56]

But in truth, they added, there was no hope in this or any other plan except independence: "Men who know they deserve nothing from their Country, and whose hope is on the arm that hath sought to enslave ye, may hold out to you . . . the false light of Reconciliation. There is no such thing. 'Tis gone! 'Tis past! The grave hath parted us, and death, in the persons of the slain, hath cut the thread of life between *Britain* and *America*."[57]

Thus were the ideas and proposals of Tories and conservative Whigs alike swept away in a torrent of propaganda. Whigs were not content, however, with a mere refutation of Tory arguments. Where possible, they were actually suppressed or censored.

Suspect individuals were closely watched, and as early as the Stamp Act period their correspondence was investigated. Even after Jared Ingersoll had resigned his office of stamp distributor for Connecticut, he was kept under surveillance by the Sons of Liberty, who opened his letters, prevented his writing English friends, and even watched the correspondence of his friends.[58] The committees set up later acted almost as modern boards of censors, and the correspondence of those under their ban was read and occasionally withheld. Andrew Miller, boycotted by a North Carolina committee, wrote a friend: "Its the freedom of the times; because I refuse to Sign the Association, I have not a letter from Britain dated later than July [1774] tho' I am Absolutely certain of some having come to Virga. of a later date."[59]

Tory preachers, writers, and printers all were the objects of actual violence and coercion, and their writings were suppressed.

[56] *Ibid.*, pp. 96 ff., 1133 ff. (Mar. 7, 1776; Apr. 29, 1776).
[57] *Ibid.*, p. 1020 (Apr. 22, 1776); *Pa. Evening Post*, June 13, 1776; *Boston Gazette*, Mar. 18, 1776; *Conn. Gazette*, Mar. 8, 1776; *N. Y. Journal*, Feb. 22, 1776. Paine devoted a great deal of *Common Sense* to the refutation of this idea.
[58] *Boston Gazette*, Jan. 13, 1766; "A Selection from the Correspondence and Miscellaneous Papers of Jared Ingersoll," New Haven Hist. Soc., *Papers*, IX, 362, 366, 377, 381; Louis H. Boutell, *The Life of Roger Sherman*, p. 54.
[59] *Col. Rec. N. C.*, IX, 1097.

Samuel Seabury's capable pamphlets attacking the Continental Congress were tarred and feathered by some committees, burned by others, and condemned by all.[60] Whig propagandists were determined to control the press. To John Adams, for instance, one of the material advantages of a declaration of independence was that tests for Toryism could be legally applied and the unfriendly papers stopped. Thereafter, "the presses will produce no more seditious or traitorous speculations. Slanders upon public men and measures will be lessened."[61]

The Sons of Liberty began the intimidation of the printers. They were determined that all business should continue as usual, that the courts and customhouses should remain open, and that the newspapers should be printed regularly. There were no stamps and no stamp distributors when the act was to go into force on November 1, but there were heavy fines for those who disobeyed the act. The Sons of Liberty insisted, however, that the printers keep their presses going. It was reported in New York that the Boston printers had been told to continue or their offices would be torn down, and the New York Sons of Liberty openly threatened those in New York. "May not any Printer, who before a Proclamation of the Governor, issued *by and with the Advice of his Majesty's Council*, stop his Press from the mere Panic of the pretended Act, fear the indignation of the Public, and the Resentment of the Populace?"[62] A placard threatening the printers was posted at one of the coffeehouses on October 31, and later a letter was thrown in John Holt's window:

"As you have hitherto proved yourself a friend to liberty, by publishing such compositions as had a tendency to promote the cause we are engaged in, we are encouraged to hope you will not be deterred from continuing your useful paper, by groundless fear of the detestable stamp act.

"However, should you at this critical time shut up the press, and basely desert us, depend upon it, your house, person, and effects will be in imminent danger. We shall therefore expect your paper on Thursday as usual; if not on Thursday evening, Take CARE.

[60] E.g., *Minutes of the Provincial Congress of New Jersey*, pp. 95 ff.; 4 Force, *Amer. Arch.*, I, 1100, 1183; *Va. Gazette* (Dixon and Hunter), Apr. 15, 1775.

[61] John Adams to John Winthrop, June 23, 1776.—Burnett, *Letters of Members of Cont. Cong.*, I, 502.

[62] *N. Y. Gazette, or, Weekly Post-Boy*, Oct. 31, 1765.

"Signed in the name, and by the order, of a great number of the Free Sons of New York.

"On the Turf, the 2nd November, 1765.

"JOHN HAMPDEN."[63]

Andrew Steuart, printer of the Wilmington *North Carolina Gazette*, printed no paper after November 1, and was threatened almost immediately by the local Sons of Liberty. They threatened his press, his person, even his life, so he claimed, and on November 20 the *Continuation of the North Carolina Gazette* appeared.[64] Only James Johnston of the *Georgia Gazette* resisted the popular demand for any length of time. The paper was discontinued from November 14, 1765, to May 31, 1766.

During later periods of the controversy, Whig committees vigilantly watched the papers. John Mein of the *Boston Chronicle* was boycotted and actually attacked during the agitation in 1769 over the Townshend Acts, and it was finally considered necessary, other measures having failed, to destroy the press of James Rivington, the most capable of the Tory printers.

Normally less violent measures were sufficient. The Georgia Whigs, for example, had been out of patience with Johnston ever since the days of the Stamp Act. He was in a difficult position, for he was faced on the one side by an increasingly aggressive Whig minority, and on the other by a strongly conservative group in control of affairs down to 1775. He printed some protests against a meeting called by the Whigs in 1774, and Lyman Hall, chairman of the committee of correspondence of St. John's Parish, wrote him: "We observe that several pieces of interesting news respecting Boston, such as their resolutions & also speeches relating to the present state of affairs, find no place in your papers, and hereby inform you, that, if you cannot find room for such things, we are determined to find one that will, and soon."[65] Early in 1776 the Council of Safety established a virtual censorship of the *Gazette* by appointing a committee to see to it that nothing appeared that might "endanger the public safety."[66]

---

[63] Leake, *Life of Lamb*, p. 13 n.   [64] *Col. Rec. N. C.*, VII, 124.

[65] *Ga. Gazette*, Oct. 26, 1774. Johnston included much more Boston material after this threat, although he said he despised it and would pay no attention to it.

[66] *Rev. Rec. Ga.*, I, 100. This may have related just to the week of January 16, 1776, but there is little doubt but that the policy was consistently pursued.

The editor of the *New Hampshire Gazette*, Daniel Fowle, was also under the close supervision of the committees. He was reported to the Provincial Congress of New Hampshire for printing an article in January, 1776, against the establishment of an independent government in New Hampshire. He was severely censured and warned never again to print anything reflecting upon the Continental Congress or the cause of American independence.[67]

The censorship of the Whig committee members was effective. The official British account of Lexington, drawn up by General Gage, appeared in very few Whig papers. Green's *Maryland Gazette*, Dixon's *Virginia Gazette*, and the *Cape Fear Mercury*, the only southern Whig papers to print the account, feared they would lose government printing if they did not. Governor Colden of New York sent Gage's account to Hugh Gaine, printer of the *New York Mercury*, on a Saturday to appear on Monday. Gaine agreed, provided he would be allowed to state who had sent it in. On Sunday he notified Colden that he could not publish it. Colden wrote Gage: "Hancock and Adams came to town on Saturday, and were probably consulted by some of the Party here, and with them determined still to suppress every account but their own. A Method by which they had so successfully deluded the people."[68]

Thus by refutation and suppression the Whig propagandists had adroitly met the necessities of the period before the Declaration of Independence. The selection of appeals had been admirable; equally important was the method of presenting them to the people.

[67] The following statement appears in the *Documents N. H.*, VIII, 24: "Upon reading an Ignominious Scurrilous & Scandalous Piece Printed in the New Hampshire Gazette & Historical Chronicle No. 1001, of Tuesday, Jany 9th 1776—Directed or Addressed to the Congress at Exeter: Voted That Daniel Fowle Esqʳ. the Supposed Printer of said Paper be forewith Sent for and ordered to Appear before this house and give an account of said Piece, So much Derogatory to the Honour of this Assembly, as well as of the Honble Continental Congress and Injurious to the cause of Liberty Now Contending for. Sent up by Capt Waite." Fowle suspended the *Gazette* on January 17, and Benjamin Dearborn began printing the *Freeman's Journal* on May 25, 1776.

[68] *Colden Letter Books*, II, 414.

X

DEMONSTRATIONS, SONGS, AND PLAYS

THE VEHICLE of the suggestion is almost as important as the suggestion itself. Appeals may be roughly divided into two types—dramatic, oral, and pictorial, reaching the literate and illiterate alike, and written, reaching directly only the literate. The choice depends upon the group to be reached and the opportunities for reaching it. Visual or oral suggestions require primary—face to face—situations and are of particular value in dealing with the illiterate or poorly educated.

It is manifest that there were serious limitations on primary contacts in eighteenth-century America. Opportunity for personal contact was limited to a comparatively restricted area, especially in the South; the bulk of the people went through life without leaving their immediate neighborhood, knowing nothing but the most rudimentary facts about the more distant colonies.[1] In the North a network of roads had been constructed, but beyond a radius of forty or fifty miles around the larger towns they were wretched. Between the more important centers there were at least one or two well-traveled roads, but not of such quality as to tempt the traveler except under stress of necessity. Two highways extended from Portsmouth down into Virginia, and one continued on into Georgia, but even in the North these were in poor condition, and in the South great stretches of highway were impassable in wet weather. It took three weeks to carry the news of Lexington to Savannah, and that was under unusual conditions; six weeks was a better average for the trip. In the South the principal lines of communications were up the rivers to the piedmont, but the roads, often little more than wide trails along the banks, stopped short at the mountains, and there was practically no contact between the older communities along the coastal rivers and the newer settlements in the mountain valleys to the west. The lines of communication for the valley settlers were not eastward but northward toward Philadelphia. This state of

[1] Michael Kraus, *Intercolonial Aspects of American Culture on the Eve of the Revolution.*

affairs as late as 1775 is startlingly revealed in the report of the Moravian settlement in Salisbury, North Carolina, on the impossibility of working with the Georgia Moravians in Savannah: "it is too far from Wachovia—can get letters more often from Europe."[2] Roads being what they were, rivers were used wherever possible and, of course, the trading vessels along the coast offered the most satisfactory means of transportation north and south. The simple fact is, that in spite of increasing travel on the roads and the establishment of a regular stage coach between New York and Philadelphia in 1758, the propagandist was limited in his personal contacts to his own neighborhood, and few tried to make more.

Within that area, however, there were many opportunities for mass appeal. After all, there were seven hundred towns, more than five hundred of them in New England. Market days, fairs, muster days (when the local militia met to drill), election days, court days, all brought the country people to town and gave the propagandist the opportunity he needed for mass appeal. There were no radios, no moving pictures, no billboards, and no skywriting, but there were plenty of other ways to make an effective and perhaps a fresher appeal. Demonstrations, celebrations, songs, plays, public addresses, and pulpit oratory, all spread the messages of the propagandists in telling form.

DEMONSTRATIONS AND CELEBRATIONS

The public demonstrations and celebrations staged by Whig leaders effectively united the people who participated, and those occasioned by events common to all the colonies had a unique value in promoting a community of sympathies and antagonisms throughout America. Of them all, those associated with the Stamp Act were the most important in creating common attitudes. From the summer of 1765 until well after the repeal of the Act there was a succession of planned demonstrations from one end of the colonies to the other. "It is remarkable," wrote the historian Ramsay, "that the proceedings of the populace on these occasions, were carried on with decorum and regularity. They were not the ebullitions of a thoughtless mob, but for the most part planned by leading men of character and influence, who were friends to peace and order. These, knowing well that the bulk of mankind are more led by their sense than by their

[2] *Moravian Records*, II, 921.

reason, conducted the public exhibitions on that principle, with a view of making the stamp act and its friends both ridiculous and odious."[3]

The first of the long series was designed to arouse people against the stamp distributors. On the morning of August 14 an animated effigy swung from a tree near Boston Common, and no one with goods to sell was allowed to pass until the figure had gone through the motions of stamping them with the "mark of the Beast." Here the propagandists appealed to two of the New Englander's vital interests—his Bible and his pocketbook—for here were combined a particularly apt Biblical phrase and a striking portrayal of the direct cost of the Act to all, rich and poor alike.[4] Equally pointed demonstrations in Connecticut prepared the people to resist Jared Ingersoll and his stamps and at the same time promoted in easily understood form the American legal arguments. In New London the usual effigy of the stamp distributor was paraded through the streets and executed on the edge of town, while everyone shouted: "There hangs a Traitor, there's an Enemy to his Country." A mock court in Lebanon denied the prisoner—again an effigy of Ingersoll—all the rights of Englishmen and allowed only his "virtual" representative to plead for him.[5] In Windham his effigy was suspended between earth and heaven, as fit for neither (a reference to the English treason law), and in Middletown an elaborate stage setting, lighted by lanterns at night, showed effigies of Bute and Grenville being kicked by a third figure, while an actor recited the lines,

> "This is the D—l we know full well,
> He's come to kick Lord B— to h—."[6]

[3] *History of the American Revolution,* I, 69 f.

[4] *Boston Gazette, Supplement,* Aug. 19, 1765. The town was crowded all day with people from neighboring villages. The Biblical reference is to Revelation 13:15-17: "And he that had power to give life unto the image of the beast, that the image of the beast should both speak, and cause that as many as would not worship the image of the beast should be killed. And he causeth all, both small and great, rich and poor, free and bond, to receive a mark in their right hand, or in their foreheads: And that no man might buy or sell, save he that had the mark, or the name of the beast, or the number of his name." It was an easy matter for the New Englander in reading this to substitute Bute or Grenville for the beast, and perhaps degenerate England for degenerate Rome.

[5] *Conn. Gazette,* Sept. 6, 1765.

[6] *Ibid.,* Nov. 15, 1765, Aug. 30, Sept. 13, 1765. Samuel Peters, *General History of Connecticut,* pp. 250 f., describes another demonstration in Lebanon in which effigies of Ingersoll, Grenville, and the Devil were carted. Grenville and the Devil were quite friendly in the cart, but the Devil had nothing but sneers and frowns for Ingersoll, for the "fawning reverence of the latter gave his infernal highness such offence, that he turned up his breech and discharged fire, brimstone, and tar, in Ingersoll's face; setting him all

The demonstrations in New London, Windham, and Lebanon occurred on the same day, August 26, and several others came within a week or so of them. Much the same buffoonery was carried out in both Rhode Island and New Hampshire, except that in Newport there were effigies of two local villains, Martin Howard and Thomas Moffat, instead of the usual figures of Grenville or Bute. With few variations effigies of the local distributor, Grenville, North, Bute, or the Devil, were pelted, burned, hanged, or buried from New York to Georgia. Inscriptions, "Liberty and No Stamps," "Liberty, Property, and No Stamp Duty," and like conceits were fastened on most of them and repeated in the toasts drunk at the execution.

The demonstrations in Charleston were typical of those in other southern towns. On October eighteenth a ship from London came in, carrying, it was believed, both stamps and the new distributor. On the morning of the nineteenth effigies were hung with placards "Liberty and No Stamp Act" and "Whoever shall dare attempt to pull down these effigies had better been born with a millstone about his neck and cast into the sea." All day the muffled bells of St. Michael's Church tolled. At night the effigies were taken down and carried in the funeral procession of American Liberty, who was to be buried. On the way to the burying ground the house of George Saxby, one of the distributors, was ransacked, but no stamps were found. The effigies were then burned, but American Liberty revived in her coffin at the moment of interment.[7] The burial of American Liberty thereafter became a common ceremony. Henry Laurens said of this affair, "some of our folks were wise enough to exhibit effigies on Saturday last" but he must have changed his mind the day after writing this, because his own house was visited by a mob looking for the stamps.[8]

Most of these demonstrations took place where the stamp distributors were located, the seat of government in each colony; there were demonstrations in other towns in New England but only occasional ones outside the principal cities in the South.[9]

---

in a blaze; which, however, Mr. Grenville generously extinguished with a squirt." Peters also avers that Trumbull gave one of his suits of clothes for this performance and thereby won an election, but Peters although highly entertaining is untrustworthy.

[7] Accounts are in *S. C. Gazette*, Oct. 19 to Oct. 31, 1765; *Ga. Gazette*, Oct. 24, 1765; *N. C. Gazette* (Steuart), Nov. 27, 1765; McCrady, *S. C. under Royal Government*, pp. 565 ff. [8] Quoted in *ibid.*, p. 565.

[9] Affairs were staged in New York; Philadelphia; New Brunswick; Baltimore; Fred-

There was another series of demonstrations on or about the first of November, the day the act was to go into effect. Portsmouth, Newport, Baltimore, and Wilmington, North Carolina, all carried out practically the same program staged on October 19 by the Charleston Liberty Boys—the burial of American Liberty, aged one hundred and forty-five years. With all the paraphernalia of a funeral service the coffin was taken to the grave, but at the moment of interment Liberty revived amid great rejoicing.[10] Effigies of Colden on a gallows with a boot over one shoulder and the Devil peeping over the other accompanied the rioters in New York.[11] The fifth of November (Guy Fawkes Day) was usually disgraced in Boston by a fight between two rival mobs, the North End led by Swift and the South End by Mackintosh, but in 1765 these two joined in a demonstration against the Stamp Act. A pageant with effigies of Tyranny,

---

ericktown; Dumfries; Williamsburg; Newbern, Cross Creek, and Duplin county, North Carolina; Charleston; and Savannah. See *Ga. Gazette*, Oct. 10, 1765; *Md. Gazette*, Dec. 10, 1765; *Col. Rec. N. C.*, VII, 123 ff. Boston and Philadelphia crowds celebrated the change in ministry in England which had taken place on July 10. In Philadelphia "the mob made a bonfire and burnt an effigy for our Stamper, and surrounded his house, whooping and hollooing, which caused him to load his arms."—Edward Burd to his father, Sept. 18, 1765, quoted in T. Balch, ed., *Letters and Papers Relating Chiefly to the Provincial History of Pennsylvania*, p. 207. In Boston the crowds assembled at Liberty Tree and raised a flag which carried on one side "PITT the Supporter of Liberty and the Terror of Tyrants," and on the other,

> To B——e and G——n——e, mark the event,
> Both Heaven and Earth are Foes,
> While Curses on each Wretch are sent
> By every Wind that blows.

—*Boston Gazette, Supplement*, Sept. 16, 1765. David Ogden, Speaker of the New Jersey Assembly, was burned in effigy in New Brunswick because he had refused to sign the petition of the Stamp Act Congress.—*N. Y. Gazette, or, Weekly Post-Boy*, Oct. 31, 1765; and R. R. Livingston Papers, I, 26.

[10] *Boston Gazette*, Nov. 11, 1765; *Newport Mercury*, Nov. 4, 1765; *Col. Rec. N. C.*, VII, 123 f. A notice was put in the *Newport Mercury*, Oct. 28, 1765, of the proposed funeral; all true-born Sons of Liberty were asked to meet at the Coffee House at eleven-thirty. The Baltimore Sons of Liberty had their celebration on November 30.—*Md. Gazette*, Dec. 10, 1765.

[11] Becker, *Political Parties*, p. 31; Abbott, *New York in the American Revolution*, pp. 54 ff. There was another effigy of Colden in the coach. The demonstrations on the first of November in Boston also included the Governor as well as the stamp distributor. Bernard felt keenly the insult and had tried vainly to prevent the affair.—Hutchinson, *History of Massachusetts Bay*, III, 135 f. There were effigies of Huske and Grenville also. One stanza of the poem pinned on Grenville's effigy read:

> "Take heed my Brother Rogues, take heed,
> In me your honest Portion read:
> Dear Cousin PETER [Oliver] no excuse,
> Come down with me without your shoes;
> 'Tis G[renvil]le calls, and sink or swim,
> You'd go to H——L to follow him."
> —*Boston Gazette*, Nov. 4, 1765.

Slavery, Oppression, and the like, was paraded through the town, and the effigies were burned at night.[12]

A third series of demonstrations used the stamps themselves as the visible symbol of oppression, just as the first had used effigies of the distributors and the second had used American Liberty. A stamped Barbados newspaper of November 2 was discovered in Philadelphia in December, exhibited at the Coffee House, and then burned, but most of the affairs took place later because stamps were scarce and came into the colonies from the West Indies slowly. The best example is the planned demonstration in several towns on February 20, 1766. The Boston Sons of Liberty wrote those in Portsmouth on February 17:

> "Enclosed you will find a Portion of that detestable Paper mark'd with AMERICA'S OPPRESSION it being half that we obtain'd of a Brother of ours from another Colony which we intend to exhibit with chains &c. next Thursday in a Public Manner on Liberty Tree—The Occasion of our delaying is, that we may have them exhibited at one Time—It will be taken down at 12 Oclock by a common Execution[er] and burnt—Let us show as much abhorrence as possible—After which We propose to have the following Toasts drank—George the third, our gracious, rightful and Lawful Sovereign—Succession to the Royal House of Hanover—Confusion to its Enemies—Success to the Foes of the Stamp-Act—A perpetual Itching without the Benefit of Scratching to the Friends of the same—Long Life Health & Prosperity to all the Sons of Liberty on the Continent."[13]

The *Massachusetts Gazette* stated that the twentieth of February had been fixed upon by the Sons of Liberty in each province for burning one of the stamps in the several principal towns, and there is every likelihood that the plan was carried out.[14]

The joy which swept the colonies on the news of the repeal was unaffected and spontaneous, but the celebrations which followed,

[12] *Ibid.*, Nov. 11, 1765.   [13] Belknap Papers, III, 116.

[14] *Mass. Gazette*, Feb. 20, 1766. *Boston Gazette*, Feb. 24, 1766, gives an account of the exhibitions in Boston and Plymouth. Others were staged at different times in Boston early in February. *Ibid.*, Feb. 3, 1766. Philadelphia Liberty Boys had an exhibition on February 14.—Lamb Papers, p. 8a. The Liberty Boys in New York burned some stamps and playbills in front of the Coffee House, "all to prevent their Spirits to flag."—*Montresor Journals*, p. 358.

though perfectly natural exhibitions of this joy, were carefully arranged. In Portsmouth the people gathered in procession and marched up Liberty Hill, on top of which a bonfire attracted still more supporters of Liberty; a discharge of cannon, followed by toasts and a speech by Dr. David Purcell, closed the exercises, and all Sons of Liberty then met for entertainment at one of the taverns.[15] The Boston Liberty Boys constructed a pyramid, the three sides of which were covered with poetry all too hastily composed for the occasion, and at night fireworks were set off from its top. As everywhere else, all the bells in town rang, cannon were fired, and flags displayed. Otis and Hancock kept open house at night for the Sons of Liberty. Nathaniel Appleton added to the usual celebration in Cambridge a carefully prepared thanksgiving sermon, and in Northampton one of the local poets composed a triumphant epic on base submission and glorious resistance.[16] As a prelude to the festivities in Newport the people were awakened before one in the morning by the ringing of bells and on arising found the town covered with signs and paintings, all conducive to the noblest sentiments.[17] New York and Philadelphia viewed the same scenes of joy, and no one attempted to restrain the hundreds of little boys who swarmed the streets to the great disgust of those older folk who kept their emotions under better control.[18] The assembly and council in Annapolis had a private celebration of their own the last of May, and the mayor of the town ordered June 11 to be observed as a day of feasting by the townspeople. In Anne-Arundel County, Maryland, a Liberty Pillar was erected, under which were optimistically buried the elements of discord.[19] Elsewhere in the South gentlemen attended a supper and ball, while outside, the commonalty repeated around a bonfire the toasts which gentlemen offered within. The streets of Norfolk were filled with color and noise; some of the

[15] N. H. Gazette, May 30, 1766; and Va. Gazette (Purdie), May 23, 1766; Belknap Papers, III, 128.

[16] Boston Gazette, May 26, 1766, Supplement, June 2, 1766; N. Y. Gazette, or, Weekly Post-Boy, July 3, 1766; Works of John Adams, II, 195; and Rowe's Diary, 2 Mass. Hist. Soc., Proceedings, X, 62.

[17] Newport Mercury, June 2, 1766. Two celebrations in Connecticut are described in Conn. Gazette, May 31, 1766, and N. Y. Gazette, or, Weekly Post-Boy, June 12, 1766.

[18] Ibid., May 29, June 5, 1766; Pa. Gazette, May 22, 1766; and Montresor Journals, p. 367. The Governor joined in the celebration in Burlington, New Jersey, and in Woodbridge the Sons of Liberty had roasted ox and ale under the Liberty Tree.—Pa. Gazette, May 29, 1766; and N. Y. Gazette, or, Weekly Post Boy, Supplement, June 19, 1766.

[19] Md. Gazette, May 29, June 12, 1766.

wondering crowd viewed an involved picture while others heard a discourse from Reverend Mr. Davis on Proverbs 25:4-5, but all met at the Courthouse for a collation and toasts.[20] The people of New-bern, Charleston, and Savannah, as well as of many other towns, had their balls and their bonfires, too, no doubt feeling as did everyone else that discord was buried and that George III now ruled a happy and united people.[21]

The triumphant success of the radicals in defeating the Stamp Act by the united efforts of all the colonies and almost all classes of people provided, as we have seen, one of the most effective types of appeal, and the opportunity to use it was offered in the significant anniversaries of the Stamp Act period. The Boston Sons of Liberty elected to commemorate August 14, the birthday of the society. On the first and second anniversaries there was no agitation under way against Great Britain, and there was simply a dinner at noon when the King's health was drunk. In 1768, however, Pascal Paoli—the Corsican liberal—and John Wilkes, his English counterpart, were added to the forty-five toasts, and in 1769 the largest and most important celebration was held. Three hundred odd Sons of Liberty in one hundred and thirty-nine carriages rode to Dorchester, Otis leading the way and Hancock bringing up the rear. After dinner there were forty-five toasts, as before, and the crowd broke up after singing the chorus of John Dickinson's Liberty song. The scene was not disgraced, said John Adams, by a single drunken Son of Liberty, and he added, "This is cultivating the sensations of freedom. There was a large collection of good company. Otis and Adams are politic in promoting these festivals; for they tinge the minds of the people; they impregnate them with the sentiments of liberty; they render the people fond of leaders in the cause, and averse and bitter against all opposers."[22] The anniversary in 1775, when the field officers of

---

[20] *Va. Gazette* (Purdie), June 6, 1766.

[21] *Ibid.*, June 13, June 20, 1766; Samuel A'Court Ashe, *History of North Carolina*, I, 325.

[22] *Works*, II, 218. See also *Boston Gazette*, Aug. 15, Aug. 22, 1768; Rowe's Diary, 2 Mass. Hist. Soc., *Proceedings*, X, 72. The names of those who attended the celebration are in 1 Mass. Hist. Soc., *Proceedings*, XI, 140. Accounts of other celebrations are in *Boston Gazette*, Aug. 18, 1766; and 2 Mass. Hist. Soc., *Proceedings*, X, 63. The celebration in 1770 was held at James Allen's house. Tickets were on sale by Caleb Davis, Thomas Chase, Paul Revere, and at the office of Edes and Gill. *Boston Gazette*, Aug. 6, 1770. The account of the dinner is *ibid.*, Aug. 20, 1770. The leaders each wrote John Wilkes a full account of the Boston Massacre.—Mass. Hist. Soc., *Proceedings*, XLVII, 190-

the 6th brigade met in Cambridge for dinner at the home of Jonathan Hastings, was apparently the last.[23]

August 14 was a significant date only in Boston, but the eighteenth of March, the anniversary of the repeal, was a common heritage. Until the eve of Lexington and Concord, when, as Ezra Stiles said, the colonists found that "the Repeal of the Stamp Act 1766 was not done on generous fraternal principles, as America at first conceived,"[24] the day was commemorated in every colony. Various groups co-operated in planning the festivities; some towns declared it a legal holiday and in a few cases even provided the entertainment,[25] and in others some organization or private individual arranged the affair. The Sons of Liberty planned numbers of them, for they considered themselves largely responsible for the repeal of the Act. When Nicholas Ray wrote the New York Liberty Boys after the repeal proposing a permanent society, he recommended that on the eighteenth of March or the first of May the organization should remind people of their deliverance: "I am firmly of opinion," he said, "that it will have such effect as you wish."[26] Sears and Lamb thereafter planned the programs in New York, as did the Sons of Liberty in other towns. Naturally much the same plan was followed everywhere. There was a celebration with bells, cannon, and a bonfire, sometimes a speech, usually a parade with the local militia company or the Sons of St. Patrick, and always a dinner at one of the taverns. These dinners were given by the Sons of Liberty, a social club, or "other select company," or by private individuals. Metcalf Bowler, for example, gave a dinner in Newport to the Sons of Liberty in 1767, and Hancock frequently entertained them in Boston.[27] These demonstrations served to keep fresh in the

---

215. The celebration of 1773 is briefly described in *Mass. Gazette, and Boston Post-Boy*, Aug. 23, 1773.

[23] *N. Y. Gazette and Weekly Mercury*, Aug. 28, 1775. The New York Sons of Liberty met at De La Montaigne's house on November 1, 1769, the only instance of commemorating that day found.—N. Y. *Journal*, Nov. 2, 1769.

[24] *Literary Diary*, I, 527 (Mar. 18, 1775).

[25] E.g., *Boston Town Records, 1758-1769*, p. 205; *Pa. Journal*, Apr. 12, 1770.

[26] Leake, *Life of Lamb*, p. 36.

[27] *Newport Mercury*, Mar. 23, 1767. See also *S. C. Gazette*, Mar. 22, 1773; and Rowe's Diary, 2 Mass. Hist. Soc., *Proceedings*, X, 63, 66. Examples of the celebration are plentiful. The first anniversary in Charleston was observed by ringing the bells and decorating houses and boats. There were several dinner parties, and afterward there was a "grand illumination." In 1769 the mechanics took a more prominent part; they met in the evening and marched with lights to Dillon's Tavern, where they had dinner with Peter Manigault, Speaker of the Assembly, and the newly elected representatives.—*S. C. Gazette*,

minds of the people their most signal success in the ten years before the Revolution; their victory had been complete and its memory was a constant source of inspiration to the Whigs.

The other demonstrations and celebrations which took place in the colonies down to the Declaration of Independence did not have the common background of a national experience, but they were none the less valuable in uniting people within a locality. One series of celebrations during the agitation over the Townshend duties did, however, have a common source in the struggles of John Wilkes and Pascal Paoli, the English and Corsican liberals. New Haven celebrated the election of Wilkes to the House of Commons in 1768, and Boston the birthday of Paoli.[28] In 1770 Boston, Queen Anne County, Maryland, and Charleston all staged demonstrations on the day Wilkes was to be released from prison (April 18), and in all of these affairs parallels were made between the treatment of liberals in England and in America.[29]

Other demonstrations grew out of local conditions or events; their number depended upon the alertness and ingenuity of the leaders in seizing opportunities. In Boston Governor Bernard was the object of several. He was effigied in 1768, and when he finally left for England, a flag was hoisted on Liberty tree, the bells were rung and small cannon fired, and two great bonfires were built—one in King's Street and one on Fort Hill.[30]

Much more important in Boston, however, were the anniversaries of the fifth of March. The town had voted in 1770 that annually thereafter a speech should be delivered on the massacre, and these speeches were always followed by a public exhibition in King's Street, the scene of the massacre. The exhibition depicted the scene of the murder, the troops, and the slaughtered victims. Inscriptions,

---

Mar. 23, 1767; Mar. 23, 1769. On the anniversary in 1774 Colonel Pinckney led the militia in parade.—*Ibid.*, Mar. 21, 1774. Lewestown, Pennsylvania, had planned for the anniversary in 1770 a satirical play burlesquing the authors of the Stamp Act, but it rained.—*Pa. Journal*, Apr. 12, 1770. Typical examples in other colonies may be found in *N. H. Gazette*, Mar. 25, 1768; *N. Y. Journal*, Mar. 23, 1769, Mar. 29, 1770, Mar. 26, 1772; *Pa. Journal*, Mar. 23, 1769; Stiles, *Literary Diary*, I, 437.

[28] *N. Y. Journal, Supplement*, July 9, 1768; *Pa. Journal*, Apr. 13, 1769.

[29] *Boston Gazette*, Apr. 23, 1770; *Md. Gazette*, Apr. 26, 1770; *S. C. Gazette; and Country Journal*, Apr. 24, 1770. These affairs were closely modeled, as in the Stamp Act period, on similar ones in England, one of which is described in *Ga. Gazette*, June 29, 1768.

[30] *N. Y. Journal*, Nov. 17, 1768; Rowe's Diary, 2 Mass. Hist. Soc., *Proceedings*, X, 72; and Mass Hist. Soc., *Proceedings*, XLVII, 209.

"The fatal effect of a standing Army, posted in a free City," or similar ones, were painted around the top. To vitalize the memory of the day still more a collection was taken each year for Christopher Monk, wounded that night and still languishing. These demonstrations were continued down to the end of the war, and, witnessed as they were by huge crowds, the combined effect of the oration, the placards, and the exhibition, was impressive.[31]

There were demonstrations in several of the colonies against violators of the nonimportation associations, tea consignees, and other public enemies. In the summer of 1770 there were effigies in Charleston representing violators of the association, and in 1773 there were effigies in New York of the tea consignees. Philadelphia burned effigies of Wedderburn and Hutchinson, who had combined to mistreat its beloved Ben Franklin, and when Governor Tryon of New York ill-advisedly issued a proclamation in March, 1776, promising speedy relief to the friends of government, his effigy, covered with insulting placards, was hung on the gallows and later burned by a huge crowd of people.[32] In the sympathetic demonstrations on the first of June, 1774, in protest against the Boston Port Act, effigies of North, Hutchinson, Gage, the Devil, and the Pope figured prominently.[33]

South Carolina leaders also showed alertness in arranging special demonstrations. Even such occasions as one of William Henry Drayton's speeches to the Grand Jury called forth an entertainment, and when the delegates to the Continental Congress returned, they were greeted with a public reception and dinner. "This had a good effect," wrote John Drayton later, "in supporting patriotic measures; and in

[31] E.g., *Boston Gazette*, Mar. 9, 1772, Mar. 8, 1773, Mar. 7, 1774; *Boston Town Records, 1770-1777*, p. 150, authorizing the collection for Christopher Monk; and Hutchinson, *History of Massachusetts Bay*, III, 135 f. The burial of those killed was attended by ten thousand people, it has been said, and the burial of Christopher Snider, killed by Richardson, was attended by two thousand or more.—Rowe's Diary, 2 Mass. Hist. Soc., *Proceedings*, X, 73, 74; *Boston Gazette*, Mar. 5, 1770; *Works of John Adams*, II, 227 f. Adams saw the funeral of Snider: "A vast number of boys walked before the coffin; a vast number of women and men after it, and a number of carriages. My eyes never beheld such a funeral; the procession extended further than can be well imagined. This shows there are many more lives to spend, if wanted, in the service of their country."
[32] *S. C. and Amer. Gen. Gazette*, July 4, 1770; *S. C. Gazette*, June 21, 1770; N. Y. *Journal*, Nov. 18, 1773; *Extracts from the Diary of Jacob Hiltzheimer, of Philadelphia, 1765-1798*, p. 30; Moore, *Diary of the Revolution*, I, 223 f.; and Diary of William Smith, Mar. 21, 1776.
[33] E.g., *Boston Gazette*, June 27, 1774; 4 Force, *Amer. Arch.*, I, 365 n.; Stiles, *Literary Diary*, I, 470.

putting down domestic opposition from crown officers, and other ill-disposed persons."[34] But in the spring of 1775 it was even more important to arouse the people, and it was determined "to bring forth something calculated to arrest the public attention; to throw odium on the British Administration; to put down the Crown Officers in the Province; and to invigorate the ardor of the people. And nothing was deemed more likely to affect the same, than some public exhibition, which might speak to the sight and sense of the multitude."[35] Accordingly, the people of Charleston were greatly amused one day by the antics of several effigies mounted on a box prominently placed on Market Street. The Pope and the Devil, as the principal actors, with Grenville and Lord North in close attendance, bobbed and danced as Edward Weyman inside the box manipulated the figures. The device demonstrated the evil origins of English legislation, for the Devil prodded the Pope, who prodded Grenville, who prodded Lord North, and all bowed to the King's men as they passed.[36]

The last of the demonstrations in this period were those which accompanied the proclamation of the Declaration of Independence. In the larger towns provision was thoughtfully made for its first public reading, so that the shouts of the Whigs might drown the groans of the Tories. In one Virginia town a collection was taken for the soldiery, who gratefully responded with a parade and toasts, and in other places, since the Declaration was an official document, the state or local officials staged an elaborate parade of all civil and military officers, with salutes, flags, and drums, after which the Declaration was read to the people. For the first time effigies of George III appeared, and these were burned—exploded in Huntington, New York—just as other effigies had always been burned.[37]

SYMBOLIC REPRESENTATIONS

Closely associated with the demonstrations were the symbolic representations of the propagandists' appeals. The two most com-

---

[34] Drayton, *Memoirs of the Revolution*, I, 154. *S. C. Gazette*, Dec. 12, 1774, describes the entertainment for Drayton.

[35] Drayton, *Memoirs*, I, 226.   [36] *Ibid.*, I, 226 f.

[37] *Huntington Records*, III, 6 f.; 5 Force, *Amer. Arch.*, I, 428, 476, 549, 582, 719, 847, 972; William Wirt, *Sketches of the Life and Character of Patrick Henry*, p. 213 (quoting from Purdie's *Virginia Gazette*); Jones, *History of Georgia*, II, 242 f.; Drayton, *Memoirs*, II, 315, "Diary of Landon Carter," *William and Mary College Quarterly*, XXI, 172.

mon forms were the effigies that always accompanied the demonstra
tions and Liberty Trees or Poles. The effigies symbolized oppression
or slavery, the trees freedom, and one was as common as the other,
for most demonstrations began or ended at the Liberty Tree. In
fact, the raising of a Liberty Pole or the dedication of a Liberty
Tree was often itself the occasion for a celebration. These visible
and permanent reminders of the struggle with England were found
practically everywhere by 1775. The first recorded Liberty Tree in
America was dedicated in Boston on September 11, 1765. With
appropriate ceremony a copper plate was affixed to the tree under
which Oliver had been burned in effigy less than a month before,
and thereafter it was the scene of much revolutionary activity.[38]
Other towns soon began to adopt the idea, especially after the repeal
of the Act. Dedham erected a Liberty Pillar, a tall wooden pedestal
surmounted by a bust of Pitt, and on the first anniversary of the
repeal the Newport Sons of Liberty marked a large tree with the
inscription, "THE TREE OF LIBERTY. STAMP ACT RE-
PEALED MARCH 18, 1766." The Petersham Liberty Boys
planned a dedication for September 19, 1768, and prior to it so
pruned the tree that at the exercises seventeen branches could be cut
off and ninety-two left, another reminder of the famous vote by
which the Massachusetts Assembly had refused to rescind the circular letter.[39]

The Plymouth Liberty Boys had a unique idea. They tried to
move Plymouth Rock to the center of the town, but unfortunately
the rock split. Only the top half could be moved to what was called
Liberty Pole Square, where this truncated memento of a brave struggle for Liberty remained until 1834.[40]

The New York Sons of Liberty had a trying time with their
Liberty Pole. One was erected in 1766 on city property but was
later destroyed, and the city officials refused to allow another to be
set up, even if it was given to the city. The Liberty Boys then
bought a piece of ground and raised one, but the troops quartered
there cut it down. A third was put up, and again the troops attacked

[38] *Boston Gazette, Supplement,* Sept. 16, 1765.
[39] *Ibid., Supplement,* Sept. 26, 1768; *Newport Mercury,* Mar. 23, 1767. William Reed
donated a tree and a piece of land.—*Boston Gazette,* Apr. 28, 1766.
[40] 2 Mass. Hist. Soc., *Proceedings,* III, 441.

it. This time the Liberty Boys were on hand, and a fight ensued, the Golden Hill affair, in which several people were hurt.[41]

The Charleston Sons of Liberty dedicated a whole pasture to the services of Liberty. They had frequently met with Christopher Gadsden under a live oak tree in Mazyck's pasture, and in 1768 the place was formally set apart for their use. Savannah did not dedicate a Liberty Tree until 1774,[42] and in general Liberty Trees were much less common in the South than in the North.

Somewhat similar in purpose were the statues and pictures of those Englishmen who had fought America's battles in Parliament. Two years after the dedication of Liberty Tree in Charleston, it was decided to add another reminder of the glorious resistance to the Stamp Act, and a statue of Pitt was ordered from England. The boats in the harbor flew their colors when it arrived, and a large body of people carried the statue to the center of town. The unveiling took place some weeks later. There was the usual play upon the numbers associated with the English liberal, Wilkes. Club 45 together with members of the assembly were in charge of the affair. Peter Manigault, speaker of the assembly, sat on the scaffold with twenty-six assemblymen. Two members of the club, numbered 26 and 92, raised the statue, and the assemblymen read the patriotic inscription. There was a discharge of cannon, and at the entertainment around the statue forty-five toasts were drunk.[43] New York also had a statue of Pitt,[44] but most of the patriots could not afford the expense of a statue. Pictures were cheaper. As early as September, 1765, a Boston town meeting voted to place a picture of Isaac Barré in Faneuil Hall, but it was not until January, 1767, that it came.[45] A portrait of Pitt by Charles Wilson Peale was placed in the Westmoreland County Courthouse in Virginia, and the Virginia House

---

[41] See a notice to the Sons of Liberty, Feb. 3, 1770, Amer. Antiq. Soc., Broadsides; and Becker, *Political Parties*, p. 82. This affair occurred just a few months before the Boston Massacre. Liberty Poles or Trees were so common in the North that it is not necessary to list them all. The people of South Kingston, Rhode Island, erected a pole eighty-five feet high with a banner carrying the word LIBERTY at the top; around the pole at the base was carved "LIBERTY IN OPPOSITION TO ARBITRARY TAXATION."—*Newport Mercury*, Nov. 14, 1774. See also William R. Staples, *Annals of the Town of Providence*, p. 222.

[42] Jones, *History of Georgia*, II, 176, says the first pole was erected in Savannah on June 5, 1775, but the call for the meeting of July 20, 1774, mentions the Liberty Pole by Tondee's Tavern. Governor Wright first mentions the liberty pole, it is true, on June 17, 1775.—Col. Rec. Ga. (Rhodes Memorial Home), Vol. XXXVIII, pt. 1, p. 466.

[43] *S. C. Gazette*, May 24, May 31, July 5, 1770.

[44] N. Y. *Journal*, Sept. 13, 1770.   [45] *Boston Gazette*, Jan. 26, 1767.

of Burgesses raised seventy-six pounds for a portrait of Camden, but as he refused to sit the money was returned to the subscribers. Later a picture of Camden was placed in the courthouse in Williamsburg, and the Burgesses continued their efforts to obtain a real portrait for their own hall.[46] The South Carolina Assembly asked its three delegates to the Stamp Act Congress—Thomas Lynch, Christopher Gadsden, and John Rutledge—to sit for their portraits.[47]

Other methods of visualizing dominant suggestions in symbolic form were even less common. There was nothing comparable to the modern cartoon or poster, and the sum total of cartoons and pictures used during the revolutionary period makes a very unimpressive list. Franklin's snake device, known as the first cartoon, which showed a snake cut into several parts with the caption "Join or Die," was used only once between 1765 and 1774, but thereafter it was frequently seen on newspapers and broadsides.[48] Other cartoons or illustrations also appeared occasionally on broadsides. A broadside concerning the Boston Massacre carried a picture of the troops firing on the luckless people, and one of the handbills of the Declaration on Taking up Arms showed a picture of Boston "when in its purity, and out of the Hands of the Philistines," but such illustrations were the exception. The magazines and almanacs were usually illustrated, however. The engravings in the *Royal American Magazine* (published for a little over a year) combined in different attitudes both the friends and enemies of America—the Pope, the Devil, or George III (who was caricatured in these pictures long before he was burned in effigy)—and Liberty, Minerva, Samuel Adams, John Hancock, or some other well-known patriot. The Boston Port Act, the Quebec Act, Magna Carta, or the Bill of Rights figured somewhere in nearly everyone of them.[49] But the magazines were so few and the circulation so limited that the effect of these cartoons was negligible.

[46] *Va. Gazette* (Purdie), Apr. 20, 1769; *Letters of Richard Henry Lee*, I, 22 ff., 36, 394. The subscription money was returned.

[47] McCrady, *S. C. under Royal Government*, p. 586.

[48] Albert Matthews, "Snake Devices, 1754-1776, and the Constitutional Courant, 1765," Colonial Soc. Mass., *Publications*, XI, gives an adequate account of this device.

[49] One or two illustrations will suffice: The issue of October, 1774, had an engraving called the Mitred Minuet; it showed four bishops dancing over the Quebec Act while George III looked on with the Devil peering over his shoulder. Another in the issue of May, 1774, showed two English ministers of State holding down an Indian while George III with the Boston Port Act in his pocket, forced him to drink tea. Soldiers with drawn swords stand ready to prevent interference, and Liberty standing by turns away her face.

More important were the pictures on the almanacs, for nearly every home had an almanac. The title page of Bickerstaff's almanac for 1770, for example, showed Otis, supported by Liberty and Hercules, with a coiled snake at their feet. Frequently the almanacs were illustrated with nothing more than a picture of one of the popular figures of the moment.[50] Occasionally prints or pictures on timely subjects were offered for sale. On November 1, 1765, there was offered for sale in Boston a complicated print in which Liberty, Pandora's Box, Liberty Tree, Bute, and many other items rivaled for attention, its chief virtue being that it included nearly all the objects of popular interest.[51]

Much more important were the transparencies made by the Liberty Boys. Few celebrations of any moment were held without one or more of these pictures, painted on thin paper pasted over a framework and lighted from within. The crowds which attended the celebration in Norfolk on the repeal of the Stamp Act, for instance, were attracted by an elaborate set, illuminated at night, which showed a complicated arrangement of George III, the Sun, Pitt, America, Agriculture, Manufacturing, Tyranny, Slavery, and Oppression.[52] The Boston Sons of Liberty on the anniversary of the fifth of March always constructed an elaborate one with crude scenes from the massacre, made more pointed by inscriptions and poetry. These transparencies, usually quite large, were placed on a balcony overlooking the site of the massacre, and in addition to the candle within, fireworks were set off from the top. Illuminated devices of a similar character were carried in the parades of the Liberty Boys or were hung on Liberty Tree before the demonstrations.[53]

SONGS

Songs as a medium of revolutionary sentiment were not extensively used, and those written were not of a very high order. There

---

[50] Reproductions of these may be found in B. J. Lossing, *The Pictorial Field-book of the Revolution,* I, 480.

[51] *Boston Gazette,* Nov. 11, 1765. A caricature called "The Repeal" is described in 1 Mass. Hist. Soc., *Proceedings,* XIV, 169.   [52] *Va. Gazette* (Purdie), June 6, 1766.

[53] In western North Carolina the Whigs wore bucktails, "which shows they are for freedom," but no other instances of the Whigs wearing symbols of their party were found. —*Moravian Records,* II, 904. The term "Bucktail" became common later, especially in New York, where it was used to refer to a member of the Tammany Society.—J. K. Paulding wrote a play called *Bucktails, or Americans Abroad.* A variant, "Buckskin," was also used.—*The Address of Liberty, to the Buckskins of Pennsylvania,* Library Company of Philadelphia, Broadsides.

was nothing like the French Marseillaise or the American "There" of the World War. Many tried to compose war songs no Julia Ward Howe appeared—not one. War songs did not appear, of course, until 1775, but before that there were attempts to put in song the basic ideas behind American resistance. The model for some of the best was David Garrick's "Hearts of Oak," a sailor's song with a real swing. In 1766 a nameless poet Americanized the words and started a series of poems set to this tune. The last stanza is by far the best of the seven:

"With Loyalty, LIBERTY let us entwine,
Our blood shall for both, flow as free as our wine.
Let us set an example, what all men should be,
And a toast give the world, *Here's to those* [who]
  dare to be free.
  Hearts of oak are we still;
  For we're sons of those men
  Who always are ready—
  Steady, boys, steady—
To fight for their freedom again and again."[54]

On the repeal of the Stamp Act another was written to the same tune; but John Dickinson curiously enough wrote the words that had the greatest appeal and the longest life. His "American Liberty Song" was composed in 1768 while he was writing the "Farmer's Letters." He sent it to James Otis for approval, and Otis had it printed in the *Boston Gazette* for July 18, 1768. The ten stanzas summed up more completely than any of the other songs the common elements of contemporary propaganda—slavery or freedom, the sufferings of the first settlers in defense of liberty, the penalties of submission, the necessity for union, and the rewards of victory. A few of the stanzas will show how these ideas were developed:

"Come join hand in hand, brave Americans all,
And rouse your bold hearts at fair Liberty's call;

[54] *Boston Post-Boy & Advertiser*, Apr. 14, 1766; Hist. Soc. Pa., Broadsides, I, 121. The other, called *A New Song*, was probably nothing more than a poem; it carried out identically the same ideas expressed in the demonstrations against the Act:
  "A bumper ye Sons of Liberty all,
  Let's drink and let's pray, ye great and ye small,
  May the *gout* and the *stone* and whatev'r ye will,
  Leave the GOOD patriot PITT, and take root in Gr.nv.ll."
  —Amer. Antiq. Soc., Broadsides.

No tyrannous acts shall suppress your just claim,
Or stain with dishonor America's name.
(Chorus:) In freedom we're born, and in freedom we'll live;
Our purses are ready,—
Steady, friends, steady,—
Not as slaves, but as freemen, our money we'll give!

.   .   .   .

"Our worthy forefathers—let's give them a cheer—
To climates unknown did courageously steer;
Thro' oceans to deserts for freedom they came
And dying bequeath'd us their freedom and fame.
In freedom, etc.

.   .   .   .

"How sweet are the labors that freemen endure,
That they shall enjoy all the profit secure;
No more such sweet labors Americans know,
If Britons shall reap what Americans sow.
In freedom, etc.

.   .   .   .

"Swarms of placemen and pensioners soon will appear,
Like locusts deforming the charms of the year;
Suns vainly will rise, showers vainly descend,
If we are to drudge for what others shall spend.
In freedom, etc."[55]

This song, reprinted in many newspapers, quickly became one of
the most popular of the day. It was the inspiration for many imitations. One of these written in Boston, called "A New Liberty Song,"
was addressed to the Sons of Liberty and particularly to the "illustrious, glorious and never to be Forgotten *Ninety-Two* of *Boston*":

"Come jolly Sons of LIBERTY—
Come ALL with Hearts UNITED
Our Motto is "WE DARE BE FREE,"
Not easily affrighted!
Oppression's Band we must subdue,
Now is the time or never.

[55] In full in Frank Moore, *Illustrated Ballad History of the American Revolution, 1763-
1783*, pp. 20 f. See also Tyler, *Literary History*, I, 240 f. A broadside of it is listed
in Evans, *Amer. Biblio.* No. 10,880. Maurice Hewlings of Virginia wrote another, called
"American Hearts of Oak," in 1775.—Tyler, *Literary History*, II, 169.

> Let each man PROVE this motto true,
> And SLAVERY from him sever."[56]

There were other Liberty Songs but none that had the popularity of the original. Joseph Warren, according to his biographer,
Frothingham, wrote one to the tune of the "British Grenadiers," the
last stanza of which expressed the current belief that America, the
land of freedom, would rule the world:

> "The land where Freedom reigns shall still be master of the main,
>   In giving laws and freedom to subject France and Spain;
>   And all the isles o'er ocean spread shall tremble and obey
>   The prince who rules by Freedom's laws in North America."[57]

Two other propagandists of the Revolution also attempted songs,
Thomas Paine and Benjamin Franklin. Paine's, to the tune "The
Gods of the Greeks," was called "The Liberty Tree." The last
stanza was unique in that it openly blamed the King for the troubles;
it was a definite forecast of *Common Sense,* which did not appear
until some time later:

> "But hear, O ye swains ('tis a tale most profane)
>   How all the tyrannical powers,
>   Kings, Commons and Lords, are uniting amain,
>   To cut down this guardian of ours;
>   From the east to the west, blow the trumpet to arms,
>   Thro' the land let the sound of it flee,
>   Let the far and the near—all unite with a cheer,
>   In defence of our *Liberty Tree.*"[58]

The one by Franklin, called "The King's own Regulars, and
Their Triumph over the Irregulars; a New Song, to the Tune of
'An Old Courtier of the Queen's, and the Queen's Old Courtier'"
was less of a song than a chant as we have already seen.

Two war songs frequently met with in the press of the day may
well close this discussion of heroics in poetry. One, simply entitled
"A Song," was written to the tune "The Echoing Horn":

---

[56] Mass. Hist. Soc., Broadsides, 1768.

[57] *Life of Joseph Warren,* p. 405. Two were printed on a broadside headed "Two
Favorite Songs."—Mass. Hist. Soc., Broadsides, 1776. Another, written in 1770, was called
"A New Massachusetts Liberty Song."

[58] *Pa. Evening Post,* Sept. 16, 1775.

"Hark! 'tis Freedom that Calls, come patriots awake!
　　To arms, my brave boys, and away:
'Tis Honour, 'tis Virtue, 'tis Liberty calls,
　　And upbraids the too tedius delay.
What pleasure we find in pursuing our foes;
　　Thro' blood and thro' carnage we'll fly;
Then follow, we'll soon overtake them, huzza!
　　The tyrants are seized on, they die."[59]

The other, "The Pennsylvania Song" was inappropriately set to an old tune "I winna marry ony Lad but Sandy O'er the Lea"; it is a good one to stop on:

"We are the troop that ne'er will stoop
　　　　To wretched slavery,
Nor shall our seed by our base deed
　　　　Despisèd vassals be!
Freedom we will bequeathe to them,
　　　　Or we will bravely die;
Our greatest foe ere long shall know
　　　　How much did Sandwich lie.
　　　　　　(Chorus:) And all the world shall know,
　　　　　　　　　　Americans are free;
　　　　　　　　　　Nor slaves nor cowards we will prove—
　　　　　　　　　　Great Britain soon shall see.

.　　.　　.　　.　　.　　.　　.　　.

"What! Can those British Tyrants think
　　　　Our Fathers cross'd the main;
And savage Foes and Dangers met,
　　　　To be enslav'd by them?
If so, they are mistaken,
　　　　For we will rather die;
And since they have become our Foes,
　　　　Their Forces we defy.
　　　　　　　　And all the world shall know, etc."[60]

PLAYS

Dramatic presentations of the propaganda themes were even less successful than the songs and much rarer. Plays were written but

[59] *N. H. Gazette*, May 26, 1775.
[60] *Ibid.*, Sept. 12, 1775. The entire poem is in Moore, *Ballad History of the Revolution*, pp. 90 f.

not played; there was no presentation during this period of a play for propaganda purposes. David Douglass managed a troup of players called the American Company, which put on shows in New York, Philadelphia, and Boston, but from 1763 to 1775 its repertoire did not include a single play that treated the dispute with England. In the sporadic intervals when economy and frugality were being urged, plays were definitely frowned upon. The eighth resolution of the Continental Association, adopted on October 20, 1774, bound the signers to "discountenance and discourage every species of extravagance and dissipation, especially all horse-racing, and all kinds of gaming, cock-fighting, exhibitions of shews, plays, and other expensive diversions and entertainments," and there is every reason to think that this was strictly adhered to. Douglass sailed with his troup for the West Indies on February 2, 1775.[61] Even before 1774, however, there had been opposition to plays. The Sons of Liberty in New York tore up handbills advertising plays and broke up one play during the second act.

The plays which were written, therefore, really constituted written appeals. Mrs. Mercy Otis Warren, sister of James Otis and wife of James Warren, wrote two plays. The first, called the *Adulateur*, dealt with the events in Massachusetts from 1770 to 1773, and the second, *The Group*, was a satire on the leading Tory figures of Massachusetts in 1775. John Adams had urged her to write a satirical piece on the tea episode, writing to her husband, "I wish to see a late glorious event celebrated by a certain poetical pen which has no equal that I know of in this country,"[62] but *The Group*, which followed about a year later, attacked English policy in its entirety.

[61] A. H. Quinn, *A History of the American Drama from its Beginnings to the Civil War*, has a good chapter on the drama of the period. A list of plays is printed in the back.
[62] *Works of John Adams*, IX, 335. There is no evidence that these plays were ever staged.

XI

PUBLIC ADDRESSES AND PULPIT ORATORY

THE MOST important forms of oral propaganda were public addresses and sermons. Naturally enough, little remains of what must have been stirring revolutionary speeches. Here and there hints may be found which give an insight into this phase of the leaders' work, but we can only guess at what Ebenezer Mackintosh said to his followers on the eve of a demonstration against the stamp distributors, or what Samuel Adams said to turn the temper of a town meeting. We hear of wild and inflammatory speeches, of violent harangues to raise a mob, of inspiring appeals for resistance against the encroachments of British tyranny, but of these impromptu efforts only fragments remain. There was rarely a planned demonstration which did not include a speech by a leading Whig, but most of these were never printed.

It must be remembered, however, that the resolutions adopted in town meeting and the circular letters received by the committees of correspondence were always publicly read.[1] Grand jury presentments and charges were also media for oral propaganda. William Henry Drayton, James Iredell, Thomas McKean, and others used their position as judges to charge their juries on the state of the dispute with Great Britain. In none of these charges did they confine themselves to the legal argument; rather the principal justification given was the depravity and cruelty of the British government and the injustice as well as the illegality of imposing taxes on America.[2]

The public addresses of which we have record were carefully prepared for a set occasion and were subsequently printed. In the hundreds of extant pamphlets are the remains of many fine revolutionary appeals.

PUBLIC ADDRESSES

An excellent illustration of the type of speech made to the laboring classes is one delivered in Boston on February 14, 1766, to

[1] The town of Marblehead ordered the town clerk to read at each annual meeting the Boston statement "The State of Rights of the Colonies."—Roads, *Marblehead*, p. 90.

[2] One of Drayton's charges may be found in Drayton, *Memoirs*, II, 259-274, and one of Iredell's in McRee, *Life and Correspondence of James Iredell*, I, 382 ff. The presentment of a Pennsylvania grand jury is in *Pa. Journal*, Sept. 27, 1770.

the Sons of Liberty. The speaker, using the analogy adopted on August 14, 1765, compared Bute to the seven-headed beast mentioned in the thirteenth chapter of Revelation and Grenville to the second mentioned further on;[3] the latter brought forth the Stamp Act, "that mark of slavery, the perfection and sum total of all his wickedness." He continued:

> "He has ordained that none amongst us shall buy or sell a piece of land, except his mark be put upon the deed, and when it is delivered, the hands of both buyer and seller must infallibly become branded with the odious impression: I beseech you then to beware as good Christians and lovers of your country, lest by touching any paper with this impression, you receive the mark of the *beast*, and become infamous in your country throughout all generations."

The worst enemy of America, and the only advocate of submission, he said, was the merchant who thought more of his profit than of his country's honor and would submit in order to have the trade with the West Indies opened: "A curse light on his selfish policy; if there is a wretch crawling upon the soil of *North-America*, who can approve of this advice, it is no matter how soon he [is] put six foot below the surface of it." In this game of imperial relations, he explained, the Americans were but raw innocents pitted against the shrewdest sharpsters—the statesmen and the merchants; their only salvation was to walk out, to leave the game entirely. The speaker explained his metaphor simply by saying that home industry alone could save the people—a warning to the extravagant and a note of hope to the unemployed: "Whatever you may think, this conduct, and no other, can bring about our deliverance; as long as our backs are clothed from *Great-Britain*, they will lay what burthens upon them they please;—industry is our best barrier against slavery; we have lived long enough for the profit of others, and it is high time that we begin to live for ourselves."[4]

[3] "And I stood upon the sand of the sea, and saw a beast rise up out of the sea, having seven heads and ten horns, and upon his horns ten crowns, and upon his heads the name of blasphemy."—Rev. 13:1. "And I beheld another beast coming up out of the earth; and he had two horns like a lamb, and he spake as a dragon."—Rev. 13:11. The speech was published in pamphlet form under the title *A Discourse, Addressed to the Sons of Liberty, At a Solemn Assembly, near Liberty-Tree, in BOSTON, February 14, 1766.*

[4] Few of the published speeches were so forthright. Silas Downer's speech at the dedication of the Liberty Tree in Providence on July 25, 1768, for example, was the usual

Another address, delivered ten years later to an entirely different group and under entirely different conditions, was equally well adapted to the task in hand, the justification of independence. This speech was made at the State House in Philadelphia, and is closely modeled upon Tom Paine's *Common Sense*. The speaker began, as did Paine, with an attack on the monarchy: "We have explored the temple of Royalty, and found that the Idol we have bow'd down to has Eyes which see not, Ears that hear not our Prayers, and a heart like the nether Mill-Stone." Like Paine he emphasized the cruelty and depravity of the English, finding in what English statesmen had done something that affected every section of the country; in one brief paragraph he united in fear and hatred the easterner, the frontiersman, the southerner, and the Protestant:

"Countrymen! the Men who now invite you to surrender your rights into their hands are *the Men* who have let loose the merciless Savages to riot in the Blood of their Brethren— who have dared to establish Popery Triumphant in our Land; who have taught treachery to your *Slaves*, and courted them to assassinate your wives and children."

And he closed, as did Paine, with a statement of the advantages of independence and the fact that America had been formed to be free: "Nature points the path, and our Enemies have obliged us to pursue it."[5]

The most important series of addresses in published form today were those prepared for the anniversaries of the Boston Massacre. Sam Adams said of these orations, "This Institution in a great Measure answers the Design of it, which is, to preserve in the Minds of the People a lively Sense of the Danger of standing Armies." The town of Boston added a further design: to impress upon the people "the necessity of such noble Exertions in all future times as the Inhabitants of the Town then made, whereby the Conspirators against the Publick Liberty may still be frustrated."[6] These annual orations administered fuel to the fire of liberty, wrote Ramsay later, "and kept it burning with an incessant flame."[7]

appeal to stand fast in the defense of rights confirmed by charter and the English constitution.

[5] *An Oration Delivered at the State House, Philadelphia, 1776.*

[6] *Writings of Sam Adams,* II, 104; *Boston Town Records, 1770-1777,* p. 48.

[7] *History of the Revolution,* I, 91.

James Lovell was the first of the anniversary orators, speaking in 1771; he developed a straightforward legal argument to show that no obedience was due Parliament and pleaded at the close for peaceful methods of resistance. Joseph Warren, the second orator, was much more restrained than he was three years later, but still made a good deal of the bloodstained streets, dying children, and mistreated women. Benjamin Church in 1773 followed almost identically the same course, and Hancock in 1774, reading a speech said to have been written by Samuel Cooper, abandoned wholly the constitutional argument and dealt entirely with the emotional aspects of the massacre.

Of all delivered on those days, the most emotional was Joseph Warren's on the anniversary in 1775. His temper was so well known that even John Adams professed uneasiness for the result. The day before the oration he wrote Samuel Savage, "Peoples expectations are alive for the Oration and Exhibition next Monday; I own myself the Companion of fear and anxiety, and *sincerely wish* the day and evening happily over—I know the undaunted spirit and fire which animates our friend and fear some expression that's *high seasoned* may draw on him more malice and influence some dirty tool to stir up to revenge and bloodshed—"[8] The day went off fairly well, however, in spite of these fears. The mob applauded while the "people of understanding groaned." When he mentioned for the first time the words, "the Bloody Massacre," someone shouted "Oh fie!" and the gallery, thinking there was a fire, jumped out of the windows and ran into a parading regiment of soldiers, whose drums and fifes made it seem to those inside that another massacre was about to be perpetrated.[9]

The speech itself was all that could have been expected. Starting with the proposition, "That personal freedom is the natural right of every man and that property, or an exclusive right to dispose of what he has honestly acquired by his own labor, necessarily arises therefrom, are truths which common sense has placed beyond the reach of contradiction," he then examined the early history of Massachusetts to discover wherein, if possible, England acquired any right to dispose of American property. Finding none, he concluded that the present assumption was a gross violation of the rights of the

[8] Savage Papers, II, 154.   [9] *N. Y. Gazetteer*, Mar. 16, 1775.

colonists, the project of an avaricious minister of state, not of the benign George III. When troops were sent to enforce laws "which placemen and pensioners were found unable to support," all the elements of the fatal tragedy of March 5, 1770, were gathered. The stage is now set, he continued, for just such another scene. Troops fill the streets and ships the harbor, but these cannot intimidate; you need not fear the arm of Britain, you too have fought, and if the only way to safety is through fields of blood, you will not hesitate until tyranny be trodden under foot:

> "Having redeemed your country, and secured the blessing to future generations, *who*, fired by your example, shall emulate your virtues, and learn from *you* the heavenly art of making millions happy; with heart-felt joy—with transports all your own, YOU CRY, THE GLORIOUS WORK IS DONE. Then drop the mantle to some young ELISHA, and take your seats with kindred spirits in your native skies."

In the same temper and with the same arguments, Peter Thatcher urged his hearers in 1776 to the same end. He added the nineteenth of April to the fifth of March, and Warren and Montgomery to the victims of the Boston Massacre, and made an even stronger plea for independence. Possessed of such strength that England could never defeat her, America could not be false to her God-given trust of freedom:

> "Freedom is offered to us, she invites us to accept her blessings; driven from the other regions of the globe, she wishes to find an asylum in the wilds of America; with open arms let us receive the persecuted fair . . . and when the earthly scene shall be closing with us, let us expire with this prayer upon our quivering lips, O GOD LET AMERICA BE FREE."[10]

---

[10] These orations may be conveniently found in Niles, *Principles and Acts of the Revolution*, pp. 1-59. Other towns in New England commemorated the day occasionally. Braintree voted in 1772, with the massacre in mind, that "an oration relative to the civil & religious rights & privileges of the People" be delivered at the annual town meeting. —*Records*, p. 435. Oliver Noble delivered an oration on the fifth of March, 1775, in the course of which he said: "O Americans! awake, arise, and stand for your life. You have a grant to do so, against all that *assault* you, from the King of Heaven; from NATURE and from NATURE'S GOD. To *repel* armed force, by force of the same kind, is lawful by Heaven's decree . . . STANDING ARMIES MUST BE REMOVED, or they will reduce us to a State of Slavery worse than DEATH."—*A Discourse delivered at Newbury-port*, p. 28.

Other orations of which we have record were much of the same type—they emphasized, that is, the unusual and the brutal in England's treatment of the colonies. Thomas McKean and Thomas Mifflin, both of Pennsylvania, were primarily speakers rather than writers, and both made many speeches after the passage of the Boston Port Act. McKean made two speeches in Delaware which are said to have had marked effect in stimulating the people. The first was at Newcastle, June 29, 1774, at a meeting called by McKean himself to consider methods of relieving Boston, and the second was at Lewestown, now Lewes, in July, when it had become clear that Sussex County was definitely holding back. This speech was one of the really fine efforts of McKean's career. He followed the same method that Adams had followed in planning the documents first sent out by the Boston committee of correspondence. He first listed the rights of the colonists and then under twenty-seven heads listed the violations of those rights. The first grievances he listed were those which concerned manufacturing, not commerce, as was common in New England. The first three listed were restraint of iron manufacturing, restraint of the hat industry, and restraint of wool manufacturing by prohibiting farmers from carrying their own wool, even across a ferry.[11]

Leaders in two colonies—North and South Carolina—made unusual effort to win over doubtful areas by planned speaking tours. North Carolina Whigs were much disturbed by the indifference and actual hostility in several of the western counties. As we have already seen, Joseph Hewes had prevailed on the Presbyterian synod in Philadelphia to write an open letter to the ministers and congregations of the church in North Carolina. He followed this up by inducing the Continental Congress to adopt a resolution on November 28, 1775, authorizing the appointment of two men at forty dollars a month to go among the Regulators and Scots Highlanders to inform them of the nature of the dispute with England and the "rectitude of those who advocate the American side of the question." Hewes selected on the recommendation of George Duffield two men, both ministers, the Reverend Elihu Spencer and the Reverend Alexander McWhorter, and drafted a letter of instructions to them:

[11] Printed in *Pa. Journal*, Aug. 3, 1774. See also William Rawle, "A Sketch of the Life of Thomas Mifflin," *Memoirs*, Hist. Soc. Penn., Vol. II, pt. 2, pp. 107-126. Perez Morton's *An Oration on Joseph Warren* was the usual type of emotional appeal.

"We know that the education of most of these men have been religious, that they look to their Spiritual pastors with great respect and that truths from their mouths come with redoubled influence upon their minds, could one or more of this [sect?] be prevailed upon to exert his good offices to give them information and stimulate them to their duty the most beneficial consequence would result."[12]

What they accomplished does not appear.

Hewes may have got the idea for this tour from an earlier attempt made by the South Carolina council of safety. On July 3, 1775, the council appointed George Wagner and Felix Long "to take a Journey among the German settlers in the *Back Country*, in order to explain to them the present situation of American affairs." They asked that Herman Nufer be allowed to accompany them, but the expedition was most unsuccessful and soon returned. On July 23 two much more influential men were appointed—William Henry Drayton and the Reverend William Tennent. Three days later the Baptist preacher Oliver Hart, Colonel Richard Richardson, and Joseph Kershaw were asked to join the party.[13] Drayton and Tennent planned the tour and did most of the speaking during this prolonged and systematic effort to win converts.

The primary purpose of the trip was to get as many as possible to sign an agreement to support the cause of America. The methods of the five men demonstrate all the forms of pressure short of violence that can be brought to bear in a community. The region they covered was between the Broad and the Saluda, where there were large numbers of Irish and German settlers who were out of sympathy with the activities of the eastern leaders.

There was so much disaffection that it was even difficult to get an audience together. At the first meeting they called not a German appeared, for they had all been told that they would lose their lands if they aided the Whigs. Drayton and Tennent then engaged a

[12] This letter, dated Dec. 8, 1775, is in Papers of Samuel Johnston. The resolution of congress is in *Journals*, III, 438. See also Hewes to Johnston, Jan. 4, Jan. 6, 1776, in Burnett, *Letters of Members of Cont. Cong.*, I, 296, 300 f. Spencer and McWhorter were admirable choices because they had been sent by their church in 1764 to organize churches in North Carolina.—Caruthers, *Caldwell*, p. 96.

[13] *Journal of the Council of Safety of the Province of South Carolina, 1775*, S. C. Hist. Soc., *Collections*, II, 31, 57, 64. See also McCrady, *History of S. C. in Revolution, 1775-1780*, p. 41; and Drayton, *Memoirs*, I, 324.

German minister to call a meeting. He was to preach but was to give one of the other two a chance to say something. At another place where they had trouble getting a hearing, they induced the leader of a local militia company to call it together. Those who failed to appear were to be ousted from the company. Barbecues were even more successful in getting people together.

Gathering audiences by such means, Drayton and Tennent harangued them on the nature of the disputes with England, the justice of the American cause, and their duty to their country, and tried to awaken their honor "by contrasting their personal value and importance against the importance of the British troops." They showed the people how much better off they were than the British and reassured them that no lands would be lost by joining the Whigs. They offered to give gold for the continental currency, which the people wisely distrusted. They also declared that no nonsubscriber could trade at the store on the Congaree or at any in Charleston, and issued orders that no miller who had signed the agreement could grind corn for any nonsubscriber. This was a shock to the farmers, but still they remained unconvinced.

After three weeks of traveling, the party of propagandists found that instead of quieting the people and winning converts, they were arousing active hostility. Colonel Thomas Fletchall, Patrick and Robert Cunningham, and Moses Kirkland were steadily undermining their work. These men followed Drayton and Tennent and cleverly killed the effect of their speeches with pro-British propaganda. They distributed copies of Dalrymple's *Rights of Great Britain Asserted*, and actually read it aloud at meetings that Drayton had called. Tennent, who had split off for a time from the rest of the party to make a tour through the Irish settlements north of the Broad, reported that Gage's account of the battle of Lexington "rages through the district and is greedily read."

The people had become so hostile by the end of August, 1775, that an actual uprising was feared, and Drayton urged the council of safety to send military assistance. The council decided against military action, and Drayton and Tennent finally signed a treaty with Thomas Fletchall on September 16, 1775. This treaty simply stated that the people in the region did not intend to show unfriendliness to the Whig cause by refusing to sign the agreement—

they wished simply to live in peace. They engaged not to assist the British troops and to deliver to the council of safety any person who reflected upon, condemned, or opposed the provincial congress. Drayton pledged in return for the council of safety and the general committee in Charleston that any associator who molested any non-associator would be punished. To this treaty the Cunninghams refused to agree, and in 1776 there was an actual military invasion of the region.[14]

SERMONS

The heavy burden of speech-making was carried by the preachers. The two men sent in to the North Carolina back country and two of five who went on the South Carolina expedition were preachers. As Hewes said, people looked to their "Spiritual pastors with great respect and . . . truths from their mouths come with redoubled influence upon their minds." The great contribution the ministers could make, of course, was the application of Christian principles to the problems of the present. The preachers were, moreover, the historians and keepers of the Puritan tradition, especially in New England; who better than they could relate the problems of the present to the heroic past of America? From every point of view, sermons or addresses by ministers were admirable vehicles of propaganda.

The first public appearances of ministers in any number were in the celebrations which followed the repeal of the Stamp Act. The committees which arranged the celebrations in each locality almost invariably asked one of the preachers to deliver an address. Throughout the country during May and June, 1766, preachers gloried in the triumphant resistance to "slavery and her ten thousand chains," a resistance condoned, nay demanded by Scripture. Jonathan Mayhew, preaching on the text, "Our Soul is escaped as a bird from the snare of the fowlers" prematurely congratulated the people on the glorious decision of the British government "whereby these colonies are emancipated from a slavish, inglorious bondage; are reinstated in the enjoyment of their ancient rights and privileges, and a foundation is laid for lasting harmony between Great Britain and them."[15]

---

[14] McCrady, *History of S. C. in Revolution, 1775-1780*, p. 51.

[15] *The Snare Broken*, p. 2. Connecticut appointed a fast day for December, 1765, and Stephen Johnson preached a sermon, published under the title *Some Important Observations*.

One preacher, the Reverend Mr. Emerson, saw in the defeat of the Act sure proof that Americans were born to be free; in America's triumph was a lesson for all future generations, a lesson which parents should pass on to their children. Tell them, he said, of the great and wondrous things of the past, of the sufferings of their forefathers in defense of their liberties, and *"aggravate* to them the many sufferings which they endured before they found a shelter from the storm in these ends of the earth."[16]

John Adams, always concerned about his pastor in Braintree, got a report of his sermon on this occasion; it used the text, "But as for you, ye thought evil against me; but God meant it unto good, to bring to pass, as it is this day, to save much people alive." "America is Joseph," wrote Adams in his diary, "the King, Lords, and Commons, Joseph's father and brethren. Our forefathers sold into Egypt, that is, persecuted into America, &c. Wibird shone, they say."[17] The Reverend Mr. Davis of Norfolk, requested by the committee which arranged the celebration to preach a sermon on the repeal, chose as his text a verse from Proverbs which aptly summed up the prevailing attitude that corrupt counsel had misled the King: "Take away the wicked from behind the king, and his throne shall be established in righteousness."[18]

During the next few years the clergy in the North were particularly concerned about the establishment of an American episcopate, while the merchants were more disturbed about the new trade legislation. As a result, the sermons of the period from 1767 to 1774 made a joint appeal for resistance to both civil and religious tyranny. A striking example is the Reverend Mr. Holly's sermon, entitled "GOD Brings about his Holy and Wise Purposes," preached in Suffield the Sunday after the news arrived of the destruction of the tea in Boston. He was unconcerned by the violation of property

---

He considered the Stamp Act under four heads: the enslavement of a free people is a great iniquity in the sight of God; Pharaoh's oppression of the Israelites is an example; the good influence this oppression had on them should be an example to Americans; God will deliver America as He delivered Israel. Most of the published sermons were in thanksgiving for the repeal.

[16] Joseph Emerson, *A Thanksgiving Sermon on the Repeal of the Act,* p. 30. See also William Patten, *A Discourse . . . for the Repeal of the STAMP ACT,* p. 19: "Since we are by nature free, and since by the agreement of political society, we are invested with liberty, we should be indeed unpardonable, if through our own default, we should become entangled with a yoke of bondage."

[17] *Works of John Adams,* II, 197.   [18] *Va. Gazette* (Purdie), June 6, 1766.

rights in the Tea Party but was deeply agitated by the threat to religion if civil encroachments were not prevented. If Great Britain were successful in binding the colonies in secular affairs, "then perhaps our religious privileges and liberties will be called for next, and in lieu thereof Popery enjoin'd."

> "But wo to the colonies, wo to New-England, if this should ever come to pass! and who can say we are out of danger. Not only to have temporal property at the disposal of arbitrary power, but conscience bound by Popish chains, which, when thoroughly fastened upon us, away must go our bibles, and in lieu thereof, we must have imposed upon us, the superstitions and damnable heresies and idolatries of the church of Rome. Then we must pray to the Virgin Mary, worship images, believe the doctrine of Purgatory, and the Pope's infallibility, and such like. And last of all, the deepest plot of hell and Rome, the holy inquisition, must guard the Catholic faith of the Church of Rome, and bind us thereto with all its terrors and cruelty."[19]

After the Boston Massacre the pulpits "rang their Chimes upon blood Guiltiness," as Peter Oliver put it, and sermons were preached from the text, "The voice of thy brother's blood cryeth unto me from the ground."[20] It was after the Boston Port Act had gone into effect, however, that the finest propaganda efforts of the ministry were exerted. At no other time in the entire period from 1763 to 1783 were the ministers in greater demand for public addresses and at no other time did they have a greater effect. The published sermons show that in New England ministers disseminated revolutionary propaganda on such special occasions as the day the Boston Port Act was to go into effect, on significant anniversaries, on fast and election days in the spring and thanksgiving days in the fall, on muster days, and on the days of humiliation and prayer. Elsewhere, as we have seen, ministers normally took a less active part in political affairs, and the published sermons were delivered almost entirely on special days of fasting, humiliation, and prayer. The sermons on these occasions were particularly important as propaganda, however, because they were outside the usual course of events, they came at

---

[19] Pp. 21 f.

[20] The Origin & Progress of the American Rebellion, p. 128. John Lathrop preached from this text on the Sunday after the Massacre, and the sermon was printed in Boston and London and reprinted in 1771.

a time of unusual gravity, many people participated, and the people were in a highly suggestive state. Particularly apt texts and a striking statement of basic principles characterized nearly all of these sermons.

William Gordon, for example, using the text, "It is of the Lord's mercies that we are not consumed, because his compassions fail not," recounted the glorious mercies of God in saving the people of New England from destruction and argued from them that, with all the other advantages America possessed, defeat was impossible; not even the horrors of war could prevent the fulfillment of God's promise to it:

> "And how will the surviving inhabitants and their posterity, together with the refugees who have fled from oppression and hardships whether civil or sacred, to our American sanctuary, daily give thanks to the Sovereign of the universe that this general asylum was not consumed! How oft will they, with raptures, think upon that noble exertion of courage that prevented it, celebrate the praises of those that led and suffered in the common cause, and with glowing hearts bless that God who owned the goodness of it, and at length crowned it with success!"[21]

When to these sure promises of God's support there was added the cruelty and depravity of the oppressors, who could resist the sword in defense of his country? Such thoughts as these prompted one of the finest examples of war propaganda delivered by a minister, the sermon by the Reverend William Stearns on the battle of Lexington and Concord.

This sermon throughout was an attack on the depravity of the British troops stationed in Boston, who were to blame for all that had happened. It closed with a violent appeal to do God's work in clearing the land of these minions of tyranny:

[21] *Religious . . . Liberty, A Discourse, Dec. 15, 1774.* Gordon preached two sermons, one in the morning and one in the afternoon. This is the afternoon sermon. Both were published. Dr. Samuel Langdon took an unusually apposite text in his sermon delivered to the Massachusetts assembly in 1775: "And I will restore thy judges as at the first, and thy counsellors as at the beginning: afterward thou shalt be called, The city of righteousness, the faithful city." Isaiah 1:26. He showed that if the people remained faithful to God, He would remain faithful to them. Dr. Lathrop preached in Springfield on the news of the Boston Port Act. He used the text "Why should ye be stricken any more? ye will revolt more and more: the whole head is sick, and the whole heart faint." Isaiah 1:5.—Boston Committee Records, p. 886.

"We trust that all, whose circumstances will admit of it, will go—that none such will refuse to enlist in defence of his country. When God, in his providence, calls to take the sword; if any refuse to obey, Heaven's dread artillery is levelled against him, as you may see . . . CURSED BE HE THAT KEEPETH BACK HIS SWORD FROM BLOOD; cursed is the sneaking coward who neglects the sinking state, when called to its defence—O then, flee this dire curse—let America's valorous sons put on the harness, nor take it off till peace shall be to Israel."[22]

Unlike the New England ministry, the clergymen of other sections did not have as many opportunities for making public appeals, nor did they have the actual presence of troops and the immediate threat of war as did those in Massachusetts in 1774. Days of fasting and prayer were appointed by civil leaders to give them an opportunity to make a public appeal and the most effective pulpit propaganda came from the sermons on these fast days.

George Duffield, Presbyterian New Light of Philadelphia, preached from the text "The wilderness and the solitary place shall be glad for them; and the desert shall rejoice, and blossom as a rose." America was the desert, which under God's care would soon rejoice and blossom, for "Behold, your God will come with vengeance, even God with a recompense; he will come and save you."[23] Even the Episcopalian William Smith in a sermon on June 23, 1775, made a long comparison between the plight of the oppressed Israelites and the oppressed Americans, concluding, with the pacifists in mind, "A continued submission to violence is no tenet of our church. . . . The doctrine of absolute non-resistance has been fully exploded among every virtuous people."[24] Silas Deane reported to his wife that afternoon, "This is stolen from Sunday, after hearing

[22] Stearns, *A View of the Controversy Subsisting between Great Britain and the American Colonies,* p. 31. The artillery company sermons after the battle were also excellent war propaganda, as were those preached to the new companies as they took the field. See particularly Webster, *Rabshakeh's Proposals Considered,* preached to new soldiers just before the outbreak of hostilities, in which he told them that war was inevitable. The text "Cursed be he that keepeth back his sword from blood" was a favorite one with ministers preaching to artillery companies. Samuel Davies had used it during the French and Indian War.

[23] *Familiar Letters of John Adams,* p. 35.

[24] Pp. 20 f. See also Joseph Montgomery, *A Sermon, Preached . . . The 20th of July 1775,* preached at Christiana Bridge, Newcastle County, Delaware.

two elegant war sermons."[25] Jacob Duché was likewise constrained to preach on the occasion of a public fast, and he, like so many others, took the familiar text from Galatians, which best summarized the scriptural authority for resistance to oppression: "Stand fast therefore in the liberty wherewith Christ hath made us free, and be not entangled again in the yoke of bondage." But Duché had little heart for his task, and the result was but a poor affair.

Dr. Archibald Laidlie of New York took the same text and made a splendid revolutionary appeal.[26] In another New York sermon,[27] the minister made modern application of the old Biblical story of King Ahasuerus and Haman, with particular emphasis upon Haman's punishment for having falsely led the King by his advice: "There is a certain people scattered abroad and dispersed among the people in all the provinces of thy kingdom; and their laws are diverse from all people; neither keep they the king's laws: therefore it is not for the king's profit to suffer them. If it please the king, let it be written that they may be destroyed."[28] The improvement, as the application of the text was then called, is obvious.

The pulpit in the southern colonies was far less prominent in the development of revolutionary sentiment: "few or no pulpits resound, or are in a foam with politics," wrote a Tory in November, 1774.[29] This was hardly a fair judgment, however, for the Anglican ministers took active part when called upon, and increasingly after 1774 the southern ministry aided in stimulating the movement. The Reverend Paul Turquand of Charleston was asked to address the first meeting of the provincial congress, and Dr. Percy preached the sermon at the first public reading of the Declaration of Independence in Charleston. The Congregationalist William Tennent and the Baptist Oliver Hart were selected by the council of safety to accompany Drayton on his tour of the back country, and both preached frequently during the trip. David Caldwell in western North Carolina also spoke for the Whig cause after 1774; in

[25] *Deane Papers*, I, 77. Several ministers held services on request in Philadelphia the day the Port Act was to go into effect. Alison, Duffield, and Spront of the Presbytery preached suitable sermons, according to Christopher Marshall.—*Diary*, p. 6.

[26] *N. Y. Gazette and Weekly Mercury*, Dec. 4, 1775. Duché's sermon was called *The Duty of Standing Fast in our Spiritual and Temporal Liberties*.

[27] N. Y. *Journal*, Sept. 1, 1774.

[28] The story of Haman and Ahasuerus as told in the Book of Esther, Chap. 3, was easily applicable to the crisis.

[29] *Mass. Gazette, and Boston Weekly News-Letter, Supplement*, Nov. 10, 1774.

the spring of 1776 he delivered a sermon called "Sloth under Tribute," from the text in Proverbs, "The hand of the diligent shall bear rule; but the slothful shall live under tribute." Even at that late date, however, Caldwell was still doubtful about independence and preferred some form of compromise based upon parliamentary renunciation of the right of taxation.[30] Although actual sermons are not available, it seems clear that the influence of the southern church, where exerted, was actively in favor of the Whigs. Articulate loyalists were rare.

From this survey it is evident that the greatest use of visual, oral, and pictorial propaganda was made in New England, where the greatest opportunities for it existed, and that elsewhere it was largely limited to the seaboard area, and particularly to the port towns. Its greatest effect, therefore, was on the lower classes, especially the mechanic class in the cities. Within these limits the use of this medium was effective: although later years have developed to a high degree propaganda of this type, the improvement has come largely through increased opportunities for primary contacts. The Revolutionary propagandist was limited in his opportunities, and even failed in many cases to make full use of those he had, but his technique, especially in demonstrations and public addresses, was excellent.

[30] Caruthers, *Caldwell*, pp. 273 ff. McCrady, *S. C. under Royal Government*, pp. 450 ff.; Alexander Garden, *Anecdotes of the Revolutionary War, with Sketches of the Character of Distinguished Men* (Charleston, 1822), pp. 199 ff.

XII

PAMPHLETS AND BROADSIDES

WRITTEN propaganda both complements and supplements oral propaganda. It not only reinforces by repetition suggestions given in another form, but it reaches those untouched directly by oral appeals. The influence of a sermon or public address was more than doubled when printed in a pamphlet or newspaper. The written word, moreover, carries an authority of its own—people believe what they read.[1]

There were, of course, limitations to the use of written propaganda. Only about half the men and only one quarter of the women could read, and the reading public was of course much smaller than that. The propagandists were not greatly inhibited by the fear of libel trials. Such trials were still possible, of course, and Alexander McDougall was put in jail for printing an inflammatory broadside in December, 1770. Southern governors still exercised a close supervision over the press, but in the northern colonies the freedom of the press had been well established. Printers were reasonably free to print what they would, barring the publication of official material without permission, and even that was done on occasion. There was at least one press in every colony (except Delaware and New Jersey), and of these the Whig propagandists made excellent use, for they were even more fully aware of the power of the written than of the spoken word. Five vehicles of suggestion came from these presses—pamphlets, newspapers, broadsides, almanacs, and magazines.

The thousands of pamphlets extant attest the fact that it was the accepted medium on both sides of the Atlantic for the dissemination of ideas. The careful writer preferred its greater dignity, and the thoughtful reader preferred its greater length. The best thought of the day expressed itself in this form.

The pamphlet in the prerevolutionary period was vitally and peculiarly the medium through which was developed the solid

---

[1] Doob, *Propaganda*, Chaps. XVIII, XXI, has a discussion of the psychological aspects of written propaganda.

framework of constitutional thought. The function of the constitutional arguments in the development of public opinion was primarily to unify the thinking of the leaders; a detailed, often obtuse, political argument did not have a popular appeal. Although the Sons of Liberty publicly thanked Richard Bland for his pamphlet, *An Inquiry into the Rights of the British Colonies,* it is doubtful that they understood a word of it, for a more involved and inconsistent essay is hard to find. Perhaps they did understand that he was one of the first to proclaim the doctrine that America was united to England only through the Crown, and that therefore Parliament had no authority over the colonies.

The pamphlet, when used to develop the constitutional argument, appealed to the intellectual classes and was the best possible type of propaganda for that specific purpose. Samuel Adams and Benjamin Franklin, for instance, whose appeal was primarily to the average reading public, relied almost entirely upon the newspaper, whereas Oxenbridge Thacher, Stephen Hopkins, James Otis, James Wilson, Alexander Hamilton, Thomas Jefferson, and many others of the outstanding intellectuals published their more important contributions in pamphlets. The basic elements of American political thought of the revolutionary period appeared first in this form. Each step in the development of the constitutional argument was taken in the pamphlet.

Political pamphlets of the more serious type appeared in numbers in only two periods of the controversy with England. The first was during the agitation over the Grenville Acts, the second at the time of the Boston Port Act, and the writers of the two periods were entirely different.

The important arguments of the first period were set forth in pamphlets by Oxenbridge Thacher, Stephen Hopkins, Daniel Dulany, James Otis, Richard Bland, and John Dickinson. The contribution of the six consisted in showing first, that the acts were unjust and unreasonable, and second, that Parliament had no right to tax the colonies, which by the very nature of things could not be represented in the British Parliament.[2] These are among the most fa-

[2] Thacher, *The Sentiments of a British American,* 1764; Hopkins, *The Rights of the Colonies Examined,* 1765; Dulany, *Considerations on the Propriety of Imposing Taxes in the British Colonies,* 1765; Otis, *The Rights of the British Colonies Asserted and Proved. A Vindication of the British Colonies,* and others. Otis suggested the possibility of American

miliar pamphlets of the entire period, and their influence was immense. The arguments they used set the form of the debate with England for the next eight or nine years.

The Townshend Acts constituted no change in basic principle, for as Dickinson pointed out in his "Farmer's Letters," a tax was a tax, wherever laid. No further development of the constitutional argument was necessary to combat the acts; the legal principles set forth in the earlier period still covered the case. The pamphlets published between 1767 and 1770 were therefore primarily either emotional attacks on the British administration or popularizations of ideas already laid down.

Conditions had materially changed, however, by the middle of 1774, and Parliament had exercised authority not covered by pamphleteers of the earlier period. Nothing in the writings of Thacher, Hopkins, or Dulany could be used to combat the right of Parliament to close the port of Boston, to change the government of Massachusetts Bay, or to alter the methods of trial. Thacher had protested against the injustice but not the authority of Parliament. Hence a new position was necessary, another step must be taken. Thus it was that a new group of serious thinkers propounded the doctrine that Parliament had no legislative authority whatever over the colonies.

In anticipation of the meeting of the Continental Congress, several pamphlets were written which attacked in direct form the right of Parliament to legislate for the colonies. Thomas Jefferson, William Henry Drayton, Alexander Hamilton, and James Wilson all wrote able arguments against the authority of Parliament and even began to attack the King's authority. Drayton held that the King's prerogative power over America was not greater than over England, and Jefferson boldly asserted that "he is no more than the chief officer of the people, appointed by the laws, and circumscribed with definite powers, to assist in working the great machine of government erected for their use, and consequently subject to their superintendence."[3] This pamphlet was first written in the form of notes

---

representation in Parliament. Solid economic arguments opposing the wisdom rather than the legality of the trade acts were intended to influence English merchants. E.g., *An Essay on the Trade of the Northern Colonies*, 1764, and *Observations on Several Acts of Parliament, passed in the 4th, 6th, and 7th Years of his present Majesty's Reign*, Boston, 1769.

[3] *A Summary View of the Rights of British America.* Some others were: James Wilson, *Considerations on the Nature and the Extent of the Legislative Authority of the British Parliament*; Alexander Hamilton, *A Full Vindication of the Measures of Congress*, and

for the consideration of the Continental Congress, and when Peyton Randolph presented it in manuscript to the members, they were so impressed by it that they had it printed in a pamphlet.[4]

After the battle of Lexington and Concord no more of the substantial, reasoned arguments appeared in pamphlet form. Not a single pamphlet advancing the argument was printed until Paine's *Common Sense*, and that was far from a reasoned, legal argument. It was, in fact, the culmination of a long series of pamphlets which had popularized the thought of the logicians.

These popularizations ranged all the way from light, humorous satires to bitter invectives against the British administration. The principal method in all of these was attack rather than defense, and the attack in nearly every instance was directed against specific officials. The method, the style, and the content were totally different from those which dealt with the legal problems. The difference is perfectly seen in Otis' *Rights of the British Colonies Asserted and Proved* and in his last attack on Martin Howard, in which he referred to Howard and his friends as that "little dirty, drinking, drabbing, contaminated knot of thieves, beggars, and transports."[5]

The colonial governors were the subject of several of these pamphlet attacks. Benjamin Church vilified Governor Bernard in a pamphlet published in 1769, *An Address to a Provincial Bashaw. O Shame; where is thy blush?*, and two years later Bernard's successor, Thomas Hutchinson, was the object of *A Ministerial Catechise, Suitable to be Learned by all Modern Provincial Governors, Pensioners, Placemen, &c.*, which showed in glaring and distorted form his mistakes. Two others used parodies of the Old Testament to undermine the authority of Sir Henry Moore in New York and Thomas Gage in Massachusetts. They are almost identical in form. The first, called *Some Chapters of the Book of Chronicles of Isaac the Scribe, Written on his Passage from the Land of the Amerikites to the Island of the Albionites*, and published some time early in the 1770's,

---

The Farmer Refuted; William Henry Drayton, *A Letter from Freeman of South-Carolina to the Deputies of North-America.* N. Y. *Journal,* Sept. 21, 1774, noted a pamphlet by "Granville Sharp," *Truth Triumphant, in a Vindication of the Colonies from Subjection to a Foreign Legislation.*

[4] Several versions of this may be found in *Writings of Thomas Jefferson* (Ford, ed.) I, 421 ff.

[5] *Brief Remarks on the Defence of the Halifax Libel on the British-American Colonies,* p. 5.

praises the friends of America in England and condemns Moore out of hand. The second, *The First Book of American Chronicles,* was so popular that two Boston printers published it, and editions were separately printed in Philadelphia and Newport.[6] The pamphlet concerned itself almost entirely with Gage and the troops. Two passages will indicate the character of both the pamphlets. The ministers of state urged the King:

> "Now, therefore, make a decree that their harbours be blocked up, and ports shut, that their merchants may be broke, and their multitudes perish, that there may be no more the voice of merchandise heard in the land, that their ships that goeth upon the waters, may be sunk in the depths thereof, and their marines dwindle away to naught, that their cods and their oil may stink, and the whale, the great Leviathan, may be no more troubled, for that they have rebelled against thee."

The King took this advice and commanded Thomas, captain of the Gageites:

> "Choose thou the valiant men of Britain, by hundreds and by thousands, and get ye together the ships, even the ships of war, the terror of the nations round about, and make your way towards the coasts of the Americanites, the land of the Bostonians, that lieth on the other side of the sea westwards, and cut off [all their men] and utterly destroy all their cities with fire and with sword, for they have rebelled against me."

Entirely different, but still in the vein of humorous satire, was Francis Hopkinson's *A Pretty Story, by Peter Grievous, an allegory of the Old Farm and the New Farm.* It recounted the trials of the colonists for the past ten years in such fashion that the acts of Parliament were made ridiculous and absurd.

The sprightly if malicious writings of Charles Lee and the plays of Mercy Warren made their principal contribution in the form of ironical comments on the power of the British to defeat the colonies. In satirical and not too delicate farces Mercy Warren dramatized the ineptness of the British officials and ridiculed the friends of the administration in America. The first canto of Trumbull's "M'Fin-

---

[6] It appeared in six chapters, each separately printed. It has been attributed to Hopkinson, but Hastings, *Hopkinson,* pp. 199-203, says after a careful study of the internal evidences that Hopkinson positively did not write it.

gal," printed in Philadelphia in January, 1776, and *The Fall of British Tyranny: or American Liberty Triumphant,*[7] both pamphlets, further popularized the propagandists' argument that the opponents of the Whigs were incompetent and corrupt.

Totally different in temper were the histories of the colonies written by preachers. They were written to prove two commonly asserted statements: the one, that by the nature and origin of colonial settlement the Americans were entitled to the rights they claimed, the other, that for more than a hundred years the colonists had served the selfish interests of Great Britain and had never received the least aid from the mother country. Amos Adams' *A Concise, Historical View of the Difficulties, Hardships, and Perils, which attended the Planting and Progressive Improvements of New-England,* and Judah Champion's *Brief View of the Distresses, Hardships and Dangers our Ancestors Encounter'd, in settling New-England,* are by their titles obvious examples.

Much more revolutionary were two pamphlets, so much alike that they were almost certainly written by the same person.[8] The first was *The American Alarm, or the Bostonian plea, For the RIGHTS, and LIBERTIES, of the PEOPLE,* addressed on its title page to the Sons of Liberty. It was directed against the attempt to establish an independent judiciary in Massachusetts in 1772. In the most violent language it denied the power of Parliament to pass such laws, limited the power of the King by the British Constitution, and asserted the right to overthrow a tyrannical monarch. The second, *An Oration, Upon the Beauties of Liberty, Or the Essential Rights of the Americans,* was even more violent in its defense of the right of revolution: "I declare it before God, the congregation, and all the world, and I would be glad if it reached the ears of every Briton and every American. . . . Shall a man be deemed a rebel that supports his own rights? it is the first law of nature, and he must be a rebel to God, to the laws of nature, and his own conscience, who will not do it."

One of the strongest attacks on the policies of Great Britain was

---

[7] John Leacock or Laycock is the supposed author.

[8] Israel Evans and Joseph Sabin both attribute these to Isaac Skillman. They note, however, that they have also been attributed to John Allen. John Adams thought Allen wrote the *Oration, Upon the Beauties of Liberty* (*Works,* II, 320), and Evans notes a newspaper statement that Allen preached a sermon on the beauties of liberty.

the publication in Massachusetts of three pamphlets, factual in character, on the activities of the troops. Two were published by order of the town of Boston after the massacre, *A Short Narrative of the Horrid Massacre*, and *Additional Observations on a Short Narrative*. These were designed to show that the attack was utterly unprovoked and that since 1768 the troubles with the soldiery had been caused by them—not by the citizens of Boston. The third, *A Narrative of the Excursion and Ravages of the King's Troops Under the Command of General Gage, on the Nineteenth of April, 1775*, published by authority of the provincial congress with the same intent, constituted the official Whig account of the engagement. The harrowing account of the devastation committed by the troops on their retreat was followed by sworn depositions that Gage and his men were responsible for the entire affair.

But the finest example of a pamphlet argument in popular form is Tom Paine's *Common Sense*. It is in a class by itself; its bold argument, trenchant phraseology, and universal appeal mark it as one of the best pieces of propaganda produced during the revolutionary period. Its power was immediately recognized by Whig leaders, and delegates to the Continental Congress sent numbers of copies back home. Francis Lightfoot Lee sent a copy to Landon Carter, known to be in opposition to independence, and a number to Colonel Tayloe for him to distribute. Gadsden took the first copy to Charleston on his return early in February, 1776. Joseph Hewes, one of the North Carolina delegates, decided against sending any, but John Penn, the other delegate, sent a copy to Thomas Person, out in the back country. Henry Wisner, delegate from New York, sent a copy to John McKesson, secretary of the provincial council, with the request that he consult "Mr. Scott and such of the Committee of Safety as you think proper, particularly Orange and Ulster, and let me know their and your opinion of the general spirit of it."[9] Thus even the more timid delegates could use the reaction to *Common Sense* as a barometer of public opinion and guide themselves accordingly.

Alert Whig leaders reprinted many of the better English pam-

[9] Quoted in Moncure D. Conway, *The Life of Thomas Paine*, I, 62. For the other references see Lee Transcripts, II, 89; Burnett, *Letters of Members of Cont. Cong.*, I, 344 f.; Drayton, *Memoirs*, II, 172; John Penn to Thomas Person, Feb. 14, 1776, John Penn Papers.

phlets in defense of America. Three went through several American editions. Jonathan Shipley's *A Speech Intended to have been Spoken on the Bill for Altering the Charters of the Colony of Massachusetts-Bay*, was twice printed in Boston, Salem, and Philadelphia, and once in Hartford, Lancaster, New York, and Newport, all in 1774. Joseph Priestley's *An Address to Protestant Dissenters . . . with Respect to the State of Public Liberty in General, and of American Affairs in Particular*, was reprinted in Philadelphia and Wilmington (North Carolina), and twice in Boston in 1774; Dr. Richard Price's *Observations on the Nature of Civil Liberty*, London, 1776, was reprinted in Boston, New York, and Charleston.[10] *The Crisis*, the most bitter of all the English pamphlets denouncing the King and Parliament, appeared in ninety-two separate numbers in England. Before 1776 presses in New York, Philadelphia, Newport, New London, Norwich, Hartford, and Williamsburg had printed twenty-eight numbers and an extraordinary issue.

The best of the speeches and sermons were printed in pamphlets after delivery in public. Literally hundreds of sermons originally delivered to comparatively small groups of people were ordered printed by the town or congregation; very few were printed at private expense.[11]

Frequently material which originally appeared in the newspapers or on broadsides was reprinted in pamphlets. John Dickinson's "Letters from a Pennsylvania Farmer" went through many editions, as did John Adams' essays signed "Novanglus." James Allen's poem on the Boston Massacre was reprinted by order of the town of Boston, and collections of the best songs of the period were put out in pamphlets.[12]

Broadsides, almanacs, and magazines were of less importance as vehicles of propaganda. Broadsides were used before 1765 only for notices, proclamations, and special news accounts. Newspapers frequently published on a single sheet an "Extraordinary" or "Supple-

[10] This pamphlet was passed from hand to hand; Trumbull sent it to Schuyler, for example.—Schuyler Papers, Aug. 23, 1776. See also Charles F. Jenkins, *Button Gwinnett, Signer of the Declaration of Independence*, pp. 92 f.

[11] The list of sermons and addresses in the bibliography is ample evidence.

[12] Rind published *The Storm, or the American Syren, being a Collection of the Newest and most Approved Songs*, 1773. Holt republished in 1770, when McDougall was being tried for libel, the report of the libel trial in 1734 of John Peter Zenger. Franklin's examination in England was reprinted in Williamsburg in 1766.

ment" to the weekly issue, but sometimes these special accounts appeared without the imprint of any paper. Election notices and lists of candidates, with occasionally some election propaganda, were struck off on single sheets, and newsboys ran off little poems to help in filling their New Year's boxes.

These familiar uses of the broadside continued during the pre-revolutionary period and were made to serve the interests of the propagandists. The speeches of Pitt, Conway, and others in favor of repealing the Stamp Act, were put on a broadside in New York, and the King's speech at the opening of Parliament in November, 1768, was published in Boston that everyone might read and know what he thought of the town: "Boston," the King had said, "appears to be in a state of disobedience to all law and government, with circumstances that might manifest a disposition to throw off its dependence on Great Britain."[13] "Junius's" remarks in 1770 in favor of the colonies were put on two folio pages in Boston, and a Hartford printer published Gage's letter to Joseph Trumbull on Lexington and Concord, together with Trumbull's reply. The selectmen of Boston issued a broadside calling for the convention of September 22, 1768, and the results of the convention were later published in the same fashion. An account of the mass meeting of November 29, 1773, at which the people of Boston determined that the tea should not be landed, was put on a broadside in both Boston and New York.[14] The resolutions of the different county conventions in Massachusetts were also printed in this way. Acts of the colonial assemblies or provincial congresses, the resolutions and addresses of the Continental Congress, the form of the nonimportation associations and the voluntary defense associations, and important acts of the British government were all put on broadsides. Particularly striking extracts from private letters were put out in this form,[15] and songs and poems were printed on single sheets. Some of the songs were widely distributed—Dickinson's "Liberty Song," for instance, and

[13] N. Y. Hist. Soc., Broadsides, Mar. 1766; and Ford, *Massachusetts Broadsides*, No. 1483.

[14] Mass. Hist. Soc., Broadsides, Sept. 14, Sept. 22, 1768.

[15] E.g., in the Library of Congress, Broadsides, New York, July 25, 1774, is a statement that there were many men in New York who were likely to be bought over by pensions and that one printer had been offered five hundred pounds to support the measures of the British government. The people were warned to discover these people if possible. See also N. Y. Hist. Soc., Broadsides, *The Plot Discovered*, and *A Genuine Letter*, both 1775.

a long song to the tune of Yankee Doodle, called "The Procession," which was pushed under the doors of houses all over New York. Most of the poems were too long for the papers and too short for a pamphlet; one of them, in seventy-two stanzas, covered a full folio page, and many others were almost as long.[16]

The propagandists found, however, a much more important use for the broadside. One of the clearest examples of their activity is the fact that they took what had once been a mere handbill and made of it a medium of the most violent anti-British propaganda. They made their most effective written appeal to the lower classes on the broadside. Here is its newest and most significant use.

The broadside was particularly suited to the more radical and inflammatory type of propaganda directed to the lower classes. No identifying marks gave clue to printer or author, it reached a far larger group than the newspaper or pamphlet, and it attracted far more attention. Tacked at night on the door of town house or tavern, on trees or posts, left on the doorsteps or handed out secretly, the broadsides were read to the groups who gathered around them next day, and thus their influence spread far beyond the confines of the literate public. Consequently they were used not by the intellectual leaders but by those nearer the people.

The most violent attacks on public enemies were printed on broadsides. One of the most common forms was simply a list of names of those who had violated one of the nonimportation agreements. Usually this was accompanied by some such statement as the following: "The Friends to Liberty and their Country's Cause are desired to paste this up over the Chimney Piece of every Public House, and on every other proper Place, in every Town, in this and every other Colony, there to remain as a monument of the Remembrance of the detestable Names above mentioned."[17] These

---

[16] Ford, *Massachusetts Broadsides*, No. 1434; N. Y. Public Library, Broadsides, Mar. 15, 1770; Mass. Hist. Soc., Broadsides, New Haven, 1773. An elegy on Warren was published in Watertown.—Pa. Hist. Soc., Broadsides, III, 366. Two poems, *A Dose for the Tories*, and *A Song Composed by the British Butchers, after the Fight at Bunker Hill*, both 1775, are in N. Y. Hist. Soc., Broadsides. A broadside list of the toasts drunk at the entertainment given the delegates to the first Continental Congress was published in Philadelphia. A copy is in Carroll Papers.

[17] Mass. Hist. Soc., Broadsides, Jan. 23, 1770. Another broadside list of those who signed the address to Hutchinson listed occupations, places of business, and home addresses, "that every Friend to his Country may know who is assisting to carry the execrable Purposes of the British Administration into Execution."—Ford, *Massachusetts Broadsides*, No. 1699. Two other lists were issued, *ibid.*, No. 1700, No. 1701. Handbills of the thirty-one non-

lists were often authorized by the local committees of inspection to give as much publicity as possible to their published boycott. Many of the posted warnings were violent enough to raise a mob against the victims. "Insolent" placards, said John Montresor, covered New York during the agitation over the Stamp Act, threatening the property and lives of those who issued or received a stamp, or who interfered in any way with the efforts to annul the Act.[18] When the ship carrying a cargo of tea was thought to be nearing Philadelphia, three warnings were issued to the Delaware pilots, who would have to bring it into the harbor. The first of these expounded the true principles of the tea tax, and warned the pilots not to assist in any way:

> "Now it is clear, that if the *Americans* buy ANY of THIS TEA, they *must* Pay the *Parliament's Duty,* and *acknowledge* their *Right* to TAX US as often as and as high as they think *proper,* than which nothing can be more disgraceful and injurious to A FREE PEOPLE."

And if any pilot should assist in landing the tea, "such Pilot will be marked for his Treason . . . and be forever recorded as the *damned traitorous Pilot,* who brought up the *Tea Ship.*"[19]

When it was reported in Boston that the customs officers were going to grant a permit for landing the tea, a warning was promptly posted:

> "As the aiding or assisting in procuring or granting any such Permit for landing the said Tea . . . or in offering any Permit when obtained to the Master or Commander of the said Ship . . . must betray an inhuman Thirst for Blood, and will also in great Measure accelerate Confusion and Civil War: This is to assure such public Enemies of this Country that they will be considered and treated as Wretches unworthy to live, and will be made the first Victims of our Just Resentment.
> "THE PEOPLE."[20]

---

associators in Charleston were issued, and the list was copied in *S. C. Gazette,* Sept. 14, 1769.

[18] *Journals,* pp. 336, 342, 346.

[19] Library of Congress, Broadsides, Pennsylvania, p. 143, reprinted in N. Y. *Journal,* Dec. 2, 1773. The two other broadsides were descriptions of the ship.

[20] Mass. Hist. Soc., Broadsides, Dec. 2, 1773.

A month or so later, the tea commissioners were the object of another warning:

"BRETHREN, AND FELLOW CITIZENS!

"You may depend, that those odious Miscreants and detestable Tools to the Ministry and Governor, the TEA CONSIGNEES, (those Traitors to their Country, Butchers, who have done, and are doing every Thing to Murder and destroy all that shall stand in the Way of their private Interest,) are determined to come and reside again in the Town of Boston.

"I therefore give you this early Notice, that you may hold yourselves in Readiness, on the shortest Notice, to give them such a Reception, as such vile Ingrates deserve.

"JOYCE, JUN.

"Chairman of the Committee of Tarring and Feathering"[21]

After Governor Tryon had escaped to a British ship in the harbor he continued to gather information for the British government from loyalists on shore, and in an attempt to stop this, a broadside signed "Sentinel" exposed his designs and closed with the command: "Shoot the first Traitor, be he who, or what he may, that shall attempt to go to this nest of sycophants; this is not the season to be mealy mouthed or to mince matters; the times are precarious and perilous."[22]

Articles or essays, more inflammatory than those in the newspapers, began to appear on broadsides as early as the Stamp Act, but the number greatly increased after 1770; here was a new use for the broadside, developed by the propagandist for his particular purposes. Such broadsides appeared in large numbers at the time of the Tea Act. A series of articles called "The Alarm" was running in the New York *Journal* in the fall of 1773, and both the first and

[21] Reprinted in. *Boston Gazette*, Jan. 17, 1774, and subsequently in Col. Soc. Mass., *Proceedings*, VIII, 89 f.

[22] N. Y. Hist. Soc., Broadsides, Jan. 27, 1776. "Sentinel" issued another the same day against giving help to the enemy.—Library of Congress, Broadsides, New York, Jan. 27, 1776. Two months later *The Speech of William Tr[yo]n, Esq.* appeared on a broadside in New York: "REBELS and TRAITORS behold me now and take warning by this my deserved Death.—Had I but tarried in my *Native Country* when there last, I might, for a little while longer, have escaped this ignominious Death; but by the Persuasion of *Bute* and the *Devil*, I returned to *America*, to pursue my old Practice of Shedding the Blood of the Innocent, the Fatherless and Widow.—But alas, the Devil hath forsaken me, as he will all such Traitors; wherefore I beseech you *Gage, Burgoyne, Howe, Clinton, Dunmore*, and *Vandeput* . . . to quit the Steps you are now treading, and let my shameful End be the Means of turning you from following the damnable Advice of North and the cursed Ministry."—*Ibid.*, Mar. 18, 1776. This, of course, is the speech of the effigy of Tryon.

fourth numbers were put on broadsides. So many of the fourth, which dealt with the dangers of submitting to the act and stated that the annual loss would be at least twenty-eight thousand pounds a year, were distributed around New York that Holt did not even print it in the *Journal*.[23] Others on all of the major problems appeared throughout the period in the principal northern cities.[24] The most violent of them all, however, related to the troops, and unquestionably they did much to develop a war psychosis among the lower classes.

As early as 1768 Boston broadsides attacked the troops in provocative language:

"Whoever has candidly traced the rapid growth of these Colonies from their little Beginnings to their present flourishing State in Wealth and Population, must eye the distinguished Hand of Heaven, and impress every Mind with a humble Confidence that 'no Design formed against us shall prosper.' The poor devoted Town of Boston has suffered, and is still suffering, all that the unmerited Malice of Men and Devils could invent for her Destruction; but although impoverished and distressed, she is not yet subjugated and enslaved; though immured within the Fortresses of their enemies, the free and generous Bosoms of the Inhabitants beat strongly in the cause of Liberty: But it appears that the Measure of ministerial Wrath is not yet full: That detested Parricide Hutchinson, has vaunted to his few Friends, that should the People submit to the villainous Exactions of the present governmental Knot of Tyrants. . . . 'yet still the Town of Boston would forever remain a garrisoned Town,' as a check upon the Country. . . . Will the People sit tame and inactive Spectators of the hostile Designs of our inveterate Enemies, and exercise such Degrees of Moderation and Forbearance as to suffer those Enemies to compleat their Works, and so far effect their dangerous Purpose, that Resistance would finally be in vain?   "The WATCHMAN."[25]

---

[23] In N. Y. *Journal*, Nov. 4, 1773. Another, signed "A Mechanic," took four pages to explain the Tea Act.—Pa. Hist. Soc., Broadsides, I, 149. Another dated Nov. 13, 1773, to the same purpose, was printed in *N. Y. Gazetteer*, Nov. 18, 1773.

[24] E.g., in Hist. Soc. Pa., Broadsides, I, 118, is an article on the Stamp Act, the earliest of this type I found. See also *A Wonderful Dream*, in which the author describes life under the laws of Cromwell. That would be the situation in America, he said, if England's laws went into effect in the colonies. Needless to say, this was published in New York, not Boston.—N. Y. Hist. Soc., Broadsides, Mar. 3, 1775.

[25] Mass. Hist. Soc., Broadsides, 1768.

When Alexander McDougall wanted to rouse New York against the assembly's granting supplies to the troops, he covered the city with a violent tirade in broadside form, *To the Betrayed Inhabitants of the City and Colony of New York*, which charged that the assemblymen, particularly James De Lancey, had sold out to the court party and were traitors to their constituents.

The radicals outdid themselves in the broadsides on the troops. The Boston Massacre was recalled in 1772 with *A Monumental Inscription on the Fifth of March*, which contained an account of the massacre and the subsequent trial and acquittal of the troops, together with a few "LINES on the Enlargement of EBENEZER RICHARDSON" (the customs officer who had killed Snider). A woodcut of the firing headed a column which began in these fervid words: "AMERICANS! Bear in Remembrance The HORRID MASSACRE! Perpetrated in King-Street, Boston, New-England, On the Evening of March the Fifth, 1770. When FIVE of your fellow countrymen, GRAY, MAVERICK, CALDWELL, ATTUCKS, and CARR, Lay wallowing in their Gore!" The "LINES on the Enlargement of Ebenezer Richardson" began as follows:

> "AWAKE my drowsy Thoughts! Awake my muse!
> Awake O earth, and tremble at the news!
> In grand defiance to the laws of God,
> The Guilty, Guilty murd'rer walks abroad."[26]

Bloody Butchery by the British Troops: or the Runaway Fight of the Regulars, which told the story of Lexington and Concord in most affecting manner, with the ubiquitous lines of wretched poetry at the end, was embellished with coffins across the top and the names of the slain under them. Two lists of the damages done by the troops after April 19, 1775, with pointed comments, were printed by order of the town of Boston.[27]

The broadside was thoroughly exploited by the northern propagandists. It played a large part in arousing the people, but because it was primarily adapted to the centers of large population where there was a strong working class, it was little used in the South.

---

[26] A poem, published on a broadside soon after the event, began:
> "Mourn O my Friends let solemn numbers flow,
> From thy sad thoughts, fit for the scene of Woe:
> For in *King-Street* their breathless Bodies lay:
> For Dead, ah! Dead for ever Dead are they."
> —N. Y. Public Library, Broadsides, 1770.

[27] Mass. Hist. Soc., Broadsides, Nov. 18, 1775; Nov. 18, 1776.

A MONUMENTAL INSCRIPTION

ON THE

Fifth of March.

Together with a few LINES

On the Enlargement of

EBENEZER RICHARDSON,

Convicted of MURDER.

A M E R I C A N S!
BEAR IN REMEMBRANCE
The HORRID MASSACRE!
Perpetrated in King-street, Boston,
New-England,
On the Evening of March the Fifth, 1770.
When FIVE of your fellow countrymen,
GRAY, MAVERICK, CALDWELL, ATTUCKS,
and CARR,
Lay wallowing in their Gore!
Being basely, and most-inhumanly
M U R D E R E D!
And SIX others badly WOUNDED!
By a Party of the XXIXth Regiment,
Under the command of Capt. Tho. Preston.
R E M E M B E R!
That Two of the MURDERERS
Were convicted of MANSLAUGHTER!
By a Jury, of whom I shall say
NOTHING,
Branded in the hand!
And dismissed,
The others were ACQUITTED,
And their Captain PENSIONED!
Also,
BEAR IN REMEMBRANCE
That on the 22d Day of February, 1770.
The infamous
EBENEZER RICHARDSON, Informer,
And tool to Ministerial hirelings,
Most barbarously
M U R D E R E D
CHRISTOPHER SEIDER,
An innocent youth!
Of which crime he was found guilty
By his Country
On Friday April 20th, 1770;
But remained Unsentenced
On Saturday the 22d Day of February, 1772.
When the GRAND INQUEST
For Suffolk county,
Were informed, at request,
By the Judges of the Superior Court,
That EBENEZER RICHARDSON'S Case
Then lay before his MAJESTY.
Therefore said Richardson
This day, MARCH FIFTH! 1772,
Remains UNHANGED!!!
Let THESE things be told to Posterity!
And handed down
From Generation to Generation,
'Till Time shall be no more!
Forever may AMERICA be preserved,
From weak and wicked monarchs,
Tyrannical Ministers,
Abandoned Governors,
Their Underlings and Hirelings!
And may the
Machinations of artful, designing wretches,
Who would ENSLAVE THIS People,
Come to an end,
Let their NAMES and MEMORIES
Be buried in eternal oblivion,
And the PRESS,
For a SCOURGE to Tyrannical Rulers,
Remain F R E E.

AWAKE my drowsy Thoughts! Awake my muse!
  Awake O earth, and tremble at the news!
  In grand defiance to the laws of God,
The Guilty, Guilty murd'rer walks abroad.
That city mourns, (the cry comes from the ground,)
Where law and justice never can be found:
Oh! sword of vengeance, fall thou on the race
Of those who hinder justice from its place.
O MURD'RER! RICHARDSON! with their latest breath
Millions will curse you when you sleep in death!
Infernal horrors sure will shake your soul
When o'er your head the awful thunders roll.
Earth cannot hide you, always will the cry
Of Murder! Murder! haunt you 'till you die!
To yonder grave! with trembling joints repair,
Remember, SEIDER'S corps lies mould'ring there;
There drop a tear, and think what you have done!
Then judge how you can live beneath the Sun.
A PARDON may arrive! You laws defy,
But Heaven's laws will stand when KINGS shall die.
Oh! Wretched man! the monster of the times,
You were not hung " by reason of old Lines,"
Old Lines thrown by, 'twas then we were in hopes,
That you would soon be hung with new made Ropes;
But neither Ropes nor Lines, will satisfy
For SEIDER'S blood! But GOD is ever nigh,
And guilty souls will not unpunish'd go
Tho' they're excus'd by judges here below!
You are enlarg'd but cursed is your fate
Tho' Cushing's eas'd you from the prison gate
The --Bridge of Tories, it has borne you o'er
Yet you e'er long may meet with HELL's dark shore.

A Boston Broadside on the Boston Massacre.
By courtesy of the Massachusetts Historical Society.

Leaders in Boston, New York, Philadelphia, and to a lesser extent Charleston and Savannah, were the only ones who used this medium on a large scale, but there it was of real value.

The almanac, the most widely read of all the printed material in the colonial period, was of little value to the propagandist, and the scattered bits on timely questions are more the efforts of the editor to make a popular almanac than the efforts of propagandists to influence thought. Nearly every almanac had an engraving on the front cover, and in addition to the astronomical data there was occasionally an article on some aspects of the political situation, and frequently short poems headed the pages. The *Essex Almanac* for 1769 had a short poem on a patriotic subject at the top of each page— Liberty, Oppression, Magna Carta, and so on. Bickerstaff's almanac for the same year carried on its cover an elaborate engraving which combined many of the ideas popular at the time: a likeness of Wilkes was held up by Hercules and Mars, who stood upon the Cross of St. George, Locke's Works, and Sydney on Government. The application to America was obvious. Within were several anecdotes of Wilkes and a poem on Liberty. Ames's almanac for 1772 had on the cover a cut showing John Dickinson holding the "Farmer's Letters," with his elbow resting on Magna Carta; below was a short poem:

> " 'Tis nobly done to Stem Taxations Rage,
> And raise the Thoughts of a degenerate Age
> For Happiness and Joy, from Freedom Spring
> But Life in Bondage is a worthless Thing."

Low's *Astronomical Diary* for 1775 showed a picture of "The Virtuous PATRIOT at the Hour of Death," and the editor, Nathaniel Low, had written an account of British depravity as seen in the actions of the troops. These pictures and poems no doubt were a constant reminder of the principles upon which the radicals based their action, but the almanac was not an important medium of propaganda. Events moved too swiftly after 1774 for even "The Virtuous PATRIOT at the Hour of Death" to hold attention long. An essential of propaganda is that it be timely, and the almanac came out only once a year; a six months' old appeal even in that age had little value. Yet the almanac reached the country people in a way that newspaper, pamphlet, and broadside never did.

The short-lived magazines were also of little use to the propagandists. Had they enjoyed a more stable existence, they might have served a real purpose. Discussions which would otherwise have had to appear in an expensive pamphlet edition might have found their way into the magazines, but their circulation was so limited, and they all came to such an abrupt end that they did the propagandist little good. The first magazine during the prerevolutionary period was the *American Magazine or General Repository*, published for nine months in 1769, but the first of any importance was the *Royal American Magazine*, published from January, 1774, to March, 1775. Isaiah Thomas originally edited it, and naturally carried over his Whig propaganda from the *Massachusetts Spy*. In addition to the articles on such topics as "Liberty in General," or "The Character of an American Patriot," Thomas reprinted Hancock's "Fifth of March Oration," and extracts from John Lathrop's "Artillery Company Sermon." One piece, "The Future Greatness of America," was reprinted in at least two newspapers. Each number contained a section headed "General History of America," an account of the current events of the month. It was here that Thomas showed himself and his opinions and indicated his ability as a propagandist. His connection with Samuel Adams is clearly seen by the insertion at the request of "A.B." in the August number of the resolutions of Monson, Massachusetts, addressed to the Boston committee of correspondence. Paul Revere's numerous engravings appearing here constituted the first important use of the political cartoon. Paul Revere did more for the cause of independence with his stylus than by any midnight ride, even if he did make one.

The *Pennsylvania Magazine*, edited by Robert Aitken with Thomas Paine as the contributing editor, was the most original magazine published up to 1775. Although it was for the greater part nonpolitical in character, Paine and President Witherspoon contributed a few stirring articles on the war, and a great many patriotic poems were printed, among them Tom Paine's "Liberty Tree." In common with most of the Pennsylvania propaganda there were numerous references to the defensive nature of the war, but in spite of Paine's close association with the editorial staff, it cannot be said that the *Pennsylvania Magazine* was a medium of propaganda to any important extent.

XIII

NEWSPAPERS

THE FINEST instance of the propagandists' activity was the development of the colonial newspaper press. In their hands the newspapers became the most effective organ for the dissemination of written propaganda.

In contrast to the words of an early writer that the newspapers were "petty, dingy, languid, inadequate affairs,"[1] is the intense interest taken in them by the leaders in both parties, who awaited impatiently their weekly appearance and sent batches of them, carefully marked, to their friends in other colonies. "I entirely agree with you," wrote Andrew Eliot to a friend, "that an interest in the public prints is of great importance. The spirit of liberty would soon be lost & the people would grow quite lethargic, if there were not some on[e] on watch, to awaken and rouse them."[2] These small, badly printed, and expensive sheets, in spite of their limited circulation, had an extensive appeal and exercised a vital influence on the minds of the reading public. Although the news might be anywhere from three to eight weeks old, it was fresh to its readers; although editorials were nonexistent, their place was more than taken by the contributions of others far more intelligent than the editors. Many other defects equally obvious have been noted, usually with the modern newspaper in mind, but from the standpoint of the eighteenth-century propagandist the greatest handicaps he faced were the limited circulation, the poor facilities for distribution, and the great number of illiterates in the population.

There were twenty-one papers published in America in 1763, and by 1775 the number had grown to forty-two. Of these, fifteen were in New England, thirteen in the middle colonies, and fourteen in the southern colonies,[3] about an average of one paper published

---

[1] Tyler, *Literary History*, I, 18.

[2] Eliot, Mayhew, Hollis Correspondence, Nov. 14, 1766.

[3] The papers were distributed as follows in the first part of 1775: New Hampshire, 2; Massachusetts, 7; Connecticut, 4; Rhode Island, 2; New York, 5; Pennsylvania, 8; Maryland, 3; Virginia, 5; North Carolina, 2; South Carolina, 3; Georgia, 1. There was none in New Jersey or Delaware.

for every sixty to sixty-five thousand people, almost exactly the average in the United States today. The modern papers, of course, are dailies, and the colonial papers were weeklies. Circulation figures are difficult to obtain. Edes of the *Boston Gazette* claimed two thousand copies were sold weekly from the middle of 1774 to the battle of Lexington and Concord, and Rivington of the *New York Gazetteer* in October, 1774, claimed thirty-six hundred, but such figures were unusual. Three hundred copies a week was a much more common average for a colonial paper.

One of the most striking facts of the entire revolutionary movement is the extent to which the Whigs controlled the press. Not a single paper prior to 1774 was exclusively an organ of pro-British propaganda, and even after 1774 there were only a few. Three main explanations account for this state of affairs.

In the first place, perhaps, the Stamp Act bound every printer to the patriot side at the outset of the controversy with England. As the historian David Ramsay said,

"It was fortunate for the liberties of America, that newspapers were the subject of a heavy stamp duty. Printers, when uninfluenced by government, have generally ranged themselves on the side of liberty, nor are they less remarkable for attention to the profits of their profession. A stamp duty, which openly invades the first, and threatened a great diminution of the last, provoked their united zealous opposition."[4]

In the second place, Tory propagandists were slow to come to the defense of the British government in the colonies. As we shall see later, it was not until 1774 that there was a widespread Tory propaganda campaign.

Finally, those editors who did not sympathize with the Whig program were more likely to attempt a neutral attitude than to turn Tory; it was safer.

In spite of these substantial reasons for supporting the Whig cause, there was considerable variation in the degree of support. The sympathies and abilities of the printer made a great difference. Editorials he did not write, but we have today far less belief in the

---

[4] *History of the American Revolution*, I, 61 f. There is a splendid discussion of the newspapers and the Stamp Act in Schlesinger, "Colonial Newspapers and the Stamp Act," *New England Quarterly*, VIII, 63-83.

power of editorials to influence than had Horace Greeley or James Gordon Bennett. Manipulation of news items is generally conceded to be much better propaganda technique. The choice of what went into the weekly paper was his, and in that choice the eighteenth-century editor could show his real interests. Some of the printers were really propagandists in themselves, so alert were they in making their papers channels of Whig propaganda. The interest and ingenuity of the local Whigs also made a great difference to the printer. He was largely dependent on voluntary contributions or other papers for what he printed and thus welcomed all the help he could get. Sam Adams spent nearly every Sunday in Edes' office helping him with Monday's *Gazette*, but Daniel Fowle got practically no help from the Portsmouth Whigs.

A survey of some of the papers published during the period, even though the Tory ones are omitted, will show the wide variations that existed.

There never was a really satisfactory Whig paper in New Hampshire, for example. *The New Hampshire Gazette*, published in Portsmouth by Daniel Fowle, ran with only a few breaks during the entire twenty years, but even in the middle of the war it was a very poor medium of propaganda. The nascent Whigs were so dissatisfied with it as early as January, 1765, that they set up the rival *Portsmouth Mercury and Weekly Advertiser*, but even with that support the paper lasted only three years. Daniel Fowle was a good newspaper man, and in his defense it must be said that he got almost no help from the local Whigs. Few essays originated in Portsmouth, and in general the temper of the community was against aggressive journalism.

The best Whig paper in the country was one of the seven Massachusetts papers—the *Boston Gazette, and Country Journal*. Benjamin Edes, one of the printers, had been a member of the Loyall Nine from its first beginnings and throughout the controversy was in close touch with the Boston radicals. John Adams tells the familiar story of spending a Sunday afternoon in company with the editors and several local leaders preparing for the Monday's *Gazette* —"a curious employment, cooking up paragraphs, articles, occurrences, &c., working the political engine!"[5] This was peculiarly Sam

[5] *Works of John Adams*, II, 219 f.

Adams' paper, and as a result of his influence and association with it, it was the only one on the continent which kept up the fight against England in the interludes between periods of agitation. Even during the long period of peace from 1771 to 1773, every issue contained articles, usually written by Adams, against the proposed civil list for the payment of crown officers or other parliamentary laws. It was this paper which so outraged English officials in Massachusetts. Governor Bernard, had he dared, would have arrested the editors and closed their office, for he blamed the riots of August 14 on the paper and charged it with "raising that flame in America which has given so much trouble."[6] Governor Hutchinson sadly reported that seven eighths of the people in Boston read none but "this infamous paper, and so are never undeceived,"[7] and a certain McGilchrist charged that the "ferment" into which the people had been thrown had been raised and kept up for some years "by six inflammatory Newspapers weekly printed in this Province, which (liberty being only allowed on one side) it is perilous to contradict by word or writing, as I have found by experience."[8]

The *Massachusetts Spy*, published by Isaiah Thomas in Boston from 1770 to 1775, was just as radically anti-British. Thomas stated that part of the design of the *Spy* was "to assist in detecting, and exposing to public view, those miscreants who, for the sake of public or private advantage to themselves, would sacrifice both their King and Country. And to help, as much as possible, in maintaining and supporting that LIBERTY for which our Fathers suffered in transferring it to us."[9]

The *Boston Evening-Post*, on the contrary, attempted a more impartial attitude. Although Sam Adams and other radicals published in it, essays from their opponents frequently appeared in the adjoining columns, and five days after the battle of Lexington and Concord the paper expired. Outside of Boston there were two papers, both Whig—the *Essex Gazette*, published by Sam and Ebenezer Hall at Salem after 1768, and the *Essex Journal*, first published by

---

[6] British Museum Transcripts, C.O. 5, vol. 3, f. 56, p. 97; Frothingham, *Warren*, p. 48 n.

[7] Quoted in Wells, *Sam Adams*, I, 244.

[8] Perry, *Collections of the American Church*, III, 555.

[9] Dec. 7, 1770.

Isaiah Thomas and Henry-Walter Tinges at Newburyport after 1773.[10]

Rhode Island and Connecticut papers with one exception were all pro-Whig down to 1776. One of the best newspapers in the colonies was Solomon Southwick's *Newport Mercury*, which consistently carried more American news in the early days than any of the others. Few of the essays in it originated in Newport, but because Southwick clipped items liberally from papers published all over the country, its readers got a splendid cross section of the American press. The *Providence Gazette and Country Journal*, sponsored by Stephen Hopkins and printed by John Carter, was likewise strongly Whig throughout the period.

Four of the five papers published in Connecticut between 1763 and 1776 were good Whig papers. The *Connecticut Courant*, the *New London Gazette*, and the *Connecticut Journal* lasted until well after 1776, but the *Connecticut Gazette* ceased publication in 1767. Members of that famous family of printers, the Greens, published the New London and New Haven papers. The fifth paper, the *Norwich Packet*, was edited by the Robertsons, who later became Tories.

The best Whig paper in New York was the *Journal*, published by John Holt. In 1765 a leading Tory merchant, John Watts, wrote a friend: "You will find the printers all mad, Holt particularly, who has been cautioned over and over again, and would have been prosecuted, but the people's minds are so inflamed about this stamp act, it would only have been exposing Government to attempt it."[11] Holt, though not so closely associated with the radical leaders as was Benjamin Edes, was nevertheless a good Whig, and his office became a training school for other Whig printers. Both James Parker and William Goddard served in his shop, later setting up their own papers. He was not so alert in realizing possibilities as was Edes, though he can hardly be blamed for the fact that local contributions failed him except at the high points of the fight. When local material was lacking, he filled his columns with essays printed in Boston, so that Colden could say of the *Journal*, during a period when local writers were quiet, "The People are familiarized to read

[10] John Mycall took over the paper in October, 1775, and published it for about twenty years.

[11] 4 Mass. Hist. Soc., *Collections*, X, 576.

Seditious if not treasonable Papers."[12] In common with nearly every other colonial paper, issues during 1770-1773 contain practically no revolutionary propaganda. Holt made nothing of the Golden Hill affair, a brush with the troops in New York on January 18, 1770, much like the Boston Massacre and with the same possibilities for arousing the people. Yet he carried full accounts of the events in Boston just a few months later. From the Tea Act to Lexington and Concord the *Journal* was as radical as any colonial paper; writers were active and the pages were full of their contributions. It was the only strong Whig paper in New York during those years, for the *New York Gazette, or, the Weekly Post-Boy* stopped publication in 1773, and the other two papers were published by Tory sympathizers—Hugh Gaine and James Rivington. John Anderson's *Constitutional Gazette* was not started until August, 1775, and ran only until June, 1776, so that it figured only slightly in the movement.[13]

The two most important Whig papers in Pennsylvania were the *Pennsylvania Journal*, edited by William and Thomas Bradford, father and son, and the *Pennsylvania Gazette*, edited by Hall and Sellers. William Bradford has been called "the printer of the Revolution," and he and his son greatly increased the influence of the paper by their interest in politics. He was the secretary of the Philadelphia Sons of Liberty and, like Benjamin Edes, was in close contact with the political leaders of the colony, especially Charles Thomson, the Morrises, and George Clymer. As a result of these contacts he could publish with pride the statement that the Sons of Liberty read the *Journal* more than any other paper.[14] During the dispute over the Townshend Acts the Bradfords were more concerned about the imaginary dangers of an American episcopate, printing long essays against it to the exclusion of those on the political questions of the day. From March, 1768, to January, 1769, not a political essay of any importance appeared in the *Journal*, while during the same period Hall and Sellers of the *Pennsylvania Gazette* had no trouble in finding plenty of spirited essays to print. The Bradfords were made printers to the Continental Congress, but later Hall and Sellers were given a good deal of the work.[15]

[12] *Colden Letter Books*, II, 135.
[13] The *Albany Gazette*, printed by Alexander and James Robertson, lasted from 1771 to 1774. *Weyman's New York Gazette* was printed from 1763 to 1767.
[14] *Pa. Journal*, Feb. 1, 1775. [15] *Letters of Richard Henry Lee*, I, 333.

William Goddard edited a strong Whig paper, the *Pennsylvania Chronicle*, from 1767 to 1774, and Dunlap's *Pennsylvania Packet* also supported the patriot side; the others were of less importance. The *Evening Post*, later important, the *Mercury*, and the *Ledger*, were all new ventures in 1775. The *Mercury* and the *Ledger* were Tory papers. There were two German papers, the *Staatsbote*, printed by Henry Miller, and Christoph Saur's *Germantauner Zeitung*. Saur's paper appealed largely to the pacifist sects, but Miller's *Staatsbote* was strongly Whig. Miller had agents as far south as Augusta County, Virginia, and his paper circulated extensively among the Germans in the Valley.[16]

The editors of the three Maryland papers were all associated with papers in other colonies as well. Dunlap of the *Baltimore Gazette* printed the *Packet* in Philadelphia; Rind, of Green and Rind's *Annapolis Gazette*, later edited a paper in Virginia; and William Goddard of the *Maryland Journal* was almost a transient, having printed papers in Providence, New York, and Philadelphia. Of the three, Green's *Maryland Gazette* was the important Whig paper, for Goddard did not start the *Journal* until 1773, and Dunlap did not set up his paper until May 2, 1775. The *Gazette* was strongly Whig throughout, but Green did not always make the best use of its columns.

Articles against the Stamp Act began as early as April, 1765; most of them were taken from other papers and by January, 1766, interest had practically died down. It revived slightly with the printing of the "Farmer's Letters," and in 1768 and 1769 Green printed Boston letters, the Boston "Journal of Occurrences," and a few scattered essays. Even in the crisis of 1774 it was weak on essays but carried good news items.

At the start of the period in Virginia there was only one paper— the *Virginia Gazette*, published at Williamsburg by John Royle; not until 1766 was another paper established. In that year Thomas Jefferson, dissatisfied with the old *Gazette*, now edited by Alexander Purdie and John Dixon, brought William Rind from Maryland, and the second *Virginia Gazette* was begun. In 1774 William Duncan began printing the third *Virginia Gazette*, this one at Norfolk; it

---

[16] Faust, *German Element*, I, 291. On Goddard and the *Chronicle*, see A. M. Schlesinger, "Politics, Propaganda, and the Philadelphia Press, 1767-1770," *Pa. Magazine of History and Biography*, LX, 309-322.

was this paper that Dunmore later printed as a royal paper. Two more were established in 1775. Purdie split with Dixon and on February 2, 1775, published his own paper, and on April 22, 1775, Clarkson and Davis added to the confusion of names by printing the fifth *Virginia Gazette*. Purdie was appointed Constitutional Postmaster by Benjamin Franklin in 1775, and after the Declaration of Independence he became the printer to the Commonwealth of Virginia. One of the best of the five was Dixon and Hunter's *Gazette*. It had more local contributions on the dispute with England, and it republished the best of the political pamphlets. Throughout the years before the Declaration it made only one bad slip—it published Gage's account of the battle of Lexington and Concord instead of the patriot account.

The two North Carolina papers most useful to the Whigs were the *North Carolina Gazette*, published at Newbern by James Davis from 1768 to 1778, and Adam Boyd's *Cape Fear Mercury*, begun in Wilmington in 1769. It was suspended in the fall of 1774, and was not revived until the spring of 1775. The Wilmington committee of safety encouraged Boyd to renew the paper, but even with the support of the committee Boyd could not carry on after September, 1775.[17]

The best Whig paper in the southern colonies, and the nearest approach to the *Boston Gazette*, was the *South Carolina Gazette*, edited by Peter Timothy, whose father had learned his trade under Benjamin Franklin. Timothy was in close contact with the Whig leaders in Charleston, particularly William Henry Drayton and the Middletons, and wrote letters for the Sons of Liberty. He corresponded with Samuel Adams, and there was a much larger amount of Boston material in his paper than in any other southern paper. He began early in 1765 copying material from the northern papers against the Stamp Act and continued with good accounts of the demonstrations and riots in New England. Even during 1766 and 1767 he printed articles in praise of American goods and in favor of domestic economy, and all through the Townshend controversy he carried the best of the northern essays and full accounts of the troubles with the troops in Boston. He was the only southern editor to

[17] *Col. Rec. N. C.*, IX, 1118 f.

issue a black-bordered sheet with a full page account of the Boston Massacre in 1770. Even in the dead years of 1771 and 1772 he printed extracts from the *Boston Gazette* on the agitation there over the salaries of the judges. In 1772 he was made Deputy-Postmaster-General for the southern colonies and turned the *Gazette* over to Thomas Powell. Excellent articles appeared in 1773 and 1774, and the Boston Port Act was published in a black-bordered issue. Boston material increased after June, 1774, and in 1775 he printed Warren's "Oration on the Fifth of March." The paper was discontinued in May, 1775, and was not revived until 1777. Charles Crouch began the *South Carolina Gazette; and Country Journal* on December 17, 1765, right in the midst of the Stamp Act difficulties. Born in one of the most successful periods of newspaper agitation against the government, it continued to be a good Whig paper throughout the controversy.[18]

The only paper in Georgia, the *Georgia Gazette*, was a most unsatisfactory paper, for it attempted almost the impossible, a neutral attitude. Governor Wright exercised a strong influence over it, but the Whigs could not afford to desert it, because there was no other and no money to set up a new one, and they made the best use of it they could.[19]

In short, there were only a few printers—Edes, Thomas, Goddard, Holt, Bradford, the Greens perhaps, and Timothy—who took the initiative in making vehicles of propaganda of their papers. The others took their tone from the local Whig leaders and the demands of the community. Newspapers influence readers by the method of presenting the contents and by the contents themselves. In both of these particulars Whig propagandists showed their adeptness in making the newspapers fight their battles.

[18] The third paper, the *South Carolina and American General Gazette*, was a colorless paper. Robert Wells, the publisher, later became a loyalist and his paper was always open to loyalist propagandists. He left for England after the outbreak of the war, and the paper was continued by his son John. According to McMurtrie, *History of Printing in the United States*, II, 327, he did not return. The *South Carolina and American General Gazette* became the *Royal Gazette* in 1781, and according to its title page it was published by R. Wells and Son, but this does not mean, of course, that Robert Wells was actually in Charleston.

[19] James Habersham resented the Whig use of the paper: "Some people," he said, "have fed our Gazette with inflammatory Doctrines, in order to keep up the Spirit of Party and Opposition."—*Letters*, Ga. Hist. Soc., *Collections*, VI, 197. In the fall of 1774 there were three or four Tory items to every Whig piece. The word gazette was so frequently

The make-up of the papers—the technical presentation of material—judged by modern standards was extremely poor. Judged by the practices of papers prior to 1763, however, it was good. There was rarely anything sensational in the appearance of the papers, nor did the printers have more than a hazy notion of what constituted effective placing of material. A striking essay might be hidden in the back column of an inside page while advertisements (as until recently in modern English newspapers) covered the front. Since the paper was read and re-read until even its tough rag composition was weakened, these faults were of little import. There were only four small pages of three columns each to the papers, and as they came out only once a week everything in them was carefully read.

On occasion some editors did attract attention by the front page of the paper. At the time of the Stamp Act several appeared on November 1 with black-bordered columns, mourning for the death of Liberty, while others affixed the symbolic skull and crossbones in lieu of the required stamp. The *Boston Gazette*, the *Essex Gazette* of Salem, and the *Massachusetts Spy* commemorated the Boston Massacre with a page in mourning, decorated with appropriate cuts of soldiers and dying victims.[20] Timothy gave the massacre sensational treatment at the time. The entire front page of the *South Carolina Gazette*, with the columns bordered in black and the colophon in solid black, was given over to it.

A more common method of attracting attention and evidencing editorial attitudes was in patriotic captions. The *South Carolina Gazette; and Country Journal*, the *Boston Post-Boy & Advertiser*, and the *New York Gazette* all used the same one during the latter part of the Stamp Act controversy: "The United Voice of His Majesty's *free* and *loyal* Subjects in AMERICA, —LIBERTY and PROPERTY, and NO STAMPS." The *Connecticut Gazette* declared in its heading after 1767 "Every Man has a Right (by the Law of Nature) to the *Defensive*," and as early as 1769 the *Newport Mer-*

---

inserted in the title of colonial newspapers because many of the colonies provided that the government printing was to be inserted in the "Gazette."

[20] The *Spy* made this a practice for several years. In 1772 the "Centinel," No. XXXVII, closed its inflammatory discussion of the massacre with the prediction that if a similar instance of depravity ever occurred again, the Biblical text "HE THAT SHEDDETH MAN'S BLOOD, BY MAN SHALL HIS BLOOD BE SHED" would be verified, a prophecy not long in the fulfilling. A. M. Schlesinger, "The Colonial Newspapers and the Stamp Act" (*New England Quarterly*, VIII, 63-83) has a good discussion of the printers' devices used on and after November 1, 1765.

THURSDAY, April 5, 1770.

BOSTON, February 26.

BOSTON, March 8.

BOSTON, March 12, 1770.

First News of the Boston Massacre. South-Carolina Gazette, *April 5, 1770.*
By courtesy of the Charleston Library Society.

cury was sufficiently determined to proclaim as its faith, "Undaunted by TYRANTS,—We'll DIE or be FREE."[21]

The content of the papers was far more important in influencing opinion than the appearance. About one fourth of the papers was taken up with advertising, about one fourth with crime and tragedy (which the printers called "melancholy incidents"), and the rest with foreign and domestic news, political essays, republished material, and features—philosophical and humorous essays, poems, problems in navigation, and the like.

The propaganda content differed materially from present-day papers. The judicious handling of "spot" news—including certain items and excluding others, exaggerating some accounts, and toning others down—is a much more common technique now. At best, news —especially intercolonial news—was hard to get. Prior to 1763 foreign news alone was printed to any extent; people in most of the colonies were not greatly concerned with events in other colonies except in time of war. It was an exceptional paper which printed before 1763 as much as a column of American news. After 1763, however, people began to take a lively interest in the progress of events in other colonies, and editors were hard put to it to find sufficient accounts. By the help of more colonial post riders, who were often members of one of the committees of correspondence or safety, and a new postal service after 1775, they gradually built up the news service of the papers. By the opening of the war domestic news was easier to obtain and was more authentic than foreign. This development of the colonial news service was of the greatest importance to the propagandists, for it aided immensely in creating a community of ideas and attitudes and hence in unifying action. The similarities of action in widely separated colonies, such as identical demonstrations, can be explained by the full accounts of the demonstrations in the different papers. The suggestive influence of the news items was unmistakable.

The first real attempt by the editors to cover events in different colonies came in 1765. Factual accounts of the rioting in Boston and Newport in August were in nearly every northern newspaper and in many of the southern ones. The fortunes of the stamp distributors

[21] The *Va. Gazette* (Purdie), in 1775 carried the statement, "Always for Liberty, and the Public Good."

were closely followed, and the demonstrations during the nine months' agitation were well reported. Again the northern papers had better accounts than those in the South. The Virginia resolves of 1765 were printed in many papers, those of the Pennsylvania assembly were printed in the *New York Mercury*, the resolves of Connecticut in the *Boston Gazette*, and those of New Jersey in the *Newport Mercury*. Many of the papers carried the Stamp Act itself, and in one specimen list of the duties printed in the *New York Gazette*, the *Newport Mercury*, and the *South Carolina Gazette*, the smallest sum listed was twenty-four pounds and the largest a hundred and twenty, although the largest sum listed in the act itself was ten pounds. The penalties ran higher, of course.

The quantity of news increased with each period of agitation, as did its quality as propaganda. A unique example of what is almost modern handling of news is the "Boston Journal of Occurrences," written in large part by Samuel Adams, Samuel Cooper, perhaps Edes, and one or two others of the Boston radicals. This was begun in the New York *Journal*, October 13, 1768, and was reprinted in many of the principal papers. It consisted of a diary of events in Boston during the military occupancy of the city, beginning September 28, 1768, and ending August 1, 1769. The development of the opposition to the Townshend Acts was treated briefly, but the relations of the citizens and troops were given minute detail. It was in fact part of the propaganda against the troops begun in the late summer of 1768. On November 23, 1768, this statement, remarkable for its disrespect of English officials (remarkable anywhere except in Boston in 1768), appeared: "What may we not expect after seeing that Lord Hillsboro had dared to write that infernal firebrand G—— B——d, that the military is to be called into assistance of the Civil Magistrate; by which our brothers and fellow citizens of Boston are to be sacrificed to the unrelenting vengeance of that merciless tyrant?"

From that time on, there were daily accounts of clashes between the people and the troops—exaggerated incidents which always put the troops in the worst possible light. The "Journal" told how they constantly insulted quiet, respectable merchants in the taverns and coffeehouses and rudely pushed them off the streets. It described how they mistreated children and leered at the women, so that no one felt either comfortable or safe on the streets. Peaceable Boston had become a garrisoned town, so ran the "Journal." Thomas Hutchinson said of it, "Nine tenths of what you read in the Journal of Occurrences in Boston is either absolutely false or grossly misrepresented."[22] Had this "Journal" been confined to Boston, its importance would have been purely local, but it generally covered the country. It appeared not only in the *Boston Evening Post*, but in the *New London Gazette*, the *Pennsylvania Journal*, Green's *Maryland Gazette*, both Purdie's and Rind's *Virginia Gazette*, and the *South Carolina Gazette* as well, a more than representative group of Whig papers. The "Journal" was the most sustained effort to spread ideas through news items that was made in the entire twenty years.

Very few papers carried any of the news relating to Adams' fight in 1772 on the new regulations for the judiciary. The *Boston Gazette*, of course, faithfully printed letters of the various towns in answer to Boston's circular letter of November, 1772. The committee of correspondence selected the ones to be published and was careful to pick only those in sympathy with its position; outside of Massachusetts, only the New York *Journal*, the *Newport Mercury*, and the *South Carolina Gazette* printed any of this material. By 1774, however, papers were beginning to print all the news they could get. Town and county resolutions, both local and domestic, assembly activities, the formation of new agencies of government, and the events in Massachusetts spread through the papers. Riders sent out by local committees carried the news of the battle of Lexington and Concord; no sooner did a rider arrive than another was sent out, but, fast as they were, the news did not reach Savannah until the tenth of May, 1775, twenty-two days later. Soon after the first reports had been published, the official account, together with the depositions hastily gathered for the Boston committee, began to appear in the different papers. Gage's account found its way into very few papers, and none at the time. Thereafter the early war news received full attention, to the exclusion, in fact, of many of the essays which had previously filled the papers.

The accounts of these early engagements were hopelessly at variance. This resulted in part from the uncertain and inaccurate in-

[22] Quoted in Andrews, "Boston Merchants and the Non-Importation Movement," *loc. cit.,* p. 196 n. Dickerson, *Boston under Military Rule,* gives the "Journal" in full. The author says many of the incidents reported in the "Journal" are founded on fact.

formation available and in part from the desire of each editor to print the most favorable account. Of Breed's Hill it was stated in one paper that fifteen hundred colonials held off two thousand regulars until a mistaken order caused a retreat, and in another, two days later, that two thousand colonials held the hill against five thousand regulars and retreated only when their ammunition gave out. Rivington's *New York Gazetteer,* however, had an entirely different version: after emphasizing the difficulties inherent in attacking the position, the writer closed his account with the words: "This action has shown the bravery of the king's troops, who under every disadvantage, gained a complete victory over three times their number, strongly posted, and covered by breastworks."[23]

The technique of the propagandist is more clearly seen in the frequent publication of private letters, or extracts from them. Some of these letters were what would be printed today in a "Voice of the People" column, but in that form they were either political essays or news accounts. The extracts meant here were taken from letters to private individuals, who permitted their publication. Whig propagandists, on receiving letters from correspondents in other colonies or in England, extracted those parts most likely to influence opinion favorably and had them published. These extracts supplemented the uncertain news service and in addition had much greater value as propaganda than the publication of straight news. Only those favorable to the Whig cause were printed, and the information they contained was always colored by the predilections of the author.

These letters came from all parts of the colonies and from abroad throughout the entire twenty years and had a really important effect. Joseph Warren wrote Samuel Adams in 1774 that he had taken the liberty of publishing parts of his letter: "These publications, I think you would approve, if you were sensible of the animation they give to our dejected friends."[24] And John Adams wrote another friend a little later, "Pray write me, by every opportunity—and beseech my Friends to write—Every Letter I receive does great good.—The

[23] July 13, 1775. It is significant that all three accounts appeared in Tory papers. The first appeared in *N. Y. Gazette and Weekly Mercury,* July 3, 1775, and the second and third were both in *N. Y. Gazetteer,* June 29, July 13, 1775. The *Pa. Packet,* June 26, 1775, printed the first.
[24] Frothingham, *Warren,* p. 382.

Gentm [Sam Adams?] to whom most Letters from our Province is addressed, has not Leisure to make the best use of them."[25]

In the main the American letters contained information of cheering and exhortatory character. News from Virginia, for example, was at a premium in the summer of 1765, and the *Newport Mercury* capitalized on several letters describing the adoption of the famous resolutions of May. The first of these letters described their adoption and enclosed a copy. Other letters described the efforts being made to prevent the enforcement of the act, and a final letter, printed on August 5, analyzed the position of Virginians with regard to the payment of the duties. The planters owed over two hundred and fifty thousand pounds, the writer said, with no possible hope of ever paying it, for paper money was illegal, and the Stamp Act if enforced would drain the colony of what little specie was in circulation. The people were eschewing luxuries, he said, but saw little hope for the future unless the Act was repealed. For their part, they were determined never to pay the duties. Further letters from Maryland, Philadelphia, and Boston supported these contentions and added weight to the Virginia protests.[26] Examples abound, for at every period of agitation letters of this same type were published.

The London letters were of equal, if not greater, importance. They were written either by Americans resident in England or by English friends of the colonies, but in either case they were excellent propaganda. To anyone who has read the letters of William Lee, Arthur Lee, or Benjamin Franklin, it is apparent that they were the authors of many of these extracts. The extracts urged perseverance and unity in resistance to the various acts of Parliament, warned of impending dangers, and sent cheering news of dissensions in England in favor of America. These writers were unhampered by fact, and rumor abounded in their letters. Three apposite examples will demonstrate how effectively this method was used. The vagueness of the following extract, written early in 1774, which appeared in

[25] To Moses Gill, June 10, 1775.—Revolutionary Letters, Mass. Arch., CXCIII, 350.

[26] See especially, Dec. 16, 1765, an extract of a letter written by a Virginian and originally printed in Lloyd's *Evening Post* and copied in the *Newport Mercury*. Charles Carroll received a letter from Daniel Barrington, then in London, containing an account of a speech, delivered in the House of Commons, in favor of the colonies. Carroll wrote Barrington, "Jonas Green has ye letter, and intends to insert some extracts he has made out of it in his newspaper."—*Unpublished Letters of Charles Carroll*, p. 111.

both a Massachusetts and a North Carolina paper, was admirably adapted to its purposes:

> "Thirteen different letters are sent to such men as adminis-
> tration thinks will accept of presents and favours, with addresses
> for each man to do his utmost to influence and cajole the ig-
> norant, to deceive and mislead the wise. Money is sent to some
> one printer in each colony to be faithful to their interest; use
> your best endeavours to find them out and expose them; watch
> your newspapers and be prudent, do not be rash in anything;
> be firm and steady."[27]

Contrasted to the above, but equally suited to his particular purpose, are the exact statements and names used by another writer in
1775, after the Tories were out in the open. After stating that commerce was to be banned among all the colonies, just as it had been
prohibited in Boston, the letter reported the rumor that greatly increased numbers of troops were to be sent to New England and New
York, "where they have it is said, been requested to be sent, by
Delancey and his band of traitors—*Cooper, White, Colden,* and
Watts— to aid them in securing *New-York* for the Ministry. This,
it seems, they have undertaken to do, with Military assistance."[28]
The third letter was from a man in London to his friend in North
Carolina; it urged him to sell his slaves as soon as possible, for he
had been told that one of the important Ministers of State had
hinted that all slaves on the continent were to be seized and sold
in Spain, France, and the West Indies.[29]

The editors also republished certain materials they considered to
have propaganda value. Colonial charters, even as early a one as
Raleigh's patent of 1584, were printed to give concrete proof to the
accompanying essays, which claimed that in these documents Parliament had reserved no right of monopolizing trade, imposing taxes,
or legislating for the colonies in any instance. The Bill of Rights

---

[27] The Boston News column of *N. C. Gazette* (Davis), Sept. 2, 1774. The letter was
dated Apr. 29, 1774.

[28] 4 Force, *Amer. Arch.*, II, 25.

[29] *N. C. Gazette* (Davis), July 7, 1775. Part of a letter written before the news of
the Boston Port Act reached America was published because it fitted so perfectly the theme
of Boston propaganda: "I hope there is no necessity of admonishing you to unite in the
defence of the liberty of *America*. The stroke may first be felt in *Boston*, but the man
who does not perceive it meant against the whole line of Colonies must be blind indeed.
Trust me, the views of the Administration are to subdue and enslave you."—4 Force,
Amer. Arch., I, 248.

and Magna Carta were printed for obvious reasons.[30] The Virginia resolutions of 1765, Dickinson's broadside issued in November, 1765, Franklin's "Edict of the King of Prussia," and Warren's "Fifth of March Oration," were other reprints which appeared more or less frequently.[31]

More important was the serial republication of the better pamphlets. Stephen Hopkins' *Rights of the Colonists Examined* ran in the *New York Gazette, or, Weekly Post-Boy*, beginning January 24, 1765, just a month after its first publication; and James Otis' *Letter to a Noble Lord* was reprinted in the *Boston Gazette* from July 22 to September 2, 1765. The *Boston News-Letter* on June 13, 1765, printed a long extract from Jenyns' *Objections to the Taxation of Our American Colonies Considered*. The *Boston Gazette* printed Mercy Warren's *Adulateur* in installments in July, 1773, and the New York *Journal* copied Jefferson's *Summary View* in October, 1774. Numbers of the *Crisis* appeared in newspapers, and Dr. Richard Price's *Observations on the Nature of Civil Liberty* was reprinted in both Gill's *Continental Journal* and the *Connecticut Courant*.[32] Both Dixon's *Virginia Gazette* and the *Connecticut Courant* printed Paine's *Common Sense*.

Opportunities for propaganda also could be found in the poets' corner, frequently found in the papers. Songs and poems of a patriotic nature were printed here in number. Dickinson's "Liberty Song" appeared in almost as many papers as his "Farmer's Letters," and at least three papers copied a parody on the famous soliloquy:

> "Be taxt, or not be taxt, that is the question:
> Whether 'tis nobler in our minds to suffer
> The flights and cunning of deceitful statesmen,
> Or to petition 'gainst illegal taxes,
> And by opposing end them?"[33]

[30] *Boston Gazette*, Aug. 17, Aug. 24, 1767, Jan. 8, 1770; *Pa. Evening Post*, May 30, 1776.

[31] *Pa. Gazette*, Dec. 5, 1765; *Conn. Gazette*, Dec. 20, 1765; N. Y. *Journal, Supplement*, Apr. 2, 1768; *S. C. Gazette*, Dec. 13, 1773; *Pa. Journal, Supplement*, Mar. 29, 1775. The *Ga. Gazette* on request published on Aug. 23, 1769, an extract from Jason Haven's Massachusetts election sermon of that year.

[32] Parts of the "Crisis" were printed in *N. E. Chronicle*, June 8, 1775, and in *N. H. Gazette*, Oct. 17, 1765. Zubly's *Short Account of the Struggle of the Swiss for Liberty*, originally appended to a sermon he had preached, was reprinted in full in *Pa. Evening Post*, beginning Oct. 19, 1775, and in *Cont. Journal*, June 13, June 20, 1776.

[33] *Mass. Spy*, Aug. 14, 1770, and *S. C. Gazette*, Mar. 16, 1769—copied from *Ga. Gazette*, Mar. 1, 1769.

The political essay, however, was the most important form of newspaper propaganda. Such essays, written almost entirely by others than the editors, correspond to nothing in the modern paper except perhaps the editorials; they appear today only in magazines or separate tracts. The articles were always signed by a pseudonym —Vindex, Brittanus, Americus, Freeman, Cato, and the like—both to avoid the charge of libel or treason, and to make it appear that more than one person was writing. Samuel Adams is said to have used at least twenty-five different pseudonyms, and William Livingston wrote under a variety of names because, he said, it discouraged his opponents, who magnified "in their own imagination the strength of their adversaries beyond its true amount."[34]

Great numbers of these essays appeared after 1763, but naturally they were far more numerous at times of stress. They began in protest to the Stamp Act in 1764, died out after the repeal of the act, reappeared in the fall of 1767 or early 1768, began to disappear in late 1770, started again in the fall of 1773, and in the year following the passage of the Boston Port Act, two thousand or more must have been printed, for there was at least one or more in each week's issue of every colonial paper.[35]

These essays were comparatively short, straightforward appeals— serious, humorous, satirical, or allegorical, depending upon the fancy and ability of the writer. A good many appeared in a series, but most of them were complete in one issue. A common form was the controversial letter, which attacked, line by line, often word by word, the writings of an opponent. The intent was to make the opponent and his arguments ridiculous and to advance the cause by controverting or neutralizing his propaganda. Christopher Gadsden attacked William Henry Drayton in this fashion, and they carried on a newspaper war for nearly three months, back and forth in each issue of the *South Carolina Gazette*.[36] Mein's writings in the *Chronicle* were treated in the same fashion, and John Adams' most famous contribution to the writings of the Revolution was the series of letters signed

[34] Sedgwick, *Life of Livingston*, p. 282. Paine wrote in the papers under the name "The Forester," Warren used "True Patriot," Quincy, "Hyperion" and "Independent," Benjamin Greenleaf and Thomas Mifflin both used "Scaevola," and Rush wrote under the name "Hampden." Scaevola was a legendary Roman hero of the sixth century, B.C.

[35] Two to a paper, including duplicates and Tory pieces and counting individual numbers of a series separately, would total four thousand or more. The *Boston Gazette* averaged three or four an issue. [36] Aug. 3 to Oct. 18, 1769.

"Novanglus," which answered Daniel Leonard's letters of "Massachusettensis." Such letters frequently became abusive and scurrilous, but at other times, as in Adams' letters, the method was more impersonal and dignified. In either case they are extremely difficult to follow, for as a usual thing both writers lost sight of their original purpose early in the series and became involved in petty bickering, word play, charge and countercharge, to such an extent that only a complete knowledge of both sides can ever untangle them. The essay type fortunately was much more common.

The political essay resembled in shorter form the political tract, except that it began where the serious, argumentative pamphlet left off. The author assumed, that is, the rights which others had attempted to prove, stated them in the baldest fashion, and then applied them to the case in point. Some of the finest examples of constructive thinking, however, appeared in the columns of these "petty, dingy," newspapers. John Dickinson's "Letters from a Farmer in Pennsylvania," unsurpassed in literary merit during the period, first appeared in the *Pennsylvania Chronicle*, December 2, 1767, and were soon reprinted in twenty-one of the twenty-five papers of the day. They began, for example, in the *Boston Gazette* on December 21, 1767, and in the *Georgia Gazette* on January 27, 1768. Two of John Adams' most important contributions—"A Dissertation on the Canon and Feudal Law," and the letters of "Novanglus"—were first written for the newspapers and only later were published as pamphlets.[37]

Most of the articles were not of such quality. They were often loosely constructed, even disconnected, and depended for their appeal either upon the force of their language, the repetition of ideas, or the novelty of the presentation. The "Book of America," for instance, which was printed in the *Boston Gazette* in May, 1766, was identical in form with the *First Book of American Chronicles* and was probably the inspiration for it. The "Guardian Angel of America" wrote a chapter from her reminiscences in Heaven and mailed it down to Edes, who obligingly inserted it on February 10, 1766.

[37] Tyler, *Literary History of the Revolution*, I, 57, says the pamphlet *Some Thoughts on Improving and Securing the Advantages which Accrue to Great Britain from the Northern Colonies*, first published in London, had previously appeared in a New York paper in August, 1764. Six essays originally published in *Pa. Packet*, June-August, 1776, entitled "A Few Political Reflections Submitted to the Consideration of the British Colonies," were collected in a pamphlet later in the year.

These reminiscences concerned the early struggles of the first set-tlers, the solemn charter engagements and their subsequent flagrant violation, and ended with an urgent request to withstand these in-fractions of agreements long since sealed and ratified. These two are typical of many others. Humorous stories, allegories, vitupera-tive articles—every form of literary expression was used to spread the typical propaganda themes.

The influence of these essays, or at least of the more popular ones, was by no means confined to the subscribers of the papers which originally published them. One of the most common practices of the day was the copying of material from other papers. Paper after paper carried the same news accounts, the same essays, the same extracts from pamphlets, and even the same poems. Some editors frequently complained that local contributions were almost impos-sible to obtain and that they were forced to fill their columns with extracts from other papers, but others copied material as a matter of policy. The *Newport Mercury*, the *Connecticut Gazette*, the *Con-necticut Journal*, and the *South Carolina Gazette* made a constant practice of it. The first opposition to the Tea Act in the *South Caro-lina Gazette*, for example, was in the form of several essays from New England, New York, and Philadelphia papers, inserted by Peter Timothy because his readers would be interested, he said, in the disturbance which the act had created there.[38]

An exact list of all the duplications would not be worth the trou-ble it would take to accomplish it; a few examples will illustrate the extent and importance of this practice.

Many of the better essays were extensively copied, but most of them were copied in only one or two other papers. Arthur Lee's "Monitor" series, originally published in the *Virginia Gazette*, was reprinted by the New York *Journal* in April, 1768, and by the *South Carolina Gazette* in June. The New York *Journal* and Green's *Maryland Gazette* copied a radical piece signed "Atticus" from one of the Virginia gazettes, and several southern papers in 1769 carried an article called "The Case of Great Britain and Amer-ica." Paine's articles signed "The Forester" and William Smith's

---

[38] Nov. 15, 1773. Sam Adams was constantly selecting material for the *Boston Gazette* from other papers, and others did the same thing. Alexander McDougall, for example, was so impressed with Jonathan Shipley's *Speech* that he sent it to Adams with the suggestion that it be reprinted in the Philadelphia papers.—Adams Papers, Sept. 3, 1774.

replies under the name "Cato" were published in the *Pennsylvania Gazette*, the *Pennsylvania Journal* in April and the *Norwich Packet* in May, 1776.

This duplication of essays, far more extensive than the few illustrations above prove, was one of the essential features of the newspapers and one of the most important. It kept the leaders in touch with the thought of other colonies, it increased the influence of the pieces copied, and it aided materially in providing the basis for common attitudes and common actions.

II

THE TORY COUNTERATTACK
1763-1783

PROPAGANDISTS AND PROBLEMS

THE ENGLISH officials in the colonies and their supporters, commonly called the Tories, were on the defensive from 1763 to 1776. Their point of view, in so far as it stood for loyalty to George III and union with the British Empire, was the normal attitude of most Americans down to 1775. The burden of proof, of conversion, of forming a coherent party, was on the Whigs, but the English officials relied too much upon legal pressures and unintentional propaganda to maintain the existing system. That is, they expected the regular agencies of government to maintain the King's authority and the traditional attitudes and values to prevent the spread of the revolutionary propaganda. In this naïve hope they were sadly mistaken. The regular agencies of government were adroitly used by Whig propagandists to spread their revolutionary ideas, and the traditional values of the old system were rapidly being swept away by the floods of Whig propaganda.

The King's cause, however, was not without its friends, and throughout every stage of the controversy with England there were those who spoke "publicly in favor of government." The number who engaged in intentional propaganda activities was never very large; there were many colonies which did not produce a single propagandist of importance. The Whigs controlled so many of the agencies of government, and closed so many avenues of approach to the people, that the circumscribed contacts greatly limited the effect of the Tories' efforts. Fear detained many would-be Tory propagandists, and coercion cut short the activities of the fearless.

The best Tory propagandists, as might be expected, were Anglican clergymen—five in particular: Samuel Seabury, Miles Cooper, and Charles Inglis, all of New York; Thomas Bradbury Chandler of New Jersey; and Jonathan Boucher of Maryland.

Samuel Seabury, the greatest of the five, was in the prime of his life when the controversy broke out. He had been born in Groton, Connecticut, in 1729, and after four years at Yale he was sent by the Society for the Propagation of the Gospel to Brunswick, New Jersey. There he defended the cause of the society and the church against the aspersions of those attacking the idea of an American episcopate. In 1765 he went to Westchester County, New York, where he remained until the Revolution. It was at this time that he entered into an engagement with three of his brother clergymen—Cooper, Inglis, and Chandler—to defend the cause of the church and the monarchy against all attacks. This engagement is the clearest and most significant piece of evidence we have that these men thoroughly understood the necessity for arousing public opinion. Seabury stated in his petition to the Loyalist Claims Commission that when it was evident to him from the continued publications and the uniting of all the "Jarring Interests of the Independents & Presbyterians from Massachusetts bay to Georgia under Grand Committees & Synods that some mischievous Scheme was meditated against the Church of England and the British Gov't in Am^a your Memor^t did enter into an engagement with the Rev^d Dr. T. B. Chandler then of Elizth Town, New Jersey and with the Rev^d Dr. Inglis, the present Rector of Trinity Church in the City of New York, to watch all publications either in News papers or Pamphlets and to obviate the evil influence of such as appeared to have a bad tendency by the speediest answers."[1] He faithfully carried out his part of the agreement in so far as it concerned the interests of the church and joined with his associates in their attack on Livingston's "American Whig." He did not enter the political dispute, however, until 1774.

The evident designs of the Whigs after the passage of the Coercive Acts so disturbed him that he began an active campaign against them. Together with Isaac Wilkins he led protest meetings in Westchester County against the provincial councils of New York and the Continental Congress, and when these failed he began his written appeals. Using the pseudonym "A Westchester Farmer," he published four of the ablest pamphlets written during the entire controversy. The first of these, *Free Thoughts on the Proceedings of the Continental Congress*, was addressed to the farmers of New York. The second, directed particularly to the merchants of the city, was *The Congress Canvassed*. The third was an answer to one of

---

[1] Transcripts of the Manuscript Books and Papers of the Commission of Enquiry into the Losses and Services of the American Loyalists (hereinafter cited Loyalist Transcripts), XLI, 560. Seabury did not list Myles Cooper, but Charles Inglis did.

Hamilton's pamphlets. This third pamphlet, *A View of the Contro-versy between Great Britain and her Colonies,* presented the con-structive side of the loyalist argument, proposing constitutional re-forms which should at once guarantee American rights and preserve the Empire. The fourth was addressed, said Seabury, not to the provincial council, nor to the Continental Congress, but to the duly elected representatives of the people of New York. It was called *An Alarm to the Legislature of New York* and was an earnest appeal to it to regain its lost authority and to settle the dispute upon terms of justice to both parties. These four pamphlets appeared within two months, from November 16, 1774, to January 17, 1775. A fifth, planned as a direct attack on the republicanism of the Whigs, was advertised the day after Lexington and Concord but was never pub-lished.

These pamphlets were so effective that mere answers were in-sufficient. Seabury heard it rumored just after the opening of the war that a crowd was coming to take him, and he and Isaac Wilkins left their homes temporarily. On November 20, 1775, Isaac Sears and a band of people from Connecticut (the same crowd which de-stroyed Rivington's press), invaded his house while he was away, and finally captured him. He was taken to New Haven and held as a prisoner until December 23, when the local committee released him because it could not prove that he was the author of the West-chester pamphlets. He was constantly molested thereafter by pass-ing bands of troops, who, he said, frequently went five miles or more out of their way to insult him, and, finally, on the first of September, 1776, after the battle of Long Island, he fled behind the British lines. Although he took an active part in the war as chaplain to an American loyalist regiment after 1778, he never wrote again for the cause. That this man was made the first bishop of the American Episcopal Church, and so soon after the Revolution, is striking testi-mony to the fact that even his enemies recognized his courage and his abilities.[2]

No other propagandist equalled the two months' record of Sam-uel Seabury. The three others closely associated with him, Cooper, Inglis, and Chandler, are all suspected of having done a great deal

[2] Seabury's own account of his troubles is *ibid.,* pp. 559-570. A good summary of his pamphlets is in Tyler, *Literary History of the Revolution,* I, 334 ff. See also, E. E. Beardsley, *Life and Correspondence of the Right Reverend Samuel Seabury, D.D.*

to further the loyalist cause, and to each of them certain pamphlets have been attributed.

Myles Cooper, English born, was President of King's College after 1763 and took an active part in the defense of the church in 1768, even touring the South seeking support for an American episcopate. Like Seabury, he took no part in the growing political dispute until after the meeting of the first Continental Congress. He is said to have done a good deal of writing. A poem, newspaper articles, and two pamphlets have been ascribed to him. The poem was called "The Patriots of North America," and the two pamphlets were *The American Querist*, a series of assertions in question form, and *A Friendly Address to all Reasonable Americans*, in which he urged a solution of the problem not unlike that proposed by Galloway. These were all published between June, 1774, and April, 1775. There is no certainty that they were by Cooper, but it was so assumed at the time, and it is certain that the forms of an essay by him were destroyed at Rivington's printing office. So furious was the Whig resentment against him that he narrowly escaped mob discipline in May, 1775. Only the timely services of young Alexander Hamilton, who harangued the crowd while he fled to the harbor, saved him. Fifteen days later, on May 25, 1775, he sailed for England.[3]

Thomas Bradbury Chandler of Elizabethtown, New Jersey, had much the same record. He was born in Connecticut and studied at Yale, as did Seabury, and confirmed his Anglicanism by studying with President Samuel Johnson of King's College. He went to St. John's in Elizabethtown in 1747 and remained there until he left America. He was one of the parties to the engagement described by Seabury and faithfully carried out his pledge. At the time of the Stamp Act he wrote the secretary of the S.P.G.: "Such an universal spirit of clamour and discontent, little short of madness . . . as I believe was scarcely ever seen on any occasion . . . I really detest it, and do endeavour to traverse and counteract it to the utmost of my ability."[4] In 1768 he bore the brunt of the fight with Livingston and Charles Chauncy over the establishment of an American bish-

---

[3] Tyler, *Literary History*, I, 392 ff. Moore, *Diary of the Revolution*, I, 8, ascribes a series of essays signed "A New York Freeholder" to him. Cf. note 7, this chapter.

[4] Quoted in Albert H. Hoyt, "The Reverend Thomas Bradbury Chandler, D.D., 1726-1790," *New England Historical and Genealogical Register*, XXVII, 227-236.

opric. He wrote two major pamphlets in defense of the plan, *An Appeal to the Public*, and *An Address to the Clergy of New York*. Again, however, he was another Tory propagandist who failed to enter the political disputes until 1774. In 1775 he published an attack on the measures of Congress, called *What Think Ye of the Congress Now?*, but so menacing did he consider the situation after the battle of Lexington and Concord that he left for England. Gage wrote the Earl of Dartmouth on June 12 recommending to him both Cooper and Chandler, "who have distinguished themselves greatly in the Cause of Government and on that Account obliged to fly from New York."[5]

The fourth of these associates was Charles Inglis, assistant rector of Trinity Church, New York City. Irish born, he came to America in 1755. Shortly thereafter he was ordained in London and sent to Dover, Delaware. From there he went to Trinity parish, New York, as the assistant to the Rector, the Reverend Samuel Auchmuty. In his petition to the Loyalist Claims Commission, Inglis gives his version of the agreement with the other Anglican clergymen:

"That your Memorialist observing a restless and seditious spirit to prevail in some parts of America long before the proceedings there occasioned any public Alarm, had formed a resolution in conjun[n] with some of his intimate friends particularly the Rev[d] Dr. Thomas Bradbury Chandler the Rev[d] Dr. Myles Cooper and Rev[d] Dr. Samuel Seabury to watch all publications that were disrespectful to Government or the parent State, or that tended to a breach between Great Britain and her Colonys and to give them an immediate answer and refutation, which resolution he and they punctually adhered to as often as an occasion was offered."[6]

He began his public agitation against the Whigs in 1774, when many were in doubt about the Continental Congress. He wrote, according to his petition to the Claims Commission, a series of newspaper essays signed "A New York Farmer,"[7] but when the Suffolk

---

[5] *The Correspondence of General Thomas Gage with the Secretaries of State*, I, 404 (June 12, 1775). Quoted by permission of Yale University Press. Chandler's activities in the matter of the episcopate are fully detailed in Cross, *Anglican Episcopate*, especially Chap. VII. See also Johnson Papers, p. 163.

[6] Loyalist Transcripts, XLII, 543.

[7] No articles signed "A New York Farmer" appear in either the *N. Y. Gazette and Weekly Mercury* or the *N. Y. Gazetteer*. A series signed "A New York Freeholder," however, ran in the *N. Y. Gazette and Weekly Mercury*, Sept. 12 to Oct. 10, 1774, inclusive.

resolves were adopted by the Continental Congress he realized, he said, that independence was designed, and he gave up further newspaper activity. He did visit extensively in Dutchess and Ulster counties during the years 1774 to 1776, "to warn his Friends in the Country as well as City of the evils that were approaching . . . and he could name many whom he confirmed in Loyalty when wavering or whom he prevented from joining in the rebellion." "In this Interval," he continued in his petition, "also he frequently afforded assist^{ce} in forwarding the publications of his Friends in support of Government and also wrote several Occasional papers when Circumstances required it."[8]

When Paine's *Common Sense* appeared, Inglis felt impelled to counteract its influence. He wrote an answer to it, first called "The Deceiver unmasked, or Loyalty and Interest united, in Answer to a pamphlet falsely called Common Sense." Governor Tryon, then on board a British ship of war in the harbor, urged its publication, and at his request David Mathews, Mayor of New York, carried it to a printer. But no sooner was it advertised than a mob gathered and demanded a copy; after a brief examination the pamphlet was condemned and the whole edition burned. Some weeks later Inglis learned that it might be published in Philadelphia, and he sent several copies. It finally was published there under the new name *The True Interest of America Impartially Stated*. When Washington took New York, Inglis went to Flushing and thereafter followed the British army, but, unlike Seabury, he continued his writing for the cause.[9]

The fifth of the outstanding Anglican propagandists was Jonathan Boucher, of Annapolis. He was born in Cumberland County, England, of rather poor parents. His father was a small landholder at one time, but died in poverty, and much of Jonathan's early career was blighted, at least in his own mind, by lack of money. He was determined to raise himself in the world, but preferred to do it by the help of others rather than by his own exertions; he was the

----

They also appeared in the *Mass. Gazette, and Boston Weekly News-Letter*, Oct. 6, Oct. 20, Oct. 27, Nov. 10, 1774. This pseudonym was used by Inglis in 1782, and the essays are in his style. There is little doubt but that these are the articles to which he referred. —Loyalist Transcripts, XLII, 564.

[8] Loyalist Transcripts, XLII, 546 f.

[9] *Ibid.*, pp. 541-567. The biography by John Wolfe Lydekker contains several of Inglis' letters.

confirmed placeman. As he admitted himself, "Determined always to raise myself in the world, I had not patience to wait for the slow savings of a humble station; and I fancied I could get into a higher, only by my being taken notice of by people of condition."[10] He had an ambitious, restless spirit, a great contempt for plain and humble people, and a marked distaste for a world in which there were no people of condition to help a poor man on his way. He sought in America the opportunities which eluded him in England, but various plans for his future failed, and he finally resorted to the church. After his ordination in 1762 he obtained a parish in Maryland, and at the time of the Revolution he was in Queen Anne's Parish, where he had for some time been ingratiating himself with Governor Eden and other people of prominence in the community. His entire attitude toward the Revolution is almost comprised in a statement he made regarding his life in Annapolis, which he had found delightful; this pleasant life lasted, he said, until "the troubles began and put an end to everything that was pleasant and proper."[11]

In the early part of the controversy, like so many ultimate loyalists, he objected to undue parliamentary legislation for the colonies and said as late as 1769, "I do think the American opposi'n the most warrantable, generous, & manly, that History can produce."[12] But like all the others, the events of 1774-75 changed his entire attitude, and, as he said in his *Reminiscences*, "I endeavoured in my sermons, and in various pieces published in the Gazettes of the country, to check the immense mischief that was impending, but I endeavoured in vain."[13] Boucher's sermons were not published at the time, but much later he published in England a volume containing thirteen sermons which he claimed to have delivered in Maryland. These may not be in the exact form in which he delivered them—in all probability they are not—but there can be no question that they reflect his attitude at the time, for his preaching and the occasional

[10] *Reminiscences of an American Loyalist, 1738-1799* (ed. Jonathan Bouchier), p. 31. This is an apology of sorts for his incurable habit of contracting debts he could not pay. In his early youth he once lived near a family of gentle people who befriended him and gave him both clothes and money. "I saw here a little of something which looked like genteel life, and which, while it inspired me with some taste and longing for it, rendered me not quite so awkward and uncouth as I must needs have been without it."—*Ibid.*, p. 12. These and subsequent quotations from this work are quoted by permission of Houghton-Mifflin Company.

[11] *Ibid.*, p. 67.

[12] "The Letters of Jonathan Boucher," *Maryland Historical Magazine*, VIII, 44.

[13] Pp. 104 f.

pieces he published aroused intense antagonism. The press was soon closed to him, and he was forcibly restrained from preaching. Even before the actual events which led to his flight from Maryland he wrote the Reverend Dr. Smith of Philadelphia:

"I write to you now, however, more immediately, with the View of drawing from you some acc't of the sad convulsions which are about to rend in Pieces this once happy Country. . . . Will you then, my dear Sir, submit to be persuaded by me, who think not to prevail by my much Speaking to step forth? . . . Were I not, as Shakespeare says, *a Fellow of no Mark nor Liklihood*, something even I wou'd certainly have done; but I have so bad a Name, and am Moreover so sure to be found out, and of course to be maul'd by the Committees. I am not ashamed to own to you, I have been deterr'd thro' Fear."[14]

He had good reason to fear the power of the committees, for he had had difficulty with them before. He first ran afoul of the patriots when asked to deliver a sermon in behalf of the suffering of Boston. He refused, he said, because it was simply a means of raising money for the purchase of arms and ammunition. Shortly thereafter he refused to sign the Continental Association of October 20, 1774, and thus came under the jurisdiction of the committee of inspection as a violator of Article XI. The Annapolis committee examined and acquitted him. But he was in an embarrassing position on July 20, the day set aside in 1775 by the Continental Congress as a day of fasting and prayer. He wanted to preach, but the crowd refused, and his friends finally persuaded him not to enter the pulpit, alleging that he would surely be killed. The crowd, led by Osborn Sprigg, a member of the local committee, became still more menacing, and finally Boucher was fully surrounded by his enemies:

"Seeing myself thus circumstanced, it occurred to me that things seemed now indeed to be growing alarming, and that there was but one way to save my life. This was by seizing Sprigg, as I immediately did, by the collar, assuring him that if any violence was offered to me I would instantly blow his

---

[14] "Letters of Jonathan Boucher," *Md. Hist. Mag.*, VIII, 238 ff. He sent a piece or so to one of the Virginia papers, but the printer showed them to Carter, who recognized the handwriting; this was what led the mob to attack him, he thought.—*Reminiscences*, pp. 110 f.

brains out, as I most certainly would have done. I then told him that if he pleased he might conduct me to my horse, and I would leave them. This he did, and we marched together upwards of a hundred yards, I with one hand fastened in his collar and a pistol in the other, guarded by his whole company, which he had the meanness to order to play on their drums the Rogue's March all the way we went, which they did. All farther that I could then do was to declare, as loud as I could speak, that he had now proved himself to be a complete coward and scoundrel."[15]

The attacks became more frequent, each more furious, he thought, than the previous one, and he determined to leave America before the Continental embargo on exports should stop all vessels. He sailed on September 10, 1775, and resumed in England his efforts to lift himself in the world by the help of men of "rank and condition."

Jonathan Odell, the finest satirist among the loyalist propagandists, took no active part in the early movement. He was a native of New Jersey and was graduated from the College of New Jersey in 1759. After a brief career as an army surgeon, he turned to the ministry. Ordained in 1766, he was sent by the S. P. G. to Burlington, New Jersey. He felt it the duty of the Anglican ministers, even after the battle of Lexington and Concord, "to promote as far as in them lies, a spirit of peace and good order among the Members of their Communion,"[16] and it was not until the late spring of 1776 that he began his satirical attacks on the Whigs. A song of his was sung by the British prisoners in the local jail on the King's birthday in 1776, and this so incensed the local Whig committee that it arrested him. The provincial council confined him to the neighborhood of Burlington, but in December he broke his parole and escaped behind the British lines. It was some time after Independence was declared that he did his best work as a poet of the loyalists.

The other ministers of the Anglican communion were less important as writers. Most of them either tried to remain neutral or followed the dominant element in their communities. Their sermons,

---

[15] *Ibid.*, pp. 122 f. He has a slightly different version in one of his letters, *Md. Hist. Mag.*, VIII, 243 f. He was proscribed by the Virginia House of Burgesses and prohibited from preaching. See W. W. Hening, comp., *The Statutes at Large: being a Collection of all the Laws of Virginia*, IX, 170.

[16] George W. Hills, *History of the Church in Burlington, New Jersey*, p. 308. See also Tyler, *Literary History*, II, 80, 100 f.

so far as we have any record of them, were not pointed to the political problems, but dealt with the general problems of loyalty, obedience to government, and purity of life in time of trouble. Whenever one in a strong Whig section did attempt more he was summarily treated. The Reverend John Bullman, for example, assistant rector of St. Michael's, Charleston, preached only one strong Tory sermon. It was preached on August 14, 1774, called "The Christian Duty of Peaceableness," but it ridiculed the Whig leaders, and he was immediately ordered out of his pulpit.[17] Both John Agnew and John Wingate of Virginia were early suppressed by the Whigs, and it was only in occasional sermons and in private conversation that other ministers attempted to win converts.

Outside the Anglican Church, the Tory propagandists were relatively scarce. The four most important men who showed a conscious determination to win public support for the administration were Joseph Galloway, Daniel Leonard, Jonathan Sewall, and Joseph Stansbury.

Joseph Galloway came from a wealthy trading family which owned large estates in Maryland. Galloway studied for the bar and early showed marked political ambitions. He was a member of the Pennsylvania Assembly from 1756 to 1776, except for one term, when he was not returned because of his opposition to the Paxton rioters. This dislike of disorder led him to oppose the Whig movement, but at the same time he thought Parliament was exercising power beyond its authority. He saw the true solution of the imperial problem in a written constitution for America. A definite plan was drawn up by him for the first meeting of the Continental Congress, and on its rejection he presented the whole matter to the people in a pamphlet called *A Candid Examination of the Mutual Claims of Great Britain and the Colonies*. He retired to the country during the worst of the troubles in Pennsylvania, hoping to remain neutral, but was finally forced to seek safety behind the British lines. He aided in the administration of Philadelphia during the British occupation, and with the withdrawal of the army he fled to England. His only serious attempt, therefore, to influence the public mind was the pamphlet published in 1775. He did write another pamphlet in answer to a published attack on his *Candid Examination*,

---

[17] Loyalist Transcripts, LIV, 85, and McCrady, *S. C. under Royal Government*, p. 752.

and Rivington printed it in 1775. Fear of mob action deterred Rivington from publishing the pamphlet at that time, and it did not appear until 1777.[18]

Daniel Leonard, as a further example, made only one important popular appeal. The Leonards for years had dominated southern Massachusetts, and Daniel was one of the outstanding citizens of the colony, wealthy, aristocratic, conservative, and highly regarded. He was a Harvard graduate and by 1774 had made a substantial reputation for himself at the bar. His natural inclinations toward a stable social order and strong government, as well, perhaps, as his love for a prominent position, predisposed him against the extreme Whig demands, and Hutchinson had no difficulty in securing his support in 1774 at the meeting under the so-called "Tory pear tree" at Taunton. Leonard became one of the new councilors provided for in the Massachusetts government act and was soon forced to defend himself against the angry crowds. He went to Boston and there wrote seventeen letters to the *Massachusetts Gazette,* signed "Massachusettensis." These letters constituted a reasonable, at times even an eloquent, defense of the Tory position. Although he admitted that he did not entirely approve of all that the government had done,[19] Leonard, unlike most of the better Tory propagandists, did not present in extended form constructive suggestions for solving the problem. He was content with a thoroughgoing defense and counterattack. These letters were his only important contribution to the propaganda of the period. He stayed with the British army in Boston until its evacuation, and then went to Halifax in March, 1776, and from there to England.

Jonathan Sewall, the third of these political propagandists, came from a Massachusetts family even more distinguished than that of the Leonards. A friend of John Adams and a Harvard graduate, it would seem that Sewall had every reason to adopt the Whig side, but on the contrary he became one of the strongest of Hutchinson's supporters in Massachusetts. It has been said that the refusal of the general court to give him financial aid in the settlement of his uncle's estate so irritated him that when Hutchinson offered him an official position he did not hesitate to accept and was thereafter bound to

[18] Evans, *Amer. Biblio.,* No. 14,060. For further information on Galloway, see Tyler, *Literary History,* Vol. I, Chap. XVII, and *Dictionary of American Biography.*

[19] Third letter of *Massachusettensis.*

the Tory cause. He became convinced of the certain defeat of America and is said to have written extensively in the newspapers in an effort to convert people to his way of thinking. He used the pseudonyms "Philanthropos" and "Long J.," and one writer asserts that he wrote Gage's proclamation of 1775. John Adams believed almost until his death that Sewall was the author of the Massachusettensis letters, but no such long pieces have ever been shown to be his. A dramatic colloquy, however, *The Americans Roused, in a Cure for the Spleen,* a hard-hitting attack on the Continental Congress, has been attributed to him. Like so many others, he left for England early in 1775.[20]

Joseph Stansbury, the only real poet of the loyalist side other than Jonathan Odell, was London born and did not come to America until 1767. He was the songster of the Tories and united in his own attitudes and in his songs real love for both England and America. His early poems consequently reflect his objection to the impolicy of much that the British ministry proposed. A song written in 1771 illustrates admirably his point of view:

> "Though party contentions awhile may run high,
> When danger advances, they'll vanish and die;
> While all with one heart, hand, and spirit unite,
> Like Englishmen think, and like Englishmen fight.

> "Then here's to our king—and oh, long may he reign,
> The lord of those men who are lords of the main!
> While all the contention among us shall be,
> To make him as happy, as we are made free."[21]

His was a peaceful nature. He opposed both the disorderliness of the Whigs and the coercive measures of the British government, but he always stood for opposition from within the empire, and after the Declaration of Independence he stayed with the British army. He was arrested by the Whigs in Philadelphia and was imprisoned for a short time in 1776. He signed the oath of allegiance, but when the British took Philadelphia, he returned to his former faith and remained with the army when it retreated to New York. It was during this period that he did his best work for the cause of the

King. He was arrested again in 1780 on well-grounded suspicions of treason (he had aided, it appears, both André and Arnold) and never reinstated himself in the confidence of the people.

Several others made individual contributions of less importance. One of the earliest was Martin Howard, the Rhode Island pamphleteer and literary opponent of Stephen Hopkins and James Otis. Howard's first pamphlet, *A Letter from a Gentleman at Halifax*, was an answer to Hopkins' *The Rights of the British Colonies Examined*. His second and last pamphlet was his rebuttal of a counterattack written by James Otis. These two statements of the right of Parliament to levy taxes in America were ably done. They were so influential, in fact, that the Rhode Island assembly debated the best method of suppressing them, and a Newport mob in August, 1765, gutted Howard's house and even injured the man himself.[22]

Then there were the Reverend Henry Caner of King's Chapel, Boston, who wrote several very "sensible publications upholding the authority of parliament," and Dr. Thomas Bolton, who published a satire on Hancock's "Fifth of March Oration."[23] Provost William Smith of Philadelphia, although previously a moderate Whig, wrote a series of newspaper articles in 1776 opposing independence. These seven essays, which began in the *Pennsylvania Gazette* on March 13, 1776, constituted one of the ablest attacks on *Common Sense*. Two newspaper men, John Mein and James Rivington, were such capable opponents of the Whigs that they, too, were propagandists in their own right.[24]

The purpose of the Tory propagandists was obviously not to support blindly all the acts of the Crown or of Parliament. There are instances, of course, of outright defense of British acts, but there were many more instances of Tories who doubted their expediency.[25]

Succinctly put, the program of the Tory propagandists was threefold: to uphold the authority of King and Parliament, not the wis-

---

[22] *Boston Gazette*, Sept. 2, 1765; *Newport Mercury*, Sept. 2, 1765.

[23] E. Alfred Jones, *The Loyalists of Massachusetts, Their Memorials, Petitions and Claims*, pp. 76 ff., 218 f.

[24] Some of the governors were adept at persuasion, Hutchinson of Massachusetts, for example, and Wright of Georgia.

[25] As Jonathan Boucher put it: "The want of policy in those of Great Britain is acknowledged in its fullest extent. . . . That the Parent State has been unwise, I readily grant; contending only that she has never been unjust: for, it has again and again been proved, that she has been right in her intentions, and, I think, right also in her principles."—*A View of the Causes*, p. 372.

dom of any particular act; to combat what they termed the riotous and illegal methods of the Whigs; and finally, to propose alternate methods of redress, or more fundamentally, to propose a permanent solution of the difficulties.

In its entirety, this program was anything but the program of obstructionists or negationists; the more enlightened Tories had the rights of America much at heart. Down to 1774 the Tories differed from the Whigs primarily on the method of redress, but after 1774 they differed from them on the ultimate purpose of resistance—the Whigs sought safety and liberty in flight from the empire, the Tories sought the same objects within a reconstructed empire. Thus the Whigs looked down one avenue to the future and saw at the end a glorious and independent republic, great in its strength, but the Tories looked down another avenue and saw an extensive and powerful empire, made up of self-governing but mutually dependent parts. The one saw the United States of America of 1929, the other the British Commonwealth of Nations. Joseph Galloway's plan of an American constitution, with an American parliament and a governor-general appointed by the crown, with full authority over the internal affairs of the country, while the British government regulated imperial affairs, clearly foreshadowed the Durham report of 1839 and the subsequent development in imperial relations. Less specific suggestions, frequently little more than the statement that an American constitution should be formed, were constantly offered for the consideration of the Whigs and together constitute impressive evidence that the Tories had far more in mind than the mere assertion of parliamentary authority.[26]

The problem faced by those who would support the administration by unofficial measures was to weaken the Whigs by detaching as many as possible, to win the alliance of those not committed to

[26] Inglis suggested that Parliament relinquish its claims of taxation, that the colonies contribute a fair share of the expenses of protection, and that American merchants be given guarantees that their trade would not be infringed upon.—*True Interest of America.* Seabury advocated Dickinson's position of 1768.—*A View of the Controversy.* Boucher held the same view.—*N. Y. Gazetteer,* Sept. 8, 1774. For similar suggestions, see *N. Y. Gazette and Weekly Mercury,* Aug. 15, 1774; and *N. Y. Gazetteer,* Nov. 2, 1775. There were also suggestions that America be represented in Parliament, and some that a constitution for America be drawn up. See *Boston Weekly News-Letter,* Jan. 19, 1769; and *N. Y. Gazetteer,* July 7, 1774. A common suggestion, thoroughly scouted by the Whigs, was to rely on dutiful petitions to the "father of his people," the King.

the Whig program, and to substitute for a state of mind a course of action. The solid nucleus of the Tory group consisted of the English officials and the Anglican clergymen in the North. In addition, there were other groups dependent on or allied to the administration who could be unified in coherent opposition to the Whig proposals.

There were those positively tied to the British government by direct benefits. Many colonists had received land grants or bounties from the home government. Not only the landed proprietors such as the Wentworths, the Penns, the Fairfaxes, were indebted to the British government for their holdings. Many small farmers newly arrived had received their land from the same source and feared that to rebel meant to lose it. Many of them had come over under the plan whereby they were given free passage, tax exemption for five years, and a grant of land and five pounds sterling as bounty. Many of the Irish who came over after 1763, as well as most of the Highland Scots, were thus indebted to what they conceived to be the bounty of the King. Many of the Germans in the southern back country, especially in South Carolina, were in the same position.[27] Direct bounties would confirm the loyalty of many. Georgians alone had received ten thousand pounds in bounties for the production of certain items.

A variety of interests would hold the allegiance of others. Positively tied to the imperial system were the commission merchants, most of whom were in the southern port towns. As agents of British firms and as creditors of the planters they doubly needed the connection with Great Britain. Anglicans in the northern colonies obviously depended upon the power of the British government. The church was making real gains (there were sixty-eight Anglican churches in Connecticut in 1775, for example) and the more powerful it became, the more intense the opposition. The cause of the King could also attract to itself those who would be in danger of attack in the event of war either from the Indians on the frontier or from English navy on the seacoast. Those of a strongly conservative frame of mind, who disliked the extra-legal and riotous activities of the Whigs, could easily be held for the Crown. Finally, there

[27] McCrady, *History of S. C. in the Revolution, 1775-1780*, pp. 33 ff.; C. A. Hanna, *The Scotch-Irish, or the Scot in North Britain, in North Ireland, and in North America*, II, 34; David Ramsay, *The History of the Revolution in South-Carolina*, I, 64 f.

were those who had such grievances against the local governments that they might prefer, if properly rewarded, English domination as the lesser of evils. Adroit methods might hold the allegiance of many in the oppressed classes in every colony.

The task in each instance was not to gain converts—that was the Whig problem—but to hold the allegiance of people. When the Tory leaders became fully aware that legal pressures and the old values were insufficient to hold the colonists, they became intentional propagandists and began an active campaign for the support of the empire.

THE MACHINERY OF PROPAGANDA

The Tories were never able to effect an organization for the dissemination of propaganda that compared to the system set up by their opponents. The Whigs had sufficient control over the legal agencies of government to prevent their use by the Tories, and through their coercive agencies they were able to break up Tory attempts to form extra-legal or voluntary organizations.

Thus legal agencies of government were used to undermine British authority in the colonies, not to maintain it. The Tories obtained no assembly resolutions supporting the Crown and Parliament; the Whigs controlled the assemblies. The town governments were also of little use to the Tories, for they, too, were under Whig control. As the party of the proposition, the Whigs could call a town meeting, and through their agency, the committee of correspondence, they could obtain favorable resolutions. The Tories, the party of the opposition and always one step behind their opponents, could do little more than obtain a protest against the meeting. The advantage was thus entirely with the Whigs. They would have formal resolutions, adopted at a legal meeting, whereas the Tories would have only a protest signed by a relatively few people.

Many attempts were made, nevertheless, to obtain public protests against the Whig program. A few towns in New England, where the Tories were in a majority, adopted formal resolutions protesting against the activities of the patriots. From Hatfield, Worcester, Marblehead, Marshfield, and Petersham in Massachusetts, and from Ridgefield, Reading, Fairfield, New Milford, and Newton in Connecticut, came such protests. Most of these were small towns in western Massachusetts, eastern Connecticut, and coastal Massachusetts.[28]

Seabury's influence in the outlying districts of New York City aided in producing dissent against the Association in Ulster, Queens, Westchester, and Dutchess counties; the resolutions of all of them concurred with the statement of some inhabitants of Rye, Westchester County, that "we also testify our dislike to many hot and furious proceedings, in consequence of said disputes, which we think are more likely to ruin this once happy country, than remove grievances, if any there are."[29]

The first protests of any moment in New Jersey came in opposition to independence. Thirty-two merchants of Burlington petitioned the provincial congress in 1775 not to vote for independence as it would close the door to reconciliation and peace. The congress replied that the merchants' fears were groundless and urged them to combat the rumor whenever they heard it. On June 4, 1776, when there was no longer much doubt about the matter, another group in Burlington petitioned again, pleading "we trust you will be too deeply impress'd with the Recollection of the peculiar Happiness and Prosperity heretofore enjoyed by the Inhabitants of this Continent, connected with and subject to the government of Great Britain, not to dread the Consequences of a declar'd Separation from that Country."[30]

Protests against the Whig program in North Carolina and Georgia, however, appeared much earlier and are more typical of those elsewhere. From Rowan, Surry, Guilford, and Anson counties, North Carolina, came a series of petitions or protests to Governor Martin in 1775. Samuel Bryan and a hundred and ninety-four residents of Rowan and Surry counties protested against the Continental Association, the committees, and all attempts to violate the King's laws or the peace of his realm. In almost the same words— identical phrases in parts—three hundred and twenty-seven people

---

[28] *Mass. Gazette*, Oct. 6, 1768; *Mass. Gazette, and Boston Weekly News-Letter*, May 13, 1773; *N. Y. Gazetteer*, Mar. 16, 1775; 4 Force, *Amer. Arch.*, I, 1177, 1202, 1215, 1249, 1259, 1270. The number of signers varied considerably; there were two hundred in Ridgefield, 162 in Newton, 141 in Reading, and 120 in Milford. Nathaniel Ray Thomas said it was by his efforts that Marshfield remained loyal.—Jones, *Loyalists of Massachusetts*, p. 274.

[29] *N. Y. Gazetteer*, Aug. 11, Nov. 10, 1774; Jan. 12, Apr. 6, 1775.

[30] *N. Y. Gazette and Weekly Mercury*, June 24, 1776; *Minutes of the N. J. Prov. Cong.*, pp. 292, 300.

of Anson County made the same complaints. John Fields and a hundred and sixteen old Regulators of Guilford County objected to the Association, and a few people in Dobbs asked Martin whether they were paying taxes to help the King or to defeat him.[31] It is reasonably clear that these protests were concerted by an individual or group of individuals among the North Carolina Tories. They came within a short time of each other and followed each other so closely in form and content that it is probable they had a common source.

The Georgia protests against the Savannah meeting at Tondee's Tavern on August 10, 1774, and the resolutions then adopted bear even stronger evidence of careful planning. The influence of Governor Wright is clearly seen. He called a convention or meeting of the people of Savannah shortly after the tenth of August, and it is said by one authority that nearly a third of the residents attended. They drew up a protest against the meeting simply on the ground that it did not properly represent the people of the city or colony. Many were present who were not properly constituted delegates, the place of meeting had changed without notice, and the tavern keeper had refused admittance to many whose names were not on his list. The protest, in other words, was an open protest against the methods the Whigs had used and an implied protest against what they had done.

Soon the *Georgia Gazette* began to publish protests from the outlying districts. The signed dissent from the Kyoka and Broad River settlements in St. Paul's Parish did not differ greatly from that of the Savannah group, but other settlements in the same parish demanded that the only method of redress be petitions from the provincial assembly. Any other method, they said, would complicate getting help against the Indians from the home government. Wrightsboro protested because it knew nothing about the meeting, and some of the inhabitants of Augusta objected because of the manner of holding the meeting, because not to object would imply consent, and because such resolutions might affect the British government's attitude toward them when they needed protection. People in the two little parishes of St. George and St. Matthew declared that they had been sadly deceived and had sent delegates to the meeting under the apprehension that unless they did so the Stamp

---

[31] *N. Y. Gazetteer,* Apr. 6, 1775; *Col. Rec. N. C.,* IX, 1127, 1160 ff.

Act would be enforced.[32] Early in 1775 two identical petitions from Christ Church and St. George Parishes were presented to the assembly urging that no other means of redress be attempted than petitions by the assembly to the King and Parliament.[33]

This is not an impressive record, especially when compared with the flood of town resolutions produced by the Whigs. Even more unimpressive compared with the Continental Association and its spawn of committees was the Tory attempt to develop counterassociations. The attempt to associate people together simply by a written statement of loyalty was first used to an important extent in Massachusetts in 1774, where the Tories felt more secure now that Gage was about to arrive with four regiments of troops.

Several groups drew up addresses to Hutchinson and Gage, assuring them of their loyalty to the King and of their appreciation for the services of the administration. The Episcopal ministers of Boston on May 23, 1774, drew up the first one of the series, and the Justices of the Peace in Suffolk County followed the next day with a welcome to Gage. Thereafter similar addresses came rapidly for a time—thirty-three people in Marblehead, one hundred and twenty-three in Boston and the neighborhood, twenty-four lawyers, thirty-one magistrates of Middlesex County, and several merchants of Boston.[34] These addresses for the most part simply acknowledged gratitude to Hutchinson and welcomed Gage. They did not bind the signers to any course of action and did not present a constructive view of the difficulties. They were complete in themselves and would lead to no further action, nor would they be likely to influence others except mildly. They were poor propaganda.

The idea of forming an actual association of Tories, bound together by a written agreement, was a much more fruitful one. Brigadier Timothy Ruggles of Massachusetts drew up the first association. As soon as he heard of the Continental Association, he proposed an agreement in which the signers were bound to defend each other's life, liberty, and property, and to uphold the right of every person to act as he pleased, to buy or sell from or to whom he wished, and

---

[32] *Ga. Gazette,* Sept. 7, Oct. 12, and Nov. 30, 1774. The protest from St. Paul's is misdated Aug. 5, 1774. See also *Rev. Rec. Ga.,* I, 18 ff. It was frequently asserted that the governor paid liberally for signatures to these protests, but there is no supporting evidence. [33] *Ga. Gazette,* Feb. 1, 1775.

[34] *Mass. Gazette, and Boston Post-Boy,* May 30, 1774.

to eat, drink, and wear whatever he desired, so long as he did not violate the laws of God or the realm. Each signer promised to encourage obedience to the King, and to maintain his personal rights by force if necessary.[35] Whether or not this agreement was ever signed by any of the Tories does not appear, and it may have been merely an ironical suggestion. Gage suggested the idea of a loyalists' association to Thomas Gilbert, who made much more effective use of the plan. He is reputed to have organized three hundred men in Massachusetts and many others in both Rhode Island and Connecticut, and he actually attempted armed resistance to the Whigs. He and some of his followers cut down liberty poles in various places, but his party was soon broken up by the militant Whigs, and its only effect was to add a few more refugees in Boston and a few more loyalist volunteers to the British army.[36]

There was an even finer opportunity in the back country of North and South Carolina for associations of this sort, and something was attempted in South Carolina by Thomas Fletchall. Fletchall, Robert and Patrick Cunningham, and Moses Kirkland, all of whom had been in active opposition to the coastal aristocracy for some time, successfully opposed the efforts of William Tennent and William Henry Drayton. The Drayton-Tennent tour almost ended in open hostilities, but a temporary truce, it will be remembered, was agreed upon. Had Governor Campbell earlier formed an actual association of those loyal to the government, much might have been done to prevent the development of the revolutionary movement; as it was, the best that could be accomplished was the formation of military associations in the fall of 1775. By that time the Whig movement was too strong to be stopped.[37]

In North Carolina not even that much was accomplished. The Earl of Dartmouth suggested to Governor Martin that he form an association against the Whigs and sent him a bundle of his own pamphlets supporting the government's position and actions. Martin distributed the pamphlets but complained bitterly that his communi-

---

[35] *Journals Mass. Prov. Cong.*, p. 68. The association was proscribed by the provincial congress.—*Ibid.*, p. 69. The plan was printed in *Mass. Gazette, and Boston Weekly News-Letter*, Dec. 23, 1774, and in *N. Y. Gazette and Weekly Mercury*, Jan. 9, 1775.

[36] *Newport Mercury*, Feb. 27, Apr. 3, 1775; Lorenzo Sabine, *Biographical Sketches of Loyalists of the American Revolution*, I, 468 ff.

[37] McCrady, *History of S. C. in Revolution*, *1775-1780*, pp. 37 ff., 88; Gibbes, *Documentary History*, I, 129, and *passim*.

cation with the back country was so cut off that he could do no more. Helplessly he saw what might have been an aggressive loyalist movement among the old Regulators and new Highlanders dwindle into a passive attitude of neutrality.[38]

Other organizations of influence and authority open to the Tories were almost nonexistent. The Anglican Church as an organization was so divided that no joint action could be taken. The Society for the Propagation of the Gospel, which alone gave unity to the work of the church, would simply have split the organization had it demanded anything other than the maintenance of peace and order and the observance of the usages of the church. Charles Inglis reported with quiet pride that the clergy, "amidst this Scene of Tumult & Disorder, went on steadily with their Duty; in their Sermons, confining themselves to the Doctrines of the Gospel, without touching on politics."[39]

Other institutions were of even less value. The Charleston Chamber of Commerce, formed on December 9, 1773, effectively united the pro-British merchants, but even when organized, they did not have sufficient power to defeat the planters and the mechanics organized in the General Committee. The merchants had representation on the Committee, but they were steadily outvoted.[40] Four Tory clubs were said to meet frequently in Philadelphia,[41] but of their work we know nothing.

With little machinery and with few organizations at their serv ice, the Tory propagandists had to rely upon their individual efforts. They did remarkably well.

[38] *Col. Rec. N. C.*, IX, 1176, 1241; X, 244, 266.
[39] Quoted from Lydekker, *Life of Charles Inglis*, p. 158, by permission of The Macmillan Company.
[40] *S. C. Gazette*, Dec. 13, 1773; Schlesinger, *Colonial Merchants*, pp. 296 f.
[41] *Diary of Christopher Marshall*, p. 80. Joseph Galloway said in his examination before Parliament that he knew of none in Pennsylvania.

XV

TORY PROPAGANDA: SUGGESTION

FROM THE beginning of the controversy there were open attacks on Whig professions and activities. There were disagreements within the Whig party itself, and diversities of opinion were numerous; indeed it is arbitrary to speak of Whig and Tory in the first years of the dispute. A strong line of cleavage in the body of opinion is clearly discernible long before 1774, however, and what we might call the government side of the question was presented at each stage of the altercation. The Tory method was primarily to refute directly Whig statements, but the obverse of the Tory rebuttal, always by implication but usually by positive statement, was the constructive Tory argument. With that argument we are now concerned.

JUSTIFICATIONS

The Whigs had justified their position by asserting that British acts violated the legal rights of the colonists as subjects of the British government, of the colonies as members of the British Empire, and of men as members of civil society. To defend their claims they asserted an American, eighteenth-century view of the British Constitution and of the legal relations within the empire, and presented a new philosophy of government. These claims the Tories branded as innovations and to them opposed the English, seventeenth-century view of the Constitution, the empire, and the nature of government.

The Tories categorically denied that the British Constitution guaranteed to every man the right to be taxed only by a representative which he himself had elected. They cheerfully admitted that the Constitution guaranteed to every Englishman, whether at home or in the colonies, personal rights—the rights to life, liberty, and property. These, said Martin Howard, "are secured to us by the common law, which is every subject's birthright, whether born in Great Britain, on the ocean, or in the colonies; and it is in this sense we are said to enjoy all the rights and privileges of Englishmen."[1]

[1] *A Letter from a Gentleman at Halifax*, p. 8.

These rights they refused to admit had been invaded. But the claim that the colonists could be taxed only by their own duly elected representatives they declared to be a new and totally false application of the old maxim, no taxation without representation. They pointed out that the colonists were demanding rights which not even Englishmen at home enjoyed. Every writer on the subject showed concretely that nowhere within the empire was the Whig proposition true. Every writer demonstrated the falsity of the Whig position; two examples will suffice. Wrote Martin Howard in 1765:

"Let me ask, is the Isle of Man, Jersey, or Guernsey represented? What is the value or amount of each man's representation in the kingdom of Scotland. . . ? Let us take into the argument the moneyed interest of Great Britain, which, though immensely great, has no share in this representation. A worthless freeholder of forty shillings per annum can vote for a member of parliament, whereas a merchant, though worth one hundred thousand pounds sterling, if it consists in personal effects has no vote at all. But yet let no one suppose that the interest of the latter is not equally the object of parliamentary attention with the former."[2]

An English pamphlet by Soame Jenyns, reprinted in the *Massachusetts Gazette, and Boston News-Letter*, gave even more pertinent and striking denial to the statement. Jenyns began with the general statement that "every Englishman is taxed, and not one in twenty is represented," and continued with specific illustrations:

"Copyholders, leaseholders, and all men possessed of personal property only, choose no representatives. Manchester, Birmingham, and many more of our richest and most flourishing trading towns send no members to parliament; consequently, cannot consent by their representatives, because they choose none to represent them. Yet are they not Englishmen, or are they not taxed? . . . if the towns of Manchester and Birmingham, sending no representatives to parliament, are notwithstanding there represented, why are not the cities of Albany and Boston equally represented in that assembly? Are they not alike British subjects? Are they not Englishmen? Or, are they only Englishmen when they solicit for protection, but not Eng-

[2] *Ibid.*, p. 12.

lishmen when taxes are required to enable this country to protect them?"[3]

The American colonists were thus represented in Parliament to precisely the same extent as their fellow subjects in Great Britain, not by their actual, but by their virtual representatives, and this system safeguarded their rights just as much as if they had been actually represented: "In truth, my friend, the matter lies here: the freedom and happiness of every British subject depends, not upon his share in elections, but upon the sense and virtue of the whole British parliament; and these depend reciprocally upon the sense and virtue of the whole nation."[4]

The Tories thus accepted the Whig proposition that the colonists were Englishmen, entitled to all the rights and privileges of Englishmen, and heartily agreed that the Constitution guaranteed to the colonists identically the same rights as to subjects resident in England. They turned this argument against the Whigs, for to the Tories the violation of the Constitution came not from Parliament but from the Whigs. Their rights under the Constitution, to which they steadily appealed, were being violated in every particular by the Whigs, the Tories asserted. Some indeed held that the colonists had no just grievances whatever,[5] but all steadfastly maintained their assertion that the Whigs had been guilty of far more illegality than the British government and had created a far greater tyranny than any they opposed.

Whig measures and institutions they condemned as "unconstitutional, illegal, and wholly unjustifiable . . . subversive of government, [and] destructive of that Peace and good Order which is the Cement of Society."[6] The poem "Liberty" aptly put the Tory case:

---

[3] *The Objections to the Taxation of our American Colonies*, pp. 7, 9. Also in *Mass. Gazette, and Boston News-Letter*, June 13, 1765. See also Cooper, *A Friendly Address*, pp. 9, *passim*, among others. This is the most familiar aspect of the controversy, and further examples are unnecessary.

[4] Howard, *A Letter from a Gentleman at Halifax*, p. 13.

[5] See *N. Y. Gazetteer*, Nov. 10, 1774; *S. C. Gazette*, July 13, 1769; *Mass. Gazette, and Boston Weekly News-Letter*, Feb. 16, 1775.

[6] The protest of the town of Hatfield, Massachusetts, against the actions of the town of Boston.—*Mass. Gazette*, Oct. 6, 1768. "I am sorry to say, gentlemen, we have seen but too many unconstitutional measures adopted among ourselves."—Broadside, dated July 25, 1774, bound with *Ga. Gazette*. "Your proceedings, therefore, are much more tyrannical and unjust than those you complain of!"—John Laird, *An Englishman's Answer*, p. 25.

"Quoth the Rabble make Way for great Cato's Descendants!
Lo! these are the Men aptly called Independents!
Quaint Patriots indeed! of Old Noll's Institution,
So Free—they'd demolish the whole Constitution;
So madly licentious, and fond of a Name,
They'd set the whole Empire at once in a Flame:
K—g, N-b-s, and C-mm-ns would gladly disown,
And contemn ev'ry Law can be fram'd, but their own."[7]

Tory propagandists charged specifically that the institutions established by the Whigs—committees, conventions, and congresses—were illegal in their nature and defied all law in their actions. They turned against the Whigs their own argument that government should be by duly elected representatives; by that test, they said, these institutions were far more tyrannical than the government of Great Britain. A broadside published in Georgia in protest against the rump meeting in Savannah denied the legality of the proceedings on the grounds that, "as there can be no TAXATION without REPRESENTATION, so there can be no REPRESENTATION without ELECTION."[8] The committees, it was commonly charged, were appointed by county or town meetings, "where, it is notorious, not one fourth of the freeholders attend."[9] Of the Continental Congress, the most commonly attacked institution, it was said by Samuel Seabury that the Whigs had no right to call such a congress in the first instance, that the assemblies had no right to send delegates, and that where the delegates had been elected by county meetings, not a hundredth of the people had consented to the choice.[10]

The author of the pamphlet, *What Think Ye of the Congress Now?* [Chandler?] declared that the delegates did not legally represent the people: "a very great part of the Americans are not their *constituents* in any sense at all, as they never voted for them, nor ever signified any approbation of their acting in behalf, and in the

[7] *Boston Weekly News-Letter*, Dec. 22, 1768.

[8] *To the Worthy Freeholders and Others, Inhabitants of the Province of Georgia*, broadside, bound with the *Ga. Gazette*, July 27, 1774.

[9] *N. Y. Gazetteer*, July 28, 1774. Another cited the case of some Whigs who wanted to appoint a committee but could not get a warrant for a town meeting. They took a handful of people two miles out of town and got them to appoint a committee.—*Ibid.*, Dec. 22, 1774. See also *S. C. Gazette*, July 19, 1770, for an attack on the General Committee of Charleston as unrepresentative. Every writer made this charge and documented it with numerous illustrations.

[10] Seabury, *The Congress Canvassed*.

name of the colonies."[11] Furthermore, he continued, the Congress exceeded its authority; its sole purpose was "to obtain for the colonies an exemption from taxation by the British Parliament," and hence, "all that was done or projected by the congress, in the way of hostility against Great Britain (and little was done or projected by them in any other way) was uncommissioned and unauthorised, and cannot be binding even upon their constituents."[12]

Illegal in their nature and unrepresentative of the people, the acts of such institutions, even though they should conform to law, were not binding upon the colonists, the Tories claimed. As a matter of fact, they said, their acts, instead of conforming to law, grossly violated rights long guaranteed by the British Constitution. The Association, ran a typical Tory attack, "is subversive of, inconsistent with, the wholesome laws of our happy Constitution; it abrogates or suspends many of them essential to the peace and order of Government; it takes the Government out of the hands of the Governour, Council, and General Assembly; and the execution of the laws out of the hands of the Civil Magistrates and Juries."[13] The Massachusetts Whigs, said another account, "have violently seized upon almost every department of government civil and military; the regular courts of justice are shut up; the Judges by force prevented from doing their duty, and obliged to resign; the Members of the Council compelled by threats and the most cruel violence to resign their seats. . . . Such are a few of the outlines of the conduct of the people you are called upon to abet and support."[14]

The Tories proceeded from such general condemnations of Whig tyranny to a detailed recital of violated rights. First of all were violated property rights. Merchants under the ban of the local committees during the Townshend controversy complained bitterly that their property was being destroyed,[15] and when the tea was destroyed in Boston, the accusation was common. One of the extracts of letters written in England and printed in the *Massachusetts Gazette, and Boston News-Letter* expressed the Tory attitude:

"Whenever a factious set of People rise to such a Pitch of Insolence, as to prevent the Execution of the Laws, or destroy the Property of Individuals, just as their Caprice or Humour leads them; there is an end of all Order and Government, Riot, and Confusion must be the natural Consequence of such Measures. It is impossible for Trade to flourish where Property is insecure."[16]

The Continental Congress had complained against the trade laws, and yet its committees at the same time "arraign the highest authority on earth, insolently trample on the liberties of their fellow-subjects; and without the shadow of a trial, take from them their property, grant it to others, and not content with all this, hold them up to contempt, and expose them to the vilest injuries."[17] Referring to the Boston committee of correspondence, a writer in the *Massachusetts Gazette* asserted that it had been appointed for a specific purpose and that purpose had been accomplished. "If this is true," he asked, "can there be any stronger instance of tyranny and usurpation, than for a number of men under the cloak of an obsolete and expired authority to continue themselves in office, and decide upon the property of their fellow citizens? . . . *I have no notion that freedom can be established by opposing arbitrary principles in one instance, and tamely submitting to them in another.*"[18]

The constitutional guarantees of freedom of opinion and freedom of press were likewise violated, accused the Tories. To require oaths by illegal means "is extremely arbitrary and oppressive, utterly inconsistent with every Principle of Liberty and the Constitution, and tending to the establishment of Tyranny by the very Instrument we are opposing to it."[19] A licentious, not a free, society seemed to be the aim of the Whigs: "How near are we approaching to such a State, from the general Clamour of some Persons, who seem to have weight with the Populace, and are for enslaving every one to their

[16] Nov. 17, 1774. Cooper, *A Friendly Address*, p. 24. Even a Boston jury would convict the perpetrators of the Tea Party said a Georgia broadside, *To the Public*, bound with *Ga. Gazette*, July 27, 1774.

[17] *N. Y. Gazetteer*, Dec. 1, 1774.

[18] *Mass. Gazette, and Boston Weekly News-Letter*, June 16, 1774. "Individuals are deprived of their liberty; their property is frequently invaded by violence, and not a single Magistrate has courage or virtue enough to interpose."—Seabury, *Free Thoughts on the Congress*, p. 3. "Shall free-born English lose their *Right*, To *rob* and *plunder* others?" Two lines from a long poem, *The Association, &c.* of the Delegates. See also *Va. Gazette* (Purdie), Jan. 20, 1774, and *Ga. Gazette*, Aug. 24, 1774.

[19] *Mass. Gazette, and Boston Weekly News-Letter*, July 7, 1774; *S. C. Gazette*, Aug. 3, 1769; *Md. Gazette*, Feb. 16, 1775.

own Opinions?"[20] The Tories charged in all fairness that the Whigs had closed the press to them. After some Whig remarks about the liberty of the press, they satirically suggested that the Whigs adopt the following resolution: "That whoever, as an instrument of tyranny, or the leader or abettor of a mob, shall go about, either by threats, or any other method, to violate the liberty of the press, is an enemy to everything for which a man of sense would think it worth his while to live."[21] A poem explained the Whig fear of an open press:

> "They tremble at an equal press,
> For reasons every dunce can guess.
> Without one single grain of Merit,
> Devoid of honour, sense and spirit;
> Treating all men as mortal foes,
> Who dare their high behests oppose."[22]

The Constitution had thus been completely subverted by the Whigs, but, not content with destroying the rights of others, they demanded additional privileges for themselves. Here, said the Tories, was the central fallacy of the Whig argument, "that the colonies have rights independent of, and not controlled by, the authority of parliament," to which all Englishmen were subject.[23] At this point the Tories moved into their attack on the Whig view of the legal relationships within the empire, with its doctrine of divided authorities.

The Tories' view of the government of the empire comprehended a central authority in London, its power fixed by the Constitution and divided among what they called the three branches of the whole legislature—King, Lords, and Commons. Supreme legislative authority was vested in Parliament, and that authority was of necessity coextensive with the empire.[24] Each branch, however, had its constitutionally determined duties which none of the others could invade. In the preservation of this balanced structure was the only

---

[20] *Mass. Gazette*, Aug. 18, 1768. See also *N. Y. Gazetteer*, Dec. 2, 1773; Myles Cooper, *The American Querist*, p. 9. [21] *N. Y. Gazetteer*, Sept. 2, 1774.

[22] *Ibid.*, Dec. 8, 1774. Further examples abound. See *Boston Weekly News-Letter*, July 21, 1768; *N. Y. Gazetteer*, Dec. 22, 1774, Feb. 23, 1775; Galloway, *Candid Examination*, p. 1.

[23] Howard, *A Letter from a Gentleman at Halifax*, p. 6.

[24] E.g., Leonard, *Massachusettensis*; Cooper, *A Friendly Address*, p. 9, and *passim*; Cooper, *American Querist*, p. 13; Seabury, *A View of the Controversy*, and *An Alarm to the Legislature*.

safety for the empire. As "Ironicus" wrote in 1770 of the Tory aims·

> "They desire to see their own Rights, and those of their Fellow Subjects, inviolably preserved; and are ready to take all proper Measures for the Redress of any unjust Encroachments. They are willing also that the Crown should enjoy its legal Prerogatives; *weakly* imagining that an equal Balance of the several Branches of the Legislature is the surest Way to preserve the Happiness and Safety of the Whole."[25]

This was what the Tories meant, they said, when they proclaimed themselves supporters of Revolutional principles—"an equal zeal for the prerogatives of the crown, and for the just liberties of the people."[26] This was the structure that Locke had defended in 1688 —the supreme legislative authority of Parliament and the supreme executive power of the Crown—so ran the Tory argument. But the Whigs, who applied Locke's principles to colonial assemblies and demanded liberty on the strength of his writings, were hopelessly perverting and distorting his meaning, for he had asserted the authority of the *British* Parliament:

> "Behold a vain, deluded Race,
> Thy venerable Name, disgrace;
> As Casuists false, as Savage rude,
> With Glosses weak, with Comments crude,
> Pervert thy fair, instructive Page,
> To Sanctify, licentious Rage."[27]

The Tories, in fact, cited Locke on the power of Parliament and Montesquieu on the necessity for checks and balances almost as much as did the Whigs. Paine indeed ridiculed the idea of checks and balances in *Common Sense* as additional evidence of the impossibility of trusting a king if he had to be checked by another authority. The principle was stoutly defended by Tory writers,[28] who always referred to the central authority in London, and never receded from their position that the power of Parliament was supreme

---

[25] *N. Y. Gazette and Weekly Mercury*, May 7, 1770.

[26] Boucher, *A View of the Causes*, p. 98.

[27] Myles Cooper, *Patriots of North America*, p. 22.

[28] "To say that the Constitution of England is a *union* of three powers, reciprocally *checking* each other, is farcical; either the words have no meaning, or they are flat contradictions."—*Works of Paine*, II, 5. In contrast, see Inglis, *True Interest of America*, pp. 21-33.

throughout the empire. They suggested compromises which should limit this power, but the concessions were always to be made by Parliament itself, the only competent authority.

Holding such unequivocal views of the power of Parliament, the Tories naturally condemned the Whig attempts to limit or deny that authority as legally unsound and politically dangerous. As early as 1765, nine years before the body of Whig opinion had come to deny it, Martin Howard perceived the real basis of the Whig objection to parliamentary taxation and contradicted it flatly. Personal rights were secured to the colonists, he agreed, but the "political rights of the colonies, or the powers of government communicated to them, are more limited." These powers, he declared, "depend altogether upon the patent or charter which first created and instituted them . . . as corporations created by the crown, they are confined within the primitive views of their institution."[29] These charters in no instance exempted the colonies from the jurisdiction of Parliament. But if they had, added Soame Jenyns, the exemption was illegal, for the King had no authority to set aside the powers of the legislature:

> "Nor is there any charter that ever pretended to grant such a privilege to any colony in America; and had they granted it, it could have had no force,—their charters being derived from the crown, and no charter from the crown can possibly supersede the right of the whole legislature. Their charters are undoubtedly no more than those of all corporations, which impower them to make by-laws and raise duties for the purposes of their own police, forever subject to the superior authority of parliament."[30]

When the issue was squarely raised by the Whigs, the Tories stated flatly their position—two independent legislatures cannot exist in the same state. Or as Isaac Hunt put the proposition: "Two distinct *independent powers* in *one civil state* are as inconsistent as *two hearts* in the same natural body. . . . A due subordination of the less parts to the greater is therefore necessary to the *existence* of BOTH."[31]

---

[29] *A Letter from a Gentleman at Halifax*, p. 8.

[30] *Objections to the Taxation of our American Colonies*, pp. 10 f.

[31] *The Political Family*, pp. 6 f. Almost identical statements are in *Ga. Gazette*, Dec. 7, 1774; and Galloway, *Candid Examination*, p. 4.

The empire was thus viewed as a single state, geographically but not politically divided, with its government established by the Constitution; to deny the established authority of any part of that government was to destroy the whole. Daniel Leonard clearly saw, he wrote in 1774, that to deny the authority of Parliament was to destroy the framework of the Constitution and with it the "priceless claim" to all the rights guaranteed by that Constitution.[32] On the same reasoning, Samuel Seabury labeled the Whig contention that the colonists owed allegiance not to Parliament but to the King a self-contradictory heresy:

> "It is a distinction made by the American republicans to serve their own rebellious purposes,—a gilding with which they have enclosed the pill of sedition. . . . The king of Great Britain was placed on the throne by virtue of an act of parliament. . . . And if we disclaim that authority of parliament which made him our king, we, in fact, reject him from being our king,—for we disclaim that authority by which he is king at all."[33]

The Tory view of the legal outlines of the empire and the supremacy of the central government was bolstered up by and comprehended in their larger philosophy of the nature of government and man's relation to it. Here was their answer to the Whig compact, natural rights philosophy of government. It was the view of the sixteenth- and seventeenth-century political theorists, who buttressed the state with a political philosophy founded upon the proposition that governments were instituted by God and that kings were His commissioned agents. Central in the theory of the Tories, therefore, was the doctrine that the laws of man and God forbade treason, for obedience was commanded of God and demanded by the nature of man.[34] Kings and princes, said Jonathan Boucher, "receive their commission from Heaven; they receive it from God, the source and original of all power." When therefore, "Christians are disobedient to human ordinances, they are also disobedient to God."[35] One of the characters in Jonathan Sewall's *The Americans Roused, in a Cure for the Spleen*, was made to say, "Treason is an

[32] *Massachusettensis*, pp. 41 f.
[33] *The Congress Canvassed*, p. 26; *Va. Gazette* (Dixon and Hunter), Feb. 18, 1775.
[34] A. C. Flick, *Loyalism in New York during the American Revolution*, p. 9. As applied in England in the seventeenth century, this idea was intended to strengthen the King in his fight with Parliament, but the American Tories applied it directly to the Whig attack on the British government.   [35] *View of the Causes*, pp. 508, 534.

odious crime in the sight of God and men; may we none of us listen to the suggestions of Satan, but may the . . . spirit lead us in the way of truth, and preserve us from all sedition, privy conspiracy and rebellion."[36] And Jonathan Boucher quoted the old Anglican homily which declares, "A rebel is worse than the worst prince, and a rebellion worse than the worst government of the worst prince that hath hitherto been."[37] So serious a crime was treason that the faithful and loyal would be cautious of advocating any change in the existing order lest they be guilty of it. Has God given anyone any authority to refuse obedience where due? asked Cooper; "whether, on the contrary, he does not command us to *submit to every ordinance of man for the Lord's sake* . . . whether it be not a matter of worldly wisdom, and of indisputable Christian duty, in every American, to *fear the Lord and the King,* and to meddle not with them that are GIVEN TO CHANGE."[38] In fact, Boucher warned his congregation, any change, even though desirable, was dangerous: "No change, in a settled state of things, can be a matter of indifference; for, the mere act of changing, even when it is allowedly for the better, is hazardous, by the countenance and encouragement it affords to those who are *given to change.*"[39]

This doctrine of submission to authority, scornfully called by the Whigs the doctrine of passive nonresistance to oppression, was preached by the Anglican ministers, who supported it with Biblical texts drawn from both testaments. Allegories of the parent England and the child America popularized the idea in the press and simplified its complexities. There was the story, for instance, of John Bull and his disobedient daughter, Bett. He tried reasoning with her and failed; he tried starving her and failed; then he beat her so heartily that he was sorry. He wiped her nose, and she wept with affection and promised never to disobey her father again.[40] Why, said Charles Inglis, if the colonies should declare independence after a little brush like the battle of Lexington, "it would resemble the conduct of a rash, froward stripling, who should call his mother a

---

[36] P. 32.   [37] *View of the Causes,* pp. 485 ff.
[38] *American Querist,* pp. 54 f.; *N. Y. Gazetteer,* Mar. 16, 1775.
[39] *View of the Causes,* pp. 209 f. The text to which these men referred is Proverbs 24:21—"My son, fear thou the Lord and the king: and meddle not with them that are given to change."   [40] *Norwich Packet,* Nov. 20, 1775.

d—mn—d b—ch, swear he had no relation to her, and attempt to knock her down."[41]

The equalitarian concepts of man and the sequential idea of government by compact were as ridiculous, said the Tories, as the idea of the equality of the parent and child and of family rule by consent. It was manifestly absurd, Jonathan Boucher told his Maryland congregation, to believe "that the whole human race is born equal; and that no man is naturally inferior or in any respect, subjected to another; and that he can be made subject to another only by his own consent." He continued: "Man differs from man in every-thing that can be supposed to lead to supremacy and subjection. . . . Without government, there can be no society; nor without some relative inferiority and superiority, can there be any government."[42] Hooker and Hobbes supplied the Tories with their theories, and they agreed with these writers that government was essential to the happiness of men, who, like children, need discipline and control for their own good. Hence it was, wrote Charles Inglis, that government was agreeable to God, who wills the happiness and order of man.[43] With this proposition Boucher was in strong agreement:

"It was not to be expected from an all-wise and all-merciful Creator, that, having formed creatures capable of order and rule, he should turn them loose into the world under the guidance only of their own unruly wills; that, like so many wild beasts, they might tear and worry one another in their mad contests for preeminence. . . . We are, indeed, so disorderly and unmanageable, that, were it not for the restraints and the terrors of human laws, it would not be possible for us to dwell together."[44]

With government decreed by God and obedience to it commanded by Him, wherein did liberty exist? The Tories were prepared for this question. The Whig concept of liberty they defined as "liberty to do whatever a man pleases," and they did not hesitate to call that license. "It has been proved," said one Tory writer, "that liberty can have no existence without obedience to the laws."[45] Jonathan Boucher, who dealt with these problems more in detail

[41] *True Interest of America*, p. 39.　　[42] *A View of the Causes*, pp. 514 f.
[43] *True Interest of America*, Section I.　He cites Hooker, Harrington, Sydney, and Montesquieu in support of his contentions.
[44] *View of the Causes*, p. 521.　　[45] *Norwich Packet*, Dec. 9, 1773.

than any of the Tory writers, recurred frequently to this problem of civil liberty. His best statement was in a sermon delivered in 1774:

> "The only rational idea of civil liberty, or (which is the same thing) of a legitimate and good government, as to this point, is, when the great body of the people are trained and led habitually to submit to and acquiesce in some fixed and steady principles of conduct. It is essential, moreover, to Liberty, that such principles shall be of power sufficient to controul the arbitrary and capricious wills of mankind. . . . The primary aim, therefore, of all well-framed Constitutions is, to place man, as it were, out of the reach of his own power, and also out of the power of others as weak as himself, by placing him under the power of the law."[46]

The whole problem of government was summed up in one of Boucher's last sermons, using the Whig text "Stand fast therefore in the liberty wherewith Christ has made us free" for his own:

> "Having, then, my brethren, thus long been *tossed to and fro* in a wearisome circle of *uncertain traditions,* or in speculations and projects still more uncertain, concerning government, what better can you do than, following the Apostle's advice, to *submit yourselves to every ordinance of man, for the Lord's sake; whether it be to the King as supreme, or unto governors, as unto them that are SENT by him for the punishment of evil-doers, and for the praise of them that do well? For, so is the will of God, that with well-doing ye may put to silence the ignorance of foolish men: as free, and not using your liberty for a cloke of maliciousness, but as servants of God. Honour all men: love the brotherhood: fear God: honour the king!* . . . . *As long as I live,* therefore, yea, *whilst I have my being,* will I proclaim . . . God save the King!"[47]

[46] *View of the Causes,* p. 363. In the same work he said, "True liberty, then, is a liberty to do everything that is right, and the being restrained from doing anything that is wrong"—(p. 511). Cf. John J. Zubly, *Great Britain's Right to Tax her Colonies,* p. 55: "*Those whom God hath joined together,* (Great Britain *and* America, *Liberty* and *Loyalty*) let no man put asunder."

[47] *View of the Causes,* p. 560. Boucher was, of course, quoting the familiar text from the first epistle general of St. Peter 2:13-17. This text was as frequently cited by the Tories as was St. Paul's text, "Stand fast in the liberty," by the Whigs. Of that passage Boucher said: "The passage cannot, without infinite perversion and torture, be made to refer to any other kind of liberty [than freedom from sin]; much less to that liberty of which every man now talks, though few understand it."—*Ibid.,* p. 504. Liberty in the sense of civil liberty, he said, did not occur in all Scripture, except perhaps in one or two doubtful passages.

Having demonstrated that the Whigs, not Parliament, had aggressively violated the legal rights of the colonists, the Tory propagandists proceeded to justify opposition to the Whig program on the grounds of colonial self-interest.

The Tory writers appealed to the economic interests of nearly every element in colonial society in protest against the Whig methods of opposition to Great Britain. Their most important attack was made on the nonimportation agreements. John Mein in 1769 declared that the sole purpose of the Boston agreement was to crush all the small traders so that a few large ones could monopolize the commerce of the colony. The merchants who refused to sign the agreements of that year, of course, protested violently.[48] In 1774 the propagandists directed their fire against the Continental Association. It was called "a base, wicked and illegal measure, calculated to distress and ruin many merchants, shopkeepers and others," and the inevitable result would be a "total stagnation to all business."[49] Cooper in his *Friendly Address* drew a dismal picture of the effects of nonimportation: ships would rot in the harbors, shipbuilders and those in allied trades would be ruined, sailors would be turned ashore without employment to create riots and disturbances, iron works must stop, and the business of shopkeepers and merchants would be totally destroyed.[50] No country ever obtained greatness by internal trade alone, wrote "Mercurius" in the *Georgia Gazette*, and the proposals of the Whigs would forever prevent the development of commercial prosperity in the colonies.[51] England with her extensive commerce would be unhurt by the Association, and its only effect would be to ruin American commerce.

The farmers would suffer from the effects of the Continental Association as much as would the merchants. In Georgia and South Carolina it was commonly said that the rice planters were spared at the expense of those who raised indigo and corn, and who made their living from lumber or cattle raising.[52] Samuel Seabury in *Free Thoughts on the Proceedings of the Congress* made the most effective appeal to farmers. The proposals, he wrote, would no doubt

---

[48] Schlesinger, *Colonial Merchants*, pp. 167, 170.

[49] *N. Y. Gazetteer*, July 14, 1774; *Mass. Gazette, and Boston Weekly News-Letter, Supplement*, Nov. 10, 1774, and June 16, 1774.

[50] Pp. 39 ff.

[51] Sept. 28, 1774; Dec. 14, 1774.   [52] *Ga. Gazette*, Dec. 14, 1774.

force Great Britain to block up all the colonial ports, but in any case the nonexportation agreement would have the same effect, and then "we shall have no trade at all, and consequently no vent for the produce of our farms." "Such part of our wheat, flaxseed, corn, beef, pork, butter, cheese, as was not consumed in the province," he continued, "must be left to rot and stink upon our hands. . . . From the day that the exports from this province are stopped, the farmers may date the commencement of their ruin." With no markets, how can debts be paid? "Blessed fruits of non-importation and non-exportation! The farmer that is in debt will be ruined. The farmer that is clear in the world, will be obliged to run into debt, to support his family; and while the proud merchant, and the forsworn smuggler, riot in their ill-gotten wealth, the laborious farmers, the grand support of every well-regulated country, must all go to the dogs together. Vile, shameful, diabolical device!"[53]

No one would profit from the association. Prices would soar despite the promises of the merchants not to be extortionate; in the honor of the merchants was no security: "confound their honour—it obliged me—it obliged many of you, to take old moth-eaten clothes that had lain rotting in the shops for years, and to pay a monstrous price for them."[54] Land values would fall, creditors could never collect their just debts, and essentials like medicines could not be imported. If a man's child should be sick and there was no medicine then what would he think of the wisdom of Congress?[55] These calamities were inevitable if the proposals were adopted. They were designed to obtain relief from parliamentary taxation, but the effect would be just the reverse: "By driving matters to an extremity, we shall oblige Great-Britain to do the very thing that we are endeavouring, at least are *pretending* to endeavour, by our mad schemes, to *prevent*. We shall oblige her to raise a revenue upon us to support an army, to retain us in our dependence on her *imperial* authority."[56]

Independence, even if gained, would cost far more than a continued alliance with England. A navy of only a hundred and nine ships (and England had two hundred and twenty-four) would cost £2,190,300 to construct and £2,252,120 annually to maintain; the

[53] P. 9, and *passim.* [54] *Ibid.,* p. 10.
[55] Chandler, *What Think Ye,* pp. 27 f.
[56] Seabury, *Alarm to the Legislature,* p. 11.

army would cost another £750,000 annually, and another quarter of a million would be needed for the civil administration. This cost, together with the "prodigious sums of paper currency which the several colonies have struck, and must hereafter strike, will make a load of debt, that must prove ruinous to this continent."[57]

Civil and religious liberty were equally endangered, accused the Tory propagandists. Early in 1770 it was prophesied that if the riotous and implacable spirit of the Whigs was allowed to go unchecked, it must "eradicate every social and benevolent Sentiment, and snap asunder those Bands of Union which alone constitute our Strength and Defence against the Encroachment of lawless Power."[58] The growing spirit of lawlessness endangered everyone, wrote a Virginian:

> "Is there no Danger to Liberty when every Merchant is liable to have his House, Property, and even Life, invaded or threatened by a mob, who may be assembled at any Time, at the Call of unknown Leaders, by Ringing of the Bells (of all the Meeting Houses) and hanging out a Flag? Are their Leaders sure they can always train them to fly at such as they may be directed to, in the Name of Liberty (I am sure not of Law or Order) or in the Name of the Lord!"[59]

Samuel Seabury in two of his pamphlets warned forcefully of the threat. In his *Free Thoughts on the Proceedings of the Congress* he urged the people of New York not to elect the committees called for in the Association:

> "Will you be instrumental in bringing the most abject slavery on yourselves? Will you choose such Committees? Will you submit to them, should they be chosen by the weak, foolish, turbulant part of the country people?—Do as you please: but, by HIM that made me, I will not.—No, if I must be enslaved, let it be by a King at least, and not by a parcel of upstart, lawless Committee-men. If I must be devoured, let me be devoured by the Jaws of a lion, and not *gnawed* to death by rats and vermin."[60]

[57] Inglis, *True Interest of America*, pp. 59 f.

[58] *N. Y. Gazette and Weekly Mercury*, May 28, 1770. "Portius" also attacked the "licentious and dissatisfied spirit which is so prevalent among us, and which threatens a subversion of the order and harmony of government."—*Ibid.*, Aug. 13, 1770.

[59] *Va. Gazette* (Purdie), Jan. 20, 1774.   [60] P. 18.

In *The Congress Canvassed* he made a devastating attack on them:

"But remember;—your liberties and properties are now at the mercy of a body of men unchecked, uncontrouled by the civil power. You have chosen your committee;—you are no longer your own masters:—you have subjected your business, your dealings, your mode of living, the conduct and regulation of your families, to *their* prudence and discretion. . . . Violence is done to private property, by riotous assemblies, and the rioters go unpunished; nay more;—are applauded for those very crimes which the laws of the government have forbidden under severe penalties . . . *You* that spurned at the thought of holding your rights on the precarious tenure of the *will* of a British ministry . . . can *you* submit to hold them on as precarious a tenure, the *will* of a New York committee, of a Continental Congress?"[61]

The abuses of the past were but a sample of those to be expected in the future. "Independence and slavery are synonymous terms" wrote the author of *Plain Truth*.[62] And the Tories to a man forbodingly declared: "The surest Way to lose Liberty is to abuse it."[63]

But there were far more serious dangers ahead if England should be provoked into war with the colonies. Long before the Whigs had come out openly for independence, the Tories had accused them of the intention, and had appealed to the loyalty of the people to resist the aims of those whose purpose at bottom was an independent republic.[64] They made a sentimental appeal to the colonists to stand by the empire which had done so much for them. "But if love be a voluntary offering," said Jonathan Boucher, "gratitude is a debt."[65] Later he explained more fully the reasons behind this statement: "owing almost solely to the protection and patronage of the Parent State, we have rapidly risen to a degree of respectability, and 'an height of felicity, scarce ever experienced by any other people.' "[66]

---

[61] P. 16. See also Galloway, *Candid Examination*, p. 62.

[62] P. 37.

[63] "A New York Freeholder," *Mass. Gazette, and Boston Weekly News-Letter*, Oct. 27, 1774. See also, among many examples, *ibid.*, June 16, 1774, and *Md. Gazette*, Jan. 19, 1775.

[64] E.g., *OUT-LINES*, Feb. 9, 1770, New York Hist. Soc., Broadsides; Grotius, *Pills for the Delegates*, p. 31; Chandler, *What Think Ye*, pp. 28 ff.

[65] *View of the Causes*, p. 374.

[66] *Ibid.*, pp. 475 f. He was refuting statements by Provost William Smith that the colonies had achieved their present status by their own efforts, and the closing words are from Smith's sermon.

"Let us remember," wrote another, "our duty to the parent state, the terms on which our forefathers settled, lived and prospered, under which we ourselves have grown rich, and lived happily."[67] The plans and actions of the Whigs, instead of prolonging this ideal situation, simply tended "to raise jealousies, to excite animosities, to foment discords between us and our mother country."[68] A declaration of independence was deplorable because it would forever close the door to a just reconciliation with Great Britain. The petition of some New Jersey inhabitants to the provincial council urged against a declaration for this very reason:

> "We trust that you will be too deeply impress'd with the Recollection of the peculiar Happiness and Prosperity heretofore enjoyed by the Inhabitants of this Continent, connected with and subject to the government of Great-Britain, not to dread the Consequences of a declar'd Separation from that Country. . . . a change of government will prevent a safe, honourable, and lasting Reconciliation with Great-Britain on constitutional Principles."[69]

It was this happy situation that the Whigs were threatening to destroy; the consequences, avowed the Tories, were frightening to imagine. In the first place, they said, it was incredible that anyone in America should challenge the power of England. In 1768 an English letter in the *Massachusetts Gazette* set the tone for later Tory propaganda on this point. Speaking of the bombast in the colonial newspapers, the writer said, "whatever men in garrets may write, Gentlemen in Parliament will not bear to see its Authority trampled on, or suffer a *Boston* Town-meeting to threaten and bid defiance to the Government of Great-Britain."[70]

As the crisis approached, Tory writers presented all the horrors of a war with England and the certainty of defeat. Why, said Seabury, "a single campaign, should she exert her force, would ruin us

---

[67] *N. Y. Gazetteer*, Sept. 8, 1774. See also Cooper, *Friendly Address*, p. 4.

[68] Seabury, *The Congress Canvassed*, p. 5. One writer, referring to the "wise and prudent" resolutions of the Continental Congress, declared, "instead of *wise* and *prudent*, I find nothing but rude, insolent and absurd resolves, calculated to answer no end, but to stir up strife and increase confusion among us, and to unite every spirited Briton against us."—*N. Y. Gazetteer*, Jan. 5, 1775.

[69] *N. Y. Gazette and Weekly Mercury*, Jan. 24, 1776.

[70] Nov. 3, 1768. See also *Loyal Verses of Stansbury and Odell*, p. 3.

effectually."[71] England was the greatest naval power in the world and could crush colonial opposition "like a moth"; not a seaport town would be safe from devastation. England had an unlimited supply of troops and could send as many as necessary; her wealth and her strength were overpowering.[72] Indeed, said Chandler, "if there should be no miraculous interposition of heaven to defeat the natural power of the mother country, should we go on to enrage it, it must at last fall upon us with an irresistible impetuosity."[73]

Actually no aid was to be expected, either from God or from any earthly power. "God is a God of order and not of confusion, he commands you to submit to your rulers, and to be obedient to the higher powers for conscience sake." The colonist who died in rebellion, they said, was damned: "Under all these Circumstances, and upon no better Grounds, if we madly rebel against our Sovereign, and cruelly let slip the Dogs of civil war, may we not justly expect, that for these Things, GOD . . . will, one Day, bring us into Judgment?"[74] Nor was there any help to be expected from Europe. France, the only power at all likely to aid, was in serious financial straits and stood to lose her colonies near America should it become independent. In fact, said one writer, "France and Spain have *actually made an offer of their assistance* to Great-Britain, in the present contest with the Colonies."[75]

On the contrary, instead of allies, the colonists would find only additional enemies. Without the protection of England, who would defend the frontiers from the Indians? From Georgia came constant complaints that the action of the Whigs was endangering the colony:

> "We have an enemy at our backs, who but very lately put us into the utmost consternation. We fled at their approach; we left our property at their mercy; and we have implored the assistance of *Great-Britain* to humble these haughty *Creeks*. And yet, no sooner is our panic a little subsided, but we insult

[71] *Free Thoughts*, p. 6.

[72] "A New York Freeholder," *Mass. Gazette, and Boston Weekly News-Letter*, Oct. 20, 1774. "A Yeoman of Suffolk County" distributed a handbill throughout Boston on Feb. 6, 1775, which played up the power of the mother country and the crime of rebellion.—Frothingham, *Warren*, p. 413. "A Suffolk Yeoman" had a similar piece in *Mass. Gazette, and Boston Weekly News-Letter*, Dec. 29, 1774. See also Hunt, *Political Family*, p. 32; and *N. Y. Gazetteer*, Sept. 22, 1774.   [73] *What Think Ye*, p. 27.

[74] *Mass. Gazette, and Boston Weekly News-Letter*, Nov. 24, 1774; Jan. 26, 1775.

[75] Inglis, *True Interest of America*, p. 66. He told this as a secret, without giving his authority. See also "Z" in *N. Y. Gazette and Weekly Mercury*, May 14, 1770.

our best and only friend, from whom alone we can expect protection. *Carolina* it is certain, will give us none."[76]

A Boston broadside signed "Monitor" made the same plea to the Massachusetts provincial congress. Hostile action toward England, said "Monitor," "would bring Fifteen or Eighteen Thousand Canadians and Indians upon the Frontiers of this and Connecticut Government."[77]

Without the power of England the colonies were defenseless:

"What have the Americans to oppose such mighty power! is it a defenseless coast without a navy, a country without manufactures, a treasury without money, an army without cloathing, arms, ammunition or discipline, and lastly councils without unanimity, in which defection from the cause must be the inevitable consequence of usurpation, folly and rashness?"[78]

And should they fail, then, "after the most dreadful scenes of violence and slaughter,—CONFISCATIONS and EXECUTIONS must close the HORRID TRAGEDY."[79] But even if they should by some wild chance succeed in breaking away from England, the colonists would destroy themselves in civil war, so divided were they. As Chandler wrote:

"Even a final victory would effectually ruin us; as it would necessarily introduce civil wars among ourselves, and leave us open and exposed to the avarice and ambition of every maritime power in Europe or America. And till one part of this country shall have subdued the other, and conquered a considerable part of the world besides, this peaceful region must become, and continue to be, a theatre of inconceivable misery and horrour."[80]

The War Between the States verified part of his prophesy. Seabury in his direful view almost hit another truth:

"But horrid indeed would be the consequence of our success! We should presently turn our arms on one another, prov-

[76] *Ga. Gazette*, Aug. 10, 1774. "In a word, that there is great danger of an Indian war I think certain, and that the event of it, should we, by our conduct, forfeit the protection of our Mother Country, must be inevitable ruin to this province is as certain."— *Ibid.*, July 27, 1774. See also *ibid.*, Oct. 12, 1774, for the protests of Wrightsborough, Kyoka, and Broad River settlements against the action of the Savannah meeting.
[77] N. Y. Public Library, Broadsides. See also *Mass. Gazette, and Boston Weekly News-Letter*, Oct. 6, 1774.
[78] *Va. Gazette* (Pinkney), Feb. 3, 1776. See also *Mass. Gazette, and Boston Weekly News-Letter*, Oct. 6, 1774.
[79] Seabury, *The Congress Canvassed*, p. 27.   [80] *What Think Ye*, p. 25.

ince against province, and destruction and carnage would desolate the land. Probably it would cost the blood of a great part of the inhabitants of America to determine what kind of a government we should have, whether a monarchy or a republic. Another effusion of blood would be necessary to fix a monarch, or to establish the commonwealth."[81]

An early statement in the *Massachusetts Gazette, and Boston News-Letter* well summarized the attitude of the Tories throughout this discussion:

"Recede then, my dear countrymen, before it is too late. Beware of drawing down upon yourselves such complicated misery and ruin. Do not excite to this extreme the judgments of your reluctant sovereign. Speak peace to yourselves and be still. *Agree with thine adversary quickly;* and provoke not the Almighty to say to you, *I also will laugh at your calamity, I will mock when your fear cometh.*"[82]

ADVANTAGES OF VICTORY

In contrast to the dismal outlook if the Whig plans were successful, the Tories presented the positive advantages of their program. In the early days of the controversy they had occasionally adduced advantages from English legislation. In a rare instance one writer defended the Stamp Act on the grounds that "the sums of money arising from the new stamp duties in North America, for the first five years are chiefly to be applied towards making commodious post roads from one province to another, erecting bridges where necessary, and other public measures equally important, to facilitate an extensive trade."[83]

Few pointed to any colonial advantages to be derived from the Townshend legislation,[84] but a great many showed how the Tea Act would be positively beneficial. The Tea Act, they stated, in no way invaded the liberties of the colonists, for the tax was not to be paid,[85] and the whole issue was simply whether the English company

---

[81] *The Congress Canvassed,* p. 27.

[82] Dec. 29, 1774.   [83] *Ga. Gazette,* June 30, 1765.

[84] It was said by one writer that the new customs board would cost far less than the old system and that the money collected by the board would stay in America.—*Mass. Gazette,* Nov. 19, 1767.

[85] This was a common statement, incorrect, and vigorously refuted by the Whigs. See N. Y. *Journal,* Nov. 4, 1773; *To the Agents of the High Mightiness,* Oct. 28, 1773, N. Y. Hist. Scc., Broadsides; *N. Y. Gazetteer,* Nov. 18, 1773.

or the Dutch company should sell tea in America. This being so, "can any of her subjects, who profess the character of patriots, hesitate a moment in determining whether it is their duty to prefer the interest of the English company to that of its rivals?"[86] It was not only a patriotic measure to support the British East India Company, it would pay good dividends. As English tea would be sold at auction, any merchant could get what he wanted and there would be no monopolizing; a two per cent tax on the gross sales would reduce taxes in New York alone eighteen hundred pounds a year.[87] Finally, everyone would be able to get much better tea at half the former price. A New York broadside (it was in New York and Philadelphia that most of these arguments were current), written as if by a Dutch trader to show the mercenary alliance of the Dutch East India Company and the Whigs, summarized the Tory position: "the people here will have an opportunity of buying good English Tea, for half the price we expected to extort from them, for the trash lodged in your hands from Holland. Our partner, Sammy Sedition, has wrote, published, threatened, prayed, and lied, to delude the inhabitants from buying English Tea: Duty, or no duty, he tried to make the people believe that their liberties were alike affected; but all will not serve to call the people together. The consumers of Tea in this city, will no longer be blinded to their own interest; therefore, dispatch our Dutch Tea immediately, that we may get it sold before the English arrives. Oh! Donder unblexin! Dispatch! Dispatch! or we are undone!"[88]

The advantages of reconciliation with England on some acceptable terms were less discussed than the obvious penalties of failure to reach an agreement, but there were some who dealt concretely with them. *Common Sense* challenged the Tory writers to show a single advantage from reconciliation, and Inglis accepted the challenge; his statement was a powerful appeal to the moderates and conservatives throughout the colonies:

1. The calamitous war would be stopped.
2. Peace would be restored.

[86] *Norwich Packet*, Dec. 2, 1773.
[87] *A Letter to the Inhabitants of the City of New York*, Nov. 22, 1773, N. Y. Hist. Soc., Broadsides; *Mass. Gazette, and Boston Weekly News-Letter*, Oct. 28, 1773.
[88] *To the Agents of the High Mightiness*, Oct. 28, 1773, *loc. cit.*; *A LETTER found on board the sloop ILLICIT, Captain Perjury, wrecked at Oyster Bay*, July 3, 1773, *ibid.*; N. Y. *Gazetteer*, Nov. 18, 1773; *Norwich Packet*, Dec. 9, 1773.

3. Agriculture, commerce, and industry would assume their wonted vigor.

4. Trade would have the protection of the greatest naval power in the world.

5. Protection would cost just a fiftieth of what it would if the colonies were independent.

6. England would pay a bounty on exports, and the colonists would be able to get the best manufactured goods in the world at lower prices than if independent.

7. Everything would return to its pristine state of prosperity. Immigration and population would increase with increased prosperity.[89]

Within the empire was the sole hope for the colonies; as it grew in strength and power, so would the colonies. Its interests were paramount, and even at the expense of some temporary disabilities, the colonists' real interest lay with it; the greatest crime they could commit would be to endanger the empire. "Yet, let me die!" exclaimed Samuel Seabury, born and bred in America, "but I had rather be reduced to the last shilling, than that the imperial dignity of Great Britain should sink, or be controlled by any people or power on earth."[90]

DEPRAVITY OF THE ENEMY

Tory propagandists knew as surely as did the Whigs that hatred of individuals must be aroused before action could be demanded, and their most characteristic appeal during the prerevolutionary period was an attack on the character of the Whigs. It was at once an attempt to arouse the hatred of their own class for the Whigs and to discredit the Whig leaders with their own party. Unfortunately for them, however, they couched this appeal in such terms as to alienate rather than to enlist the sympathies of the average man in America. It was admirably phrased to appeal to the conservative, moderate elements in society, but it unquestionably failed in its effect when read by the common man. The Whig appeal that the profligate, corrupt rich were oppressing the poor and downtrodden was much

[89] *True Interest of America*, pp. 47 ff. See also Hunt, *Political Family*, p. 32; Laird, *Englishman's Answer*, p. 26; *N. Y. Gazetteer*, Nov. 2, 1775.

[90] *View of the Controversy*, p. 23. "For my own part, I think the lopping off half a dozen of these colonies *forever*, would be of less consequence to the *British Empire*, than that Great Britain should be reduced to the necessity of making a single concession, unbecoming to her honour and dignity."—*N. Y. Gazetteer*, Aug. 18, 1774.

more telling than the Tory appeal that "silly clowns and illiterate mechanics" were promoting social rebellion and deluding the people. Yet that was the characteristic suggestion.

The Tories never wearied of ridiculing the common origin of Whig leaders. The Reverend John Bullman's sermon of August, 1774, is an apt illustration:

> "In short, it is from this unhappy temper that every idle projector, who perhaps cannot govern his own household, or pay the debts of his own creating, presumes he is qualified to dictate how the state should be governed, and to point out means of paying the debts of a nation. Hence, too, it is that every silly clown and illiterate mechanic will take upon him to censure the conduct of his Prince or Governor, and contribute as much as in him lies to create and ferment those misunderstandings which, being brooded by discontent and diffused through great multitudes, come at last to end in schism in the church, and sedition and rebellion in the state; so great a matter doth a little fire kindle."[91]

A South Carolina poem comprehensively condemned the entire Whig leadership:

> "Not only our money from nothing appears,
> From nothing our hopes, and from nothing our fears,
> From nothing our statesmen, our army, our fleet,—
> From nothing they came, and to nought they'll retreat,
> And no arms they handle so well as their feet.
> Down at night a bricklayer or carpenter lies,
> With next sun a Lycurgus or Solon doth rise;
>
> .   .   .   .
>
> Priests, tailors, and cobblers fill with heroes the camp,
> And sailors, like crawfish, crawl out of each swamp."[92]

"Our danger," wrote Jonathan Boucher, "arises from rash and daring ignorance; from the pertness and self-sufficiency of men who are

---

[91] Quoted in McCrady, S. C. under Royal Government, p. 752.

[92] The Loyalist Poetry of the Revolution, pp. 59 f. Those who directed the movement against the Tea Act, wrote a Tory, "must not, they cannot, they *shall* not have to escape the animadversions of a lover of constitutional Liberty; but a sworn foe to *Coblers* and *Taylors*, so long as they take upon their *everlasting* and *unmeasureable* shoulders the power of *directing* the *loyal* and *sensible* inhabitants of the CITY and PROVINCE of NEW YORK."—N. Y. Gazetteer, Apr. 28, 1774.

so illiterate as even to despise learning."[93] Cooper's long poem, "The Patriots of North America" contained lines which castigated the folly, stupidity, and knavery of the Whig leaders:

> "The Men deprav'd, who quit their Sphere,
> Without Remorse, or Shame, or Fear,
> And boldly rush, they know not where;
> Seduc'd, alas! by fond Applause,
> Of gaping Mobs, and loud Huzzas.
> Unconscious all, of nobler Aim,
> Than sordid Pelf, or vulgar Fame;
> Men undefin'd by any Rules,
> Ambiguous Things, half Knaves, half Fools,
> Whom God denied the Talents great
> Requir'd, to make a Knave, complete;
> Whom Nature form'd, vile paltry Tools,
> Absurder much, than downright Fools,
> Who from their own dear Puppet-Show,
> The World's great Stage, pretend to know."[94]

In "The Congress," a Tory ballad published in the spring of 1776, there is buried a stanza which offers a typical prayer:

> "O goddess, hear our hearty prayers;
> Confound the villains by the ears;
> Disperse the plebeians—try the peers,
> And execute the Congress."[95]

These men of low and common origin, these professed patriots, were deluding the good people of America for their own selfish aims. The opposition to the establishment of an American episcopate came, it was said, "from an ambitious, disappointed faction."[96] The first and principal instigators of the agitation against the Tea Act, wrote a Georgian, "are those very persons who were lately concerned in the illicit trade which these acts were intended effectually to put a stop to."[97] The unpopular phraseology of much of this part of

---

[93] *View of the Causes*, p. 214.

[94] P. 3. The poem works out the story of a school boys' rebellion against their master and says of the Whig leaders,
> "With all this Bullying, Rant, and Noise,
> They're giddy, thoughtless, helpless Boys."

[95] *Loyalist Poetry of the Revolution*, pp. 70 ff.

[96] *N. Y. Gazette and Weekly Mercury*, Apr. 4, 1768.

[97] A broadside dated July 25, 1774, bound with the *Ga. Gazette*. See also *N. Y. Gazette and Weekly Mercury*, Sept. 3, Oct. 15, 1770.

Tory propaganda is admirably illustrated in the further remarks of this Georgian on the riots in Boston, "where the populace, inflamed and misled by the artifices and misrepresentations of some interested and designing men" destroyed the tea: "such is, unfortunately, the ignorance and infatuation of mankind, that, let but any mad-man, enthusiast, or worse, set up the standard of faction, and give it the specious name of liberty, let him but bellow out death and freedom, chains and slavery, and a few other sounding words, to delude and misguide the minds of the unthinking multitude, and thousands will immediately enlist under his treacherous banner, and be desperate enough to second whatever he may be base enough to attempt."[98]

Some saw in the controversy nothing but the efforts of a few disappointed politicians attempting to oust those in power, who with others sought their own welfare even at the expense of wrecking the empire:

> "Would you know what a Whig is, and always was,
> I'll show you his face, as it were in a glass,
> He's a *rebel* by nature, a villain in grain,
> A *saint* by profession, who never had grace:
> *Cheating* and *lying* are puny things,
> *Rapine* and *plundering* venial sins,
> His great occupation is ruining *nations,*
> *Subverting of Crowns,* and *murdering Kings*."[99]

Self-seeking debauchees and prostituted priests composed the leadership of the Whig party as another saw it:

> "It is a remark that the high sons of Liberty consist of but two sorts of men. The first are those who by their debaucheries and ill conduct in life, are reduced almost to poverty, and are happy in finding a subsistence, though it is even on the destruction of their country; for on the turbulence of the times, and the heated imaginations of the populace, depends their existence. The latter are the ministers of the gospel, who, instead of preaching to their flocks meekness, sobriety, attention to their

[98] A broadside dated July 25, 1774, bound with the *Ga. Gazette*.
[99] *N. Y. Gazetteer*, Jan. 26, 1775. The Massachusetts "Liberty Song" was parodied in 1770, N. Y. Hist. Soc., Broadsides. See also two broadsides in *ibid*.: *The Times*, Jan. 27, 1770; and *To John M. S[cott] Esq.*, July 23, 1774. This latter accuses Scott of attempting to split the mechanics and the merchants in his own interests. A similar attack was made on Alexander McDougall: *To the Inhabitants of the City and County of New York*, July 12, 1774, N. Y. Hist. Soc., Broadsides.

different employments, and a steady obedience to the laws of Britain, belch from the pulpit liberty, independence, and a steady perseverance in endeavoring to shake off their allegiance to the mother country."[100]

Born in obscurity and destined to die in obscurity unless a social earthquake spewed them to the top, to such leaders "every change in the affairs of government must be a desirable object; the more confusion they can create . . . the greater chance have they of enriching themselves by the spoils of their country."[101] Indeed, wrote "Phileirene," "The whole system of popular manoeuvres has been dictated and directed, by *unprincipled, factious, designing men,* whose *interest* it has been to keep alive the coals of sedition, and blow the popular discontents into a flame, who have *nothing* to lose by failing in their enterprize, and *everything* to hope from success."[102]

More serious still, the propagandists charged, Whig leaders were actually cruel and depraved. The atrocity stories of the war were not common until later, of course, but as early as the Boston Massacre it was frequently stated that the Whigs had planned to provoke the massacre in order to remove the troops. As Bernard wrote Hutchinson: "It is put out of all doubt, that the attacking the soldiers was preconcerted in order to oblige them to fire, and then made it necessary to quit the town, in consequences of their doing what they were forced to do. It is considered by thinking men wholly as a manoeuvre to support the cause of non-importation."[103] So also did they accuse the Whigs of provoking the first clash of arms at Lexington and Concord. A circular was distributed on April 21 which threw all the blame on them, and Gage's account was sent to the governor of each province with instructions to have it printed in the local gazette.[104]

The coercion of the Tories, however, provided much more ma-

---

[100] *N. Y. Gazetteer,* Mar. 9, 1775. There is the same attack on the ministers in *The Two Congresses Cut Up,* p. 13. [101] *N. Y. Gazetteer,* Aug. 11, 1774.

[102] *Mass. Gazette, and Boston Weekly News-Letter,* Jan. 12, 1775. See also *N. Y. Gazette and Weekly Mercury,* Nov. 19, 1770; *Norwich Packet,* Dec. 2, 1773.

[103] Quoted in Frothingham, "Sam Adams Regiments," *Atlantic Monthly,* XII, 616. See also 4 Mass. Hist. Soc., *Collections,* IV, 372, and Mass. Hist. Soc., Manuscript Collections, 1761-1776, pp. 61-74.

[104] *S. C. and Amer. Gen. Gazette,* July 28, 1775. For the broadside, see *A Circumstantial Account of the Attack . . . on His Majesty's Troops,* April 21, 1775, Mass. Hist. Soc., Broadsides; and 4 Force, *Amer. Arch.,* II, 538. "Grotius" in his first letter defended Gage for preparing his troops because of the open statements of the rebels that they were planning an attack.—*Pills for the Delegates,* pp. 1-13.

terial for such charges than the military activities. The South Carolina Whigs were accused of giving the Indians of the back country powder with instructions to kill every man who refused to sign the Association,[105] and the Tory papers in the North carried numerous accounts of the suffering from mobs, riots, and committeemen. One in particular summed up the accusation against the Whigs admirably. It was a petition to the Massachusetts provincial congress, calling to its attention the plight of those "who, from a sense of their duty to their King, and a reverance for his laws, have behaved quiet and peaceable; and for which reason they have been deprived of their liberty, abused in their persons, and suffered such barbarous cruelties, insults and indignities, besides the loss of their property by the hands of lawless mobs and riots, as would have been disgraceful even for savages to have committed."[106]

[105] Ramsay, *History of the Revolution of South Carolina*, I, 70 f. The Indians were given powder, but the Whigs indignantly denied that it was to be used for killing non-associators.—*Ibid.*, pp. 71 ff.   [106] 4 Force, *Amer. Arch.*, I, 1260 f.

XVI

TORY PROPAGANDA: MEDIA

THE TORY appeal was a written appeal; the dearth of oral, dramatic, and pictorial suggestions is striking. The Whig propagandists explored the possibilities of every available contact, and although some were inadequately used, the number and variety of their activities become the more impressive as the puny record of the Tories is set forth. For this failure to exploit the possibilities of primary contacts there were good reasons. In the first place, the Tories appealed primarily to what they called the "thinking, reasonable, part of mankind," and were contemptuous of the buffoonish efforts of the Whigs to influence the lower classes. In the second place, the Whigs, especially after 1774, narrowly circumscribed Tory activities. Whigs broke up their meetings, persecuted their speakers, and drove their preachers from their pulpits. As a result, it would be only an exaggeration to say that there were no Tory demonstrations, no public addresses, no pictures, no "loyalty" poles or trees.

VISUAL AND ORAL APPEALS

Tory demonstrations and celebrations are conspicuously missing in the records of prerevolutionary America, and almost necessarily so. What would the Tories celebrate?—perhaps the King's birthday, but everyone was supposed to celebrate that. By 1774, however, only British troops marked the day, wrote one Tory poet:

> "Here we now lament to find
> Sons of Brittain, fierce and blind
> Drawn from Loyal Love astray,
> Hail no more this welcome Day!"[1]

The Tory calendar had no such days as the fifth of March, the eighteenth of March, and the nineteenth of April, and after 1774 a Tory demonstration enlivened with effigies of Sam Adams, or Gadsden, or Sears, would have been immeasurable folly. Even so, some people of Ulster County, New York, raised in 1775 a seventy-five-

---

[1] Loyalist Rhapsodies, No. 3.

foot pole, carrying the royal standard and an inscription of loyalist sentiments, but that was in the heart of the loyalist country, and it was soon cut down.[2] The time for demonstrations of loyalty was gone after 1774, and no one had thought of them before.

The public address, so important a feature of modern propaganda, and one used with considerable effect by the Whigs of Massachusetts, played little part in disseminating Tory suggestions. Samuel Seabury spoke of assembling four hundred people in White Plains, New York, in 1775, to protest against the acts of Congress, but no record of his talk remains. The persecution of the Tories made formal meetings except in churches almost impossible after the summer of 1774, and only in private conversation and informal gatherings was there much opportunity for face-to-face contacts. Seabury rode his parish almost daily during the crisis of 1774, urging people to oppose the acts of the first Continental Congress, and when ratification of the Association was being debated in the New York Assembly, he influenced, according to his own claim, nearly a third of the members.[3] Charles Inglis was active in the same way; he wrote the Loyalist Claims Commission that "he endeavoured by persuasion and every other method consistent with his function, in public & private to discourage the rising Spirit of revolt and he ceased not to stimulate his numerous acquaint[ces] to exert themselves in extinguishing a Flame which was likely to involve them and everything dear to them in universal ruin."[4]

Doubtless the sermon was the most effective vehicle of propaganda that the Tories had. Tory sermons were not printed as were those of the Whigs, and the Anglican Church as a whole took no official stand in the colonies. The general policy of individual churches as far north as Philadelphia was to avoid a cleavage. Even in the more aggressive northern churches the ministers did not face the issue until forced to it by the Whigs. It was not until 1774 that Anglican clergymen began to preach openly against the Whigs, and, as those who did were soon suppressed, the majority of the preacher propagandists carried on their work either in private conversation or under pseudonyms in the press. John Bullman, assistant rector of St. Michaels, as we have already seen, preached only one Tory ser-

[2] C. H. Van Tyne, *The Loyalists in the American Revolution,* p. 75.
[3] Loyalist Transcripts, XLI, 561 f.   [4] *Ibid.,* XLII, 545.

mon, "The Christian Duty of Peaceableness," and was immediately forced to resign. Jonathan Boucher, whose sermons contain some of the finest propaganda of the period, did not take politics into his pulpit until 1774 and was allowed to preach thereafter less than a year; his sermons were not published until long after he had returned to England. Such experiences were typical. Under such circumstances the comparatively limited amount of pulpit propaganda and its few remains are not surprising.

It was the task of the Tory clergyman, just as it was that of the Whig, to apply Christian principles to the political problem of the time, and to the Whig text from St. Paul, "Stand fast therefore in the liberty wherewith Christ hath made us free," they opposed the words of St. Peter: "Submit yourselves to every ordinance of man for the Lord's sake." That was the dominant theme of Tory sermons throughout the period. In the early days of the controversy, sermons were mild exhortations to fear God and honor the King. After June, 1774, the ministers added to this persistent theme an attack on the character, methods, and purposes of the Whigs as directly contrary to basic principles of human action. Too severe an attack on Whig personalities, however, was dangerous, and the sermons usually stuck to fundamentals. Ezra Stiles recorded in his diary that the Reverend Mr. Bisset had preached on a fast day a "high Tory Sermon inveighing (by Allusions) against Boston & N. England as a turbulent ungoverned people."[5]

Jonathan Boucher's sermons attacked more directly the principles of the Whigs and less directly their characters, although these he did not spare in his conversation. In his published sermons he opposed to the eighteenth-century ideas of the Whigs the seventeenth-century doctrines of submission to authority and the divine origin of government in a more fundamental way than was commonly done.[6] Inglis constantly urged his flock to remain loyal, and only a few deserted the King, he wrote the Claims Commission,[7] but of his prewar sermons little record remains; and so with Seabury, Chandler, Cooper, and Odell.

There was only one outstanding song writer of the period, Joseph Stansbury, and songs were of little importance in spreading

[5] I, 447 f. (June 30, 1774).
[6] *View of the Causes.*
[7] Loyalist Transcripts, XLII, 551.

Tory ideas. Stansbury's best work was done after the war started and only a few songs of his had any popularity before then. He usually wrote a song for the annual banquet of the Sons of St. George, and one of them, to the popular tune "Hearts of Oak," is typical of his ideas before Independence was proclaimed. It is little more than a plea for the unity and strength of the empire against her common enemies:

"When good Queen Elizabeth governed the realm,
 And Burleigh's sage counsels directed the helm,
 In vain Spain and France our conquests opposed,—
 For valor conducted what wisdom proposed.
     Beef and beer was their food;
     Love and truth armed their band;
     Their courage was ready—
     Steady, boys, steady—
 To fight and to conquer by sea and by land. .

"But since tea and coffee, so much to our grief,
 Have taken the place of strong beer and roast beef,
 Our laurels have withered, our trophies been torn,
 And the lions of England French triumphs adorn.
     Tea and slops are their food—
     They unnerve every hand;
     Their courage unsteady
     And not always ready—
 They often are conquered by sea and by land.

.   .   .   .

"While thus we regale, as our fathers of old,—
 Our manners as simple, our courage as bold,—
 May vigor and prudence our freedom secure,
 Long as rivers, or ocean, or stars shall endure.
     Beef and beer are our food;
     Love and truth arm our band;
     Our courage is steady
     And always is ready
 To fight and to conquer by sea and by land."[8]

WRITTEN APPEALS

The Tories, it is clear, depended upon a written rather than a spoken appeal, but their opportunities for using the press were

[8] Sargent, *Loyal Verses of Stansbury and Odell,* pp. 4 f.

sharply limited. There were few declared Tory printers—Richard and Samuel Draper of Boston, Alexander and James Robertson, Hugh Gaine, and James Rivington of New York were the only important ones prior to 1776. Limited as their facilities were, however, the Tories made good use of them after 1773.

Tory printers used the pamphlet as a vehicle of propaganda to any great extent only in the fall of 1774. The defense of Parliament in 1765 had been carried on principally by English pamphleteers. Martin Howard's two in 1765, *A Letter from a Gentleman at Halifax*, and *A Defence of the Letter from a Gentleman at Halifax*, were the most important American pamphlets upholding parliamentary authority. In 1774, however, the first Continental Congress and its actions produced a major pamphlet war.

Every important Tory writer except Jonathan Boucher published a pamphlet attack on the Continental Congress. Seabury, Cooper, Chandler, Inglis, and Galloway, all wrote in this form.[9] Other individuals joined temporarily in the fight against the rapidly developing Whig program. Harrison Gray, treasurer of Massachusetts and loyalist refugee, published through Draper's press in Boston *The Two Congresses Cut Up*, an attack on the first Continental Congress and the Massachusetts Convention of 1774.[10] Isaac Hunt saw the coming movement for independence and combated it in his long pamphlet, *The Political Family: or a Discourse, pointing out the Reciprocal Advantages, which Flow from an Uninterrupted Union between Great Britain and her American Colonies.*[11] Reprinted in America and widely circulated at this time was Sir John Dalrymple's *The Rights of Great Britain Asserted against the Claims of America.* This was one of the pamphlets that Governor Martin distributed in the North Carolina back country. Two other pamphlets used some-

---

[9] Three editions of Cooper's *Friendly Address* appeared in New York, and there were two printings by Rivington of his *American Querist*, and one by Mills and Hicks. Leonard's *Massachusettensis* was first published in pamphlet form by Mills and Hicks and was twice reprinted by Rivington. Galloway wrote another pamphlet, replying to a critic of his *Candid Examination*, and Rivington printed it in April, 1775. Just as the last sheets were struck off, a crowd surrounded the shop and destroyed the entire edition, according to one account. According to another, Rivington was afraid to publish it. It was published in 1777 when Rivington returned.—Evans, *Amer. Biblio.*, No. 14,060.

[10] Rivington reprinted this under a slightly different title in 1774.

[11] This was originally written for a prize essay contest in 1766; it did not win. Another pamphlet of similar import, *The Advantage which America Derives from her Commerce, Connexion, and Dependance on Britain*, published in 1775, has been attributed to Lieutenant Henry Barry.—Evans, *Amer. Biblio.*, No. 13,822.

what different methods of attack on the Continental Congress. The first was a satire written by a pretended Whig: *The Triumph of the Whigs: or T'other Congress Canvassed*. It damned the Congress as being wholly unrepresentative and the Whigs as being wholly licentious. The other, *Pills for the Delegates*, was a series of four letters which had originally appeared in the *Boston News-Letter*. These letters were addressed to Peyton Randolph, president of the Continental Congress and were signed "Grotius." The common theme of the four was that the Whigs had been the aggressors throughout.

These pamphlets were written in opposition to the Continental Congresses, but there was no pamphlet attack of such proportions against *Common Sense* and the proposals for independence. The Tory pamphleteers were gone. Seabury and Galloway were under close watch, and Cooper, Chandler, Leonard, and Sewall had left America. Boucher was never a pamphleteer, but he too was gone.[12] Of the old pamphlet writers only Inglis remained, safe on a British warship. With great difficulty he finally published his refutation of *Common Sense*, *The True Interest of America Impartially Stated*, which took up Paine's arguments in order and attacked them one by one. Similar in method but atrociously written was *Plain Truth Addressed to the Inhabitants of America*, published in Philadelphia by an unknown author.[13]

These pamphlets were straightforward, controversial essays; only in rare instances did the Tory propagandists use the pamphlet for a different type of appeal. The Whigs had published long poems, plays, histories, and sermons in this form, but there were few such Tory pieces. Myles Cooper is credited with a long poem, *The Patriots of North America*, throughout a scurrilous attack on the Whig leaders, and to Jonathan Sewall has been attributed one of the rare Tory dramas, *The Americans Roused, in a Cure for the Spleen*, written probably in the winter of 1774. This is in the form of conversations on the times and is distinguished by the crude vigor with which the colloquists attack the Continental Congress. It was not

[12] Evans, *Amer. Biblio.*, attributes to Boucher a pamphlet published in New York in 1774, *A Letter from a Virginian, to the Members of the Congress, to be held in Philadelphia*. Mills and Hicks reprinted this in Boston, and there were two other Boston editions, printers not given.

[13] James Humphreys published two editions of *The True Interest of America*, but *Plain Truth*, a much poorer pamphlet, went through three Philadelphia editions, all by Robert Bell, one London edition, and one Dublin edition. It has been attributed to several of the Tory writers.

intended to be staged, of course, and the actual plays put on by the British troops were a later development.[14]

Tory propagandists, like the Whigs, developed the newspaper as a channel of propaganda to a remarkable extent. The number of actual Tory printers was small, but first and last there were several papers which would print anti-Whig articles from 1765 to 1774, for most of the printers adopted the motto, "Open to all Parties, Influenced by None." In practice, however, this ideal was never reached, and as a paper came to be identified with one party the other withdrew its support. It is an interesting fact that the most impartial papers in the country, those in short that most nearly lived up to the ideal of a newspaper, were the ones that later became Tory papers because the Whigs refused to deal with them. The number of really impartial papers was small. The universal uprising of the printers against the Stamp Act had identified them to a certain extent with the Whig movement, and increasingly thereafter the Whigs tightened their control on the colonial press, using violence where necessary. Even so, there were several papers open to the Tories.

Four of these Tory papers were published throughout the decade preceding the Revolution: *The Massachusetts Gazette, and Boston News-Letter*, *The New York Gazette and Weekly Mercury*, the *South Carolina and American General Gazette*, and the *Georgia Gazette*. Of the four, the *Massachusetts Gazette* was the most important. It was the first paper established in the colonies; begun in 1704 under the imprint *The Boston News-Letter*, it was continuously published with varying titles and editors until March, 1776. In 1765 it was called the *Massachusetts Gazette, and Boston News-Letter*, published by Richard and Samuel Draper, and continued under this name, except for a short period in 1768 and 1769.[15] Publication was suspended from April 20 to May 19, 1775, and from September 7 to October 13, 1775. John Howe took over the paper about October, 1775, and in March he fled with the British troops from Boston.

---

[14] Another poem, author unknown, satirized the Congress: *The Association &c. of the Delegates . . . Versified and Adapted to Music*, Philadelphia, 1774. A burlesque oration, said to have been delivered by Thomas Bolton, was published in Boston in 1775: *An Oration delivered March fifteenth 1775, at the Request of a Number of Inhabitants of the Town of Boston.*

[15] From May 23, 1768, to October 2, 1769, the *Massachusetts Gazette* was printed on Mondays as one sheet of the *Boston Post-Boy*, and on Thursdays as part of the *Boston News-Letter*. This gave in effect a semiweekly official paper. The plan has been interpreted as a propaganda device of the Governor and Council.—Arthur M. Schlesinger,

The paper, by policy, was impartial. It carried excellent news accounts in 1765 and printed many articles on the Stamp Act. It did not carry an account of the resignation of Andrew Oliver (the Massachusetts stamp distributor) on August 14, 1765, and Draper was charged by the *Boston Gazette* with wilfully omitting it; he answered that, being impartial, he was not favored with first-hand news from the radical party. He then printed an account of the affair taken from another paper. The only piece in the *Massachusetts Gazette* in 1765 which upheld the government side of the question was the reprint of a pamphlet, *Objections to the Taxation of Our American Colonies . . . Briefly Considered*. This was one of the few items, incidentally, which defended the Stamp Act.[16]

The paper became more identified with those opposed to the Whigs during the controversy over the Townshend Acts and the nonimportation agreements of 1768. It was one of the few papers which did not print John Dickinson's "Letters from a Pennsylvania Farmer," and it, with Mein's *Boston Chronicle*, was the only place where those who refused to sign the nonimportation agreement could state their case.

In common with the great majority of colonial newspapers, the *Massachusetts Gazette* printed practically no controversial material from 1770 to 1773, but in the spring of 1773 it defended Governor Hutchinson and attempted to nullify the effect of his letters by showing that there was little harm in them. It defended the tea consignees just as it had defended the importers in 1769, and by 1774 it had become definitely a Tory paper. Jonathan Sewall and Daniel Leonard wrote essays for it, and Samuel Waterhouse, Joseph Greenleaf, and John Vardell published their satires in its pages. It was called the "Court Gazette" by the Whigs, and until the spring of 1775 it continued as an effective organ of Tory propaganda. Thereafter its publication was interrupted, and it finally ceased in March, 1776.

The *New York Mercury*, its title changed on January 25, 1768, to the *New York Gazette and Weekly Mercury*, was published continuously by Hugh Gaine until 1783. As early as 1754, William

---

"Propaganda and the Boston Newspaper Press, 1767-1770," Col. Soc. Mass., *Publications*, XXXII, p. 404.

[16] *Mass. Gazette, and Boston News-Letter*, June 13, Aug. 22, 1765.

Livingston had said of Gaine, "He is a fickle fellow, and easily intimidated by our opponents";[17] and that remark is typical of the contemporary charges against him. It was commonly held that Gaine was an unprincipled fellow, who either through fear or a desire for profits, or both, set his type according to the prevailing sympathies. Gaine certainly changed about enough to give some point to these charges, but he was after all a newspaper man and a good one. He was industrious and alert and wanted to publish a real newspaper. William Livingston had printed the "Watch Tower" in Gaine's *Mercury,* but in 1768 Livingston's opponents published their pieces in the *Mercury.* It published the "Whip for the American Whig" and similar pieces by T. B. Chandler and others. In 1770 it was the vehicle of those who opposed the non-importation agreement, but in the crisis of 1774 it was used by the Whigs. Not until after the Declaration of Independence did Gaine definitely side with the Tories.

The *South Carolina and American General Gazette* published in Charleston by Robert Wells, was an impartial, colorless paper until the British took Charleston in 1780 and made the *Royal Gazette* of it. Robert Wells left for England shortly after the news of the battle of Lexington and Concord reached Charleston, and the paper was continued by his son John Wells. Local Tory contributions were lacking, and Wells did not reprint Tory pieces from other papers. Nor did he print any except occasional Whig pieces. The *Gazette* did not carry the "Farmer's Letters," but it did run some of the Boston letters in the spring of 1768. There was practically nothing on the disturbance from 1768 to 1770. In 1774 it printed the addresses to Hutchinson, but from April, 1774, to June, 1775, there was not a single political essay, local or clipped, in the paper, and then the first one was from the Whig side. John Wells stated in the *Gazette* for August 25, 1775, that no anonymous publication, referring to public events or characters, could ever find a place in his *Gazette,* and it was not until August, 1776, that one appeared. Both Gage's and the patriot account of Lexington appeared in the *Gazette.* It has been listed here with the Tory papers only because it was open to the Tories in the early days, and because the paper did not actively serve the Whigs. Since the burden was upon the Whigs to

[17] Sedgwick, *Life of Livingston,* p. 105.

overcome inertia, a colorless paper such as the *General Gazette* in effect aided the Tories.

The fourth and last of the papers open to the Tories throughout the ten years preceding the Revolution was the *Georgia Gazette,* published in Savannah by James Johnston. It was the only paper in Georgia and, like Wells' paper, was used by both Whigs and Tories. Of all the papers in the colonies it more nearly approached the idea of complete impartiality, but its effect, on the whole, was to advance the Tory case. The *Georgia Gazette* was one of the very few papers which published any statements in favor of the Stamp Act,[18] and in 1774 the columns of the paper were filled with town protests against the meeting in Savannah in August and with Tory essays supporting the coercive measures of the British government. Johnston closed up his paper in the spring of 1776, after the flight of Governor Wright, but when the British retook Savannah, he returned and printed for a time a Tory paper, the *Royal Georgia Gazette.*

There was, in addition to the four English papers open to the Tories, a German paper which appealed to the pacifist sects. Christoph Saur's *Germantauner Zeitung,* 1762-1777, gave expression to the ideas of passive nonresistance upheld by those who supported the government, and the paper circulated extensively among the Mennonites, Dunkards, and other pietistic sects. After 1777 Saur moved his press to Philadelphia and published the *Pennsylvanische Staats Courier,* which continued the same policy.[19]

Prior to 1773 there was one short-lived paper that more vigorously upheld the government side than all the papers put together. Mein and Fleeming's *Boston Chronicle,* published in Boston from 1767 to 1770, was a much finer propaganda organ than even the official *Massachusetts Gazette.* Mein led the attack on the nonimportation agreements and so successfully that he was personally threatened. A concerted drive against the *Chronicle* ended satisfactorily for the Whigs on June 25, 1770, when Mein (who for some time had either been in hiding or out of the city) stopped publication.

The Tory propagandists seriously began their newspaper campaign against the Whigs in 1773. No less than eight Tory news-

[18] June 30, 1765, an article which stated that for five years the revenue from the Stamp Act would be used chiefly for internal improvements in the colonies.
[19] Faust, *German Element,* I, 286.

papers were established between 1773 and 1775, and increasingly Tory arguments began to appear even in Whig newspapers.

The first and most important of the new papers established in 1774 was James Rivington's *New York Gazetteer*. He began publication on April 22, 1773, and continued printing it, under varying titles, with only one interruption until 1783. He maintained what he called an uninfluenced press, but his paper early became identified with the Tories. The *Gazetteer* within six months of its founding printed articles in defense of the Tea Act, and thereafter practically nothing but Tory items appeared in it. Rivington was a newspaper man, however, and he published not only Tory protests against the town resolutions of the Whigs, but he usually published the resolutions themselves. The Whigs disliked it, nevertheless, more than any of the Tory papers and on November 20, 1775, raided the shop and destroyed the type. Rivington had tried to make peace with the Whigs, but after this he left for England, and the *Gazetteer* was not reissued until October 4, 1777. It was certainly the most influential of the Tory papers. The Whigs charged that Gage bought four hundred copies weekly for distribution to the troops,[20] and Rivington claimed in October, 1774, that he had a circulation of thirty-six hundred copies and that his paper reached Tories in every colony.

The *Massachusetts Gazette, and Boston Post-Boy and Advertiser* was the first paper financially aided by the Tories. It had previously been published by Green and Russel, but in April, 1773, Nathaniel Mills and John Hicks, with funds partially supplied by the local Tories, bought Fleeming's old office and the rights to the *Post-Boy*.[21] It lasted almost exactly two years, the last known issue being that of April 17, 1775. In addition to publishing a Tory paper, Mills and Hicks printed editions of nearly all the local Tory pamphlets and thus for two years at least were important in the dissemination of Tory propaganda.

The third Tory paper founded in 1773, *The Norwich Packet*, was another product of the Robertsons, Alexander and James. Two years previously they had begun printing the *Albany Gazette*, which was continued until 1775. *The Norwich Packet, and the Connecticut, Massachusetts, New Hampshire, and Rhode Island Weekly Adver-*

[20] N. Y. *Journal, Supplement*, Mar. 30, 1775.
[21] Evans, *Amer. Biblio.*, No. 12,858.

tiser, first appeared on September 30, 1773. John Trumbull, a distant cousin of the two more famous John Trumbulls, was associated with the Robertsons, and the partnership was continued until June, 1776. The Robertsons then sold their interest to Trumbull, who continued the paper throughout the Revolution. When the Robertsons dominated the editorial policy, the paper was strongly Tory, but Trumbull turned it into a Whig paper.

Two Tory papers were established in Pennsylvania in 1775, but both had short lives. James Humphreys began printing the *Pennsylvania Ledger* on January 28, 1775, and continued it without interruption until November 30, 1776. He printed Charles Inglis' *The True Interest of America Impartially Stated*. The other paper, Enoch Story and Daniel Humphrey's *Pennsylvania Mercury* began on April 17, 1775, but the building burned just after the issue of December 27, 1775, and that ended the career of the *Mercury*.

A Tory paper was set up in New Hampshire just before the Declaration of Independence. Robert Fowle, a nephew of Daniel Fowle, began publication at Exeter of the *New Hampshire Gazette* in late 1775. It was a very unsatisfactory paper. The title and the day of publication changed frequently, and the paper was published irregularly for only two years. In the summer of 1777 Robert Fowle fled to the British army for protection.[22]

In addition to the papers definitely identified with the government side, there were some Whig papers that even in the crisis of 1774-75 would print Tory items. Southern governors exercised considerable influence over the press and undoubtedly forced the publication of this material. The Virginia gazettes all published Tory pieces even after 1774, and Green's *Maryland Gazette* carried some in 1775.[23] William Smith published his letters against *Common Sense* in the *Pennsylvania Gazette*, and Tory items are met with in other papers as well.

The Tories did not vary their appeal in the newspapers. They limited it, in fact, almost exclusively to controversial essays and satir-

[22] The twelfth paper was the *Virginia Gazette*, published by Governor Dunmore from his headquarters at Gosport, near Norfolk. He had seized the press of John Holt (who had succeeded William Duncan) in September, 1775. No copies are known to exist.— H. J. Eckenrode, *The Revolution in Virginia*, p. 64; Evans, *Amer. Biblio.*, No. 14,607.

[23] E.g., *Md. Gazette*, Jan. 19, Feb. 16, 1775; *Va. Gazette* (Purdie), Jan. 20, 1774; *Va. Gazette* (Dixon and Hunter), Feb. 18, 1775; and *Va. Gazette* (Pinkney), Feb. 3, 1776.

ical poems. The colored or exaggerated news account did not appear to any great extent in Tory papers until after the war was under way.[24] The Whig papers printed, with considerable effect, a great many extracts from private letters, either from colonists or from American friends in England, but Tory papers were supplied with little of this material.[25] The Whig editors frequently reprinted the better pamphlets and made a practice of clipping striking essays from other papers, so that five or six papers sometimes carried the same series of articles. The *Massachusetts Gazette, and Boston News-Letter* did reprint one pamphlet in 1765 and obtained more of its material from other papers than any of the other Tory papers, but the practice was not general; it is uncommon to find the same essay in more than two papers.

The most important type of propaganda appeal in the Tory as in the Whig papers was the political essay. Such articles appeared sparingly prior to 1773. For the most part, the early ones did not attempt a defense of British legislation, and no doubt many of them were written by socially conservative Whigs who objected to the violence of some of their fellow Whigs. Many were from merchants and their friends who opposed the nonimportation agreements of 1768. The constant warning of the Tories, "while we are watchful against external attacks on our freedom, let us be on our guard, lest we become enslaved by dangerous tyrants within," is recurrent in these early essays. But they were neither numerous nor outspokenly Tory prior to 1773.

The Tea Act was the first British act to be defended openly to any considerable extent, and the essays of this period assumed the positive tone which was maintained throughout the remainder of the controversy. In 1774 and in the early part of 1775, the Tory papers were filled with essays, but with the flight of many leading Tories in the summer of 1775 and the closing down of several of the best Tory papers, the number declined rapidly. When the debate over independence occurred, only five of the old Tory papers were still being published, and of these only Humphreys' *Pennsylvania Ledger* was really effective.

The broadside, used so well by the Whigs, was neglected by the

[24] E.g., *N. Y. Gazetteer,* Jan. 20, 1774.
[25] There were some, of course; see *ibid.,* Feb. 23, 1775; and *Mass. Gazette, and Boston Weekly News-Letter,* Nov. 3, 1768.

abler Tory writers, although it was the answer to their problem of anonymous publication—not even the printer could be identified. Several broadsides appeared in New York during the broadside war in 1770 that might be considered Tory products, in that they presented what later were typical Tory arguments. So many good Whigs were involved on both sides of the controversy raging around the nonimportation agreements that Whig and Tory were almost indistinguishable. The first definitely Tory use of the broadside came in 1773, when it was used to present pro-British ideas in the conventional essay form. Articles defending the Tea Act were printed on a single sheet and distributed in New York and Philadelphia, and to a less extent in Boston.[26] A good many were printed in Savannah.[27] Occasionally the appeal varied. *The Address of Liberty, to the Buckskins of Pennsylvania, on hearing of the intended Provincial Congress*,[28] however, is a type rarely met with in Tory broadsides. One or two Tory accounts of Lexington and Concord were printed on broadsides and distributed in New England,[29] but the Tory use of the broadside on the whole was neither significant nor effective.

The other issues of the colonial press, the magazine and the almanac, were not used by the Tories at all to further their ideas. There was not a single Tory magazine, and, although the Tory printers each published an almanac, it does not appear that they inserted any Tory propaganda. Rivington's almanac for 1775 (printed in 1774, of course) actually reprinted John Hancock's March Fifth Oration, which does not speak very well for Rivington as a Tory propagandist. He was more concerned about the sale of his almanac.

[26] E.g., N. Y. Hist. Soc., Broadsides, Oct. 28, 1773, July 3, 1773.

[27] These are bound with the *Ga. Gazette*, and may have been extra, unnumbered sheets of the *Gazette*, although most of them are unquestionably broadsides issued independently of the paper.

[28] Library Company of Philadelphia, Broadsides.

[29] Mass. Hist. Soc., Broadsides, Apr. 21, 1775; and 4 Force, *Amer. Arch.*, II, 538.

XVII

LOYALIST PROPAGANDA, 1776-1783

THE WAR and the Declaration of Independence sharply divided
Whig and loyalist. The Whigs, now in power, could use legal pressures to maintain their position against any attack from within. The
loyalists, dependent on the British army, could only hope to demoralize the enemy by suggestion. The great body of the indifferent
and the doubtful within America could be reached by them with
difficulty. Only by suggestion could their loyalty to America be
undermined. Pro-British propaganda during the war, however, was
narrowly circumscribed; its sources were limited in time and place
to those areas under control of the British army. New York City
throughout the war, Newport from December, 1776, to October,
1779, Philadelphia from October to June, 1777-1778, and the seacoast of South Carolina and Georgia after 1779-1780, were thus the
narrow limits within which British propaganda could originate during the war. The task of the propagandists under such conditions
was twofold: to maintain the morale of the loyal within the area
controlled by the British and to demoralize the enemy.

Only those propagandists who had stayed in America under the
protection of the British army were left to do the task. Charles Inglis, Joseph Stansbury, and Jonathan Odell of the old writers were
the most important ones still active, the others were gone.

Charles Inglis returned to his old post at Trinity Church with
the arrival of the British troops in New York in the summer of
1776. During the war he contributed even more to inspire his fellow
loyalists and to discourage the patriots than he had before the Declaration of Independence. *The Christian Soldier's Duty briefly Delineated,* a sermon preached in 1777, was printed in pamphlet form,
as was another sermon, *The Duty of Honouring the King.* His series
of letters signed "Papinian" was printed in both Rivington's and
Gaine's papers and later in a pamphlet, and in 1782 his last writing
for the cause, a newspaper series signed "A New York Freeholder,"

was published. Unquestionably he did other writing for the papers, but nothing else has been definitely identified as his.

Jonathan Odell also stayed in New York, where he had fled in 1776, and although his identified satires published during the war number but four, there can be no doubt but that many short pieces in the local papers were by him. Joseph Stansbury, the other able poet of the loyalist side, remained in Philadelphia after the Declaration and greeted the British army when it arrived in October, 1777. He wrote for the British papers during the occupation, and when the city was evacuated he went to New York, where he published his humorous songs and satires. Joseph Galloway remained in Philadelphia until 1778 but did no public writing. He co-operated with Isaac Ogden and some leading loyalists and loyalist sympathizers in forming a loyalist association or club, and after he reached England he did some pamphlet writing. The old loyalist writers had earlier transferred their activities to London and there formed an association which agitated for the continuance of the war and the protection of the loyalists in America. Others took their places in New York, Philadelphia, Savannah, and Charleston, filling the papers with their satires and comments, but not a single individual made so great a contribution as had Seabury, Cooper, Chandler, or Boucher.

The British propagandists had few contacts with those outside the areas controlled by the British army. Considerable effort was expended by army officials in forming volunteer military associations of pro-British sympathizers, and General Clinton in the late winter of 1780 created a board to direct the energies of those who wished to aid in suppressing the rebellion. The Anglican Church was maintained in those cities held by the British, and its ministers aided in confirming obedience and loyalty. Other organizations which could be used to affect opinion, or through which suggestions could be disseminated, were few. In Philadelphia there was formed in the autumn of 1777 a Loyal Association Club, and it was continued in the early part of 1778 under the name the Refugee Club. Isaac Ogden, son of David Ogden of New Jersey, wrote Joseph Galloway, who had left for England: "We have established a Refugee Club, composed of the first Characters from the different Provinces. Govr Franklin thinks it will be attended with good consequences, I fancy it will be respectable. You will perceive by the Address to the Commissioners & by some late Publications in the Papers, that the friends to government dare begin to speake &c."[1]

The war propaganda of the loyalists was carried on by few individuals, but it was cleverly conceived and well executed. Almost all of the suggestions both inspirited the loyalists and demoralized the Whigs. As the one was bolstered, so was the other depressed, for in spite of the war, loyalist propaganda circulated to a surprising degree in patriot areas.

SUGGESTION

The legal justification was unchanged—the colonists were engaged in rebellion and the laws of God and man forbade it. The long series of acts committed by the New England leaders, pro-British propagandists asserted, could be viewed in no other light than as "deep designed, premeditated rebellion," and loyal and religious people in America were urged to remember "that obedience to legal authority is the positive command of God, and the constant doctrine of his word."[2] Charles Inglis' sermon, *The Duty of Honouring the King,* preached on the fast day commemorating the martyrdom of Charles I, rehearsed the old controversy on the nature of government and the necessity for it, and then turned to the war, which originated, he said, "from those who dishonoured the King, traduced his Government, trampled on his Authority, and imputed to him Designs which had not the least foundation in Truth." In *The Christian Soldier's Duty,* Inglis appealed to the soldiers' love of George III to urge them on: "Your generous efforts are required to assert the just rights of your amiable, insulted Sovereign—a Sovereign whose numerous Virtues add Lustre to his Throne." In a footnote in the pamphlet edition of this sermon he added, "There is scarcely a Circumstance attending the present unnatural Rebellion which can excite more Indignation in a generous Mind, than the insolent Abuse and scurrilous Invectives that are flung out, by the Abettors of it, against our gracious Sovereign."[3] That is typical of the manner in which the legal argument was changed into a sentimental

---

[1] *Pa. Evening Post,* Oct. 16, 1777; Balch Papers, Oct. 15, 1778.

[2] *N. Y. Loyal Gazette,* Nov. 1, 1777; *Royal Gazette,* Oct. 21, 1778.

[3] *The Christian Soldier's Duty,* p. 18. A refugee, said another, was one who, "from a delicate sense of honour, and a tender regard to the dictates of conscience, have refused to abjure his faith to the King . . . or to take up arms with a view to overset the laws and constitution of his country."—*Royal Gazette,* June 19, 1779.

appeal to the loyalty of the subjects. Many of Jonathan Odell's poems emphasized this feature of British propaganda:

> "Tho' Knaves do combine,
>   With Belzebub join,
>   To aim our Downfall and undo us;
>   By George's fam'd shield,
>   We never will yield,
>   To the pimps or the Armies of Louis.
>
> True Souls drink and sing,
> Remember the King,
>   With Loyalty, good Will and fervour;
> So while we can stand,
> The Flaggon command,
>   To George and his Empire for ever."[4]

Another, perhaps by Stansbury, was written for the King's birthday:

> "While rebel sons with ruffian hand,
>   And trait'rous force oppose their king,
>   Come join with me, ye loyal band,
>   In chorus loud with rapture sing.
>   Hail, hail, all hail,
>   Great George's natal day,
>   Loyal hearts the tribute pay.
>
> .   .   .   .   .   .
>
> "Though treason raise her impious arm,
>   And envy roll her haggard eyes,
>   Revenging heaven shall rage disarm,
>   And waft this chorus to the skies.
>   Hail, hail, all hail,

---

[4] N. Y. Hist. Soc., Broadsides, Apr. 23, 1779. A broadside giving four poems or songs for St. George's Day was published in 1777. Odell was given as the author. A song to the tune of "Smile Brittania" was more militant:

> "But lo! What Furies rise,
> O'er this once happy Shore!
> Thy Sons, o Britain, prize,
> Thy wonted Love no more.
> Rebellion proudly Stalks, and flings
> Defiance at the best of Kings!
>
> "Britons strike home!
> Let Vengeance, Vengeance arm your Hands!
> Haste, haste to pursue, Haste haste to pursue,
> And quell the frantic Bands!
> Now, Seize and destroy! Seize, Seize and destroy!
> Destroy, destroy, the frantic bands."

Great George's natal day,
Loyal hearts the tribute pay."[5]

The familiar appeal to the self-interest of the people emphasized during the war the inevitable consequences of living under the control of the abandoned republicans in America, who were leagued with the equally abandoned Catholic absolutists of France. "In the revolted Colonies," wrote a New York loyalist, "life, liberty, and property is undeniably at command of every despot in power in or out of Congress."[6] "Where is that Peace, that Ease, that Affluence, Security and Freedom which formerly resided in, and distinguished America? They are fled. Oppression, Violence and Usurpation prevail in their Stead." Thus lamented Charles Inglis.[7] The colonists were commonly called the slaves of Congress,[8] and were warned that submission to it would entail far greater burdens on them than ever subjection to Great Britain could. In the matter of taxes alone the people of America would be far more burdened. Of the present debts, warned a writer in the *Pennsylvania Evening Post*, Pennsylvania's alone was a quarter of a million pounds, the payment of which would require a tax of twenty-one shillings on the pound on real and personal estates outside of Philadelphia (held by the British). The tax would still be one of fourteen shillings if Philadelphia were included. The whole value of the national income was twenty-three million pounds less than the debts. Why, asked this writer, allow what amounts to complete confiscation of private property, when England will welcome back the revolted colonies and pay the debts?[9] Congress was deceiving the people as to the real state of the debts, and its promises of redeeming the currency, which Congress itself was inflating, were meaningless pledges, made without the "remotest idea of attempting ever to fulfill the promise."[10] "Beggary and ruin Stare you in the face," concluded the propagandists. Only an immediate reconciliation with Great Britain could save America.[11]

---

[5] *Pa. Evening Post*, Dec. 11, 1777.
[6] *Royal Gazette*, Aug. 5, 1780.   [7] *Duty of Honouring the King*, p. 26.
[8] There are illustrations in plenty, the charge was so common.
[9] *Pa. Evening Post*, Mar. 20, 1778, taken from *Pa. Ledger*. The figures on the debt varied so greatly that it almost seems as if the writers made them up. Five days later another writer stated that the total debt was fifty-six million, five million more than the whole value of the property in the country.—*Pa. Evening Post*, Mar. 25, 1778, taken from the *Pa. Ledger*. A year later another set the debt at three hundred million.—*Royal Gazette*, June 16, 1779.
[10] *Ibid.*, Feb. 27, 1779. Congress said the debt was a hundred and twenty-three million.
[11] *Ibid.*, June 12, 1779. See also *S. C. and Amer. Gen. Gazette*, Feb. 17, 1781.

Life was as insecure as property under the rule of Congress and its troops. By the defeat of the rebels at Camden, two provinces were saved from the horrible scenes which would have followed a rebel victory:

"Bloody, dark, and deep plots, and machinations were *in embryo* by obdurate rebels, in all quarters of the town and country, ready to spring forth into action, whenever Gates should give the decisive blow. Scenes of tyranny, robbery, persecution, and distress, even unto death, more intolerable and abominable, if possible, than ever, would have instantly followed. Cruel and relentless tyrants of the Congress and mankind, were in greedy expectation, to satiate their unbounded malice and resentment, and even imbue their wicked hands afresh in the blood of the loyalists, and again subject us to the accursed domination of the *miscreant* Congress; a system so abhorredly infamous, as not to be equalled in any age or nation under heaven."[12]

Congress had bartered away or endangered in the French alliance every right the colonists possessed, asserted British propagandists.

It was charged that France was actually given rights to the territory of America:

"The solemn ceremony of delivering the turf and twig, performed by Mr. Deane . . . to Mr. Gerard . . . the people in general believe, was a transfer of some right, either absolute or conditional, to the territory of America, in pursuance of some of the six articles of their treaty, which Congress have perfidiously concealed from their constituents. This belief seems founded on very good reasons, because this ceremony was the ancient and almost universal mode of conveying real estate in England . . . which yet prevails in France, and has never been made use of on any other occasion."[13]

[12] *Royal Gazette,* Jan. 3, 1781. "We have our wives, children, parents, friends, property, liberty, lives, and religion, to fight for.—Rouse then, my friends, from your languid inactivity, equip yourselves for the fight, prepare with alacrity for your defence. . . ." *Ibid.,* Nov. 8, 1777.

[13] *Ibid.,* Aug. 22, 1778. "The ceremony observed at the landing of the French ambassador and Mr. Silas Deane, has created a good deal of uneasiness in the minds of the spectators. . . . If this be considered as the cession of the whole or part of America, in consequence of the late treaty, the Congress have acted wisely in keeping back from the people's view the secret articles which related to it; for we believe that however fond their constituents may *now* be of their *great* and *good ally* . . . they are hardly yet so

Congress, by not denying the truth of this assertion, and by maintaining profound secrecy as to six of the articles in the treaty made suspicion positive truth, continued the "American Freeman." The people of the back country were told that they and their land had been sold to France, and it was said that many of them in consequence joined the British army.[14] Even if no actual grants were made, said others, France had joined the conflict simply to aggrandize herself, and in the event of a rebel victory, she would take what she wanted of American soil as her share of the spoils. "We believe," ran a loyalist version of the creed of French rulers, "that conquerors ought to provide for the future destroying every thing that may hurt them; and that we ought to have no law but the sword, the appetite of governing, and the glory to be had by aggrandizing ourselves at the cost of our neighbors."[15] Surely, the propagandists said, Americans had reason to fear the restless and enterprising spirit of France. In the code of France and her rulers "justice is a phantasm, reason a chimera, marriage a trifle, the faith of treaties an illusion, peace but a bait."[16] Said a short poem,

> "Let Washington now from his mountains descend
> Who knows but in George he may still find a friend
> A Briton although he loves bottle and wench,
> Is an honester fellow than parle vous French."[17]

Whatever else might happen to the colonists under French domination, asserted the loyalists, one thing was certain: popery was to be established in America. "We not only run a manifest risque of becoming slaves ourselves, under the treacherous title of independency" wrote a New Yorker, "but we are doing everything in our power to overturn the protestant religion and extinguish every spark both of civil and religious freedom in the world!"[18] Charles Inglis in both of his printed sermons to the troops, stressed the danger:

infatuated as to choose Louis for their master."—*Ibid.*, July 29, 1778. See also *ibid.*, Oct. 24, 1778.

[14] John Henderson was told that sixty thousand colonials had joined the King's army —Harrell, *Loyalism in Virginia*, pp. 50 f.

[15] *Royal Gazette*, June 24, 1778. See also *ibid.*, Jan. 2, 1779.

[16] *Ibid.*, June 24, 1778. "Is it possible that we can *now* wish for a final separation from Britain . . . for the sake of upholding a little longer, at the expense of our lives and fortunes, the arbitrary power of that Congress, who without even asking our consent have *disposed of us*, have mortgaged us like vassals and slaves . . . by entering into a treaty with that ambitious and treacherous power, whose religious and political maxims have so often disturbed the peace and invaded the rights of mankind?"—*Pa. Ledger*, May 13, 1778.

[17] *Royal Gazette*, Oct. 24, 1778.   [18] *Ibid.*, June 13, 1778.

"Unsatisfied with this accumulated Evils, the Leaders of Rebellion would plunge this devoted Country still deeper in Ruin. They have leagued with the Popish, inveterate Enemies of our Nation, of our Religion and Liberties—they have virtually, so far as in them lay, delivered this Country into the Hands of a despotic Power—a Power which has extinguished Liberty, and extirpated the Protestant Religion from all its Dominions; and would, doubtless, gladly avail itself of the Opportunity, now offered, to exterminate Both in this Country also."[19]

Holding up particularly the danger of popery, the loyalists, agreed Sam Adams and James Warren, were practising every art that "Wickedness and weakness can devise" to prejudice the people against France.[20] Just as the Whig propagandists had listed before the war the taxes that might be imposed should England gain her point, so a loyalist propagandist listed the orders that France might give when she had gained control of America. As if copying from an American newspaper of 1789 he made an effective summary of the dangers from the French alliance: item one, Count Tyran established the inquisition in Boston; item two, the Old South meeting house has been converted into a cathedral; item three, "Samuel Adams read his recantation of heresy, after which he was presented at mass"; item four, Louis çonferred exclusive fishing rights in American waters upon a company of Havre de Grace merchants; item five, the making of rum was prohibited, as it injured the sale of French brandy; item six, the act abolishing the English language and prohibiting trial by jury in all courts will go into effect on November 20; item seven, a cargo of rosaries, mass books, and indulgences has just arrived in Philadelphia; item eight, George Washington this day executed as possessing a dangerous influence in the country; item nine, the King has been pleased to parcel out the land to noblemen of distinction, who will let it out to the peasantry on leases at will; item ten, large revenues are expected from the salt gabelle of thirty livres per bushel; item eleven, Obadiah Standfast, the Quaker who refused to recant, was burned this day; item

---

[19] *Duty of Honouring the King*, p. 26. Congress, he told them again, "would rend you from the Protection of your Parent State, and *eventually* place you—astonishing Infatuation and Madness!—place you under the Iron Rule of our inveterate and popish Enemies—the inveterate Enemies of our Religion, our Country, and our Liberties."—*Christian Soldier's Duty*, p. 20.   [20] *Warren-Adams Letters*, II, 9, 15.

twelve, the new capitation tax caused some disturbance in Williams
burg, but a company of troops promptly suppressed it, killing fifty
on the spot; item thirteen, all trade hereafter shall be in French
bottoms, manned by French sailors.[21] France, another put it suc
cinctly, would swallow the colonists whole:

> "Say, *Yankees*, don't you feel compunction,
> At your unnat'ral, rash conjunction?
> Can love for you in him take root,
> Who's Catholic, and absolute?
> I'll tell these croakers how he'll treat 'em;
> *Frenchmen*, like *Storks*, love *frogs*—to eat 'em."[22]

The whole situation was canvassed in an article in Rivington'
Royal Gazette for October 7, 1778, in which the writer contrasted
the condition of the colonists in 1773 and 1778, clearly implying
the advantages of a return to the safety and prosperity of the
empire:

GOVERNMENT: 1773—the government of the colonies was just
like the most excellent English government; 1778—now under dem
ocratic and popular governments, "which all experience has shown
. . . are the worst, and pregnant with innumerable mischiefs."

PROTECTION: 1773—secure under the most powerful nation in
the world; 1778—"groaning under a debt . . . enormous beyond
expression . . . her trade and commerce destroyed, her labourers
mechanics and artists, for the most part lost by sickness or in battle
her lands not one half of them cultivated, her manufactures ruined
and her territories laid waste by the ravages of the war."

LAWS: 1773—governed by the laws of England which guaran
teed the security of life and property; 1778—the laws which now
govern the people are without model or parallel, and the arbitrary
edicts "surpass in cruelty those of the rankest despotism."

RELIGION: 1773—toleration was complete, and the rights of con
science were preserved inviolate; 1778—New England Presbyterian
are now in alliance with Romanism!

[21] *Royal Gazette*, Mar. 17, 1779. See also *ibid.*, Oct. 10, 1778, Oct. 14, 1778, Jan. 24
1781; and *Mass. Spy*, Nov. 12, 1778, citing *Royal Gazette*.
[22] *Royal Gazette*, Dec. 5, 1778. "Nothing therefore seems clearer, in human affairs
than, that the revolted colonies, unaided by Great Britain, can never shake off the yok
of France, and that dependence on that kingdom must ruin America."—*Ibid.*, Aug. 5, 1780

SECURITY OF PERSON: 1773—Legal government and justice was faithfully administered; 1778—"Legal government is destroyed and force and violence prevail in its stead. All is anarchy and war."

SECURITY OF PROPERTY: 1773—enjoyed by all; 1778—"The Right of property is entirely derainged."

AGRICULTURE AND COMMERCE: 1773—increasing daily, and happier people were not to be found; 1778—"Our foreign Commerce and internal traffic are ruined" and poverty and want face the people on every hand.

TAXES: 1773—equally imposed by our own representatives, men of wealth, who knew the problem; 1778—"Our taxes are now laid by men, a great majority of whom have started up into power like mushrooms from the dunghill, without principle, without property, the most profligate and abandoned, and by no means the representatives of the people."

ADVANTAGES AND ILLUSIONS OF VICTORY

To do away at once with these distressing and dangerous conditions, nothing more was needed than a return to the protection of the British government: "Look forward, Americans! Compare the secure, prosperous, and truly free and independent state which is now most certainly and immediately in your offer, to the hazzards, intermediate distresses, and probable consequences of the projects into which the Congress wish to plunge you."[23] So great were the advantages to the colonists from a restoration of British rule that any methods were admissible to accomplish this end:

"The employing German Protestant Troops . . . is a Measure at this Critical Juncture full of true Wisdom and good policy: The deluded Colonists running wildly after the Shadow of Liberty have lost the Substance. The present Armament will restore the Americans to Freedom—to that Freedom which is enjoyed under a BRITISH Constitution. It will relieve them from the most degrading Species of Tyranny, Republican Tyranny. Every dispassionate and well disposed American, must despise the Idea of Republicanism."[24]

[23] "Concord" in *ibid.*, Oct. 3, 1778. See also *ibid.*, Jan. 13, 1779.

[24] Library of Congress, Broadsides, New York, p. 109, "Camillus," Oct. 18, 1776. See also *Royal Gazette*, Nov. 7, 1778. When Charleston was taken, the loyalists exclaimed over the contrast between the two governments: "the beams in the wall everywhere proclaim that there has been more tranquility, order and justice, these few months since the restora-

To save the Americans from themselves and from their leaders, to substitute the "happiness and freedom" of life with Great Britain for the misery and slavery under Congressional rule, was their sole aim, so the loyalists said. And never for a moment did they doubt but that they would. "I will not point out to you the dismal consequences which would ensue to themselves, as well as to us," said a typically confident loyalist, "should these blindfolded people obtain the independency they wish for, because I have not an idea of their establishing it. Every one who is acquainted with *our* strength, and *their* weakness, must know they cannot."[25] As late as October 3, 1781, when Cornwallis was making his last stand, a writer in Rivington's *Royal Gazette* surveyed the situation and found it full of hope: one defeat would discourage the French, so ephemeral their character, the Dutch would unquestionably discover shortly that they were being duped, and the British navy was just beginning to fight; the time now demanded added exertions, not despair.[26]

This unbounded confidence displayed itself throughout the war in constant references to the power of the British navy and her armies, to the steady increase in the number of loyalists, and to the military successes. "Britain is prepared," said "A Citizen" in 1778, "to meet her enemies;—her fleets are numerous;—her armies are disciplined, and bravely determined for the conflict. We, the friends to her government, are many, in every Province,—we have tasted the sweets of it, and felt the pangs inflicted by the usurpers."[27] Actual victories cheered them on as proof of what could be done with spirited exertions, and the puny efforts of the rebels were the subject of endless merriment. Schuyler's invasion of Tryon County, New York, where there was no British army, was cleverly satirized in poetry,[28] and Gaine in his *Gazette* reported in October, 1776, that

tion of legal government, than during the whole period it was interrupted. . . ."—*S. C. and Amer. Gen. Gazette*, Jan. 31, 1781. [25] *Royal Gazette*, June 6, 1778.

[26] Cornwallis himself mentioned some cheering news for publication. He reported that he and his army were in good health and that in two recent engagements "we are informed two hundred and forty more of the enemy were killed; our loss hitherto is trifling, a very few having been killed, and about twenty wounded."—*Ibid.*, Oct. 17, 1781.

[27] *Ibid.*, June 6, 1778. "The loyalists increase hourly, scarce a day passes without fugitives to this place, from the barbarities perpetrated by the usurpers in the upper parts of this, as well as from the neighboring provinces."—*Ibid.*, Aug. 26, 1780.

[28] Loyalist Rhapsodies, No. 2; *Royal Gazette*, Aug. 15, 1778. From *Pa. Evening Post*, Dec. 4, 1777:
"The rebels retreat and their bulwarks they shun,
To the woods nimbly skulk with their brave Washington.
HOWE boldly advances, and tempts them to fight;
The rebels know better, their safety's in flight."

though not a hundred regulars had been killed in the campaigns around New York, four or five thousand rebels had. Five years later, Wells in South Carolina was printing scornful remarks about the great General Sumter, who was disgracefully beaten off "by a small party of sequestered negroes."[29]

Propagandists amused themselves and attempted to demoralize the enemy by gibes and jeers at the tottering, bankrupt, rebel government. "The Feu de Joie" by Odell was more earnest in its appeal than most:

> "Your Congress every moment weaker grows,
>   Rags are its treasure, honest men its foes,
>   Its building cracks, tho' buttress'd by the Gaul,
>   It nods, it shakes, it totters to its fall.
>   O save yourselves before it is too late!
>   O save your country from impending fate!
>   Leave those, whom justice must at length destroy.
>   Repent, come over, and partake our joy."[30]

The colonial currency was a never failing source of ridicule. "The account that we have had that the grand American Congress could make no more dollars for want of rags, proves altogether a mistake, for *independent* of the large supply expected from Washington's army as soon as they can be spared, we have reason to believe the country in general never abounded more in that article."[31] Rivington announced the following news item as the most accurate account he had yet obtained of the annihilation of the currency, and this was in May, 1781:

> "The Congress is finally bankrupt! Last Saturday a large body of the inhabitants with paper dollars in their hats by way of cockades, paraded the streets of Philadelphia . . . with a DOG TARRED, and instead of the usual appendage and ornament of feathers, his back was covered with the Congress' paper dollars. This example of disaffection, immediately under the

[29] *Royal S. C. Gazette*, Mar. 31, 1781; *Conn. Courant*, Oct. 21, 1776.

[30] *Royal Gazette*, Nov. 24, 1779. Stansbury's poem in the same year was different in temper:

> "Last Year King Congo, through the land,
>   Displayed his thirteen stripes to fright us;
>   But GEORGE'S power, in CLINTON'S hand,
>   In this New Year shall surely right us.
>   —*Ibid.*, Jan. 2, 1779.

[31] *N. Y. Gazette and Weekly Mercury*, Feb. 23, 1778.

eyes of the rulers of the revolted provinces, in solemn session at the State House assembled, was directly followed by the jailer, who refused accepting the bills in purchase of a glass of rum, and afterwards by the traders of the city, who shut up their shops, declining to sell any more goods but for gold or silver. It was declared also by the popular voice, that if the opposition to Great Britain was not in future carried on by solid money instead of paper bills, all further resistance to the mother country were vain, and must be given up."[32]

Divisions within the patriot ranks were weakening them, th loyalists hopefully pointed out to their fellows. "Mutual animosit and reviling have risen to such a height between the French an rebels since they were defeated," wrote a resident of Savannah afte the failure of the expedition against that town, "that they were a most ready to cut one another's throats." A street ballad capitalize the same incident:

"To Charleston with fear,
The rebels repair;
D'Estaing scampers back to his boats, sir;
Each blaming the other,
Each cursing his brother,
And—may they cut each other's throats, sir."[33]

Adams and Hancock were at odds, the Deanes and the Lees wer fighting each other, and everywhere "distrust, discontent and distres very generally prevail."[34] Rumors were circulated that officers o high rank were implicated with Arnold, and Rivington printed pamphlet of letters purporting to be by Washington, which showe that he had opposed the war from the start and was now thoroughl despondent. These letters, first printed in the *Royal Gazette* o February 14, 1778, and then printed in a pamphlet, were early de tected as spurious and thus did little damage.[35] Isaac Ogden wrot Galloway that he had seen some discouraged letters of Silas Deane': but that the holder would not publish them in America, where a present (1779) they would be of great importance. "They woul

[32] *Royal Gazette*, May 12, 1781. See *ibid.*, Feb. 21, 1778, for an earlier instance of t same method. There Washington is shown to have refused paper money.
[33] *Ibid.*, Nov. 20, 1779; Moore, *Songs and Ballads of the American Revolution*, p. 27
[34] *Royal S. C. Gazette*, July 21, 1781; *Pa. Ledger*, Mar. 7, 1778.
[35] *Letters of General Washington to several of his Friends in the Year 1776* [Rivin ton], 1778.

let the people at large know their melancholy & distressed Situation."[36] And on January 31, 1781, Rivington's paper carried from the pen of a still confident loyalist the last will and testament of Congress, which "being weak in body, low in credit, and poor in estate," did give its soul to the devil and the country to England.[37]

The final theme was the depravity of the enemy, the familiar appeal to hatred and contempt. Important as it was in the propaganda of the Whigs, it formed a still larger proportion of loyalist propaganda during the war.

The loyalist text might well have been a statement in Gaine's *New York Gazette* on the condition of some deplorably ragged and distressed deserters: "Pity is due to these poor deluded People, but Indignation to the cruel and designing Leaders."[38] When the peace proposals of 1778 were offered, loyalists insistently warned the people that they were being duped into continuing the war, simply to "pursue a PHANTOM OF INDEPENDENCY; or, in other Words, to support at the Expense of her own Blood and Treasure; *the* POWER *and Consequence of a Set of Men, who oppose Peace merely because such an event would sink them into Obscurity.*"[39]

The ills of the present were due entirely to the leaders of the rebellion, who, "callous to the prayers of the widow, the tears of the orphan, and the earnest supplications of creditors of all denominations," were the first to set the example of depreciating the currency, and the first to work its annihilation.[40] Those who had said to the brambles, come thou and reign over us, had to take the consequences; "Let such lay their hands to their bosoms, and solemnly declare, how happy they have been during their bramble govern-

---

[36] Balch Papers, Feb. 6, 1779. Much joy was caused among the loyalists by the revolt of the Pennsylvania troops.—*Royal Gazette*, Jan. 6, 1781.

[37] *Ibid.*, Jan. 31, 1781.

[38] Feb. 18, 1777. This was a favorite theme of allied propaganda during the World War.

[39] *Royal Gazette*, June 3, 1778. The address by Sir George Collier and William Tryon on July 4, 1779, spoke of the "ungenerous and Wanton Insurrection against the Sovereignty of Great-Britain, into which this Colony, has been deluded by the Artifices of desperate and designing Men for private Purposes."—N. Y. Hist. Soc., Broadsides. The leaders had "no other idea than aggrandizing themselves," Congress throughout had deceived and was still deceiving the people, the unthinking multitudes were cheated out of their property and liberty by the pitiful production of scheming men—these are typical statements. See *Royal Gazette*, Jan. 6, 1779; Apr. 21, 1779; May 9, 1778.

[40] *Royal S. C. Gazette*, May 5, 1781; *Royal Gazette*, Apr. 15, 1780.

ment."[41] The lawlessness, the tyranny, the privation and suffering were all caused by men of low origin and still lower characters: "Is there a man among them of distinguished honour and probity? . . . Were they not all people of doubtful origin, of desperate fortune, and of suspicious character?"[42]

The loyalist attack ranged from satirical fiction to factual statement. In August, 1776, there was printed the drama, *The Battle of Brooklyn, a Farce,* the most indecent of all the loyalist publications. The men and women who led the Whigs were treated as lustful and indecent people who saw in the war simply an opportunity to satisfy their lust for the pleasures of the flesh. In origin black-legs, jockeys, bar tenders, cobblers, in morals no better than the pimps of brothels, and in ability and courage incompetent and cowardly—such were the leaders. In 1778 and again in 1780 the members of Congress were listed with their occupations—fisher, tavern keeper, shopkeeper, artisan, farmer—and at the end of the list printed in 1780 the contributor appended a note: "I am one of those who always had that contempt for the Congress that their former characters and insignificance must inspire every one with that has any knowledge of this country, and the origin and connection of its inhabitants."[43]

Sometimes the method was slightly humorous in outward form, but underneath even such pieces there was a strong undertone of bitterness. In Major André's dream, for example, in which the judges of the nether world sentenced the patriot leaders, Thomas McKean was compared to Jeffries of English fame. Deane was simply a vain, monkeyish man, while Livingston, whose black soul was fit for *"treason, sacrilege, and spoil,* and polluted with every species of murder and iniquity," was condemned to howl in the body of a wolf, its tongue "still red with gore." Jay, "a mixture of the lowest cunning and most unfeeling barbarity," and "indefatigable in the pursuits of ambition and avarice, by all the ways of intrigue, perfidy, and dissimulation," was transformed into a rattlesnake. Washington, crowing and strutting as if meditating a combat, immediately began to brush his wings and ruffle his feathers on the

[41] *S. C. and Amer. Gen. Gazette,* Dec. 27, 1780.

[42] *Royal Gazette,* Oct. 21, 1778.

[43] *N. Y. Gazette and Weekly Mercury,* May 23, 1778; a more general statement, and a detailed statement are in *Royal Gazette,* Mar. 8, 11, 1780. Tyler found this list in the correspondence of a resident of Germany.—*Literary History,* II, 57 f.

approach of a few cropplecrowned Dame Partlets. As a final fling, André saw the whole continental army transformed into hares, and saw Washington, their commander, wearing a collar with the words written on it, "They win the fight, who win the race."[44] In another dream, attacking the French alliance, Louis XVI was turned into a cat, D'Estaing into a village cur, and Gerard into an owl.[45] Washington was accused of having an illegitimate child by Betsy Sidmouth, and of living with the wife of a corporal, whom he pacified by promoting to a sergeant's rank.[46]

Acts of extreme cruelty distinguished the prosecution of war by such men. Plundering, burning, and devastation marked the route of the rebel army, and extreme misery the fate of those who fell into its hands. Gaine's account of the fate of the De Lanceys was good propaganda:

> "On Wednesday Morning, the 26th of November, a Party of Rebel Troops landed at Bloomendale . . . near Brigadier General De Lancey's, robbed and plundered his House of the most valuable Furniture and Money, set the House on Fire before Mrs. De Lancey, her two Daughters, and two other young Ladies could remove out of it, which was effected through the Flames in only their Bed-Dresses; when they were most cruelly insulted, beat, and abused, and what Money they had, taken from them; an Infant Grandchild in a most barbarous Manner thrown on the Ground. . . . The Whole exhibited such

---

[44] *Royal Gazette*, Jan. 23, 1779. It is said that this was read to a group of people at Deane's home in New York.—Moore, *Diary of the Revolution*, II, 120. Hamilton, it was said, was writing a book on the Revolution, and among the illustrations was "a rear view (by far the most intelligent and pleasing) of the titular Lord Stirling, on his return from one of his nightly *feu de joies* at Bergen, in Jersey, and supposed to be mumming his usual boast in a strain something like this:—

> "Peer's blood I have—
> Toddied and brave—
> Who-o-o'd be a sla-a-a-ve?"
> —*Ibid.*, p. 124.

[45] *Royal Gazette*, Jan. 30, 1779.

[46] *Ibid.*, Nov. 15, 1780. He was commonly charged with murdering André.—*Ibid.*, Mar. 14, July 11, 1781. See *Royal S. C. Gazette*, Oct. 31, 1781, for an attack on Governor Rutledge, and *Royal Gazette*, May 6, 1780, for one on Governor Reed of Pennsylvania. The leaders were attacked, as was the army, but the people as a whole infrequently. The following is rarely met with as a type:

> "If Souls are sav'd as Parsons tell,
> By FAITH and WORKS together,
> The Rebels sure must go to H——,
> For d—n 'em they hold neither."
> —*Ibid.*, June 9, 1779.

a Scene of Savage Barbarity as is scarcely to be met with in History or Romance."[47]

The mistreatment of prisoners was not nearly so prominent in loyalist propaganda as in patriot, but more concrete examples were given of the abuse and murder of noncombatants. Some skulking rebels, it was reported in 1776, had "slyly" fired on a little boy and killed him, but on seeing the approach of some British troops, "they gave three Cheers and retired."[48] Loyalists were tied to trees, marks made on their breasts for targets, and the troops allowed to amuse themselves shooting at them; others were threatened with being pulled apart by horses and were actually badly beaten and mauled. Three loyalists were hanged in Monmouth County, New Jersey, their sole crime having been "an *unfortunate attachment* to the old Constitution." This and many other instances of depravity were committed by men "who have decorated their standard with the specious names of *Liberty* and *Justice*."[49]

NEUTRALIZING INCONVENIENT SUGGESTIONS

Certain American suggestions were directly refuted, particularly those intended to inspire confidence. The rebel victories were minimized in part by pointing to the martial power of England in the past; Burgoyne's failure was disappointing, admitted "Marcellus," but, he continued, "I will only hint to the honest part of my countrymen, that the spirit, strength and resources of this nation are immense, and I appeal to past experience for the proof, though they are seldom fully exercised, until called forth by absolute occasion."[50] Some Whig claims they flatly contradicted. Washington's report of a victory was picked to pieces and called the "most extravagant piece of Jesuitical quackery that has been exhibited during the present rebellion."[51] His claim of a victory at Monmouth was treated with hilarious raillery—what sort of a victory was it when the victor retreated four miles on the double-quick? Sullivan's report that he

---

[47] Quoted in *The Journals of Hugh Gaine*, II, 57. See also *Royal Gazette*, May 24, 1780, Sept. 26, 1781; *S. C. and Amer. Gen. Gazette*, Jan. 24, 1781; *Royal S. C. Gazette*, Feb. 20, 1782; and Inglis, *Christian Soldier's Duty*, p. 19.

[48] *N. Y. Gazette and Weekly Mercury*, Oct. 21, 1776. See also *ibid.*, Feb. 23, 1778; *Royal Gazette*, May 20, 1778; and *Royal S. C. Gazette*, Feb. 20, 1782.

[49] *N. Y. Gazette and Weekly Mercury*, Apr. 14, 1777; *Royal Gazette*, Jan. 6, 1781; *Royal S. C. Gazette*, Apr. 11, 1781.

[50] *Royal Gazette*, Apr. 4, 1778; Jan. 5, 1780.

[51] *Ibid.*, Nov. 22, 1777.

had silenced the guns at Newport and driven in the British lines was answered by a witness who said that Sullivan was so far away that the British could hardly reach him with their guns, and he himself could kill only one man.[52] Many a patriot suggestion was printed and followed by some such statement as the one which accompanied the assertion that Burgoyne had violated the articles of capitulation: "By such villainous assertions, which have no foundation in truth, they mask their infernal perfidy, which is of so enormous a magnitude that it absorbs every idea of punic faith."[53]

The most important idea the loyalists tried to offset was the prevalent and well-founded argument that France would come to the aid of the revolting colonies. This the loyalists scouted, even more vigorously as the alliance seemed more certain. In October, 1777, it was said that France could not afford to join the colonies, for a war would ruin her; in January, 1778, another propagandist printed two French letters to show her pacific intentions and the extent to which the leaders were duping the people. In February the public was assured "it is an undoubted fact that the court of France is positively, and has in earnest determined, that they will show no countenance whatever to the rebellion in America—have given the most satisfactory assurances that they will not assist the Americans in any manner, or suffer their vessels to trade at their ports." On March 21, 1778, six weeks after the alliance was made, the *Pennsylvania Ledger* made the following statement: "And yet this long looked for French assistance is only to be seen by the eyes of faith, and those eyes begin to grow very dim! The people begin to be ashamed of their past credulity; and their deceivers, if they had any shame, or any regard for the welfare of the people, would cease the repetition of those falsehoods in which they have been so often detected."[54] Once the alliance was formed, the loyalists did their best, as we have seen, to undermine the confidence of the people in the new ally, and their well-taken gibes at the fruits of the alliance must have been galling to the patriots.

[52] *Ibid.*, July 29, Aug. 1, Sept. 26, 1778.
[53] *Pa. Ledger*, Mar. 11, 1778. "Such are the means taken by this people to impose upon the credulous and unwary; that to give their intelligence the appearance of truth they have either a *feu de joie* with a gill of whiskey in their camp, or some other kind of rejoicings."—*Ibid.*, Mar. 7, 1778.
[54] *Royal Gazette*, Oct. 11, 1777; *Pa. Evening Post*, Jan. 3, 1778; *N. Y. Gazette and Weekly Mercury*, Feb. 23, 1778; and *Pa. Ledger*, Mar. 21, 1778. News of the alliance reached America in April, 1778.

Finally, certain things were done directly to demoralize the enemy, with no thought of inspiring the loyalists except by amusing them. Richard Henry Lee reported to Jefferson in May, 1777, that some evilly disposed persons had industriously propagated among the North Carolina troops the statement *"that the plague rages in our army"*; in consequence of this, he said, "the recruiting business stops, and dissertions are frequent. There never was a more infamous and groundless falsehood. . . ."[55] At almost the same time, Samuel Johnston reported that the British sympathizers had put out the notice that Washington's army was full and southern troops were not needed.[56] In the spring of 1778 two false resolves of Congress were audaciously printed in loyalist papers. These resolves declared that all future enlistments would be for the duration of the war, that those now in the army must stay there until the end of the war, and that any who left because their terms had expired would be punished as deserters. These resolutions were promptly denied by the Continental Congress, who had received notice of them from Washington, with the advice that it "pursue proper steps for counteracting this wicked publication." Governor Livingston was testimony that the forgeries had slowed up enlistments in New Jersey.[57] Papers were distributed among the troops urging them to desert, rumors were circulated in the South that the northern states were about to abandon them, and letters of the leaders were fabricated. Washington, a frequent victim, found some of these letters most embarrassing.[58]

MEDIA OF SUGGESTION

Loyalist propaganda as before was almost entirely a written appeal. There were a few celebrations, most of them on the King's or the Queen's birthday, which were usually observed by the troops. In 1776 some Hessians on Staten Island prepared effigies of Washington, Lee, Putnam, and Witherspoon, arranged in a scene showing Witherspoon reading an address to the generals. The effigies were

---

[55] *Letters of Richard Henry Lee*, I, 292.

[56] Johnston to Thomas Burke, Apr. 19, 1777, Governor Thomas Burke's Letter Book, 1774-1781.

[57] These resolves were printed in at least the *N. Y. Gazette and Weekly Mercury*, and the *Pa. Evening Post*. The statement of the Continental Congress is in *Pa. Packet*, May 6, 1778. Washington's comments are in his *Writings* (Ford, VI), 475 n., 493 f.

[58] McCrady, *History of S. C. in Revolution, 1775-1780*, p. 540; Washington, *Writings* (Ford), VIII, 292, IX, 226.

burnt after a heavy rainstorm, but Washington's, not having been tarred before the rain, refused to burn, to the fright of the superstitious troops.[59] More dignified were the Masonic celebrations in New York on St. John's day, at one of which at least, "loyal and Masonic" toasts were given.[60]

The record of printed sermons is small, and there is no other way of knowing what was propagated from the pulpit or the rostrum. Unquestionably the Anglican ministers in those cities held by the British and the chaplains in the army preached appropriate sermons. If Inglis' two sermons are typical, they all emphasized, as did those of their fellow clergymen across the line, the help of God and the depravity of the enemy.[61]

The songs of Joseph Stansbury were of some importance in spreading loyalist themes. One of his best was a sea song, designed for the British sailors:

"When Faction, in league with the treacherous Gaul,
      Began to look big, and paraded in state,
A meeting was held at Credulity Hall,
      And Echo proclaimed their ally good and great.
            By sea and by land,
            Such wonders are planned—
No less than the bold British lion to chain!
            'Well hove!' says Jack Lanyard,
            'French, Congo, and Spaniard,
Have at you!—remember, we're Lords of the Main.
Lords of the Main, aye, Lords of the Main;
The Tars of Old England are Lords of the Main.'

.   .   .   .

"Then, Britons, strike home—make sure of your blow:
      The chase is in view—never mind a lea shore.
With vengeance o'ertake the confederate foe:
      'T is now we may rival our heroes of yore!
            Brave Anson, and Drake,
            Hawke, Russell, and Blake,

[59] Moore, *Diary of the Revolution*, I, 277 f.

[60] The toasts were all loyal in thought.—Moore, *Diary of the Revolution*, II, 443. A Masonic celebration in Philadelphia, however, did nothing so far as the account goes which could be construed as showing sympathy either to England or to America.—*Ibid.*, p. 113.

[61] Thomas O'Beirne preached a sermon to Howe's troops in September, 1776, which listed the churches damaged in the rebel attempt to burn New York.—*An Excellent Sermon Preached at St. Paul's Church.*

With ardor like yours, we defy France and Spain!
    Combining with treason,
    They're deaf to all reason;
Once more let them feel we are Lords of the Main.
Lords of the Main, aye, Lords of the Main—
The first-born of Neptune are Lords of the Main!"

Another of his cheerful songs, written in 1781, exhibits the outward confidence of the loyalist propagandists even at that late date:

"Friends, push round the bottle, and let us be drinking,
While Washington up in his mountains is slinking:
Good faith, if he's wise he'll not leave them behind him,
For he knows he's safe nowheres where Britons can find him.
When he and Fayette talk of taking this city,
Their vaunting moves only our mirth and our pity.

.   .   .   .

Today a wild rebel has smoked on the table;
You've cut him and sliced him as long as you're able.
He bounded like Congo, and bade you defiance,
And placed on his running his greatest reliance;
But fate overtook him and brought him before ye,
To shew how rebellion will wind up her story."[62]

But the song ended with a stronger plea:

"Then cheer up, my lads! if the prospect grows rougher,
Remember from whence and for whom 't is you suffer:—
From men whom mild laws and too happy condition
Have puffed up with pride and inflamed with sedition;
For George, whose reluctance to punish offenders
Has strengthened the hands of these upstart pretenders."

The written appeal was practically a newspaper appeal. Very few pamphlets were published by loyalist presses during the war—an occasional sermon or a reprint of an English publication was almost the only example of propaganda published in this form.[63] Broadsides infrequently appeared. Used for official proclamations,

---

[62] Both are from the *Loyal Verses of Stansbury and Odell*, pp. 61 f., 79 f. "The Royal Oak," 1781, and "The Tradesman's Song," written for the King's birthday in 1777, are other good examples of Stansbury's songs.

[63] Propaganda originating in England and not reprinted in America is not dealt with. Many of the refugee loyalists wrote pamphlets which were sent to America.

of course, its use for propaganda purposes was limited to the publication of songs.[64]

Fifteen loyalist newspapers were published at one time or another following the Declaration of Independence: the largest number in any one year was eight in 1778, the smallest, five in 1779. In
only four cities—New York, Philadelphia, Charleston, and Savannah
—were there pro-British papers, and in 1779 the only ones published
in America were printed in New York City.[65] Not a single one was
published continuously from the Declaration of Independence to
the end of the war.

The longest-lived and the best loyalist papers were in New York
City. The oldest was Hugh Gaine's *New York Gazette and Weekly
Mercury*, which had been open to the Tories before the war. In
September, 1776, Gaine moved one of his presses to Newark and
published there a Whig paper from September 21 to November 2,
but as a result of British bribes, patriot antagonism, or his personal
inclinations, he returned to New York and resumed publication of
the *Gazette* there on November 9. The last issue of the Newark
paper contained one account of an engagement in which "our" troops
beat the regulars and another in which "our" troops beat the rebels,[66]
but after his return to New York, Gaine necessarily stuck to the
British side. After the war he abandoned his paper but stayed in
New York and tried to make his peace with America.

During Gaine's absence, the British authorities in New York took
over his remaining press and authorized Ambrose Serle to publish
a paper, which lasted from September 21 to October 28. Serle well
knew the power of the press and urged the British government to
establish superintendents of the press in different colonies, because,
he said, among the methods of raising the present commotion, "next
to the indecent harangues of the preachers, none has had a more extensive or stronger influence than the newspapers of the respective
colonies."[67]

[64] "Camillus" on Oct. 18, 1776, published a loyalist broadside urging attention to the
proposals of Lord Howe.—Library of Congress, Broadsides, New York, p. 109.
[65] The *Royal Georgia Gazette* was published in Savannah but was probably printed in
New York.   [66] Payne, *Journalism in the United States*, pp. 127 f.
[67] B. F. Stevens, Facsimiles of Manuscripts in European Archives Relating to America,
1773-1783, Nos. 2044-2046. This was a report to Lord Dartmouth. He added: "Ever
since the press here has been under my direction (from the 30th of September) I have
seen sufficient reason to confirm this opinion and have had the pleasure to hear that the
papers, which have been circulated as extensively as possible, have been attended with the
most promising effects."

Gaine returned after the battle of Long Island, and Serle's paper was stopped. Shortly thereafter, the third paper was founded in New York, *The Royal American Gazette*, published by Alexander Robertson from January 16, 1777, to the end of the war.

The most important loyalist paper was established near the end of the year by James Rivington. On October 4, 1777, he revived the *New York Gazetteer* and shortly thereafter gave it its final name of the *Royal Gazette*.[68] This paper was the official gazette of the city and was the best paper published there. Rivington tried to make his peace with the patriots at the close of the war, but on December 31, 1783, his old enemy, Isaac Sears, raided his place again, and Rivington's printing career was over.[69]

The fifth and last loyalist paper published in New York was William Lewis' *New York Mercury*, the first issue of which appeared on September 3, 1779. With its appearance, the British authorities arranged a daily newspaper service in the city. Gaine's paper was published on Mondays, Rivington's *Gazette* on Wednesdays and Saturdays, Robertson's *Royal American Gazette* on Thursdays, and Lewis' *Mercury* on Fridays.

The only loyalist papers in Pennsylvania, with the exception of the Saurs' *Germantauner Zeitung*, which ceased publication about the middle of March, 1777, were published in Philadelphia during the British occupation of the city. Two—the *Pennsylvanische Staats Courier*, published by Saur after he left Germantown, and the *Zeitungs Blatt*—were German and lasted only a short time.[70] Three were English—the *Evening Post*, the *Ledger*, and the *Royal Pennsylvania Gazette*. The *Pennsylvania Evening Post* was a Whig paper published by Benjamin Towne, who suspended publication for two weeks when the British took Philadelphia but continued thereafter to publish a pro-British paper; after the evacuation of the city, he switched back again to the patriot side. The *Pennsylvania Ledger*, edited by James Humphreys, was a revival of the old *Ledger* discontinued the previous year. It lasted only during the occupation—

---

[68] *N. Y. Gazetteer*, Oct. 4-18, *New York Loyal Gazette*, Oct. 25-Dec. 6, *Royal Gazette*, Dec. 13, 1777-1783.

[69] It has been said that he was one of Washington's spies in New York during the last year of the war, but the evidence is not considered conclusive by some. See Hastings, *Hopkinson*, pp. 312 f.

[70] *Staats Courier*, October (?), 1777-May, 1778, no copies known; *Zeitungs-Blatt*, Feb. 4-June 24 (?), 1778.

October 11 to May 23, 1778, in fact. The *Royal Pennsylvania Gazette* had an even shorter life—March 3 to May 26, 1778.

The remaining loyalist papers are easily disposed of. When the British took Savannah, they published the *Royal Georgia Gazette*, January 21, 1779, subsidized by the British government and edited by John D. Hammerer. It was probably printed in New York until the issue of March 21, 1781. The first loyalist paper in Charleston was the *South Carolina and American General Gazette*, published by Robert and John Wells, although Robert Wells was probably in England. With the capture of Charleston in May, 1780, the paper became pro-British, but in the next year the policy of publishing an official gazette was extended to Charleston, and John Wells issued on March 3 the first copy of the *Royal Gazette*, which lasted until December 10, 1782.[71]

The technique of the propagandists is best seen in their manipulation of news accounts. Accounts were falsified, distorted, or omitted, and the effect of patriot accounts was nullified by interpolated refutation. A comparison of the journals of Hugh Gaine and the corresponding items in the *Gazette and Weekly Mercury* provides excellent examples of his methods. A particularly good instance is the treatment of Tarleton's defeat at Cowpens. On February 13, 1781, Gaine noted in his journal the defeat of Tarleton, but in the *Gazette* he inserted the following notice:

> "*The following is an Extract of a Letter from Staten Island, Dated February 11, 1781:* By a late Letter from Virginia we are informed, that Lord Cornwallis had defeated General Green, and taken 1600 Prisoners. This advice arrived last Evening from Jersey from a Person who saw the Letter, and who may be relied on."[72]

The Battle of Guilford Court House, when Cornwallis did defeat Greene, took place a month after this account—March 15. In other instances he greatly exaggerated the sparse accounts he received, and

[71] Wells had published the *S. C. and Amer. Gen. Gazette* continuously during the war but had printed no pro-British items, of course, and very few patriot ones for that matter. There was another British paper, John Howe's *Newport Gazette*, fifteen issues of which appeared from January 16 to April 24, 1777, during the British occupation. It was unusual for the British not to publish a paper in every city they occupied throughout the period of occupation.

[72] *Journals of Hugh Gaine*, II, 110 and n. Gaine, of course, rarely wrote any of the accounts he published; he simply selected those he printed.

in still others—as in the case of Burgoyne's surrender—he simply failed to print the news. Both Gaine and Rivington, probably acting under instructions, inserted the following statement in their papers on November 3 and November 1, 1777, respectively:

> "As no accounts, properly authenticated, of the Situation of the Northern Army, have yet been brought to this City, the Printer entreats the Public to excuse his inserting any of the Reports that have been circulated, until he may be warranted by Intelligence derived immediately from General Burgoyne."

Yet on the twenty-sixth Gaine had recorded in his journal: "What shall I say? Poor Burgoyne is at last a Prisoner! He and his whole army taken by a Capitulation about the 15th by the Troops under the command of Ge. Gates."[73]

The news accounts in loyalist papers emphasized those features favorable to the British, and not an account but was written in a manner to influence opinion. Typical is the account of Camden which was printed in Rivington's *Gazette*. After a straightforward statement of the engagement itself, the writer appended several paragraphs of pure propaganda:

> "Lord Cornwallis's whole force, including Tarleton's legion, did not exceed twenty-four hundred, most of whom were in a low state of health, which is the only reason that can be ascribed for Gates' meeting them in the open field, for it is notorious that no other instance can be adduced during the whole course of the war, of any of the rebel generals coming to fair action with the royalists.
>
> "About five hundred of Burgoyne's soldiers that had enlisted in the rebel service, were in the action; their superior discipline and bravery rendered it so obstinate and bloody."[74]

---

[73] *Ibid.*, p. 53 and n. A good instance of the exaggeration is the following from *ibid.*, p. 122: "An Account of an Action, in the West Indies, between the British and French Fleets to the Loss of the latter but not much credited." The *Gazette:* "By the Gentlemen just arrived last night from Havanna, we are informed that on the 20th of June a brigantine arrived there from Windward, by which information was brought that an action at sea had been fought between Admiral Rodney and the Count de Grasse, the event of which terminated greatly in favour of the British; Sir George Rodney took six 70 and two 64 gun ships; the British lost two ships. . . . Should the above stand in need of a corroboration we will add from the same authority, that all the French ships . . . *immediately departed for Martinique.*"—*Ibid.*, p. 122 and n.

[74] Jan. 3, 1781.

Accounts of that nature, interspersed with atrocity stories and refutations of patriot news items, formed the bulk of the propaganda in the papers. The older device of reprinted pamphlets or sermons was rarely used.[75] A good many poems and songs were printed in all of the northern papers but only a few appeared in the southern ones. Some of the satirists wrote allegories or dreams as vehicles of suggestion, but such methods were unusual.[76]

The essay form of propaganda, as in the Whig papers, declined during the war. More political essays were printed in Rivington's *Gazette* than in the others. Only one, for instance, was ever printed in the *Royal Georgia Gazette*. There were few in the South Carolina papers but relatively more in the ephemeral Philadelphia papers. In the longer-lived papers, the number of essays varied from time to time, just as they did in the patriot press. There was a marked increase in the fall and winter of 1777, another in the spring and summer of 1778, a third in the late winter and early spring of 1779 and there were slight increases in the summers of 1780 and 1781. The largest number was written in 1778, just as in patriot papers, and in general the ups and downs in both sets of papers corresponded to each other. Like the patriot essays, the loyalist articles during the war were primarily satirical and hortatory rather than argumentative; as Jonathan Odell aptly put it, "Reason has done her part, and therefore this is the legitimate moment for satire."[77]

The loyalist papers had a larger influence than might be supposed. Aside from person to person contacts, they were the only important contacts the loyalists had, and that their suggestions were effective is apparent from the earnestness with which the patriots refuted them. More tangible evidence exists, however, in the complaints of their baneful effects. Taking all the difficulties into consideration, it is evident that the loyalists did a more effective job with the limited resources at their command than did the Whigs, whose opportunities were greater.

[75] William Pultney, *Considerations on the Present State of Public Affairs*, was reprinted in *Royal Gazette*, beginning Oct. 13, 1779.

[76] Most of these have been mentioned above—André's Dream, the last will and testament of Congress, the satire on the French alliance, depicting the future of America under French rule, and so on.

[77] *The Loyal Verses of Stansbury and Odell*, p. 152.

III

PATRIOT PROPAGANDA
1776-1783

XVIII

CHANGED CONDITIONS

ON THE first Fourth of July a private in the army encamped at New York wrote home:

"Honer'd Father & Mother,

"The time is now near at hand which must probably determine wether Americans are to be free men or slaves; whether their houses & farms are to be pillaged & destroyed and they confined to a state of wretchedness from which no human effort will deliver them. The fate of unborn millions will now depend, under God on the courage and conduct of this army. Our cruel and unrelenting foe leaves us no choice but a brave resistance, or the most abject submission. This is all we can expect. We have therefore to resolve to conquer or die. Our own & our country's honor all calls upon us for a vigorous and manly exertion, & if we now shamefully fail, we shall become infamous to the whole world. Let us therefore rely upon the goodness of our cause, and the aid of the Supreme Being, in whose hand the decree is to animate and encourage us to great and noble actions. The eyes of all our countrymen are upon us, and we shall have their blessings and praises, if happily we are the means of saving them. Let us therefore animate and encourage each other,—and shew the whole world, that freemen contending for liberty on their own ground are superiour to any slavish mercenary on earth. The Genl recommends to the officers great coolness in time of action, & to the soldiers strict attention & obedience, with a becoming firmness of spirit. I would proceed to write more, but the drum beats, I must turn out the fatigue men & the main guard. 'Tis, thanks be to God, pretty healthy in the army.

"I remain your healthy & dutiful son

"Hezekiah Hayden."[1]

That letter is as good an illustration of the results of the propagandists' efforts as one would want. It was as good a result as the propagandists themselves could have wanted; if they could imbue enough

[1] Connecticut Papers (New York Public Library), pp. 433 f.

people with such sentiments, they would have no trouble with disaffection or indifference. And they had done surprisingly well in the two years prior to the Declaration; with the help of British blunders and inadequate Tory propaganda, they had fashioned a revolutionary machine of vast dimensions. The parts were badly fitted and crudely joined, but a fair body of hope hid the internal weaknesses, and the machine looked strong enough to stand the wrack and strain of war. The people of western Massachusetts, who in 1774 were willing to take up the old charter and remain under the protection of England, had been won over to the idea of independence by the Massachusetts Government Act and the outbreak of war.[2] The disaffection in Dutchess, Queens, and Ulster counties in New York had been put down with military force,[3] and in both Pennsylvania and New York the Whig party had taken over the central government. In North Carolina, the Highlanders declared themselves neutral, to Governor Martin's dismay, and in September, 1775, he wrote Dartmouth of the general situation:

> "The spirits of the loyal and well affected to Government droop and decline daily; they despair, my Lord, of succour and support, and for the preservation of their persons from insult, and their property from confiscations . . . they indignantly and reluctantly yield to the over bearing current of revolt rather than side with it, or oppose themselves to it, at the hazard of everything that is dear, without the least prospect of successful resistance. . . ."[4]

In Georgia, where there had been such coolness to the warm ideas of the Whigs, the situation was completely changed by the news of Lexington and Concord. The people were in a turmoil in May, 1775, and in the upheaval the Whigs emerged the victors. Only in South Carolina was there open rebellion against the Whig program. The loyalists outnumbered the Whigs in the region between the Broad and the Saluda, and in the winter of 1776 there was open fighting in the so-called Snow Campaign, and only apparently were the loyalists defeated.[5]

---

[2] See letter of Joseph Warren to Sam Adams, Sept. 12, 1774, quoted in Frothingham, *Warren*, p. 376.

[3] Becker, *Political Parties*, p. 265.   [4] *Col. Rec. N. C.*, X, 244, 266, 325.

[5] McCrady, *History of S. C. in Revolution, 1775-1780*, pp. 88-97; Col. Rec. Ga. (Rhodes Memorial Home), Vol. XXXVIII, pt. 1, pp. 444 f.

The official ruling class had been broken up, and the triumphant Whigs ascended to its old position in the affairs of the new states. Positions long denied Whig politicians were now open to them and were seized with the avidity of the politically hungry. For the first time Whigs could be governors; for the first time they could elect their own members to the upper house of the legislature.[6] No longer would crown attorneys and English appointed judges bar the path of ambitious lawyers, no longer would English appointees hold the lucrative customs offices. For English pensioners and placemen could be substituted the beneficiaries of a Whig patronage. Many of the wealthier merchants, dismayed by the violence of the times and distrustful of independence, joined the loyalist exodus, and a new merchant aristocracy composed of loyal Whigs took their places; there was land too for the Whigs—confiscated estates of the great and little loyalist landholders were at the disposal of the new state governments. The socially prominent, the first families, were now the leading Whigs; the Leonards and the Sewalls, the De Lanceys, the Brewtons, gave way to a new social aristocracy.

But the Whig party was not a unit in 1776 and never had been; with the break-up of the official ruling class, against which it had been negatively united, the rift within the party became even more important. Still outwardly united in the prosecution of the war against England, the party wrangled within itself over local issues, so much so that the success of the war was endangered. There was still the internal fight between the socially radical and the conservative elements of the party, a fight in which the conservatives were not always successful. In common with all wars, furthermore, the Revolution brought to the top men of lesser ability, and many of the new leaders were of poorer quality than the older ones. As one group of leaders moved out and another took its place, so its place too was taken by those below; the whole body of Whig politicians, their relative positions unchanged, moved up in the scale. This elevation of the lesser Whig politicians, and their very number, would seem almost disastrous to the conservatives of the old day. As John Eliot wrote of the situation in Boston: "*O Tempora, O mores*, is at present the universal cant: Paul Revere haranguing in town meeting, the

---

[6] Rhode Island and Connecticut are constant exceptions to such statements, and in some of the colonies the council had been in the hands of the Whigs before the Revolution.

commandant of every particular company, the gentlemen in his domestic circle, & every drabbling dishclout politician, however various their opinions, have all some kind of observation to make upon the times."[7] Paul Revere and drabbling, dishclout politicians might harangue town meetings, but John Hancock was Governor of Massachusetts.

But even the apparent smoothness of the process by which Whig politicians ascended the political scale was badly marred by bitter political feuds within the ranks of the Whigs. As a result relative changes in position did take place. John Hancock fought Sam Adams, Patrick Henry fought Jefferson, and in every colony there were sharp factional contests.

More serious still was the distressing amount of indifference and defeatism within the country. Active loyalists were few, except in the neighborhood of the British troops, but every state had its share of indifferents, many of whom changed their allegiance to suit the nearest or most successful army. These people the active Whigs continued to call Tories, and so they shall be called here. In the Carolinas and Georgia the issue between the patriots and the loyalists had not been so sharp in 1775 as in the northern colonies where the war was in progress, and what amounted almost to a truce was declared. It was not until the real crisis came in 1779 that the internal fight between patriot and loyalist took place. In Virginia the government was plagued with indifference and actual discontent throughout the war,[8] and in the eastern shore counties of Somerset and Worcester, Maryland, and in Delaware, active loyalists were under arms in 1778.[9] Pennsylvania was so full of disaffection that it was the despair of the patriot party. New York City, the former stronghold of the Whigs, was in the hands of the British throughout the war; upstate New York had long been indifferent, and Tories abounded. Even of Boston James Warren could write: "I wish it was in my power to tell you that the Number and Influence of the Tories here were reduced, but I think they gain ground fast."[10] Every colony had its troubles with malingerers, if not with actual loyalists.

[7] John Eliot to Jeremy Belknap, May 9, 1777, Belknap Papers, Vol. III. Hancock was not elected governor until the next year.
[8] Eckenrode, Revolution in Virginia, p. 174; Harrell, Loyalism in Virginia, Chap. II.
[9] Burnett, Letters of Members of Cont. Cong., II, 233 f.; III, 179, 185 f., 197 ff.
[10] Warren-Adams Letters, II, 51 (Oct. 7, 1778). On Rhode Island see Burnett, op. cit., II, 327, 330 f.

Under such circumstances propagandists were certainly as necessary, if not more so, than in the prerevolutionary period, for, as Woodrow Wilson once aptly remarked, "the campaign of mind is as hard as the campaign of arms." It is a curious fact, however, that beginning with the summer of 1775 there was a progressive decline in propaganda activity. The decline was abruptly checked in January, 1776, and there was a marked increase in the volume of propaganda that lasted until about August, 1776, and then another long decline set in. Complaints of this lethargy were frequent, not only from the propagandists but from others as well, who missed the lift in spirits given by propagandists. One of the North Carolina delegates to the Continental Congress wrote Cornelius Harnett: "we have searched almost every Booksellers shop in this City for pamphlets but have made a poor Collection, few are Written, none read, since the appeal to arms."[11] And that was written just a month after *Common Sense* was published. During that same period, when writing was on the increase, Sam Adams fretfully wrote James Warren of the plans for raising new troops:

"But what will avail the ordering additional Battalions if men will not inlist? Do our Countrymen want Animation at a Time when all is at Stake! Your Presses have too long been silent. What are your Committee of Correspondence about? I hear nothing of *Circular Letters*, of *Joynt Committees*, etc., etc. Such Methods have in times passed raised the Spirits of the People, drawn off their Attention from *picking up pins*, and directed their Views to great objects."[12]

After the public agitation over independence had died down, complaints were even more frequent and plaintive. Jonathan Dickinson Sergeant was one of those who missed the propagandist's work. He wrote Sam Adams of the disturbing signs of renewed Tory activity, occasioned largely, he said, by "the Want of proper Information by Pamphlets News Papers &c as formerly on this Subject." "But why are the presses silent at this critical period?" he continued, "they certainly rouzed the People at first, they led them on to concur in the Independence of this Country & they alone can do more than any other Means to keep alive that Zeal which is absolutely necessary

[11] Hayes Collection (Feb. 10, 1776).
[12] *Warren-Adams Letters*, I, 245 (May 10, 1776).

to save us from Ruin."[13] There was a man who really understood the necessity for propaganda.

This curious relaxation of effort is perhaps not so curious after all; at least it can be explained. The war and the Declaration of Independence had, of course, exactly reversed the position of Whig and Tory. The Whigs were now in control of the government and could use legal pressures to command obedience. They could rely upon the values they had inculcated in the preceding dozen years. They thus became unintentional propagandists. The loyalists, on the contrary, were now the intentional propagandists. The patriot propagandists, that is, could now make the mistake so many Tories had made from 1765 to 1773. And they did.

It was natural, in view of the first enthusiasm and the great self-confidence of the Whigs, for the leaders to count heavily upon military success, to throw themselves into the work of organizing the Revolution and to wait for obvious signs of weakening before inspiriting the people. It was not wise, but it was somewhat natural. The Tory opposition, so intense in 1774, had been silenced; the Tory writers had been driven out and their party broken up. Whig propagandists, therefore, may have felt as if they were shadowboxing; until taught by experience, they did not realize, as does the modern propagandist, the need for maintaining the morale of the public. Important local and national problems employed their time. Many of the best leaders were organizing their own state governments, several were in the army, and others were deeply involved in congressional activities. When Congress failed to make public comments on its reports, Francis Lightfoot Lee wrote a friend, "this was not my opinion, & always hoped some private hand wou'd have done it, but alas! *constitutions* employ every pen."[14]

The losses in the ranks of the propagandists moreover were serious. The old Massachusetts quadrumvirate was a thing of the past. Quincy and Warren were dead, and John Adams, never the propagandist his cousin was, figured but slightly in the war propaganda,

---

[13] Adams Papers (Oct. 9, 1776). Jefferson wrote Adams on May 16, 1777, "Our people, merely for want of intelligence which they may rely on, are becoming lethargic and insensible of the state they are in."—*Writings of Thomas Jefferson*, II, 131. Samuel Chase explained the failure of the people in Maryland to raise the state's quota of troops by saying that "the Gentlemen of this County have not yet assisted, by public meetings and associations, to carry any public Measures into Execution."—Burnett, *op. cit.*, II, 267 f.

[14] Lee Transcripts, II, 102 (Nov. 9, 1776).

so engaged was he in Congress. Sam Adams was almost pathetic in his decline after independence was adopted.

Burdened with the uncongenial routine of committee work in the Continental Congress, and with much less interest in sustaining than in fomenting revolution, he was not nearly so active as he had been. Adams loved the secrecy, the excitement, and the danger of intrigue. He was buoyed up by both the condemnation of his enemies and the applause of his friends, but with independence achieved, he lacked the incentive and the enthusiasm for continued propagandizing. For years at a time he did not write for publication. In 1778 he joined in the hastily organized campaign against the peace commissioners, and in 1780 he rather wistfully headed a solitary communication to the *Boston Gazette*, "An Old Correspondent begs room for a few Words in your next."[15] He urged others to write and frequently showed his old perspicacity in selecting the critical issue to be met, but he took very little part himself. In his bitterness against his old ally John Hancock, now intriguing against him, he was too inclined to identify his personal enemies with the enemies of his country. He wrote querulously in 1778:

"The Tories will try their utmost to discredit our new Alliance. You know how much depends upon our cultivating mutual Confidence. It is not in the Power of the undisguisd Tories to hurt our Cause. Injudicious tho honest Whigs may & too often do injure it. Those whose chief aim is to establish a Popularity in order to obtain the Emoluments of places or the Breath of Applause will think they may serve *themselves* by declaiming on this Subject, or prompting others to do it; and they will not fail doing it though they essentially wound their Country.

"If there be any of my virtuous & *publick* spirited fellow Citizens who pay the least Regard to my Opinions I wish they would particularly regard what I say on this Occasion."[16]

The Sam Adams of 1774 would never have said, "it is not in the Power of undisguisd Tories to hurt our Cause" in the sense in which

---

[15] June 12, 1780. The essay is printed in his *Writings*, IV, 188-191. Two unsigned articles, headed "Extracts of Letters from the Southward," either written or copied by Sam Adams, were published in the *Boston Gazette* in 1781. Both deal with Massachusetts politics.

[16] *Writings of Sam Adams*, IV, 62. Almost the same words were used in two other letters.—*Ibid.*, pp. 60, 64.

he meant it here. Political feuds embittered him, and orderly congressional duties damped his spirit. His afflatus was gone.

Other propagandists of the earlier period also were either gone or diverted from their former activities. Alexander Hamilton and Mifflin were in the army, and Franklin had left America in October, 1776. The old provincial leaders—Dickinson, Chase, the Lees, Hooper—were in Congress and were thus out of touch with the local problem. Their work had been of prime importance in the individual colonies, where they were in relatively close contact with the people. Dealing with national problems, they gave less attention to local propaganda, but local propaganda was still of more importance than national. The same situation would not exist today, of course. The old leaders of the lower classes were also removed from agitation for they too were in the army—Avery, Crafts, Trott, Hughes, Mott, McDougall, Lamb, Sears, Gadsden—all were gone to the war.

Still other reasons explain the decline in the volume of propaganda. In the South, of course, there was a decline because the war in the early days was fought almost entirely in the North. Finally, some of the presses were stopped by the war, and others stopped, ridiculously enough, because of the war.[17] The real reason for the temporary let-down was what must have been the belief of many leaders that the war was now primarily a military problem; in their emphasis upon this phase of it, they, for the time, neglected the equally important task of keeping alive the spirit of the troops and of those behind the lines. Whatever the reason, when indifference and defeatism reached alarming proportions, when the army itself was in a desperate plight, the propagandists started the presses, called on the orators, and began anew to stage their demonstrations.

It is not to be supposed, however, that there was at any time a total cessation of activity. There were a number of propagandists who perceived from the start of the war the necessity for continued effort, there were others who joined in the movement as the occasion demanded, and there were still others far more active during the war than before.

The two ablest war propagandists were William Livingston and Thomas Paine. Livingston had gone to live in Elizabethtown,

---

[17] Paper was scarce and the newspapers were expensive, but greater efforts should have been made to keep them going.

New Jersey, in 1772, and, after an active career in local revolutionary circles, was elected the first governor of the new state. In spite of his heavy duties he found time to do a surprising amount of active propagandizing. His speeches as governor were so good that they were frequently printed and reprinted and attracted comment even in Europe.[18] In February, 1777, he published in Dunlap's *Pennsylvania Packet* "The Impartial Chronicles" satirizing Gaine's *New York Mercury*. Later in the year, the New York *Journal* printed his parody of Burgoyne's proclamation; in 1778 he led the propagandist's attack on the peace proposals, writing extensively for the papers and urging others to do the same. He established the first newspaper in New Jersey and knew the value of fast days and celebrations, for he urged both the legislature of New Jersey and the Continental Congress to adopt them.[19]

Objections from members of the New Jersey legislature to his activities, objections made by men blind to the prime importance of his work, are said to have induced him to cease his literary warfare.[20] Whether or not that was the reason, he did stop most of his writing in 1780, but he had carried the people through a trying period. It was unfortunate that he could not have carried on during the dismal year of 1780.

Thomas Paine's single contribution to the propaganda of the war is sufficient to mark him as one of the really inspired manipulators of public opinion. Paine joined the army in August, 1776, and in the retreat across New Jersey in the winter of 1776 he began to inspirit the people with a series of essays which continued throughout the war. On December 19, 1776, there appeared in the *Pennsylvania Journal* the first number of the "American Crisis," which was almost immediately issued in three pamphlet editions. Twelve of these essays and four extra numbers appeared between December, 1776, and December, 1783. The later numbers dealt with internal problems and were not war propaganda. In April, 1777, Paine was made secretary to the committee of Congress on foreign affairs, and from then on held various posts in the state or national government or in the

---

[18] *Pa. Gazette*, Oct. 1, 1776; *Warren-Adams Letters*, II, 38 (a letter of John Adams to James Warren, Aug. 4, 1778). A speech to the militia is in *Pa. Evening Post*, Nov. 28, 1776.

[19] Burnett, *op. cit.*, I, 388, 395; Sedgwick, *Life of Livingston*, pp. 297 f.

[20] *Ibid.*, pp. 327 f.

army. But wherever he was, he constantly had in mind the state of public opinion and timed his writing shrewdly.

A third capable propagandist was the president of the College of New Jersey—the Reverend John Witherspoon. He had taken the lead in bringing New Jersey into the patriot ranks and had stimulated the Whigs to declare independence, which he considered not only inevitable but providentially inspired. He was an active member of Congress during the war, and in the first years of it he used his abilities to inculcate right attitudes. He was the author of several of the congressional fast day proclamations, and in spite of his opposition to the vituperation of the King and his ministers, he was chosen on the committee to investigate the reports of British depravity in New Jersey. He personally collected much of the evidence and wrote most, if not all, of the final report, which was widely circulated.[21] In 1778 he was the author of other attacks on British cruelty—the resolutions of Congress of December 19, 1777, and January 21, 1778—and in October, 1778, he had a part in the published manifesto which threatened reprisals if the treatment were continued. He also wrote a satire on Benjamin Towne's apostasy in printing a pro-British paper during the British occupation of Philadelphia, but this apparently is his only voluntary contribution to the propaganda of the period. Busy for the next three years, he did almost no writing. He was on the congressional committee appointed to mediate the revolt in the Pennsylvania troops in 1781 and wanted to start by preaching them a sermon, believing that "religious admonition might be attended with powerful effect," but his colleagues objected.[22] He did write the report, however, which emphasized the fine attitude of the soldiery in not selling out to the British. Two fast-day proclamations in 1781 and 1782 closed his propaganda activities.

Less important and more intermittent services were performed by a number of leaders. William Henry Drayton, who unfortunately died in 1779, published a pamphlet in October, 1776, "*To their Excellencies Richard Viscount Howe, Admiral, and William Howe, Esq.*" in which he attacked the proposals for reconciliation.

[21] Varnum L. Collins, *President Witherspoon, A Biography*, II, 21, 198. Collins says that in Witherspoon there was little of the sentimentalist, less of the reckless enthusiast, and least of the ranting demagogue. [22] *Ibid.*, II, 18.

In 1778 he returned to the same problem in a series of newspaper essays signed "W. H. D." These were particularly well received throughout the country. Gouverneur Morris also wrote a series at the same time, and later, at Washington's request, contributed articles on domestic problems.[23] James Iredell, like Drayton reluctantly converted to independence, supported it ably with his writing. In March, 1777, he wrote a piece headed "To his Majesty, George the Third," and another in 1778, "To the Commissioners of the King of Great Britain," both able expositions of the Whig position on the suggested compromises. His addresses to the grand juries of Edenton and other North Carolina towns contained equally effective war propaganda. Alexander Hamilton wrote little during the war, but he did contribute one series signed "Publius" in 1778, and he occasionally sent embellished accounts of military engagements to the papers.[24] Of the preachers, Samuel Cooper, Charles Chauncy, and William Tennent were particularly active, but Tennent died in 1777. There were a good many others who served as chaplains in the army, and still others who stayed with their congregations and whose published sermons added to the volume and effectiveness of war propaganda.[25]

Both Washington and Richard Henry Lee, although doing no writing themselves, knew the necessity for encouraging the people and constantly recommended pertinent opportunities to their literary friends. Washington on several occasions gave the propagandists their cue and was always conscious of the need for their activity.[26] More significant throughout the course of the war was the work of the literary propagandists—Frances Hopkinson, Philip Freneau, Hugh Henry Brackenridge, and David Humphreys.

Francis Hopkinson, always in public office, was prolific in his satirical prose and poetry. He wrote Franklin in 1778: "I have not Abilities to assist our righteous Cause by personal Prowess & Force

[23] Burnett, op. cit., III, 315; and Writings of Washington (Ford), VII, 452: "I shall conclude by observing, that it is well worthy the ambition of a patriot statesman at this juncture, to endeavor to pacify party differences, to give fresh vigor to the springs of government, to inspire the people with confidence, and above all to restore the credit of the currency."

[24] Works of Hamilton, I, 85 f. Iredell's articles are in McRee, Life and Correspondence of Iredell.

[25] These men will be dealt with as a group below.

[26] E.g., Letters of Richard Henry Lee, I, 401 f.; Writings of Washington (Sparks), III, 241 f., IV, 354; and Writings of Washington (Ford), V, 505, VI, 475 n., 485, 493 f., VII, 282.

of Arms, but I have done it all the Service I could with my Pen—throwing in my Mite at Times in Prose & Verse, serious & satirical Essays &c."[27] For some months after his election to Congress he found no time for writing, but in the fall of 1776 he wrote two letters exposing the danger from the Tories and another to Lord Howe combating by sweet reason and persuasion the peace proposals.[28] In July, 1777, he wrote an answer to Burgoyne's proclamation,[29] but because of the threat to Philadelphia he wrote nothing for several months, not, in fact, until he published his famous "Battle of the Kegs" in March, 1778. This he followed with two songs in April, and rapidly for two months his poems appeared in the local papers. In July, 1778, however, he became treasurer of loans of the Continental Congress, an arduous task, and for three years he did no writing of any moment. Four poems in 1780 were followed in 1781 by satires on Rivington, and even by a cantata, which was delivered before Washington and an assemblage of French notables in 1781. His real contribution, unlike Freneau's, was not in arousing bitter hatred against England but in humorously belittling her.

Philip Freneau was absent on a trip to the West Indies during the early years of the Revolution. After his return in 1778 he aided Hugh Brackenridge with the *United States Magazine* until the spring of 1780, when he made another trip to the West Indies. On this trip he was captured by the British for the second time. He had been quickly released after his first capture, but now he was detained for some weeks, suffering a serious illness in addition to the normal hardships of life on a prison ship. The treatment on the ship combined with the illness gave him the experience and the bitterness to make of him an inspired critic of British prison methods. In 1781 he became the editor of the *Freeman's Journal*, published by Francis Bailey in Philadelphia, and here he had a sure outlet for his morbid, corrosive poems on British depravity. Freneau supplied the venom that others lacked, and venom was as necessary as humor.[30]

Hugh Henry Brackenridge, author, jurist, playwright, and preacher, did his best work after the Revolution was under way. He had just taken the degree of Master of Arts from Princeton in 1774 and had begun to teach. He also studied divinity and later became

---

[27] Hastings, *Hopkinson*, p. 277.   [28] *Ibid.*, pp. 282 f.
[29] *Pa. Packet*, Aug. 26, 1777; *Pa. Gazette*, Aug. 27, 1777.
[30] Philip Freneau, *Poems*.

a preacher. In 1775 he had begun to write political poems. William Bradford impatiently waited for some of these, for he knew they "would serve to counterbalance several satires that have been published this way against the Congress & the patriotic party."[31] In 1776 he wrote a play, "The Battle of Bunker Hill," and another in 1777, "The Death of General Montgomery." These it is said were actually staged by his students. As a chaplain in Washington's army, he preached at least six sermons intended to inflame the hatred of the troops for the enemy.[32] He established the *United States Magazine* in 1779, gave it up after a year in disgust at the lack of support, and began to study law under Samuel Chase in Annapolis. His literary career against the English was ended, for in 1781 he moved to Pittsburgh to practice.

The last of the poets was David Humphreys, a Yale graduate of 1774. He had a brilliant military record and was an intimate of Washington. He had written poetry as a student at Yale, and during the Revolution he published some poems on the war, the most important of which was "A Poem Addressed to the Armies of the United States of America," written in 1780. His purpose in writing it was well set forth in the preface: "To inspire our countrymen now in arms, or who may, hereafter, be called into the field . . . is the object of this address. For this purpose . . . no consideration could be more effectual than the recollection of the past, and the interpretation of the future."[33] Although he wrote an atrocity poem on the burning of Fairfield, his real contribution was in his appeal to the advantages of victory, the future glory of America. Thus each of the four major poets of the period met a particular need and had a particular appeal.

These men do not account for all the propaganda of the war, for there were many lesser figures who contributed in greater or less degree to swell the amount.[34]

The objective of the propagandists was obvious—to maintain the independence of the United States. In order to achieve this objec-

---

[31] To James Madison, either January or April, 1775.—Bradford Manuscripts (Hist. Soc. Pa.).

[32] *Six Political Discourses Founded on the Scripture*, Lancaster (1778).

[33] *Poems by Col. David Humphreys, late Aid-de-Camp to his excellency General Washington*, p. 4.

[34] Franklin was at loss to identify the "new crop of prose writers" who wrote for the press in the later years of the war.—Hastings, *Hopkinson*, p. 281.

tive, it was necessary for propagandists to inspirit the troops and the public and to demoralize the enemy.[35]

These tasks were accomplished in large part through the individual efforts of the propagandists. They established no central agency for the dissemination of propaganda; they even used the agencies of government to a far less extent than they had formerly. Few concerted efforts were made to obtain resolutions from town and county meetings and from the new state legislatures. The old committee system had, of course, been made unnecessary by the establishment of new governments. There was a revival of the committee system during the financial crisis of 1779, but the committees did not carry on propaganda activities to support the war.[36]

Many of the more able propagandists were in the Continental Congress, and they made of it the most important political agency for the spreading of their ideas.

The propagandists, realizing that "greater advantage results from communicating important Events to the People, in an authentic Manner, than by unauthorized Reports," issued through the Continental Congress a good many addresses to the people of America. The address of December 10, 1776, written by Dr. John Witherspoon with the people of Pennsylvania and the adjoining states particularly in mind, was intended to stimulate them to greater efforts and to prepare them for military invasion and the possible loss of Philadelphia. Witherspoon was also on the committee which presented the report on the conduct of the war by the British. This report, presented to Congress on April 18, 1777, was in four heads: the wanton and oppressive devastation of the country and the destruction of property, the inhuman treatment of prisoners, the savage butchery of those who had submitted, and the lust and brutality of the soldiers in their abuse of women. Affidavits were to be appended substantiating the statements, and the whole was ordered printed in both German and English, but there is no evidence that the pamphlet was published.[37]

---

[35] Enlistment propaganda and appeals to allies and neutrals are not included.

[36] The revival of the committees was the subject of much criticism. Boston, New York, Philadelphia, and many of the New England towns had committees. Some of the Massachusetts committees were called committees of correspondence.—See Massachusetts Town Resolutions, 1773-1787, Division of Manuscripts, Library of Congress. Price fixing and the prevention of monopoly practices were commonly attempted by local committees and state conventions.

[37] *Journals of the Continental Congress*, VI, 1018 ff.; VII, 276 ff.; VIII, 565. Four thousand English copies and two thousand German copies were ordered.

The principal address in 1778 was issued to counteract the effect of the peace proposals; it was published on a broadside and ordered read from all the pulpits in America. Henry Miller made a German translation, but no copies are known to exist.[38] Congress commonly issued handbills of its addresses and of favorable events—military or diplomatic—and these it sent in bundles to the governors of the different states for distribution.[39]

The old practice of identifying the churches with the movement by legally appointed fast and thanksgiving days was continued. The Continental Congress appointed annually a day in the spring for fasting, humiliation, and prayer, and a day in the autumn for thanksgiving. These were proclaimed by the governors of the states and were observed throughout the country. William Livingston was convinced of their value. He wrote Laurens in 1778: "I cannot but think that such a measure is our indispensable Duty, & I dare affirm that it would be very agreeable to all pious people, who are all friends to America; for I never met with a religious Tory in my life."[40] George Mason was a bit more dubious about them. As he said to Richard Henry Lee, "I have no objection to the Fast they have recommended; these solemnities, if properly observed, and not too often repeated, have a good effect upon the minds of the people . . . I can not but think it would have good effects if a manifesto was published upon the occasion, and a particular recommendation to the different States of the Union to cause exact accounts and valuations to be made of all the private property which the British forces shall wantonly destroy, or the devastations which they shall make contrary to the practice and custom of civilized nations."[41]

[38] N. Y. Hist. Soc., Broadsides, May 9, 1778; N. Y. Journal, May 25, 1778; Burnett, op. cit., III, 225. Sam Adams wrote R. H. Lee, April 20, 1778: "As there [are] every where awful Tories enough to distract the Minds of the People, would it not be wise for Congress by a Publication of their own to set this important Intelligence in a clear Light before them, and fix in their Minds the first Impressions in favor of Truth?"—Writings of Sam Adams, IV, 22 f.

[39] Burnett, op. cit., II, 460, 473; III, 216, 225 f., 240. But Richard Henry Lee wrote Francis Lee, Jan. 10, 1779: "We sometimes have handbills published to notify some great victory obtained over the enemies of our Country, but when have we taken pains to have them penetrate every part of the U. S.?"—Letters of Richard Henry Lee, II, 2.

[40] Laurens Papers (July 23, 1778).

[41] Rowland, Life and Correspondence of George Mason, I, 320. The proclamations were printed on broadsides. Congressional fast days are noted in Journals, XIII, 343 f.; XIV, 252; XV, 1191 f.; XVIII, 950; XIX, 284; XXI, 1074. State proclamations may be found in Evans, Amer. Biblio., No. 15,267, No. 15,268; Library of Congress, Broadsides, New Hampshire, p. 88; N. Y. Hist. Soc., Broadsides, Nov. 17, 1777; Rev. Rec. Ga., II, 269.

XIX

WAR PROPAGANDA

THE PRINCIPAL method of opinion control other than legal pressure during the Revolution was propaganda, for the lump of indifference could be best leavened by suggestion. Throughout the war Whig propagandists with arguments and entreaties, with words of hope and fear and hatred tried to stimulate the people to greater firmness and greater exertions.

JUSTIFICATION

The dominant themes of revolutionary propaganda differed markedly, if naturally, from those of the prerevolutionary period. The elaborate legal justification of the Revolution was simply summarized by war propagandists, more as an assertion and a reminder than as an argument. It had long since been proved, they felt, that England had violated the rights of the people. Jacob Green, friend of John Witherspoon, in a fast day sermon in 1778 used the typical formula of the day: "We are contending for liberty. Our cause is just—is glorious; more glorious than to contend for a kingdom."[1] Another minister summarized the legal argument as applied to the war under the following heads: This land is God's possession, given to us to inherit, and England herself recognized the grant by the charters granted the settlers; no one else has any right to it; therefore British attempts to take it by force are unjust and barbarous.[2] So just was the cause of America, asserted Nathaniel Whitaker, that those who failed to support it were impious: "That indolence and backwardness in taking arms, and exerting ourselves in the service of our Country, when called thereto by the public voice, in order to recover and secure our freedom, is an heinous sin in the sight of God." This proposition he expounded at some length, applying the

[1] *A Sermon*, April 22, 1778, p. 4. See also *Boston Gazette*, May 1, 1780.
[2] *Ibid.*, Oct. 20, Oct. 27, 1777. Similar statements are *ibid.*, Mar. 31, 1777; *Pa. Evening Post, Supplement*, Feb. 4, 1777; *N. Y. Journal*, Oct. 6, 1777; Amer. Antiq. Soc., Broadsides, Jan. 26, 1777; Nathan Williams, *A Sermon Preached in the Audience of the General Assembly . . . 1780*, pp. 24 f.; Jonas Clark, *A Sermon Preached before his Excellency John Hancock*, 1781; John Murray, *Nehemiah, or the Struggle for Liberty, Never in Vain*, pp. 40 f.; William Gordon, *The Separation of the Jewish Tribes . . . A Sermon . . . July 4, 1777*, p. 34.

Biblical account of the curse of Meroz, a town, he said, that was cursed not for aiding the enemies of God, but for not aiding the friends of God. The curse of Meroz would surely fall on those who failed to support the most just of all wars, a war for liberty.[3]

National self-interest as justification for the continuance of the war was stressed much more in these years than was legal right. The penalties of defeat were itemized just as specifically as before. General statements of the fatal consequences of defeat, the reader to supply his own applications, were made in plenty. "Aesop" told the fable of the boy trying to catch a horse that had flung him, and closed with the moral: "There, thought I to myself, is the true picture of the disposition of Britain; let her once more get astride of America, and if she don't ride her to the devil, Whig and Tory without distinction, my name is not Aesop."[4] But there were plenty of writers to supply the applications. The economic consequences were specified in detail. Paine's "Crisis Extraordinary," published in 1780, stated clearly the cost of submission in terms of money. Great Britain, he wrote, intended either to establish the same taxes in America as in England or to confiscate the whole property of America. In either case, he declared, America was lost if England won: "In short, the condition of that country, in point of taxation, is so oppressive, the number of her poor so great, and the extravagance and rapaciousness of the court so enormous, that, were they to effect a conquest of America, it is then only that the distresses of America would begin." He estimated the costs of defending the country and governing it after the war as two and three-quarter millions sterling. "Can it then be a question," he concluded, "whether it is best to raise two millions to defend the country, and govern it ourselves, and only three quarters of a million afterwards, or pay six millions to have it conquered and let the enemy govern it?"[5]

Unconscionable taxes, if the propagandists could be believed, were but the lightest of the burdens the patriots would bear should

---

[3] *An Antidote against Toryism*, particularly sections III and IV. The Biblical reference is to Judges 5:23: "Curse ye Meroz, said the angel of the Lord, curse ye bitterly the inhabitants thereof; because they came not to the help of the Lord, to the help of the Lord against the mighty." Cf. Samuel Webster, *A Sermon Preached before the Honourable Council . . . 1777*, p. 16.

[4] *Mass. Spy*, Oct. 12, 1780; and Feb. 27, 1777.

[5] *Works of Thomas Paine*, II, 224 f. See also *The Continental Journal*, Feb. 27, 1777; John Lathrop, *A Discourse, Preached March 5, 1778*, p. 21; Robert Smith, *The Obligations of the Confederate States of North America to Praise God*, pp. 6 f.

England win. The following catalogue sounds very much as if it might be from the pen of William Livingston:

> "What a miserable and despised people should we be, if we were to make peace with England! We should be run over with placemen and pensioners, who like locusts would eat up the land. Corruption and bribery, like a torrent, would sweep down with everything before it. Our trade would be hampered and confined more than ever it was. For fear that we should feel our strength, and try again to make ourselves independent, they would do everything in their power to keep us poor, weak, and miserable. They would insult and trample us under foot. The whole world would despise us as a foolish mean-spirited race of men."[6]

Estates would be confiscated, industry destroyed. The merchant and the farmer alike would bear the burdens of an even more oppressive English government: "Our interest and our honor, our lives and property, the gains of the merchant and the lands of the farmer, our own freedom and happiness, and those of our posterity, are all suspended on our present efforts."[7]

The new-found positions, occupied by the Whigs since the loyalists fled, would be taken away from them and given back to the pensioners and placemen of England. Propagandists scouted the offer of England to give preference to Americans in American positions; preference for what, they asked? "Why, to become the scavengers of streets, the attendants on wharfs, cooks to transports, or stewards to privateers."[8] Every personal right that the Americans had would be destroyed. Paine's first "Crisis" concluded coarsely but vigorously: "By perseverance and fortitude we have the prospect of a glorious issue; by cowardice and submission, the sad choice of a variety of evils—a ravaged country—a depopulated city—habitations without safety, and slavery without hope—our homes turned into barracks and bawdyhouses for Hessions, and a future race to provide for, whose fathers we shall doubt of. Look on this picture and weep over it! and if there yet remains one thoughtless wretch who believes it not, let him suffer it unlamented."[9]

The life and safety of every American, Whig and Tory alike,

[6] *N. J. Gazette*, May 6, 1778; *Boston Gazette*, Feb. 3, 1777; *Mass. Spy*, July 13, 1780.
[7] *Continental Journal*, June 15, 1780; *ibid.*, Feb. 27, 1777.
[8] *Pa. Packet*, May 1, 1779.   [9] *Works of Paine*, II, 78.

were endangered by an English victory: "For there is not the least scruple in the matter" warned the Reverend Mr. Payson, "but the subjugation of these States would be followed with the most shocking scenes of hanging and gibbetting."[10] "Timothy Steadfast" made a stirring appeal to Virginians at the close of the dismal year 1780:

"Good God! what a picture of distress would a conquest of this country present to a sensible mind! . . . A life of infamy dragged out in chains, and rendered forever miserable by severe and bitter reflections, the epithet of rebel eternally crammed down our throats by some haughty Scotchman, or imperious Briton, a confiscation of property, the pains of bondage, and the disgrace of the gibbet to ornament the black catalogue of consequences, would attend our downfall. Virginians, think of the danger that threatens a bleeding country! Awake to public virtue, and sleep no more in the arms of indifference and supineness."[11]

ADVANTAGES OF VICTORY

Such, on the one hand, were the penalties of submission; on the other were the positive gains of victory. Here was the categorical yes and no situation the propagandist must present.

Again, as before the war, the propagandists took refuge in generalities, but there were also statements sufficiently precise to influence large groups without alienating others. The essential idea, then as now, in such an appeal is that everyone wins and no one loses. The Continental Congress in its long address in 1778 included in its varied appeal a strong statement of the promise of the future: "The sweets of a free commerce with every part of the earth, will soon reimburse you for all the losses you have sustained. The full tide of wealth will flow in upon your shores, free from the arbitrary impositions of those whose interest, and whose declared policy it was, to check your growth."[12] Benjamin Rush inspired Mad Anthony Wayne to continued victories with the words, "Britain I hope will soon enjoy the heroic pleasure of dying in *the last ditch*. Are not

[10] *A Memorial of Lexington Battle*, 1782, pp. 19 f. See also *Pa. Packet, Postscript*, Apr. 25, 1778; and *N. J. Gazette*, June 2, 1779: "And while we contemplate the numberless tortures inflicted on our brave and virtuous citizens, we shall naturally consider what our portion would be, should Heaven in wrath permit the accursed foe to prevail over us."
[11] Quoted in Moore, *Diary of the Revolution*, II, 359 f., taken from one of the Virginia gazettes, Dec. 30, 1780.
[12] N. Y. Hist. Soc., Broadsides, May 9, 1778; also in N. Y. *Journal*, May 25, 1778.

peace—liberty—& independance before us?—There will be no end to our commerce—freedom—and happiness."[13] The end of the war, the people were told, would see the restoration of the value of money, depreciated by the nefarious arts of the Tories; taxes would be reduced, commerce restored, and there would be an end to avarice and speculation. The new state, freed from the restrictions of a waning power, would learn the industrial arts and would soon outdistance the old empire.[14] So great were the advantages of independence that it would almost seem, said Nathan Strong in a thanksgiving sermon, that God had planned the Revolution, knowing full well that the future welfare of America depended upon freedom from England: "We had received every possible benefit from the connection, and were beginning to be endangered—we had learned the British arts—had drank at her fountains of science—made her most valuable improvements, our own—were rich enough for a virtuous and free State;—and were beginning to import her luxury, effeminacy and irreligion."[15] Why do we continue still to struggle under such difficulties? asked a New Jersey writer. "This we ought to consider and keep in mind, that it is for LIBERTY; the glorious cause of *Liberty*, that we may be a free people; that we may enjoy the natural rights of mankind; that we may not be reduced to a state of mean and abject slavery."[16] Nathan Fiske's thanksgiving sermon on the defeat of Cornwallis summed up the hope of the future:

"Happy Country! the scene of such wonders, the nurse of such heroes, the defender of liberty, and the care of Jehovah. . . . Soon, we trust, will commence the era of our quiet enjoyment of those liberties which our fathers purchased with the toil of their whole lives, with their treasure, with their blood. Safe from the enemy of the wilderness, safe from the griping hand of arbitrary sway, here shall be the late-founded seat of peace and freedom. Here shall arts and sciences, the companions of tranquillity, flourish. Here shall dwell uncorrupted faith, the pure worship of God in its primitive simplicity—unawed, unrestrained, uninterrupted. Here shall religion and liberty extend their benign influences to savage, enslaved, and benighted na-

[13] Wayne Manuscripts, VII, 83.
[14] This statement from the Pennsylvania Executive Council was signed by Joseph Reed. —*Pa. Packet*, Aug. 8, 1780; *Mass. Spy*, Feb. 27, 1777; *Freeman's Journal*, June 21, 1777.
[15] *The Agency and Providence of God Acknowledged*, p. 12.
[16] *N. J. Journal*, May 3 and May 10, 1780, two letters on liberty by "Eumenes."

tions. How can we forbear rejoicing in such happy prospects!"[17]

In short, said the propagandists, "We are contending for the rights of mankind, for the welfare of millions now living, and for the happiness of millions yet unborn."[18] Were it not for the exertions of America, said Paine, "there had been no such thing as freedom left throughout the whole universe."[19]

Tom Paine knew that the public morale must be kept up by confidence; there must be, as one writer has called it, the illusion of victory. "It is always dangerous to spread an alarm of danger unless the prospect of success be held out with it, and that not only as probably, but naturally essential."[20] The privations of the war and defeats dispirited many, even among the leaders. The French alliance of 1778 gave point to the confident boasting of the propagandists, but there were many times even after 1778 that the words of the propagandists were the only cheerful sounds in the land.

Propagandists cheered the despondent with much the same appeals that had counteracted the confident assertions of the Tories before the war. The power and resources of the country, its extent, its distance from England, were still good arguments. As each year passed without final defeat, the propagandists became still surer that ultimate victory would reward them. They emphasized the growth of the United States during the war as an added proof of strength. James Dana's Connecticut election sermon of 1779 aptly put the case:

"The American confederacy, from the circumstances of its' formation—the necessity impelling to it—the situation of the confederate States, with the common interest European nations will have in protecting them—and the strength it will acquire by improvements in husbandry, manufactures and commerce, new settlements in the wilderness, other states joining in the

---

[17] Quoted in Tyler, *Literary History*, II, 306 f.

[18] Abraham Keteltas, *God Arising and Pleading His People's Cause*, p. 19. "Our COUNTRY, our LIVES, our LIBERTIES, our PARENTS, our CHILDREN & our WIVES, &c. are the SACRED PLEDGES for which we are now contending," and if America should lose, it would lose the "inestimable blessings of LIBERTY, PEACE and INDEPENDENCE."—*Freeman's Journal*, Apr. 12, 1777.

[19] "The Crisis" (Mar. 21, 1778), *Works of Paine*, II, 161. See also Webster, *A Sermon Preached before the Honourable Council*, p. 26.

[20] To Joseph Reed, June 4, 1780, quoted in Conway, *Life of Paine*, I, 159. This referred particularly to financial difficulties.

union, &c. bids fair to endure, when the power now armed against it shall be *broken in pieces*."[21]

Each year this strength increased, it was urged: "when we reckon up the encrease of inhabitants and improved skill in carrying on war, and established order in the several governments, and more settled commerce of the continent, it cannot be a doubt that America has now more strength and ability, to resist the enemy, than she had some time ago."[22] Even after the first year of the war, said a writer, America was nineteen times as strong on land and a hundred and ninety-nine times as strong on the sea as at the start.

Eulogies of American commanders, on the contrary, to make them seem the greater, minimized the resources at their command and multiplied their difficulties. "But with what anxiety did we dread a disunion," exclaimed "Theophilus," "until we saw a WASHINGTON raised by Heaven to lead our armies . . . and how remarkable has he been supported amidst the toils, fatigues, and dangers incident to his high station!"[23] The closing lines of a short panegyric on Washington contain common sentiments:

"But none the laurel, can more justly claim,
Than WASHINGTON the great, inroll'd in fame,
Whose virtues, future history shall write;
And ev'ry page, far distant age delight."[24]

Other American officers were lauded, and their exploits recounted, but none so frequently or so loudly as were those of Washington; the natural and frequent criticism of him produced an even more bombastic defense:

"When God t' effect some great designs,
Plants a new world with Freedom's sons,
Full flowing raptures swell our minds,
He gives the world his Washington."[25]

[21] *A Sermon Preached before the General Assembly of the State of Connecticut*, p. 12.
[22] *Pa. Packet*, July 18, 1780; *Conn. Gazette*, Oct. 18, 1776; *Mass. Spy*, Mar. 7, 1782.
[23] *Freeman's Journal*, Mar. 24, 1778, and *ibid.*, Apr. 12, 1777, April 7, 1778.
[24] *Conn. Journal*, Apr. 21, 1778. See also, *N. J. Gazette*, Aug. 18, 1779; *Pa. Evening Post*, Jan. 7, 1777. From *Cont. Journal*, Jan. 30, 1777:
"Britain shall cease to plague mankind,
With sister tyrants strive to bind,
and check the freeborn soul:
To WASHINGTON her trophies yield,
FREEDOM shall triumph in the field,
and rule from pole to pole."
[25] *Pa. Packet*, Dec. 24, 1778; Library of Congress, Broadsides, Massachusetts, p. 40.

The French alliance of 1778, the fulfillment of the most promised reward of a declaration of independence, gave the propagandists their strongest factual argument for confidence. They could cite but one major military success down to that time, but the alliance was sure proof of victory. At least so it must have seemed. Immediately upon hearing the news, writers began to frame their paragraphs of joy: "Aided by that powerful and illustrious nation, under the benign influence of all-glorious providence, America will persist in her firm resolution to encounter every peril and difficulty rather than return to the humiliating state of dependance on that haughty state."[26] To their amazement, they were immediately put upon the defensive by Tory propagandists, who scouted the value of the alliance and forced the patriot writers to defend their new ally. Each year the Tory attack was more founded in fact, as campaign after campaign passed without effective aid; each year patriot propagandists made more and more promises. Even Washington took a hand and actually wrote out a newspaper paragraph for Lafayette to insert in the papers:

"We have it from good authority, that the Marquis de Lafayette brings the important and agreeable intelligence of a very considerable naval and land force, intended to be sent by his Most Christian Majesty to the succor of these States; and that the Campaign will open with a combined operation against New York. This, there is every reason to hope, with proper exertions on our part, will put a happy period to the war; nor can there be any room to doubt that the glorious opportunity will be effectually improved. This instance of the friendship of our ally is a new claim to the lasting affection and gratitude of this country."[27]

That was in the spring of 1780, and in July, Count Rochambeau and six thousand troops landed in Newport; this heartened the friends of France, and thereafter accounts of French aid as sureties of victory were more boldly put.[28]

Favored by such native resources, commanded by such generals, and aided by such powerful allies, America could not lose; it was obvious to the cloudiest intellect, avowed the propagandists, that

[26] *Continental Journal*, Apr. 23, 1778. [27] *Writings* (Ford), VIII, 282.
[28] E.g., *Cont. Journal*, Feb. 15, 1781; *Mass. Spy*, Nov. 8, 1781.

God had decreed the independence of America. At every stage He had intervened on behalf of the United States. At Lexington the British troops retreated in a panic, "which the Lord of Hosts suffers to fall upon self-sufficient creatures"; even the fall of Ticonderoga and Crown Point was planned by Him to draw Burgoyne deeper into the country.[29] At critical times He sent supplies of arms and ammunition; He brought France and Spain into the conflict and sustained Washington throughout the terrible years of the war. In the growth of the population, in the increase of manufacturing, in every favorable circumstance was His hand seen. "In the rise, and in the whole progress of the unnatural controversy between Great Britain, and the now United Independent American States, the hand of God has been, I must think, very conspicuous." These words of the Reverend Mr. Whittelsey were echoed in a sermon by Phillips Payson, who prematurely declared in 1778: "A kind and wonderful providence has conducted us, by astonishing steps as it were, within sight of the promised land."[30]

Propagandists contrasted this inspired power with the weaknesses, the divisions, the discouragements of Great Britain. Bankruptcy and ruin faced her; with no trade, no money, and no credit, she could not long continue the conflict. "If the brave Americans can support themselves this campaign," said an extract of a private letter from Amsterdam, printed in New York in 1777, "I consider them as free and independant, for England this summer will be ruined."[31] Desertions among the British troops, it was said, increased constantly. It was reported that fifteen hundred, mostly Hessians, had left the army within a few months after the retirement from Philadelphia.[32] Satires on English pretensions exposed the weaknesses of the enemy and bolstered up the hopes of the patriots.

> "But my Lords do not fear,
> Before the next year,

[29] John Devotion, *The Duty and Interest of a People*, p. 21. See also Samuel West, *An Anniversary Sermon, Dec. 22, 1777*, pp. 42 f.; *Freeman's Journal*, June 7, 1777; Israel Evans, *A Discourse . . . Dec. 18, 1777*, pp. 21 f.

[30] Chauncey Whittelsey, *The Importance of Religion in a Civil Ruler*, p. 15; Phillips Payson, *A Sermon Preached before the Honorable Council* (1778), p. 28. See also Henry Cumings, *A Sermon . . . April 19, 1781*, p. 24; *Georgia Revolutionary Records*, II, 211 f.; *Conn. Gazette*, June 24, 1777, reporting a sermon by William Tennent.

[31] *N. Y. Journal*, Aug. 18, 1777. See also *Pa. Evening Post, Supplement*, Feb. 4, 1777.

[32] *Boston Gazette*, Feb. 2, 1778; *Pa. Packet*, July 4, 1778. The frequent disputes between Hessians and regulars seriously weakened the British army, the patriots were told. See *Pa. Packet*, May 5, 1781.

(Altho' a small Island could fret us)
The Continent whole
We shall take by my soul—
If the *cowardly Yankees will let us*."[33]

A poem of David Humphreys, written in 1780, pictured England, defeated but still bloodthirsty, sullenly drawing off in search of other victims:

"Chang'd are the scenes. Now fairer prospects rise,
And brighter suns begin to guild our skys.
Th' exhausted foe, his last poor efforts try'd
Sees nought remain, save impotence and pride:
His golden dream of fancied conquest o'er,
(And Gallia thundering round his native shore,
Iberia aiding with Patosi's mines,
While brave Batavia in the conflict joins)
Reluctant turns, and deep involv'd in woes,
In other climes, prepares for other foes."[34]

DEPRAVITY OF THE ENEMY

The most important theme of the war propaganda was the depravity and cruelty of the English; in the prerevolutionary period other themes had been relatively more important, but during the war no other suggestion received so much emphasis. By arousing hatred and disgust for the British, the propagandists hoped not only to spur the people on to greater efforts in support of the army but also to prevent a possible settlement short of independence.

The indictment against the British comprehended their method of waging war and their national character; it was directed against the people as a whole, as well as against individuals.

The English waged a cruel and predatory war, fought with bitterness and malice; from their lust and rapacity no one, nothing, was safe. Wherever the troops went, devastation and ruin were left behind. Villages were burned and farm dwellings razed. Troops pillaged the houses, leaving not even food for the children. They

---

[33] *Mass. Spy*, Mar. 27, 1777; Jan. 17, 1782. See also N. Y. *Journal*, May 17, 1779; Library of Congress, Broadsides, New York, p. 109.

[34] *Poems of David Humphreys*, pp. 13 f. See also *Boston Gazette*, Jan. 20, 1777: "Britannia—sinks beneath her Crimes, She dies—she dies—Let Empire rise, And Freedom cheer the Western Skies."

wantonly burned Charlestown, charged Thomas McKean, and seized on the ships and vessels in the harbor, and "by fire, sword and famine spread destruction and desolation around them."[35] The pillaging of troops was but the individual expression of a national necessity; with a debt of a hundred and ninety million pounds, said a North Carolinian, "we may gather the Necessity of that Country making War, and letting loose her Band of Robbers, to plunder the Earth, and enlarge her Dominions."[36]

Ignorant and malicious savages, the troops plundered and desecrated, not from military necessity, but from wanton pleasure. One of William Livingston's addresses to the New Jersey legislature summed up this charge:

"They have committed hostilities against the possessors of literature; and the ministers of religion: Against public records; and private monuments; and books of improvement; and papers of curiosity; and against the Arts and Sciences. They have . . . disfigured private dwellings of taste and elegance; and in the rage of impiety and barbarism, profaned edifices dedicated to Almighty God."[37]

Not even graves were safe from their covetous hands:

"These monsters exceed even the most barbarous nations. With them the ashes of the dead have ever been sacred. But under the patronage of a British tyrant and his general, snuffing the tainted gale, they have ransacked the silent repositories, and the remains of one that was once amiable and captivating, flung about as food for the birds of the air. O GOD, where is thy Vengeance? O Virtue, honor, religion, humanity, where, where are ye fled!"[38]

[35] *A Charge Delivered to the Grand-Jury, 1778*, p. 8. See also *Mass. Spy*, Feb. 5, 1778; N. Y. *Journal*, Aug. 3, Nov. 23, 1778; *Conn. Gazette*, Oct. 31, 1777.

[36] *N. C. Gazette*, Oct. 24, 1777. David Humphreys wrote a poem on the burning of Fairfield.—*Poems*, pp. 1 f.

[37] *Archives of N. J.*, ser. 2, Vol. I, p. 301. Another, using the same incidents, declared that they had degraded themselves "by wantonly destroying the curious water works at New York, an elegant public library at Trenton, and the grand orrery, made by the celebrated Rittenhouse . . . a piece of mechanism which the most untutored savage, staying the hand of violence, would have beheld with wonder, reverence, and delight! Thus are our cruel enemies warring against liberty, virtue, and the arts and sciences."—*Freeman's Journal*, Jan. 28, 1777.

[38] Jonathan W. Austin, *Oration, Delivered at Boston, March 5, 1778*, p. 110 (!). This statement was inspired and almost copied from a piece which appeared in the *Freeman's Journal*, Feb. 18, 1777. The original (which may, of course, have been written by Austin) follows: "The repositories of the dead have ever been held sacred by the most barbarous

Wanton destruction of property was overmatched by wanton abuse of innocent noncombatants, so continued the indictment. On the poor excuse that the troops had been fired on from private homes, citizens were shot, their houses and contents destroyed, and the women and children stripped of their clothing and forced into the wilderness. Without provocation, old men and women had been shot or stabbed, and still others mutilated.[39]

The Caldwell case aroused great indignation, indignation that grew as the accounts grew. The wife of the Reverend James Caldwell was killed during Knyphausen's Connecticut campaign. The English stated that the killing was accidental and that there was even evidence to show that the stray bullet came from the rebel army. The patriot accounts, however, made the most of the distressing affair:

> "Soon after their possessing themselves of the neighborhood, a soldier came to the house, and putting his gun to the window of the room where this worthy woman was sitting, (with her children, and a maid with an infant in her arms, along side of her), he shot her through the lungs dead on the spot. Soon after an officer with two Hessians came in, and ordered a hole dug and her body thrown in, and the house to be set on fire. At the earnest request of an officer of the new levies, and with some difficulty, the body was suffered to be carried to a small house in the neighborhood, and Mr. Caldwell's dwelling-house immediately set on fire, and every thing belonging to him consumed together."[40]

Compare the following account, written six weeks later:

> "And Oh! that unequalled act of guilt and cruelty! We cannot forget it, nor are we willing it should be forgotten. Defended by every personal charm; protected by a complete collection of the softest and most charming virtues; guarded by a sucking infant and a large family of depending babes, and who, sitting still in her own house, might thereby claim, at least, life

and savage nations. But here, not being able to accomplish their accursed purposes upon the living, they wreaked their vengeance on the dead. . . . At Morrisania, the family vault was opened, the coffins broken, and the bones scattered abroad. At Delancey's farm, the body of a beautiful young lady, which had been buried for two years, was taken out of the ground, and exposed for five days in a most indecent manner."

[39] N. Y. *Journal*, July 19, 1779, Aug. 2, 1780; *Pa. Evening Post*, Jan. 7, 1777; *Pa. Packet*, June 13, 1780; *Mass. Spy*, July 13, 1780.

[40] *Pa. Packet*, June 13, 1780.

from the enemy in whose power she had put hers;—yet she falls by the deliberate aim of an instigated soldier! What then can we expect if fully in their power? Some of the enemy affect to say her death was accidental. There is sufficient proof to the contrary. But suppose some of the enemy thought so, did they show one mark of grief, pity, or humanity? Did one officer, or one soldier, protect the corpse, or save any property for the bereaved babes? Not one; General Robertson's wagon was brought to the door, and loaded by his own servants with the beds and family goods. . . . And her corpse, which was in part stripped, must have been consumed in the flames had it not been for the humanity of some persons who were not of the army."[41]

That is a typical example of the way propaganda accounts, then and now, grow with the telling.

To the familiar catalogue was inevitably added sex atrocities. One account in particular spread through the states. It concerned the rape of women during the occupation of New Jersey. Women of Maidenhead, Hopewell, and Woodbridge were attacked; one was seventy years old, another was pregnant, and still another was a very young girl. Nor was it just the common soldier who committed such atrocities, "but officers, even British officers four or five . . . went about the town by night, entering into houses, and openly enquiring for women."[42] The same account appeared in the *Freeman's Journal*, the *Massachusetts Spy*, and the *Connecticut Journal*, and was printed in broadside form at Peekskill.[43] Most of the references to such cases, however, were simple statements to the effect that women were commonly ravished. The Continental Congress amplified section IV of its report, written by Witherspoon in 1777, "The lust and brutality of the soldiers in abusing women" as follows:

"The committee had authentic information of many instances of the most indecent treatment, and actual ravishment of married and single women; but, such is the nature of that most irreparable injury, that the persons suffering it, and their relations, though perfectly innocent, look upon it as a kind of reproach to have the facts related, and their names known. They

[41] *N. J. Journal*, Aug. 2, 1780.   [42] *Freeman's Journal*, June 21, 1777.
[43] *Conn. Journal*, Jan. 1, 1777; *Mass. Spy*, Jan. 2, 1777; and *Freeman's Journal*, Jan. 7, 1777.

have, however, procured some affidavits, which will be published in the appendix."[44]

In every paper, in a variety of forms—reports, poems, newspaper accounts by women, by ministers, by soldiers—the repetition of these atrocities spread the doctrine of hate:

"The late conduct of the *British demons* in New Jersey, in the robberies, burnings, ravishments and murders, with a long catalogue of crimes as black as *hell!* is a call louder than thunder, more piercing than lightening and more affecting than firebrands, arrows and death.—He that is not moved with compassion to the suffering citizens, and with heroic fire against the *tyrant* and his *bloody butchers*, is *dead while he lives* . . . like *Cain*, he ought to be haunted from the society of men. . . . The dying hopes of the enemy revive by the reduction of Charlestown, and as on former occasions, they grow more brutal with any success; this affords instruction to the Americans, and marks their *future designs*—were they to succeed, every species of malice is in their hearts; *laid up for us*—can there be a more powerful incentive to preserving exertions?—Then let us NOW act as becometh MEN in our distinguished situation, on whom are the eyes of GOD and the world. Every sentiment in our souls should be energy, and every nerve strained in the highest tone of exertion, until our COUNTRY is secured in LIBERTY, PEACE, and SAFETY."[45]

The treatment of prisoners was but another instance of the barbarity of the English, continued the propagandists, and accounts of the inhuman abuse of prisoners constitute one of the most common features of the war propaganda. Prisoners were brutally mistreated on the field of battle when asking for quarter. Hessians used them as screens for themselves, and the wounded were shot, stabbed, or knocked on the head: "They have butchered the wounded, asking for quarter; mangled the dying, weltering in their blood," said William Livingston.[46] Sworn depositions that the troops were instructed to take no prisoners but to kill those who surrendered, appeared in

[44] *Journals of the Continental Congress,* VII, 278.

[45] *Cont. Journal,* July 13, 1780. The greater part of this literature relates to the war in New Jersey in the winter of 1776, the Knyphausen campaign in Connecticut, and to the campaigns in Long Island. The Committee of Safety of New Jersey, George Bickham, secretary pro tem., published an account of the ravages in New Jersey.—*Pa. Evening Post,* Dec. 28, 1776.

[46] *Archives of New Jersey,* ser. 2, Vol. I, p. 301.

several papers, but the Continental Congress refused to accept completely the truth of the assertions; it simply declared in its report:

> "The committee found it to be the general opinion of the people in the neighbourhood of Princeton and Trenton, that the enemy, the day before the battle of Princeton, had determined to give no quarter.—They did not, however, obtain any clear proof, that there were any general orders for that purpose; but the treatment of several particular persons at and since that time, has been of the most shocking kind, and gives too much countenance to the supposition. Officers wounded and disabled, some of them of the first rank, were barbarously mangled or put to death. A minister of the gospel in Trenton, who neither was nor had been in arms, was massacred in cold blood, though humbly supplicating for mercy."[47]

Those who were mercifully killed were far better off than those who dragged out miserable existences in the British prison ships. "General Howe has discharged all the privates, who were prisoners in New York; one-half he sent to the world of spirits for want of food—the other he hath sent to warn their countrymen of the danger of falling into his hands, and to convince them by ocular demonstration, that it is infinitely better to be slain in battle, than to be taken prisoners by British brutes, whose tender mercies are cruelties."[48] Prisoners were kept in putrid holes, with no fresh air or water, little food and that spoiled; they were never allowed on deck, and the accumulated filth below deck was never removed. From inadequate clothing in winter, from the sweltering heat in the holds in summer, unequalled even by the Black Hole of Calcutta,[49] from neglect when sick, thus did the prisoners die by the hundreds. Of those who lived, continued one account, "the greater part, as far as I can learn, are dead and dying. Their constitutions are broken, the stamina of nature worn out, they cannot recover—they die."[50]

It was the unquestioned policy, in fact, said patriot writers, to kill the prisoners. The *Pennsylvania Packet* quoted in proof a letter

---

[47] *Journals*, VII, 276 ff.

[48] *Freeman's Journal*, Feb. 18, 1777. There are many statements about the cruel treatment of prisoners in New York, yet Elias Boudinot, American commissary of prisoners, was "well satisfied" in February, 1778, with the treatment they received.—Jones, *Loyalists of Massachusetts*, p. 200.

[49] *Pa. Journal*, Nov. 6, 1776. Among many examples, see *Boston Gazette*, Mar. 17, Mar. 24, 1777; *Mass. Spy*, Aug. 19, 1779; *Conn. Gazette*, Nov. 17, 1779.

[50] *Conn. Journal*, Jan. 30, 1777.

from Howe to Germain in which Howe stated that he hoped to be relieved of the burden of part of the prisoners by an exchange, "which once being effected, I SHALL SOON RID MYSELF OF THE REMAINING INCUMBRANCE."[51] Another asserted that many of the released prisoners died of smallpox, for "our enemies determined that even those whom a good constitution and a kind Providence had carried through unexampled sufferings, should not at last escape death, just before their release from imprisonment infected them with that fatal distemper."[52]

The British, not content with their own brutalities, called to their aid the most vicious and savage allies. The Hessians, it was asserted and reasserted, were guilty of the foulest crimes imaginable for they were by their nature depraved and ferocious. The outlook for the future was horrible to imagine when once the Hessians came, "whose native ferosity, when heightened and whetted, by the influence and malice of the sceptered savage of Great-Britain, thirsting for the blood of his faithful American subjects, will exhibit such a scene of cruelty, death and devastation, as will fill those of us who survive the carnage, with indignation and horror; attended with poverty and wretchedness."[53] They indulged themselves in "rapine and bloodshed"; they protected themselves from shellfire with American prisoners; they delighted in torture. Yet Washington wrote Congress, apropos of its projected report on their activities, "One thing I must remark in favor of the Hessians, and that is, that our people, who have been prisoners, generally agree that they received much kinder treatment from them, than from the British officers and soldiers. The barbarities at Princeton were all committed by the British, there being no Hessians there."[54]

Indian allies were naturally attacked by patriot propagandists, and numerous accounts of their barbarities, directly attributed to

[51] *Pa. Packet*, Jan. 25, 1780.
[52] *Conn. Journal*, Jan. 30, 1777. The article, signed "Miserecors," on the suffering and death of prisoners in New York, the alleged number varying between five hundred and fifteen hundred, appeared in *Freeman's Journal*, Mar. 22, 1777; and in *Conn. Journal*, Jan. 30, 1777. [53] *Norwich Packet*, July 8, 1776.
[54] *Writings of Washington* (Ford), V, 220 n.; *Conn. Journal*, Feb. 5, 1777. The report of the Continental Congress in April made the following statement: "Freemen and men of substance suffered all that a generous mind could suffer from the contempt and mockery of British and foreign mercenaries . . . sometimes the common soldiers expressed sympathy with the prisoners, and the foreigners more than the English. But, this was seldom or never the case with the officers. . . ."—*Journals*, VII, 278. See also *ibid.*, VI, 1018 ff.

British instigation, were printed. The most striking instance was the death of Jenny M'Crea in the summer of 1777. She was to be married to a Tory, and she herself inclined toward the British side, but in the skirmishing around Fort Edward, where General Burgoyne was stationed, she was captured by some Indians, scalped, and shot. The propagandists emphasized three features of this incident—the savagery of the Indian allies, the tacit or expressed consent of the British in such atrocities, and the fact that Jenny was friendly to the English:

"She and an old woman were taken by the savages, who generally serve as an advance guard or flanking parties to the regulars . . . and then, with a barbarity unheard of before, they butchered the poor innocent girl, and scalped her in the sight of those very men who are continually preaching up their tender mercies, and the forbearance of their more than Christian King. Is not this sufficient to congeal the heart of humanity with horror, and even oblige a Tory of liberal sentiments to curse the cause which approves or winks at such worse than hell-like cruelties? . . . What renders this affair more remarkable is, that Miss M'Crea has a brother an officer in the British service . . . and she herself leaned to that side of the question; but thus they treat their friends as well as their enemies."[55]

A poem by Wheeler Case, deservedly forgotten, stresses the culpability of the British:

"Oh, cruel Savages! what hearts of steel!
O cruel Britons! who no pity feel!
Where did they get the knife, the cruel blade?
From *Britain* it was sent, where it was made.
The tom-hawk and the murdering knife were sent
To barbarous Savages for this intent.
Yes, they were sent, e'en from the *British throne*."[56]

[55] *Pa. Evening Post*, Aug. 12, 1777. See also *Boston Gazette*, Jan. 20, 1777; *Cont. Journal*, Aug. 6, 1778; N. Y. *Journal*, May 31, 1779. The *Pa. Packet*, June 24, 1780, carried an article signed "Anti-Britannus," which listed the M'Crea and Caldwell cases.

[56] *Revolutionary Memorials, Embracing Poems by the Rev. Wheeler Case*, p. 39. The British were also accused of inciting the slaves to insurrection. E.g., Keteltas, *God Arising and Pleading his People's Cause*, p. 25; *Freeman's Journal*, Oct. 29, 1776. Lord Dunmore was attacked on this point. Just before the war, rumors of a Negro uprising filled New York. A man overheard his servant discussing the details of a plot to set fire to houses and kill people as they came out. Another account increased the number of Negroes involved and added that five or six hundred Indians were to help. The magistrate's examination of the rumor disclosed no further details.—N. Y. *Gazette and Weekly Mercury*, Mar. 6, 1775; *Pa. Journal*, Mar. 8, 1775.

Equally depraved were the internal friends of England, the Tories. They were the principal cause of the depreciation of the currency, a charge commonly made but rarely explained: "We are all crying out against the depreciation of our money . . . while the Tories, who are one principal cause of the depreciation, are taken no notice of. . . ."[57] They threw the country into disorder and confusion by counterfeiting its currency, and they refused to accept the regular currency—these were the only explanations offered.[58] They monopolized goods and caused an exorbitant rise in prices, they discouraged enlistment, and openly traded with the enemy. They were spies aiding the invasion of the country.[59] When before in the history of warfare did a people allow open and professed enemies to live within their borders, "to break their laws—destroy their currency—monopolize the necessaries of life—correspond with the enemy—discourage their soldiers—move from town to town where they can do the most mischief—hold consultations with the prisoners of war—and after all, say publicly, That the indulgence ariseth from timidity?"[60]

Just as Thomas Jefferson in the Declaration of Independence had fastened the blame for the whole trouble on George III, so in later years the sins of the British were loaded on his shoulders. Hate was given a concrete object. George was a fool:

> "O George! thou tyrant of the earth!
> I curse the day that gave thee birth:
> Thou'lt be the laughing-stock and scorn
> Of millions who are yet unborn.
> From your destruction may we all
> Learn this good lesson by your fall;
> Never to raise to public rule
> So great a dunce as *George the fool*."[61]

George was a murderer: "Think, O monster in human form! Think how many dying groans you have caused—how many widows

---

[57] *Pa. Packet*, Aug. 5, 1779.

[58] *Freeman's Journal*, May 31, 1777; *Pa. Packet*, Feb. 15, 1780.

[59] *Pa. Evening Post*, May 8, 1777; *Pa. Packet*, July 8, 1779.

[60] *Boston Gazette*, Apr. 28, 1777. Paine said of the Tories in the first "Crisis": "And what is a tory? Good God! what is he? I should not be afraid to go with a hundred Whigs against a thousand tories, were they to attempt to get into arms. Every tory is a coward; for servile, slavish, self-interested fear is the foundation of toryism; and a man under such influence, though he may be cruel, never can be brave."—*Works of Paine*, II, 73.   [61] *Boston Gazette*, Aug. 17, 1778.

& children are weeping for the death of husbands and fathers, whose blood you have shed."[62] Dishonored and disgraced, he had obstinately wrecked an empire:

> "Thus I'll drive on, in spite of *Mars*,
> With *Nero's* rage, to act *North's* farce;
> 'Till *ways* and *means* shall d—n the nation,
> Or bring it to—*accomodation*."[63]

In him and his associates were united injustice, obstinacy, folly, and treachery. His printers lied, his officers seduced and bribed.[64] In them were the traits of the nation exemplified.

The British people and the British King, "sullied with every crime that can deform their souls and offend their god," were enemies to "virtue and mankind."[65] And with the last year of the war, the *Massachusetts Spy* delivered its valedictory to the English:

"The free Americans of the United States utterly deny themselves to be Englishmen in any respect. Although these

[62] *Ibid.*, Oct. 9, 1780. Cf. "A Merry Song about Murder," *ibid.*, May 22, 1780:
> "Swords, hatchets and knives he prepared,
> To slaughter his people like sheep;
> Man woman or child, he ne'er spar'd
> Which makes even Savages weep.
> Then, like a great lubberly calf,
> On his marrow bones down he did fall;
> I have killed of my people but half,
> Lord, help me to murder them all!"

[63] *Pa. Journal*, Mar. 15, 1780; *Boston Gazette*, Mar. 9, 1778.

[64] All the British officers were attacked, of course. They were charged with bribing American officers and troops and treacherously deceiving prisoners.—*Cont. Journal*, Sept. 27, 1781; *N. Y. Journal*, Nov. 9, 1778. John Sullivan published a letter which urged him to turn over Ticonderoga, and it was later charged that the British tried to buy out the governor of Vermont.—*Freeman's Journal*, Aug. 30, 1777; *Mass. Spy*, Sept. 13, 1781. Arnold, who did take a bribe, was the victim of popular fury. A typical poem reflects the general attitude:
> "ARNOLD, thy name as heretofore,
> Shall now be *Benedict* no more;
>
> .   .   .   .   .
>
> 'Tis fit we brand thee with a name,
> To suit thy infamy and shame;
> And since of treason thou'rt convicted,
> Thy name should now be *maledicted*;
> Unless by way of contradiction,
> We style thee BRITAIN'S *Benediction*."

—*Cont. Journal*, Oct. 26, 1780. See also *ibid.*, Oct. 5, 1780. Galloway was particularly abused in Pennsylvania. Wrote "Incognitas": "The cries of ruined families and the curses of the distressed composed the grand chorus that attended your triumphant progress to the city of your residence—The hoofs of your horses were drenched in gore, and the bones of your slaughtered brethren crackled under the wheels of your carriage—*Let the remembrance of these things sit heavy on thy soul*."—*Pa. Packet*, Jan. 21, 1778.

[65] *Pa. Packet*, July 29, 1780; *Boston Gazette*, Mar. 5, 1781.

gentlemen are fond of honouring us with the appellation of children and brethren we beg leave to dispense with the compli-
ment; as we should reckon it the greatest disgrace to be thought
to be any way related to that wretched blood-thirsty people."[66]

NEUTRALIZING INCONVENIENT SUGGESTIONS

There were, during the war, certain ideas promulgated by loyalist propagandists that were dangerous to the common safety. These
were met by the united efforts of many of the propagandists. Three
problems in particular troubled them: the military defeats, which
had to be minimized; the French alliance, which had to be defended;
and the peace proposals, which had to be rejected.

In spite of all the bombast about the power of America and the
weakness of England, defeats came, and these had to be explained
away as much as possible. Breed's Hill was easily explained, as we
have already said—one wing unfortunately mistook an order to advance as an order to retreat, throwing the whole army into confusion; furthermore, all the soldiers were out of ammunition.[67] Years
later the defeat at Camden was explained in the same way. This
time it was the Maryland regiment which confused its orders and
precipitated a rout: all went well at first and the day was almost
won, "when by an unfortunate accident the first Maryland Regiment (in front) got into some disorder, which, by a mistake of
orders, was communicated to the second. . . . Our army retired
about two miles, without any loss of artillery, ammunition or bag-
gage, and notwithstanding this little repulse are in high spirits!"[68]
The loss of some vessels off Penobscot in the same year was interpreted as, in reality, a piece of clever strategy. England was deceived into thinking that she had destroyed the whole American
fleet, and acting on this favorable conjecture, "out pops the Quebec
fleet; *the most, if not the whole of which, are fallen into our hands.*
That's the cream of the jest. Now this fleet is so valuable that it
will not only pay for what we lost at Penobscot, but amounts to as

[66] *Mass. Spy,* Jan. 3, 1782.

[67] Conn. Hist. Soc., Broadsides, *Fresh News, 1775.*

[68] *Royal S. C. Gazette,* Aug. 11, 1781. An earlier account mentioned no confusion,
only great firmness and bravery borne down by the weight of superior numbers. This
account closes, "The British loss hath been much more considerable than the Americans.
Lord Cornwallis, or some other British General, *it is conjectured,* is amongst the slain."
—*Pa. Gazette,* Sept. 6, 1780.

much as all the expense of the war besides."[69] Somehow the sale price did not measure up to the expectations.

The smashing attacks of the British in the South, which resulted in the loss of Savannah and Charleston, were more difficult to explain away. Let the loss of Charleston be exaggerated as much as the Tories would wish, said one, the fact remained that no one but a few craven spirits were dejected by this "small, very small misfortune."[70] In fact, said another, the loss will simply serve to inspirit the people of the South, purge the territory of those unfriendly to America, and awaken the spirits of the northern army; already "the fall of Charles-Town, and the distresses of our brave friends in that quarter, have infused fresh vigour into the Councils of America."[71] It was of little importance in any event, wrote a third, and was sure evidence of the incapacity of Sir Henry Clinton, who should have taken it much sooner; if this was the best he could do, America had little to fear.[72] The loss was but another call to renewed action:

> "And ye who are now chap fallen at the loss of a single city in *Carolina*, may view that event as a summons necessary to rouse ye, lest that lost lethargy shou'd overtake ye, and ye shou'd sleep the sleep of death. . . . A French squadron will soon be on the coast with eight or ten thousand troops on board; —their monarch expects that we have a band of bathers ready to join them; that, united we may take vengeance, and silence, at a blow, the common enemy."[73]

Satisfaction was found even in some features of the revolt in the Pennsylvania troops which occurred in the winter of 1780-81. They were dissatisfied, it was said, with evidences of discrimination among them, and rioting broke out. An officer was killed and the troops began to break up and return to Pennsylvania. They marched through the country "with great regularity and good conduct, and perhaps less damage than is common on the passing of troops." On their march they were tempted by British spies to join the English, but these they turned over to Anthony Wayne, who hanged them. A commission later settled the dispute. "Upon the whole," con-

---

[69] *Cont. Journal*, Aug. 17, 1780. [70] *Ibid.*, Aug. 24, 1780.
[71] *Md. Gazette*, July 14, 1780. See also *Pa. Packet*, Feb. 27, 1779 (referring to the loss of Georgia); July 4, 1780.
[72] *Pa. Packet*, Oct. 21, 1780. [73] *Cont. Journal*, June 22, 1780.

cluded the newspaper summary of Witherspoon's report to Congress, "this affair, which at first seemed so alarming, has only served to give a new proof of the inflexible honor of the soldiery, and their inviolable attachment to American liberty; and will teach General Clinton, that though he could bribe such a mean toad-eater as Arnold, it is not in his power to bribe an American Soldier."[74] Of such defeats and disasters there was, in truth, little to be said, but the propagandists did their best.

The French alliance, hailed with such joy in America, was promptly attacked by the Tories and the British commissioners, who arrived within a month of the news of it; the aggrieved patriots found themselves forced to defend what they considered one of their crowning achievements. It was said that France came into the war simply to prevent a reconciliation with England and not from any love of America, that the alliance was an unnatural one because France was the ancient and natural enemy of America, and that it was actually dangerous since France was seeking simply to regain her lost colonies and to impose popery upon the colonists. To these charges the propagandists replied with spirit.

English perfidy, not French perfidy, was to be feared. England provoked France into war, and France had only the welfare of America at heart:

> "Let others toil, their empire to extend
> By baneful conquest, for a selfish end.
> Let Britain's Monarch aim at lawless pow'r,
> And on our western world his vengeance show'r;
> Or send his servile minions to destroy,
> What Heav'n's decree forbids him to enjoy.
> While you great *LOUIS*, with a God-like mind,
> Persist in your resolve to save mankind."[75]

[74] *Boston Gazette*, Feb. 12, 1781; *N. J. Gazette*, Jan. 17, 1781; and a variant in *Conn. Courant*, Feb. 20, 1781. The committee report in full is in *Journals of the Continental Congress*, XIX, 79-83; it was summarized for the press.

[75] *Pa. Packet*, Sept. 4, 1779. See also *ibid.*, Aug. 6, 1778; Feb. 18, 1779. Joel Barlow in "The Prospect of Peace," written in 1778, explained that France was simply trying to bring peace to America. "Peace" was floating over Europe—

> "This LEWIS view'd, and reach'd a friendly hand,
> Pointing her flight to this far-distant land;
> Bade her extend her empire o'er the West
> And Europe's balance tremble on the crest!"

The alliance was a perfectly natural one. "France, tho' a monarchy, has been the nurse and protectress of free republics," and in the present issue her interests and those of America were identical.[76] Furthermore, said others, alliances should be not with a similar state or race, but with as different a nation as possible in order to preserve the identity and independence of each. If America were allied with England, "all her train of national, domestic and private vices would have insinuated themselves among us, and destroyed all that republican simplicity, industry, and virtue, both public and domestic which have been introduced into our country by the present glorious struggle for liberty."[77]

Nor was the alliance dangerous. France acted solely from magnanimous motives, and American territory was safe. The danger of popery was chimerical. France was but moderately Catholic, and America, allied to a Catholic country, would be even more on the alert against its establishment. "Perhaps," it was even suggested, "our alliance with France may prove hereafter the means of introducing liberty, and the Protestant religion into that country in exchange for the protection and independence she hath afforded this."[78] God Himself had brought France into the conflict; there could be no danger: "The chief wonder of all is yet to be told—In the magnanimity of the generous MONARCH of FRANCE, Heaven has brought on the stage the CYRUS of the church in gospel-times. . . . does the bigot give credit to the tory's tale—and dream it unlawful to accept such aid?"[79]

The alliance, finally, was wholly new and was not encumbered with old claims and disputes: "America and France have met in the early walks of a first acquaintance. There are no seeds of difference between us. Our mutual confidence exists perfect. Let it not be interrupted in the smallest instance, lest it may not again be perfect."[80] Cherish the French alliance and remember the depravity of England —this was the propagandist's command: "let us rather cherish our resentments. Let us instill them into the minds of our children; and let the first lessons we teach them be, that to love liberty and to hate

---

[76] Samuel Cooper, *A Sermon Preached before his Excellency John Hancock*, 1780, p. 43.

[77] *Pa. Packet*, Aug. 1, 1778. See also *ibid.*, Aug. 24, 1779.

[78] *Ibid.*, Aug. 1, 1778.

[79] Murray, *Nehemiah, Or the Struggle for Liberty*, p. 50.

[80] *Boston Gazette*, Mar. 6, 1780, clipped from the *Pa. Gazette*.

Englishmen mean one and the same thing."[81] "Away then," wrote a good American, "with all national prejudices (a due partiality in favour of our own country excepted) and let us learn to look on those who bring fire and sword into our land, and unprovoked exert every power for our ruin, as base and degenerate, the enemies of us and mankind; and let us esteem those who act by the dictates of true honour and sound policy, as worthy of our friendship, as worthy of our admiration and imitation."[82] And at the close of the war, on the anniversary of the battle of Lexington, the Reverend Mr. Payson said the final word on the French alliance: we had learned to look with distrust on France in former years, but after our associations with them, "we are now induced to view and esteem the French by far the most polished, humane, and generous people in the world."[83]

As to the far more serious problem of reconciliation, although there was no disposition among the leaders to stop short of independence, they had to prevent a popular demand for a compromise. Every suggestion of the propagandists—the penalties of submission, the positive advantages of victory, confidence in success, and the depravity of the enemy—all, of course, tended and were meant to build up resistance to defeatist attitudes. There were, however, direct attacks upon the particular propositions.

There had been tentative proposals from the British in 1775 (the North resolutions), and periodically afterward there were either official or unofficial offers or suggestions of peace. British generals frequently issued proclamations urging the people to return to their former loyalties and offering pardon for those who did. These too had to be counteracted. Burgoyne issued in the summer of 1777 a proclamation which so disturbed Washington that he wrote Philip Schuyler: "General Burgoyne, I have no doubt, will practise every art, which his Invention shall point out, to turn their [the people in northern New York] minds and seduce them from their allegiance. He should be counteracted as much as possible, as it is of the last importance to keep them firm and steady in their attachments."[84] Livingston, Washington's right-hand propagandist, parodied the proclamation, as did several others, but his was the cleverest. It was a long poem and appeared in print over the signature, "A New

[81] *Pa. Packet*, Aug. 24, 1779.
[82] *Ibid.*, Nov. 19, 1778.
[83] *A Memorial of Lexington Battle*, p. 14.
[84] *Writings* (Ford), V, 505.

Jerseyman." One stanza stressed Burgoyne's threat to use Indians to pacify the people:

> "If any should so hardened be,
> As to expect impunity,
> Because *procul a fulmine*,
> I will let loose the dogs of hell,
> Ten thousand Indians, who shall yell,
> And foam and tear, and grin and roar,
> And drench their maukeskins in gore;
> To these I'll give full scope and play
> From Ticonderog to Florida;
> They'll scalp your heads, and kick your shins,
> And rip your guts, and flay your skins,
> And of your ears be nimble croppers,
> And make your thumbs tobacco stoppers."[85]

The most serious threat of reconciliation came in the spring and summer of 1778. The British government agreed to repeal the distasteful laws, such as the duty on tea, the coercive measures of 1774, and the law which excluded New Englanders from the Newfoundland fisheries, and to remove the ban on colonial commerce. It gave up the right of taxation, except for the regulation of trade, and promised to use any money collected from a colony within that colony. It guaranteed that no bill altering the charter or government of any colony would be considered except at the request of the colony. The colonists could elect their own governors, judges, and other civil officials. The government promised, moreover, to consider "amicably" and seriously a request for representation in Parliament, and it agreed to put the credit of the British treasury behind the colonial currency issued to prosecute the war. Finally it offered full pardon to everyone engaged in the rebellion. The commissioners were authorized to treat with the commander in chief of the army, or any agency the colonies might elect, and to address it in any style it might desire. Three commissioners were sent to present the offer, Lord Carlisle, Sir George Johnstone, and William Eden.[86] The concessions came too late. Burgoyne's defeat, the French alli-

---

[85] *N. Y. Journal*, Sept. 8, 1777. The original is in Livingston Papers (Mass. Hist. Soc.). See also *Conn. Courant*, Nov. 4, 1776, on Carleton's kindness to Americans in his power: "O Americans! beware of such delusive bait, remember that absolute power is sufficient to corrupt the best man human nature ever produced."

[86] See Philip G. Davidson, "Whig Propagandists of the American Revolution," *Amer. Hist. Rev.*, XXXIX, 447-453.

ance, news of which reached America just a little before the English offer, and the retreat of the British from Philadelphia shortly thereafter greatly cheered the people. But the determined leaders took no chances; until the commissioners left in October, 1778, they kept up a constant fight against them and their proposal.

They flatly denied the alleged advantages of accepting the terms. Representation in a British Parliament had been totally useless to Scotland. What profit could Americans expect? England could not discharge her own debts, much less those of the United States. What conceivable advantage could there be in allowing a foreign country to regulate American trade? Protection and security? These America already had. Nothing in the past indicated that England could protect her American colonies; they had always protected themselves, and now, with the powerful aid of France, security was doubly secure.[87] Financial advantages? Livingston wrecked that idea:

> "And what can be more provoking than for Great Britain, after acknowledging the superiority of our arms, to propound such a controul over our commerce as we remonstrated against before the commencement of the war; and which would infallibly render us and our remotest posterity the slaves and tributaries of a nation venal, corrupt, abandoned, and rushing headlong into inextricable perdition? But to palliate this ruinous measure, it is sugar'd over with 'that the net-proceeds of such duties shall be always paid and applied to and for the use of the colony, &c. in which the same shall be respectively levied'; that is, in plain English, to maintain legions of hungry ministerial dependents, who are to be sent amongst us to accumulate fortunes, and then re-cross the Atlantic to dissipate in luxury what they amassed by iniquity, and thus make room for another set equally penurious and rapacious. For my own part, I would rather pay the tax immediately into the English exchequer, as I think it infinitely more eligible to support a number of rogues in London than in America."[88]

The advantages were illusory, and the proposals were insincere, insidious, and dangerous. England, having failed to win by force of arms, was simply trying by cunning to discourage and divide the

[87] W. H. Drayton in N. Y. *Journal*, July 13, 1778; *Mass. Spy*, Oct. 8, 1778; N. Y. *Journal*, Oct. 5, 1778.   [88] *N. J. Gazette*, May 6, 1778.

country, with no thought of relinquishing her control. Fitzhugh MacKay warned his congregation:

> "Be not deceived by any specious pretenses of friendship that may be offered you by Britain; justly may you suspect the root from whence they spring, hypocrisy and inability conjoined. Were they able to subdue you, they would delight to trample you to mortar, and the crackling of your bones under their horse's hoofs, would be to them an agreeable sound."[89]

"What faith," asked another propagandist, "can be placed in men, who in the very moment of making proposals of reconciliation, could commit the most wanton depredations, and the most horrid barbarities,—*wounds of deadly hate have pierced so deep,* that it is now become impossible ever to effect a cordial reconciliation."[90]

Sir George Johnstone issued a statement interpreted by patriot propagandists as evidence of an attempt to bribe congressional leaders, and Henry Laurens promptly wrote Livingston, "Mr. Johnstone's Declaration in particular cannot escape in New Jersey the correction it deserves, when the proper time shall come of which due notice shall be given, it ought to be bated everywhere."[91] On September 14, "Bob Centinel" warned the people of the threat:

> "ATTENTION!—to British commisaries; British insinuations, and British arts, and take care that their *gold* be not more fatal to you than their *lead*. The *last* has slain its thousands, the *first* may purchase chains for millions. Observe where it is like to go; mark its effects in every order; and let the sovereign remedy be ever kept, a wakeful attention in *the body of the people.*"[92]

The principal argument against a compromise was thus not so much an argument as an emotional appeal based on the depravity of the enemy, a method typical of war propaganda.[93] Instead of returning to a fatal alliance with a degraded and broken empire, propagandists urged redoubled efforts to maintain the independent position of the United States. The introduction to the series of articles signed "An Independent Whig" stated the case fairly:

[89] *American Liberty Asserted,* p. 14. Compare this with the attack on Galloway cited above, Chap. XIX, n. 64. [90] *Mass. Spy,* June 18, 1778.
[91] Laurens Letter-Book, Mar. 6-Sept. 23, 1778. The letter was written early in September. [92] N. Y. *Journal,* Sept. 14, 1778.
[93] E.g., Paine, "Crisis" No. IV; *N. J. Gazette,* June 17, 1778; N. Y. *Journal,* Aug. 3, 1778; *Pa. Packet,* Nov. 5, 1778.

"I intend in the course of a few numbers to prove, that the proposals of reconciliation, which the British Ministry are now making, can proceed only from a conviction of the impossibility of succeeding in the war—That it would be ruin to America to come to an Accomodation with Britain—That our Independence is either already ratified and a war declared in Europe, or that both the one and the other must very speedily happen—That instead of listening to terms of compromise with Britain, our honor, interest and duty demand we should redouble our efforts to give the finishing blow to the remains of British power in America, and to secure to our country, Peace, Safety, and Independence."[94]

Propagandists taunted the commissioners with the weakness of British arms and pointed scornfully to the fact that after three years of war their forces did not command a foot of soil on the continent of America—"Staten Island, York Island, a small part of Long Island, and Rhode Island, circumscribe your power."[95] On the contrary, "our resources are yet far from being exhausted—our cause is just and righteous and is acknowledged as such by almost all the powers of Europe—we have a good and increasing army, with a General at their head, in whom the affections of this extensive continent are united—these combin'd circumstances will enable us by the blessings of Heaven, to expel from our country those lawless invaders."[96] English officials themselves recognized the inevitability of defeat, for, said the propagandists, a British handbill, distributed on the authority of Lord North himself, contained the words, "All hope of conquest is . . . over. *America stands on high ground; France and England must now court her.* We have no possible chance of making peace with her, but by an immediate act of parliament, giving her perfect independence."[97] But one thing remained for the commissioners to do, concluded the propagandists: "Away with your fleets and your armies, acknowledge the independence of America, and as Ambassadors, not Commissioners, solicit a treaty of peace, amity, commerce and alliance with the rising Stars of this

---

[94] *Pa. Packet, Postcript,* Apr. 25, 1778.

[95] Paine, "Crisis" No. VI. [96] *Mass. Spy,* June 18, 1778.

[97] N. Y. *Journal,* Sept. 7, 1778. Cf. Paine, "Crisis" No. VI: "There was a time when Britain disdained to answer, or even hear a petition from America. But that time is passed, and she in her turn is petitioning our acceptance. We now stand on higher ground, and offer her peace; and the time will come when she perhaps in vain, will ask it from us." This was dated October 20, 1778. Paine evidently read the newspapers.

western world. Your nation totters on the brink of a stupendous precipice, and even delay will ruin her."[98]

Subsequent proclamations offering pardon to those who would return to their allegiance, and other proposals of settlement met with the same treatment. The proclamations were parodied, and the terms ridiculed.[99] Each instance was used as a further incentive to renewed efforts:

"The only hope of the enemy is bounded in the idea that we shall not persevere with spirit, and they mean to *murder freedom* while we are *slumbering*. . . . May we now annihilate that hope by such united exertions as shall convince and confound all our enemies . . . THE DAY *IS* COME that DEMANDS such exertions; we now hear the call of GOD in his *Providence*, and *reason* and *nature* join their voice."[100]

Until American soil was freed from the British invader, urged the leaders at every proposal, no settlement was possible. Every foot she held at the time of making the treaty meant just that much more she would get in the final settlement. "Are you willing," asked "The Sentinel" in 1781, "that New-York, and several other of your sea-ports, which they now hold, should be annexed to the Crown of Britain forever?" If so, America would never be free, for England could then control American commerce just as if America still belonged to her, and revenues from imports would go to her, not to the United States.[101]

They dismissed the proclamators and the commissioners with the words: "Trouble us no more with impertinence, but if you wish for an object so desirable as peace, let AMERICAN INDEPENDENCE, from under your master's hand, be amply displayed in the front of your declaration."[102]

[98] N. Y. *Journal*, July 6, 1778.
[99] E.g., *Boston Gazette*, Apr. 5, 1779:

> "Whereas the Congress leagued with France,
> Has led us many a Hellish dance,
> And did with studied disrespect,
> Our peaceful overtures reject;
> And to disgrace of human nature,
> Still persecutes their fellow creatures,
> Hanging the honest hearted Tory,
> Who dared oppose their rising glory:
> We publish this our proclamation,
> To every man in every station."

[100] *Boston Gazette*, July 17, 1780. See also *ibid.*, Oct. 2, 1780; *Pa. Packet*, Nov. 4, 1780; *Conn. Courant*, Mar. 6, 1781; *Mass. Spy*, Jan. 18, Jan. 24, 1781.
[101] *Conn. Courant*, July 3, 1781. See also *Pa. Packet*, Mar. 25, Apr. 1, Apr. 15, 1780.
[102] *Conn. Courant*, Mar. 20, 1781.

XX

VEHICLES OF PROPAGANDA

THE SUGGESTIONS of the Revolutionary period were not so industriously propagated as those which came before. Visual, oral, dramatic, and pictorial appeals were relatively less important in disseminating Revolutionary propaganda than were the written appeals. The need for economy; the fact that the lower-class leaders, who had aided materially in staging the former demonstrations, were now in the army; and the general feeling, before mentioned, that such measures were not so necessary as before—all contributed to lessen the number of demonstrations and to diminish the use of other vehicles of suggestion.

The only prewar anniversaries still celebrated during the Revolution were the two Massachusetts days, the fifth of March and the nineteenth of April. An address was annually delivered by a local minister in Boston, and occasionally elsewhere, but the elaborate demonstrations of former years were no longer staged. The important celebrations during the war were those on the Fourth of July, on the anniversary of the French alliance, and on the news of a victory.

The Fourth of July celebrations, which began in 1777, were usually managed by the militia, who generally planned a salute of thirteen guns, an address, and an entertainment followed by thirteen toasts. Congress arranged an unusually magnificent celebration in 1778 with a great display of fireworks and a parade. The local patriots in Philadelphia dressed up a woman of the town in a caricature of the huge headdresses affected by the Tory women, to their great mortification.[1]

The celebrations on the news of the French alliance, particularly in Boston, were considered necessary by some to counteract the Tory propaganda against it. The Massachusetts Council gave an "Elegant Entertainment" at Marston's House for the officers of the newly

[1] *The Letters of Richard Henry Lee*, I, 421. For other celebrations see *Gazette of the State of S. C.*, July 7, 1777, July 8, 1778; *N. J. Gazette*, July 8, 1778; *Boston Gazette*, July 6, 1778; *Mass. Spy*, July 16, 1778, recounting a dinner given by General Gates at White Plains; and *Conn. Courant*, July 21, 1778.

arrived French frigate, and James Warren reported to Sam Adams his doubtful approval: "this was attended with the fireing of cannon, etc. and seemd to give great Satisfaction, and if not quite conformable to the rigid rules and Oeconomy of a Young Republic may under our Circumstances be good policy."[2] Hancock, dubious about the alliance, absented himself, and some time later Adams worriedly wrote Warren: "In my opinion, it is in a great Degree impolitick at this Juncture to suffer an Odium to be cast on the Count D'Estaing. If there should be a Disposition to do it I am perswaded Men of Discretion & Influence will check it."[3] When the alliance had proved sufficiently popular, Hancock joined the procession and gave a series of public and private dinners for the French officers. The General Court gave an elaborate dinner for them in Faneuil Hall in September; afterward there was a military parade and a series of toasts.[4] The Continental Congress and the town of York celebrated the alliance in a spontaneous burst of enthusiasm, and Washington's little army shot off some of its much needed powder, cheering its commander and his new allies in a public review.[5] On the first anniversary of the alliance a celebration was carefully prepared to hearten the troops. There were the usual fireworks for everybody and a ball for the officers, but an unusual feature was added. A set of thirteen illuminated scenes depicted the high lights of the struggle for independence. Well chosen, they dramatized nearly every aspect of Revolutionary propaganda: the battle of Lexington, the burning of Charlestown, the separation of the colonies from England (shown by a broken arch), England as a decaying empire, America as a rising empire, Louis XVI, the leaders in Congress, Franklin, the battle of Saratoga, the convention at Saratoga, a sea fight, representations of the dead heroes—Warren, Montgomery, Mercer, Wooster, Nash—and finally, Peace and her blessings—harvest, ships, cities, and commerce.[6]

Celebrations of military victories were natural expressions of joy and were hastily arranged. Occasionally, however, plans were made.

[2] *Warren-Adams Letters*, II, 9.

[3] *Writings of Samuel Adams*, IV, 60.   [4] *Warren-Adams Letters*, II, 48 f.

[5] N. Y. *Journal*, June 15, 1778; *Mass. Spy*, May 26, 1778; Burnett, *Letters of Members of Cont. Cong.*, III, 223 n.; and *Conn. Journal*, May 6, 1778.

[6] N. Y. *Journal*, Mar. 15, 1779. Major General David Wooster of the Connecticut militia was killed on April 27, 1777, when Tryon raided Danbury. Brigadier General Francis Nash was killed at Germantown, and Brigadier General Hugh Mercer was killed at Princeton.

The officers in camp at Peekskill in 1781 celebrated the anniversary of Burgoyne's surrender, and Charles Wilson Peale executed a large number of transparent scenes to welcome Washington after the surrender at Yorktown; these scenes showed the foundations of independence—the Stamp Act, the duties on tea, and the battles of Lexington and Breed's Hill.[7] They were exceptions, however.

The old demonstrations of the Sons of Liberty with their effigies were practically gone. When Arnold was caught in treason, effigies were displayed—Arnold in a cart with the Devil, Arnold in a coffin with the Devil, Arnold on a gallows with the Devil. Philadelphia staged a parade with effigies of Arnold and the Devil and with transparencies showing the enormity of Arnold's crime. Continental officers, militia, and the city guard, together with leading officials on horseback, formed the procession.[8]

Public addresses and sermons were relatively as important in disseminating propaganda during the war as before. Opportunity was given for persons of authority to influence the people on such occasions as the anniversary celebrations and fast and thanksgiving days, and in sermons or addresses to the troops. Ministers as usual carried the burden of this work, especially in the North, but one of the finest examples of Revolutionary oratory was delivered in Charleston on the second anniversary of independence by the historian, David Ramsay. It merits detailed analysis.[9]

The twenty-seven-year-old patriot enumerated in detail the advantages which would accrue from independence. After extolling the virtues of republican simplicity as opposed to monarchical extravagance, idleness, and false refinement (a popular theme in America), he enlarged upon the great boon independence would confer upon the arts and sciences and then turned to the important matters of commerce and manufacturing. Unfettered by a throttling British monopoly, "we may expect to see the colors of France, Spain, Holland, Prussia, Portugal, and those of every other maritime power, waving on our coasts; whilst Americans unfurl the thirteen stripes

[7] *N. J. Gazette*, Dec. 12, 1781. See also *Conn. Journal*, Nov. 5, 1777; *Mass. Spy*, Nov. 8, 1781, Nov. 22, 1781—accounts of the celebrations in the army camps on the news of Yorktown. In Brookfield the Sons of Liberty, meaning simply the local patriots, staged the affair. The unlighted windows in Philadelphia were broken the night the news reached there.—*Diary of Jacob Hiltzheimer*, p. 46.

[8] *Pa. Packet*, Oct. 3, 1780, Jan. 16, 1781; *N. J. Gazette*, Oct. 28, 1780.

[9] Conveniently found in Niles, *Principles and Acts of the Revolution*, pp. 64-72.

in the remotest harbors of the world." And here followed naturally the appeal which has stirred millions to patriotic fervor: "Our stately oaks, the greater part of which would probably have withered in their native spots, had we remained subjects, will now be converted into ships of war, to ride triumphant on the ocean, and to carry American thunder around the world."

Returning after this brief interlude of nascent jingoism to the oppressive effects of British trade restrictions, he exhibited the particular advantages of independence to Carolina. The restrictions on rice were particularly burdensome, he contended, for England did not consume more than five thousand barrels a year; the charge for unloading, reloading, and shifting each cask was immense, "though it served no other purpose, but to procure jobs for British coopers and wharfingers." But the crowning iniquity was not the system, but the origin of the system: a certain ship captain, prevented from getting a cargo in the colonies because the wharfs were all taken up by ships loading rice for Portugal, returned to England in a high dudgeon, representing to officials there that the shipment of rice to Portugal was prejudicial to British trade. "How could our trade flourish, or our produce bring its full value, while restricted by a legislature so regardless of our interest, that a petty captain, to secure himself a cargo, could prevent our staple from being sent directly to a foreign market?" By thus placing the whole burden of blame upon the shoulders of one man and a reckless legislature, Ramsay showed himself well versed in the art of dealing with a crowd; a public speech designed to influence opinion is no place for a reasoned discussion of commercial complexities.

Throughout the entire speech he appealed to each interest of the people. The millions of acres of western lands were to be sold to new settlers to defray the cost of the war; the annual quit rents, formerly paid to the King, would obviate taxation in the future; the thrones of despotism and tyranny would totter when their subjects saw by the example of America that the happiness of the people is the end of all government. From the new state constitutions, which, "formed on the justest principles, promise fair to give the most perfect protection to life, liberty and property, equally to the poor and the rich," from these even England might profit. So grand was the prospect, so signal the present successes, that the special interposition

REPRESENTATION of the FIGURES exhibited and paraded through the Streets of Philadelphia, on *Saturday*, the 30*th* of *September*, 1780.

DESCRIPTION of the FIGURES.

A STAGE raised on the body of a cart, on which was an effigy of General ARNOLD fitting; this was dressed in regimentals, had two faces, emblematical of his traiterous conduct, a mask in his left hand, and a letter in his right from Beelzebub, telling him that he had done all the mischief he could do, and now he must hang himself.

At the back of the General was a figure of the Devil, dressed in black robes, shaking a purse of money at the general's left ear, and in his right hand a pitchfork, ready to drive him into hell as the reward due for the many crimes which the thief of gold had made him commit.

In the front of the stage and before General Arnold, was placed a large lanthorn of transparent paper, with the consequences of his crimes thus delineated, i. e. on one part, General Arnold on his knees before the Devil, who is pulling him into the flames—a label from the General's mouth with these words, "My dear Sir, I have served you faithfully;" to which the Devil replies, "And I'll reward you." On another front, two papers from a gallows, inscribed, "The Traitor's reward." And on the front of the lanthorn was wrote the following:

"MAJOR, GENERAL BENEDICT ARNOLD, late COMMANDER of the FORT WEST-POINT. THE CRIME OF THIS MAN IS HIGH TREASON." "He has deserted the important post WEST-POINT, on Hudson's River, committed to his charge by His Excellency the Commander in Chief, and is gone off to the enemy at New-York."

"His design to have given up this fortress to our enemies, has been discovered by the goodness of the Omniscient Creator, who has not only prevented his carrying it into execution, but has thrown into our hands ANDRE, the Adjutant-General of their army, who was detected in the character of a spy.

"The treachery of this ungrateful General is held up to public view, for the exposition of infamy; and to proclaim with joyful acclamation, another instance of the interposition of bounteous Providence.

"The effigy of this ingrate is therefore hanged (for want of his body) as a Traitor to his native country, and a Betrayer of the laws of honour."

The procession began about four o'clock, in the following order:

Several Gentlemen mounted on horse-back.
A line of Continental Officers.
Sundry Gentlemen in a line.
A guard of the City Infantry.
Just before the cart, drums and fifes playing the Rogues March.
Guards on each side.

The procession was attended with a numerous concourse of people, who after expressing their abhorrence of the Treason and the Traitor, committed him to the flames, and left both the effigy and the original to sink into ashes and oblivion.

'TWAS *Arnold's* post fir *Harry* fought,
  Arnold ne'er enter'd in his thought,
How ends the bargain? let us fee,
The fort is fafe, as fafe can be,
ı is favouring *per force* muft die,
His view's laid bare to ev'ry eye;
His money's gone—and lo! he gains
One fcoundrel more for all his pains.
ANDRE was *juſt*, *true*, and *brave*,
And in his room, he buys a knave.
'Tis fure ordain'd, that *Arnold* cheats
All thofe, of courfe, with whom he treats.
Now let the *Devil* fufpect a bite
Or *Arnold* cheats him of his right.

Mothers fhall fill their children, and fay—Arnold!—
Arnold fhall be the bug-bear of their years,
Arnold!—wild, treacherous, and leagued with Satan.

A Philadelphia Broadside on Arnold's Treason.
By courtesy of the New York Public Library.

of Providence was manifest, making it "impious to disbelieve the final establishment of our heaven-protected independence."

And in one final galaxy of generalities, he brought hope to all before him, hope that was vague and intangible, but beautiful in its unreality: "Our sun of political happiness is already risen, and hath lifted its head over the mountains, illuminating our hemisphere with liberty, light, and polished life. Our independence will redeem one quarter of the globe from tyranny and oppression, and consecrate it the chosen seat of truth, justice, freedom, learning and religion."

Ministers usually delivered the patriotic addresses on fast days and anniversaries. Although they naturally adapted their remarks to the particular occasion, they always laid stress on two themes—the evidences of divine guidance and the depravity of the enemy. The sermons preached on the anniversaries of the Boston Massacre and the battle of Lexington laid the whole blame for the war on George III and used the depredations of the troops as sufficient justification for independence and the continuance of the war. "The shocking massacre," said John Lathrop in 1778, "may be consider'd as the commencement of hostilities by the British troops in America, and the inhabitants of these States, must have been justified by the impartial world, had they resolved from that moment, never to suffer one in the livery of George III to walk this ground."[10]

Jacob Cushing in his sermon in 1778 on the battle of Lexington stated clearly, perhaps without realizing it, the function of the war propagandist: others he said, had described the events, "I have only to stir up your pure minds, by way of remembrance of the transactions of that awful day."[11]

Election sermons in New England, dealing with the familiar topic of the duty of the rulers to the people and the duty of the people to the rulers, naturally showed how George III had been faithless to his duty and had exercised his power to his subjects' detriment, and dwelt upon the duty of the people to defend their rulers and George Washington. These sermons, with few exceptions, also stressed the justice of the war, begun by British tyranny, and were powerful appeals to action. Jonas Clark, for example, in 1781, was still talking as he had talked so many years ago at Lexington:

[10] *A Discourse, Preached March the Fifth, 1778*, p. 11. Jacob Green delivered one in Princeton in 1778, and Fitzhugh MacKay one to the soldiers near Lancaster in 1778.
[11] *Divine Judgments upon Tyrants*, p. 21.

the enemy was preparing a crushing blow, "May GOD AL-MIGHTY defeat and disappoint them!!" but Americans must rouse themselves by the greatness of the cause and the distresses of the bleeding country: "O my fathers and brethren! ALL! all is yet at stake!—All may yet be lost, if we rise not, as one man, to the noble cause!"[12]

Fast and thanksgiving sermons varied little from the others. Several of them were delivered to soldiers. On the public thanksgiving ordered after the surrender of Burgoyne, Israel Evans preached a sermon which emphasized, as did all the others on that day, the evident hand of God in American affairs. Printed copies of this sermon were distributed without charge to the soldiers who were there.[13]

The sermons contained two other themes of importance. The ministers were naturally asked if the French alliance endangered the protestant religion in America, and in these sermons they answered wholeheartedly in favor of the alliance; they interpreted it, indeed, as another of Heaven's special dispensations. The second theme is aptly summed up in the text they used so frequently: "Cursed be he that keepeth back his sword from blood." These sermons, nearly everyone of them by a Congregational or Presbyterian minister, were of prime importance in maintaining a war psychosis.

Revolutionary songs, judged at least by modern standards, were definitely poor in quality, although contemporary evidence has it that some of them were sung and enjoyed. A few of these were written in an elevated, ennobled tone; others like Nathaniel Niles' "The American Hero" were deeply religious. The majority, however, were either light, satirical ditties gibing at the British, or heavier songs lauding America and her leaders.

"Yankee Doodle," the only one that has held its place as a war song, appears to have been unintentionally popularized by some British troops in Boston. The air was an old one, dating from Cromwellian England, and the words, satirizing the Americans, may have been written at the time of the French and Indian War and adapted to the later period. However that may be, in March, 1775,

---

[12] *A Sermon Preached before his Excellency John Hancock* (1781), p. 68.

[13] *A Discourse, December 18, 1777.* He delivered another one to the soldiers on the anniversary of the surrender. David Avery, *The Lord is to be Praised for the Triumphs of his Power,* preached on the same day, stressed the same themes.

some troops in Boston tarred and feathered a man for buying a gun from a soldier. They pinned a label on his back, "AMERICAN LIBERTY, OR A SPECIMEN OF DEMOCRACY," and then played "Yankee Doodle" as they rode him through the streets.[14] The Whigs took it up after some British troops (who had gone to the aid of their compatriots just after the first engagement at Lexington), had played Yankee Doodle, which, said the account, "had become their favorite tune ever since that notable exploit, which did so much honor to the troops of Britain's king, of tarring and feathering a poor countryman in Boston."[15] In November, Sears and his mob marched out of New York playing the tune after destroying Rivington's press, and thereafter it became almost the national war song.[16]

There were several songs which ridiculed the British. A song to the tune "Smile Britannia," written in 1778, is a fair example:

> "We laugh at war's alarms,
>   Its' toils and arts we know,
> And how to wield our arms,
> And when to charge the foe:
> Fam'd Britain (in the trade compleat)
> Excell us only in—retreat."[17]

A song called "The Hatchet & Block, or L—d B—'s Triumph," to the tune of "There was a Magpie," was printed on a broadside and distributed among the troops. Two of its twenty-six stanzas are a sufficient sample:

> "Old England protector of freedom and trade,
>   No more shall her power dispute;
> As a province to France to[o] soon will be made,
> Thru the obstinate maxims of B—
>
> .   .   .   .   .   .
>
> "One hope still remains on America's shore,

[14] N. Y. *Journal*, Mar. 30, 1775.
[15] *Pa. Journal*, May 24, 1775.   [16] *Ibid.*, Dec. 6, 1775.
[17] *Cont. Journal*, Feb. 12, 1778. "A Song, On the Surrender of General Burgoyne" contained forty-six stanzas. The forty-fifth:
> "Brave boys we'll now go & visit Lord Howe,
>   With powder and ball we will line him,
> With courage hold out & we shall without doubt,
> Before the next winter Burgoyne him."
—New York Public Library, Broadsides. At least some of the songs written before 1776 were still being sung.

Which thousands of BRITONS will suit;
To fly there to live when freedoms no more,
And curse the remembrance of B—"[18]

The songs which lauded Washington were numerous and, unhappily, for the most part very poor. Jonathan Mitchell Sewall's "War and Washington," written in 1775, was sung by the troops everywhere, and Benjamin Towne issued it on a broadside in 1779. Less familiar is a song entitled "GENERAL WASHINGTON"; the sheet on which it was printed called it "A New Favorite Song, at the American CAMP":

"Your dark unfathom'd Councils, our weakest Heads defeat,
Our Children rout your Armies, our Boats destroy your Fleet;
And to complete the dire Disgrace, cooped up within a Town,
You live the Scorn of all our Host, the Slaves of
WASHINGTON.

.   .   .   .

"Yet think not thirst for Glory, unsheathes our vengeful
Swords,
To rend your Bands asunder, and cast away your Cords;
'Tis Heav'n-born FREEDOM fires us all, and strengthens
each brave SON,
From him who humbly guides the Plough, to God-like
WASHINGTON.

.   .   .   .

"Should George too choice of Britons, to foreign Realms apply,
And madly arm half Europe, yet still we would defy,
Turk, Russian, Jew, or Infidel, or all these Powers in one,
While HANCOCK crowns our Senate, our Camp great
WASHINGTON."[19]

And finally, there were the numerous variants of "God Save the King." Two of these were written by friends of America in Holland and sent by one of them to America "with the most hearty wish that they may be a fuel to the precious fire, which is burning in every American heart." One of them follows:

[18] *Ibid.* The reference is to Lord Bute, still being vilified; why not have spelled his name out this late?
[19] N. Y. Hist. Soc., Broadsides. This was published in Massachusetts; it is listed in Ford, *Massachusetts Broadsides*, No. 2038.

> "God save the Thirteen States!
> Long rule the United States!
> God save our States!
> Make us victorious;
> Happy and glorious;
> No Tyrants over us;
> God save our States!"[20]

The stage was a poor vehicle of propaganda. Dramatic literature appeared, but there is little evidence that even the best examples of Revolutionary propaganda in the list were ever staged. Mercy Warren's third play, *The Motley Assembly* (at least it has been with some reason attributed to her)[21] resembled closely the *Group;* this time she satirized, not the Tory leaders, but typical members of the Tory society in Boston. There is no evidence to show that any of the dramas was staged during the period. When Addison's "The Tragedy of Cato" was played in Portsmouth, New Hampshire, in 1778, an actor read an epilogue, written by Jonathan Mitchell Sewall, comparing Rome and America:

> "Rise, then, my countrymen! for fight prepare,
> Gird on your swords, and fearless rush to war!
> For your grieved country nobly dare to die,
> And empty all your veins for liberty.
> No pent up Utica contracts your powers,
> But the whole boundless continent is yours!"[22]

It may have been that similar instances occurred, but the need for economy and the old dislike of plays in the North make it unlikely.

WRITTEN SUGGESTIONS

The written appeal was relatively much more important, but there was still a decline. The number of publications listed in Evans' *American Bibliography* decreases steadily, except for one year, from

---

[20] *Pa. Packet,* Jan. 1, 1780. The other was much like it:
> "God bless the thirteen States,
> And save for ev'r our fates
> From tyranny."

[21] See Quinn, *American Drama,* p. 53.

[22] Quoted in Tyler, *Literary History,* II, 225. Even so close a student of the American drama as Professor Quinn could find few instances of staged productions.

1775 to 1783, the largest drop being from the high number 852 in 1775, to 590 in 1776. Only 360 items are listed for 1782.[23]

The pamphlet literature of the Revolution, for example, is markedly inferior in both quantity and quality to that of the pre-revolutionary years. With the exception of Paine's first *Crisis*, no really great piece of Revolutionary writing appeared in this form. The pamphlet was still valued by some above the newspaper; the New York council of safety wrote the delegates to the Continental Congress that the report on the depravity of the enemy, written in 1777, should be published and widely distributed, "which they think cannot be so well done by parcels in a News Paper, as altogether in a Pamphlet."[24] The Massachusets General Court in 1781 printed an address to the people in a pamphlet, and one of Thomas McKean's charges to a grand jury was so published at its request.[25] Some of the longer prison accounts—*A Narrative of Colonel Ethan Allen's Captivity*, and *A Narrative of the Capture and Treatment of John Dodge by the English at Detroit*, for instance—and the dramatic literature described above, were published in pamphlets. However, the most important single use of the pamphlet during the Revolution was for the publication of sermons. These sermons, of course, were public addresses, delivered on some special occasion; rarely were ordinary pulpit sermons published. Very few of the pamphlets were issued in more than one edition, and the controversial pamphlets of the earlier days simply were not written during the Revolution.

The newspapers carried the bulk of the revolutionary propaganda, but even the use of the newspapers decreased. The number of papers dropped from the prewar high of forty-two in 1775 to a low of thirty-five in 1780 and went back to forty-one in 1782. A few papers became semiweekly—one or two of the German papers and the *Pennsylvania Journal*, for example—but many were reduced in size, and several had to suspend for lack of paper or lack of support. A good many changes took place during the seven years; the Tory papers were almost all brought to an abrupt end by the battle

---

[23] In 1775, 852; 1776, 590; 1777, 487; 1778, 461; 1779, 512; 1780, 387; 1781, 371; 1782, 360. Many items are not in Evans, of course; however, these figures are sufficiently accurate to show proportions.

[24] William Duer Papers, I, 45.

[25] *An Address to the People of Massachusetts-Bay*, and McKean, *A Charge Delivered to the Grand-Jury . . . April 21, 1778*.

of Lexington, and several of the Whig papers were interrupted, a few permanently. Some doubtful papers switched back and forth with the swing of the armies.

The one New Hampshire paper of any value to the Whigs was the old *New Hampshire Gazette*. Daniel Fowle had been censured by the provincial congress, and there was no paper from January 17 to May 25, 1776. On May 25, Benjamin Dearborn began to publish the *Freeman's Journal* but transferred the paper back to Fowle later in the year. The effect of the rebuke had been good. The new paper was, as Sam Adams would have said, serviceable to the cause. Local contributions were few, but nearly every issue contained an essay or so from other papers, a far better average than most others maintained. In 1778 Fowle reverted to the old name, the *New Hampshire Gazette*, and for a time the paper was printed in both Exeter and Portsmouth. After 1779 the paper resumed its former lethargy and was of little value in the dissemination of propaganda.[26]

Important changes occurred in the Massachusetts papers. The *Boston Gazette* of the old days was now quite different. Edes and Gill broke up a long-standing partnership in April, 1775, and the *Gazette* was temporarily suspended until June, 1775. Sam Adams went to Philadelphia, and without him the *Boston Gazette*, continued by Edes, lacked the fire of the old paper; fuel and bellows were lacking. Edes took the *Gazette* to Watertown when the provincial congress fled from Boston, and thereafter he was the official printer of the congress. The *Boston Gazette* was better supplied with local contributions than most of the papers, and, as it borrowed a good many items, it was reasonably well filled with political and exhortatory essays. There was a marked falling off in 1779, but there was a distinct revival in 1780 which lasted until 1782. Gill established the *Continental Journal* in May, 1776; it was about the same sort of paper as the *Gazette*. Its militant heading—"The entire prosperity of every state, depends upon the discipline of its armies. *The King of Prussia*"—was reflected in the articles which appeared with fair regularity in its columns. It too was serviceable to the patriots through the early years of the war, fell off in 1779, as did the *Gazette*, but revived its publication of essays on the war in 1780.

[26] Two other papers were begun during the war—the *Exeter Journal*, published by Zechariah Fowle from Feb. 17, 1778 to Mar. 23, 1779 (last known issue), and the *Hanover Dresden Mercury*, from Mar. 4 to Aug. 9, 1779 (last known issue). Both were weeklies.

The best newspaper propaganda was in the *Massachusetts Spy,* published in the first part of the war at Watertown by Isaiah Thomas. The paper was taken over by two other printers in 1776, and in August, 1777, by still a third, but on June 18, 1778, Thomas returned as editor. In spite of Thomas' personal patriotism, which had made the *Spy* such a good revolutionary paper in 1775, the change of editorship did not materially affect the paper as a medium of propaganda. His return, indeed, made little change in this regard, and even he switched in 1779 from war propaganda to the controversial essays on the Lee-Deane argument which filled every paper for almost a year. The *Spy* was an even better revolutionary organ in 1780 and 1781 than either the *Gazette* or the *Journal.*

Massachusetts had more papers than any other state except Pennsylvania; at least seven others were published at one time or another during the war. The old *Essex Gazette* was moved to Cambridge in 1775, and its name changed to the *New England Chronicle.* In 1776 it underwent another transformation; moved to Boston, it became on September 19, 1776, the *Independent Chronicle,* published by Powars and Willis. John Mycall was still publishing the *Essex Journal,* and in 1778 the *Independent Ledger* and the *Evening Post* were established; the latter became the *Morning Chronicle* in 1780. Mary Crouch started the *Salem Gazette* in 1781, and a year later, too late to influence the war, the first paper published in Springfield appeared, the *Massachusetts Gazette.*[27]

The four Connecticut papers published in 1775 went through the war with only one major change. Alexander Robertson left the *Norwich Packet* in 1775; under Trumbull's sole direction the paper became a patriot organ. The *Courant,* the *Gazette,* and the *Journal,* published at Hartford, New London, and New Haven, respectively, were about of equal value as agencies. All depended largely upon other than local contributions, but they borrowed extensively. Essays on the war were printed uniformly but not in great quantities during the seven years. The *Packet* was not so important a paper from this standpoint as were the others.[28]

The Whigs lost a good revolutionary organ in Rhode Island

[27] *American Gazette,* Rogers and Russel, a weekly, was published just from June 18, 1776, to July 30, 1776.
[28] Only scattered numbers of the *Norwich Packet* have been consulted, but if those numbers were typical the paper was less used as a medium of propaganda.

when the arrival of the British in 1776 forced the removal of Solomon Southwick and his *Newport Mercury*. No paper was published there until the British withdrew in 1780 and Southwick returned, except for fifteen issues of the *Newport Gazette*, published by John Howe from January to April, 1777. The *Providence Gazette* was continuously published, however, and in 1779 the *American Journal and General Advertiser* was started, which lasted two years.

The Whig papers of New York, excluded from the city, were published in various places during the war. Holt kept up the *Journal*, moving as the occasion demanded, with breaks from August, 1776, to July, 1777, and from October, 1777, to May, 1778. It was suspended on November 6, 1780, because of the scarcity of paper and the lack of support; it began again in July, 1781, but ran only until January, 1782, and was not revived until after the war. In the intervals, however, Holt published an excellent war paper. He printed a great deal of military news, items from other newspapers, comments on conditions in the army, and hortatory articles. The paper was particularly useful to the patriots in 1778; nearly every one of the major series of articles on the peace proposals appeared in it, as did a good many single essays. There were fewer in 1779, but more than were found in most of the other papers. Samuel Loudon's *New York Packet* was first printed in January, 1777, and continued through the war. Loudon was disciplined by the provincial congress for reprinting some articles which had appeared in Gaine's *New York Gazette and Weekly Mercury*. The chairman of the committee of safety, which heard his explanation and apology, declared that although the congress did not desire to restrict the liberty of the press it would not employ any person "who shall do things inimical to the cause of American freedom."[29] These were the only patriot papers printed in New York until 1782, when the *New York Gazetteer* was set up in Albany and the *New York Morning Post* was published in New York City; these came too late to have any effect on the war.[30]

Pennsylvania had more papers than any of the states, and they changed bewilderingly. The occupation of the city by the British made some of the printers leave, but others preferred to change

[29] *Journals of the New York Provincial Congress*, I, 781.

[30] John Anderson published a short-lived paper, the *Constitutional Gazette*, which ran for a year after August, 1775.

their policy rather than their place of business. The three best patriot papers were the *Packet,* the *Gazette,* and the *Journal.* The *Gazette* and the *Journal* suspended publication during the occupation of the city, but the *Packet* followed the government to Lancaster. It was one of the best vehicles the propagandists had in any state. It printed all of the essays on the British commissioners in 1778, and all through 1779 and 1780 it was very serviceable; a large number of its pieces were against the numerous local Tories. The *Journal,* on the contrary, which had been one of the best of the prewar agencies, was definitely poor in this regard during the war. It suspended publication during the British occupation of Philadelphia, and even after it began again its propaganda was confined chiefly to the poets' corner. The *Pennsylvania Gazette,* revived at York on the request and at the expense of the Continental Congress,[31] was its official organ, and in it were published the communications of the Congress to the people. Benjamin Towne's *Pennsylvania Evening Post* was published as a British paper in Philadelphia during the stay of the troops there, but before and after that period it occasionally, but only occasionally, printed war propaganda in the form of essays or articles. The only other patriot paper of any importance was the *Freeman's Journal,* printed by Francis Bailey under the editorship of Philip Freneau. This paper began publication in April, 1781, and was an excellent medium. Of the numerous and ephemeral German papers, the most important patriot one was Henry Miller's *Pennsylvanischer Staatsbote,* which, after suspending publication during the British occupancy, began again in September, 1778, only to stop permanently in May, 1779.[32]

Delaware had no papers in this period, but two were established in New Jersey. Governor Livingston was responsible for the first paper in New Jersey, which had suffered before because of its proximity to New York and Philadelphia. He recommended to the legislature in October, 1777, that a paper be printed, the government to underwrite the expenses of an issue of seven hundred copies. The legislature passed a bill to that effect, and Isaac Collins issued the

[31] Burnett, *Letters of Members of Cont. Cong.,* II, 523; *Letters of R. H. Lee,* I, 333.
[32] Six others were printed at one time or another, most of them lasting less than a year. Several were Tory. In 1782 the *Independent Gazetteer* was begun. The other Pennsylvania papers were pro-British.

first copy of the *New Jersey Gazette* on December 5, 1777.[33] The paper was supplied with articles in 1778 by Livingston himself, and under his guidance Collins reprinted some from other papers. After Livingston gave up his public writing, however, the paper contained little war propaganda. The second paper was published at the suggestion of Washington, who wanted a paper for his troops at Morristown. General Knox mentioned the matter to Shepard Kollock, who began publishing the *New Jersey Journal* in February, 1779. The soldiers subscribed liberally to it, and, as a result of its military sponsorship, the paper contained excellent war news and good accounts of activities in other states.[34]

No southern paper equalled the *Boston Gazette*, the New York *Journal*, or the *Pennsylvania Packet*. The *Maryland Journal* was the only Maryland paper that lived through the war, but it suffered an eclipse because William Goddard, its publisher, took up Charles Lee's fight with Washington. Dunlap's *Maryland Gazette* stopped in 1779. The paper most used by the propagandists was Green's *Maryland Gazette*. It had suspended publication in 1777 for want of paper, but Fred and Sam Green revived it in 1779, and in 1780 it was full of exhortatory articles. The Virginia papers had troubled histories and were little used by the propagandists. Three—Purdie's, Dixon's, and Clarkson's—held the field until 1779, when Purdie's ended. The other two lasted only a short time longer. Clarkson's ceased about December, 1780, and Dixon's was probably destroyed by the British in May, 1781. Richard Henry Lee was much distressed by this unfortunate situation and complained frequently of the lack of printers and newspapers in Virginia.[35] The invasion of the state made it difficult to arrange for a press, but in December, 1781, John Dunlop and James Hayes issued a new *Virginia Gazette*. The state had refused the contract to Dixon and Nicolson, publishers of the last *Gazette*, because doubtful of their loyalty, but Dixon's

[33] James Melvin Lee, *History of American Journalism*, pp. 59 f.

[34] *Ibid.*, pp. 60 f.

[35] *Letters of R. H. Lee*, II, 230, 238. He wrote Arthur Lee, apropos of a British proclamation: "Have Congress seen the very artful and dangerous proclamation lately published. . . . It is published at N. York the 27th of december and is now most diligently circulating in the Southern States, whilst we have no Press & no means of counteracting its malignity—Surely Congress will publish such an answer as it easily admits of and cause a sufficiency of Hand bills to be printed for dispersion, especially in these southern parts where a want of Presses renders us in a great measure a prey to such artifices as this proclamation—I think that no time is to be lost in doing this."—*Ibid.*, II, 225.

paper had been at one time a good Whig paper, much used by the propagandists.

The *North-Carolina Gazette,* published by James Davis at New-bern, was the only paper in the state, and it stopped in November, 1778. Even during the period of its publication it was little used as a medium, although occasional propaganda pieces did appear. For three years there was no paper at all in Georgia. Johnston stopped printing the *Gazette* early in 1776, and the British *Royal Georgia Gazette* was not published until 1779.

The South Carolina papers were likewise little used as vehicles of propaganda. Powell's old *Gazette* had stopped in 1775, but in 1777 Peter Timothy revived it under the name *The Gazette of the State of South Carolina.* It lasted until May, 1780, when the British took Charleston, but it contained only comparatively few items in the nature of propaganda. The *South Carolina Gazette; and Country Journal,* which ceased to appear after December, 1779, was of little import as a medium. The *South Carolina and American General Gazette,* slightly used by either Whig or Tory, stopped in May, 1780, but Wells stayed in Charleston and printed the British paper, the *Royal Gazette.*[36]

It is evident from this brief survey of the newspapers available to the propagandists that they had more opportunities than they used; not a single paper during the Revolution was as important in the development of favorable attitudes as several of the prerevolutionary ones. The northern papers were more extensively used than the southern, but over the country as a whole only a dozen or so were more than moderately active disseminators of propaganda, even at periods of crisis.

When the papers were used, they were used effectively; the dominant themes of revolutionary propaganda were repeated and emphasized in a variety of forms. The propagandists comprehended the method of handling news accounts. It must be remembered that inadequate news facilities and low standards of journalism insured inaccuracy. Conflicting, imperfect accounts were inevitable; there is,

---

[36] *The Vermont Gazette, or Green Mountain Post Boy,* published by Judah Spooner and Timothy Green at Westminster, was the first paper in Vermont. It lasted, however, only from February to about December, 1781, perhaps a bit longer. Its heading was a two-line poem: "Pliant as reeds, where streams of freedom glide; Firm as the Hills, to stem oppression's tide."

however, this peculiarity about the conflicting accounts—the conflict was invariably most marked, not between two American (or two British) accounts of the same event, but between an American and a British account.

Compare, for example, the accounts of the battle of Princeton. Except that the names of the officers and the location of the battle are the same, the two descriptions are at such variance that they seem to refer to two entirely different battles. The patriot account stated: "It is difficult precisely to ascertain the loss we have sustained in the two engagements, but we think we have lost about forty men killed, and had near double the number wounded." The enemy loss was much greater, and there were at least four hundred wounded and taken prisoner.[37] Gaine's version described the heroic feat of the 17th regiment, less than three hundred men, who engaged the rebel army of five or six thousand and forced its retreat. The loss was twenty killed and eighty wounded, whereas the rebels lost near four hundred.[38] The accounts of Wayne's attack on Stony Point are equally at odds. The American estimate of losses listed twenty-five killed and fifty wounded on the patriot side, while the British losses included sixty killed, sixty wounded, and four hundred and five taken prisoner.[39] Rivington's estimate did not include a statement as to the American losses—"The loss of the enemy, though considerable, is not yet known"—but gave the British losses as thirty killed, forty-eight wounded, and two hundred and six prisoners.[40] Monmouth was both a British victory and an American one, and the losses on the other side were very severe, but very light on this side—depending upon which side the writer was on.[41] These are typical examples. Moreover, no account wholly unfavorable to the patriot cause was allowed in the papers, and every account, even of the greatest distresses, always minimized the extent of the disaster and closed on a note of hope. Even the loss of Ticonderoga, of

[37] *Pa. Journal*, Feb. 5, 1777.
[38] *N. Y. Gazette and Weekly Mercury*, Jan. 13, 1777.
[39] N. Y. *Journal*, Aug. 2, 1779.   [40] *Royal Gazette*, July 21, 1779.
[41] "Had we been possessed of a powerful body of cavalry on the field, there is no doubt the success would have been much more complete."—N. Y. *Journal*, July 13, 1778. Certain divisions of the British army, said Gaine, "distinguished themselves in a particular manner, having opposed the whole of Mr. Washington's army and pursued them several miles. . . . It is certain the rebels have not suffered so heavy a loss as on this occasion, in any engagement since their defeat on Long Island."—*N. Y. Gazette and Weekly Mercury*, July 6, 1778.

which Washington wrote, "The evacuation of Ticonderoga and Mount Independence is an Event of Chagrin and surprise, not apprehended nor within the compass of my reasoning. . . . This stroke is severe indeed, and has distressed us much," was softened in the accounts. One of them, although not glossing over the mistakes, yet closed vigorously:

> "This is a candid statement of facts, and for this conduct we are told our country calls us either knaves or cowards; I conceive they ought to be grateful to our general, for had we stayed we very certainly should have been taken, and then no troops could have stood between the enemy and the country. Our affairs now are not desperate in this quarter, as they would certainly have been; we have destroyed Fort George and its appendages, and shall soon be able, I hope, to make head against our enemies, as we are gathering strength and re-collecting ourselves."[42]

Each side accused the other of intentionally distorting facts and bluntly called each other liars—good propaganda technique, and there is no doubt but that exaggeration was commonly practiced in writing newspaper accounts. Hamilton admitted to it, and Cornelius Harnett complained "We are generally too apt to lessen the number of the Enemies Army & exaggerate that of our own, which is bad policy,"[43] but that was done only between battles—the accounts of battles reversed the distortion.

Factual accounts of atrocities fortified the patriot suggestions. All of the newspapers carried them. The narrative of John Dodge's captivity was printed in both the *Continental Journal* and the *Pennsylvania Journal*, and Robert Sheffield's story of his imprisonment was printed in the *Connecticut Courant* and reprinted in the *Pennsylvania Packet* as well as in the New York *Journal*.[44] The descriptions of the treatment of women in New Jersey were printed in at least two papers. The men in Captain Baylor's regiment, defeated at Hackensack in 1778, claimed that the British had killed those who surrendered, and their depositions were printed in the New York

[42] *Pa. Evening Post*, Aug. 9, 1777; Washington's *Writings* (Ford), V, 485.
[43] Cornelius Harnett to William Wilkinson, Nov. 20, 1777, *Colonial and State Records of N. C.*, XI, 809; *Works of Hamilton*, I, 85 f.
[44] *Pa. Journal*, Feb. 3, 1779; *Cont. Journal*, Dec. 30, 1779, Jan. 6, Jan. 13, 1780; *Pa. Packet*, July 23, 1778; N. Y. *Journal*, Sept. 7, 1778.

Journal and the *Massachusetts Spy.*[45] Of these, or similar atrocity accounts, Andrew Eliot said, "There are various accounts of their cruelty to several persons; but none that I can depend upon. Some I find to be false."[46]

Rumor was commonly propagated through the printed extracts of letters, foreign or domestic. These extracts did not appear so frequently or in so great numbers as before the war, but they were used in about the same way as formerly. They were usually letters from friends of America abroad urging firmness in the cause and describing favorable conditions in Europe; several, of course, were from American agents abroad. An example of the method used by the Continental Congress in handling such items exhibits its technique in spreading a badly needed bit of encouraging information of doubtful authenticity without endangering the reputation of Congress, should the news prove false. A letter was published in the early summer of 1777, which stated that a war between France and England was inevitable, and of this letter Charles Carroll wrote his father:

"The letter, of which an extract is published under the sha [*sic*] head from a gentleman of eminence & character in ye West Indies comes from Mr. Bingham the continental agent at Martineco, and therefore altho' the name of Charles Thompson [*sic*] is not signed, you may look when the intelligence is authentick;—There is a possibility that ye answer of their High Mightiness may not be strictly true, and therefore it was thought prudent not to publish the intelligence as coming from Congress. . . ."[47]

Aside from news and rumors, the propagandists' suggestions were presented in the press in the form of satires, parodies, or direct refutation of British actions and statements. Parodies in verse or prose invariably followed a British proclamation,[48] and the King's speeches were usually published with interpolated comments. Sam Adams wrote Samuel Cooper a letter in February, 1777: "I send you the

[45] *Freeman's Journal*, Jan. 7, 1777; *Mass. Spy*, Jan. 2, 1777. See also *ibid.*, Nov. 26, Dec. 3, 1778; N. Y. *Journal*, Dec. 14, 1778.

[46] Belknap Papers, Vol. III, John Eliot to Jeremy Belknap, May 20, 1777.

[47] Carroll Papers, IX, 405. A similar letter from Amsterdam was printed in N. Y. *Journal*, Aug. 18, 1777.

[48] E.g., *Cont. Journal*, Jan. 2, 1777; *Pa. Packet*, Nov. 5, 1778; N. Y. *Journal*, Aug. 2, 1779; *Boston Gazette*, Apr. 5, 1779, May 8, 1780; *Pa. Journal*, Mar. 15, 1780.

inclosd Speech for your Amusement. One or two Remarks you will observe are made upon it. There is Room for many more. I wish some ingenious Pen might be employd."[49] His own ingenious pen would have been employed three years before, but as it was, Cooper published the parts of the letter which commented on the speech, and reported a month later, "The remarks you sent in your letter were extremely Pertinent & adapted to Public Use they were accordingly—with some few additional ones—printed in Power & Willis paper & thence reprinted in several N. E. States."[50]

A similar method of newspaper propaganda was to reprint leading British articles with satirical remarks; sometimes the remarks offered no proof in denial but distracted attention from the original charge by a countercharge—also good propaganda technique. Observe the method of "O" in refuting the statement made in New York that twenty-seven of the thirty nurses in a Philadelphia hospital died while caring for the sick:

"The death of twenty-seven of the thirty nurses in the Philadelphia hospital, is probably a wilful mistake. That it is not true is certain. If the account had been, that of thirty sick persons who had been prisoners at New York, twenty-seven had died under the care of the nurses in the Philadelphia hospital, we might have believed the relation to be true; because it is well known that those poor prisoners were generally starved to death, or from want of food and through barbarous usage in many respects, died in nearly the above proportion, after they were released in exchange for prisoners in our hands, who were well kept, and returned in health and good order."[51]

He concluded his comments on this and other items in the article with the statement that many other articles of the same sort "ought not to appear in any of our papers without proper notes to guard the unwary reader from deception and false impressions."

[49] *Writings of Sam Adams*, III, 353 (Feb. 4, 1777).

[50] Samuel Adams Papers, Cooper to Adams, Mar. 24, 1777. Cooper was referring to Powars' and Willis' *Independent Chronicle*. The King's speech of the next year was treated in the same fashion.—*Boston Gazette*, Mar. 9, 1778. Paine's "Crisis" No. XI did the same for the speech in 1781.

[51] N. Y. *Journal*, Sept. 15, 1777. Cf. *Mass. Spy*, Sept. 27, 1781, among many examples. The "Address of the Quakers" in 1778 was replied to in the same way.—*Pa. Packet*, Aug. 15, Aug. 20, 1778; Feb. 27, 1779. In their petition the Quakers spoke of their conscience making them oppose war, and "Philadelphiensis" answered, attacking their consistency: the Quaker assembly had once passed a militia law, he wrote, but once had refused wood for the soldiers' canteens. "I never knew before," he said, "that a canteen was a *warlike instrument;*—I suppose it has been such only since the *battle of the kegs.*"—*Pa. Packet*, Aug. 20, 1778.

The poetic suggestions were published almost exclusively in the newspapers. Several of the papers had a poets' corner, so that there were weekly contributions, but more commonly poems were printed as received, and few were received by the southern papers. The Boston and Philadelphia papers were well supplied, but those elsewhere printed poems on revolutionary subjects only at irregular intervals. Occasionally a poem would be reprinted in several papers. A piece called "Honour I Obey Thee" was published in the *South Carolina Gazette*, the *Continental Journal*, and the *Pennsylvania Evening Post*, and the satirical "Expedition to Danbury," in which General Tryon says,

> "In cunning and canting, deceit and disguise,
> In cheating a friend, and inventing of lies,
> I think I'm a match for the best of my species,
> But in this undertaking I feel all in pieces;
> So I'll fall in the rear, for I'd rather go last;—
> *Come, march on, my boys,* let me see you all past;
> For his Majesty's service (so says my commission)
> Requires that I *bring up* the whole expedition."

was printed in at least three papers.[52]

The most important form, however, in which propaganda suggestions were printed was the newspaper article—hortatory, satirical, abusive, and sometimes argumentative. The rise and fall in the number of these articles is a measure of the propaganda activity of each year, for this was the most characteristic form of suggestion. After the fight over independence there was a distinct lull in all forms of propaganda activity and the articles were few in number until the first of the year. Then from January to about June or July, 1777, there was a marked revival in newspaper writing, which reached its peak about April. After July, 1777, the number fell off rapidly until April, 1778, when it began to increase steadily to its maximum in June, and then began to decline again until, by November, 1778, few were appearing. From that time until the early summer of 1780 paper after paper appeared without a single essay in the nature of war propaganda. There was a slight increase from June to

[52] *Pa. Evening Post*, May 22, 1777; *S. C. Gazette*, July 23, 1777; *Pa. Gazette*, May 14, 1777. The poem "Honour I Obey Thee" was on the greatness of Washington. —*Cont. Journal*, Mar. 20, 1777; *Pa. Evening Post*, Apr. 5, 1777, taken from *S. C. Gazette*; *Norwich Packet*, Apr. 7, 1777. A poem on Arnold was in both *Pa. Packet*, Oct. 24, 1780, and *Cont. Journal*, Oct. 26, 1780. There are many other instances.

August, 1779, but it was very slight. About May, 1780, the number rose sharply to a maximum in June and July, began to decrease in August, and fell off steadily until there was another brief rise in the spring of 1781. Through the summer of 1781, until the surrender at Yorktown, the number of articles was small but fairly uniform, but after October they almost disappeared.

It will readily be discerned that the maxima and minima vary in direct ratio to war activity, but not always in proportion to the importance of the campaigns. The three highest points were the winter of 1777, during and after the Jersey campaign, the period from April to October, 1778, when the peace proposals were under consideration, and the summer of 1780, when affairs were so critical in the South. The absolute bottom was 1779. Francis Hopkinson wrote Franklin in September, thanking him for a piece of satire: "In Return for your Rocket I send you a few of my political Squibs. Ammunition of this kind hath been rather scarce with us. Most of our Writers have left the great field of general Politics, wherein they might have been of considerable Service to skirmish & bush-fight in the Fens & Thickets of Party Dispute—for which I blame them much."[53] The papers were filled with the letters in the Lee-Deane dispute, and similar personal and public quarrels were so fully aired that the letters of principals and partisans absorbed the space of the papers and the attention of the leaders. So intense was the excitement over the Lee-Deane affair, that one issue of the *Pennsylvania Evening Post* was sold out immediately upon publication.[54] The letters on this affair filled the papers for months. The serious conditions in local affairs—scarcity of goods, exorbitant rise in prices, lack of credit, and the depreciation of the currency—were thoroughly and acrimoniously discussed in the papers. There are several instances of writers abandoning the field of war propaganda to write on the domestic economic problems, which were considered of equal importance.[55] Political essays by no means disappeared from the

[53] Quoted from George E. Hastings, *The Life and Works of Francis Hopkinson*, p. 279, by permission of the University of Chicago Press.

[54] Carroll Papers, XII, 536. Hastings, *Hopkinson*, p. 309, mentions such a controversy between two Quakers which lasted three years and so filled the papers that Hopkinson finally intervened, his brother-in-law being involved.

[55] Hamilton and Gouverneur Morris both wrote on local issues rather than on war problems. William Hooper wrote Iredell on December 17, 1778, "Are we to ascribe it to a dearth of genius, or the restraint imposed upon the press, that no pen appears to lash the private and public vices of this licentious State?"—McRee, *Life and Correspondence of James Iredell*, I, 404.

papers. The subject matter simply changed, and more attention was paid local problems after 1778.

As before the war, the papers copied from each other extensively; many pieces appeared in two papers, and the best ones were frequently reprinted. Tom Paine's "Crisis" essays were printed in most of the northern papers and in some of those in the South, and the essays which attacked the peace plan of 1778 were widely copied.[56] This policy was encouraged by several of the propagandists, but in the case of less significant articles it usually resulted from printers' needs.[57] English and foreign essays favorable to America were also reprinted in American papers, frequently at the suggestion of American agents or friends abroad. The English essays usually scored the administration for its errors and were reprinted to show the growing sentiment in favor of the republic; the European essays usually dealt with the likelihood of war between England and one of the European countries.[58]

The practice of reprinting leading pamphlets was much less extensive than before the war, if for no other reason than that there were few leading pamphlets. An essay on the future greatness of America, which had appeared in the *Royal American Magazine* for January, 1774, was reprinted in the *Pennsylvania Packet*, June 15, 1779, and in the *Connecticut Gazette*, July 1, 1779. An extract from William Gordon's "Fourth of July Oration" was printed in the

---

[56] For example, William Henry Drayton's series signed "W. H. D." and the article signed "An American" appeared in the following papers: N. Y. *Journal*, July-Aug., 1778; *Conn. Journal*, July-Aug., 1778; *Pa. Packet*, July, 1778, Feb. 1779; *Pa. Evening Post*, July, 1778; *N. J. Gazette*, July, 1778, Mar., 1779; *N. C. Gazette*, July, 1778; *S. C. and Amer. Gen. Gazette*, Apr., 1779; *Cont. Journal*, July-Oct., 1778; *Mass. Spy*, Oct., 1778. "Bob Centinel," a single number, was printed in *Mass. Spy*, July 23, 1778; N. Y. *Journal*, Sept. 14, 1778; *Pa. Packet*, Sept. 26, 1778; *Boston Independent Ledger*, clipped in *Conn. Courant*, Nov. 3, 1778. Paine's "Crisis" essays were generally reprinted: *Boston Gazette*, *Mass. Spy*, *Cont. Journal*, *Freeman's Journal*, N. Y. *Journal*, *Pa. Journal*, the four Connecticut papers, *Va. Gazette* (Dixon), *S. C. Gazette*, and others.

[57] E.g., Arthur Lee to James Warren, Dec. 12, 1782, *Warren-Adams Letters*, II, 184; *Works of John Adams*, IX, 509.

[58] E.g., two articles from London in *Cont. Journal*, Dec. 19, Dec. 26, 1776, which placed the blame on the ministers; two in the *Boston Gazette*, May 26, 1777, which attacked the incompetence of the administration; twelve letters from the *London Remembrancer* in the *Pa. Packet*, Oct. 16, Oct. 19, 1779, which pointed out the necessity of granting independence; the first chapter of the "American Acts," a satire on Burgoyne, in N. Y. *Journal*, May 17, 1779, and *Mass. Spy*, Apr. 1, 1779; a favorable sketch of Washington in *ibid.*, Jan. 11, 1781; and the "Scourge," attacking the abandoned ministry which had wrecked the empire, in *Mass. Spy*, Aug.-Sept., 1780, *Conn. Courant*, Aug., 1780, *Boston Gazette*, July-Aug., 1780. The *Boston Gazette* took articles from the *Leyden Gazette*, sent in by John Adams.—See especially *Boston Gazette, Supplement*, Mar. 13, 1780; and *Mass. Spy*, Apr. 13, 1780.

Continental Journal on October 23, 1777, but there are few other instances.

The dominant themes of revolutionary propaganda were also presented in such forms as dreams, fables, and allegories. A letter from Belzebub to his servant, Benedict Arnold, urged him to get rid of Washington, a dialogue between the Devil and George shows how hellishly conceived were George's plans, and the "Ghost" of General Montgomery returned to urge on his former associates.[59] Francis Hopkinson's "Advertisement" was a list of James Rivington's effects for sale after the defeat of Cornwallis, and in it he cleverly repeated many of the dominant suggestions. Among the books for sale was "Miss M'Crea, a Tragedy," and "A New System of Cruelty: Containing a Variety of modern Improvements in that Art. Embellished with an elegant Frontispiece, representing an inside View of a Prison Ship." There were also for sale "An Elegant Map of the British Empire in North America, upon a very small Scale," and a variety of patent medicines—Sp. Men. Or, the genuine spirit of Lying. Extracted by distillation from many hundreds of "The Royal Gazette of New York." At the end was this note, "To every purchaser to the value of five Pounds, will be delivered gratis, one quire of counterfeit Continental Currency. Also, two quires of Proclamations offering Pardon to Rebels."[60]

The use of broadsides as a medium of war propaganda fell off even more sharply than did the use of pamphlets. Their primary use during the war was to communicate important news which came too late for the weekly paper or items which some governmental authority wanted widely known. Congress, for instance, published handbills of the victory at Bennington, "for the more easy dispersion thro the army, that the troops may be made acquainted with, and emulate the conduct of their brave northern and eastern brethren."[61] Acts and resolutions of the different governments, as well as appeals for supplies from committees, were printed on handbills, but their use for war propaganda was much more limited. The official addresses of Congress and of the state legislatures were printed on

[59] *Pa. Packet*, Oct. 7, 1780; *Boston Gazette*, Oct. 8, Nov. 19, 1781; *Pa. Packet*, Nov. 4, 1780. See also *Boston Gazette*, Jan. 27, 1777; *Mass. Spy*, Oct. 12, 1780.

[60] *Boston Gazette*, Dec. 3, 1781. A satirical piece on Rivington made him petition Congress for pardon, offering to write America into independence. To this Rivington protested.—*Mass. Spy*, Dec. 14, 1781.

[61] Burnett, *Letters of Members of Cont. Cong.*, II, 473. See also *ibid.*, II, 460; III, 240.

broadsides, and many of the revolutionary songs for obvious reasons were so published. But the old appeals to the lower classes and the inflammatory essays of the prerevolutionary days in Boston, New York, and Philadelphia were no longer written. Occasionally, however, an article on the current economic and financial problems would appear on a broadside, but rarely on the war issues.[62]

Only one magazine was published after the adoption of the Declaration of Independence, the *United States Magazine*, edited by Hugh Henry Brackenridge, assisted by Philip Freneau. During its short life it was filled with essays on the war, accounts of battles, atrocity accounts, and revolutionary poems. In addition it reprinted David Ramsay's "Fourth of July Oration" and two fast day sermons. Freneau contributed numerous poems—two of them satires on George III—"A Dialogue between His Britannic Majesty and Mr. Fox," and "George the Third his Soliloquy for 1779." An engraving in the first number, similar to those of Paul Revere in the old *Pennsylvania Magazine*, fortified the revolutionary suggestions which abounded in that issue.

The most varied appeal was made in this first number; thereafter the magazine for lack of suitable contributions was forced to rely largely on military news, poems, and even on the state constitutions, several of which were copied in the later issues. But the magazine had a short career, only twelve months, and Brackenridge's statement on giving it up tends to diminish considerably its importance as a medium of propaganda—he confessed by implication that the magizine simply was not read. But, as he said, his publication had angered the Philadelphia Tories: "These have been sorely pricked and buffeted with the sharp points of whiggism, which, like arrows from the great machines of Archimedes, have been darted out from it. They have been sorely injured by these points, and will be ready to believe, that in the suspension of the work is accomplished that prophesy of the Apocalypse, *And Satan shall be bound a thousand years*."[63]

[62] Even the sketchiest glance at Evans, *Amer. Biblio.*, will convince. Only scattering ones are listed during the war. One of those on local economic problems is a good example of the application of revolutionary sentiments to the hardships of the times: *A New Touch on the Times, Well adapted to the distressing situation of every Sea-port Town. By a Daughter of Liberty.*—N. Y. Hist. Soc., Broadsides, 1779.
[63] Quoted from Claude M. Newlin, *Life and Writings of Henry Hugh Brackenridge.* p. 53, by permission of Princeton University Press.

CONCLUSIONS

The work of the propagandists has spoken for itself; by their fruits we have known them. Without their work independence would not have been declared in 1776 nor recognized in 1783.

British legislation was, of course, the immediate occasion for rebellion. The provincial ruling class, threatened in its position, used legal agencies of government and already established social institutions to undermine and ultimately to overthrow the British control. Through propaganda they spread the alarm to all classes. The propagandists identified the interests of the provincial ruling class with national interests and created a war psychosis. It was the propagandists who made inchoate feelings articulate opinion and provided the compulsive ideals which led to concrete action.

A movement originating in the necessities of the provincial class thus became in the capable hands of its leaders a dominant national movement. The ideas and interests of those who wished to remain within the empire were ultimately overwhelmed and their leaders discredited by patriot propaganda, but not before the pro-British advocates had made an effective counterattack.

As a result, much of what we know of the Revolution has been learned from revolutionary propaganda. The patriots were not all of the lower classes, frontiersmen and buckskins as Tory propaganda had it; the friends of England were not all aristocrats and oppressors of the downtrodden, as Whig propaganda had it. Nationalism was not the cause of the revolution, nor was it democratic in its origin, but the work of the revolutionary propagandists aided in developing the feeling of nationalism and in stimulating the ideals of a new democracy.

The propagandists thus gave expression to ideals that had been germinating for years; the appeals to a common history and a common destiny and the ideas they presented expressed clearly what the people had but dimly sensed. The fears the propagandists aroused and the hopes they enkindled became the national fears and national hopes. The national ideals of American life, slowly maturing through the colonial period, thus came clearly into the consciousness of the American people through the effects of war propaganda.

BIBLIOGRAPHY

BIBLIOGRAPHY

Primary Sources: Manuscripts

Adams, Samuel. Samuel Adams Papers. New York Public Library.

Allen, James. The Allen Papers. Historical Society of Pennsylvania.

Balch, Thomas. Balch Papers. New York Public Library.

Belknap Papers, 1745-1776. Massachusetts Historical Society.

Boston. Minutes of the Committee of Correspondence, November, 1772-December, 1774. 13 vols. New York Public Library.

——. Records of the Committee of Correspondence, 1772-1775. 3 vols. New York Public Library.

Bradford, William. Bradford Manuscripts. Historical Society of Pennsylvania.

Burke, Thomas. Governor Thomas Burke's Letter Book, 1774-1781. North Carolina Historical Commission.

Charles Carroll of Carrollton Papers, 1731-1832. Maryland Historical Society.

Dickinson, John. Dickinson Papers. Historical Society of Pennsylvania.

Duer, William. William Duer Papers. New York Historical Society.

Eliot, Andrew. Andrew Eliot, Jonathan Mayhew, Thomas Hollis Correspondence, 1761-1766. New York Public Library.

Emmett Collection. 65 vols. New York Public Library.

Force, Peter. Miscellaneous Correspondence. Division of Manuscripts, Library of Congress.

Georgia. Colonial Records of Georgia, Vols. XXXVII, XXXVIII. Rhodes Memorial Home, Atlanta, Georgia.

Gist, Mordecai. The Mordecai Gist Papers. Maryland Historical Society.

Hawley, Joseph. Joseph Hawley Manuscripts. 2 vols. New York Public Library.

Hayes Collection, 1748-1806. North Carolina Historical Commission.

Hutchinson, Thomas. Hutchinson's Correspondence. Massachusetts Archives, Vols. XXV, XXVI, XXVII. State House, Boston.

Johnson, Sir William. Johnson Papers. Division of Manuscripts, Library of Congress.

Johnston, Samuel. Papers of Samuel Johnston, 1763-1803. North Carolina Historical Commission.

Lamb, John. Lamb Papers. New York Public Library.

Laurens, Henry. Henry Laurens Papers. South Carolina Historical Society.

Lee Transcripts. 5 vols. Virginia Historical Society. Letters to and from the five Lee brothers.

Livingston, Robert R. R. R. Livingston Papers. New York Public Library.

Livingston, William. Livingston Papers. Massachusetts Historical Society.

Loyalists. Transcripts of the Manuscript Books and Papers of the Commissioner of Enquiry into the Losses and Services of the American Loyalists. 59 vols. New York Public Library.

Loyalist Rhapsodies. Division of Manuscripts, Library of Congress.

McDougall, Alexander. The Alexander McDougall Papers. 7 vols. New York Historical Society.

Massachusetts. Town Resolutions, 1773-1787. Division of Manuscripts, Library of Congress.

Oliver, Peter. The Origin & Progress of the American Rebellion to the year 1776 in a letter to a Friend. Massachusetts Historical Society.

Penn, John. The Penn Papers. North Carolina Historical Commission.

Reed, Joseph. Reed Papers. New York Historical Society.

Revolutionary Letters. Massachusetts Archives, Vol. CXCIII.

Rhode Island Historical Society, Manuscript Collections, Letters and Papers, 1765-1776, Vol. XII.

Savage, Samuel Phillips. Savage Papers. 3 vols. Massachusetts Historical Society.

Schuyler, Philip. Schuyler Papers. New York Public Library.

Smith, William. Diary of William Smith. New York Public Library.

Stevens, B. F., ed. Facsimiles of Manuscripts in European Archives Relating to America, 1773-1783; with Descriptions, Editorial Notes, Collations, References, and Translations. 25 vols. London, 1889-1898.

Transcripts of Materials Relating to American History in the British Museum. Division of Manuscripts, Library of Congress.

Wayne, Anthony. Wayne Manuscripts. Historical Society of Pennsylvania.

PRINTED PRIMARY SOURCES

NEWSPAPERS AND PERIODICALS:

Connecticut. *The Connecticut Courant*, Hartford, 1764-1783. Title varies.

———. *The Connecticut Gazette*, New Haven, 1763-1767.

———. *The Connecticut Journal*, New Haven, 1767-1783. Title varies.

———. *The New-London Gazette*, 1764-1773; *The Connecticut Gazette*, 1774-1783. New London.

———. *Norwich Packet*, Norwich, 1773-1783.

Georgia. *The Georgia Gazette*, Savannah, 1763-1776.

———. *The Royal Georgia Gazette*, Savannah, 1779-1782.

Maryland. *The Maryland Gazette*, Annapolis, 1763-1783.

———. *The Maryland Journal*, Baltimore, 1773-1783.

Massachusetts. Ames, Nathaniel, *An Astronomical Diary or, Almanack*, Boston, 1765-1774.

———. *Bickerstaff's Boston Almanac*, Boston, 1767-1783.

———. *The Boston Chronicle*, Boston, 1767-1770.

———. *The Boston Evening Post*, Boston, 1763-1775.

———. *The Boston Gazette, and Country Journal*, Boston, 1763-1783. Place of publication varies.

———. *Boston News-Letter*, Boston, 1763-1776: *Massachusetts Gazette and Boston News-Letter*, 1763-1765; *Massachusetts Gazette*, 1765-1766; *Massachusetts Gazette and Boston News-Letter*, 1766-1768; *Boston Weekly News-Letter*, 1768-1769; *Massachusetts Gazette: and the Boston Weekly News-Letter*, 1769-1776.

———. *The Boston Post-Boy & Advertiser*, Boston, 1763-1775: *Green & Russel's Boston Post-Boy & Advertiser*, 1763; *Boston Post-Boy & Advertiser*, 1763-1769; *Massachusetts Gazette, and the Boston Post-Boy and Advertiser*, 1769-1775.

———. *The Continental Journal*, Boston, 1776-1783.

———. *The Essex Almanac*, Salem, 1769.

———. *The Essex Gazette*, Salem, 1768-1775; *The New-England Chronicle, or the Essex Gazette*, Cambridge, 1775-1776; *Independent Chronicle*, Boston, 1776-1783.

———. Low, Nathaniel, *An Astronomical Diary: Or, Almanack*, Boston, 1775.

———. *Massachusetts Gazette. See Boston News-Letter*.

———. *Massachusetts Spy*, Boston, 1770-1775; Worcester, 1775-1783.

————. *The Royal American Magazine, or Universal Repository of Instruction and Amusement*, Boston, Jan. 1774-Mar. 1775.

New Hampshire. *The New Hampshire Gazette and Historical Chronicle*, Portsmouth, 1763-1776; *Freeman's Journal*, Portsmouth, 1776-1778; *The New Hampshire Gazette*, Portsmouth and Exeter, 1778-1783.

New Jersey. *The New Jersey Gazette*, Burlington, 1777-1778; Trenton, 1778-1783.

————. *The New Jersey Journal*, Chatham, 1779-1783.

New York. *The New York Gazette, or, The Weekly Post-Boy*, New York, 1763-1773.

————. *New-York Gazeteer*, New York, 1773-1775, 1777-1783: *Rivington's New-York Gazetteer*, 1773-1775; *Rivington's New-York Gazetteer*, Oct. 4-Oct. 18, 1777; *Rivington's New-York Loyal Gazette*, Oct. 25-Dec. 6, 1777; *Royal Gazette*, Dec. 13, 1777-1783.

————. The New York *Journal*, New York, 1766-1776; Kingston, 1776-1778; Poughkeepsie, 1778-1780, 1781-1782.

————. *The New York Mercury*, New York, 1763-1783: *New York Mercury*, 1763-1768; *New York Gazette and the Weekly Mercury*, New York, 1768-1776, Newark and New York, 1776, New York, 1776-1783.

North Carolina. *The Cape Fear Mercury*, Wilmington, 1769-1774, 1775.

————. *North-Carolina Gazette* (James Davis), Newbern, 1768-1778.

————. *North-Carolina Gazette* (Andrew Steuart), Wilmington, 1764-1766.

Pennsylvania. *American Magazine or General Repository*, Philadelphia, 1769.

————. *The Pennsylvania Chronicle*, Philadelphia, 1767-1774.

————. *The Pennsylvania Evening Post*, Philadelphia, 1775-1783.

————. *The Pennsylvania Gazette*, Philadelphia, 1763-1776, 1777; York, 1778; Philadelphia, 1779-1783.

————. *The Pennsylvania Journal*, Philadelphia, 1763-1777, 1778-1783.

————. *The Pennsylvania Ledger*, Philadelphia, 1775-1776, 1777-1778.

————. *The Pennsylvania Magazine: or, American Monthly Museum*, Philadelphia, 1775-1776.

——. *The Pennsylvania Packet, and the General Advertiser,* Philadelphia, 1771-1773; *Dunlap's Pennsylvania Packet,* Philadelphia, 1773-1777; *Pennsylvania Packet,* Lancaster, 1777-1778, Philadelphia, 1778-1783.

——. *The United States Magazine: A Repository of History, Politics, and Literature,* Philadelphia, 1779.

Rhode Island. *The Newport Mercury, or the Weekly Advertiser,* Newport, 1763-1776.

South Carolina. *Royal Gazette,* Charleston, 1781-1782.

——. *The South-Carolina and American General Gazette,* Charleston, 1763-1780.

——. *The South Carolina Gazette,* Charleston, 1763-1775; *Gazette of the State of South Carolina,* 1777-1780.

——. *The South Carolina Gazette; and Country Journal,* Charleston, 1765-1779.

Virginia. *The Virginia Gazette,* Williamsburg, 1763-1781: Alexander Purdie, 1766; Purdie and John Dixon, 1766-1775; Dixon and William Hunter, 1775-1779; Dixon and Thomas Nicholson, 1779-1781.

——. *The Virginia Gazette,* Williamsburg, 1766-1779: William Rind, 1766-1773; Clementina Rind, 1773-1774; John Pinkney, 1774-1776.

——. *The Virginia Gazette,* Williamsburg, 1775-1779, Alexander Purdie.

BROADSIDES:

American Antiquarian Society, Broadside Collection, 1763-1783.
Connecticut Historical Society, Broadside Collection, 1763-1783.
Library Company of Philadelphia, Broadside Collection, 1763-1783.
Library of Congress, Broadside Collection, 1763-1783.
Massachusetts Historical Society, Broadside Collection, 1763-1783.
New York Historical Society, Broadside Collection, 1763-1783.
New York Public Library, Broadside Collection, 1763-1783.
Historical Society of Pennsylvania, Broadside Collection, 1763-1783.

PAMPHLETS AND SERMONS:

Adams, Amos. *A Concise, Historical View of the Difficulties, Hardships, and Perils, which attended the Planting and Progressive Improvements of New-England.* . . . Boston, 1770.

——. *Religious Liberty an Invaluable Blessing: Illustrated in two Discourses Preached at Roxbury Decr. 3, 1767. Being the Day of general Thanksgiving.* Boston, 1768.

Additional Observations to A Short Narrative. . . . See below, Boston.

An Address of the Presbyterian Ministers, of the City of Philadelphia, To the Ministers and Presbyterian Congregations, in the County of ——— *in North Carolina.* Philadelphia, 1775.

Allen, Ethan. *A Narrative of Colonel Ethan Allen's Captivity . . . Written by himself.* Philadelphia, 1779.

[Allen, James]. *The Poem which the Committee of the Town of Boston has voted Unanimously to be published with the late Oration. . . .* Boston, 1772.

The American Alarm, or the Bostonian plea, For the RIGHTS, and LIBERTIES, of the PEOPLE. Humbly Addressed to the KING and COUNCIL, and To the Constitutional Sons of LIBERTY, in AMERICA. By the BRITISH BOSTONIAN. Boston, 1773.

Appleton, Nathaniel. *A Thanksgiving Sermon on the total Repeal of the STAMP-ACT. Preached in Cambridge, New-England, May 20th, in the Afternoon preceding the Public Rejoicing of the Evening upon that great Occasion.* Boston, 1766.

The Association, &c. of the Delegates of the Colonies, at the Grand Congress . . . . By Bob Jingle, Esq. [Philadelphia], 1774.

Austin, Jonathan W. *Oration, Delivered at Boston, March 5, 1778.* Boston, 1778.

Avery, David. *The Lord is to be Praised for the Triumphs of his Power. A Sermon, preached at Greenwich, in Connecticut, on the 18th of December, 1777.* Norwich, 1778.

Baldwin, Samuel. *A Sermon, preached at Plymouth, Dec. 22, 1775.* Boston, 1776.

Barlow, Joel. *The Prospect of Peace. A Poetical Composition, delivered in Yale-College, at the Public Examination, of the Candidates for the Degree of Bachelor of Arts; July 23, 1778.* New Haven, 1778.

Bernard, Francis. *Letters to the Ministry. . . .* Boston, 1769.

Bland, Richard. *An Inquiry into the Rights of the British Colonies. . . .* Williamsburg, 1766.

Bollan, William. *A Succinct View of the Origin of our Colonies. . . .* London, 1766.

Bolton, Thomas. *An Oration delivered March fifteenth 1775, at the Request of a Number of the Inhabitants of the Town of Boston.* Boston, 1775.

Boston. *Additional Observations to A Short Narrative of the Horrid Massacre. . . .* Boston, 1770.

——. *Observations on Several Acts of Parliament, passed in the 4th, 6th and 7th Years of his Present Majesty's Reign . . . . Published by the Merchants of Boston.* Boston, 1769.

——. *A Short Narrative of the Horrid Massacre in Boston perpetrated in the Evening of the Fifth Day of March, 1770, by Soldiers of the XXIXth Regiment. . . .* Boston, 1770.

Boucher, Jonathan. *A View of the Causes and Consequences of the American Revolution; in Thirteen Discourses, preached in North America between the years 1763 and 1775, with an Historical Preface.* London, 1797.

[Brackenridge, Hugh Henry]. *The Death of General Montgomery, at the Seige of Quebec. A Tragedy. . . .* Philadelphia, 1777.

——. *An Eulogium of the Brave Men who have fallen in the Contest with Great Britain . . . delivered on Monday, July 5, 1779. . . .* Philadelphia, 1779.

——. *Six Political Discourses Founded on the Scripture.* Lancaster [1778].

Carmichael, John. *A Self-Defensive War Lawful, proved in a Sermon, preached at Lancaster . . . June 4, 1775.* Lancaster, 1775.

Champion, Judah. *A Brief View of the Distresses, Hardships and Dangers our Ancestors Encounter'd, in settling New-England, the Privileges we enjoy, and our Obligations thence arising, with moral Reflections thereupon. In two Sermons delivered at Litchfield on the general Fast, April 18, 1770.* Hartford, 1770.

[Chandler, Thomas Bradbury?]. *What Think Ye of the Congress Now? Or, An Enquiry, how far the Americans are Bound to Abide by and Execute the Decisions of the late Congress?* New York, 1775.

Chauncy, Charles. *The Accursed Thing must be Taken Away from among a People, if They Would Reasonably Hope to Stand before their Enemies. . . .* Boston, 1778.

[Chauncy, Charles]. *A Letter to a Friend. Giving a Concise, but Just, Representation of the Hardships and Sufferings the Town of BOSTON is Exposed to. . . . By T. W. A Bostonian.* Boston, 1774.

[Church, Benjamin?]. *Liberty and Property Vindicated, and the St——pm——n burnt. A Discourse Occasionally Made on Burning the Effige of the St—pm—n. In New-London. . . . By a Friend to the Liberty of his Country.* Boston, 1766.

Clark, Jonas. *The Fate of Blood-thirsty Oppressors and GOD'S Tender Care of His Distressed People. A Sermon, Preached at Lexington, April 19, 1776. . . .* Boston, 1776.

——. *The Importance of Military Skill, Measures for Defence and a Martial Spirit, in a Time of Peace. . . .* Boston, 1768.

——. *A Sermon Preached before his Excellency John Hancock. . . .* Boston, 1781.

Coombe, Thomas. *A Sermon Preached before the Congregations of Christ Church and St. Peter's, Philadelphia, On Thursday, July 20, 1775. . . .* Philadelphia, 1775.

[Cooper, Myles?]. *The American Querist: or, Some Questions Proposed Relative to the Present Disputes between Great Britain, and her American Colonies. Printed in North America,* 1774.

——. *A Friendly Address to all Reasonable Americans on the Subject of our Political Confusions. . . .* New York, 1774.

——. *The Patriots of North America: A Sketch. With Explanatory Notes.* New York, 1775.

Cooper, Samuel. *A Sermon Preached before his Excellency John Hancock. . . .* Boston, 1780.

Copy of Letters sent to Great Britain, by his Excellency Thomas Hutchinson, the Hon. Andrew Oliver, and Several other Persons, BORN AND EDUCATED AMONG US. . . . Boston, 1773.

Cumings, Henry. *A Sermon, Preached in Billerica, On the 23d of November, 1775. . . .* Worcester, 1775.

——. *A Sermon Preached at Lexington, on the 19th of April, 1781. . . .* Boston, 1781.

——. *A Thanksgiving Sermon Preached at Billerica, November 27, 1766.* Boston, 1767.

Cushing, Jacob. *Divine Judgments upon Tyrants: And Compassion to Oppressed. A SERMON, Preached at Lexington, April 20th, 1778. In Commemoration of the MURDEROUS WAR and RAPINE, Inhumanly Perpetrated, by Two Regiments of British Troops, in that Town and Neighbourhood, on the Nineteenth of April, 1775.* Boston, 1778.

[Dalrymple, Sir John]. *The Rights of Great Britain Asserted against The Claims of America . . . . Said to be written by Lord George Germaine.* London printed, Philadelphia reprinted, 1776.

Dana, James. *A Century Discourse, Delivered at the Anniversary Meeting of the Freemen of the Town of Wallingford, April 9, 1770.* New Haven [1770].

———. *A Sermon Preached before the General Assembly of the State of Connecticut. . . . May 13, 1779.* Hartford, 1779.

Devotion, John. *The Duty and Interest of a People to Sanctify the LORD of HOSTS. . . .* Hartford, 1777.

[Dickinson, John]. *The Late Regulations Respecting the British Colonies on the Continent of America Considered. . . .* Philadelphia, 1765.

A Discourse, Addressed to the Sons of Liberty, At a Solemn Assembly, near Liberty-Tree, in BOSTON, February 14, 1766. Providence, 1766.

[Downer, Silas]. *Discourse, Delivered in Providence . . . at the Dedication of the Tree of Liberty . . . . By a Son of Liberty.* Providence, 1768.

Dodge, John. *A Narrative of the Capture and Treatment of John Dodge, by the English at Detroit. Written by himself.* Philadelphia, 1779.

Drayton, William Henry. *A Charge, on the Rise of the American Empire, delivered . . . to the Grand Jury for the District of Charlestown.* Charleston, 1776.

[Drayton, William Henry?]. *A Letter from Freeman of South-Carolina, to the Deputies of North-America, assembled in the High Court of Congress. . . .* Charleston, 1774.

Drayton, William Henry. *The Speech of the Hon. William Henry Drayton, esquire, Chief-Justice of South-Carolina, January 12, 1778.* Charleston, 1778.

Duché, Jacob. *The Duty of Standing Fast in our Spiritual and Temporal Liberties, a Sermon, Preached in Christ-Church, July 7th, 1775. . . .* Philadelphia, 1775.

[Dulany, Daniel]. *Considerations on the Propriety of Imposing Taxes in the British Colonies, for the Purpose of Raising a Revenue by Act of Parliament.* 2nd ed., Annapolis, 1765.

An Elegy to the Infamous Memory of Sr. F—— B——. n.p., 1769.

Emerson, Joseph. *A Thanksgiving Sermon on the Repeal of the Act, Preach'd at Pepperrell, July 24th, 1766. . . .* Boston, 1766.

An Essay on the Trade of the Northern Colonies of Great Britain In North America. Philadelphia printed, London reprinted, 1764.

AN ESSAY upon Government adopted by the Americans. Wherein, the Lawfulness of Revolutions, are Demonstrated in a Chain of Consequences from the Fundamental Principles of Society. Philadelphia, 1775.

Evans, Israel. *A Discourse, delivered, on the 18th Day of December, 1777, the Day of Public Thanksgiving. . . .* Lancaster, 1778.

————. *A Discourse, Delivered at Easton, On the 17th of October, 1779. To the Officers and Soldiers of the Western Army. . . .* Philadelphia, 1779.

The First Book of the American Chronicles of the Times. Boston, 1774.

Fish, Elisha. *A Discourse, Delivered at Worcester, March 28th, 1775. . . .* Worcester, 1775.

————. *Joy and Gladness; A Thanksgiving Discourse, Preached in Upton . . . May 28, 1766.* Providence, 1767.

Fiske, Nathan. *An Oration Delivered at Brookfield, November 14, 1781, in Celebration of the Capture of Lord Cornwallis and his Whole Army.* Boston, n.d.

————. *The Importance of Righteousness to the Happiness, and the Tendency of Oppression to the Misery of a People. . . .* Boston, 1774.

————. *Remarkable Providences to be Gratefully Recollected, Religiously Improved, and Carefully Transmitted to Posterity. . . .* Boston, 1776.

Fitch, Elijah. *A Discourse, The Substance of which was Delivered at Hopkington . . . March 24th, 1776, being the Next Sabbath Following the Precipitate Flight of the British Troops from Boston.* Boston, 1776.

[Galloway, Joseph]. *A Candid Examination of the Mutual Claims of Great Britain and the Colonies. With a Plan of Accomodation on Constitutional Principles.* New York, 1775.

Gordon, William. *Religious and Civil Liberty, a Thanksgiving Discourse . . . December 15, 1774. . . .* Boston, 1775.

————. *The Separation of the Jewish Tribes, after the Death of Solomon, Accounted for, and Applied to the Present Day, in a Sermon Preached before the General Court on Friday, July the 4th, 1777. . . .* Boston, 1777.

————. *A SERMON Preached before the Honourable House of Representatives. . . .* Watertown, 1775.

Green, Jacob. *A Fast Sermon, Pointing out the Sins and Vices, which the Author humbly Supposes are the Principle Grounds of God's Controversy with the People of this Land.* Chatham, 1779.

Grotius. *Pills for the Delegates: or the Chairman Chastised, in A Series of Letters, addressed to Peyton Randolph. . . .* New York, 1775.

[Hamilton, Alexander]. *The Farmer Refuted: or, A More Impartial and Comprehensive View of the Dispute between Great Britain and the Colonies. . . .* New York, 1775.

Hichborn, Benjamin. *An Oration, Delivered at Boston, March 5, 1777.* Boston, 1777.

Hitchcock, Gad. *A Sermon Preached at Plymouth December 22d, 1774. . . .* Boston, 1775.

Holly, Israel. *GOD Brings about His Holy and Wise Purpose or Decree . . . Briefly Illustrated in a SERMON, Preached . . . the Next Sabbath after the Report Arrived, that the People at Boston had Destroyed a Large Quantity of TEA. . . .* Hartford, 1774.

[Hopkins, Stephen]. *The Rights of the Colonies Examined. Published by Authority.* Providence, 1765.

[Hopkinson, Francis]. *A Pretty Story. Written in the Year of our Lord 1774. By Peter Grievous, Esq. A.B.C.D.E.* Philadelphia, 1774.

[Howard, Martin]. *A Defence of the Letter from a Gentleman at Halifax. . . .* Newport, 1765.

———. *A Letter from a Gentleman at Halifax, to his Friend in Rhode Island. . . .* Newport, 1765.

Howard, Simeon. *A Sermon Preached to the Ancient and Honourable Artillery Company, in Boston . . . June 7, 1773.* Boston, 1773.

———. *A Sermon Preached before the Honorable Council . . . of the State of Massachusetts-Bay . . . May 31, 1780.* Boston, 1780.

Hunt, Isaac. *The Political Family: or A Discourse Pointing out the Reciprocal Advantages, which Flow from an Uninterrupted Union between Great-Britain and her American Colonies. . . .* Philadelphia, 1775.

Huntington, Enoch. *The Happy Effects of Union, and the Fatal Tendency of Divisions, Shown in a Sermon preached . . . April 8, 1776.* Hartford, 1776.

Huntington, Joseph. *A Discourse, Adapted to the Present Day . . . Preached at Coventry, April, 1781. . . .* Hartford, 1781.

[Inglis, Charles]. *The Christian Soldier's Duty Briefly Delineated in a Sermon Preached at Kings'-Bridge, September 7, 1777.* New York, 1777.

———. *The Duty of Honouring the King, Explained and Recommended. . . .* New York, 1780.

———. *The True Interest of America Impartially Stated, in Certain Strictures on a Pamphlet Intitled Common Sense.* Philadelphia, 1776.

Jenyns, Soame. *The Objections to the Taxation of Our American Colonies by the Legislature of Great Britain, Briefly Considered.* 2nd ed. London, 1765.

[Johnson, Stephen]. *Some Important Observations, Occasioned by, and Adapted to, The Public Fast . . . December 18th, A.D. 1765. . . .* Newport, 1766.

Jones, David. *Defensive War in a Just Cause Sinless. . . .* Philadelphia, 1775.

Keteltas, Abraham. *God Arising and Pleading His People's Cause; or the American War in favor of Liberty, against the Measures and Arms of Great Britain, shewn to be the Cause of God. . . .* Newburyport, 1777.

[Laird, John]. *An Englishman's Answer to the Address, from the Delegates, to the People of Great-Britain. . . .* New York, 1775.

Langdon, Samuel. *A Sermon Preached to the Honorable Council. . . .* Watertown, 1775.

Lathrop, John. *A Discourse Preached December 15, 1774. . . .* Boston, 1774.

———. *A Discourse, Preached March the Fifth, 1778.* Boston, 1778.

———. *Innocent Blood Crying to God from the Streets of Boston. . . .* London printed, Boston reprinted, 1771.

———. *A Sermon Preached to the Ancient and Honorable Artillery Company, in Boston . . . June 6th, 1774.* Boston, 1774.

[Lee, Charles]. *Strictures on a Pamphlet Entitled A Friendly Address to all Reasonable Americans. . . .* Philadelphia, 1774.

[Leacock, John?]. *The Fall of British Tyranny: or American Liberty Triumphant.* Philadelphia printed, Boston reprinted, 1776.

[Leonard, Daniel]. *Massachusettensis: or, a Series of Letters, Containing a Faithful State of many Important and Striking Facts which Laid the Foundation of the Present Troubles in the Province of Massachusetts-Bay. . . .* London, 1776.

MacKay, Fitzhugh. *American Liberty Asserted: or British Tyranny Reprobated.* . . . Lancaster, 1778.

McKean, Thomas. *A Charge Delivered to the Grand-Jury . . . at a Court of Oyer and Terminer . . . April 21, 1778.* Lancaster, 1778.

Mather, Moses. *America's Appeal to the Impartial World.* Hartford, 1775.

Mayhew, Jonathan. *The Snare Broken. A Thanksgiving Discourse Preached at the Desire of the West Church in Boston . . . May 23, 1766.* . . . Boston, 1766.

Meigs, Josiah. *Oration pronounced before a Public Assembly in New-Haven, On the 5th Day of November, 1781, at the Celebration of the Glorious Victory over Lieutenant-General Earl Cornwallis.* . . . New Haven, 1782.

A Ministerial Catechise, Suitable to be Learned by all Modern Provincial Governors, Pensioners, Placemen, &c. Dedicated to T—— H——, Esq. Boston, 1771.

Minot, George. *Oration Delivered at Boston, March 5, 1782.* Boston, 1782.

Montgomery, Joseph. *A Sermon, Preached at Christiana Bridge and New-Castle, The 20th of July, 1775.* . . . Philadelphia, 1775.

Morrill, Isaac. *Faith in Divine Providence the Great Support of God's People. A Sermon, Preached at Lexington, April 19, 1780.* . . . Boston, 1780.

Morton, Perez. *An Oration; Delivered at the King's-Chapel in Boston, April 8, 1776, On the Re-Interment of the Remains of the late Most Worshipful Grand-Master, Joseph Warren.* . . . Boston, 1776.

Murray, John. *Nehemiah, or the Struggle for Liberty, Never in Vain, when managed with Virtue and Patience. A Discourse Delivered at the Presbyterian Church in Newburyport, Nov. 4, 1779.* . . . Newburyport, 1779.

A Narrative of the Excursion and Ravages of the King's Troops Under the Command of General Gage, on the Nineteenth of April, 1775. Together with the DEPOSITIONS taken by ORDER of CONGRESS, to Support the Truth of it. [Worcester, 1775].

Noble, Oliver. *A Discourse delivered at Newbury-port, North Meeting House, March 5th, 1775. In Commemoration of the Massacre at Boston, March Fifth, 1770.* Newburyport, 1775.

O'Beirne, Thomas L. *An Excellent Sermon Preached in St. Paul's Church . . . Printed at the Desire of the Congregation.* [New York, 1776].

Observations on Several Acts of Parliament. See above, Boston.

Oppression: A Poem. Boston, 1765.

An Oration Delivered at the State House, in Philadelphia, to a very Numerous Audience; on Thursday the 1st of August, 1776. . . . Philadelphia, 1776.

An Oration, Upon the Beauties of Liberty, Or the Essential Rights of the Americans . . . Humbly Dedicated to the Right-Honourable the Earl of Dartmouth. Boston, 1773.

Otis, James. *Brief Remarks on the Defence of the Halifax Libel on the British-American Colonies.* Boston, 1765.

———. *The Rights of the British Colonies Asserted and Proved.* Boston, 1764.

[Otis, James]. *A Vindication of the British Colonies, against the Aspersions of the Halifax Gentlemen.* . . . Boston, 1765.

Patten, William. *A Discourse Delivered at Halifax in the County of Plymouth, July 24, 1766. On the Day of Thanksgiving to Almighty God . . . for the Repeal of the STAMP-ACT.* Boston, 1766.

Payson, Phillips. *A Memorial of Lexington Battle, and of some Signal Interpositions of Providence in the American Revolution.* . . . Boston, 1782.

———. *A Sermon Preached before the Honorable Council . . . of the State of Massachusetts-Bay . . . May 27, 1778.* . . . Boston, 1778.

Plain Truth: Addressed to the Inhabitants of America; Containing Remarks on a late Pamphlet, entitled Common Sense. . . . Philadelphia, 1776.

[Priestley, Joseph]. *An Address to Protestant Dissenters of all Denominations on the Approaching Election of Members of Parliament, with respect to the State of Public Liberty in General, and of American Affairs in Particular.* London printed, Boston reprinted, 1774.

Price, Richard. *Observations on the Nature of Civil Liberty, the Principles of Government, and the Justice and Policy of the War with America.* . . . London printed, Philadelphia reprinted, 1776.

Quincy, Josiah, Jr. *Observations on the Act of Parliament, Commonly Called the Boston Port-Bill; with Thoughts on Civil Society and Standing Armies.* Boston, 1774.

Ramsay, David. *An Oration on the Advantages of American Independance; Spoken before a Public Assembly of the Inhabitants of Charlestown . . . on the second Anniversary of that Glorious Aera.* Charleston, 1778.

Ross, Robert. *A Sermon, in which the Union of the Colonies is Considered and Recommended; and the bad Consequences of Divisions are Represented. Delivered on the Public Thanksgiving, November Sixteenth, 1775.* New York, 1776.

Rowland, David S. *Divine Providence Illustrated and Improved. A Thanksgiving Discourse . . . Occasioned by the Repeal of the Stamp Act. . . . Providence* [1766].

Sampson, Ezra. *A Sermon, Delivered at Roxbury Camp, before Colonel Cotton's Regiment, July 20, 1775. . . .* Watertown, 1775.

Scales, William. *The Confusion of Babel Discovered. Or, an Answer to Jeremy Belknap's Discourse upon the Lawfullness of War. . . . America,* 1780.

[Seabury, Samuel]. *An Alarm to the Legislature of the Province of New York, Occasioned by the present Political Disturbances in North America. . . .* New York, 1775.

———. *The Congress Canvassed; or, An Examination into the Conduct of the Delegates, at the Grand Convention held in Philadelphia, September 1, 1774. Addressed to the Merchants. By A. W. Farmer. . . .* [New York], 1774.

———. *Free Thoughts on the Proceedings of the Continental Congress, held at Philadelphia September 5, 1774: wherein their Errors are Exhibited . . . and the only Means Pointed out for Preserving and Securing our Present Happy Constitution . . . By a Farmer.* [New York], 1774.

———. *A View of the Controversy between Great Britain and her Colonies: Including a Mode of Determining their Present Disputes, finally and effectually, and of Preventing all Future Contentions . . . By A. W. Farmer. . . .* New York, 1774.

[Sewall, Jonathan?]. *The Americans Roused, in a Cure for the Spleen; or, Amusement for a Winter's Evening. . . .* New England printed, New York reprinted, n.d.

Sewall, Jonathan Mitchell. *War and Washington. A Song Composed at the Beginning of the American Revolution.* Philadelphia, 1779.

Sherwood, Samuel. *The Church's Flight into the Wilderness: An Address on the Times.* New York, 1776.

———. *A Sermon, Containing Scriptural Instructions to Civil Rulers, and all Free-born Subjects . . . Delivered on the Public Fast, August 31, 1774. . . .* New Haven, 1774.

Shipley, Jonathan. *A Speech Intended to have been Spoken on the Bill for Altering the Charters of the Colony of Massachusetts-Bay by the Rev. Jonathan Shipley, Lord Bishop of Asaph.* London printed, Boston reprinted, 1774.

Short Advice to the Counties of New York. New York, 1774.

Short Narrative of the Horrid Massacre. . . . See above, Boston.

Smith, Robert. *The Obligations of the Confederate States of North America to Praise God. Two Sermons Preached at Pequea, December 13, 1781.* Philadelphia, 1782.

Smith, William. *A Sermon on the Present Situation of American Affairs. Preached in Christ-Church, June 23, 1775. . . .* Philadelphia, 1775.

Some Chapters of the Book of Chronicles of Isaac the Scribe, Written on his Passage from the Land of the Amerikites to the Island of the Albionites, while the Ship was Tossed on the Waves of the Great and Wide Sea. New York, n.d.

Spring, Samuel. *A Sermon Delivered at the North Congregational Church in Newbury-Port on a Day of Public Thanksgiving, November 20th, MDCCLXXVII.* Newburyport, 1778.

Stearns, William. *A View of the Controversy Subsisting between Great Britain and the American Colonies. A Sermon, Preached at a Fast, in Marlborough . . . on Thursday May 11, 1775.* Watertown, 1775.

Stillman, Samuel. *Good News from a Far Country. A Sermon Preached at Boston . . . Upon the Arrival of the important News of the Repeal of the Stamp-Act.* Boston, 1766.

———. *A Sermon Preached before the Honorable Council . . . of the State of Massachusetts-Bay . . . May 26, 1779. . . .* Boston, 1779.

———. *A Sermon Preached to the Ancient and Honorable Artillery Company in Boston, New-England, June 4, 1770.* Boston, 1770.

The Storm, or the American Syren: being a Collection of the Newest and most Approved Songs. Williamsburg, 1773.

Street, Nicholas. *The American States Acting over the Part of the Children of Israel in the Wilderness, and thereby Impeding their Entrance into Canaan's Rest . . . A Sermon Preached at East-Haven, April 1777, and Occasionally at Branford.* New Haven, [1777].

Strong, Nathan. *The Agency and Providence of God Acknowledged in the Preservation of the American States. . . .* Hartford, 1780.

Story, Isaac. *The Love of our Country Recommended and En-forced, In a Sermon from Psalm CXXII. 7, Delivered on a Day of Public Thanksgiving, December 15, 1774.* Boston, 1775.

Thacher, Oxenbridge. *The Sentiments of a British American.* Boston, 1764.

Thatcher, Peter. *An Oration Delivered at Watertown, March 5, 1776. . . .* Boston, 1776.

Throop, Benjamin. *A Thanksgiving Sermon, Upon the Occasion, of the Glorious News of the Repeal of the Stamp-Act, Preached in New-Concord, in Norwich, June 26, 1766.* New London, 1766.

Triumph of the Whigs; or, T'other Congress Convened, The. New York, 1775.

Tudor, William, *An Oration Delivered at Boston, March 5, 1779. . . .* Boston, 1779.

Two Congresses Cut Up: or a Few Remarks upon Some of the Votes and Resolutions of the Continental Congress, The. . . . Boston, 1774.

[Warren, Mercy Otis]. *The Adulateur. A Tragedy as it is now Acted in Upper Servia.* Boston, 1773.

———. *The Group, As lately Acted and to be Re-Acted to the Wonder of all Superior Intelligences, nigh Headquarters at Amboyne.* Boston, 1775.

[Washington, George, spurious]. *Letters from General Washington to Several of his Friends in the Year 1776. . . .* [New York], 1778.

Webster, Samuel. *The Misery and Duty of an Oppress'd and Enslav'd People, Represented in a Sermon Delivered at Salisbury, July 14, 1774. . . .* Boston, 1774.

———. *Rabshakeh's Proposal Considered, In a Sermon, Delivered at Groton February 21, 1775. . . .* Boston, 1775.

———. *A Sermon Preached before the Honourable Council . . . of the State of Massachusetts-Bay . . . May 28, 1777.* Boston, 1777.

Welsh, Thomas. *Oration, Delivered at Boston, March 5, 1783. . . .* Boston, 1783.

West, Samuel. *An Anniversary Sermon, Preached at Plymouth, December 22, 1777. . . .* Boston, [1778].

Whitaker, Nathaniel. *An Antidote against Toryism. Or the Curse of Meroz. . . .* Newburyport, 1777.

Whitney, Peter. *The Transgression of a Land Punished by a Multitude of Rulers. Considered in two Discourses, Delivered July 14, 1774. . . .* Boston, 1774.

Whittelsey, Chauncey. *The Importance of Religion in a Civil Ruler*. . . . New Haven, 1778.

Williams, Nathan. *A Sermon Preached in the Audience of the General Assembly of the State of Connecticut . . . May 11, 1780*. Hartford, 1780.

Williams, Samuel. *A Discourse on the Love of our Country; Delivered on a Day of Thanksgiving, December 5, 1774*. Salem, 1775.

[Wilson, James]. *Considerations on the Nature and the Extent of the Legislative Authority of the British Parliament*. Philadelphia, 1774.

Witherspoon, John. *The Dominion of Providence over the Passions of Men. A Sermon Preached at Princeton, On the 17th of May, 1776*. Philadelphia, 1776.

[Zubly, John Joachim]. *Great Britain's Right to Tax her Colonies, Placed in the Clearest Light*. [Philadelphia?, 1775].

————. *The Law of Liberty, Preached at the Opening of the Georgia Provincial Congress*. . . . Philadelphia, 1775.

————. *The Stamp-Act Repealed*. Savannah, 1766.

CORRESPONDENCE, DOCUMENTS, MEMOIRS, ETC.

Adams, John. *The Works of John Adams, with a Life of the Author, Notes and Illustrations*. C. F. Adams, ed. 10 vols. Boston, 1850-1856.

Adams, John, and Adams, Abigail. *Familiar Letters of John Adams and his Wife*. . . . C. F. Adams, ed. Boston, 1875.

Adams, Samuel. *The Writings of Samuel Adams*. H. A. Cushing, ed. 4 vols. New York, 1904-1908.

Andrews, John. "The Letters of John Andrews, Esq., of Boston. 1772-1776." Winthrop Sargent, comp. 1 Mass. Hist. Soc., *Proceedings*, VIII, 316-412.

Aspinwall Papers (4 Mass. Hist. Soc., *Collections*, IX, X). 2 vols. Boston, 1871.

Balch, T., ed. *Letters and Papers Relating Chiefly to the Provincial History of Pennsylvania*. Philadelphia, 1855.

Barrington, W. W. B., and Bernard, F. *The Barrington-Bernard Correspondence . . . 1760-1770*. E. Channing and A. Coolidge, eds. Cambridge, 1912.

Boston. "Correspondence in 1774 and 1775 between a Committee of the Town of Boston and Contributors of Donations for the Relief of the Sufferers by the Boston Port Bill," R. Frothingham, Jr., ed. 4 Mass. Hist. Soc., *Collections*, IV, 1-278.

———. *Reports of the Record Commissioners of the City of Boston.* 38 vols. Boston, 1876-1908.

Boucher, Jonathan. "The Letters of Jonathan Boucher," *Maryland Historical Magazine*, VII, 1-26, 150-156, 286-304, 337-356; VIII, 34-50, 168-186, 235-256, 338-352; IX, 54-67, 232-241, 327-336.

———. *Reminiscences of an American Loyalist, 1738-1789. Being the Autobiography of the Revd. Jonathan Boucher. . . .* Jonathan Boucher, ed. Boston, 1925.

Braintree. *Records of the Town of Braintree, 1640-1793.* Samuel A. Bates, ed. Randolph, 1886.

Burnett, Edmund C., *Letters of Members of the Continental Congress.* ——— vols. Washington, D. C., 1921——.

Carroll, Charles. *Unpublished Letters of Charles Carroll of Carrollton, and of his Father, Charles Carroll of Doughoregan.* Thomas Meagher Field, ed. (The United States Catholic Historical Society, Monograph Series I). New York, 1902.

Carter, Landon. "The Diary of Landon Carter," *William and Mary College Quarterly*, XIII, 45-53, 157-164, 219-224; XIV, 38-44, 181-186, 246-253; XV, 15-20, 205-211; XVI, 149-156, 257-268; XVII, 8-18; XVIII, 37-44; XX, 173-185; XXI, 172-181.

Case, Wheeler. *Revolutionary Memorials, Embracing Poems by the Rev. Wheeler Case, published in 1778. . . .* Stephen Dodd, ed. New York, 1852.

Church, Benjamin. "An Address to a Provincial Bashaw," *Magazine of History*, extra number 74.

———. "The Times. A Poem." *Magazine of History*, extra number 84.

Colden, Cadwallader. *The Colden Letter Books, 1760-1775* (New York Historical Society, *Collections*, Vols. IX, X). New York, 1877.

Connecticut. *Public Records of the Colony of Connecticut, 1636-1776.* J. H. Trumbull and C. J. Hoadley, comps. 15 vols. Hartford, 1850-1890.

Cooper, Samuel. "Letters of Samuel Cooper to Thomas Pownall, 1769-1777," *American Historical Review*, VIII, 301-330.

Cushing, Thomas. "Letters of Thomas Cushing from 1767 to 1775," 4 Mass. Hist. Soc., *Collections*, IV, 347-366.

Deane, Silas. *The Deane Papers, 1774-1790.* New York Historical Society, *Collections*, New York, 1886-1890.

Dickinson, John. *The Writings of John Dickinson, 1764-1774* (*Memoirs*, Historical Society of Pennsylvania, Vol. XIV), P. L. Ford, ed. Philadelphia, 1895.

Ecclesiastical Records of the State of New York. Hugh Hastings, ed. 6 vols. New York, 1906.

Eliot, Andrew. "Letters from Andrew Eliot to Thomas Hollis," 4 Mass. Hist. Soc., *Collections*, IV, 398-461.

Fitch, Thomas. *The Thomas Fitch Papers* (Conn. Hist. Soc., *Collections*, Vols. XVII, XVIII). Hartford, 1919-1920.

Force, Peter, comp. *American Archives: Consisting of a Collection of authentick Records, State Papers, Debates and Letters. . . .* 9 vols. Washington, 1837-1853.

Ford, W. C., comp. *Broadsides, Ballads, etc. printed in Massachusetts 1639-1800* (Mass. Hist. Soc., *Collections*, Vol. LXXV). Boston, 1922.

Franklin, Benjamin. *The Writings of Benjamin Franklin.* A. H. Smyth, ed. 10 vols. New York, 1907.

Freneau, Philip M. *Poems; edited for the Princeton Historical Association by Fred Lewis Pattee.* 3 vols. Princeton, 1902-1907.

Gaine, Hugh. *The Journals of Hugh Gaine.* P. L. Ford, ed. 2 vols. New York, 1902.

Gage, Thomas. *The Correspondence of General Thomas Gage with the Secretaries of State, 1763-1775.* C. E. Carter, ed. 2 vols. New Haven, 1931-1933.

Georgia. *Colonial Records of the State of Georgia, 1732-1774.* A. D. Candler, ed. 17 vols. Atlanta, 1904-1906.

——. *Revolutionary Records, 1769-1784.* 3 vols. Atlanta, 1908.

Gibbes, R. W., ed. *Documentary History of the American Revolution . . . 1764-1782.* 3 vols. New York, 1853-1857.

Habersham, James. *The Letters of the Honorable James Habersham, 1756-1775* (Ga. Hist. Soc., *Collections*, Vol. VI). Savannah, 1904.

Hamilton, Alexander. *The Works of Alexander Hamilton.* J. C. Hamilton, ed. 7 vols. New York, 1850-1851.

Hening, W. W., comp. *The Statutes at Large: being a Collection of all the Laws of Virginia. . . .* 13 vols. New York, 1819-1823.

Hiltzheimer, Jacob. *Extracts from the Diary of Jacob Hiltzheimer, of Philadelphia, 1765-1798.* J. C. Parsons, ed. Philadelphia, 1893.

Humphreys, David. *Poems by Col. David Humphreys, late Aid-de-Camp to his excellency General Washington.* 2nd ed. Philadelphia, 1789.

Huntington. *Huntington Town Records, including Babylon, Long Island, New York (1653-1873).* Charles Street, ed. 3 vols. n.p. 1887-1889.

Ingersoll, Jared. "A Selection from the Correspondence and Miscellaneous Papers of Jared Ingersoll," Franklin B. Dexter, ed. New Haven Hist. Soc., *Papers*, IX, 201-472.

Jay, John. *The Correspondence and Public Papers of John Jay.* H. P. Johnson, ed. 4 vols. New York, 1890-1893.

Jefferson, Thomas. *The Writings of Thomas Jefferson.* P. L. Ford, ed. 10 vols. New York, 1892-1899.

Journals of the Continental Congress. W. C. Ford and G. Hunt, eds. 34 vols. Washington, 1904-1937.

Lasswell, H. D., Casey, R. D., and Smith, B. L. *Propaganda and Promotional Activities; an Annotated Bibliography.* Minneapolis, 1935.

Lee, Richard Henry. *The Letters of Richard Henry Lee.* J. C. Ballagh, ed. 2 vols. New York, 1911-1914.

Lee, William. *Letters of William Lee, Sheriff and Alderman of London; Commercial Agent of the Continental Congress in France; and Minister to the Courts of Vienna and Berlin. 1766-1783.* W. C. Ford, ed. 3 vols. Brooklyn, 1891.

The Loyalist Poetry of the Revolution. Winthrop Sargent, ed. Philadelphia, 1857.

Marshall, Christopher. *Extracts from the Diary of Christopher Marshall kept in Philadelphia and Lancaster during the American Revolution, 1774-1781.* William Duane, ed. Albany, 1877.

Maryland. *Archives of Maryland.* W. H. Browne, *et al.*, eds. —— vols. Baltimore, 1883——.

Massachusetts. *The Journals of Each Provincial Congress of Massachusetts in 1774 and 1775, and of the Committee of Safety.* . . . William Lincoln, ed. Boston, 1838.

——. *Speeches of the Governors of Massachusetts, from 1765 to 1775; and the Answers of the House of Representatives to the Same.* . . . Boston, 1818.

Montresor, John and James. *The Montresor Journals.* G. D. Scull, ed. (New York Hist. Soc., *Collections*, Vol. XIV.) New York, 1881.

Moore, Frank. *Illustrated Ballad History of the American Revolution. 1763-1783.* New York, 1876.

――――. *Diary of the American Revolution. From Newspapers and Original Documents.* 2 vols. New York, 1859-1860.

――――. *Songs and Ballads of the American Revolution.* New York, 1856.

Moore, Maurice. "The Justice of Taxing the American Colonies, in Great Britain, considered," *Some Eighteenth Century Tracts Concerning North Carolina.* Wm. K. Boyd, comp. Raleigh, 1927, pp. 157-175.

Moravians. *Records of the Moravians in North Carolina.* Adelaide L. Fries, ed. 4 vols. Raleigh, 1922-1930.

New Hampshire. *Documents and Records Relating to the Province [Town and State] of New Hampshire, 1623-1800.* N. Bouton, *et al.,* eds. 31 vols. Concord, etc., 1867-1907.

New Jersey. *Archives of the State of New Jersey.* W. A. Whitehead, *et al.,* eds. 30 vols. Newark, etc., 1880-1906.

――――. *Minutes of the Provincial Congress and the Council of Safety of the State of New Jersey, 1774-1776.* Trenton, 1879.

New York. *Journals of the Provincial Congress, Provincial Convention, Committee of Safety and Council of Safety of the State of New York.* 2 vols. Albany, 1842.

Niles, Hezekiah. *Principles and Acts of the Revolution in America.* . . . Baltimore, 1822.

North Carolina. *Colonial and State Records of North Carolina, 1662-1790.* W. L. Saunders, *et al.,* eds. 26 vols. Raleigh, 1886-1906.

Odell, Jonathan. *See* Stansbury, Joseph.

Paine, Thomas. *The Complete Works of Thomas Paine.* 2 vols. New York, 1922.

Pennsylvania. *Colonial Records of Pennsylvania, 1683-1790.* 16 vols. Philadelphia, 1852-1853.

Perry, William Stevens, comp. *Historical Collections Relating to the American Colonial Church.* 4 vols. Hartford, 1870-1878.

Pitkin, William. *The Pitkin Papers* (Conn. Hist. Soc., *Collections,* Vol. XIX.) Hartford, 1921.

Plymouth. *Records of the Town of Plymouth.* 3 vols. Plymouth, 1899-1903.

Rhode Island. *Records of the Colony of Rhode Island and Providence Plantations in New England, 1636-1792.* J. R. Bartlett, comp. 10 vols. Providence, 1856-1865.

Rodney, Caesar. *Letters to and from Caesar Rodney, 1756-1784.* G. H. Ryden, ed. Philadelphia, 1933.

Rowe, John. "The Diary of John Rowe," 2 Mass. Hist. Soc., *Proceedings*, Vol. X.

Sargent, Winthrop. *See* Stansbury, Joseph.

South Carolina. *Journal of the Council of Safety of the Province of South Carolina, 1775.* South Carolina Historical Society, *Collections*, II, 22-64.

Stansbury, Joseph, and Odell, Jonathan. *The Loyal Verses of Joseph Stansbury and Doctor Jonathan Odell, relating to the American Revolution.* Winthrop Sargent, ed. Albany, 1860.

Stiles, Ezra. *The Literary Diary of Ezra Stiles, D.D., LL.D.* F. B. Dexter, ed. 3 vols. New York, 1901.

Thomson, Charles. *The Thomson Papers, 1765-1816* (New York Historical Society, *Collections*, XI, 1-286). New York, 1878.

Thornton, John Wingate. *The Pulpit of the American Revolution.* . . . Boston, 1860.

Tisbury. *Records of the Town of Tisbury, Massachusetts.* . . . Boston, 1903.

Tryon County. *The Minute Book of the Committee of Safety.* New York, 1905.

Vermont. *Records of the Council of Safety and Governor and Council of the State of Vermont.* . . . 3 vols. Montpelier, 1873-1880.

Virginia. "Proceedings of the Virginia Committee of Correspondence, 1759-1770," *Virginia Magazine of History and Biography*, X, 337-356; XI, 1-25, 131-143, 345-354; XII, 157-169, 225-240, 353-364.

Warren-Adams Letters. Being Chiefly a Correspondence among John Adams, Samuel Adams, and James Warren (Mass. Hist. Soc., *Collections*, Vols. LXXII, LXXIII). 2 vols. Boston, 1917-1925.

Washington, George. *The Writings of George Washington,* W. C. Ford, ed. 14 vols. New York, 1889-1893.

———. *The Writings of George Washington, being his Correspondence, Addresses, Messages, and other Papers, Official and Private.* Jared Sparks, ed. 12 vols. Boston, 1837.

Weston. *Town of Weston Records, 1746-1803.* . . . Boston, 1893.

Wilkes, John. "John Wilkes and Boston," Mass. Hist. Soc., *Proceedings*, XLVII, 190-214.

Witherspoon, John. *The Works of John Witherspoon.* . . . 9 vols. Edinburgh, 1804-1805.

Worcester. *Worcester Town Records 1753 to 1783.* Franklin P. Rice, ed. (Worcester Society of Antiquity, *Collections,* Vol. IV.) Worcester, 1882.

Wright, James. "Letters from Governor Sir James Wright to the Earl of Dartmouth and Lord George Germaine. . . ." Ga. Hist. Soc., *Collections,* III, 157-375.

SECONDARY SOURCES

Abbott, Wilbur C. *New York in the American Revolution.* New York, 1929.

Abernethy, Thomas Perkins. *Western Lands and the American Revolution.* New York, 1937.

Adams, Charles Francis. *History of Braintree, Massachusetts (1639-1788).* Cambridge, 1891.

Adams, James Truslow. *Revolutionary New England 1691-1776.* Boston, 1923.

Adams, Nathaniel. *Annals of Portsmouth.* . . . Portsmouth, 1825.

Anderson, G. P. "A Note on Ebenezer Mackintosh," Colonial Society of Massachusetts, *Publications,* XXVI, 348-366.

Andrews, C. M. "Boston Merchants and the Non-Importation Movement," Colonial Society of Massachusetts, *Publications,* XIX, 159-259.

Arnold, S. G. *History of the State of Rhode Island.* 2 vols. New York, 1859-1860.

Ashe, Samuel A'Court. *History of North Carolina.* 2 vols. Greensboro and Raleigh, 1908-1925.

Austin, James T. *The Life of Elbridge Gerry, With Contemporary Letters.* 2 vols. Boston, 1828-1829.

Baldwin, Alice M. *The New England Clergy and the American Revolution.* Durham, 1928.

Bassett, J. S. "The Regulators of North Carolina (1765-1771)," American Historical Association, *Report 1894,* pp. 141-212.

Beardsley, E. E. *Life and Correspondence of the Right Reverend Samuel Seabury, D.D.* Boston, 1881.

Becker, Carl. *The History of Political Parties in the Province of New York, 1760-1776.* Madison, 1909.

Bouton, Nathaniel. *The History of Concord.* Concord, 1855.

Boutell, Lewis H. *The Life of Roger Sherman.* Chicago, 1896.

Bradford, Alden. *Memoir of the Life and Writings of Rev. Jonathan Mayhew, D.D.* Boston, 1838.

Brown, E. Francis. *Joseph Hawley, Colonial Radical.* New York, 1931.

Caruthers, Eli W. *A Sketch of the Life and Character of the Rev. David Caldwell, D.D. . . . Including two of his Sermons. . . .* Greensborough, 1842.

A Century of Meriden. Bancroft Gillespie and George Munson, comp. Meriden, 1906.

Collins, Varnum L. *Princeton.* New York, 1914.

――――. *President Witherspoon, A Biography.* Princeton, 2 vols., 1925.

Connor, R. D. W. *Cornelius Harnett.* Raleigh, 1909.

――――. *Revolutionary Leaders of North Carolina.* Greensboro, 1914.

Conway, Moncure D. *The Life of Thomas Paine. With a History of his Literary, Political, and Religious Career in America, France, and England.* 2 vols. New York, 1892.

Cross, Arthur Lyon. *The Anglican Episcopate and the American Colonies* (Harvard Historical Studies, Vol. IX). Cambridge, 1924.

Davidson, Philip G. "Sons of Liberty and Stamp Men," *North Carolina Historical Review*, IX, 37-55.

――――. "The Southern Back Country on the Eve of the Revolution," in *Essays in Honor of William E. Dodd.* Chicago, 1935.

――――. "Whig Propagandists of the American Revolution," *American Historical Review*, XXXIX, 442-453.

Dickerson, Oliver M. *Boston under Military Rule (1768-1769): As Revealed in a Journal of the Times.* Boston, 1936.

Doob, Leonard W. *Propaganda, Its Psychology and Technique.* New York, 1935.

Drayton, John. *Memoirs of the American Revolution, From its Commencement to the year 1776, inclusive; as Relating to the State of South-Carolina; and occasionally Referring to the States of North-Carolina and Georgia.* 2 vols. Charleston, 1821.

Eckenrode, H. J. *The Revolution in Virginia.* Boston, 1916.

The Era of the American Revolution. Studies Inscribed to Evarts Boutell Greene. Richard B. Morris, ed. New York, 1939.

Evans, Israel. *American Bibliography. . . .* 12 vols. Chicago, 1903-1904.

Farrand, Max. "The West and the Principles of the Revolution," *Yale Review*, Old Series, XVII, 44-58.

Faust, Albert B. *The German Element in the United States.* . . . 2 vols. Boston, 1909.

Faÿ, Bernard. *Revolution and Freemasonry 1680-1800.* Boston, 1935.

Fisher, E. J. *New Jersey as a Royal Province, 1738 to 1776* (Columbia University Studies, Vol. XLI). New York, 1911.

Flick, A. C. *Loyalism in New York during the American Revolution* (Columbia University Studies, Vol. XIV, no. 1). New York, 1901.

Frothingham, Richard. "The Sam Adams Regiments in the Town of Boston," *Atlantic Monthly*, X, 179-203; XII, 595-616.

Frothingham, Richard, Jr. *The History of Charlestown, Massachusetts.* Charlestown, 1845-1849.

———. *Life and Times of Joseph Warren.* Boston, 1865.

Gipson, Lawrence H. *Jared Ingersoll: A Study of American Loyalism in Relation to British Colonial Government.* New Haven, 1920.

Gordon, William. *The History of the Rise, Progress, and Establishment of the Independence of the United States of America.* 3 vols. New York, 1794.

Goss, Elbridge H. *The Life of Colonel Paul Revere.* 2 vols. Boston, 1891.

Hanna, C. A. *The Scotch-Irish, or the Scot in North Britain, in North Ireland, and in North America.* 2 vols. New York, 1902.

Harlow, R. V. *Samuel Adams, Promoter of the American Revolution. A Study in Psychology and Politics.* New York, 1923.

Harrell, Isaac S. *Loyalism in Virginia. Chapters in the Economic History of the Revolution.* Durham, 1926.

Hastings, George E. *The Life and Works of Francis Hopkinson.* Chicago, 1926.

Headley, Joel T. *The Chaplains and Clergy of the Revolution.* Springfield, 1861.

Hildeburn, Charles R. *A Century of Printing. The Issues of the Press in Pennsylvania 1685-1784.* 2 vols. Philadelphia, 1886.

———. *Sketches of Printers and Printing in Colonial New York.* New York, 1895.

———. "Loyalist Ladies of the Revolution." Typed MS., Historical Society of Pennsylvania.

Hills, George W. *History of the Church in Burlington, New Jersey.* 2nd ed. Trenton, 1885.

Hollister, G. H. *The History of Connecticut.* . . . 2 vols. Hartford, 1857.

Howe, George. *History of the Presbyterian Church in South Carolina.* Columbia, 1870.

Hoyt, Albert H. "The Reverend Thomas Bradbury Chandler, D.D., 1726-1790," *New England Historical and Genealogical Register*, XXVII, 227-236.

Hudson, Charles. *History of the Town of Lexington.* Boston, 1868.
———. *History of the Town of Marlborough.* Boston, 1862.

Hudson, Frederic. *Journalism in the United States, from 1690 to 1872.* New York, 1873.

Humphrey, Edward Frank. *Nationalism and Religion, 1774-1789.* Brookline, 1924.

Hutchinson, Thomas. *The History of the Colony [and Province] of Massachusetts Bay.* 3 vols. Boston and London, 1795-1828.

Jenkins, Charles Francis. *Button Gwinnett, Signer of the Declaration of Independence.* New York, 1926.

Johnson, Joseph. *Traditions and Reminiscences, chiefly of the American Revolution in the South, particularly of the Upper Country.* Charleston, 1851.

Jones, Charles Colcock, Jr. *History of Georgia.* 2 vols. Boston, 1883.

Jones, E. Alfred. *The Loyalists of Massachusetts, Their Memorials, Petitions, and Claims.* London, 1930.
———. *Loyalists of New Jersey, Their Memorials, Petitions, Claims, etc., from English Records* (New Jersey Historical Society, *Collections*, Vol. X). Newark, 1927.

Jones, Thomas. *History of New York during the Revolutionary War.* . . . Edward F. De Lancey, ed. 2 vols. New York, 1887.

Kimball, James. "The One Hundredth Anniversary of the Destruction of Tea in Boston Harbor," Essex Institute, *Historical Collections*, XII, 197-239.

Kraus, Michael. *Intercolonial Aspects of American Culture on the Eve of the Revolution. With Special Reference to the Northern Towns.* New York, 1928.

Larned, Ellen D. *History of Windham County, Connecticut.* 2 vols. Worcester, 1874-1880.

Lasswell, H. D. *Propaganda Technique in the World War.* New York, 1927.

Leake, Isaac Q. *Memoir of the Life and Times of General John Lamb*. . . . Albany, 1850.

Lecky, W. E. H. *The American Revolution, 1763-1783*. . . . J. A. Woodburn, ed. New York, 1916.

Lee, James Melvin. *History of American Journalism*. Boston, 1923.

Lincoln, Charles H. *The Revolutionary Movement in Pennsylvania, 1760-1776*. Philadelphia, 1901.

Lingley, Charles R. *The Transition in Virginia from Colony to Commonwealth*. New York, 1910.

Lippmann, Walter. *Public Opinion*. New York, 1922.

Lossing, Benson John. *The Pictorial Field-book of the Revolution*. . . . 2 vols. New York, 1860.

Love, W. Deloss, Jr. *The Fast and Thanksgiving Days of New England*. Boston, 1895.

Lumley, Frederick E. *The Propaganda Menace*. New York, 1933.

Lydekker, John Wolfe. *The Life and Letters of Charles Inglis*. London, 1936.

McCrady, Edward. *The History of South Carolina under the Royal Government, 1719-1776*. New York, 1899.

———. *The History of South Carolina in the Revolution*, Vol. I, 1775-1780; Vol. II, 1780-1783. New York, 1901-1902.

McMurtrie, Douglas C. *A History of Printing in the United States*. . . . Vol. II, *Middle and South Atlantic States*. New York, 1936.

McRee, Griffith J. *Life and Correspondence of James Iredell, One of the Associate Justices of the Supreme Court of the United States*. 2 vols. New York, 1857-1858.

Matthews, Albert. "The Snake Devices, 1754-1776, and the Constitutional Courant, 1765." Colonial Society of Massachusetts, *Publications*, XI, 409-452.

Metzger, Charles Henry. *The Quebec Act; a Primary Cause of the American Revolution*. New York, 1937.

Miller, John C. *Sam Adams, Pioneer in Propaganda*. Boston, 1936.

Morse, Sidney. *Freemasonry in the American Revolution*. Washington, D. C., 1924.

Newlin, Claude M. *Life and Writings of Hugh Henry Brackenridge*. Princeton, 1932.

Palfrey, J. G. *History of New England*. 5 vols. Boston, 1858-1890.

Paullin, Charles O. *Atlas of the Historical Geography of the United States*. Washington, 1932.

Payne, George Henry. *History of Journalism in the United States*. New York, 1929.

Peters, Samuel. *The Rev. Samuel Peters' Ll.D. General History of Connecticut. . . .* S. J. McCormick, ed. New York, 1877.

Propaganda Analysis. Vol. I, no. 1, October, 1937. New York, 1937-.

Quincy, Josiah. *The History of Harvard University.* 2 vols. Cambridge, 1840.

————. *Memoir of the Life of Josiah Quincy, Junior, of Massachusetts Bay; 1744-1775.* Boston, 1875.

Quinn, A. H. *A History of the American Drama From its Beginnings to the Civil War.* New York, 1933.

Ramsay, David. *The History of the American Revolution.* Two vols. in one. London, 1793.

————. *The History of the Revolution of South-Carolina, from a British Province to an Independent State.* 2 vols. Trenton, 1785.

Rawle, William. "A Sketch of the Life of Thomas Mifflin" (*Memoirs,* Historical Society of Pennsylvania, Vol. II, pt. 2, pp. 107-126). Philadelphia, 1830.

Roads, Samuel. *The History and Traditions of Marblehead.* Boston, 1880.

Rowland, Kate Mason. *The Life of Charles Carroll of Carrollton, 1737-1832. With his Correspondence and Public Papers.* 2 vols. New York, 1898.

————. *Life and Correspondence of George Mason, 1725-1792.* 2 vols. New York, 1892.

Sabine, Lorenzo. *Biographical Sketches of Loyalists of the American Revolution.* 2 vols. Boston, 1864.

Sanderson, John, *et al. Biography of Signers to the Declaration of Independence.* 9 vols. Philadelphia, 1823-1827.

Schlesinger, Arthur M. *The Colonial Merchants and the American Revolution, 1763-1776* (*Columbia University Studies,* Vol. LXXVIII). New York, 1918.

————. "The Colonial Newspapers and the Stamp Act," *New England Quarterly,* VIII, 63-83.

————. "Politics, Propaganda, and the Philadelphia Press, 1767-1770," *The Pennsylvania Magazine of History and Biography,* LX, 309-322.

————. "Propaganda and the Boston Newspaper Press, 1767-1770," Colonial Society Massachusetts, *Publications,* XXXII, 396-416.

Sedgwick, Theodore, Jr. *Memoir of the Life of William Livingston.* New York, 1833.

Smith, J. E. A. *The History of Pittsfield (Berkshire County) Massachusetts*. Boston, 1869.

"The Stamp Act and New Jersey's Opposition to it," New Jersey Historical Society, *Proceedings*, April, 1924.

Staples, William R. *Annals of the Town of Providence*. Providence, 1832.

Stillé, C. J. *The Life and Times of John Dickinson, 1732-1808* (*Memoirs*, Historical Society of Pennsylvania, Vol. XIII). Philadelphia, 1891.

Stillson, Henry L., ed. *History of the Ancient and Honorable Fraternity of Free and Accepted Masons. . . .* Boston and New York, 1900.

Stuart, I. W. *Life of Jonathan Trumbull, Sen., Governor of Connecticut*. Boston, 1859.

Teele, A. K., ed. *The History of Milton, Massachusetts. 1640 to 1887*. Boston, 1887.

Thatcher, James. *History of the Town of Plymouth. . . .* Boston, 1835.

Tryon, Rolla Milton. *Household Manufactures in the United States, 1640-1860; a Study in Industrial History*. Chicago, 1917.

Tudor, William. *The Life of James Otis, of Massachusetts: Containing also, Notice of Some Contemporary Characters and Events from the year 1760 to 1775*. Boston, 1823.

Tyler, Moses Coit. *The Literary History of the American Revolution, 1763-1783*. 2 vols. New York, 1897.

Upton, R. F. *Revolutionary New Hampshire*. Dartmouth, 1937.

Van Tyne, Claude H. *The Loyalists in the American Revolution*. New York, 1929.

Wallace, D. D. *The Life of Henry Laurens. . . .* New York, 1915.

Wells, W. V. *The Life and Public Services of Samuel Adams*. 3 vols. Boston, 1865.

Wirt, William. *Sketches of the Life and Character of Patrick Henry*. Hartford, 1854.

INDEX

INDEX

ABINGTON, town resolutions of, 40 n

Adams, Amos, 214

Adams, John, as a propagandist, 6-7; and Sons of Liberty, 6, 69; and independence, 39, 170; writes instructions of the town of Braintree, 54; attacks Stamp Act, 123; approves anniversary celebrations, 180; and Braintree pastor, 203; "Novanglus," 216, 242-43; and *Boston Gazette*, 227; and Jonathan Sewall, 259, 260; mentioned, 197, 238, 346

Adams, Samuel, as a propagandist, 3-6, 347-48; relations with lower classes, 5-6; relations with Joseph Hawley, 10; relations with John Dickinson, 15; relations with Samuel Cooper, 22; relations with Thomas Young, 26; and independence, 39; unifies colonial assemblies, 49-50; and letter to Lord Hillsborough, 52; organizes committees of correspondence, 56-58; and Sons of Liberty, 72-73; proposes union of writers, 73; and Congregational ministers, 84; appeals to British Constitution, 106; appeals to 18th century compact philosophy, 112; defends civil and religious liberty, 123; obtains Hutchinson's letters, 147; and *Boston Gazette*, 227-28; contributes to "Boston Journal of Occurrences," 236; condemns propaganda decline, 345; counteracts King George's speech, 403-4; mentioned, 37, 319, 355 n

Additional Observations on a Short Narrative, 215

Address of Liberty, The, Tory broadside, 311

Address to a Provincial Bashaw, An, 212

Address to Protestant Dissenters, An, 216

Addressors, address Hutchinson and Gage, 267

Administration of Justice Act, terms, 43; Whig attack on, 107. *See also* Intolerable Acts

Advantages of victory, Tory appeal to, 290-92, 321-22; Whig appeal to, 131-38, 359-61

Agnew, John, 258

Aiken, Benjamin, 113

Albany Gazette, 308

Alison, Francis, 90

Allen, James, 216

Allen, John, 214 n

Allen, Thomas, as a propagandist, 23-24

Allicocke, Joseph, 67 n

Almanacs, pictures in, 188; Whig use of, 223; Tory use of, 311

American Alarm, The, 214

American bishopric, *see* American episcopate

American episcopate, Livingston's attack on, 11; opposed by Congregationalists, 84; opposed by Presbyterians, 86; Whig attack on, 122-24; mentioned, 57

American Gazette, 396 n

American Journal and General Advertiser, 397

American liberty, burial ceremony, 176, 177

"American Liberty Song," John Dickinson, 15, 189, 217, 241

American Magazine, 224

Ames, Nathaniel, almanacs, illustrations in, 223

Amicable Society of Georgia, 100

André's dream, 326-27

Anglicans, *see* Church of England

Annapolis Gazette, 231

Anniversaries, March 5, 182-83, 385; March 18, 181-82; April 19, 385, 389; July 4, 385; August 14, 180-81; King's birthday, 298

Anson County, inhabitants of, protest Whig actions, 265

Appleton, Nathaniel, on committee of correspondence, 57

Arnold, Benedict, poetic attack on, 374 n; effigies of, 387; mentioned, 324

Artisans, *see* Lower classes

Ashe, John, and Sons of Liberty, 67

[445]